Contents at a Glance

Italian
ALL-IN-ONE

FOR DUMMIES

A Wiley Brand

by Antonietta Di Pietro with
Francesca Romana Onofri, Teresa Picarazzi,
Karen Möller, Daniela Gobetti, and
Beth Bartolini-Salimbeni

FOR DUMMIES
A Wiley Brand

Italian All-in-One For Dummies®

Published by: **John Wiley & Sons, Inc.,** 111 River Street, Hoboken, NJ 07030-5774, www.wiley.com

Copyright © 2013 by John Wiley & Sons, Inc., Hoboken, New Jersey

Media and software compilation copyright © 2013 by John Wiley & Sons, Inc. All rights reserved.

Published simultaneously in Canada

For general information on our other products and services, please contact our Customer Care Department within the U.S. at 877-762-2974, outside the U.S. at 317-572-3993, or fax 317-572-4002. For technical support, please visit www.wiley.com/techsupport.

Wiley publishes in a variety of print and electronic formats and by print-on-demand. Some material included with standard print versions of this book may not be included in e-books or in print-on-demand. If this book refers to media such as a CD or DVD that is not included in the version you purchased, you may download this material at http://booksupport.wiley.com. For more information about Wiley products, visit www.wiley.com.

Library of Congress Control Number: 2013942766

ISBN 978-1-118-51060-5 (pbk); ISBN 978-1-118-51057-5 (ebk); ISBN 978-1-118-51062-9 (ebk); ISBN 978-1-118-51053-7 (ebk)

Manufactured in the United States of America

10 9 8 7 6 5 4 3 2 1

Table of Contents

Book IV: Mastering Italian Verbs and Tenses 345

Chapter 1: Jumping into Action with Italian Regular Verbs 347

Chapter 2: Talking in the Present Tense with Irregular Verbs 361

Chapter 3: Using Reflexive Forms and the Imperative Mood 375

Introduction

*I*f you're reading this introduction, you're likely interested in learning a foreign language. You're surely aware of the importance of knowing how to communicate in every circumstance and situation because world views, ideas, and people travel and meet in a borderless space. Why you're choosing Italian is a question with many possible answers. You may want to refresh your memory of the Italian you learned in school, or perhaps you're preparing for a full immersion into the arts, fashion, and design. Maybe you're studying Italian so you can surprise an Italian friend or to get ready for a business trip to Italy. Or you may simply want to know the "language that sings." Whatever the reason, this book will help you do it.

Italian All-in-One For Dummies isn't a language course. This book deconstructs the Italian language and culture in chapters that complement each other but that you can read in the order you prefer and at your own pace. Rather than a vertical scaffolding of cultural topics, vocabulary, and grammar, *Italian All-in-One For Dummies* is a collection of what you need to successfully communicate in Italian. The accompanying audio tracks will help improve your pronunciation and intonation, and the online resources provide additional references.

About This Book

Italian All-in-One For Dummies presents aspects of the Italian culture and daily life as well as the grammatical framework of the language as it's spoken today. Each section in the book has a theme. You can choose where you want to begin and how you want to proceed. You can skip the sidebars (shaded text boxes) without remorse, or simply leave them for another time. *Italian All-in-One For Dummies* lets you read at the pace and in the order you prefer.

English translations are *italicized* when they accompany Italian words and sentences. The phrases and idiomatic expressions in Books I and II come with pronunciation guidelines. Within the Italian pronunciations, you see *italic* on the stressed syllables in words with two or more syllables. In addition, dialogues built around specific topics and real-life situations will enrich your vocabulary and your speech. Those who can't speak a language unless they comprehend its syntax and grammar will be satisfied by the thorough clarifications presented in *Italian All-in-One For Dummies*. The appendixes provide quick references to specific grammar points (such as verbs) and translations of important words that appear throughout the book. The audio tracks help you practice your spoken Italian whenever and wherever you like! And because Italian is the "language that sings," all you have to do is repeat after the audio track and join the chorus!

Within this book, you may note that some web addresses break across two lines of text. If you're reading this book in print and want to visit one of these web pages, simply key in the web address exactly as it's noted in the text, pretending as though the line break doesn't exist. If you're reading this as an e-book, you've got it easy — just click the web address to be taken directly to the web page.

Foolish Assumptions

Italian All-in-One For Dummies makes the following assumptions about you, dear reader:

- ✔ You're an Italian student looking for an in-depth, easy-to-use reference.
- ✔ You know very little or no Italian — or if you took Italian back in school, you remember very little of it.
- ✔ Your goal is to expand your knowledge of Italian. You don't want to be burdened by long-winded explanations of unnecessary grammatical terms, nor do you care to hold a scholarly discussion in Italian about Dante's *Inferno*. You just want to express yourself in clear and reasonably accurate Italian.
- ✔ You're enthusiastic about having fun while honing your Italian skills.

If any or all of these statements describe you, then you're ready to start using this book.

Icons Used in This Book

You may be looking for particular information while reading this book. To make certain types of information easier to find, the following icons appear in the left-hand margins throughout the book.

This icon highlights tips that can make learning Italian — and using it correctly — easier.

This icon points out interesting information that you shouldn't forget.

This icon highlights potential linguistic, grammatical, and cultural errors to avoid.

Languages are full of quirks that may trip you up if you're not prepared for them. This icon points to discussions of these peculiar grammar rules. Because Books III, IV, and V are nearly all grammar, you see this icon only in Books I and II.

If you're looking for information and advice about Italian culture and travel, look for this icon.

This icon marks the Talkin' the Talk dialogues in Books I and II that you can listen to in order to get a better understanding of what Italian sounds like.

Beyond the Book

In addition to the plethora of Italian language information you find in the print book or e-book you're reading right now, this product also comes with some access-anywhere goodies on the web. Check out the eCheat Sheet at www.dummies.com/cheatsheet/italianaio for common idiomatic expressions that use the verbs **fare** (*to do; to make*), **avere** (*to have*), **essere** (*to be*), and **andare** (*to go*); the scoop on using capital letters properly in Italian; and more.

This book comes with 29 audio tracks that allow you to hear many of the Talkin' the Talk dialogues spoken by Italian speakers. If you've purchased the paper or e-book version of *Italian All-in-One For Dummies,* just go to www.dummies.com/go/italianaio to access and download these tracks. (If you don't have Internet access, call 877-762-2974 within the U.S. or 317-572-3993 outside the U.S.)

Where to Go from Here

Before you start reading *Italian All-in-One For Dummies,* answer the question "how much Italian do I know?" If your answer is "not much," "nothing," or "just a little," start with Book I. If you have a foundation of Italian but find that grammar always trips you up, you may want to jump to Book III. To test your understanding of tenses and how to use them properly, Book V is the place for you. You decide your priorities, so go ahead and make your choice — there's plenty to browse and to select. **Buon divertimento**! (bwohn dee-vehr-tee-*mehn*-toh!) (*Have fun!*)

Book I

Speaking Italian in Everyday Settings

Contents at a Glance

Chapter 1

Exploring Pronunciations and Italian You May Already Know

In This Chapter

▶ Taking note of the little Italian you know

▶ Becoming familiar with basic Italian pronunciation

▶ Putting the emphasis on the right syllable

*Y*ou probably know that Italian is a Romance language, which means that Italian, just like Spanish, French, Portuguese, and some other languages, is a "child" of Latin. There was a time when Latin was the official language in a large part of Europe because the Romans ruled so much of the area. Before the Romans came, people spoke their own languages, and the mixture of these original tongues with Latin produced many of the languages and dialects still in use today.

If you know one of these Romance languages, you can often understand bits of another one of them. But just as members of the same family can look very similar but have totally different personalities, so it is with these languages. People in different areas speak in very different ways due to historical or social reasons, and even though Italian is the official language, Italy has a rich variety of dialects. Some dialects are so far from Italian that people from different regions can't understand each other.

Despite the number of different accents and dialects, you'll be happy to discover that everybody understands the Italian you speak and you understand theirs. (Italians don't usually speak in their dialect with people outside their region.)

You Already Know Some Italian!

Although Italians are very proud of their language, they have allowed some English words to enter it. They talk, for example, about gadgets, jogging, feeling, and shock; they often use the word *okay;* and since computers have entered their lives, they say **cliccare sul mouse** (kleek-*kah*-reh soohl mouse) (*to click the mouse*). Finally, there's **lo zapping** (loh *zap*-ping), which means switching TV channels with the remote. These are only a few of the flood of English words that have entered the Italian language.

In the same way, many Italian words are known in English-speaking countries. Can you think of some?

How about . . .

- **pizza** (*peet*-tsah)
- **pasta** (*pahs*-tah)
- **spaghetti** (spah-*geht*-tee)
- **tortellini** (tohr-tehl-*lee*-nee)
- **mozzarella** (moht-tsah-*rehl*-lah)
- **espresso** (ehs-*prehs*-soh)
- **cappuccino** (kahp-pooh-*chee*-noh)
- **panino** (pah-*nee*-noh) (singular) or **panini** (pah-*nee*-nee) (plural)
- **biscotti** (bees-*koht*-tee) (*cookies* [plural]) or **biscotto** (bees-*koht*-toh) (singular)
- **tiramisù** (tee-rah-mee-*sooh*) (Literally: *pull me up,* a reference to the fact that this sweet is made with Italian espresso)

You may have heard words from areas other than the kitchen, too, such as the following:

- **amore** (ah-*moh*-reh): This is the word *love* that so many Italian songs tell about.
- **avanti** (ah-*vahn*-tee): You use this word to mean *Come in!* It can also mean *Come on!* or *Get a move on!*
- **bambino** (bahm-*bee*-noh): This is a male child. The female equivalent is **bambina** (bahm-*bee*-nah).
- **bravo!** (*brah*-voh!): You can properly say this word only to one man. To a woman, you must say **brava!** (*brah*-vah!), and to a group of people, you say **bravi!** (*brah*-vee!) unless the group is composed only of women, in which case you say **brave!** (*brah*-veh!).

✔ **ciao!** (chou!): **Ciao** means *hello* and *goodbye.* **Ciao** comes from the Venetian expression *sciào vostro,* or **schiavo vostro** (*skyah*-voh *voh*-stroh) (*[I am] your slave*) in Italian; servants used this phrase in the 18th century when they addressed their lords.

✔ **scusi** (*skooh*-zee): This word stands for *excuse me* and *sorry* and is addressed to persons you don't know or to whom you speak formally. You say **scusa** (*scooh*-zah) to people you know and to children.

Getting to the root of cognates

In addition to the words that have crept into the language directly, Italian and English have many cognates. A *cognate* is a word in one language that has the same origin as a word in another one and may sound similar. You can get an immediate picture of what cognates are from the following examples:

✔ **aeroporto** (ah-eh-roh-*pohr*-toh) (*airport*)

✔ **attenzione** (aht-tehn-*tsyoh*-neh) (*attention*)

✔ **comunicazione** (koh-mooh-nee-kah-*tsyoh*-neh) (*communication*)

✔ **importante** (eem-pohr-*tahn*-teh) (*important*)

✔ **incredibile** (een-kreh-*dee*-bee-leh) (*incredible*)

You understand much more Italian than you think you do. Italian and English are full of cognates. To demonstrate, read this little story with some Italian words and see how easy it is for you to understand.

It seems **impossibile** (eem-pohs-*see*-bee-leh) to him that he is now at the **aeroporto** (ah-eh-roh-*pohr*-toh) in Rome. He always wanted to come to this **città** (cheet-*tah*). When he goes out on the street, he first calls a **taxi** (*tah*-ksee). He opens his bag to see whether he has the **medicina** (meh-dee-*chee*-nah) that the **dottore** (doht-*toh*-reh) gave him. Going through this **terribile traffico** (tehr-*ree*-bee-leh *trahf*-fee-koh), he passes a **cattedrale** (kaht-teh-*drah*-leh), some **sculture** (skoohl-*tooh*-reh), and many **palazzi** (pah-*laht*-tsee). He knows that this is going to be a **fantastico** (fahn-*tahs*-tee-koh) journey.

Picking up popular expressions

Every language has expressions that you use so often that they almost become routine. For example, when you give something to somebody and he or she says, "Thank you," you automatically reply, "You're welcome." This type of popular expression is an inseparable part of every language. When you know these expressions and how to use them, you're on the way to really speaking Italian.

Italian slang

Dialects and other deviations from "standard" Italian are also used in different social contexts. You may hear words such as **zecche** (*dzehk*-keh) (*young Italians politically engaged on the left side and dressed in a "trashy" manner*), **rimastini** (ree-mah-*stee*-nee) (*meaning leftovers, the term is used to jestingly refer to chain-smokers, or what's left of them!*), **pariolini** (pah-ryoh-*lee*-nee) (*young people from the upper middle class, politically engaged on the zecche's opposite side*), and **truzzi** (*trooht*-tzsee) (*youth who listen to dance, techno, and house music*). You may also hear **bella** (*behl*-lah) instead of **ciao** (chou) (*hi*), **tajo** (*tah*-lyoh) (*fun*), **tanato** (tah-*nah*-toh) (*caught; discovered*), or **evaporato** (eh-vah-poh-*rah*-toh) (*disappeared*). Don't bother to memorize these words; they'll be outdated by the time you've managed to pronounce them.

The following are some of the most common popular expressions in Italian:

- **Accidenti!** (ahch-chee-*dehn*-tee!) (*Wow!*) (*Darn it!*)
- **Andiamo!** (ahn-*dyah*-moh!) (*Let's go!*)
- **Che c'è?** (keh cheh?) (*What's up?*)
- **D'accordo? D'accordo!** (dahk-*kohr*-doh? dahk-*kohr*-doh!) (*Agreed? Agreed!*)
- **E chi se ne importa?** (eh kee seh neh eem-*pohr*-tah?) (*Who cares?*)
- **È lo stesso.** (eh loh *stehs*-soh.) (*It's all the same.*) (*It doesn't matter.*)
- **Fantastico!** (fahn-*tahs*-tee-koh!) (*Fantastic!*)
- **Non fa niente.** (nohn fah nee-*ehn*-teh.) (*Don't worry about it.*) (*It doesn't matter.*) You say **Non fa niente** when someone apologizes to you for something.
- **Non c'è di che.** (nohn cheh dee keh.) (*You're welcome.*)
- **Permesso?** (pehr-*mehs*-soh?) (*May I pass/come in?*) Italians use this expression every time they cross a threshold entering a house or when passing through a crowd.
- **Stupendo!** (stoo-*pehn*-doh!) (*Wonderful!*) (*Fabulous!*)
- **Va bene!** (vah *beh*-neh!) (*Okay!*)

Mouthing Off: Basic Pronunciation

Italian provides many opportunities for your tongue to do acrobatics. This is really fun, because the language offers you some new sounds. This section includes some basic pronunciation hints that are important both for surfing through this book and for good articulation when you speak Italian.

Next to the Italian words throughout this book you find the pronunciation in parentheses. The following sections help you figure out how to read these pronunciations — that is, how to pronounce the Italian words. In the pronunciations, the syllables are separated with a hyphen, like this: **casa** (*kah*-zah) (*house*). Furthermore, the stressed syllable appears in italics, which means that you put the stress of the word on the italicized syllable. (See the section "Stressing Syllables Properly," later in this chapter, for more information about stresses.) If you master the correct pronunciation in this chapter, starting with the alphabet, you may even forego the pronunciation spelling provided, and read like a real Italian.

Starting with the alphabet

What better way is there to start speaking a language than to familiarize yourself with its **alfabeto** (ahl-fah-*beh*-toh) (*alphabet*)? Table 1-1 shows you all the letters as well as how each one sounds. Knowing how to pronounce the Italian alphabet is essential to pronouncing all the new words you learn. Note that the Italian alphabet has only 21 letters: Missing are *j, k, w, x,* and *y* (which have crept into some Italian words now used in Italy).

Listen to the alphabet on Track 1 as many times as you need to in order to get down the right sounds. In the long run, this will help you be understood when you communicate in Italian.

Table 1-1		The Italian Alphabet	
Letter	*Pronunciation*	*Letter*	*Pronunciation*
a	ah	b	bee
c	chee	d	dee
e	eh	f	*ehf*-feh
g	jee	h	*ahk*-kah
i	ee	j	ee *loohn*-gah

(continued)

Table 1-1 *(continued)*

Letter	Pronunciation	Letter	Pronunciation
k	*kahp*-pah	l	*ehl*-leh
m	*ehm*-meh	n	*ehn*-neh
o	oh	p	pee
q	kooh	r	*ehr*-reh
s	*ehs*-seh	t	tee
u	ooh	v	veeh
w	*dohp*-pyah vooh	x	eeks
y	*eep*-see-lohn	z	*dzeh*-tah

Vowels

When it comes to vowels, the sounds aren't that new, but the connection between the written letter and the actual pronunciation isn't quite the same as it is in English.

Italian has five written vowels: **a, e, i, o,** and **u.** The following sections tell you how to pronounce each of them.

The vowel "a"

In Italian, the letter **a** has just one pronunciation. Think of the sound of the *a* in the English word *father.* The Italian **a** sounds just like that.

To prevent you from falling back to the other *a* sounds found in English, the Italian **a** appears as (ah) in this book, as shown earlier in **casa** (*kah*-sah) (*house*). Here are some other examples:

- ✔ **albero** (*ahl*-beh-roh) (*tree*)
- ✔ **marmellata** (mahr-mehl-*lah*-tah) (*jam*)
- ✔ **sale** (*sah*-leh) (*salt*)

The vowel "e"

To pronoun the **e,** try to think of the sound in the word *day,* which comes very close to the Italian **e.** In this book, you see the **e** sound as (eh). For example:

✔ **sole** (*soh*-leh) (*sun*)

✔ **peso** (*peh*-zoh) (*weight*)

✔ **bere** (*beh*-reh) (*to drink*)

The Italian **e** actually has two pronunciations: an open **e** and a closed **e**. The open **e** sounds like the *e* in the English words *exit* and *bet* and in the Italian **ecco** (*ehk*-koh) (*here we go*) (*here it is*), **è** (*eh*) (*he/she/it is*), and **festa** (*feh*-stah) (*party*). You pronounce the closed **e** like the *a* in the English words *late* and *day*, such as in the Italian words **e** (eh) (*and*), **nemico** (neh-*mee*-koh) (*enemy*), and **nome** (*noh*-meh) (*name*). How do you know when to pronounce the open or closed **e?** You listen to many Italian songs and native Italian speakers and follow their lead.

The vowel "i"

The Italian **i** is simply pronounced (ee), as in the English word *see*. Here are some examples:

✔ **cinema** (*chee*-neh-mah) (*cinema*)

✔ **bimbo** (*beem*-boh) (*little boy*)

✔ **vita** (*vee*-tah) (*life*)

The vowel "o"

The Italian **o** is pronounced as the *o* in the English (from the Italian) *piano,* and the pronunciation appears as (oh). Try it out on the following words:

✔ **domani** (doh-*mah*-nee) (*tomorrow*)

✔ **piccolo** (*peek*-koh-loh) (*little; small*)

✔ **dolce** (*dohl*-cheh) (*sweet*)

Just as the **e** has two pronunciations for the open or closed **e,** so does the **o.** You pronounce the open **o** in Italian like the *o* in the English word *soft:* **buono** (*bwoh*-noh) (*good*), **notte** (*noht*-teh) (*night*), and **nove** (*noh*-veh) (*nine*). The closed **o** sounds like the English word *cold,* which you see in Italian words like **sole** (*soh*-leh) (*sun*), **voto** (*voh*-toh) (*vow*), and **torta** (*tohr*-tah) (*cake*). Again, the best way to get familiar with the two pronunciations is to listen to native Italian speakers and practice.

The vowel "u"

The Italian **u** always sounds like the English (ooh), as the *oo* in *zoo*. Here are some sample words:

- ✔ **tu** (tooh) (*you*)
- ✔ **luna** (*looh*-nah) (*moon*)
- ✔ **frutta** (*frooht*-tah) (*fruit*)

Pronunciation peculiarities

You'll come across some sounds and spellings that aren't so familiar, for example:

- ✔ ohy as the *oi* in *oink:* **noi** (nohy) (*we*)
- ✔ ahy as the *i* in *ice:* **dai** (dahy) (*you give*)
- ✔ ee as in *feet:* **diva** (*dee*-vah) (*diva*)
- ✔ ehy as the *ai* in *aid:* **lei** (lehy) (*she*)
- ✔ ou as in *out:* **auto** (*ou*-toh) (*car*)

Consonants

Italian has the same consonants that English does. You pronounce most of them the same way in Italian as you pronounce them in English, but others have noteworthy differences.

- ✔ **b:** As in **bene** (*beh*-neh) (*well*)
- ✔ **d:** As in **dare** (*dah*-reh) (*to give*)
- ✔ **f:** As in **fare** (*fah*-reh) (*to make*)
- ✔ **l:** As in **ladro** (*lah*-droh) (*thief*)
- ✔ **m:** As in **madre** (*mah*-dreh) (*mother*)
- ✔ **n:** As in **no** (noh) (*no*)
- ✔ **p:** As in **padre** (*pah*-dreh) (*father*)
- ✔ **t:** As in **treno** (*treh*-noh) (*train*). Make certain to exaggerate the **t** when it's doubled, like in the word **spaghetti** (spah-*geht*-tee).
- ✔ **v:** As in **vino** (*vee*-noh) (*wine*)

Some consonants don't really exist in Italian except in some foreign words that have entered the language.

- ✔ **j:** It sounds like the *j* in *jam* and exists mostly in foreign words such as **jogging, jet,** and **jeans.**

- **k:** You find it in words like **okay, ketchup,** and **killer.**

- **w:** You find it in some foreign words (for the most part English words), like **whiskey, windsurf,** and **wow.**

- **x:** As with **j, k,** and **w, x** doesn't really exist in Italian, with the difference that "**x** words" derive mostly from Greek. Examples include **xenofobia** (kseh-noh-foh-*bee*-ah) (*xenophobia*) and **xilofono** (ksee-*loh*-foh-noh) (*xylophone*).

- **y:** The letter **y** normally appears only in foreign words, like **yogurt, hobby,** and **yacht.**

The consonants in the following sections are pronounced differently than they are in English.

The consonant "c"

The Italian **c** has two sounds, depending on which letter follows it:

- **Hard c:** When **c** is followed by **a, o, u,** or any consonant, you pronounce it as in the English word *cat,* indicated by the pronunciation (k). Examples include **casa** (*kah*-sah) (*house*), **colpa** (*kohl*-pah) (*guilt; fault*), and **cuore** (*kwoh*-reh) (*heart*).

  To get the (k) sound before **e** and **i,** you must put an **h** between the **c** and the **e** or **i.** Examples include **che** (keh) (*what*), **chiesa** (*kyeh*-zah) (*church*), and **chiave** (*kyah*-veh) (*key*).

- **Soft c:** When **c** is followed by **e** or **i,** you pronounce it as you do the first and last sounds in the English word *church;* therefore, the pronunciation is (ch). Examples include **cena** (*cheh*-nah) (*dinner*), **cibo** (*chee*-boh) (*food*), and **certo** (*chehr*-toh) (*certainly*).

  To get the (ch) sound before **a, o,** or **u,** you have to insert an **i.** This **i,** however, serves only to create the (ch) sound; you don't pronounce it. Examples include **ciao** (chou) (*hello; goodbye*), **cioccolata** (chok-koh-*lah*-tah) (*chocolate*), and **ciuccio** (*chooh*-choh) (*baby's pacifier*).

This pronunciation scheme sounds terribly complicated, but in the end, it's not that difficult. Here it is in another way, which you can take as a little memory support:

cera, **ci**bo, **ce**leste, **ci**nesei, **ce**nere = (ch)

Mi**che**le, **chio**do, **chia**ve, **che**, **che**rubino = (k)

The consonant "g"

The Italian **g** behaves the same as the **c,** so it's presented here the same way:

✔ **Hard g:** When **g** is followed by **a, o, u,** or any consonant, you pronounce it as you pronounce the *g* in the English word *good,* and the pronunciation looks like (g). Examples include **gamba** (*gahm*-bah) (*leg*), **gomma** (*gohm*-mah) (*rubber*), and **guerra** (*gweh*-rah) (*war*).

To get the (g) sound before **e** or **i,** you must put an **h** between the letter **g** and the **e** or **i.** Examples include **spaghetti** (spah-*geht*-tee) (*spaghetti*), **ghiaccio** (*gyahch*-choh) (*ice*), and **ghirlanda** (geer-*lahn*-dah) (*wreath*).

✔ **Soft g:** When **g** is followed by **e** or **i,** you pronounce it as you do the first sound in the English word *job;* therefore, the pronunciation is (j). Examples include **gentile** (jehn-*tee*-leh) (*kind*), **giorno** (*johr*-noh) (*day*), and **gelosia** (jeh-loh-*zee*-ah) (*jealousy*).

To get the (j) sound before **a, o,** or **u,** you have to insert an **i.** The **i** serves only to indicate the proper sound; you don't pronounce it. Examples include **giacca** (*jahk*-kah) (*jacket*), **gioco** (*joh*-koh) (*game*), and **giudice** (*jooh*-dee-cheh) (*judge*).

Here's another little pattern to help you remember these pronunciations:

gamba, **go**mma, **gu**erra, **ghia**ccio, spa**ghe**tti = (g)

gentile, **gio**rno, **gia**cca, **gio**co, **giu**dice = (j)

The consonant "h"

The consonant **h** has only one function: namely, to change the sound of **c** and **g** before the vowels **e** and **i,** as described earlier. It also appears in foreign expressions such as *hostess, hit parade,* and *hobby,* and in some forms of the verb **avere** (ah-*veh*-reh) (*to have*), but it's always silent.

The consonant "q"

Q exists only in connection with **u** followed by another vowel; that is, you always find **qu.** The **q** is pronounced like (k), and **qu** is, therefore, pronounced (kw). Examples include **quattro** (*kwaht*-troh) (*four*), **questo** (*kwehs*-toh) (*this*), and **quadro** (*kwah*-droh) (*painting; framed art*).

The consonant "r"

The Italian **r** is not pronounced with the tongue in the back, as it is in English, but trilled at the *alveolar ridge,* which is the front part of your palate, right behind your front teeth. You have to practice it. In the beginning, you may not find this pronunciation manageable, but practice makes perfect!

Here are some words to help you practice:

✔ **radio** (*rah*-dee-oh) (*radio*)

✔ **per favore** (pehr fah-*voh*-reh) (*please*)

✔ **prego** (*preh*-goh) (*you're welcome*)

Using gestures

Italians love to emphasize their words with gestures. For example, they use gestures to express the following feelings: **Ho fame** (oh *fah*-meh) (*I'm hungry*), **Me ne vado** (meh neh *vah*-doh) (*I'm leaving*), and **E chi se ne importa?** (eh kee seh neh eem-*pohr*-tah?) (*Who cares?*). Needless to say, a flood of rude gestures exist as well.

Unfortunately, describing gestures in words is too difficult, because Italian body language is a science and is hard for non-Italians to copy. You also have to make the right facial expressions when performing these gestures.

These gestures generally come naturally and spontaneously, and you're sure to see some as you observe Italian life. Still, there are some practical, useful gestures that you may want to make when you're with Italians. Greeting and saying goodbye, for example, are accompanied by a common gesture — hugging and kissing. Italians seek direct contact when greeting one another. When you're not very familiar with a person, you shake hands. But when you know a person well or you have an immediate good feeling, you kiss cheek to cheek; that is, you don't really touch with your lips, but only with your cheek.

The consonant "s"

S is sometimes pronounced as the English *s*, as in *so*. In this case, the pronunciation is (s). When in between vowels, it's pronounced like the English *z*, as in *zero;* in these cases, you'll see (z) as the pronunciation. Examples include **pasta** (*pahs*-tah) (*pasta*), **solo** (*soh*-loh) (*only*), **chiesa** (*kyeh*-zah) (*church*), and **gelosia** (jeh-loh-*zee*-ah) (*jealousy*).

The consonant "z"

A single **z** is pronounced (dz) — the sound is very similar to the English *z* in *zero,* with a (d) sound added at the beginning, as in **zero** (*dzehr*-oh) (*zero*). Just try it. When the **z** is doubled, you pronounce it more sharply, like (t-ts), as in **tazza** (*taht*-tsah) (*cup; mug*). Furthermore, when **z** is followed by the letter **i,** it also has a (ts) sound, like in the word **nazione** (nah-*tsyoh*-neh) (*nation*).

Double consonants

When you encounter double consonants in Italian, you have to pronounce each instance of the consonant or lengthen the sound. The difficult part is that there's no pause between the consonants.

Doubling the consonant usually changes the meaning of the word. So, to make sure that your Italian is understandable, emphasize doubled consonants well. To help you pronounce words with double consonants correctly, the pronunciations include the first consonant at the end of one syllable and the other one at the beginning of the following one, as in these examples:

- **nono** (*noh*-noh) (*ninth*)
- **nonno** (*nohn*-noh) (*grandfather*)
- **pala** (*pah*-lah) (*shovel*)
- **palla** (*pahl*-lah) (*ball*)

Try it once again:

- **bello** (*behl*-loh) (*beautiful*)
- **caffè** (kahf-*feh*) (*coffee*)
- **occhio** (*ohk*-kyoh) (*eye*)
- **spiaggia** (*spyahj*-jah) (*beach*)

Consonant clusters

Certain consonant clusters have special sounds in Italian. Here they are:

- **gn** is pronounced as the English (ny). The sound is actually the same as in the Spanish word **señorita** (seh-nyoh-*ree*-tah) (*miss*), or better yet, an Italian word like **gnocchi** (*nyohk*-kee).

- **gl** is pronounced in the back of the throat like the English word *million* in words like **gli** (lyee) (*the*) and **famiglia** (fah-*mee*-lyah) (*family*). It doesn't sound anything like the English *g*.

- **sc** follows the same rules of the soft and hard **c** from the previous section. It's pronounced as in the English *scooter* when it comes before **a, o, u,** or **h** — that is, as in **scala** (*skah*-lah) (*scale*), **sconto** (*skohn*-toh) (*discount*), and **scuola** (*skwoh*-lah) (*school*). Before **e** and **i**, it's pronounced like the *sh* in *cash*. Examples of this pronunciation include **scena** (*sheh*-nah) (*scene*), **miscela** (mee-*sheh*-lah) (*mixture*), and **scimmia** (*sheem*-myah) (*monkey*).

Stressing Syllables Properly

Stress is the audible accent that you put on a syllable as you speak it. One syllable always gets more stress than all the others. (A reminder: In this book, stressed syllables appear in *italic*.)

Some words give you a hint as to where to stress them: They have an accent grave (ˋ) or acute (ˊ) above one of their letters. Here are some examples:

- **caffè** (kahf-*feh*) (*coffee*)
- **città** (cheet-*tah*) (*city*)
- **lunedì** (looh-neh-*dee*) (*Monday*)

   ✔ **perché** (pehr-*keh*) (*why*)

   ✔ **però** (peh-*roh*) (*but*)

   ✔ **università** (ooh-nee-vehr-see-*tah*) (*university*)

   ✔ **virtù** (veer-*tooh*) (*virtue*)

Book I

Speaking Italian in Everyday Settings

Differences between dialects and the Italian language

The different peoples living in the Italian peninsula have only recently been united under the common banner of "Italian." Indeed, a long period of political and social disunity characterized much of Italy's history. Following the fall of the Roman Empire in 476 CE, the Italian peninsula was disjointed by repeated invasions that ushered in an era of internal division that would last until the 18th century. After the Middle Ages, merchants, artists, and artisans from the Italian peninsula were recognized as "Italian" by outsiders, but they identified themselves based on their city of origin and spoke regional dialects. In the 1500s, the issue of having a literary Italian language was addressed, and it was in part resolved by the choice of adopting the language from Florence of the 1300s. But the provincialism of Italy was exhibited even more distinctly by illiterate peasants, who composed 80 percent of the Italian population in the 19th century. When Italy was politically unified in 1861, the Italian government promoted national literacy and the adoption of a standard Italian language to build a cohesive social identity.

In the proper context, the use of regional words or expressions helps to express particular nuances of meaning and to render communication playful. Italian dialects correspond to the geographical areas that characterize Italy. It's possible to distinguish among a northern Italian area, an Italian Tuscan area, an Italian central area, and a southern Italian area. Each of these areas is home to several regional dialects.

For example, you can say **ragazza** (rah-*gaht*-tsah) (*girl*) in ten different ways, as you can see in this table.

Dialect	*Region*
carosa (kah-*roh*-zah)	Puglia
carusa (kah-*rooh*-zah)	Sicilia
ciumachella (choo-mah-*kehl*-lah)	Lazio
fiola (*fyoh*-lah)	Umbria
guagliona (gwah-*lyoh*-nah)	Campania
putela (pooh-*teh*-lah)	Trentino Alto Adige
mata (*mah*-tah)	Piemonte
suéna (*sweh*-nah)	Liguria
tosa (*toh*-sah)	Veneto
vagnona (vah-*nyoh*-nah)	Puglia

Only vowels can have accents, and in Italian, all vowels at the end of a word can have this accent (ˋ). If there's no accent in the word, you're unfortunately left on your own. A rough tip is that Italian tends to have the stress on the *penultimate* (next-to-last) syllable. But there are too many rules and exceptions to list them all here!

Fortunately, only a few words have the same spelling and only an accent to distinguish them. But it can be a very important distinction, as in the following example: **e** (eh) (*and*) and **è** (eh) (*he/she/it is*) are distinguished only by the accent on the vowel and from a closed and opened sound in the pronunciation.

Chapter 2

Dealing with Numbers, Dates, and Time

*N*umbers crop up in all aspects of conversation, from counting, to telling someone your phone number, to putting things in order ("I went to Rome first, then Bologna second"). The good news is, in Italian, numbers are reliably straightforward, even though using them for dates, for example, may not seem so. This chapter gets you up-to-speed on counting, chatting about time and date, and using numbers with confidence in Italian.

Counting from Zero to a Billion: Cardinal Numbers

To express how many glasses of wine or scoops of gelato you want, you have to know your numbers. Table 2-1 provides some of the more useful cardinal numbers, from zero to a billion. Listen to Track 2 to hear a selection of numbers in Italian: 0 to 25, 30, 40, and 50.

Table 2-1	Counting from Zero to a Billion	
Number	**Italian**	**Pronunciation**
0	zero	*dzeh*-roh
1	uno	*ooh*-noh
2	due	*dooh*-eh
3	tre	treh
4	quattro	*kwaht*-troh
5	cinque	*cheen*-kweh
6	sei	sey
7	sette	*seht*-teh
8	otto	*oht*-toh
9	nove	*noh*-veh
10	dieci	*dyeh*-chee
11	undici	*oohn*-dee-chee
12	dodici	*doh*-dee-chee
13	tredici	*treh*-dee-chee
14	quattordici	kwaht-*tohr*-dee-chee
15	quindici	*kween*-dee-chee
16	sedici	*seh*-dee-chee
17	diciassette	dee-chahs-*seht*-teh
18	diciotto	dee-*choht*-toh
19	diciannove	dee-chahn-*noh*-veh
20	venti	*vehn*-tee
21	ventuno	vehn-*tooh*-noh
22	ventidue	*vehn*-tee-*dooh*-eh
23	ventitré	*vehn*-tee-*treh*
24	ventiquattro	*vehn*-tee-*kwaht*-troh
25	venticinque	*vehn*-tee-*cheen*-kweh
26	ventisei	*vehn*-tee-*sey*
27	ventisette	*vehn*-tee-*seht*-teh
28	ventotto	vehn-*toht*-toh
29	ventinove	*vehn*-tee-*noh*-veh
30	trenta	*trehn*-tah

Number	Italian	Pronunciation
40	quaranta	kwah-*rahn*-tah
50	cinquanta	cheen-*kwahn*-tah
60	sessanta	sehs-*sahn*-tah
70	settanta	seht-*tahn*-tah
80	ottanta	oht-*tahn*-tah
90	novanta	noh-*vahn*-tah
100	cento	*chen*-toh
101	centouno	*chen*-toh-*ooh*-noh
200	duecento	*dooh*-eh-*chehn*-toh
300	trecento	treh-*chehn*-toh
400	quattrocento	*kwaht*-troh-*chehn*-toh
500	cinquecento	*cheen*-kweh-*chehn*-toh
600	seicento	*sey*-*chehn*-toh
700	settecento	*seht*-teh-*chehn*-toh
800	ottocento	*oht*-toh-*chehn*-toh
900	novecento	*noh*-veh-*chehn*-toh
1,000	mille	*meel*-leh
2,000	duemila	*dooh*-eh-*mee*-lah
10,000	diecimila	*dyeh*-chee-*mee*-lah
100,000	centomila	*chehn*-toh-*mee*-lah
105,000	centocinquemila	*chehn*-toh-*cheen*-kweh-*mee*-lah
1,000,000	un milione (di)	oohn mee-*lyoh*-neh
1,000,000,000	un miliardo (di)	oohn mee-*lyahr*-doh

Book I

Speaking Italian in Everyday Settings

Building numbers in Italian

Before you can get very far with using numbers in Italian, you have to know how to build them. For example, say you have a powerful appetite and want to order 12,640 scoops of gelato. How do you convey that specific number? You'll be happy to know that you build Italian numbers in a direct manner, similar to English. When building Italian numbers, you spell out large numbers as one word, without the use of *and* (**e**) to connect them. So *12,640* is written (and spoken) as **dodicimilaseicentoquaranta** (*doh*-dee-chee-*mee*-lah-sey-*chehn*-toh-kwah-*rahn*-tah).

To build numbers in Italian, simply add the larger number at the beginning, as in the following examples:

2	**due**
22	**ventidue**
122	**centoventidue**
422	**quattrocentoventidue**
1,422	**millequattrocentoventidue**
3,422	**tremilaquattrocentoventidue**

Here are some other specifics you need to know about using numbers in Italian:

✔ Some handwritten numbers, such as 1, 4, 7, and 9, look different in Italian from their English counterparts. See Figure 2-1.

Figure 2-1: Handwritten Italian numbers 1, 4, 7, and 9.

Illustration by Wiley, Composition Services Graphics

✔ Italian uses periods and commas in numbers differently from English. For example, **1.200** in Italian is *1,200* in English. Remembering this difference is particularly important when looking at bills. A dinner that costs €36,00 differs greatly from one that costs €36.00!

✔ Telephone numbers are usually separated by periods rather than hyphens and are broken into units of two rather than three. Italian speakers often say the units of two digits as one number; for example, 21.30.52 would be said **ventuno, trenta, cinquantadue** (vehn-*tooh*-noh, *trehn*-tah, cheen-*kwahn*-tah-*dooh*-eh). A seven-digit number may be given as 4.21.30.52, or **quattro, ventuno, trenta, cinquantadue** (*kwaht*-troh, vehn-*tooh*-noh, *trehn*-tah, cheen-*kwahn*-tah-*dooh*-eh). However, nothing can stop you from simply saying each individual digit to relay a phone number, such as **due, uno, tre, zero, cinque, due** (*dooh*-eh, *ooh*-noh, treh, *dzeh*-roh, *cheen*-kweh, *dooh*-eh).

Speaking numbers like a native

When speaking numbers in general, you want to maintain the fluid nature of spoken Italian. To this end, from 20 through 90, the numbers 1 (**uno**) and 8 (**otto**) *contract,* meaning they drop the final vowel from **venti** (*vehn*-tee), **trenta** (*trehn*-tah)**,** and so on, before adding **uno** (*ooh*-noh) or **otto** (*oht*-toh).

So although some numbers follow the counting pattern, such as 22 (**venti- due**) (vehn-tee-*dooh*-eh) or 75 (**settantacinque**) (seht-*tahn*-tah-*cheen*-kweh), others, like 21 (**ventuno,** rather than **ventiuno**) (vehn-*tooh*-noh) and 68 (**ses- santotto,** not **sessantaotto**) (sehs-sahn-*toht*-toh), drop the final vowel from the tens and flow directly into **uno** and **otto.**

Read the following numbers, paying close attention to the *musicality,* or the flow of sound, in each example.

> **ventotto** (vehn-*toht*-toh)
>
> **trentuno** (trehn-*tooh*-noh)
>
> **cinquantuno** (cheen-kwahn-*tooh*-noh)
>
> **sessantotto** (sehs-sahn-*toht*-toh)
>
> **novantuno** (noh-vahn-*tooh*-noh)
>
> **quarantotto** (kwah-rahn-*toht*-toh)

Also, numbers ending in 3 require the use of an accent when written out. Thus, the number **tre** (treh) when added onto one of the tens becomes **tré,** as in **ventitré** (vehn-tee-*treh*).

One (**uno**) is the only cardinal number that agrees in number (only singular) and gender with words it modifies. It works in the same way as the indefinite article.

> **un ragazzo** (oohn rah-*gaht*-tsoh) (*a boy*)
>
> **una ragazza** (*ooh*-nah rah-*gaht*-tsah) (*a girl*)
>
> **uno studente** (*ooh*-noh stooh-*dehn*-teh) (*a male student*)
>
> **una casa** (*ooh*-nah *kah*-sah) (*a house*)
>
> **uno zio** (*ooh*-noh *dzee*-oh) (*an uncle*)
>
> **un'amica** (ooh-nah-*mee*-kah) (*a female friend*)

Cardinal numbers with special meanings

Certain cardinal numbers, accompanied by the masculine singular definite article **il** (eel) or **l'**, have specialized meanings, particularly when making historical, literary, or art historical references. **Il Trecento** (eel treh-*chen*-toh), **Il Quattrocento** (eel *kwaht*-troh-*chen*-toh), and so on, refer to the *1300s,* the *1400s,* and so on, which is certainly easier than the English naming of centuries, where the 14th century refers to the 1300s. For example, Petrarch (**Petrarca**), inventor of the sonnet form of poetry, lived during the **Trecento** (also written as '**300**). Michelangelo lived during both the **Quattrocento** (*1400s*) and the **Cinquecento** (*cheen*-kweh-*chen*-toh) (*1500s*).

The High Renaissance refers to that time in the **Cinquecento** (*1500s*) when the focus of effort and artists moved from Florence to Rome. A study of 20th-century literature would be a study of the literature of the **Novecento** (*noh*-veh-*chen*-toh) (*1900s*).

Other nouns that derive from the cardinal numbers include references to large quantities (*hundreds* = **centinaia** [chen-tee-*nah*-yah]; *thousands* = **migliaia** [mee-*lyah*-yah]). Also, by dropping the final vowel from a number and adding **-enne,** you can refer to a person of a certain age. A **diciottenne** (dee-choht-*tehn*-neh) is an 18-year-old; a **ventenne** (vehn-*tehn*-neh) is a 20-year-old.

Making sense of addresses

Like dates, which are covered later in this chapter, Italian reverses the order of street numbers and zip codes from the typical pattern in English. In Italian, numbers *follow* street names and *precede* city names, so an address may read something like this:

> **Dott. Duilio Falcone**
>
> **Via Verdi, 86**
>
> **20000 Firenze (FI), Italia**

This reverse order isn't the only thing that can make street addresses confusing in Italian. Occasionally, business addresses include a number and a color (such as **rosso** [*rohs*-soh] [*red*]), and residential numbers are followed by a different color (**blu** [blooh] [*blue*], for example). A street may have two buildings with the same number but with a color added. For example, **Via Verdi, 86blu** (*vee*-ah *vehr*-dee, oht-*tahn*-tah-sey blooh) may indicate a residence; **Via Verdi, 86rosso** (*vee*-ah *vehr*-dee, oht-*tahn*-tah-sey *rohs*-soh) may indicate a store. These same numbers can be on different buildings, blocks apart, with only the color indicating the correct site.

Putting Things in Order: Ordinal Numbers

To express the order, placement, or sequence of things (such as first, fourth, and eighth), you use *ordinal numbers.* Unlike cardinal numbers, ordinal numbers agree in gender with the nouns or pronouns they modify.

Table 2-2 lists examples of ordinal numbers in Italian. Note that for numbers one through ten, the ordinal numbers are irregular, meaning they don't follow the pattern of simply adding **-esimo** (*eh*-see-moh) to their cardinal form. You'll have to memorize these.

From 11 to infinity, you form ordinal numbers by dropping the final vowel of cardinal numbers and adding **-esimo,** with stress on the **e.** Here are some examples:

dodicesimo (*12th*) (doh-dee-*cheh*-see-moh)

trentaquattresimo (*34th*) (*trehn*-tah-kwaht-*treh*-see-moh)

centesimo (*100th*) (chehn-*teh*-see-moh)

The only exception to this rule is a cardinal number that ends in **-tré.** In this case, you retain the final vowel, but the stress doesn't change:

ventitreesimo (*23rd*) (*vehnt*-tee-treh-*eh*-see-moh)

cinquantatreesimo (*53rd*) (cheen-*kwahn*-tah-treh-*eh*-see-moh)

Table 2-2	Ordinal Numbers	
Italian	*Pronunciation*	*Translation*
primo/prima	*pree*-moh/*pree*-mah	*first*
secondo/seconda	seh-*kohn*-doh/seh-*kohn*-dah	*second*
terzo/terza	*tehr*-tsoh/*tehr*-tsah	*third*
quarto/quarta	*kwahr*-toh/*kwahr*-tah	*fourth*
quinto/quinta	*kween*-toh/*kween*-tah	*fifth*
sesto/sesta	*sehs*-toh/*sehs*-tah	*sixth*
settimo/settima	*seht*-tee-moh/*seht*-tee-mah	*seventh*

(continued)

Table 2-2 *(continued)*

Italian	Pronunciation	Translation
ottavo/ottava	oht-*tah*-voh/oht-*tah*-vah	*eighth*
nono/nona	*noh*-noh/*noh*-nah	*ninth*
decimo/decima	*deh*-chee-moh/*deh*-chee-mah	*tenth*
undicesimo/undicesima	oohn-dee-*cheh*-see-moh/ oohn-dee-*cheh*-see-mah	*eleventh*
quindicesimo/quindicesima	kween-dee-*cheh*-see-moh/ kween-dee-*cheh*-see-mah	*fifteenth*
ventesimo/ventesima	vehn-*teh*-see-moh/ vehn-*teh*-see-mah	*twentieth*
ventunesimo/ventunesima	vehn-tooh-*neh*-see-moh/ vehn-tooh-*neh*-see-mah	*twenty-first*
ventitreesimo/ventitreesima	vehn-tee-treh-*eh*-see-moh/ vehn-tee-treh-*eh*-see-mah	*twenty-third*
trentesimo/trentesima	trehn-*teh*-see-moh/ trehn-*teh*-see-mah	*thirtieth*
sessantesimo/sessantesima	sehs-sahn-*teh*-see-moh/ sehs-sahn-*teh*-see-mah	*sixtieth*
centesimo/centesima	chehn-*teh*-see-moh/ chehn-*teh*-see-mah	*hundredth*
millesimo/millesima	meel-*leh*-see-moh/ meel-*leh*-see-mah	*thousandth*
milionesimo/milionesima	mee-lyoh-*neh*-see-moh/ mee-lyoh-*neh*-see-mah	*millionth*

Here are several things to keep in mind when using ordinal numbers:

✓ You want to make sure the ordinal number that precedes a noun agrees in number and gender with that noun. For example:

> **È la quarta persona nella fila.** (eh lah *kwahr*-tah pehr-*soh*-nah *nehl*-lah *fee*-lah.) (*He is the fourth person in line.*)

> **Questo è il nono figlio!** (*kweh*-stoh eh eel *noh*-noh *fee*-lyoh!) (*This is the ninth son!*)

> **prima donna** (*pree*-mah *dohn*-nah) (*first lady*)

> **i primi libri** (ee *pree*-mee *lee*-bree) (*the first books*)

✔ To indicate something that has happened for the umpteenth time, you can use **ennesimo/ennesima.** Note that in the following example, **ennesima** is feminine and singular, as is the noun it modifies, **volta.**

> **È l'ennesima volta che me ne parla.** (eh lehn-*neh*-see-mah *vohl*-tah keh meh neh *pahr*-lah.) (*It's the umpteenth time he has talked to me about it.*)

✔ To refer to someone whose title carries a number (such as a king like Henry II), you use Roman numerals in English and say, "Henry the Second." In Italian, you may also use a Roman numeral, but you don't use the article.

> **Enrico Secondo** (ehn-*ree*-koh seh-*kohn*-doh) (*Henry the Second; Henry II*)

> **Carlo Quinto** (*kahr*-loh *kween*-toh) (*Charles the Fifth; Charles V*)

✔ You can abbreviate ordinal numbers by placing an **o** or an **a** in a raised, or superscript, position to agree in gender with what you're talking about. For example:

> **1º piano** (*pree*-moh *pyah*-noh) (*1st floor*)

> **5ª casa** (*kween*-tah *kah*-sah) (*5th house*)

Looking at the Calendar: Days, Months, and Seasons

In this day and age, to keep track of appointments or social events (for yourself and others), you need a calendar. To talk about when an event occurs or what date marks a special anniversary, you need to know the days of the week and months of the year in Italian. This section provides all the info you need to know to navigate the calendar and the seasons in Italian.

Days of the week

In English, you generally start naming the days of the week with Sunday, and you end the week with Saturday. In Italian, however, you begin with *Monday* (**lunedì**) (looh-neh-*dee*) and end with *Sunday* (**domenica**) (doh-*meh*-nee-kah), which is how the days are organized in Table 2-3. Note that in Italian, the days aren't capitalized as they are in English, unless they begin a sentence.

Table 2-3	Days of the Week	
Italian	*Pronunciation*	*Translation*
lunedì	looh-neh-*dee*	*Monday*
martedì	mahr-teh-*dee*	*Tuesday*
mercoledì	mehr-koh-leh-*dee*	*Wednesday*
giovedì	joh-veh-*dee*	*Thursday*
venerdì	veh-nehr-*dee*	*Friday*
sabato	*sah*-bah-toh	*Saturday*
domenica	doh-*meh*-nee-kah	*Sunday*

All the days except **domenica** (doh-*meh*-nee-kah) (*Sunday*) are masculine. Using the definite article with the day names changes their meaning, a specific day to "every" one of those days. For example:

> **La domenica andavamo dalla nonna.** (lah doh-*meh*-nee-kah ahn-dah-*vah*-moh *dahl*-lah *nohn*-nah.) (*Every Sunday, we used to go to Grandmother's.*)

> **Il lunedì vado a scuola.** (eel looh-neh-*dee vah*-doh ah *skwoh*-lah.) (*Every Monday, I go to school.*)

> **Il sabato non lavorano.** (eel *sah*-bah-toh nohn lah-*voh*-rah-noh.) (*They don't work on Saturdays.*)

> **Chiuso il mercoledì.** (*kyooh*-soh eel mehr-koh-leh-*dee*.) (*Closed Wednesdays.*)

Months and seasons of the year

Being able to express the day will get you only so far; you also need to know the months of the year, which are listed in Table 2-4. As with days of the week, the months aren't capitalized in Italian.

Table 2-4	Months of the Year	
Italian	*Pronunciation*	*Translation*
gennaio	jehn-*nah*-yoh	*January*
febbraio	fehb-*brah*-yoh	*February*
marzo	*mahr*-tsoh	*March*
aprile	ah-*pree*-leh	*April*

Italian	Pronunciation	Translation
maggio	*mahj*-joh	May
giugno	*jooh*-nyoh	June
luglio	*looh*-lyoh	July
agosto	ah-*gohs*-toh	August
settembre	seht-*tehm*-breh	September
ottobre	oht-*toh*-breh	October
novembre	noh-*vehm*-breh	November
dicembre	dee-*chehm*-breh	December

To remember which months have 31, 30, or 28 (sometimes 29) days, this children's rhyme can help:

> **Trenta giorni ha novembre, con aprile, giugno e settembre. Di ventotto ce n'è uno. Tutti gli altri ne han trentuno.** (*trehn*-tah *johr*-nee ah noh-*vehm*-breh kohn ah-*pree*-leh *jooh*-nyoh eh seht-*tehm*-breh. dee vehn-*toht*-toh cheh neh *ooh*-noh. *tooht*-tee lyee *ahl*-tree neh ahn trehn-*tooh*-noh.) (*Thirty days hath November, with April, June, and September. With twenty-eight days there is but one. All the others have thirty-one.*)

Half of the seasons in Italian are feminine, and the other half are masculine. And, like the days of the week and months of the year, they're not capitalized.

- **la primavera** (lah pree-mah-*veh*-rah) (*spring*)
- **l'estate** (leh-*stah*-teh) (*summer*)
- **l'autunno** (lou-*toohn*-noh) (*fall; autumn*)
- **l'inverno** (leen-*vehr*-noh) (*winter*)

To say *during the summer* or *winter* or whichever season, you say

- **in estate** (een eh-*stah*-teh) (*during/in the summer*)
- **in inverno** (een een-*vehr*-noh) (*during/in the winter*)

Specific dates

In Italian, you use cardinal numbers to express a specific date, except for the first day of the month. For example:

> **Oggi è il primo settembre.** (*ohj*-jee eh eel *pree*-moh seht-*tehm*-breh.) (*Today is September 1st.*)

Domani sarà il due. (doh-*mah*-nee sah-*rah* eel *dooh*-eh.) (*Tomorrow is the 2nd.*)

Il mio compleanno è il quattro settembre. (eel *mee*-oh kohm-pleh-*ahn*-noh eh eel *kwaht*-troh seht-*tehm*-breh.) (*My birthday is September 4th.*)

Loro si sposano l'otto giugno. (*loh*-roh see *spoh*-sah-noh *loht*-toh *jooh*-nyoh.) (*They are getting married June 8th.*)

Here are a few more specifics on how to note dates in Italian:

✔ The day and numbers always precede the name of the month.

> **Lunedì, 12 maggio, è il suo compleanno.** (looh-neh-*dee*, doh-dee-chee *mahj*-joh, eh eel *sooh*-oh kohm-pleh-*ahn*-noh.) (*Monday, May 12th, is his birthday.*)

> **Ma il suo onomastico è il 4 novembre.** (mah eel *sooh*-oh oh-noh-*mah*-stee-koh eh eel *kwaht*-troh noh-*vehm*-breh.) (*But his Saint's Day is November 4th.*)

✔ When you make a date or an appointment in Italian, as in English, you want to specify the day, the month, and the date. For example, you may want to fill in your own calendar with appointments as you discover how to say the dates.

> **Domenica, undici maggio, vado a una festa.** (doh-*meh*-nee-kah, *oohn*-dee-chee *mahj*-joh, *vah*-doh ah *ooh*-nah *feh*-stah.) (*Sunday, May 11th, I'm going to a party.*)

✔ To add a year to a date, put it after the day, number, and month.

> **giovedì, 4 settembre 1947** (joh-veh-*dee*, *kwaht*-troh seht-*tehm*-breh *meel*-leh-noh-veh-*chen*-toh-kwah-rahn-tah-*seht*-the) (*Thursday, September 4, 1947*)

> **l'undici ottobre 2006** (*loohn*-dee-chee oht-*toh*-breh dooh-eh-*mee*-lah-sey) (*October 11, 2006*)

To place something *in* a specific year, you use the contracted preposition **nel** (*in the*).

> **Luisa è nata nel 1983.** (looh-*ee*-sah eh *nah*-tah nehl *meel*-leh-noh-veh-*chen*-toht-than-tah-*treh*.) (*Luisa was born in 1983.*)

Generally, you abbreviate dates in the same order you write them. In Italian, that means day/month/year. Sometimes, you may see the month written with a Roman numeral. Also, periods are often used instead of slashes. So you can write December 10, 2012, as

10 dicembre, 2012

10/12/2012 or **10.12.2012**

10/XII/2012 or **10.XII.2012**

To ask questions about dates, the following expressions may prove useful.

Che giorno è oggi? (keh *johr*-noh *eh ohj*-jee?) (*What day is today?*)

E domani? (eh doh-*mah*-nee?) (*And tomorrow?*)

E ieri? (eh *yeh*-ree?) (*And yesterday?*)

E l'altro ieri? (eh *lahl*-troh *yeh*-ree?) (*And the day before yesterday?*)

E dopo domani? (eh *doh*-poh doh-*mah*-nee?) (*And the day after tomorrow?*)

Quando è il tuo compleanno? (*kwahn*-doh *eh* eel twoh kohm-pleh-*ahn*-noh?) (*When is your birthday?*)

Talkin' the Talk

Sarah is doing a home stay with an Italian family in Castellaneta. They are getting to know each other. (Track 3)

Host Mom:	**Sarah, quanti fratelli hai?** *sah*-rah, *kwahn*-tee frah-*tehl*-lee ahy? *Sarah, how many brothers and sisters do you have?*
Sarah:	**Ho un fratello e due sorelle.** oh oohn *frah*-tehl-loh eh *dweh* soh-*rehl*-leh. *I have one brother and two sisters.*
Host Mom:	**Quanti anni hanno?** *kwahn*-tee *ahn*-nee *ahn*-noh? *How old are they?*
Sarah:	**Mio fratello David ha dodici anni.** *mee*-oh frah-*tehl*-loh David ah *doh*-dee-chee *ahn*-nee. *My brother David is 12.* **Mia sorella Rebecca ne ha diciannove, e mia sorella Naomi ne ha 21.** *mee*-ah soh-*rehl*-lah Rebecca neh hah *deech*-ahn-*noh*-veh, eh *mee*-ah soh-*rehl*-lah Naomi neh ah vehn-*tooh*-noh. *My sister Rebecca is 19, and my sister Naomi is 21.*
Host Mom:	**E quando è il tuo compleanno?** eh *kwahn*-doh eh eel *tooh*-oh kohm-pleh-*ahn*-noh? *And when is your birthday?*
Sarah:	**Il ventidue maggio.** eel *vehn*-tee-*dweh mahj*-joh. *May 22.*

Host Mom:	**Quanto dista casa tua da New York?**
	kwahn-toh *dee*-stah *cah*-sah *tooh*-ah dah New York?
	How far is your house from New York?
Sarah:	**Centoventi chilometri più o meno.**
	chehn-toh-*vehn*-tee kee-*loh*-meh-tree pyooh oh
	meh-noh.
	120 kilometers, more or less.

Words to Know

quanti	kwahn-tee	how many
quanto	kwahn-toh	how much
numero	nooh-mehr-oh	number
anni	ahn-nee	years
quando	kwahn-doh	when
compleanno	kohm-pleh-ahn-noh	birthday
giorno	johr-noh	day
mese	meh-zeh	month

Telling Time

After getting familiar with the numbers in Italian (see the earlier sections in this chapter), you can use them to tell time. For telling time, you need to be able to count to 60.

To ask the time, you can say, **Che ora è?** (keh *oh*-rah eh?) or **Che ore sono?** (keh *oh*-reh *soh*-noh?) (*What hour is it?*) (*What hours?*) For 1:00, noon, or midnight, the answers are **È l'una** (eh *looh*-nah), **È mezzogiorno** (eh *medz*-oh-*johr*-noh), and **È mezzanotte** (eh *medz*-ah-*noht*-teh), respectively. All other hours need **sono** (*it is*) before the hour(s), as shown in the following examples.

✔ **Che ora è?** (keh *oh*-rah eh?) (*What time is it?*)

✔ **Sono le due.** (*soh*-noh leh *dooh*-eh.) (*It's 2:00.*)

✔ **Sono le tre.** (*soh*-noh leh treh.) (*It's 3:00.*)

✔ **Sono le quattro.** (*soh*-noh leh *kwaht*-troh.) (*It's 4:00.*)

✔ **Sono le cinque.** (*soh*-noh les *cheen*-qweh.) (*It's 5:00.*)

✔ **Sono le sei.** (*soh*-noh les sey.) (*It's 6:00.*)

✔ **Sono le sette.** (*soh*-noh leh *seht*-teh.) (*It's 7:00.*)

✔ **Sono le otto.** (*soh*-noh leh *oht*-toh.) (*It's 8:00.*)

✔ **Sono le nove.** (*soh*-noh leh *noh*-veh.) (*It's 9:00.*)

✔ **Sono le dieci.** (*soh*-noh les *dyeh*-chee.) (*It's 10:00.*)

✔ **Sono le undici.** (*soh*-noh leh *oohn*-dee-chee.) (*It's 11:00.*)

✔ **Sono le dodici.** (*soh*-noh leh *doh*-dee-chee.) (*It's 12:00.*)

✔ **È mezzogiorno.** (eh *medz*-oh-*johr*-noh.) (*It's noon.*)

✔ **È mezzanotte.** (eh *medz*-ah-*noht*-teh.) (*It's midnight.*)

✔ **È l'una.** (eh *looh*-nah.) (*It's 1:00.*)

If you're following the 24-hour clock, used for anything official — office hours; train, bus, plane arrivals and departures; or theater opening times — continue counting through **ventiquattro** (vehn-tee-*kwaht*-troh) (*twenty four*). Thus, 5:00 in the morning remains **le cinque** (leh *cheen*-kweh), but, 5:00 in the afternoon becomes **le diciassette** (leh dee-chahs-*seht*-teh) (*seventeen*). Another way to make clear the difference between morning and afternoon or evening is to add **di mattina** (dee maht-*tee*-nah) (*morning*) or **del pomeriggio** (dehl poh-meh-*reej*-joh) (*early afternoon*) or **di sera** (dee *seh*-rah) (*evening*). These divisions are somewhat arbitrary: **Mattina** (maht-*tee*-nah) (*morning*) usually lasts until lunch; **pomeriggio** (poh-meh-*reej*-joh) (*afternoon*), until 4:00 or 5:00 p.m.; and **sera** (*seh*-rah) (*evening*), until one goes to bed.

One easy way to convert time is to subtract 12 from it. So 19.00 – 12.00 gives you 7, which is the time on the 12-hour clock.

When times are written numerically, Italian uses a period to separate the hour from the minutes, so the English *2:15* becomes **2.15**.

Here are a few other considerations to keep in mind when telling time in Italian:

✔ In general, you add the first 30 minutes of the hour to that hour.

    Sono le due e dieci. (*soh*-noh leh dweh eh *dyeh*-chee.) (*It's 2:10.*)

> **Sono le quattro e venti.** (*soh*-noh leh *kwaht*-troh eh *vehn*-tee.) (*It's 4:20.*)

✔ You subtract the second half hour's minutes from the top of the hour.

> **Sono le dieci meno venti.** (*soh*-noh leh *dyeh*-chee *meh*-noh *vehn*-tee.) (*It's 9:40.*) (*It's 20 until 10.*)

✔ Instead of saying **quindici** (*kween*-dee-chee) (*15 minutes*), you can add on **un quarto** (oohn *kwahr*-toh) (*a quarter of an hour*).

> **Sono le cinque e un quarto.** (*soh*-noh leh *cheen*-kweh eh oohn *kwahr*-toh.) (*It's 5:15.*)

✔ When referring to half past the hour, you can say **mezzo** (*meh*-dzoh) (*half*) instead of **trenta** (*trehn*-tah) (*thirty*), although more and more, one hears **mezza** (*meh*-dzah) instead of **mezzo** (*meh*-dzoh), evidently referring to the feminine **ora** (*oh*-rah).

> **È l'una e mezzo.** (eh *looh*-nah eh *meh*-dzoh.) (*It's 1:30.*)

✔ You may hear times that continue counting past 30 minutes and not simply with reference to the 24-hour clock.

> **Sono le due e quarantacinque.** (*soh*-noh leh dweh eh kwah-*rahn*-tah-*cheen*-kweh.) (*It's 2:45.*)

✔ To ask at what time something is to happen, you say, **A che ora . . . ?** (ah keh *oh*-rah . . . ?) (*At what time . . .?*) The reply is **all'** (ahl) (for **una**) (*ooh*-nah), **a** (ah) (for **mezzanotte** or **mezzogiorno**) (meh-dzah-*noht*-teh or meh-dzoh-*johr*-noh), or **alle** (*ahl*-leh) (all mean *at*) and a number. You can also say **verso le due** (*vehr*-soh leh *dooh*-eh) (*around two*), for example.

✔ When talking about time, you often make reference to something that has already happened, is about to happen, or will happen as a result of something else. To that end, the following expressions may prove useful.

- **Prima** (*pree*-mah) (*first*): **Prima mangiamo.** (*pree*-mah mahn-*jah*-moh.) (*First we'll eat.*)

- **Poi** (pohy) (*then*): **Poi andiamo.** (pohy ahn-*dyah*-moh.) (*Then we'll go.*)

- **Dopo** (*doh*-poh) (*after*): **Dopo parleremo.** (*doh*-poh pahr-leh-*reh*-moh.) (*Afterward, we'll talk.*)

- **Fra** (frah) (*within*): **Fra mezz'ora** (frah mehdz-*dzoh*-rah) (*Within half an hour*).

- **Più tardi** (pyooh *tahr*-dee) (*later*): **Piu tardi li vedremo.** (pyooh *tahr*-dee lee veh-*dreh*-moh.) (*Later, we'll see them.*) and **A più tardi** (ah pyooh *tahr*-dee) (*Until later*).

✔ **Il mezzogiorno** (eel *mehdz*-dzoh-*johr*-noh) (*noon; midday*) also refers to the southern regions of Italy, including the islands of Sicily and Sardinia. It's frequently used in publications (newspapers, magazines, and so forth) to refer to the area, approximately, south of Rome.

Talkin' the Talk

 Alex and Marco are waiting for Lella, Marco's sister, to go downtown to the best **gelateria** (jeh-lah-teh-*ryah*) (*ice-cream parlor*) in town. Lella is late. (Track 4)

Alex: **Come mai Lella ancora non si vede?**
koh-meh may *lehl*-lah ahn-*koh*-rah nohn see
veh-deh?
Why is Lella not here yet?

Marco: **Sai com'e' Lella; per lei l'orologio è soltanto un accessorio-moda.**
sah-ee koh-*meh lehl*-lah; pehr ley loh-roh-*loh*-joh eh
sohl-*tahn*-toh oohn ahch-chehs-*soh*-ryoh-*moh*-dah.
You know how Lella is; watches are only a fashion accessory for her.

Alex: **Ma avevamo appuntamento alle 4! Che ore sono adesso?**
mah ah-veh-*vah*-moh ahp-poohn-tah-*mehn*-toh *ahl*-
leh *kwaht*-troh! keh *oh*-reh *soh*-noh ah-*dehs*-soh?
But we were supposed to meet at 4! What time is it now?

Marco: **Le 4 o le 5, che cambia? Comunque sono le 4:35.**
leh *kwaht*-troh oh leh *cheen*-kweh, keh *kahm*-byah?
koh-*moohn*-kweh *soh*-noh leh *kwaht*-troh eh
trehn-tah-*cheen*-kweh.
4 or 5, what does it matter? If you really want to know, it's 4:35.

Alex: **Tu sarai anche abituato ai suoi ritardi, ma io no. Adesso la chiamo.**
tooh sah-*rah*-ee *ahn*-keh ah-bee-*twah*-toh ay swohy
ree-*tahr*-dee, mah ee-oh noh. ah-*dehs*-soh lah
kyah-moh.
You might be used to her tardiness, but I'm not. I'm going to call her.

Marco:	**Aspetta, ha appena mandato un messaggio . . . dice "ci vediamo direttamente in gelateria prima della chiusura. Poi vi spiego — Lella."** ah-*speht*-tah, ah ahp-*peh*-nah mahn-*dah*-toh oohn mehs-*sahj*-joh . . . *dee*-cheh "chee veh-*dyah*-moh dee-reht-tah-*mehn*-teh een geh-lah-teh-*ryah* pree-mah *dehl*-lah kyooh-*sooh*-rah. pohy vee *spyeh*-goh — *lehl*-lah." *Wait, she just sent a message . . . it says, "I'll meet you directly at the ice-cream parlor before it closes. I'll explain later — Lella."*
Alex:	**Prima della chiusura? Cioè alle 19:30! Che facciamo per tre ore?** *pree*-mah *dehl*-lah kyooh-*sooh*-rah? choh-*eh ahl*-leh dee-chahn-*noh*-veh eh *trehn*-tah! keh fahch-*chah*-moh pehr treh *oh*-reh? *Before it closes? That's at 7:30 p.m.! What are we going to do for three hours?*
Marco:	**Io una idea ce l'avrei: mangiamo gelato!** ee-oh ooh-nee-*deh*-ah cheh lah-*vreh*-ee: mahn-*jah*-moh jeh-*lah*-toh! *I have an idea: Let's eat some ice cream!*
Alex:	**Quanto gelato si potrà mangiare in 180 minuti? Boh, lo sapremo presto. Mi piace; ci sto!** *kwahn*-toh jeh-*lah*-toh see poh-*trah* mahn-*jah*-reh een *chen*-toht-*tahn*-tah mee-*nooh*-tee? boh, loh sah-*preh*-moh *preh*-stoh. mee *pyah*-cheh; chee stoh! *How much ice cream can we eat in 180 minutes? Well, we'll find it out soon. I like it; I'm in!*

Familiarizing Yourself with the Metric System

If you're like most Americans, the metric system quite simply defeats you. The decimal system is practically hard-wired into U.S. residents. It's used almost exclusively, outside of scientific fields. So what do you really need to know about the metric system? The temperature would be nice. So would knowing how much of something to buy in the food market or at the gas station. If you're cooking, being able to convert oven temperatures may be useful. Likewise, knowing how to figure out the body's temperature is helpful.

Converting the temperature to/from Celsius

To convert Fahrenheit to Centigrade, or Celsius, degrees, and Celsius to Fahrenheit, the following formula will suffice:

Fahrenheit degrees

Subtract 32

Remainder

Multiply by 0.556

Celsius degrees

So, for example, say you want to figure out how many Celsius degrees 100 degrees Fahrenheit is. Just plug the numbers into the formula to find the answer:

$$
\begin{array}{r}
100 \\
-32 \\
\hline
68 \\
\times 0.556 \\
\hline
37.7
\end{array}
$$

Then to convert Celsius degrees to Fahrenheit, you use this formula:

Celsius degrees

Add 17.8

Total

Multiply by 1.8

Fahrenheit degrees

Using the result of the earlier example, you can convert the Celsius degrees back to Fahrenheit like this:

$$
\begin{array}{r}
37.7 \\
+17.8 \\
\hline
55.5 \\
\times 1.8 \\
\hline
99.9
\end{array}
$$

This conversion works for oven temperatures (it's probably useful to know that the ever popular 350-degree Fahrenheit is about 180 degrees Celsius), for body temperatures (an Italian thermometer is normal when it reads 37 degrees Celsius), and for discussing the weather (38 degrees Celsius is *hot;* −20 degrees Celsius is way too cold to be out and walking about).

Measuring in metric units

A dual scale (in grams and ounces) and dual measuring cups are invaluable as you try to cook with metric measures. As for weights and measures, a *kilogram* is about 2.2 pounds.

When you go to the market, you'll want to be familiar with these metric conversions:

✔ If you're buying meats, fish, or cheeses and want about a pound, a **mezzo chilo** (*mehdz*-dzoh *kee*-loh) (*half kilo*) should be about right. Loaves of bread tend to weigh about the same, a **mezzo chilo.**

✔ Vegetables are a little harder to measure, so you may want to use the old standbys: **una manciata** (*ooh*-nah mahn-*chah*-tah) (*a handful*), **due manciate** (dweh mahn-*chah*-teh) (*two handfuls*), **un ciuffo** (oohn *choohf*-foh) (*a tuft*), **due ciuffi** (dweh *choohf*-fee) (*two tufts*), **un cespo** (oohn *cheh*-spoh) (*a head*), **due cespi** (dweh *cheh*-spee) (*two heads*), **un mazzo** (oohn *mahts*-tsoh) (*a bunch*), **due mazzi** (dweh *mahts*-tsee) (*two bunches*). Use **ciuffo/ciuffi** for herbs, like parsley and basil, and **cespo/ cespi** for heads of lettuce and other green-leaf vegetables. Remember that you're not the one picking out the vegetables and fruits; that is, you're not handling them — that's the greengrocer's job. You simply *do not touch* the fruit and vegetables on offer.

✔ For cold cuts, knowing that **un etto** (oohn *eht*-toh) equals 100 grams, or about 3.5 ounces, should be sufficient information. If you're especially hungry, **due etti di prosciutto crudo** (dweh *eht*-tee dee proh-*shooht*-toh *crooh*-doh) (*200 grams, or 7 ounces, of prosciutto*) is about right.

Here are a few other situations where knowing the metric system will come in handy:

✔ If you need to buy gasoline for your car (**benzina** [behn-*dzee*-nah], not **gasolio** [gah-*soh*-lyoh] which refers to *diesel fuel*), you need to know how to convert liters to gallons. One liter multiplied by 0.26420 equals about a quarter of a gallon. So four liters are a little more than a gallon. Close enough?

✔ To convert miles into kilometers, multiply the number of miles by 1.60934. For example, if you want to drive 60 miles per hour, that will come out to 96.6 kilometers per hour on your speedometer. In other words, if something is 100 kilometers away, it's only a little more than 60 miles.

✔ To know whether your weight is holding steady, 1 pound is 0.4536 kilos. If you're used to weighing 180 pounds, it can be a bit of a shock to see your weight "drop" precipitously, to its kilo equivalent of 82.

Chapter 3

Buongiorno! Salutations!

In This Chapter

▶ Saying hello and goodbye

▶ Introducing yourself and others

▶ Describing where you come from

▶ Extending and accepting invitations

Buongiorno! (bwohn-*johr*-noh!) (*Hello!*)

Have you ever counted the number of times you say hello in a single day? You probably say it more often than you realize. When you interact with people, you usually begin with a greeting — and that greeting can have an impact on the first impression you give. This chapter explains how to say hello and goodbye as well as how to supplement a greeting with some basic small talk.

Looking at Common Greetings and Goodbyes

Italians like to have social contact and meet new people. Generally, they're easygoing and receptive to people trying to speak their language. At the same time, they tend to be very respectful and polite.

To give you a good start in greeting people in Italian, the following sections provide the most common greetings and goodbyes, along with some examples.

Issuing a greeting

You can use **ciao** (chou) and **salve** (*sahl*-veh) to mean *hello,* and **ciao** can also mean *goodbye.* **Ciao** is informal; **salve** is neutral but more formal than **ciao.** For example:

Ciao Claudio! (chou *klou*-dyoh!) (*Hi/Bye, Claudio!*)

Salve ragazzi! (*sahl*-veh rah-*gaht*-tsee!) (*Hi, folks!*) (*Hey, guys!*)

Salve is a relic from Latin. In Caesar's time, the Romans used it a lot.

Buongiorno (bwohn *johr*-noh) (*good morning;* literally: g*ood day*) and **buonasera** (*bwoh*-nah-*seh*-rah) (*good afternoon/evening*) are both formal greetings — your best bet whenever you're in doubt. Which one you use depends on the time of day: Before 12 p.m., use **buongiorno**; after 12 p.m., **buonasera** is the appropriate choice. Just mind the time of day!

> **Buongiorno, Signora Bruni!** (bwohn *johr*-noh, see-*nyoh*-rah *brooh*-nee!) (*Good morning, Mrs. Bruni!*)

> **Buonasera, signor Rossi!** (*bwoh*-nah-*seh*-rah, see-*nyohr rohs*-see!) (*Good afternoon/evening, Mr. Rossi!*)

You frequently hear **Buongiorno!** when you enter an Italian shop.

Arrivederci (ahr-ree-veh-*dehr*-chee) (*goodbye*) and **buonanotte** (*bwoh*-nah-*noht*-teh) (*good night*) are parting terms. (Use **buonanotte** only when you're parting for the night and going to bed.)

> **Arrivederci, signora Eva!** (ahr-ree-veh-*dehr*-chee, see-*nyoh*-rah *eh*-vah!) (*Goodbye, Mrs. Eva!*)

> **Buonanotte, ragazzi!** (*bwoh*-nah-*noht*-teh, rah-*gaht*-tsee!) (*Good night, guys!*)

You can use the phrases **Buona giornata** (*bwoh*-nah johr-*nah*-tah) (*Have a good day*) and **Buona serata** (*bwoh*-nah seh-*rah*-tah) (*Have a good evening*) when you're leaving a friend or saying goodbye on the phone. The difference is that, according to Italian custom, **buona serata** is more appropriate after 6 p.m.

Using body language

In Italy, people who are familiar with each other, such as family and friends, commonly hug and kiss on both cheeks. Italians kiss twice: once right, once left.

Another common physical greeting is the more formal handshake. You shake hands with people you meet for the first time and with those you don't know well.

Deciding between formal and friendly

In Chapter 1 of Book III, you see some of the differences between using the **tu, voi, lei,** and **Loro** pronouns and verbs when you want to say *you*.

An important feature of Italian culture is that you can address people in one of two ways:

- ✔ **With people you don't know:** You generally use the formal form of address — **lei** (ley) (*you* [singular]) — with adults you don't know, such as businesspeople (waiters, shopkeepers), officials, and persons of higher rank (for example, supervisors, teachers, professors, older people, and so on). With children or among young people, you use the informal **tu** (tooh) (*you* [singular]).

- ✔ **With people you do know:** When you get to know someone better, depending on your relationship, you may switch to the informal form of address — **tu.** You also use the informal form with members of your family, friends, and children.

If you travel to Italy and make new friends, you may be asked these informal questions:

- ✔ **Sei appena arrivato? Di dove sei?** (sehy ahp-*peh*-nah ahr-ree-*vah*-toh? dee *doh*-veh *seh*-ee?) (*Have you just arrived? Where are you from?*)

- ✔ **Ti piace l'Italia?** (tee *pyah*-cheh lee-*tah*-lee-ah?) (*Do you like Italy?*)

- ✔ **Sei qui per la prima volta?** (sehy kwee pehr lah *pree*-mah *vohl*-tah?) (*Is this your first time here?*)

- ✔ **Sei qui in vacanza?** (sehy kwee een vah-*kahn*-tsah?) (*Are you on vacation?*)

- ✔ **Quanto rimani?** (*kwahn*-toh ree-*mah*-nee?) (*How long are you staying?*)

Replying to a greeting

When you reply to a greeting in English, you often say "How are you?" as a way of saying "Hello" — you don't expect an answer. In Italian, however, this is not the case; the greeting calls for an answer. Following are common ways to reply to particular greetings.

Book I

Speaking Italian in Everyday Settings

✔ **Formal greeting and reply:**

Greeting: **Buongiorno signora, come sta?** (bwohn-*johr*-noh see-*nyoh*-rah, *koh*-meh stah?) (*Hello, ma'am, how are you?*)

Reply: **Benissimo, grazie, e Lei?** (beh-*nees*-see-moh, *grah*-tsyeh, eh ley?) (*Very well, thank you, and you?*)

✔ **Informal greeting and reply:**

Greeting: **Ciao, Roberto, come stai?** (chou, roh-*behr*-toh, *koh*-meh stahy?) (*Hi, Roberto, how are you?*)

Reply: **Bene, grazie, e tu?** (*beh*-neh, *grah*-tsee-eh, eh tooh?) (*Fine, thanks, and you?*)

✔ **Another typical, rather informal, greeting and reply:**

Greeting: **Come va?** (*koh*-meh *vah?*) (*How are things?*)

Reply: **Non c'è male.** (nohn cheh *mah*-leh.) (*Not bad.*)

Specifying your reunion

Sometimes, you want to say more than just goodbye; you want to specify when you'll meet again. The following expressions are common and also can be used as goodbyes on their own:

✔ **A presto!** (ah *prehs*-toh!) (*See you soon!*)

✔ **A dopo!** (ah *doh*-poh!) (*See you later!*)

✔ **A domani!** (ah doh-*mah*-nee!) (*See you tomorrow!*)

✔ **Ci vediamo!** (chee veh-*dyah*-moh!) (*See you!*)

You can also combine **Ci vediamo** with other phrases. For example:

• **Ci vediamo presto!** (chee veh-*dyah*-moh *prehs*-toh!) (*See you soon!*)

• **Ci vediamo dopo!** (chee veh-*dyah*-moh *doh*-poh!) (*See you later!*)

• **Ci vediamo domani!** (chee veh-*dyah*-moh doh-*mah*-nee!) (*See you tomorrow!*)

Making Introductions

It's important to be able to introduce yourself to someone and to answer questions about who you are and where you're from.

Whether to use first or last names as well as formal and informal registers are important considerations. In a job situation, you usually use last names, whereas at private functions, people are more likely to tell you their first names. The fact that someone gives you his or her first name, however, does not necessarily mean that you should use the informal **tu** (tooh) (*you*); using a person's first name with the formal form of address is quite common. Usually, the older person proposes making the switch to the informal form.

Introducing yourself

We want to familiarize you with an important reflexive verb, **chiamarsi** (kyah-*mahr*-see) (*to call oneself*), which you use to introduce yourself and to ask others for their names. Here are the present-tense forms of this important verb.

Conjugation	Pronunciation	Meaning
mi chiamo	mee *kyah*-moh	*My name is*
ti chiami	tee *kyah*-mee	*Your name is*
si chiama	see *kyah*-mah	*Your/his/her/name is*
ci chiamiamo	chee kyah-*myah*-moh	*Our names are*
vi chiamate	vee kyah-*mah*-teh	*Your names are*
si chiamano	see kyah-*mah*-noh	*Their names are*

So that you can get the hang of the verb **chiamarsi**, practice these easy examples. Just change your intonation and word order, and you can ask others for their name instead of telling them yours.

- ✔ **Ciao** (or **Buongiorno**), **mi chiamo Eva.** (chou/bwohn-*johr*-noh, mee *kyah*-moh *eh*-vah.) (*Hello, my name is Eva.*)
- ✔ **E tu come ti chiami?** (eh too *koh*-meh tee *kyah*-mee?) (*And what's your name?*)
- ✔ **Lei, come si chiama?** (lehy, *koh*-meh see *kyah*-mah?) (*What's your name?*)
- ✔ **Piacere!** (pyah-*cheh*-reh!) (with a quick handshake) is one way of saying *Nice to meet you!*

Incidentally, as in English, you can also introduce yourself simply by saying your name: **Io sono Pietro** (*ee*-oh *soh*-noh pyeh-troh) (*I'm Pietro*). Finally, you can just state your name, without the **Mi chiamo** (*My name is*) or **Sono** (*I am*), as shown in the sample dialogue that follows.

Talkin' the Talk

The people in this dialogue are colleagues assigned to work on the same project. They introduce themselves to each other.

Mr. Messa: **Carlo Messa. Piacere!**
kahr-loh *mehs*-sah. pyah-*cheh*-reh!
Carlo Messa. Nice to meet you!

Mr. Rossi: **Piacere, Marco Rossi.**
pyah-*cheh*-reh, *mahr*-koh *rohs*-see.
Nice to meet you, Marco Rossi.

Ms. Pertini: **Piacere. Sono Paola Pertini.**
pyah-*cheh*-reh. *soh*-noh *pah*-oh-lah pehr-*tee*-nee.
Nice to meet you. I'm Paola Pertini.

Ms. Salvi: **Lieta di conoscerla. Anna Salvi.**
lyeh-tah dee koh-*noh*-shehr-lah. *ahn*-nah *sahl*-vee.
Pleased to meet you. Anna Salvi.

Mr. Melis: **Mi chiamo Carlo Melis, piacere.**
mee *kyah*-moh *kahr*-loh *meh*-lees, pyah-*cheh*-reh.
My name is Carlo Melis, nice to meet you.

Mr. Foschi: **Molto lieto, Silvio Foschi.**
mohl-toh *lyeh*-tah, *seel*-vee-oh *fohs*-kee.
Very pleased to meet you, Silvio Foschi.

Children and young people forego ceremony and introduce themselves more casually, though still politely — something like this:

Ciao! Sono Giulio. (chou! *soh*-noh *jooh*-lee-oh.) (*Hello! I'm Giulio.*)

E io sono Giulia, piacere. (eh *ee*-oh *soh*-noh *jooh*-lee-ah, pyah-*cheh*-reh.) (*And I'm Giulia, nice to meet you.*)

The following example offers a very informal introduction, used only in a very casual situation, such as on the beach or at a club:

Come ti chiami? (*koh*-meh tee-*kyah*-mee?) (*What's your name?*)

Chiara. E tu? (*kyah*-rah. eh tooh?) (*Chiara. And yours?*)

Amedeo. (ah-meh-*deh*-oh.) (*Amedeo.*)

Introducing other people

Sometimes you not only have to introduce yourself, but also introduce some-one to your friends or to other people.

The following vocabulary may be helpful in making introductions. With it, you can indicate the relationship between you and the person you're intro-ducing. Gesturing toward the person and simply saying **mio fratello** (*mee*-oh frah-*tehl*-loh) means, quite simply, *This is my brother.* Following are some other common relationships you may want to reference:

- ✔ **mia sorella** (*mee*-ah soh-*rehl*-lah) (*my sister*)

- ✔ **mia figlia** (*mee*-ah *fee*-lyah) (*my daughter*)

- ✔ **mio figlio** (*mee*-oh *fee*-lyoh) (*my son*)

- ✔ **mio marito** (*mee*-oh mah-*ree*-toh) (*my husband*)

- ✔ **mia moglie** (*mee*-ah *moh*-lyee-eh) (*my wife*)

- ✔ **mia madre** (*mee*-ah *mah*-dreh) (*my mother*)

- ✔ **mio padre** (*mee*-oh *pah*-dreh) (*my father*)

- ✔ **la mia amica/il mio amico** (lah *mee*-ah ah-*mee*-kah/eel *mee*-oh ah-*mee*-koh) (*my friend* [feminine/masculine]) Sometimes this term also means *my girlfriend* or *my boyfriend.*

- ✔ **la mia ragazza/il mio ragazzo** (lah *mee*-ah rah-*gat*-tsah/eel *mee*-oh rah-*gat*-tsoh) (*my girlfriend/my boyfriend*)

- ✔ **la mia fidanzata/il mio fidanzato** (lah *mee*-ah fee-dahn-*zah*-tah/eel *mee*-oh fee-dahn-*zah*-toh) (*my fiancée/fiancé* [feminine/masculine])

    The words **fidanzata/fidanzato** and **ragazza/ragazzo** are sometimes interchangeable for Italian people.

- ✔ **il mio collega** (eel *mee*-oh kohl-*leh*-gah) (*my colleague* [masculine])

- ✔ **la mia collega** (lah *mee*-ah kohl-*leh*-gah) (*my colleague* [feminine])

To make life easier, you can use the verb **presentare** (preh-*sehn*-tah-reh) (*to introduce*), as in these examples:

> **Ti presento mia moglie, Teresa.** (tee preh-*sehn*-toh *mee*-ah *mohl*-yeh, Teh-*reh*-sah.) (*Let me introduce you* [informal] *to my wife, Teresa.*)

> **Le presento mia suocera, Mary.** (leh preh-*sehn*-toh *mee*-ah *swoh*-chehr-ah, *Meh*-ree.) (*Let me introduce you* [formal] *to my mother-in-law, Mary.*)

Talkin' the Talk

 Friends can be informal with one another. Here Teresa bumps into her old friend Marinella. Both are married now and introduce their husbands. (Track 5)

Marinella: **Ciao, Teresa, come stai?**
chou, teh-*reh*-zah, *koh*-meh stahy?
Hello, Teresa. How are you?

Teresa: **Bene, grazie.**
beh-neh, *grah*-tsyeh.
Well, thank you.

Sono contenta di vederti!
soh-noh con-*tehn*-tah dee veh-*dehr*-tee!
I'm happy to see you!

Marinella, ti presento mio marito, Giancarlo.
mah-ree-*nehl*-lah, tee preh-*zehn*-toh *mee*-oh mah-ree-toh, jahn-*kahr*-loh.
Marinella, I'd like to introduce you to my husband, Giancarlo.

Marinella: **Ciao, Giancarlo.**
chou, jahn-*kahr*-loh.
Hello, Giancarlo.

Giancarlo: **Piacere.**
pyah-*cheh*-reh.
Nice to meet you.

Marinella: **E questo è Gianni.**
eh *kwehs*-toh eh *jahn*-nee.
And this is Gianni.

Gianni: **Piacere.**
pyah-*cheh*-reh.
Nice to meet you.

Talking about Language, Countries, and Nationalities

Introducing yourself is the first step in getting to know someone. If you get a good feeling about the person and want to speak more, a conversation usually follows the introduction. This section tells you about the different topics you may talk about to get to know each other, including the language you speak and your nationality.

Finding out whether someone speaks Italian

Of course you'll want to practice your Italian anytime you speak with someone whose native language is Italian. You have an opportunity to try out your newly acquired smattering of Italian.

> **Parla/Parli italiano?** (*pahr*-lah/*pahr*-lee ee-tahl-ee-*ah*-noh?) (*Do you speak Italian?* [formal/informal])

> **Parla/Parli inglese?** (*pahr*-lah/*pahr*-lee een-*gleh*-seh?) (*Do you speak English?* [formal/informal])

A possible response to these questions is:

> **Lo parlo un po'.** (loh *pahr*-loh oohn poh.) (*I speak a little bit.*)

Talkin' the Talk

Ilaria and Carmen have recently gotten to know each other. Because Carmen isn't Italian, although she lives in Italy, Ilaria is curious to know how many languages she speaks.

Ilaria: **Quante lingue parli?**
kwahn-teh *leen*-gweh *pahr*-lee?
How many languages do you speak?

Carmen: **Tre: italiano, spagnolo e tedesco.**
treh: ee-tah-lee-*ah*-noh, spah-*nyoh*-loh eh teh-*dehs*-koh.
Three: Italian, Spanish, and German.

Ilaria:	**E qual è la tua lingua madre?**
	eh *kwah*-leh lah *tooh*-ah *leen*-gwah *mah*-dreh?
	And which is your mother tongue?
Carmen:	**Lo spagnolo.**
	loh spah-*nyoh*-loh.
	Spanish.
Ilaria:	**Tua madre è spagnola?**
	tooh-ah *mah*-dreh eh spah-*nyoh*-lah?
	Is your mother Spanish?
Carmen:	**Sì. E mio padre è austriaco.**
	see. eh *mee*-oh *pah*-dreh eh ous-*tree*-ah-koh.
	Yes. And my father is Austrian.

Talking about where you come from

You know how interesting it can be to meet people from other countries and of different nationalities. When you do, you may be asked where you're from in the following ways:

✔ **Da dove vieni?** (dah *doh*-veh *vyeh*-nee?) (*Where are you from?* [informal])

✔ **Di dove sei?** (dee *doh*-veh sey?) (*Where are you from?* [informal])

✔ **Da dove viene?** (dah *doh*-veh *vyeh*-neh?) (*Where are you from?*) (*Where do you come from?*) (*Where are you coming from?*) (formal)

✔ **Di dov'è?** (dee *doh*-veh?) (*Where are you from?* [formal])

This question can be used to inquire about either your place of birth or your residence. The context will help you decide which information to supply.

If you want to clearly state your residence, you can answer

Vengo da . . . (*vehn*-goh dah) (*I come from/I'm from . . .*)

If you want to clearly state your place of birth and/or your nationality, you can answer

Sono di . . . (*soh*-noh dee) (*I'm from . . .*)

So, for example, if George was born in New York but is living in Bruxelles, he'd reply with an answer like this:

> **Sono di New York e vengo da Bruxelles. Sono arrivato una set-timana fa!** (*soh*-noh dee New York eh *vehn*-goh dah Bruxelles. *soh*-noh ahr-ree-*vah*-toh *ooh*-nah seht-tee-*mah*-nah fah!) (*I am from New York and come from Bruxelles. I arrived a week ago!*)

Book I

Speaking Italian in Everyday Settings

Now you can play with these phrases. You can insert the names of continents, countries, cities, or places.

If you want to talk about provenance, the adjectives denoting nationalities come in handy. As you say in English, "Are you American?" you say the same in Italian:

> **È americano/a?** (eh ah-meh-ree-*kah*-noh/nah?) (*Are you American?* [masculine/feminine, formal])

> **Sei americano/a?** (sey ah-meh-ree-*kah*-noh/nah?) (*Are you American?* [masculine/feminine, informal])

In English, you must put the pronoun (*I, you, he, she, we,* and so on) in front of the verb. You may notice that this is not the case in Italian. Because the verb form is different for each pronoun, you can easily leave out the pronoun — you understand who is meant from the verb ending and from the context. You use the pronoun only when the subject isn't clear enough or when you want to emphasize a fact, as in this example:

> **Loro sono americani, ma io sono italiano.** (*loh*-roh *soh*-noh ah-meh-ree-*kah*-nee, mah *ee*-oh *soh*-noh ee-tahl-*yah*-noh.) (*They are Americans, but I am Italian.*)

Use adjectives ending in **-o** (singular) and **-i** (plural) to refer to males, and adjectives ending in **-a** (singular) and **-e** (plural) to refer to females. Adjectives that end in **-e** in the singular and adjectives that end in **-i** in the plural refer to both males and females.

Some adjectives indicating nationality end with **-e**: This form is both feminine and masculine. Table 3-1 gives some examples.

Table 3-1	Some Nationalities and Countries	
Nationality/ Country	**Pronunciation**	**Translation**
albanese/i	ahl-bah-*neh*-zeh/zee	*Albanian/Albanians*
Albania	ahl-bah-*nee*-ah	*Albania*

(continued)

Table 3-1 *(continued)*

Nationality/Country	Pronunciation	Translation
belga/i/ghe	*behl*-gah/jee/gheh	*Belgian* (m/f, sing./m, pl./f, pl.)
Belgio	*Behl*-joh	*Belgium*
cinese/i	chee-*neh*-zeh/zee	*Chinese* (sing./pl.)
Cina	*chee*-nah	*China*
francese/i	frahn-*cheh*-zeh/zee	*French* (sing./pl.)
Francia	*frahn*-chah	*France*
giapponese/i	jahp-poh-*neh*-zeh/zee	*Japanese* (sing./pl.)
Giappone	jahp-*poh*-neh	*Japan*
greco/a/ci/che	*greh*-koh/kah/chee/keh	*Greek* (m, sing./f, sing./m, pl./f, pl.)
Grecia	*Greh*-chah	*Greece*
Inghilterra	een-geel-*tehr*-rah	*England*
irlandese/i	eer-lahn-*deh*-zeh/zee	*Irish* (sing./pl.)
Irlanda	eer-*lahn*-dah	*Ireland*
olandese/i	oh-lahn-*deh*-zeh/zee	*Dutch* (sing./pl.)
olanda	oh-*lahn*-dah	*Holland*
portoghese/i	pohr-toh-*geh*-zeh/zee	*Portuguese* (sing./pl.)
Portogallo	pohr-toh-*gahl*-loh	*Portugal*
senegalese/i	seh-neh-gahl-*eh*-zeh/zee	*Senegalese* (sing./pl.)
Senegal	*seh*-neh-gahl	*Senegal*
svedese/i	sveh-*deh*-zeh/zee	*Swedish* (sing./pl.)
Svezia	*sveh*-tsyah	*Sweden*

In other cases, nationalities have feminine, masculine, plural feminine, and plural masculine forms, and end in **-a, -o, -e,** and **-i,** as Table 3-2 shows.

Table 3-2   Gender-Specific Nationalities and Countries

Nationality/Country	Pronunciation	Translation
americana/o/e/i	ah-meh-ree-*kah*-nah/noh/neh/nee	*American/Americans (from the Americas)*
statunitense/i	stah-tooh-nee-*tehn*-seh/see	*American/Americans (exclusively from the United States)*

Nationality/ Country	Pronunciation	Translation
America	ah-*meh*-ree-kah	*The Americas*
Stati Uniti d'America	*stah*-tee ooh-*nee*-tee dah-*meh*-ree-kah	*United States of America*
australiana/o/e/i	ou-strahl-*yah*-nah/noh/ neh/nee	*Australian/Australians*
Australia	ou-strahl-*yah*	*Australia*
brasiliana/o/e/i	brah-see-*lyah*-nah/noh/ neh/nee	*Brazilian/Brazilians*
Brasile	brah-*see*-leh	*Brazil*
greca/greco/ greci/greche	*greh*-kah/koh/chee/keh	*Greek/Greeks*
Grecia	*greh*-chah	*Greece*
italiana/o/e/i	ee-tah-lee-*ah*-nah/noh/ neh/nee	*Italian/Italians*
Italia	ee-*tah*-lee-ah	*Italy*
marocchina/o/e/i	mah-*rohk*-kee-nah/noh/ neh/nee	*Moroccan/Moroccans*
Marocco	mah-*rohk*-koh	*Morocco*
messicano/a/e/i	meh-see-*kah*-nah/noh/ neh/nee	*Mexican/Mexicans*
Messico	*meh*-see-koh	*Mexico*
polacco/polacca/ polacchi/ polacche	poh-*lah*-koh/kah/kee/keh	*Polish* (sing./pl.)
Polonia	poh-*loh*-nee-ah	*Poland*
rumeno/a/i/e	rooh-*meh*-nah/noh/neh/ nee	*Romanian/Romanians*
Romania	roh-mah-*nee*-ah	*Romania*
russa/o/e/i	*roohs*-sah/soh/seh/see	*Russian/Russians*
Russia	*roos*-see-ah	*Russia*
spagnola/o/e/i	spah-*nyoh*-lah/loh/leh/lee	*Spanish* (sing./pl.)
Spagna	*spah*-nyah	*Spain*
svizzera/o/e/i	*sveet*-tseh-rah/roh/reh/ree	*Swiss* (sing./pl.)
Svizzera	*sveet*-tseh-rah	*Switzerland*
tedesca/tedesco/ tedesche/tedeschi	teh-*dehs*-kah/koh/keh/kee	*German/Germans*
Germania	jehr-*mah*-nee-ah	*Germany*

Instead of saying **sono americano** (*soh*-noh ah-meh-ree-*kah*-noh) (*I'm American*), you can also say **vengo dall'America** (*vehn*-goh dahl-lah-*meh*-ree-kah) (*I'm from America*). The same is true for all countries.

The following examples give you more practice with this construction.

Veniamo dall'Italia. (veh-nee-*ah*-moh dahl-lee-*tah*-lee-ah.) (*We come from Italy.*) (*We're from Italy.*)

Vengono dalla Spagna. (*vehn*-goh-noh *dahl*-lah spah-nyah.) (*They come from Spain.*)

Vengo dal Giappone. (*vehn*-goh dahl jahp-*poh*-neh.) (*I come from Japan.*)

Veniamo dal Canada. (veh-nee-*ah*-moh dahl *kah*-nah-dah.) (*We come from Canada.*)

Veniamo dagli U.S.A. (or Stati Uniti) (veh-nee-*ah*-moh *dah*-lyee *ooh*-sah [or *stah*-tee ooh-*nee*-tee].) (*We come from the U.S.A.* [or *United States*].)

Extending and Responding to Invitations

You may be asked to join an Italian friend for a meal in a restaurant, or even at his home after you've become friends. When you want to invite someone to dinner, you can use the following phrases:

Andiamo a cena insieme? (ahn-*dyah*-moh ah *cheh*-nah een-*syeh*-meh?) (*Should we go to dinner together?*)

Posso invitarti stasera? (*pohs*-soh een-vee-*tahr*-tee stah-*seh*-rah?) (*Can I invite you for this evening?*)

To accept an invitation, you can use the following expressions:

Volentieri, grazie! (voh-lehn-*tyeh*-ree, *grah*-tsyeh!) (*I'd like to, thank you!*)

Con piacere, grazie! (kohn pyah-*cheh*-reh, *grah*-tsyeh!) (*With pleasure, thank you!*)

Of course, you can't accept every invitation you receive. Following are expressions you can use to decline an invitation:

Mi dispiace ma non posso. (mee dees-*pyah*-cheh mah nohn *pohs*-soh.) (*I'm sorry, but I can't.*)

Magari un'altra volta, grazie. (mah-*gah*-ree oohn-*ahl*-trah *vohl*-tah, *grah*-tsyeh.) (*Perhaps another time, thank you.*)

Mi dispiace, ho già un altro impegno. (mee dees-*pyah*-cheh, oh jah oohn *ahl*-troh eem-*peh*-nyoh.) (*I'm sorry, but I already have another appointment.*)

Chapter 4

Making Small Talk

*W*hether you're speaking with someone you know or someone you just met, your conversation is likely to include some small talk. This type of back and forth chatting often involves asking and answering simple questions as well as discussing yourself, your family, and what's going on around you, like the weather. This chapter presents some of these basic essentials that deserve some space of their own, starting with interrogative pronouns (*who, what, where*) to help you find out exactly what you need to know.

Discovering Interrogative Pronouns

In Italian, at least one thing is easier than in English: forming questions. In English, you usually need a form of *to do, to be,* or *to have* to form a question. You also (mostly) have to invert part of your sentence construction. For example, "He goes to the movies" becomes "Does he go to the movies?" In Italian, you simply ask **Lui va al cinema?** (*looh*-ee vah ahl *chee*-neh-mah?) (*Does he go to the movies?*) There's no word for *does,* just as there's no word for *are* in the following sentence: **Vai alla partita?** (vahy *ahl*-lah pahr-*tee*-tah?) (*Are you going to the game?*)

In Italian, forming questions is easy: A question has the same structure as an affirmative statement. You identify a question only by the intonation in your voice and by the use of a question mark in written language. For example:

> **Luca va a scuola.** (*looh*-kah vah ah *skwoh*-lah.) (*Luca goes to school.*)
>
> **Luca va a scuola?** (*looh*-kah vah ah *skwoh*-lah?) (*Luca goes to school?*) (*Does Luca go to school?*)
>
> **Mangi la carne.** (*mahn*-jee lah *kahr*-neh.) (*You eat/You're eating meat.*)

Mangi la carne? (*mahn*-jee lah *kahr*-neh?) (*Do you eat/Are you eating [the] meat?*)

Italian also has interrogative pronouns (*when, where, what,* and so on). You use these pronouns to start questions.

- ✔ **Chi?** (kee?) (*Who?*)
- ✔ **Che?** (keh?) (*What?*)
- ✔ **Cosa?** (*koh*-sah?) (*What?*)
- ✔ **Quando?** (*kwahn*-doh?) (*When?*)
- ✔ **Quanto/a?** (*kwahn*-toh/tah?) (*How much?* [masculine/feminine])
- ✔ **Quanti/e?** (*kwahn*-tee/teh?) (*How many?* [masculine/feminine])
- ✔ **Quale/i?** (*kwah*-leh/ee?) (*Which/what?* [singular/plural])
- ✔ **Dove?** (*doh*-veh?) (*Where?*)
- ✔ **Perché?** (pehr-*keh*?) (*Why?*)
- ✔ **Come?** (*koh*-meh?) (*How?*)

TIP

Che, cosa, and **che cosa** are often used interchangeably.

Here are some sample questions, using these interrogative pronouns:

Chi è? (kee eh?) (*Who is it/this?*)

Cosa stai facendo? (*koh*-sah stahy fah-*chehn*-doh?) (*What are you doing?*)

Quando arrivi? (*kwahn*-doh ahr-ree-*vee*?) (*When do you arrive?*)

Dov'è la stazione? (doh-*veh* lah stah-*tsyoh*-neh?) (*Where is the station?*)

Perché non sei venuto? (pehr-*keh* nohn sahy veh-*nooh*-toh?) (*Why didn't you come?*)

Come stai? (*koh*-meh stahy?) (*How are you?*)

Come si dice "rain" in italiano? (*koh*-meh see *dee*-cheh "rain" in ee-tah-lee-*ah*-noh?) (*How do you say "rain" in Italian?*)

Asking simple questions

When you ask a question using an interrogative pronoun, you don't need the interrogative pronoun in the response. For example:

Dov'è la Cappella Sistina? (doh-*veh* lah kahp-*pehl*-lah sees-*tee*-nah?) (*Where is the Sistine Chapel?*)

La Cappella Sistina è a Roma. (lah kahp-*pehl*-lah sees-*tee*-nah eh ah *roh*-mah.) (*The Sistine Chapel is in Rome.*)

Quante regioni ci sono in Italia? (*kwahn*-teh reh-*joh*-nee chee *soh*-noh in ee-*tah*-lee-ah?) (*How many regions are there in Italy?*)

Ci sono 20 regioni. (chee *soh*-noh vehn-tee reh-*joh*-nee.) (*There are 20 regions.*)

Book I

Speaking Italian in Everyday Settings

The interrogatives **dove** (*doh*-veh) (*where*) and **come** (*koh*-meh) (*how*) can be contracted with the verb **essere** (*ehs*-sehr-reh) (*to be*) in the third person singular. Note that the pronunciation and stress also change. Take a look at these interrogatives with third person singular and third person plural verbs.

Dov'è Mario. (doh-*veh mah*-ryoh?) (*Where's Mario?*)

Dove sono i ragazzi? (*doh*-veh *soh*-noh ee rah-*gahts*-tsee?) (*Where are the boys?*)

Com'è quel ristorante? (koh-*meh* kwehl rees-toh-*rahn*-teh?) (*How is that restaurant?*) (*What's that restaurant like?*)

Come sono gli gnocchi? (*koh*-meh *soh*-noh lyee *nyohk*-kee?) (*How are the gnocchi?*)

Use **quale** (*kwah*-leh) (*what/which*) in the singular, **quali** (*kwah*-lee) in the plural, but **qual è** (kwahl-*eh*) when combined with the third person singular of **essere.** See these examples:

Quale (*kwah*-leh): **Quale film vuoi vedere?** (*kwah*-leh feelm vwohi veh-*deh*-reh?) (*What/which film do you want to see?*)

Qual è (kwahl-*eh*): **Qual è il mare più profondo in Italia?** (kwahl-*eh* il mah-reh pyooh proh-*fohn*-doh in ee-*tah*-lee-ah?) (*What is the deepest sea in Italy?*)

Quali (*kwahl*-ee): **Quali amici hai invitato?** (*kwahl*-ee ah-*mee*-chee ahy in-vee-*tah*-toh?) (*Which friends did you invite?*)

C'è and ci sono

Although seemingly insignificant, you just can't get around in Italian without the essential terms **c'è** (cheh) (*there is*) and **ci sono** (chee *soh*-noh) (*there are*) that are useful both for asking and answering questions. Just remember that both have a "ch" sound!

Cosa c'è nel frigo? (*koh*-zah cheh nehl *free*-goh?) (*What's in the fridge?*)

C'è un esame domani? (cheh oohn eh-*zah*-meh doh-*mah*-nee?) (*Is there an exam tomorrow?*)

Sì, c'è italiano. (see, cheh ee-tah-lee-*ah*-noh.) (*Yes, there is the Italian one.*)

Ci sono ancora dei ravioli? (chee *soh*-noh ahn-*koh*-rah dehy rah-*vyoh*-lee?) (*Are there any ravioli left?*)

Sì, ci sono. (see, chee *soh*-noh.) (*Yes, there are.*)

Taking care of basic needs

Sometimes you just need to ask for something very basic but necessary. Here are a few phrases that will take you far:

- **Scusi, dov'è il bagno per favore?** (*skooh*-zee, doh-*veh* il bah-*nyoh* pehr fah-*voh*-reh?) (*Excuse me, where is the bathroom please?*) Some people get fancy and ask for **la toilette** with a Frenchified accent; however, **bagno** gets you where you need to go (no pun intended).

- **Scusi, dov'è la farmacia più vicina?** (*skooh*-zee, doh-*veh* lah fahr-mah-*chee*-ah pyooh vee-*chee*-nah?) (*Excuse me, where's the nearest pharmacy?*)

- **Scusi, dov'è una banca?** (*skooh*-zee, doh-*veh* ooh-nah *bahn*-kah?) (*Excuse me, where is a bank?*)

- **Ho bisogno di/Mi serve/Mi servono** (oh bee-*zoh*-nyoh dee/mee *sehr*-veh/mee *sehr*-voh-noh) (*I need* [singular/plural])

  - **un parucchiere** (oohn pah-rooh-*kyeh*-reh) (*a hairdresser*)

  - **un'estetista (per fare la ceretta)** (oohn-eh-steh-*tee*-stah [pehr *fah*-reh lah chehr-*eht*-tah]) (*an esthetician [for waxing]*) (It's uncommon for Italian women to shave with a razor.)

- **Sto cercando** (stoh chehr-*kahn*-doh) (*I'm looking for*)

  - **il dentifricio** (il dehn-tee-*free*-choh) (*toothpaste*)

  - **la crema solare** (lah *kreh*-mah soh-*lah*-reh) (*sun protection lotion*)

  - **i tamponi** (ee tahm-*poh*-nee) (*tampons*)

  - **la carta igienica** (lah *kar*-tah ee-*jehn*-ee-kah) (*toilet paper*)

  - **qualcosa per le zanzare** (kwahl-*koh*-zah pehr leh dzahn-*zah*-reh) (*something for mosquitoes*)

  - **qualcosa per il mal di testa** (kwahl-*koh*-zah pehr eel mahl dee *tehs*-tah) (*something for a headache*)

- **Vorrei** (vohr-*rey*) (*I'd like*)

- **Mi può/potrebbe consigliare . . . ?** (mee pwoh/poh-*trehb*-beh kohn-seel-*yah*-reh . . . ?) (*Would you be able to recommend . . . ?*)

- **Può ripetere lentamente, per favore?** (pwoh ree-*peh*-teh-reh lehn-tah-*mehn*-teh, pehr fah-*voh*-reh?) (*Would you repeat slowly, please?*)

- **Non capisco.** (nohn kah-*pees*-koh.) (*I don't understand.*)

- **Non lo so.** (nohn loh soh.) (*I don't know.*)

Italians use **boh** (boh) to express doubt and uncertainty. Despite its colloquialism, it's what most people use and would use to answer a question.

However, avoid its use in a more formal setting, like in school, talking with a professor, in a business meeting, or during a job interview.

> **Scusi, sa a che ora arriva il treno da Siena?** (*skooh*-zee, sah ah keh *oh*-ra ahr-*ree*-vah eel *treh*-noh dah *syeh*-nah?) (*Excuse me, do you know at what time the train from Siena arrives?*)

> **Boh, dovrebbe essere gà qui.** (boh, doh-*vrehb*-beh *ehs*-seh-reh jah kwee.) (*Well, it should be here already.*)

Pronto (*prohn*-toh) means more than just *hello* when you pick up the phone. It frequently means *ready,* in which case it functions as an adjective and, therefore, changes according to the noun it describes. In other words, when the noun it modifies is masculine, the adjective ends in **-o** — **pronto.** If the noun is feminine, it ends in **-a** — **pronta** (*prohn*-tah). When modifying plural nouns, it ends in **-i** (-ee) (masculine, plural) and **-e** (-eh) (feminine, plural). Consider these examples:

> **Ragazzi, siete pronti?** (rah-*gats*-zee, *syeh*-teh *prohn*-tee?) (*Guys/kids, are you ready?*)

> **La cena è pronta.** (lah *cheh*-nah eh *prohn*-tah.) (*Dinner is ready.*)

Another use of **pronto** you should know is **pronto soccorso** (*prohn*-toh sohk-*kohr*-soh) (*first aid; emergency room*). In this context, **pronto** means *rapid.*

Presto (*prehs*-toh), on the other hand, means either *early* or *soon* and as an adverb is invariable (ending always in **-o**). For example: **Siamo arrivati presto** (*syah*-moh ahr-ree-*vah*-tee *prehs*-toh) (*We arrived early*).

Here are a few other terms to help you cover the basic needs:

- ✔ **abbastanza** (ahb-bah-*stahn*-zah) (*enough*)
- ✔ **il bagno** (il *bah*-nyoh) (*bathroom*)
- ✔ **Come ti trovi. . . ?** (*koh*-meh tee *troh*-vee. . . ?) (*How do you like. . . ?* [used only in certain situations, like a job or new city])
- ✔ **consigliare** (kohn-see-*lyah*-reh) (*to recommend; to advise*)
- ✔ **Da quanto tempo?** (dah *kwahn*-toh *tehm*-poh?) (*For how long?*) (*Since when?*)
- ✔ **ditta** (*deet*-tah) (*company; firm*)
- ✔ **gemello/a** (jeh-*mehl*-loh/lah) (*twin* [masculine/feminine])
- ✔ **partita** (pahr-*tee*-tah) (*game*)

Talking About Your Family

Italian has specific rules for using possessive adjectives with family members. For singular family members, you *don't* use the article, but plural family members *do* take the article, as in these examples:

mia sorella (no definite article) (*mee*-ah soh-*rehl*-lah) (*my sister*)

<u>le</u> **mie sorelle** (with definite article) (leh *mee*-eh soh-*rehl*-leh (*my sisters*)

Want to talk about more relatives? Use this list as your guide:

- ✔ **marito** (mah-*ree*-toh) (*husband*)
- ✔ **moglie** (*mohl*-yeh) (*wife*)
- ✔ **figlio** (*feel*-yoh) (*son*)
- ✔ **figlia** (*feel*-yah) (*daughter*)
- ✔ **figli** (*feel*-yee) (*children*)
- ✔ **nipote** (nee-*poh*-teh) (*niece, nephew, granddaughter, grandson*)
- ✔ **nipoti** (nee-*poh*-tee) (*nieces, nephews, granddaughters, grandsons, grandchildren*)
- ✔ **suocero** (*swoh*-cheh-roh) (*father-in-law*)
- ✔ **suocera** (*swoh*-cheh-rah) (*mother-in-law*)
- ✔ **genero** (*geh*-neh-roh) (*son-in-law*)
- ✔ **nuora** (*nwoh*-rah) (*daughter-in-law*)
- ✔ **zio** (*dzee*-oh) (*uncle*)
- ✔ **zia** (*dzee*-ah) (*aunt*)
- ✔ **cugina/o** (kooh-*jee*-nah/noh) (*cousin* [feminine/masculine])
- ✔ **cugine/i** (koo-*jee*-neh/nee) (*cousins* [feminine/masculine])
- ✔ **nonna** (*nohn*-nah) (*grandmother*)
- ✔ **nonno** (*nohn*-noh) (*grandfather*)
- ✔ **nonni/e** (*nohn*-nee/neh) (*grandparents, grandfathers/grandmothers*)
- ✔ **madre** (*mah*-dreh) (*mother*)
- ✔ **padre** (*pah*-dreh) (*father*)
- ✔ **genitori** (geh-nee-*toh*-ree) (*parents*)

Discussing What You Do

Che fai? (keh fahy?) (*What do you do?*) is a common Italian expression that has several nuanced meanings. The context of the conversation or your interlocutor's body language will tell you whether you're being asked the English equivalent of *What's going on; what's new; what's up?* or whether you're being asked what you do for a living. In the latter case, you answer **Faccio il (dottore, tassista, . . .)** (*fahch*-choh eel [doht-*toh*-reh, tahs-*see*-stah, . . .]) (*I'm a [doctor, taxi driver, . . .]*) or **Sono (dottore, tassista, . . .)** (*soh*-noh [doht-*toh*-reh, tahs-*see*-stah, . . .]) (*I'm a [doctor, taxi-driver, . . .]*).

Talkin' the Talk

Friends Flavio and Dino are checking in and making plans for the day. (Track 6)

Flavio: **Che fai?**
keh *fah*-ee?
What are you up to?

Dino: **Niente. Hai qualche idea?**
nyehn-teh. *Ah*-ee *kwahl*-keh ee-*deh*-ah?
Nothing. Any ideas?

Flavio: **No. Fa anche freddo, non saprei proprio . . .**
noh. fah *ahn*-keh *frehd*-doh, nohn sah-*preh*-ee *proh*-pryoh . . .
No. And it's also cold, I wouldn't know . . .

Dino: **Sai se gli altri fanno qualcosa?**
sah-ee seh lyee *ahl*-tree *fahn*-noh kwahl-*koh*-zah?
Do you know if they [our friends] have any plans for today?

Flavio: **Possiamo chiamarli. Chissà, si può andare tutti al cinema.**
pohs-*syah*-moh kyah-*mah*-reh. kees-*sah*, see pwoh ahn-*dah*-reh *toot*-tee ahl *chee*-neh-mah.
We can call them. Maybe we can all go to the movies.

Talking shop

Work is such a big part of so many people's lives, it's something you may want to be able to talk about when you're in Italy and getting to know people you've just met.

The verb **lavorare** (lah-voh-*rah*-reh) (*to work*) will be useful, as will these other key phrases:

- ✔ **Che lavoro vuoi fare da grande?** (keh lah-*voh*-roh vwohi *fah*-reh dah *grahn*-deh?) (*What work would you like to do when you are older/grow up?*)

- ✔ **Cosa vuoi diventare?** (*koh*-zah vwohi dee-vehn-*tah*-reh?) (*What do you want to be?*)

- ✔ **Che lavoro fa/fai?** (keh lah-*voh*-roh fah/fahy?) (*What work/job do you do?* [formal/informal])

- ✔ **Che mestiere fa/fai?** (keh mehs-*tyeh*-reh fah/fahy?) (*What work do you do?* [formal/informal])

You can generally answer this question in two ways (note the verbs and the use of the definite article in the first example):

Faccio il/la dentista. (*fach*-choh il/lah dehn-*tees*-tah.) (*I'm a dentist.* [masculine/feminine])

Sono dentista. (*soh*-noh dehn-*tees*-tah.) (*I'm a dentist.*)

Discussing your job

Italian has at least three words for *company* — **la compagnia** (lah kohm-pah-*nyee*-ah), **la ditta** (lah *deet*-tah) (which also means *the firm*), and **la società** (lah soh-cheh-*tah*). These words are virtually interchangeable.

L'ufficio (loohf-*fee*-choh) is Italian for *office*. The following sentences give you a taste of the phrases you hear in **uffici** (oohf-*fee*-chee) (*offices*) everywhere:

È una grande società? (eh *ooh*-nah *grahn*-deh soh-cheh-*tah*?) (*Is it a big company?*)

Non proprio, diciamo media. (nohn *proh*-pryoh, dee-*chah*-moh *meh*-dyah.) (*Not really, let's say medium-sized.*)

Lavoro per una piccola agenzia. (lah-*voh*-roh pehr *ooh*-nah *peek*-koh-lah ah-jehn-*tsee*-ah.) (*I work for a small company.*)

Mi piace il mio lavoro. (mee *pyah*-cheh eel *mee*-oh lah-*voh*-roh.) (*I like my job.*)

Table 4-1 shows some of the professions and careers with which you may be familiar.

Table 4-1	Professions/Jobs	
Profession	*Pronunciation*	*Meaning*
agronomo	ah-*groh*-noh-moh	*agronomist*
archeologo	ahr-keh-*oh*-loh-goh	*archeologist*
architetto	ahr-kee-*teht*-toh	*architect*
avvocato	ahv-voh-*kah*-toh	*lawyer*
bracciante	brach-*chahn*-teh	*farm worker*
chirurgo	kee-*roohr*-goh	*surgeon*
commesso	kohm-*mehs*-soh	*salesperson*
dentista	denhn-*tees*-tah	*dentist*
falegname	fah-leh-*nyah*-meh	*carpenter*
fornaio	fohr-*nah*-yoh	*baker*
giornalista	johr-nah-*lees*-tah	*journalist*
impiegato	ihm-pyeh-*gah*-toh	*clerk (white-collar worker)*
ingegnere	in-geh-*nyeh*-reh	*engineer*
insegnante	in-seh-*nyahn*-teh	*teacher (grades 1–8)*
meccanico	mehk-*kah*-nee-koh	*mechanic*
medico	*meh*-dee-koh	*doctor*
operaio	oh-peh-*rah*-yoh	*factory worker*
pasticciere	pah-steech-*cheh*-reh	*baker, pastry baker*
psicologo	psee-*koh*-loh-goh	*psychologist*
professore	proh-fehs-*soh*-reh	*professor, teacher (grades 6–university)*
segretaria	seh-greh-*tah*-ryah	*secretary*
stilista	stee-*lees*-tah	*designer*

Some of the following terms may also come in handy when talking about jobs in Italian:

- **capo** (*kah*-poh) (*head; boss*)
- **direttore** (dee-reht-*toh*-reh) (*manager; director*)
- **fabbrica** (*fahb*-bree-kah) (*factory; plant*)

- **lavoro** (lah-*voh*-roh) (*work; job*)
- **padrone** (pah-*droh*-neh) (*boss; owner*)
- **sciopero** (*shoh*-peh-roh) (*strike*)
- **stipendio** (stee-*pehn*-dyoh) (*salary*)
- **tasse** (*tahs*-seh) (*taxes*)
- **ti/mi interessa** (tee/mee in-teh-*rehs*-sah) (*you're/I'm interested in*)

The word **sciopero** (*shoh*-peh-roh) (*strike*) is very important in Italy, because workers go on strike all the time.

Chatting about the Weather

Talking about the weather in Italian is as easy as talking about it in English: Is it hot? Is it cold? Is it muggy? Is it raining? It's snowing. It's hailing. You can express a great deal about the weather by using one verb, impersonally: **fa** (Literally: *it makes* or *it does*). Here are some examples for how to answer the question **Che tempo fa?** (keh *tehm*-poh fah?) (*What's the weather like?*)

> **Fa caldo** (statement or question depending on your intonation) (fah *kahl*-doh) (*It's hot.*) (*Is it hot?*)
>
> **Sì, abbiamo 35 gradi!** (see ahb-*byah*-moh trehn-tah-*cheen*-kweh *grah*-dee!) (*It's 35 degrees!*) (Celsius 35 = Fahrenheit 95.)
>
> **Fa freddo** (statement or question depending on your intonation) (fah *frehd*-doh) (*It's cold.*) (*Is it cold?*)
>
> **Fa un freddo orribile, –20!** (fah oohn *frehd*-doh ohr-*ree*-bee-leh, *meh*-noh *vehn*-tee!) (*It's terribly cold, –20!*) (Celsius –20 = Fahrenheit 0.)
>
> **Fa fresco, fa freschino** (statement or question depending on your intonation) (fah *freh*-skoh, fah freh-*skee*-noh) (*It's chilly; it's a little chilly.*) (*Is it chilly?*)

Intonation makes your comments about the weather statements or questions. The following simple words allow you to remark on the weather in any condition.

- **Piove.** (*pyoh*-veh.) (*It's raining.*)
- **Tira vento.** (*tee*-rah *vehn*-toh.) (*It's windy.*)
- **Lampeggia.** (lahm-*pehj*-jah.) (*It's lightning.*)

- **Tuona.** (*twoh*-nah.) (*It's thundering.*)
- **Nevica.** (*neh*-vee-kah.) (*It's snowing.*)
- **Grandina.** (*grahn*-dee-nah.) (*It's hailing.*)
- **Che afa!** (keh *ah*-fah!) (*It's muggy!*)
- **Fa bel tempo.** (fah behl *tehm*-poh.) (*It's beautiful.*)
- **Fa brutto tempo.** (fah *brooht*-toh *tehm*-poh.) (*It's nasty weather.*)

Talkin' the Talk

Il signor Brancato and Ms. Roe, airplane seatmates, are talking about the weather.

Ms. Roe: **E l'estate a Milano com'è?**
e lehs-*tah*-teh ah mee-*lah*-noh cohm-*eh*?
What's the summer like in Milan?

Sig. Brancato: **Molto calda e lunga.**
mohl-toh *kahl*-dah eh *loohn*-gah.
Very hot and long.

Ms. Roe: **E la primavera?**
eh lah pree-mah-*veh*-rah?
And the spring?

Sig. Brancato: **La mia stagione preferita.**
lah *mee*-ah stah-*joh*-neh preh-feh-*ree*-tah.
My favorite season.

Ms. Roe: **Davvero?**
dahv-*veh*-roh?
Really?

Sig. Brancato: **Sì, perché è mite.**
see, pehr-*keh* eh *mee*-teh.
Yes, because it's mild.

Ms. Roe: **Come l'estate in Canada.**
koh-meh lehs-*tah*-teh een *kah*-nah-dah.
Like the fall in Canada.

Words to Know

umido	*ooh*-mee-doh	humid
tempo incerto [m]	*tehm*-poh een-*chehr*-toh	uncertain weather
nebbia [f]	*nehb*-byah	fog
mite	*mee*-teh	mild
gradi	*grah*-dee	degrees
primavera	pree-mah-*veh*-rah	spring
estate	eh-*stah*-teh	summer
autunno	ou-*toohn*-noh	autumn; fall
inverno	in-*vehr*-noh	winter

CULTURAL WISDOM

Weather-wise

Italy is a fortunate country, at least as far as weather is concerned. During at least three of the four seasons, it has a mild climate and gets a lot of sun.

The summers are for the most part warm — sometimes *too* hot. The winters can be very cold, but snow is rare, except for primarily in the mountains of north and central Italy, but as far south as Calabria.

Summer in the cities is generally terribly hot, so most Italians take their vacation in August and flee to cooler places: the sea or the lakes or the mountains. As a matter of fact, in August, it's hard to find actual residents in the big cities. The only people you find there are likely to be tourists and those Italians who have to work.

Chapter 5

Casa Dolce Casa: Home Sweet Home

In This Chapter

▶ Talking about where you live

▶ Touring your home

Your home is a big part of your life, and it's likely to be a popular topic of conversation. People may ask you where you live and what your home is like. This chapter introduces you to the different vocabulary and situations associated with the house and life at home.

Describing Where You Live

When someone asks you where you're from, you want to tell them the name of your country, followed by your city (or hometown) and state. You may also want to mention the type of home you have. The following sections show you how to do just that.

Stating your country and hometown

When telling where you're from, you can start by saying your country of origin; you use the word **sono** (*soh*-no) (*I am*) followed by an adjective of nationality that matches your gender, or you use **vengo** (*vehn*-goh) (*I am*) followed by a variation of the words **da** (dah) (*from*) + the definite article and a country. (See Chapter 3 of Book I for a list of countries and nationalities in Italian.) Here are some examples:

Sono americano/a; vengo dagli Stati Uniti. (*soh*-noh ah-meh-ree-*kah*-noh/ nah; *vehn*-goh dah-lyee *Stah*-tee Ooh-*nee*-tee.) (*I am American* [masculine/ feminine]; *I am from the United States.*)

Sono argentino/a; vengo dall'Argentina. (*soh*-noh ahr-jehn-*tee*-noh/nah; *vehn*-goh dahl-lahr-jehn-*tee*-nah.) (*I am Argentinian* [masculine/feminine]; *I am from Argentina.*)

Sono messicano/a; vengo dal Messico. (*soh*-noh mehs-see-*kah*-noh/nah; vehn-goh dahl *Mehs*-see-koh.) (*I am Mexican* [masculine/feminine]; *I am from Mexico.*)

Did you notice in the preceding examples that adjectives of nationality aren't capitalized in Italian? However, when nationality is used as a noun to describe the people of a country, or its language, you use capitalization. For example:

I Messicani giocano bene a calcio. (ee mehs-see-*kah*-nee *joh*-kah-noh *beh*-neh ah *kahl*-choh.) (*Mexicans play soccer well/are good at soccer.*)

Gli Americani preferiscono la pallacanestro. (lyee ah-meh-ree-*kah*-nee preh-feh-*ree*-skoh-noh lah *pahl*-lah-kah-*neh*-stroh.) (*Americans prefer to play basketball.*)

Gli Argentini adorano il tango. (lyee ahr-jehn-*tee*-nee ah-*doh*-rah-noh eel tahn-goh.) (*Argentinians love tango.*)

Italians are very sociable and love to meet foreigners. They'll certainly like to know more about you. To say your hometown and state (or province), you use **abito a . . .** (*ah*-bee-toh ah . . .) (*I live in . . .*) or **sono di . . .** (*soh*-no dee) (*I'm from . . .*). Here's an example:

Abito in Michigan, a Detroit. (*ah*-bee-toh een Michigan, ah Detroit.) (*I live in Detroit, Michigan.*)

Note that you use **in** before Michigan, the state, and **a** before Detroit, the city. One more example:

Pam abita a Louisville, in Kentucky. (Pam *ah*-bee-tah ah Louisville, een Kentucky.) (*Pam lives in Louisville, Kentucky.*)

Noting the type of home you have

Besides sharing your country and hometown, you may also want to describe the type of home in which you live. Italians usually speak of **la casa** (lah *kah*-zah) (*the house; the home*), even though they often mean **l'appartamento** (lahp-pahr-tah-*mehn*-toh) (*the apartment*). A recent study by the European

Statistics Institute shows that more than 50 percent of Italians of all social strata live in **condomini** (kohn-doh-*mee*-nee) (*condos; apartment buildings*) in small towns and large cities rather than in single-family dwellings in residential areas.

A **villa** (*veel*-lah) (*villa*) is a free-standing house, usually in the country or by the sea. The **villa** is generally someone's second home. Some people opt to live **in campagna** (een kahm-*pah*-nyah) (*in the countryside*), which isn't the same as living in the suburbs in the United States. As a matter of fact, **periferia** (peh-ree-fehr-*ee*-ah) (*suburbs which are neither country nor city*) may have a negative connotation in Italy.

Taking a Tour of Your Home

To describe your house or apartment, you need to know the names of different rooms and furnishings. The following sections take you on a tour of a typical Italian home.

Il soggiorno: The living room

Italians refer to **il soggiorno** (eel sohj-*johr*-noh) (*the living room*) as the main living area in the home. Italians spend a lot of time in the living room, sitting and watching TV, entertaining friends, and listening to music. A **soggiorno** that's large enough for a corner to be used as a dining area will also be used for lunches and dinners with guests. The American family room is the analogue to the Italian **soggiorno.** Now you know how to name the room where you keep your coziest couch, where you watch the latest shows or football, baseball, and basketball games, alone or with your friends! Here's a list of common furnishings for the living room:

- ✔ **il camino** (eel kah-*mee*-noh) (*fireplace*)
- ✔ **il divano** (eel dee-*vah*-noh) (*couch*)
- ✔ **la lampada** (lah *lahm*-pah-dah) (*lamp*)
- ✔ **la poltrona** (lah pohl-*troh*-nah) (*armchair*)
- ✔ **lo scaffale** (loh skahf-*fah*-leh) (*bookshelf*)
- ✔ **il tappeto** (eel tahp-*peht*-toh) (*rug*)
- ✔ **il tavolino** (eel tah-voh-*lee*-noh) (*coffee table*)
- ✔ **il tavolo da pranzo** (eel *tah*-voh-loh dah *prahn*-tzoh) (*dining table*)
- ✔ **il televisore** (eel teh-leh-vee-*soh*-reh) (*TV set*)

Talkin' the Talk

Valerio has found a new, **non ammobiliato** (nohn ahm-moh-bee-*lyah*-toh) (*unfurnished*) apartment. His friend Eugenia is asking him what he needs.

Valerio:	**Ho trovato un appartamento! Devo comprare dei mobili.** oh troh-*vah*-toh oohn ahp-pahr-tah-*mehn*-toh! *deh*-voh kohm-*prah*-reh deh *moh*-bee-lee. *I just found an apartment! I have to buy some furniture.*
Eugenia:	**Tutto?** *tooht*-toh? *(Do you need) everything?*
Valerio:	**No, per la camera da letto il letto e l'armadio.** noh, pehr lah *kah*-meh-rah dah *leht*-toh eel *leht*-toh eh lahr-*mah*-dyoh. *No, a bed and a wardrobe for my bedroom.*
Eugenia:	**Nient'altro?** nyehnt-*ahl*-troh? *Anything else?*
Valerio:	**Ho due comodini e una cassettiera.** oh *dooh*-eh koh-moh-*dee*-nee eh *ooh*-nah kahs-seht-*tyeh*-rah. *I have two bedside tables and a dresser.*
Eugenia:	**E per il soggiorno?** eh pehr eel sohj-*johr*-noh? *And for the living room?*
Valerio:	**Ho una poltrona. Mi mancano ancora il divano e un tavolino.** oh *ooh*-nah pohl-*troh*-nah. mee *mahn*-kah-noh ahn-*koh*-rah eel dee-*vah*-noh eh oohn tah-voh-*lee*-noh. *I have an armchair. I still need a couch and a coffee table.*

Words to Know

appartamento	ahp-pahr-tah-<u>mehn</u>-toh	apartment
mobili	<u>moh</u>-bee-lee	furniture
camera da letto	<u>kah</u>-meh-rah dah <u>leht</u>-toh	bedroom
letto	<u>leht</u>-toh	bed
armadio	ahr-<u>mah</u>-dyoh	wardrobe
cassettiera	kahs-seht-<u>tyeh</u>-rah	dresser
soggiorno	sohj-johr-noh	living room
poltrona	pohl-<u>troh</u>-nah	armchair
divano	dee-<u>vah</u>-noh	couch
tavolino	tah-<u>voh</u>-lee-noh	coffee table

La cucina: The kitchen

Much of the activity in any home occurs in **la cucina** (lah kooh-*chee*-nah) (*the kitchen*). Stereotypically, the kitchen is the most important room for Italians; is it for you as well? Whatever the answer, you'll make a good impression on native Italian speakers if you know some kitchen vocabulary. What if the nice lady who has just served you delicious food at your favorite Italian restaurant is curious about *your* kitchen? You don't want to disappoint her by not even being able to say that you use only **cibo surgelato** (*chee*-boh soohr-jeh-*lah*-toh) (*frozen food*) defrosted in the **microonde** (mee-kroh-*ohn*-deh) (*microwave oven*), and that you don't use a **lavastoviglie** (lah-vah-stoh-*vee*-lyeh) (*dishwasher*) because your food comes in plastic containers!

Here are common items found in the kitchen:

- **l'apribottiglia** (lah-pree-boht-*tee*-lyah) (*bottle opener*)
- **la caffettiera** (lah kahf-feht-*tyeh*-rah) (*coffee maker*)
- **il congelatore** (eel kohn-jeh-lah-*toh*-reh) (*freezer*)
- **i fornelli** (ee fohr-*nehl*-lee) (*stove-top burners*)
- **il forno** (eel *fohr*-noh) (*oven*)
- **il frigorifero** (eel free-goh-*ree*-fehr-oh) (*refrigerator*)
- **il frullatore** (eel froohl-ah-*toh*-reh) (*blender*)
- **la frusta** (lah *frooh*-stah) (*whisk*)
- **la lavastoviglie** (lah lah-vah-stoh-*veel*-yeh) (*dishwasher*)
- **la lavatrice** (lah lah-vah-*tree*-cheh) (*washing machine*)
- **il lavello** (eel lah-*vehl*-loh) (*sink*)
- **il microonde** (eel mee-kroh-*ohn*-deh) (*microwave oven*)
- **la padella** (lah pah-*dehl*-lah) (*frying pan*)
- **la pattumiera** (lah paht-tooh-*myeh*-rah) (*garbage can*)
- **i pensili** (ee *pehn*-see-lee) (*cabinets*)
- **la pentola** (lah *pehn*-toh-lah) (*pot*)
- **le sedie** (leh *seh*-dyeh) (*chairs*)
- **lo scolapasta** (loh skoh-lah-*pah*-stah) (*colander*)
- **la spatola** (lah *spah*-toh-lah) (*spatula*)
- **il tagliere** (eel tah-*lyeh*-reh) (*cutting board*)
- **il tavolo** (eel *tah*-voh-loh) (*table*)
- **il tostapane** (eel toh-stah-*pah*-neh) (*toaster*)

You may be wondering why **la lavatrice** (*washing machine*) is included on this list. In Italy, you often find washing machines in the kitchen; however, dryers aren't very common in Italy because of the enormous amount of electricity they consume.

La sala da pranzo: The dining room

Italians show their sense of hospitality **in sala da pranzo** (een *sah*-lah dah *prahn*-tzoh) (*in the dining room*). They set the dining table carefully and welcome their guests with refined details. Here are some items you'll likely see in the dining room:

Book I

Speaking
Italian in
Everyday
Settings

- **il bicchiera da acqua** (eel beek-*kyeh*-reh dah *ah*-kwah) (*water glass*)
- **il bicchiere da vino** (eel beek-*kyeh*-reh dah *vee*-noh) (*wine glass*)
- **il centrotavola** (eel *chehn*-troh-*tah*-voh-lah) (*centerpiece*)
- **il cestino per il pane** (eel cheh-*stee*-noh pehr eel *pah*-neh) (*bread basket*)
- **il coltello** (eel kohl-*tehl*-loh) (*knife*)
- **il cucchiaino** (eel koohk-kyah-*ee*-noh) (*teaspoon*)
- **il cucchiaio** (eel koohk-*kyah*-yoh) (*spoon*)
- **la forchetta** (lah fohr-*keht*-tah) (*fork*)
- **il piattino** (eel pyaht-*tee*-noh) (*saucer*)
- **il piatto fondo** (eel *pyaht*-toh *fohn*-doh) (*bowl*)
- **il piatto piano** (eel *pyaht*-toh *pyah*-noh) (*plate*)
- **la sedia** (lah *seh*-dyah) (*chair*)
- **il tavolo da pranzo** (eel *tah*-voh-loh dah *prahn*-tzoh) (*dining table*)
- **la tazzina da caffé** (lah taht-*tsee*-nah dah kahf-*feh*) (*cup*)
- **la tovaglia** (lah toh-*vah*-lyah) (*tablecloth*)
- **il tovagliolo** (eel toh-vah-*lyoh*-loh) (*napkin*)

Did you know that some of the most beautiful ceramics in the world are produced in Italy? Many are hand-painted works of art unto themselves. Some towns well known for their ceramics include Faenza (Emilia Romagna), Deruta (Umbria), Vietri (Amalfi Coast), Grottaglie (Apulia), and Caltagirone (Sicily). If you find yourself visiting these towns, you'll probably find yourself buying a new set of dinnerware!

Talkin' the Talk

Salvatore and his mother are preparing for dinner. Mamma asks him to set the table and sweep the floor in the **sala da pranzo** (*sah*-lah dah *prahn*-tzoh) (*dining room*) before their guests arrive.

Mamma: **Salvatore, per favore, passa la scopa prima che arrivino gli ospiti.**
sahl-vah-*toh*-reh, pehr fah-*voh*-reh, *pahs*-sah lah *skoh*-pah *pree*-mah keh ahr-*ree*-vee-noh lyee *ohs*-pee-tee. *Salvatore, please sweep the floor before the guests arrive.*

Salvatore: **Va bene, mamma.**
vah *beh*-neh, *mahm*-mah.
Okay, Mom.

Che altro?
keh *ahl*-troh?
Anything else?

Mamma: **Apparecchia il tavolo, caro.**
ahp-pah-*rek*-kyah eel *tah*-voh-loh, *kah*-roh.
Set the table, dear.

Salvatore: **Cosa ci metto?**
koh-zah chee *meht*-toh?
What should I put out?

Mamma: **Metti la tovaglia con i limoni con i suoi tovaglioli.**
meht-tee lah toh-*vah*-lyah kohn ee lee-*moh*-nee kohn
ee swohy toh-vahl-*yoh*-lee.
*Put out the tablecloth with the lemons and the
matching napkins.*

Salvatore: **Quali piatti?**
kwah-lee *pyaht*-tee?
Which dishes?

Mamma: **Quelli di Faenza, il piano e il fondo.**
kwehl-lee dee fah-*ehn*-tsah, eel *pyah*-noh eh eel
fohn-doh.
The ones from Faenza, the flat ones, and the bowls.

**Non dimenticare forchette, coltelli, e cucchiai per il
brodetto.**
nohn dee-mehn-tee-*kah*-reh fohr-*keht*-teh, kohl-*tehl*-
lee, eh koohk-*kyahy* pehr eel broh-*deht*-toh.
*Don't forget forks, knives, and spoons for the fish
stew.*

Salvatore: **Mamma, non bastano i bicchieri per l'acqua.**
mahm-mah, nohn *bahs*-tah-noh ee beek-*kyeh*-ree
pehr *lahk*-wah.
Mom, there aren't enough water glasses.

Mamma: **Non importa. Li ho qui nella lavastoviglie.**
nohn eem-*pohr*-tah. lee oh kwee *nehl*-lah
lah-vah-stoh-*veel*-yeh.
That's okay. I have them here in the dishwasher.

Aggiungiamo anche i bicchieri da vino. Grazie.
aj-joohn-*jah*-moh *ahn*-keh ee beek-*kyeh*-ree dah *vee*-noh. *grah*-tsyeh.
Let's add wine glasses, too. Thanks.

Words to Know

scopa	skoh-pah	broom
apparecchiare	ahp-pahr-ehk-kyah-reh	to set the table
tovaglia	toh-vahl-yah	tablecloth
tovagliolo/i	toh-vahl-yoh-loh/lee	napkin/s
piatto/i	pyaht-toh/ee	dish/dishes
il (piatto) piano	eel pyah-noh	flat dish
il (piatto) fondo	eel fohn-doh	bowl (for soup or pasta)
forchetta/e	fohr-keht-tah/eh	fork/s
coltello/i	kohl-tehl-loh/ee	knife/knives
cucchiaio/ chucchiai	koohk-kyahy-oh/ee	spoon/s
bicchiere/i	beek-kyeh-reh/ee	glass/glasses

La camera da letto: The bedroom

La camera da letto (lah *kah*-meh-rah dah *leht*-toh) (*the bedroom*) is the space where you get to relax and unwind, and it may have as much or as little stuff in it as you want. It's your personal space, after all! Here's what you commonly find in the bedroom:

- ✔ **l'armadio** (lahr-*mah*-dyoh) (*armoire*)

- ✔ **il comò** (eel koh-*moh*) (*dresser*)

- ✔ **il comodino** (eel koh-moh-*dee*-noh) (*nightstand*)

- ✔ **la coperta** (lah koh-*pehr*-tah) (*blanket*)

- ✔ **i cuscini** (ee kooh-*shee*-nee) (*pillows*)

- ✔ **la finestra** (lah fee-*nehs*-trah) (*window*)

- ✔ **la lampada** (lah *lahm*-pah-dah) (*lamp*)

- ✔ **il lenzuolo/le lenzuola** (eel lehn-*zwoh*-loh/leh lehn-*zwoh*-lah) (*sheet/sheets*)

- ✔ **il letto** (eel *leht*-toh) (*bed*)

- ✔ **lo specchio** (loh *spehk*-kyoh) (*mirror*)

- ✔ **la sveglia** (lah *sveh*-lyah) (*alarm clock*)

- ✔ **le tende** (leh *tehn*-deh) (*curtains*)

By the way, don't bother to provide information about the size of your bed. Chances are that Italians won't follow your explanation of royal measurements when it comes to mattresses. Do you know the saying "one size fits all"? It applies to Italian beds. You have to specify only **matrimoniale** (mah-tree-moh-*nyah*-leh) (*double bed*) or **singolo** (*seehn*-goh-loh) (*single bed*).

Il bagno: The bathroom

One important room in any home is **il bagno** (eel *bahn*-yoh) (*the bathroom*). Italian bathrooms are peculiar. Should you want to try your hand at a compare-contrast game of non-Italian versus Italian bathrooms, one item commonly found in Italian bathrooms will probably stick out for you: **il bidet** (eel bee-*deh*) (*the bidet*) — a plumbing fixture of French origin that's present in every full Italian bathroom. If you're puzzled by the bidet, then use the toilet, a half bathroom that offers the bare essentials. Here, you'll find only a **la tazza** (lah *tahts*-sah) (*toilet bowl*) and a **lavandino** (lah-vahn-*dee*-noh) (*sink*).

Here are some terms common to bathrooms:

- ✔ **l'armadietto dei medicinali** (lahr-mah-*dyeht*-toh dehy meh-dee-chee-*nah*-lee) (*medicine cabinet*)

- ✔ **l'asciugamano/gli asciugamani** (lah-shooh-gah-*mah*-noh) (lyee ah-shooh-gah-*mah*-nee) (*towel/s*)

- ✔ **il bidet** (eel bee-*deh*) (*bidet*)

- ✔ **la carta igienica** (lah *kahr*-tah ee-*jeh*-nee-kah) (*toilet paper*)

- ✔ **la doccia** (lah *doch*-chah) (*shower*)

- ✔ **il lavandino** (eel lah-vahn-*dee*-noh) (*sink*)
- ✔ **il pettine** (eel *peht*-tee-neh) (*comb*)
- ✔ **il sapone** (eel sah-*poh*-neh) (*soap*)
- ✔ **la spazzola** (lah *spaht*-tzoh-lah) (*brush*)
- ✔ **la tazza** (lah *tahts*-sah) (*toilet bowl*)
- ✔ **la vasca da bagno** (lah *vahs*-kah dah *bahn*-yoh) (*bathtub*)

Other areas around the house

The average Italian home isn't very large. Don't forget that Italy is a long, narrow, and densely populated peninsula mostly covered by mountains and hills. The living room, kitchen, bedroom, and bathroom are all typical spaces in Italian homes, but yours may have more or different rooms. Here's a list of additional terms you may use to discuss your home in Italian. Italians love to know about the customs of the people they meet. If you have pictures, show them and point to the different parts of your home, using the proper Italian terms:

- ✔ **il balcone** (eel bahl-*koh*-neh) (*balcony*)
- ✔ **la cantina** (lah kahn-*tee*-nah) (*cellar*)
- ✔ **il corridoio** (eel kohr-ree-*doh*-yoh) (*hallway*)
- ✔ **il garage** (eel gah-*raj*) (*garage*)
- ✔ **l'ingresso** (leehn-*grehs*-soh) (*entrance, entryway*)
- ✔ **la lavanderia** (lah lah-vahn-deh-*ryah*) (*laundry room*)
- ✔ **la mansarda** (lah mahn-*sahr*-dah) (*attic*)
- ✔ **la piscina** (lah pee-*shee*-nah) (*pool*)
- ✔ **la scala** (lah *skah*-lah) (*staircase*)
- ✔ **lo studio** (loh *stooh*-dyoh) (*office; study*)

Talkin' the Talk

Susan is an exchange student visiting Italy. She is showing some pictures to Laura, the host family's daughter. (Track 7)

Susan: **Ecco, la terza casa a destra è la mia.**
            ehk-koh, lah *tehr*-tsah *kah*-sah ah *deh*-strah eh lah *mee*-ah.
            Here, the third home on the right is mine.

Laura: **Ma è grandissima!**
mah eh grahn-*dees*-see-mah!
It's really huge!

Susan: **Dici? Mah, ci sono sei stanze, una cucina, e tre bagni . . .**
dee-chee? mah, chee *soh*-noh sehy *stahn*-tseh, ooh-nah koo-*chee*-nah, eh treh *bah*-nyee . . .
You really think so? Well, there are six rooms, a kitchen, and three bathrooms . . .

Laura: **Ma quanti siete in famiglia?**
mah *kwahn*-tee *syeh*-teh een fah-*mee*-lyah?
How many persons are there in your family?

Susan: **Siamo in quattro: i miei genitori, mio fratello e io. Abbiamo tre stanze da letto di sopra e un soggiorno, una sala da pranzo e una *family room* di sotto. Come si dice "family room"?**
syah-moh een *kwaht*-troh: ee *myeh*-ee jeh-nee-*toh*-ree, *mee*-oh frah-*tehl*-loh eh *ee*-oh. ahb-*byah*-moh treh *stahn*-tseh dah *leht*-toh dee *soh*-prah eh oohn sohj-*johr*-noh, *ooh*-nah *sah*-lah dah *prahn*-tzoh eh *ooh*-nah family room dee *soht*-toh. *koh*-meh see *dee*-cheh "family room"?
It's four of us: my parents, my brother, and me. We have three bedrooms upstairs, and a living room, a dining room, and a family room downstairs. How do you say "family room"?

Laura: **Family room? Non so . . . è una specie di soggiorno. . . . Ma dimmi, cosa c'è a sinistra di questa veranda?**
family room? nohn soh . . . eh *ooh*-nah *speh*-cheh dee sohj-*johr*-noh. . . . mah *deem*-mee, *koh*-sah cheh ah see-*nee*-strah dee *kweh*-stah veh-*rahn*-dah?
Family room? I don't know . . . it's like a living room. . . . But tell me, what's that on the left of the porch?

Susan: **C'è la piscina. Non è molto grande, ma mio fratello e io la usiamo molto per fare esercizio . . . e per le nostre feste.**
cheh lah pee-*shee*-nah. nohn eh *mohl*-toh *grahn*-deh, mah *mee*-oh frah-*tehl*-loh eh *ee*-oh lah ooh-*syah*-moh *mohl*-toh pehr *fah*-reh eh-sehr-*chee*-tsyoh . . . eh pehr leh *noh*-streh *feh*-steh
That's the swimming pool. It's not very big, but my brother and I use it a lot to exercise . . . and for our parties.

Laura: **Feste in piscina? Sembra divertente!**
feh-steh een pee-*shee*-nah? *sehm*-brah
dee-vehr-*tehn*-teh!
Pool parties? That sounds exciting!

Susan: **Lo è! Sei invitata alla prossima!**
loh eh! sehy een-vee-*tah*-tah *ahl*-lah *prohs*-see-mah!
It is exciting! You are invited to the next one!

Laura: **Contaci, ci sarò!**
kohn-tah-chee, chee sah-*roh*!
You bet! I'll be there.

Words to Know

a destra	ah <u>deh</u>-strah	on the right
a sinistra	ah see-<u>nee</u>-strah	on the left
sopra	<u>soh</u>-prah	on top of
sotto	<u>soht</u>-toh	under
di lato	dee <u>lah</u>-toh	on its side
festa	<u>feh</u>-stah	party
piscina	pee-<u>shee</u>-nah	swimming pool
veranda	veh-<u>rahn</u>-dah	porch
alla prossima	<u>ahl</u>-lah <u>prohs</u>-see-mah	the next (or "see you later")
contaci!	<u>kohn</u>-tah-chee	you bet!
fare esercizio	<u>fah</u>-reh eh-sehr-<u>chee</u>-tsyoh	to exercise
è una specie di	eh <u>ooh</u>-nah <u>speh</u>-cheh dee	it looks like

Contemporary Italian architects and interior designers

Imagination and laborious design character-ize Italian style. Italian designers know how to combine **funzionalità** (foohn-tsyo-nah-lee-*tah*) (*functionality*) with **estetica** (eh-*steh*-tee-kah) (*aesthetics*) and have never made qualms about taking inspiration from the world around them. In 1946, soon after the end of World War II, the Milan Triennale organized the RIMA (**Riunione Italiana per le Mostre e l'Arredamento**) (ryooh-*nyoh*-neh ee-tah-*lyah*-nah pehr leh *moh*-streh eh lahr-reh-dah-*mehn*-toh) (*Italian Exhibition of Furniture and Furnishing*) exhibition, where **giovani architetti italiani** (*joh*-vah-nee ahr-kee-*teht*-tee ee-tah-lee-*ah*-nee) (*young Italian architects*) were invited to share their designs and showcase prototypes of their projects. It was a felicitous moment, when the Italian people were swept by the desire to reconstruct and build anew. Gian Luigi Banfi, Lodovico Barbiano di Belgiojoso, Enrico Peressutti, Ernesto Nathan Rogers, Ignazio Gardella, Charles De Carli, and Vico Magistretti met at RIMA and proposed a portfolio of interior design ideas to be mass-produced for houses where space would be organized in a func-tional, premeditated fashion. This exceptionally talented cohort of architects, engineers, and artists were the fathers of Italian design and share a significant artistic legacy.

Chapter 6

Using the Phone and Talking Business

*I*n this chapter, you encounter expressions and phrases that relate to telephones and telecommunication — for example, how to behave when someone calls you and how to leave a message. In addition, you'll find some samples of common phone dialogues. This chapter also delves into life at the office, helping you get a handle on terminology for both people and things around your workplace.

Phoning Made Simple

Pronto! (*prohn*-toh!) (*Hello!*) is the first thing you hear when you talk to an Italian on the phone. In most languages, you answer the phone with the same word you use for saying hello in person, but in Italian, you use **pronto** to say hello only on the phone.

You can answer the phone and say **Pronto. Chi parla?** (*prohn*-toh. kee *pahr*-lah?) (*Hello. Who's speaking?*)

A typical response may be **Pronto! Sono Sabrina. C'è Stefano?** (*prohn*-toh! *soh*-noh sah-*bree*-nah. cheh *steh*-fah-noh?) (*Hello! This is Sabrina. Is Stefano there?*)

Or you may hear **Sono Susanna. Posso parlare con Michele per favore?** (*soh*-noh sooh-*sahn*-nah. *pohs*-soh pahr-*lah*-reh kohn mee-*keh*-leh pehr fah-*voh*-reh?) (*This is Susan. May I please speak with Michael?*)

Connecting via cellphones, texts, and video

Italians love their **cellulari** (*chehl*-looh-*lah*-ree) (*cellphones*); there's no doubt about that. They were one of the first cultures to embrace full-force the **telefonino** (teh-leh-foh-*nee*-noh) (*little phone*) back in the '80s, when they adopted this useful accessory as a fashion (and social/class) statement.

Acquiring a cellphone

When you're in Italy, you need to have your own cellphone because public phones are hard to find, and hotel phones are very expensive to use. If you take your phone with you from, say, the United States, make certain that it will work in Italy and that calls won't cost you a mint. Of course, you can buy a phone when you get there. If you buy one, phone time can be purchased two ways at the local **tabaccaio** (tah-bahk-*kah*-yoh) (*tobacconist*). You can purchase **una scheda telefonica** (*ooh*-nah *skeh*-dah teh-leh-*foh*-nee-kah) (*a phone card*), or you can ask the salesperson to charge your phone for you by putting on a specific number of minutes or euros. You can do the same thing at any branch of the phone store where you bought your cellphone.

Text messaging

Because Italians tend to text more frequently than make phone calls these days (because it's so much cheaper and also trendy), you should know how to say a couple of important things, such as **messaggino** (mehs-sahj-*jee*-noh) or **sms** (*ehs*-seh-*ehm*-meh-*ehs*-seh), two ways of saying *text message,* and **mandami un messaggino** (*mahn*-dah-mee oohn mehs-sahj-*jee*-noh) (*text me*) (Literally: *send me a text message*).

Using the Internet to connect

All cities have their share of Internet stations where you can pay a per-minute fee to use the Internet. All you have to ask is **Posso usare Internet?** (*pohs*-soh ooh-*zah*-reh *een*-tehr-neht?) (*May I use the Internet?*) whereupon you'll be asked for **un documento** (oohn doh-kooh-*mehn*-toh) (*identification*) and assigned to a computer station. There, you can make Internet calls or e-mail to your heart's content.

Here are a few more useful phone phrases:

> **Avete un telefono?** (ah-*veh*-teh oohn teh-*leh*-foh-noh?) (*Is there/Do you have a [public] telephone?*)

> **Avete schede telefoniche?** (ah-*veh*-teh *skeh*-deh teh-leh-*foh*-nee-keh?) (*Do you sell phone cards?*)

Ha un recapito telefonico? (ah oohn reh-*kah*-pee-toh teh-leh-*foh*-nee-koh?) (*Do you have a contact phone number?*) (You may hear this when you go to change money at the bank.)

Qual è il suo/tuo numero di telefono? (kwahl eh eel *sooh*-oh/*tooh*-oh *nooh*-meh-roh dee teh-*leh*-foh-noh?) (*What is your* [formal/informal] *phone number?*)

Book I

Speaking Italian in Everyday Settings

Talkin' the Talk

Giorgio is back in Naples again and decides to give an old friend of his a call. (Track 8)

Simona: **Pronto!**
prohn-toh!
Hello!

Giorgio: **Pronto, Simona?**
prohn-toh, see-*moh*-nah?
Hello, Simona?

Simona: **Sì, chi parla?**
see, kee *pahr*-lah?
Yes, who's speaking?

Giorgio: **Sono Giorgio.**
soh-noh *johr*-joh.
It's Giorgio.

Simona: **Che bella sorpresa!**
keh *behl*-lah sohr-*preh*-zah!
What a nice surprise!

Sei di nuovo a Napoli?
sey dee *nwoh*-voh ah *nah*-poh-lee?
Are you in Naples again?

Giorgio: **Sì, sono arrivato stamattina.**
see, *soh*-noh ahr-ree-*vah*-toh stah-maht-*tee*-nah.
Yes, I arrived this morning.

Simona: **Ci vediamo stasera?**
chee veh-*dyah*-moh stah-*seh*-rah?
Are we going to meet tonight?

Giorgio:	**Ti chiamo per questo!**
	tee *kyah*-moh pehr *kwehs*-toh!
	That's why I'm calling!

In Italy, when you don't know a **numero di telefono** (*nooh*-meh-roh dee teh-*leh*-foh-noh) (*phone number*), look it up in the **elenco telefonico** (eh-*lehn*-koh teh-leh-*foh*-nee-koh) (*phone book*). If it's a business number, you can also look in the **pagine gialle** (*pah*-jee-neh *jahl*-leh) (*yellow pages*).

Calling for business or pleasure

Whether you want to find out what time a show starts, make a dental appointment, or just chat with a friend, the easiest way to accomplish any of these tasks is usually to pick up the telephone. This section takes you through the nuts and bolts of talking on the telephone.

Talkin' the Talk

The following is a formal dialogue between two **signori** (see-*nyoh*-ree) (*gentlemen*) who have met only once.

Sig. Palladino:	**Pronto?**
	prohn-toh?
	Hello?

Sig. Nieddu:	**Pronto, il signor Palladino?**
	prohn-toh, eel see-*nyohr* pahl-lah-*dee*-noh?
	Hello, Mr. Palladino?

Sig. Palladino:	**Sì. Con chi parlo?**
	see. kohn kee *pahr*-loh?
	Yes. Who am I speaking to?

Sig. Nieddu:	**Sono Carlo Nieddu.**
	soh-noh *kahr*-loh *nyeh*-dooh.
	This is Carlo Nieddu.
	Si ricorda di me?
	see ree-*kohr*-dah dee meh?
	Do you remember me?

Sig. Palladino:	**No, mi dispiace.** noh, mee dees-*pyah*-cheh. *I don't, I'm sorry.*
Sig. Nieddu:	**Il cugino di Enza.** eel kooh-*jee*-noh dee *ehn*-dzah. *Enza's cousin.*
Sig. Palladino:	**Ma certo! mi scusi tanto!** mah *chehr*-toh! mee *skooh*-zee *tahn*-toh! *Why, of course! Excuse me!*

Sometimes you call just *to chat on the phone* — **fare due chiacchiere al tele-fono** (*fah*-reh *dooh*-eh *kyahk*-kyeh-reh ahl teh-*leh*-foh-noh). But the person on the other end of the line may not be prepared for a lengthy chat.

When you're really busy and don't have even one second to speak, you may need the following phrases. The first is informal, and the second is one you may use at work.

> **Ti posso richiamare più tardi?** (tee *pohs*-soh ree-kyah-*mah*-reh *pyooh tahr*-dee?) (*Can I call you back later?*)

> **La posso richiamare fra mezz'ora?** (lah *pohs*-soh ree-kyah-*mah*-reh frah mehd-*dzoh*-rah?) (*Can I call you back in half an hour?*)

Talkin' the Talk

On many occasions, your call may be quite welcome, as Monica's is this time:

Monica:	**Ciao, mamma, ti disturbo?** chou, *mahm*-mah, tee dees-*toohr*-boh? *Hello, Mom. Am I disturbing you?*
Lucia:	**No, assolutamente.** noh, ahs-soh-looh-tah-*mehn*-teh *Not at all.*
Monica:	**Volevo sentire cosa fate per Pasqua.** voh-*leh*-voh sehn-*tee*-reh *koh*-sah *fah*-teh pehr *pahs*-qwah. *I wanted to hear what you were doing for Easter.*

Lucia:	**Andiamo tutti dalla nonna.**
	ahn-*dyah*-moh *tooht*-tee *dahl*-lah *nohn*-nah.
	We're all going to Grandma's.
Monica:	**Ottimo! Buon'idea!**
	oht-tee-moh! bwohn-ee-*dee*-ah!
	Great! Good idea!

Words to Know

cellulare	chehl-looh-<u>lah</u>-reh	cellular phone
telefonino [m]	teh-leh-foh-<u>nee</u>-noh	cellphone
telefono pubblico [m]	teh-<u>leh</u>-foh-noh <u>poohb</u>-blee-koh	public phone
scheda telefonica	<u>skeh</u>-dah teh-leh-<u>foh</u>-nee-kah	phone card
messaggino	mehs-sahj-<u>jee</u>-noh	text message

Making Arrangements over the Phone

Making an appointment, reserving a table at a restaurant, and ordering tickets for a concert are all activities you usually do by phone. This section introduces you to the Italian way to handle these matters.

Talkin' the Talk

Mrs. Elmi calls her doctor's office to make an appointment. She is speaking with the doctor's nurse. (Track 9)

Sig.ra Elmi:	**Buongiorno, sono la signora Elmi. Vorrei prendere un appuntamento.**
	bwohn-*johr*-noh, *soh*-noh lah see-*nyoh*-rah *ehl*-mee. vohr-*rehy prehn*-deh-reh oohn ahp-poohn-tah-*mehn*-toh.
	Good morning, this is Ms. Elmi. I'd like to make an appointment.

Nurse: **È urgente?**
eh oohr-*jehn*-teh?
Is it urgent?

Sig.ra Elmi: **Purtroppo sì.**
poohr-*trohp*-poh see.
Unfortunately, it is.

Nurse: **Va bene oggi alle quattro e mezza?**
vah *beh*-neh *ohj*-jee *ahl*-leh *kwaht*-troh eh
mehd-dzah?
Today at four-thirty?

Sig.ra Elmi: **Va benissimo, grazie.**
vah beh-*nees*-see-moh, *grah*-tsyeh.
That's great, thank you.

Nurse: **Prego. A più tardi.**
preh-goh. ah *pyooh tahr*-dee.
You're welcome. See you later.

CULTURAL WISDOM

The Italian media

I mezzi di comunicazione di massa (ee *meht*-tsee dee koh-mooh-nee-kah-*tsyoh*-neh dee *mahs*-sah) (*media*) played a major role in Italy's cultural transformations in the years following World War II, driving and accompanying the **modernizzazione** (moh-dehr-neet-tsah-*tsyoh*-neh) (*modernization*) of the country. RAI Radiotelevisione Italiana, **emittente televisiva e radiofonica nazionale** (eh-meet-*tehn*-teh teh-leh-vee-*see*-vah eh rah-dyoh-*foh*-nee-kah nah-tsyo-*nah*-leh) (*national radio and television broadcaster*), helped nationalize the country by bringing the Italian standard language into every household, where only regional dialects had been spoken until then. Only in the early '80s did RAI lose its **monopolio** (moh-noh-*poh*-lee-oh) (*monopoly*) on Italian TV, with the advent of the first Italian private television broadcasting companies.

Besides **programmi radiofonici e televisivi** (proh-*grahm*-mee rah-dyoh-*foh*-nee-chee eh teh-leh-vee-*see*-vee) (*radio and TV programs*), Italian media include a plethora of printed and online **quotidiani** (kwoh-tee-*dyah*-nee) (*daily newspapers*), **riviste** (ree-*vee*-steh) (*magazines*) and **periodici** (peh-*ryoh*-dee-chee) (*periodicals*), and **settimanali e mensili** (seht-tee-mah-*nah*-lee eh mehn-*see*-lee) (*weekly and monthly magazines*), which contain **notizie politiche, d'attualità, sportive, economiche, e di cronaca** (noh-*tee*-tsyeh poh-*lee*-tee-keh, daht-twah-lee-*tah*, spohr-*tee*-veh, eh-koh-*noh*-mee-keh, eh dee *kroh*-nah-kah) (*political news, current events, sports, economics, and city life events*). The most important daily newspapers are distributed across the Italian regions and abroad, in the major traffic areas, such as airports and train stations.

Il Corriere della Sera (eel kohr-*ryeh*-reh *dehl*-lah *seh*-rah) was the first Italian national newspaper. Its first 1906 issue had a **tiratura** (tee-rah-*too*-rah) (*circulation*) of 106,000

(continued)

(continued)

copies! Today, **Corriere della Sera** (kohr-*ryeh*-reh *dehl*-lah *seh*-rah) and **Repubblica** (reh-*poohb*-blee-kah) are the most important Italian daily newspapers. **Gazzetta dello Sport** (gahds-*dseht*-tah *dehl*-loh sport) is a daily newspaper that has only sport news, mostly soccer news, and it sells hundreds of thousands of copies.

Some of these means of mass communication are politically oriented or influenced by economic lobbies. However, there's also independent media to guarantee **pluralità d'informazione** (ploo-rah-lee-*tah* deen-fohr-mah-*tsyoh*-neh) (*plurality of information*). Because facts can be cast in different light, well-informed Italians explore different **fonti** (*fohn*-tee) (*sources*).

The expression **a domani** (ah doh-*mah*-nee) (*see you tomorrow*) is a bit different in Italian, in that it doesn't have a verb. In English, the verb *see* indicates that you will see the other person tomorrow. Italian is more concise; you say **a domani** — literally, *until tomorrow*.

Asking for People and Getting the Message

This section offers useful terminology about asking to speak to people and leaving messages. You know how often the person you want isn't available, so you need to be comfortable getting a message across.

Or you may find yourself in this familiar situation: You're waiting for a call, but the telephone doesn't ring. Then, you have to go out. When you get back, you want to know whether anyone called for you. You can ask that question in several ways:

Ha chiamato qualcuno per me? (ah kyah-*mah*-toh kwahl-*kooh*-noh pehr meh?) (*Has anybody called for me?*)

Mi ha chiamato qualcuno? (mee ah kyah-*mah*-toh kwahl-*kooh*-noh?) (*Did anybody call me?*)

Non mi ha cercato nessuno? (nohn mee ah chehr-*kah*-toh nehs-*sooh*-noh?) (*Has anybody looked for me?*)

Talkin' the Talk

Leo wants to give Camilla a call, but she's not home. Therefore, he leaves a message for her.

Leo:	**Buongiorno, sono Leo.**
	bwohn-*johr*-noh, *soh*-noh *leh*-oh.
	Good morning, this is Leo.

Voice:	**Ciao Leo.**
	chou *leh*-oh.
	Hello, Leo.

Leo:	**C'è Camilla?**
	cheh kah-*meel*-lah?
	Is Camilla in?

Voice:	**No, è appena uscita.**
	noh, eh ahp-*peh*-nah ooh-*shee*-tah.
	No, she's just gone out.

Leo:	**Quando la trovo?**
	kwahn-doh lah *troh*-voh?
	When can I find her?

Voice:	**Verso le nove.**
	vehr-soh leh *noh*-veh.
	Around nine.

Leo:	**Le posso lasciare un messaggio?**
	leh *pohs*-soh lah-*shah*-reh oohn mehs-*sahj*-joh?
	Can I leave her a message?

Voice:	**Come no, dimmi.**
	koh-meh noh, *deem*-mee.
	Of course, tell me.

As you can see, there are different ways for asking for people as well as for saying that they're not in and asking whether you can leave a message. The preceding informal dialogue gives you one way of saying these things, and the dialogue that follows recasts the situation into a formal exchange.

Talkin' the Talk

 Mr. Marchi calls Mr. Trevi's office to talk about an upcoming meeting. Mr. Trevi's secretary picks up the phone. (Track 10)

Secretary:	**Pronto?**
	prohn-toh?
	Hello?
Sig. Marchi:	**Buongiorno, sono Ennio Marchi.**
	bwohn-*johr*-noh, *soh*-noh *ehn*-nioh *mahr*-kee.
	Good morning, this is Ennio Marchi.
Secretary:	**Buongiorno, dica.**
	bwohn-*johr*-noh, *dee*-kah.
	Good morning, can I help you?
Sig. Marchi:	**Potrei parlare con il signor Trevi?**
	poh-*trehy* pahr-*lah*-reh kohn eel see-*nyohr treh*-vee?
	Can I speak to Mr. Trevi?
Secretary:	**Mi dispiace, è in riunione.**
	mee dees-*pyah*-cheh, eh een ree-ooh-*nyoh*-neh.
	I'm sorry, he's in a meeting.
Sig. Marchi:	**Potrei lasciargli un messaggio?**
	poh-*trehy* lah-*shahr*-lyee oohn mehs-*sahj*-joh?
	May I leave him a message?
Secretary:	**Certo. Prego.**
	chehr-toh. *preh*-goh.
	Of course. Go on . . .

Sometimes you don't understand the name of the person you're talking to and you have to ask for the spelling. If someone needs you to spell your name, you may hear either of the following questions:

Come si scrive? (*koh*-meh-see *skree*-veh?) (*How do you write it?*)

Può fare lo spelling? (pwoh *fah*-reh loh spelling?) (*Can you spell it?*)

Don't worry too much about this; as long as you know the basic Italian alphabet in Book I, Chapter 1, you'll be able to spell your name and town to anyone!

Words to Know

pronto	prohn-toh	hello
chiacchierare	kyahk-kyeh-rah-reh	to chat
Attenda in linea!	aht-tehn-dah een lee-neh-ah!	Please hold!
chiamare	kyah-mah-reh	to call
chiamata [f]	kyah-mah-tah	call
informazione [f]	een-fohr-mah-tsyoh-neh	information
sorpresa [f]	sohr-preh-zah	surprise

Discussing Your Job

The world is getting smaller, and business contact with people in other countries is getting more common. Whether by phone, fax, or e-mail, knowing how to communicate to business colleagues around the world is becoming more and more important. If you happen to have business contacts with Italian companies, knowing some basic Italian business vocabulary may be useful.

Italian has at least four words for *company* — **la compagnia** (lah kohm-pah-*nyee*-ah), **la ditta** (lah *deet*-tah) (which also means *the firm*), **l'azienda** (lah-*dzyehn*-dah), and **la società** (lah soh-cheh-*tah*). These words are virtually interchangeable.

L'ufficio (loohf-*fee*-choh) is Italian for *office.* The following sentences give you a taste of the phrases you hear in **uffici** (oohf-*fee*-chee) (*offices*) everywhere:

La mia scrivania è troppo piccola. (lah *mee*-ah skree-vah-*nee*-ah eh *trohp*-poh *peek*-koh-lah.) (*My desk is too small.*)

È una grande società? (eh *ooh*-nah *grahn*-deh soh-cheh-*tah?*) (*Is it a big company?*)

Lavora per una piccola agenzia. (lah-*voh*-rah pehr *ooh*-nah *peek*-koh-lah ah-jehn-*tsee*-ah.) (*He works for a small agency.*)

Mi piace il mio lavoro. (mee *pyah*-cheh eel *mee*-oh lah-*voh*-roh.) (*I like my job.*)

Referring to coworkers

Even if you are **libero professionista** (*lee*-beh-roh proh-fehs-syoh-*nee*-stah) (*self-employed*), chances are that your **lavoro** (lah-*voh*-roh) (*job*) puts you in contact with other people. All those people have titles and names, as the following short exchanges show:

- **Il mio capo è una donna.** (eel *mee*-oh *kah*-poh eh *ooh*-nah *dohn*-nah.) (*My boss is a woman.*)

- **Hai un'assistente personale?** (ahy oohn-ahs-see-*stehn*-teh pehr-soh-*nah*-leh?) (*Do you have a personal assistant?*)

   No, il nostro team ha un segretario. (noh, eel *nohs*-troh teem ah oohn seh-greh-*tah*-ryoh.) (*No, our team has a secretary.*)

- **Dov'è il direttore?** (doh-*veh* eel dee-reht-*toh*-reh?) (*Where is the director?*)

   Nel suo ufficio. (nehl *sooh*-oh oohf-*fee*-choh.) (*In her office.*)

Interviewing

Congratulations! You've sent in your **curriculum** (koohr-*ree*-kooh-loohm) (*resumé*) and the company has invited you for a **colloquio di lavoro** (kohl-*loh*-kwyoh dee lah-*voh*-roh) (*job interview*). The job interview is a discussion in which you have to take an active part. Not only do you have to "sell" your skills, but you must also assess **le opportunità di carriera** (leh ohp-pohr-tooh-nee-*tah* dee kahr-*ryeh*-rah) (*career opportunity*) and **crescita professionale** (*kreh*-shee-tah proh-fehs-syoh-*nah*-leh) (*professional growth*) within the company.

As a **candidato** (kahn-dee-*dah*-toh) (*candidate*), you answer and ask questions, exchange **punti di vista** (*poohn*-tee dee *vee*-stah) (*points of view*), and emphasize your potential. Don't forget that the objective is to move toward a mutual, good **rapporto di lavoro** (rahp-*pohr*-toh dee lah-*voh*-roh) (*working relationship*).

In Italy, want ads often request information on an applicant's personality. Also, job advertisements don't usually contain mailing addresses. Instead, ads list fax or e-mail addresses. You send your **domanda d'assunzione** (doh-*mahn*-dah dahs-soohn-*tsyoh*-neh) (*job application*) and/or your curriculum vitae or resumé via fax or e-mail.

Here are a few other terms that may be useful when applying or interviewing for a job:

✔ **affidabile** (ahf-fee-*dah*-bee-leh) (*dependable*)

✔ **annuncio** (ahn-*noohn*-choh) (*advertisement*)

✔ **assistente** (ahs-sees-*tehn*-teh) (*assistant*)

✔ **colloquio** (kohl-*loh*-kwyoh) (*interview*)

✔ **responsabile** (reh-spohn-*sah*-bee-leh) (*responsible*)

Covering compensation and breaks

According to the Constitution of the Italian Republic (Article 36), **lo stipendio** (stee-*pehn*-dyoh) (*salary*) must be proportionate and appropriate to the duration and quality of service performed by the **lavoratore** (lah-voh-rah-*toh*-reh) (*worker*) and sufficient for a reasonably good quality of life.

In Italy, there's no **stipendio minimo** (stee-*pehn*-dyoh *mee*-nee-moh) (*minimum wage*) set by law. Usually, a pay is deemed sufficient if it corresponds to that shown in the **contratto collettivo** (kohn-*traht*-toh kohl-leht-*tee*-voh) (*collective labor agreement*) for the sector. **Il pagamento** (eel pah-gah-*mehn*-toh) (*payment*) of wages is normally **mensile** (mehn-*see*-leh) (*on a monthly basis*).

The Italian Constitution also establishes that all **lavoratori** (lah-voh-rah-*toh*-ree) (*workers*) have the right to **riposo settimanale** (ree-*poh*-soh seht-tee-mah-*nah*-leh) (*weekly rest*) and **ferie annuali retribuite** (*feh*-ryeh ahn-*nwah*-lee reh-tree-*bwee*-teh) (*paid annual holidays*).

Describing things around the office

For many of us, **l'ufficio** (loohf-*fee*-choh) (*the office*) is the place where we spend most of our day. No matter whether it's a single **stanza** (*stahn*-tsah) (*room*) and a simple **scrivania** (scree-vah-*nee*-ah) (*desk*) between two **pareti** (pah-*reh*-tee) (*walls*), with few **sedie** (*seh*-dyeh) (*chairs*), Italians will furnish it to make it **un ambiente comodo** (oohn ahm-*byehn*-teh *koh*-moh-doh) (*a comfortable environment*) for **gli impiegati** (lyee eem-pyeh-*gah*-tee) (*employees*) and **attraente** (aht-trah-*ehn*-teh) (*attractive*) for **i clienti** (*clyehn*-tee) (*customers*).

Buildings, hangouts, and other key work areas

Open spaces are increasingly prevalent. They require more flexible solutions such as **panche** (*pahn*-keh) (*benches*), **tavoli condivisi** (*tah*-voh-lee kohn-dee-*vee*-see) (*shared desks*), and **zone relax** (*dzoh*-neh reh-*lahx*) (*relaxation areas*).

In times of frenetic activity, **la pausa caffé** (lah *pah*-ooh-sah cahf-*feh*) (*the coffee break*) is very important. You can relax from **attività ripetitive** (aht-tee-vee-*tah* ree-peh-tee-*tee*-veh) (*repetitive tasks*) and deepen the relations with your **colleghi** (kohl-*leh*-ghee) (*coworkers*). Italians give great importance to the quality of personal relationships between colleagues.

Each business has a specific décor: **L'arredamento** (lahr-reh-dah-*mehn*-toh) (*furniture*) is chosen according to the services provided. **Uno studio medico** (*ooh*-noh *stooh*-dyoh *meh*-dee-koh) (*a doctor's office*), for example, needs a **lettino** (leht-*tee*-noh) (*a cot*) and **attrezzatura professionale** (aht-trehts-tsah-*tooh*-rah proh-fehs-syoh-*nah*-leh) (*professional equipment*).

Office equipment

Even the smallest offices today utilize a wide variety of equipment. Many of these technology words are the same in Italian as they are in English: *computer, fax,* and *e-mail* are used and pronounced as they are in English, and the Italian words for *photocopy* and *photocopier* are fairly intuitive — **fotocopia** (foh-toh-koh-pyah) and **fotocopiatrice** (foh-toh-koh-pyah-*tree*-cheh), respectively.

The following sentences can help you develop your Italian office vocabulary to a respectable level.

> **Posso usare la stampante, per favore?** (*pohs*-soh ooh-*zah*-reh lah stahm-*pahn*-teh, pehr fah-*voh*-reh?) (*May I use the printer, please?*)

> **Il lavoro non va bene.** (eel lah-*voh*-roh nohn vah *beh*-neh.) (*Work isn't going well.*)

> **Il fax è arrivato.** (eel *fahks* eh ahr-ree-*vah*-toh.) (*The fax arrived.*)

> **Quando ha spedito l'e-mail?** (*kwahn*-doh ah speh-*dee*-toh lee-*mail?*) (*When did you send the e-mail?*)

Keep your **cancelleria** (kahn-chel-*leh*-ree-ah) (*stationery*) well organized: **carta** (*kahr*-tah) (*paper*) inside **cassetti** (kahs-*seht*-tee) (*drawers*) and **schedari** (skeh-*dah*-ree) (*file cabinets*), **penne** (*pehn*-neh) (*pens*) and **matite** (mah-*tee*-teh) (*pencils*) in **porta penne** (*pohr*-tah *pehn*-neh) (*pencil holders*), and **forbici** (*fohr*-bee-chee) (*scissors*) and **spillatrice** (speel-lah-*tree*-cheh) (*stapler*) always handy.

Talkin' the Talk

Mr. Miller, an American businessman, has been trying unsuccessfully to send his Italian associate, il signor Tosi, some important information.

Mr. Miller:
Ha ricevuto la mia raccomandata?
ah ree-cheh-vooh-toh lah mee-ah rahk-koh-mahn-dah-tah?
Have you received the express letter I sent?

Sig. Tosi:
No, oggi non è arrivato niente.
noh, ohj-jee nohn eh ahr-ree-vah-toh nyehn-teh.
No, nothing has arrived yet today.

Mr. Miller:
Le mando subito un fax.
leh mahn-doh sooh-bee-toh oohn fahks.
I'll send you a fax immediately.

Sig. Tosi:
Purtroppo è rotto.
poohr-trohp-poh eh roht-toh.
Unfortunately, it's broken.

Mr. Miller:
Le invio un'e-mail allora.
leh een-vee-oh oohn-ee-mail ahl-loh-rah.
I'll send you an e-mail then.

Sig. Tosi:
Va bene. E può mandarmi il documento?
vah beh-neh. eh pwoh mahn-dahr-mee eel doh-kooh-mehn-toh?
Yes. And can you send me the document?

Mr. Miller:
Certo, glielo mando come allegato, ma avrò bisogno di più tempo.
chehr-toh, lyee-loh mahn-doh koh-meh ahl-leh-gah-toh, mah ah-vroh bee-zoh-nyoh dee pyooh tehm-poh.
Of course, I'll send it as an attachment, but I'll need a bit more time.

Sig. Tosi:
Va benissimo. Oggi lavoro fino a tardi.
vah beh-nees-see-moh. ohj-jee lah-voh-roh fee-noh ah tahr-dee.
That's great. I'm working late today.

Words to Know

messaggio [m]	mehs-_sahj_-joh	message
lavoro [m]	lah-_voh_-roh	work
È rotto.	eh _roht_-toh.	It's broken.
macchina [f]	_mahk_-kee-nah	machine
tempo [m]	_tehm_-poh	time
tardi	_tahr_-dee	late

Chapter 7

Food, Glorious Food, and Drink

In This Chapter

▶ Taking a look at breakfast, lunch, and dinner

▶ Surveying Italian drink selections

▶ Reserving a table and paying for your meal

▶ Going grocery shopping

Food is distinctly unique from one region to another. This chapter introduces you to essential phrases to help you enjoy eating Italian-style. **Buon appetito!** (bwohn ahp-peh-*tee*-toh!) (*Enjoy!*)

Eating, Italian-Style

Italians have three main meals: **la prima colazione** (lah *pree*-mah koh-lah-*tsyoh*-neh) (*breakfast*), **il pranzo** (eel *prahn*-zoh) (*lunch*), and **la cena** (lah *cheh*-nah) (*dinner*). You eat **uno spuntino** (*ooh*-noh spoohn-*tee*-noh) (*a snack*) when you're hungry between main meals. **La merenda** (lah meh-*rehn*-dah) is a snack-time that most children enjoy daily.

Having breakfast

Your first meal of the day is always **la prima colazione** (lah *pree*-mah koh-lah-*tsyoh*-neh) (*breakfast*).

Some Italians begin the day with **un caffè** (oohn kahf-*feh*) (*espresso*) at home, but many stop for breakfast in **un bar** (oohn bahr) (*a coffee shop*) on their way to work. Breakfast consists of coffee and **una pasta** (*ooh*-nah *pahs*-tah) (*a pastry*), which can be **salata** (sah-*lah*-tah) (*savory*), **semplice** (*sehm*-plee-cheh) (*plain*), or filled with **marmellata** (mahr-mehl-*lah*-tah) (*jam*), **crema** (*kreh*-mah) (*custard*), or **cioccolato** (chohk-koh-*lah*-toh) (*chocolate*).

Talkin' the Talk

The man behind the counter in a coffee bar in Italy is called **il barista** (eel bah-*rees*-tah) (*the barman*).

Barista:	**Buongiorno!**
	bwohn-*johr*-noh!
	Good morning!
Sig. Zampieri:	**Buongiorno! Un caffè e una pasta alla crema per favore.**
	bwohn-*johr*-noh! oohn kahf-*feh* eh *ooh*-nah *pah*-stah *ahl*-lah *kreh*-mah pehr fah-*voh*-reh.
	Good morning! One espresso and a custard pastry please.
Barista:	**Qualcos'altro?**
	qwahl-kohs-*ahl*-troh?
	Anything else?
Sig. Zampieri:	**Una spremuta d'arancia, per favore.**
	ooh-nah spreh-*mooh*-tah dah-*rahn*-chah, pehr fah-*voh*-reh.
	One fresh-squeezed orange juice, please.
Barista:	**Ecco la spremuta. Prego.**
	ehk-koh lah spreh-*mooh*-tah. *preh*-goh.
	Here's the juice. Here you go.

Eating lunch

Italians do **il pranzo** (eel *prahn*-zoh) (*lunch*) differently from many other countries. The traditional courses are

- ✔ **antipasto** (ahn-tee-*pah*-stoh) (*appetizer*): Can be either hot, such as **bruschetta** (brooh-*skeht*-tah) (*toasted bread*), **crostini** (kroh-*stee*-nee) (*croutons*), and **supplì** (soohp-*plee*) (*rice croquettes*), or cold, such as **prosciutto e melone** (proh-*shooht*-toh eh meh-*loh*-neh) (*prosciutto and cantaloupe*) or **affettato e olive** (ahf-feht-*tah*-toh eh oh-*lee*-veh) (*cold cuts and olives*). **Antipasti** vary from region to region.

- ✔ **primo piatto** (*pree*-moh *pyaht*-toh) (*first course*): Although this comes after the antipasto, it's still called a first course. The **primo** consists of all kinds of **pasta** (*pah*-stah) (*pasta*), **risotto** (ree-*zoht*-toh) (*risotto*), or **minestra** (mee-*nehs*-trah) (*soup*).

✔ **il secondo** (eel seh-*kohn*-doh) (*the second course*): This generally consists of **carne** (*kahr*-neh) (*meat*) or **pesce** (*peh*-sheh) (*fish*), prepared in a wide variety of ways.

✔ **contorni** (kohn-*tohr*-nee) (*side dishes*): Vegetables may be ordered separately.

✔ **il dolce** (eel *dohl*-cheh) (*the dessert*): Last, but certainly not least, dessert may be **un dolce** (oohn *dohl*-cheh) (*a sweet*), **frutta fresca** (*froot*-tah *frehs*-kah) (*fresh fruit*), or **una macedonia** (*ooh*-nah mah-cheh-*doh*-nyah) (*fruit salad*).

The verb **prendere** (*prehn*-deh-reh) (*to have*) (Literally: *to take*) is the verb to use when talking about food and drinks.

Conjugation	Pronunciation
io prendo	*ee*-oh *prehn*-doh
tu prendi	tooh *prehn*-dee
lui/lei prende	*looh*-ee/ley *prehn*-deh
noi prendiamo	nohy prehn-*dyah*-moh
voi prendete	vohy prehn-*deh*-teh
loro prendono	*loh*-roh *prehn*-doh-noh

Pasta is usually made with durum wheat flour and water. The different types include: **spaghetti** (spah-*geht*-tee) (*spaghetti*), **bucatini** (booh-kah-*tee*-nee) (*thick, tube-like spaghetti*), **penne** (*pehn*-neh) (*short, cylindrical pasta shaped to a point at each end*), **fusilli** (fooh-*zeel*-lee) (*spiral-shaped pasta*), **rigatoni** (ree-gah-*toh*-nee) (*short, cylindrical, grooved pasta*), and so on.

On the other hand, **pasta fresca** (*pah*-stah *freh*-skah) (*fresh pasta*) means **pasta all'uovo** (*pahs*-tah ahl-*lwoh*-voh) (*egg noodles*), also called **pasta fatta in casa** (*pahs*-tah *faht*-tah een *kah*-sah) (*homemade pasta*). These are **tagliatelle** (tah-lyah-*tehl*-leh) (*flat noodles*), **fettuccine** (feht-toohch-*chee*-neh) (*narrow, flat noodles*), and **tonnarelli** (tohn-nah-*rehl*-lee) (*tubular noodles*), to mention just a few.

On Thursdays, Italians traditionally eat **gnocchi** (*nyohk*-kee) (*soft potato dumplings*). They're not pasta, though! They make a nice change from pasta and **risotto** (ree-*soht*-toh) (*rice*) and can be served in red or white sauces.

Incidentally, when you have a bite of pasta, you should make sure that it's **al dente** (ahl *dehn*-teh) (Literally: *to the tooth*). It means that the pasta is a little hard so that you really need to use your teeth!

The following conjugation shows you the polite form of the verb **volere** (voh-*leh*-reh) (*to want*). You have another verb for when you're being polite: *to like.* Italian, however, uses a conditional to express politeness.

Conjugation	Pronunciation
io vorrei	*ee*-oh vohr-*ray*
tu vorresti	too vohr-*rehs*-tee
lui/lei vorrebbe	*loo*-ee/ley vohr-*rehb*-beh
noi vorremmo	nohy vohr-*rehm*-moh
voi vorreste	vohy vohr-*rehs*-teh
loro vorrebbero	*loh*-roh vohr-*rehb*-beh-roh

Enjoying dinner

Italians often have **la cena** (lah *cheh*-nah) (*supper*) at home, but they also eat out. In this chapter, you're introduced to the different types of eateries available to you. Supper time varies throughout the peninsula; for example, restaurants in Venice stop serving dinner earlier than those in Rome, where you can go as late as 9 or 10 p.m.

CULTURAL WISDOM

The many meanings of "prego"

Prego (*preh*-goh) has several meanings. When you say it in response to **grazie** (*grah*-tsyeh) (*thank you*), it means *you're welcome.* But clerks and servers also use it to ask you what you would like or if they can help you. You often hear **prego** when you enter a public office or shop. You also use **prego** when you give something to someone. In this case, the word translates as *here you are.* **Prego** is also a very formal answer when you ask for permission. Following are a few examples of how **prego** is used:

✔ **Grazie.** (*grah*-tsyeh.) (*Thank you.*)

Prego. (*preh*-goh.) (*You're welcome.*)

✔ **Prego?** (*preh*-goh?) (*Can I help you?*)

✔ **Posso entrare?** (*pohs*-soh ehn-*trah*-reh?) (*May I come in?*)

Prego. (*preh*-goh.) (*Please.*)

✔ **Prego, signore.** (*preh*-goh see-*nyoh*-reh.) (*Here you are, sir.*)

Grazie. (*grah*-tsyeh.) (*Thank you.*)

Talkin' the Talk

A group of friends gather at a local pizzeria for dinner. Their exchanges are quite informal. (Track 11)

Sandra: **Che cosa prendiamo?**
keh *koh*-zah prehn-*dyah*-moh?
What should we have?

Laura: **Non lo so! Guardiamo il menù.**
nohn loh soh! gwahr-*dyah*-moh eel meh-*nooh.*
I don't know! Let's look at the menu.

Silvio: **Avete fame?**
ah-veh-teh *fah*-meh?
Are you hungry?

Laura: **Ho fame; prendo una pizza margherita.**
oh *fah*-meh; *prehn*-doh *ooh*-nah *peet*-tsah mahr-gheh-*ree*-tah.
I'm hungry; I'm getting a pizza margherita.

Sandra: **Io non tanto.**
ee-oh nohn *tahn*-toh.
I'm not so hungry.

Silvio: **Allora cosa prendi Sandra?**
ahl-*loh*-rah *koh*-zah *prehn*-dee *sahn*-drah?
So what are you going to have, Sandra?

Sandra: **Vorrei qualcosa di leggero.**
vohr-*rey* kwahl-*koh*-zah dee lehj-*jeh*-roh
I'd like something light.

   Un'insalatona.
onn-een-sah-lah-*toh*-nah.
A big salad.

Silvio: **Poco originale . . .**
pohk-koh oh-ree-jee-*nah*-leh . . .
Kind of boring . . .

Most Italian pizzerias have a wide range of pizzas. They're individual servings. You can also get pasta and salads there, and afterward, a dessert.

You've certainly heard of Italian **gelato** (jeh-*lah*-toh) (*ice cream*). Go for the **gelato artigianale** (jeh-*lah*-toh ahr-tee-jah-*nah*-leh) (*homemade ice cream*) — made in a **gelateria** (jeh-lah-teh-*ree*-ah) (*ice cream parlor*). You can have it in a **cono** (*koh*-noh) (*cone*) or a **coppetta** (kohp-*peht*-tah) (*cup*). You also have to decide on the **gusto** (*goohs*-toh) (*flavor*) and size, which usually goes according to euros or **palline** (pahl-*lee*-neh) (*scoops*).

Talkin' the Talk

Laura and Silvio stop for some ice cream. (Track 12)

Server: **Prego?**
preh-goh?
What would you like?

Laura: **Due coni, per favore.**
dooh-eh *koh*-nee, pehr fah-*voh*-reh.
Two ice-cream cones, please.

Server: **Da quanto?**
dah *kwahn*-toh?
What size?

Silvio: **Uno da due euro, e l'altro da 1 euro e 50.**
oohn-oh dah *dooh*-eh *eh*-ooh-roh, eh *lahl*-troh dah oohn *eh*-ooh-roh eh cheen-*qwahn*-tah.
One two-euro size and the other one for 1½ euros.

Server: **Che gusti?**
keh *goohs*-tee?
Which flavors?

Silvio: **Fragola e limone.**
frah-goh-lah eh lee-*moh*-neh.
Strawberry and lemon.

Server: **Prego. E Lei?**
preh-goh. eh ley?
Here you are. And you?

Laura: **Crema, cioccolato, cocco, e noce.**
kreh-mah, chohk-koh-*lah*-toh, *kohk*-koh, eh *noh*-cheh.
Custard, chocolate, coconut, and walnut.

Silvio:	**3 euro e 50?**
	treh *eh*-ooh-roh eh cheen-*qwahn*-tah?
	Three and a half euros?
Server:	**Sì, grazie. Ecco lo scontrino.**
	see, *grah*-tsyeh. *ehk*-koh loh *skohn*-tree-noh.
	Yes, thanks. Here's the receipt.

In a **gelateria,** you can also find **frullati** (froohl-*lah*-tee) (*mixed fruit juice*), **frappé** (frahp-*peh*) (which can be a *fruit milk shake* or a *frozen fruit shake*), and **yogurt** (*frozen yogurt*).

Drinking, Italian-Style

This section talks about many sorts of drinks, starting, obviously, with good Italian coffee, but also covering water, tea, and some spirits.

Expressing your love for espresso

You may have to order an espresso at your favorite coffee emporium back home, but in Italy, you get the same drink by asking the **barista** (bah-*rees*-tah) (*barman*) or **il cameriere** (eel kah-meh-*ryeh*-reh) (*the waiter*) for just **un caffè** (oohn kahf-*feh*) (*a coffee*).

In addition to **caffè,** you can enjoy a nice cup of **cioccolata calda** (chohk-koh-*lah*-tah *kahl*-dah) (*hot cocoa*); **tè** (*teh*) or **tè freddo** (*teh frehd*-doh) (*cold or iced tea*); **infusi** (een-*fooh*-zee) (*herbal teas*) with **camomilla** (kah-moh-*mee*-lah) (*chamomile tea*), the perfect bedtime infusion; **succhi di frutta** (*soohk*-kee dee *frooht*-tah) (*fruit juices*); **spremute** (spreh-*mooh*-teh) (*fresh-squeezed fruit juice*); and a wide selection of **acqua** (*ah*-kwah) (*water*).

Not many Italians anywhere in Italy drink tap water. Most Italians drink **acqua minerale** (*ah*-kwah mee-neh-*rah*-leh) (*mineral water*), which can be **acqua gassata/gasata** (*ah*-kwah gas-*sah*-tah/gah-*zah*-tah) (*sparkling water*), also called **acqua frizzante** (*ah*-kwah freets-*tsahn*-teh), or **acqua liscia** (*ah*-kwah *lee*-shah) or **naturale** (nah-tooh-*rah*-leh) (*still water*).

In **estate** (ehs-*tah*-teh) (*summer*), you will seek **ghiaccio** (*ghyach*-choh) (*ice*) wherever you go because most bars will part with only one small piece.

When you order a drink in Italy, you may need to specify how much you want, such as a whole bottle, a carafe, or just a glass. Use the following words:

- **una bottiglia di . . .** (*ooh*-nah boht-*tee*-lyah dee . . .) (*a bottle of . . .*)
- **un bicchiere di . . .** (oohn beek-*kyeh*-reh dee . . .) (*a glass of . . .*)
- **una caraffa di . . .** (*ooh*-nah kah-*rahf*-fah dee . . .) (*a carafe of . . .*)
- **mezzo litro di . . .** (*mehdz*-oh *lee*-troh dee . . .) (*half a liter of . . .*)
- **un quartino di . . .** (oohn kwahr-*tee*-noh dee . . .) (*a quarter liter of . . .*)

Italy's national drink: Espresso

Use the following terms exactly as you see them when ordering your coffee at the **bar** (bahr) (*coffee shop*), and you will definitely be understood!

- **un Caffè Hag** (oohn kahf-*feh* ahg): A popular brand of instant decaffeinated coffee — every Italian knows it.
- **un caffè** (oohn kahf-*feh*): When you order **caffè,** you automatically get an espresso.
- **un caffè ristretto** (oohn kahf-*feh* ree-*streht*-toh): Very strong and concentrated espresso.
- **un caffè doppio** (oohn kahf-*feh dohp*-pyoh): Double espresso.
- **un caffè lungo** (oohn kahf-*feh loohn*-goh): Espresso with more water to make it less concentrated.
- **un caffè corretto** (oohn kahf-*feh* kohr-*reht*-toh): Espresso with a bit of cognac or other liquor.
- **un cappuccino** (oohn kahp-pooh-*chee*-noh): Espresso with frothed milk.
- **un caffelatte** (oohn *kahf*-feh-*laht*-teh): Espresso with plenty of milk.
- **un caffè macchiato** (oohn kahf-*feh* mahk-*kyah*-toh): Espresso with a touch of milk.
- **un latte macchiato** (oohn *laht*-teh mahk-*kyah*-toh): Hot milk with just a touch of espresso.

- **un caffè americano** (oohn kahf-*feh* ah-meh-ree-*kah*-noh): American coffee but stronger — this type of coffee has become a new fashion.
- **un caffè decaffeinato** (oohn kahf-*feh* deh-kahf-feh-ee-*nah*-toh): Decaffeinated coffee.
- **un caffè d'orzo** (oohn kahf-*feh dohr*-zoh): Coffee substitute made from germinated, dried, and roasted barley. You can have it strong or light.
- **un caffè freddo/shakerato** (oohn kahf-*feh frehd*-doh/sheh-keh-*rah*-toh): Iced espresso shaken like a martini with cane syrup and ice.

And here are some tips to help you order your Italian coffee:

- Super-size coffee portions don't exist in Italy, and there's one size for a **cappuccino** and a **caffellatte.**
- Italians generally have their coffee while standing at the bar. The concept of coffee "to go" is one used primarily by tourists.
- Italians don't drink **cappuccino** after breakfast (11ish at the latest), and never after a meal!
- Beware! A **latte** is precisely what it says — milk. If you're hankering for a glass of warm milk, say **Un bicchiere di latte tiepido** (oohn bee-*kyeh*-reh dee *laht*-teh *tyeh*-pee-doh) (*a glass of warm milk*).

The last three terms are generally reserved for the house wine and beer.

When do you pay for your drinks in an Italian coffee bar? It depends. Normally, you have your coffee or whatever first and pay afterward. In little Italian bars, where just one or two people work behind the bar, you simply tell the cashier what you had and pay then. In bigger bars, and especially in large cities with many tourists, you first pay at the register, get a *sales slip* called a **scontrino** (skohn-*tree*-noh), and take that sales slip over to the **barista.**

Beverages with even more of a kick

Italy is also famous for its **vini** (*vee*-nee) (*wines*) and other fermented beverages, like the popular after-dinner drinks **limoncello** (lee-mohn-*chehl*-loh) (*lemon liquor*) and **grappa** (*grahp*-pah) (*grape spirit*). Each region has many of its own varieties of wine, so make certain you try some of the wines of the regions you visit.

Talkin' the Talk

Friends eating a casual meal in a **trattoria** (traht-tohr-*ee*-ah) (*little restaurant*) are ordering wine to have with their meal. They are in Tuscany and have ordered **pappa al pomodoro** (*pahp*-pah ahl poh-moh-*doh*-roh) (*a Tuscan bread soup*) and one **bistecca alla fiorentina** (bee-*stehk*-kah *ahl*-lah fyohr-ehn-*tee*-nah) (*huge steak*) for two or more people.

Server: **Ecco la lista dei vini.**
ehk-koh lah *lees*-tah dey *vee*-nee.
Here's the wine list.

Laura: **Che cosa ci consiglia?**
keh *koh*-sah chee kohn-*see*-lyah?
What do you recommend?

Server: **Abbiamo un ottimo Chianti della casa.**
ahb-*byah*-moh oohn *oht*-tee-moh kyahn-tee *dehl*-lah *kah*-sah.
We have some great house Chianti.

Silvio: **Prendiamo un po' di vino rosso, allora, con la bistecca.**
prehn-*dyah*-moh oohn poh dee *vee*-noh *rohs*-soh, ahl-*loh*-rah, kohn lah bee-*stehk*-kah.
Let's get some red wine, then, to have with our steak.

Laura:	**Si. Quello della casa?**
	see. *kwehl*-loh *dehl*-lah *kah*-sah?
	Yes. The house wine?
Silvio:	**Perfetto!**
	pehr-*feht*-toh!
	Perfect!

In Italy, the **aperitivo** (ah-pehr-ah-*tee*-voh) (*before-dinner drink*) is usually taken at the bar, either standing or seated at a **tavolino** (tah-voh-*lee*-noh) (*small table*). **Campari** (kahm-*pah*-ree) (*alcoholic apéritif*), **prosecco** (proh-*sehk*-koh) (*a dry sparkling wine*), and the most fashionable Spritz (zpreetz) (*refreshing wine-based cocktail*) are three major **aperitivi,** but you can also get alcohol-free **aperitivi** like **un Crodino** (kroh-*dee*-noh) (*bitter aperitif*) or **un Sanbitter** (sahn beet-*tehr*) (*aperitif soda*). The **aperitivo** is frequently served with a delectable assortment of free munchies.

You may prefer to get a **birra** (*beer*-rah) (*beer*) **grande** (*grahn*-deh) (*large*), **media** (*meh*-dyah) (*medium*), or **piccola** (*peek*-koh-lah) (*small*), either in a **bottiglia** (boht-*tee*-lyah) (*bottle*) or **alla spina** (*ahl*-lah *spee*-nah) (*draft beer*).

Dining Out, from Start to Finish

One of the more enjoyable (if potentially fattening) ways to explore a new culture is to sample the native cuisine. People interested in Italian cuisine are lucky — Italian-style restaurants are plentiful in North America. You can eat in a pizza joint or enjoy a traditional, multicourse meal in a classy restaurant. And, if you're fortunate enough to actually travel to Italy, your taste buds are in for a real treat! Just be aware that pizza and pasta are different in Italy than in the United States.

This section discusses the beginnings and endings of meals — from making reservations to paying the tab.

Making reservations

Unless you're going to a pizzeria, to the **trattoria** (traht-toh-*ree*-ah) (*little restaurant*), or to an **osteria** (oh-steh-*ree*-ah) (*small places with a simple but typical menu and a discrete choice of wines and beers*) down the street, you may need to reserve a table in a nice Italian restaurant.

Talkin' the Talk

Mr. Di Leo calls for reservations at his favorite restaurant. (Track 13)

Waiter:	**Pronto! Ristorante Roma.** *prohn*-toh! rees-toh-*rahn*-teh *roh*-mah. *Hello! Roma Restaurant.*
Sig. Di Leo:	**Buonasera! Vorrei prenotare un tavolo.** *bwoh*-nah-*seh*-rah! *vohr*-rey preh-noh-*tah*-reh oohn *tah*-voh-loh. *Good evening! I would like to reserve a table.*
Waiter:	**Per stasera?** pehr stah-*seh*-rah? *For this evening?*
Sig. Di Leo:	**No, per domani.** noh, pehr doh-*mah*-nee. *No, for tomorrow.*
Waiter:	**Per quante persone?** pehr *kwahn*-teh pehr-*soh*-neh? *For how many people?*
Sig. Di Leo:	**Per due.** pehr *dooh*-eh. *For two.*
Waiter:	**A che ora?** ah keh *oh*-rah? *At what time?*
Sig. Di Leo:	**Alle nove.** *ahl*-leh *noh*-veh. *At nine.*
Waiter:	**A che nome?** ah keh *noh*-meh? *In whose name?*
Sig. Di Leo:	**Di Leo.** dee *leh*-oh. *Di Leo.*

Words to Know

tavolo [m]	<u>tah</u>-voh-loh	table
cameriere [m]	kah-meh-<u>ryeh</u>-reh	waiter
domani [m]	doh-<u>mah</u>-nee	tomorrow
prenotazione [f]	preh-noh-tah-<u>tsyoh</u>-neh	reservation
stasera [f]	stah-<u>seh</u>-rah	this evening

Paying for your meal

You don't need to use cash in all restaurants. In many restaurants, mostly higher-end ones, you can pay with your credit card, too.

You don't have to tip in Italy, not even in an elegant restaurant, even though it can be a way to reward good service. You always pay **pane e coperto** (*pah*-neh eh koh-*pehr*-toh) (*a cover or service charge*) just to sit down.

When you want **il conto** (eel *kohn*-toh) (*the bill*), you ask the server to bring it to you. She will never bring it to you unless you ask for it. Use the verbs **portare** (pohr-*tah*-reh) (*to bring*) or **fare** (*fah*-reh) (*to prepare*) and say

> **Ci porta/fa il conto, per favore?** (chee *pohr*-tah/fah eel *kohn*-toh, perh fah-*voh*-reh?) (*Will you please bring/prepare us the bill?* [formal])

Or simply say

> **Il conto, per favore!** (eel *kohn*-toh, pehr fah-*voh*-reh!) (*The bill, please!*)

Save that sales slip

Be sure to keep **lo scontrino** (loh skohn-*tree*-noh) (*the sales slip*), at least until you leave an Italian bar or any kind of shop or restaurant. This is important in Italy because **la Guardia di Finanza** (lah *gwahr*-dyah dee fee-*nahn*-tsah) (*Financial Guard*) often checks. If you leave without a sales slip and are caught, you and the owner of the establishment have to pay a fine.

Shopping for Food

Many people do their marketing in a **supermercato** (*sooh*-pehr-mehr-*kah*-toh) (*supermarket*) even if there are other places to get food. But most Italian cities have specialty shops, starting with the **alimentari** (ah-lee-mehn-*tah*-ree) (*grocery store*), where you can get many items — everything from **latte** (*laht*-teh) (*milk*) to **carta igienica** (*kahr*-tah ee-*jeh*-nee-kah) (*toilet paper*). These shops, with their specific selection of goods, provide the personal attention often lacking in supermarkets.

Dal macellaio (butcher shop)

From the **dal macellaio** (dahl mah-chehl-*lah*-yoh) (*butcher shop*) you may select items like the following:

- ✔ **agnello** (ah-*nyehl*-loh) (*lamb*)
- ✔ **bistecca** (bee-*stehk*-kah) (*steak*)
- ✔ **coniglio** (koh-*nee*-lyoh) (*rabbit*)
- ✔ **maiale** (mah-*yah*-leh) (*pork*)
- ✔ **manzo** (*mahn*-zoh) (*beef*)
- ✔ **pollo** (*pohl*-loh) (*chicken*)
- ✔ **vitello** (vee-*tehl*-loh) (*veal*)

Pesce (fish)

Not all restaurants serve fresh **pesce** (*peh*-sheh) (*fish*). To be sure, the better restaurants offer fresh (not frozen) fish, and it's usually listed as a special of the day. Getting fresh fish certainly depends on the region, such as whether you're close to the sea. If you're in doubt about the fish a restaurant offers, your best bet is to ask someone local for a recommendation. Better safe than sorry!

> **Dove si può mangiare il pesce fresco?** (*doh*-veh see pwoh mahn-*jah*-reh eel *peh*-sheh *frehs*-koh?) (*Where can we eat fresh fish?*)

Some common types of fish, depending on the region, include:

- ✔ **acciughe fresche** (ahch-*chooh*-geh *frehs*-keh) (*fresh anchovies*)
- ✔ **branzino** (brahn-*zee*-noh) (*sea bass*)

- **calamari** (kah-lah-*mah*-ree) (*squids*)
- **cozze** (*koht*-tseh) (*mussels*)
- **frutti di mare** (*frooht*-tee dee *mah*-reh) (*shellfish*)
- **gamberetti** (gahm-beh-*reht*-tee) (*small shrimp*)
- **gamberi** (*gahm*-beh-ree) (*prawns*)
- **merluzzo** (mehr-*loot*-tsoh) (*cod*)
- **orata** (oh-*rah*-tah) (*sea bream*)
- **pesce spada** (*peh*-sheh *spah*-dah) (*swordfish*)
- **polpo/polipo** (*pohl*-poh/*poh*-lee-poh) (*octopus*)
- **seppia** (*sehp*-pyah) (*cuttlefish*)
- **sogliola** (*soh*-lyoh-lah) (*sole*)
- **spigola** (*spee*-goh-lah) (*snapper*)
- **tonno fresco** (*tohn*-noh *frehs*-koh) (*fresh tuna*)
- **vongole** (*vohn*-goh-leh) (*clams*)

Common simple preparations are **al forno** (ahl-*for*-noh) (*baked*), **alla griglia** (*ahl*-lah *gree*-lyah) (*grilled*), and **in padella** (een pah-*dehl*-lah) (*in the skillet*).

At the panetteria (bread shop)

In a **panetteria** (pah-neht-teh-*ree*-ah) (*bread shop*), you can try all sorts of different kinds of **pane** (*pah*-neh) (*bread*), as well as some oven-baked **dolci** (*dohl*-chee) (*sweets*).

In some Italian bread shops, you can also find **pizza al taglio** (*peet*-tsah ahl *tah*-lyoh) (*slices of pizza*) and **focaccia** (foh-*kah*-chah) (*flatbread*), and pay according to weight.

Talkin' the Talk

A baker in a bread store waits on two customers, Mrs. Belli and Paolo.

Sig.ra Belli: **Ha del pane biologico?**
ah dehl *pah*-neh byoh-*loh*-jee-koh?
Do you have any organic bread?

Baker: **Ho dei panini, o questo tipo di Matera, tutti cotti nel forno a legna.**
oh dey pah-*nee*-nee, oh *kwehs*-toh *tee*-poh dee mah-*teh*-rah, *tooht*-tee *koht*-tee nehl *fohr*-noh ah *leh*-nyah.
I have these rolls, or this Matera-style one, all baked in our wood-burning oven.

Sig.ra Belli: **Mi dà quello rustico per favore.**
mee dah *kwehl*-loh *rooh*-stee-koh peh fah-*voh*-reh.
I'll take that hard-crust one please.

Quant'è?
kwahn-*teh*?
How much is it?

Baker: **3 euro e 50 centesimi.**
treh *eh*-ooh-roh eh cheen-*qwahn*-tah chehn-*teh*-see-mee.
Three euros and 50 cents.

Sig.ra Belli: **Grazie, e arrivederla.**
grah-tsyeh, eh ahr-ree-veh-*dehr*-lah.
Thank you, and good-bye.

Baker (to another customer):
Desidera?
deh-*zee*-deh-rah?
What would you like?

Paolo: **Un pezzo di pizza al pomodoro.**
oohn *peht*-tsoh dee *peet*-tsah ahl poh-moh-*doh*-roh.
A piece of pizza with tomatoes.

Baker: **Così va bene?**
koh-*zee* vah *beh*-neh?
Is this okay?

Paolo **Un po' più grande, per favore.**
oohn poh pyooh *grahn*-deh, pehr fah-*voh*-reh.
A little bigger, please.

Baker **Così?**
koh-zee?
Like this?

Paolo **Perfetto, grazie!**
pehr-*feht*-toh, *grah*-tsyeh!
That's perfect, thank you.

Going for an aperitivo with rinforzo

Sometimes, you don't have time for a traditional lunch or dinner, or maybe you're not that hungry. In this case, **aperitivo con rinforzo** (ah-peh-ree-*tee*-voh *kohn* reen-*fohr*-tsoh) (*reinforced aperitif*) is what you need. This is usually a drink that may consist of alcoholic or nonalcoholic cocktails, or sparkling wine, accompanied by a finger-food buffet, mini-sandwiches, and snacks. The food is arranged in an aesthetically pleasing manner, and you may choose to stand or sit while enjoying it.

REMEMBER

Items are priced according to weight, usually by **chilo** (*kee*-loh) (*kilo*). You know that when you hear **un etto** (oohn *eht*-toh), it means *100 grams.* **Mezz'etto** (meht-*tseht*-toh) is 50 grams, because **mezzo** (*meht*-tsoh) means *half.* Likewise, a **mezzo chilo** (*meht*-tsoh *kee*-loh) is *half a kilo.* Meat, fish, fruits, cheese, cold cuts, and vegetables are sold by weight.

Table 7-1 lists common fruits and vegetables that you may find at an open-air farmers' market.

Table 7-1	Fruits and Vegetables	
Italian Singular/Plural	*Pronunciation*	*Translation*
albicocca/albicocche [f]	ahl-bee-*kohk*-kah/keh	*apricot/s*
ananas [m]	*ah*-nah-nahs	*pineapple*
arancia/arance [f]	ah-*rahn*-chah/cheh	*orange/s*
asparago/i [m]	ah-*spah*-rah-goh/jee	*asparagus*
banana/e [f]	bah-*nah*-nah/neh	*banana/s*
broccoli [m]	*brohk*-koh-lee	*broccoli*
carota/e [f]	kah-*roh*-tah/teh	*carrot/s*
cavolo/i [m]	*kah*-voh-loh/lee	*cabbage/s*
ciliegia/gie [f]	chee-*lyeh*-jah/jeh	*cherry/cherries*
cocomero/i [m]	koh-*koh*-meh-roh/ree	*watermelon/s*
fico/fichi [m]	*fee*-koh/kee	*fig/s*
fragola/e [f]	*frah*-goh-lah/leh	*strawberry/strawberries*
fungo/funghi [m]	*foohn*-goh/gee	*mushroom/s*
limone/i [m]	lee-*moh*-neh/nee	*lemon/s*

Italian Singular/Plural	Pronunciation	Translation
mela/e [f]	*meh*-lah/leh	*apple/s*
melanzana/e [f]	meh-lahn-*zah*-nah/neh	*eggplant/s*
melone/i [m]	meh-*loh*-neh/nee	*melon/s*
peperone/i [m]	peh-peh-*roh*-neh/nee	*bell pepper/s*
pera/e [f]	*peh*-rah/reh	*pear/s*
pesca/pesche [f]	*pehs*-kah/keh	*peach/es*
pomodoro/i [m]	poh-moh-*doh*-roh/ree	*tomato/es*
pompelmo/i [m]	pohm-*pehl*-moh/mee	*grapefruit/s*
prugna/e [f]	*prooh*-nyah/nyeh	*plum/s*
spinaci [m]	spee-*nah*-chee	*spinach*
uva [f]	*ooh*-vah	*grapes*
zucchina/o/e/i [f/m]	dzoohk-*kee*-nah/noh/ neh/nee	*zucchini/s*

Chapter 8

Shopping, Italian-Style

. . . .

. . . .

Italy is famous throughout the world for its fashion, **la moda** (lah *moh*-dah), as well as for its **stilisti** (stee-*lees*-tee) (*designers*), such as **Armani** (ahr-*mah*-nee) and **Valentino** (vah-lehn-*tee*-noh). You may suddenly feel inspired to shop, and what better place to shop than in Italy! In Italian, a famous brand is called **la griffe** (lah greef) (a French word) or **la firma** (lah *feer*-mah) that means, literally, *the signature*. So to say that a good is designed by a famous stylist, you say it's **griffato** (greef-*fah*-toh) or **firmato** (feer-*mah*-toh) — *signed*.

Checking Out Stores

I negozi di quartiere (ee neh-*goh*-tsee dee kwahr-*tyeh*-reh) (*neighborhood stores*) are an important component of the social fabric and architecture of Italian cities and villages (although in recent years, the number of department stores is growing). Italians love to shop in stores that specialize in a particular type of **merce** (*mehr*-cheh) (*good*) or **prodotto artigianale** (proh-*doht*-toh ahr-tee-jah-*nah*-leh) (*craft*). There are **profumerie** (proh-foo-meh-*ree*-eh) (*beauty shops*), **negozi di scarpe** (neh-*goh*-tsee dee *skahr*-peh) (*shoe stores*), **negozi di abbigliamento** (neh-*goh*-tsee dee ahb-bee-lyah-*mehn*-toh) (*clothing stores*), **negozi di articoli sportivi** (neh-*goh*-tsee dee ahr-tee-koh-lee spohr-*tee*-vee) (*sportswear stores*), boutiques, and shops that sell only **borse** (*bohr*-seh) (*bags*), **borsette** (bohr-*seht*-teh) (*purses*), **cinte** (*cheen*-teh) (*belts*), **guanti** (*gwahn*-tee) (*gloves*), and **accessori** (ahch-chehs-*soh*-ree) (*accessories*).

There are also **mercati** (mehr-*kah*-tee) (*outdoor markets*) and **mercatini** (mehr-kah-*tee*-nee) (*small outdoor markets*), which are a popular destination for adventurous bargain hunters. **Mercato** (singular of **mercati**) tends to refer mostly to fresh produce; **mercatino** (singular of **mercatini**) may include fresh produce, but it implies the presence of stands with housewares, shoes, clothes, purses, linens, and so on. A visit to one of these markets is a journey into great chaos: The swarming **folla** (*fohl*-lah) (*crowds*) and sprawling **mucchi** (*moohk*-kee) (*piles*) of merchandise make for a memorable experience.

In these **mercatini,** you can find shoes, shirts, bags, and clothing for men and women at bargain prices. If you're lucky (although you may have to literally dig into the pile of items on display), you'll find fabulous items — at fabulous prices!

There are also specialized **mercatini,** like **dell'antiquariato** (dehl-lahn-tee-kwah-*ryah*-toh) (*of antiquities*) or **del libro** (dehl *lee*-broh) (*of books*).

Deciding between department stores and boutiques

North Americans have access to huge **centri commerciali** (*chehn*-tree kohm-mehr-*chah*-lee) (*shopping malls*), where you really can find everything. In Italy, people shop in **grandi magazzini** (*grahn*-dee mah-gaht-*dzee*-nee) (*department stores*), which are tiny compared to American ones. The biggest Italian department stores are **Coin** (koh-*een*) and **Oviesse** (oh-*vyehs*-seh). Both carry a variety of items; however, many Italians prefer to shop in smaller, privately owned stores where service is key (and where there's little to no browsing and self-service).

Incidentally, what's *shopping* in Italian? You say **fare la spesa** (*fah*-reh la *speh*-zah) when you buy food, and **fare spese** (*fah*-reh *speh*-seh) and **fare lo shopping** (*fah*-reh loh *shohp*-peeng) for everything else. Good news is that you have to conjugate only the verb **fare**.

Navigating the store

Following are some signs pointing to the various **reparti** (reh-*pahr*-tee) (*departments*) or individual boutiques:

- **abbigliamento da donna/da uomo** (ahb-bee-lyah-*mehn*-toh dah *dohn*-nah/dah *woh*-moh) (*women's/men's wear*)
- **intimo donna** (*een*-tee-moh *dohn*-nah) (*ladies' intimate apparel*)

- **intimo uomo** (*een*-tee-moh *woh*-moh) (*men's intimate apparel*)
- **accessori** (ahch-chehs-*soh*-ree) (*accessories*)
- **profumeria** (proh-fooh-meh-*ree*-ah) (*perfumery [including shampoo, barrettes, creams, makeup, and other related items]*)
- **casalinghi** (kah-sah-*leen*-gee) (*housewares*)
- **biancheria per la casa** (byahn-keh-*ree*-ah pehr lah *kah*-sah) (*household linens and towels*)

Talkin' the Talk

Here, a clerk is kept busy giving directions for various departments. (Track 14)

Sig.ra Verdi:	**Sto cercando l'abbigliamento da bambino.** stoh chehr-*kahn*-doh lahb-bee-lyah-*mehn*-toh dah bahm-*bee*-noh. *I'm looking for children's wear.*
Clerk:	**Al secondo piano.** ahl seh-*kohn*-doh *pyah*-noh. *On the second floor.*
Sig. Marchi:	**Dove devo andare per ritirare un paio di pantaloni?** *doh*-veh *deh*-voh ahn-*dah*-reh *pehr* ree-tee-*rah*-reh oohn *pah*-yoh dee pahn-tah-*loh*-nee? *Where should I go to pick up a pair of trousers?*
Clerk:	**Deve rivolgersi al commesso del reparto uomo.** *deh*-veh ree-*vohl*-jehr-see ahl kohm-*mehs*-soh dehl reh-*pahr*-toh *woh*-moh. *You need to see the clerk in the men's department.*
Anna:	**Dove sono i camerini, per favore?** *doh*-veh *soh*-noh ee kah-meh-*ree*-nee, pehr fah-*voh*-reh? *Where are the fitting rooms, please?*
Clerk:	**Vede l'uscita di sicurezza? I camerini sono sulla sinistra.** *veh*-deh looh-*shee*-tah dee see-kooh-*reht*-tsah? ee kah-meh-*ree*-nee *soh*-noh *soohl*-lah see-*nees*-trah. *Do you see the emergency exit there? The fitting rooms are to the left.*

In some places, you'll notice elementary signs — like the one over the door reading **uscita di sicurezza** (ooh-*shee*-tah dee see-kooh-*reht*-tsah) (*emergency exit*) — can be very useful, including the following:

- **entrata** (ehn-*trah*-tah) (*entrance*)
- **uscita** (ooh-*shee*-tah) (*exit*)
- **spingere** (*speen*-jeh-reh) (*to push*)
- **tirare** (tee-*rah*-reh) (*to pull*)
- **orario di apertura** (oh-*rah*-ryoh dee ah-pehr-*tooh*-rah) (*business hours*)
- **aperto** (ah-*pehr*-toh) (*open*)
- **chiuso** (*kyooh*-zoh) (*closed*)
- **la scala mobile** (lah *skah*-lah *moh*-bee-leh) (*escalator*)
- **l'ascensore** (lah-shehn-*soh*-reh) (*elevator*)
- **la cassa** (lah *kahs*-sah) (*cash register*)

Avere bisogno di (ah-*veh*-reh bee-*zoh*-nyoh dee) (*to need*) is a frequent expression in Italian. You use it in any kind of store. The form that you use as a speaker goes like this:

    Ho bisogno di . . . (oh bee-*zoh*-nyoh dee) (*I need . . .*)

When you're in a store and have a question or need some advice, you turn to **la commessa/il commesso** (lah kohm-*mehs*-sah/eel kohm-*mehs*-soh) (*the sales clerk* [feminine/masculine]) and say **Mi può aiutare, per favore?** (mee pwoh ah-yooh-*tah*-reh, pehr fah-*voh*-reh?) (*Can you help me, please?*) Of course, if you're just looking and a salesperson asks **Desidera?** (deh-*zee*-deh-rah?) (*Can I be of help?*) (*Can I help you?*), you can answer **Posso dare un'occhiata?** (*pohs*-soh *dah*-reh oohn-ohk-*kyah*-tah?) (*Is it all right if I just look?*)

Admiring shop displays

Guardare le vetrine (gwahr-*dah*-reh leh veh-*tree*-neh) (*window shopping*) is an Italian pastime. **Le vetrine** (leh veh-*tree*-neh) (*the shop windows*) are artistically set up to attract the attention **dei passanti** (*deh*-ee pahs-*sahn*-tee) (*of passersby*) and to inform even the most distracted person of the latest trends. Variety and color diversity are indicators of good taste and a sense of style, so watching the window displays is almost like admiring an art exhibit!

Clothing Yourself

Shopping can be an informative and fun way to learn about a culture because of the ways that colors and fabrics differ. For example, you can always tell what color is in fashion and how careful Italians are about wearing ironed **vestiti** (veh-*stee*-tee) (*clothes*) just by walking down a city street. In Italy, you can explore lots of boutiques and designer shops, as well as numerous department stores.

Checking out various items

The Italian wardrobe is generally a piece of furniture. Given the size of houses in Italy, there's often no room for walk-in closets. Looking inside one of these wardrobes, you'll likely find the following:

- **abito** (*ah*-bee-toh) (*suit*)
- **camicetta** (kah-mee-*cheht*-tah) (*blouse*)
- **camicia** (kah-*mee*-chah) (*shirt*)
- **cappotto** (kahp-*poht*-toh) (*coat*)
- **completo** (kohm-*pleht*-oh) (*outfit; suit*)
- **costume da bagno** (kohs-*tooh*-meh dah *bahn*-yoh) (*bathing suit; swimming trunks*)
- **giacca** (*jahk*-kah) (*jacket; sports jacket*)
- **gonna** (*gohn*-nah) (*skirt*)
- **impermeabile** (eem-pehr-meh-*ah*-bee-leh) (*raincoat*)
- **jeans** (jeenz) (*jeans*)
- **maglia** (*mah*-lyah) (*sweater*)
- **maglietta** (mahl-*yeht*-tah) (*T-shirt*)
- **pantaloni** (pahn-tah-*loh*-nee) (*pants*)
- **vestito** (veh-*stee*-toh) (*dress*)

Sizing up Italian sizes

When shopping for clothing, size matters. An item may be **piccolo** (*pee*-koh-loh) (*small*) or **grande** (*grahn*-deh) (*large*), and you need to be able to express the problem to get a size that fits.

Whenever you go to another country, and this is particularly true in Europe, the sizes — called **taglie** (*tah*-lyeh) or **misure** (mee-*zooh*-reh) in Italy — change and you never know which one corresponds to yours. Table 8-1 helps you with this problem by giving you the most common sizes.

Table 8-1	Clothing Sizes	
Italian Size	*American Size*	*Canadian Size*
Women's dress sizes		
40	4	6
42	6	8
44	8	10
46	10	12
48	12	14
Men's suit sizes		
48	38	40
50	40	42
52	42	44
54	44	46
56	46	48

In Italy, you won't have any difficulties with sizes like S, M, L, and XL because they're used the same way — *S* for small, *M* for medium, *L* for large, and *XL* for extra large — beware, though, that an Italian *large* often corresponds to a North American *small*.

Talkin' the Talk

Giovanna has found the skirt she's been looking for. She asks the saleswoman if she can try it on. (Track 15)

Giovanna: **Posso provare questa gonna?**
pohs-soh proh-*vah*-reh *kweh*-stah gohn-*nah*?
May I try on this skirt?

Saleswoman: **Certo. Che taglia porta?**
chehr-toh. keh *tah*-lyah *pohr*-tah?
Sure. What size do you wear?

Giovanna: **La quarantadue.**
lah kwah-*rahn*-tah-*dooh*-eh.
Forty-two.

Saleswoman: **Forse è un po' piccola.**
fohr-seh eh oohn poh *peek*-koh-lah.
Perhaps it's a little bit too small.

Giovanna: **Me la provo.**
meh lah *proh*-voh.
I'll try it on.

Giovanna returns from the dressing room.

Saleswoman: **Va bene?**
vah *beh*-neh?
Does it fit?

Giovanna: **È troppo stretta. Ha una taglia più grande?**
eh *trohp*-poh *streht*-tah. ah *ooh*-nah *tah*-lyah pyooh
grahn-deh?
It's too tight. Do you have it in a larger size?

Saleswoman: **Nella sua taglia solo in blu.**
nehl-lah *sooh*-ah *tah*-lyah *soh*-loh *een* blooh.
In your size, only in blue.

Italy is the leader in the shoe industry. You won't believe what good taste Italians have in **scarpe** (*skahr*-peh) (*shoes*). You may just find the shoes of your dreams, whether they be a regular **paio di scarpe** (*pah*-yoh dee *skahr*-peh) (*pair of shoes*), **pantofole** (pahn-*toh*-foh-leh) (*slippers*), **sandali** (*sahn*-dah-lee) (*sandals*), or **stivali** (stee-*vah*-lee) (*boots*).

When you try on footwear, you may need to use some of the following words:

- **stretta/e/o/i** (*streht*-tah/teh/toh/tee) (*tight*)
- **larga/ghe/go/ghi** (*lahr*-gah/geh/goh/ghee) (*loose*)
- **corta/e/o/i** (*kohr*-tah/teh/toh/tee) (*short*)
- **lunga/ghe/go/ghi** (*loohn*-gah/gheh/goh/ghee) (*long*)

You may notice that Italian uses **numero** (*nooh*-meh-roh) (*number*) to talk about shoes, but **taglia** (*tah*-lyah) or **misura** (mee-*sooh*-rah) (*size*) to talk about clothes.

Table 8-2 shows women's shoe sizes in North America and their conversions to European (including Italian) and U.K. sizes.

Table 8-2	Women's Shoe Sizes	
United States and Canada	*European (Italian)*	*United Kingdom*
5	35	2.5
5.5	35.5	3
6	36	3.5
6.5	36.5	4
7	37	4.5
7.5	37.5	5
8	38	5.5
8.5	38.5	6
9	39	6.5
9.5	39.5	7
10	40	7.5
10.5	40.5	8

Talkin' the Talk

If you've seen the pair of shoes of your dreams **in vetrina** (een veh-*tree*-nah) (*in the shop window*) and you want to try them on, you can follow Michela's example. (Track 16)

Michela: **Posso provare le scarpe esposte in vetrina?**
pohs-soh proh-*vah*-reh leh *skahr*-peh eh-*spoh*-steh een veh-*tree*-nah?
May I try on a pair of shoes in the window?

Saleswoman: **Quali sono?**
kwah-lee *soh*-noh?
Which ones?

Michela: **Quelle blu, a destra.**
kwehl-leh blooh, ah *dehs*-trah.
Those blue ones there, on the right.

Saleswoman: **Che numero porta?**
keh *nooh*-meh-roh *pohr*-tah?
Which size do you wear?

Michela: **Trentasette.**
trehn-tah-*seht*-teh.
Thirty-seven.

Saleswoman: **Ecco qua. Un trentasette . . . sono strette?**
ehk-koh kwah. oohn trehn-tah-*seht*-teh . . . soh-noh
streht-teh?
Here we are. A 37 . . . are they tight?

Michela: **No. Sono comodissime.**
noh. *soh*-noh koh-moh-*dees*-see-meh.
No. They are very comfortable.

    Quanto vengono?
kwahn-toh *vehn*-goh-noh?
How much do they cost?

Saleswoman: **Novanta euro.**
noh-*vahn*-tah *eh*-ooh-roh.
Ninety euros.

Talking definitely and indefinitely

When you're shopping for something, even if you're looking for something as specific as a blue skirt, you don't say, "I'm looking for *the* blue skirt." Instead, you say that you're looking for *a* blue skirt, where the indefinite article *a* shows that you don't have a specific object in mind.

You use exactly the same construction in Italian: *I'm looking for a blue skirt* becomes **Sto cercando una gonna blu** (stoh cher-*kahn*-doh *ooh*-nah *gohn*-nah blooh); **una,** here, is your indefinite article, which corresponds to the English *a* and *an*. In Italian, the article has to match the gender of the word: Feminine words (which usually end with **-a**), use **una** and **un',** and masculine words (which usually end with **-o**) use **un** or **uno**.

Coloring your words

Of course, knowing some **colori** (koh-*loh*-ree) (*colors*) is important when you're shopping for clothes, shoes, or anything! To make life a little easier for you, Table 8-3 lists the most common colors. Some colors agree in number and gender, some agree only in number, and some are invariable. The following table is organized accordingly (with the first set agreeing in number and gender).

Table 8-3	Colors	
Italian	*Pronunciation*	*Translation*
Color adjectives that agree in number and gender (o/a/i/e)		
rosso	*rohs*-soh	*red*
giallo	*jahl*-loh	*yellow*
azzurro	ahd-*dzoohr*-roh	*sky blue*
bianco/a/chi/che	*byahn*-koh/kah/kee/keh	*white*
grigio	*gree*-joh	*gray*
nero	*neh*-roh	*black*
Color adjectives that agree only in number (e/i)		
arancione	ah-rahn-*choh*-neh	*orange*
marrone	mahr-*roh*-neh	*brown*
verde	*vehr*-deh	*green*
Color adjectives that never change, invariable!		
rosa	*roh*-zah	*pink*
beige	*beh*-jeh	*beige*
blu	blooh	*blue*
viola	vee-*oh*-lah	*purple*

Choosing the right fabric

Each type of fabric has its own characteristics. You need to choose **la stoffa giusta** (lah *stohf*-fah *jooh*-stah) (*the right fabric*) for your garment. If it's an elegant piece, you'll choose **seta** (*seh*-tah) (*silk*), **velluto** (vehl-*looh*-toh) (*velvet*), or **raso** (*rah*-soh) (*satin*). **Cotone** (koh-*toh*-neh) (*cotton*) and **lino** (*lee*-noh) (*linen*) fabrics are fresh and practical, very suitable for sportswear and summer clothing. No time to iron your clothes? Then choose **acrilico e sintentico** (ah-*kree*-lee-koh eh seehn-*teh*-tee-koh) (*acrylic and synthetic*), but don't complain if you don't look glamorous in clothing made with these materials!

Talkin' the Talk

Matteo is looking for a new suit for the summer.

Salesman:	**La posso aiutare?** lah *pohs*-soh ah-yooh-*tah*-reh? *May I help you?*
Matteo:	**Sì. Cerco una giacca sportiva blu . . .** see. *chehr*-koh *ooh*-nah *jak*-kah spohr-*tee*-vah blooh . . . *Yes. I'm looking for a casual blue jacket . . .*
	. . . con i pantaloni bianchi di lino . . . kohn ee pahn-tah-*loh*-nee *byahn*-kee dee *lee*-noh. *. . . and also some white linen pants.*
Salesman:	**Benissimo. Ecco . . . provi questi.** beh-*nees*-see-moh. *ehk*-koh . . . *proh*-vee *kwehs*-tee. *Very well. Here you are . . . try these on.*

Matteo returns with a smile on his face.

Salesman:	**Va bene?** vah *beh*-neh? *Okay?*
Matteo:	**Sì, mi vanno bene. Li prendo.** see, mee *vahn*-noh *beh*-neh. lee *prehn*-doh. *Yes, they fit me well. I'll take them.*

Words to Know

camoscio [m]	kah-<u>moh</u>-shoh	suede
cotone [m]	koh-<u>toh</u>-neh	cotton
fodera [f]	<u>foh</u>-deh-rah	lining
lana [f]	<u>lah</u>-nah	wool
lino [m]	<u>lee</u>-noh	linen
pelle [f]	<u>pehl</u>-leh	leather
seta [f]	<u>seh</u>-tah	silk
velluto [m]	vehl-<u>looh</u>-toh	velvet
viscosa [f]	vee-<u>skoh</u>-zah	rayon

Accessorizing

Of course, no outfit is complete without beautiful **accessori** (ahch-chehs-*soh*-ree) (*accessories*) to give it that final touch. This list gives you an impression of the variety you can find:

- **berretto** (behr-*reht*-toh) (*cap*)
- **borsa** (*bohr*-sah) (*bag*)
- **calze** (*kahl*-tseh) (*stockings*)
- **calzini** (*kahl*-tsee-nee) (*socks*)
- **cappello** (kahp-*pehl*-loh) (*hat*)
- **cintura** (cheen-*tooh*-rah) (*belt*)
- **collant** (kohl-*lahn*) (*tights; pantyhose*)
- **cravatta** (krah-*vaht*-tah) (*tie*)
- **guanti** (*gwahn*-tee) (*gloves*)
- **ombrello** (ohm-*brehl*-loh) (*umbrella*)
- **sciarpa** (*shahr*-pah) (*scarf*)

CULTURAL WISDOM

Italian fashion

The term **moda** (*moh*-dah) (*fashion*) derives from the Latin word *modus*, which means *rule, tempo, melody, rhythm*. The present meaning of **moda** comes from a 1645 book entitled **La carrozza: ovvero del vestire alla moda** (*The Horse Carriage: or How to Dress Fashionably*) written by . . . an Italian priest!

For Italians, dressing up isn't just a means of covering up their body: accessories, colors, a simple button have meanings and reasons. **La moda** is an instrument of **emancipazione sociale** (eh-mahn-chee-pah-*tsyoh*-neh soh-*chah*-leh) (*social emancipation*) and the rise of class through the dress. Buying an Italian fashion product, therefore, doesn't mean buying **una firma** (ooh-nah *feer*-mah) (*a brand product*); it means buying a beautifully crafted idea.

Fashion is a fleeting commodity if it isn't supported by quality and **imprenditorialità** (eem-prehn-dee-toh-ryah-lee-*tah*) (*entrepreneurship*). In the last 50 years, the great Italian designers have understood this message and paired their talent with **materiali di alta qualità** (mah-teh-*ryah*-lee dee *ahl*-tah kwah-lee-*tah*) (*high-quality materials*), **cura dei dettagli** (*koo*-rah dehy deht-*tah*-lyee) (*meticulous artisanship*), and marketing. All of these attributes have contributed to the success of the *made in Italy*. Milan, the industrial center of the peninsula, became the capital of fashion and **prêt a porter** in the years 1970 through 1980, soon followed by Rome as the seat of the major Italian **sartorie** (sahr-toh-*ree*-eh) (*brands of luxury merchandise*). **Stilisti** (stee-*lee*-stee) (*designers*) such as Giorgio Armani, Missoni, Gianfranco Ferré, Gianni Versace, Fendi, Dolce & Gabbana, and Krizia started to become famous in those years.

Narrowing Your Options

Making the right choice requires critical sense and the ability to distinguish and compare quality, styles, and prices. You don't want to be **troppo sportivo** (*trohp*-poh spohr-*tee*-voh) (*too casual*) and go to an opera's premiere in blue jeans and **maglietta** (mah-*lyeht*-tah) or **troppo elegante** (*trohp*-poh eh-leh-*gahn*-teh) (*too elegant*) and go to class in a **vestito** (veh-*stee*-toh) (*suit*) and **cravatta** (krah-*vaht*-tah) (*tie*)! If you're buying clothes, you should be aware of sizes as well. Comparing prices and quality is also very important. Keep an eye on the price tag and don't pay a fortune for a cheap item. If you find something that has **la stessa qualità** (lah *stehs*-sah kwah-lee-*tah*) (*the same quality*) at **un prezzo inferiore** (ah oohn *preht*-tzoh een-feh-*ryoh*-reh) (*a cheaper price*), go for it!

Comparing items, more or less

In both English and Italian, you can compare things in three ways. You can say something possesses a quality more than, less than, or as much as something else. The two objects you're comparing are called the first and the second term of comparison. You can convey them with names, nouns, pronouns, adjectives, adverbs, and verbs.

Here are the rules for establishing comparisons in Italian:

✔ To say that one object has a quality *more than* or *less than* another object, use **più** (pee-*ooh*) to convey *more,* **meno** (*meh*-noh) to convey *less* or *fewer* (before a countable plural noun), and **di** (dee) (or a contracted form of **di**) or **che** (keh) to convey *than.* You use **di** only when the second term is a name, a pronoun without a preposition, or an adverb. Here are some examples:

> **Bianca è più elegante di Silvia.** (*byahn*-kah eh pee-*ooh* eh-leh-*gahn*-teh dee *seel*-vyah.) (*Bianca is more elegant than Silvia.*)

> **Sembra meno stretta di ieri!** (*sehm*-brah *meh*-noh *streht*-tah dee *yeh*-ree!) (*It seems less tight than yesterday!*)

✔ When the second term is a name or a noun preceded by a preposition; or when you compare two adjectives, two adverbs, or two verbs, you can use only **che** before the second term, as shown here:

> **Compriamo meno gonne che pantaloni.** (kohm-*pryah*-moh *meh*-noh *gohn*-neh keh pahn-tah-*loh*-nee.) (*We'll buy fewer skirts than pants.*)

> **Le piace provare i vestiti più che acquistare.** (leh *pya*-cheh proh-*vah*-reh ee veh-*stee*-tee pee-*ooh* keh ah kwee-*stah*-reh.) (*She likes trying on clothing more than buying.*)

With the exception of **migliore** and **peggiore, meglio** and **peggio** (*better* and *worse*), unlike English, Italian doesn't add endings to adjectives or adverbs to convey that one individual possesses a quality to a different degree than someone else. For example, **vecchio** (*vehk*-kyoh) (*old*) remains the same, and you add the words **più** or **meno** before it. In English, you add *-er* to one- and two-syllable adjectives to assert a difference of degree; for example, *old* becomes *older,* and *new* becomes *newer.*

TIP

When you want to say that the degree of a quality (or the amount of an object) keeps on increasing or decreasing, as in *more and more expensive, taller and taller,* and *less and less stylish,* in Italian you use **sempre più** and **sempre meno** (which are invariable) plus an adjective, an adverb, or a noun. For example:

> **È sempre più alto.** (*He is taller and taller.*)
>
> **Abbiamo sempre meno euro.** (*We have fewer and fewer euros.*)

To say that one object possesses a quality as much as another object, you use the expressions **tanto . . . quanto** or **così . . . come** to convey *as . . . as, as much . . . as,* or *as many . . . as.* For example, **Bianca è tanto creativa quanto Silvia** (*Bianca is as creative as Silvia*).

When you use an adjective to compare two individuals, you can omit the words **tanto** or **così,** as in **Luciano è alto quanto Carlo** (*Luciano is as tall as Carlo*). You keep **tanto** and **così** when you compare two nouns, as in **Compriamo tante sciarpe quante cravatte** (*We'll buy as many scarves as ties*); two adjectives, as in **Luisa è tanto bella quanto brava** (*Luisa is as beautiful as she's good*); or two verbs, as in **A Gianni piace tanto fare acquisti quanto andare ai grandi magazzini** (*Gianni likes shopping in department stores as much as visiting outdoor markets*).

Considering price

When you visit an Italian store, try to have a strategy. Determine what you really want to buy and look at the price. Prices are labeled in euros. Often, during **saldi** (*sahl*-dee) and **svendite** (*zvehn*-dee-teh) (*sales*), **il prezzo** (eel *preht*-tsoh) (*the price*) on the label is already reduced, but you may find tags reading **saldi alla cassa** (*sahl*-dee ahl-lah *kahs*-sah) (*reduction at the cash register*).The items are all charming and inviting, but keep in mind that **il cambio** (eel *kahm*-byoh) (*the conversion rate*) isn't always favorable. Buy goods that have a price label and do the currency conversion before you go **alla cassa** (*ahl*-lah *kahs*-sah) (*to the checkout counter*). By the way, **la fila** (lah *fee*-lah) (*the line*) in Italy isn't always very orderly! You'll often see people in groups around the cash register, waiting to pay. Keep an eye on those who arrived before you and be determined not to let anyone pass in front of you. If they try, smile and say **Mi dispiace, c'ero prima io!** (mee dee-*spyah*-cheh, *cheh*-roh *pree*-mah *ee*-oh!) (*Sorry, I was here before you!*)

Book I

Speaking Italian in Everyday Settings

Talkin' the Talk

John wants to buy a scarf for his wife. He asks the sales clerk for help.

John: **Vorrei una sciarpa rossa.**
vohr-*ray ooh*-nah *shahr*-pah *rohs*-sah.
I'd like a red scarf.

Sales clerk: **Ne abbiamo una bellissima, di cachemire.**
neh ahb-*byah*-moh *ooh*-nah behl-*lees*-see-mah, dee *kahsh*-meer.
We have a very beautiful cashmere one.

È in saldo.
eh een *sahl*-doh.
It's on sale.

John: **In saldo? Bene! Che sconto c'è?**
een *sahl*-doh? *beh*-neh! keh *skohn*-toh *cheh*?
On sale? Great! How much is the discount?

Sales clerk: **Su questo articolo facciamo il 20 per cento. Sa, certi accessori non passano mai di moda.**
sooh *kweh*-stoh ahr-*tee*-koh-loh fahch-*chah*-moh eel *vehn*-tee pehr *chen*-toh. sah, *chehr*-tee ahch-chehs-*soh*-ree nohn *pahs*-sah-noh may dee *moh*-dah.
We apply 20 percent discount on this item. You know, accessories like this one are never outdated.

John: **Vediamo . . . con il 20 per cento di sconto la sciarpa verrebbe a costare 180 euro . . . al cambio di 1.30 sono 234 dollari. No, è troppo. Forse devo cambiare articolo.**
veh-*dyah*-moh . . . kohn eel *vehn*-tee pehr *chehn*-toh dee *skohn*-toh lah *shahr*-pah vehr-*rehb*-beh ah koh-*stah*-reh chen-toht-*tahn*-tah eh-ooh-roh . . . ahl *kahm*-byoh dee *ooh*-noh eh *trehn*-tah *soh*-noh dooh-eh-*chehn*-toh-trehn-tah-*kwaht*-troh dohl-lah-ree. noh, eh *trohp*-poh. *fohr*-seh *deh*-voh kahm-*byah*-reh ahr-*tee*-koh-loh.
Let's see . . . after a discount of 20 percent, this scarf would cost 180 euros . . . at the conversion rate of 1.30, it is 234 dollars. No, it is too much. Maybe I have to find something else.

Sales clerk: **Allora guardi questi guanti. Su questi le posso fare
un prezzo veramente speciale.**
ahl-*loh*-rah *gwahr*-dee *kweh*-stee *gwahn*-tee. sooh
kweh-stee leh *pohs*-soh *fah*-reh oohn *preht*-tsoh veh-
rah-*mehn*-teh speh-*chah*-leh.
*Then look at these gloves. They have a very special
price.*

John: **Quanto speciale?**
kwahn-toh speh-*chah*-leh?
How special?

Sales clerk: **Li diamo al 50 per cento. Il colore è molto particolare,
ma se piace, fa un affarone. Sono suoi per 45 euro.**
lee *dyah*-moh ahl cheen-*kwahn*-tah pehr *chehn*-toh.
eel koh-*loh*-reh *eh mohl*-toh pahr-tee-koh-*lah*-reh,
mah seh *pyah*-cheh, fah oohn ahf-fah-*roh*-neh. *soh*-
noh swohy pehr kwah-rahn-tah-*cheen*-kweh
eh-ooh-roh.
*We let them go [we sell them] with a discount of 50
percent on the original price. The color is very particular, but if you like it, it's an incredible deal. You can
have them for 45 euros.*

John: **Meno di 60 dollari per guanti in pelle "made in Italy"
. . . li prendo. Il viola è il colore preferito da mia
moglie! Mi faccia un pacchetto regalo, per favore.**
meh-noh dee sehs-*sahn*-tah *dohl*-lah-ree pehr *gwahn*-
tee een *pehl*-leh "made in Italy" . . . lee *prehn*-doh.
eel vee-*oh*-lah *eh* eel koh-*loh*-reh preh-feh-*ree*-toh
dah myah *moh*-lyeh! mee *fahch*-chah oohn pahk-
keht-toh reh-*gah*-loh, pehr fah-*voh*-reh.
*Less than 60 dollars for leather gloves made in
Italy . . . I'll take them. Purple is my wife's favorite
color! Can they be gift-wrapped, please?*

Sales clerk: **Certo, non si preoccupi. Farà una bellissima figura.**
cehr-toh, nohn see preh-*ohk*-kooh-pee. fah-*rah ooh*-
nah behl-*lees*-see-mah fee-*gooh*-rah.
*Sure, don't worry. You will make an incredible
impression.*

Artisan craft

L'artigianato (lahr-tee-jah-*nah*-toh) (*artisan craft*) is an important marker of a country's culture and customs and in recent years has also become **una attrazione turistica** (ooh-naht-trah-*tsyoh*-neh tooh-*ree*-stee-kah) (*a tourist attraction*). Italian artisan craft has vivacity and vitality; some regions are richer than others, but each one has peculiar aspects that derive from **antiche tradizioni** (ahn-*tee*-keh trah-dee-*tsyoh*-nee) (*ancient traditions*), **ambiente naturale** (ahm-*byehn*-teh nah-tooh-*rah*-leh) (*the natural environment*), **eventi storici** (eh-*vehn*-tee *stoh*-ree-chee) (*historical events*), **retaggio artistico** (reh-*tahj*-joh ahr-*tee*-stee-koh) (*artistic heritage*), and even from the character of its inhabitants. Italy has great richness and variety of crafts. Buy **oggetti in ceramica** (ohj-*jeht*-tee een cheh-*rah*-mee-kah) (*ceramics*) in Faenza, Deruta, and Grottaglie, and **in vetro** (een *veh*-troh) (*glass*) in Venice, **articoli in legno e ferro battuto** (ahr-*tee*-koh-lee een *leh*-nyoh eh *fehr*-roh baht-*tooh*-toh) (*woodwork and metalwork*) in Abruzzo, **cesti** (*cheh*-stee) (*basket*) and objects in **sughero** (*sooh*-ghe-roh) (*cork*) and **cuoio** (*kwoh*-yoh) (*leather*) in Sardinia, **merletti** (mehr-*leht*-tee) (*laces*) in Sicily, and **gioielli** (joh-*yehl*-lee) (*jewelry*) in Arezzo. No matter where you are, you can find a special, unique object that will remind you of the places and the people you've known.

Book II
Exploring and Wandering About

DEPARTURE STATION: BOLOGNA (TUTTE LE STAZIONI)	ARRIVAL STATION: ROMA (TUTTE LE STAZIONI)				DATE: 19/1/2011		
DEPARTURE	ARRIVAL	LENGTH OF JOURNEY	TRAIN NO.	TRAIN CATEGORY	1ST CLASS*	2ND CLASS*	SELECT
10:53 BOLOGNA	13:13 ROMA TE	02:20	9413 FRECCIARGENTO		80,00€	58,00€	○
10:23 BOLOGNA	12:45 ROMA TE	02:22	9519 FRECCIAROSSA		80,00€	58,00€	○
10:38 BOLOGNA	12:55 ROMA TE	02:17	9415 FRECCIARGENTO		80,00€	58,00€	○
11:18 BOLOGNA	15:24 ROMA TE	04:06	589	IC	52,00€	38,50€	○
13:00 BOLOGNA	15:22 ROMA TE	02:22	9521 FRECCIAROSSA		80,00€	58,00€	○

Contents at a Glance

Chapter 1

Where Is the Colosseum? Asking Directions

· ·

In This Chapter

▶ Understanding directions

▶ Discovering Italian attractions

· ·

Have you ever been lost in a foreign city or country? If so, you realize how helpful it is to know enough of the native language to be able to ask for directions. Knowing the language also enables you to understand the answer. In this chapter, you find some helpful conversational tips that make finding your way around easier.

Finding Your Way: Asking for Specific Places

When asking for directions, it's always polite to start your question with one of the following expressions (which are friendly forms of the imperative mood or command tense). The expression you use depends on who (and how many people) you're talking to.

Mi scusi (mee *skooh*-zee) or **Scusi** (*skooh*-zee). (*Excuse me* [singular, formal]). You use this form when addressing someone formally, as in *Sir, Madam, Doctor, Professor*, and so forth

Mi scusino. (mee *skooh*-zee-noh.) (*Excuse me* [plural, formal]). You use this form when addressing a group formally, such as *gentlemen, ladies, doctors, professors,* and so on.

Scusa. (*skooh*-zah.) (*Excuse me* [singular, informal].) You use this form when addressing a family member or a close friend.

Scusate. (skooh-*zah*-teh.) (*Excuse me* [plural, informal].) You use this form when addressing a group of family members or close friends.

Per favore. (pehr fah-*voh*-reh.) (*Please.*)

Un'informazione. (oohn een-fohr-mah-*tsyoh*-neh.) (*I need some information.*)

Then you can continue with your questions, which may resemble the following:

Dov'è il Colosseo? (doh-*veh* eel koh-lohs-*seh*-oh?) (*Where is the Colosseum?*)

È questa via Garibaldi? (eh *kweh*-stah *vee*-ah gah-ree-*bahl*-dee?) (*Is this via Garibaldi?*)

Per la stazione? (pehr lah stah-*tsyoh*-neh?) (*How do I get to the station?*)

Può indicarmi la strada per il centro? (pwoh een-dee-*kahr*-mee lah *strah*-dah pehr eel *chehn*-troh?) (*Can you show me the way downtown?*)

Dove siamo adesso? (*doh*-veh *syah*-moh ah-*dehs*-soh?) (*Where are we now?*)

Mi sono perso. Dov'è il duomo? (mee *soh*-noh *pehr*-soh. doh-*veh* eel *dwoh*-moh?) (*I'm lost. Where is the cathedral?*)

È qui vicino la Fontana di Trevi? (eh kwee vee-*chee*-noh lah fohn-*tah*-nah dee *treh*-vee?) (*Is the Fountain of Trevi nearby?*)

Some possible answers, not in any particular order (mix and match according to the context!), to the preceding questions are

Sì, è proprio qui vicino! (see, eh *proh*-pryoh kwee vee-*chee*-noh!) (*Yes, it is very close!*)

Segua la strada principale fino al centro. (*seh*-gwah lah *strah*-dah preen-chee-*pah*-leh *fee*-noh ahl *chehn*-troh.) (*Follow the main street to the center of the city.*)

Vada sempre dritto. (*vah*-dah *sehm*-preh *dreet*-toh.) (*Go straight ahead.*)

Dopo il semaforo, giri a destra. (*doh*-poh eel seh-*mah*-foh-roh, *jee*-ree ah *dehs*-trah.) (*After the traffic light, turn right.*)

È in fondo a sinistra. (*eh* een *fohn*-doh ah see-*nees*-trah.) (*It's at the end, on the left side.*)

È vicino alla posta. (*eh* vee-*chee*-noh *ahl*-lah *pohs*-tah.) (*It's next to the post office.*)

Attraversi il ponte, poi c'è una piazza e lì la vede. (aht-trah-*vehr*-see eel *pohn*-teh, pohy cheh *ooh*-nah *pyahts*-tsah eh lee lah *veh*-deh.) (*Cross the bridge, then there's a square and there you see it.*)

È la terza strada a sinistra. (*eh* lah *tehr*-tsah *strah*-dah ah see-*nees*-trah.) (*It's the third street on the left.*)

È dopo il terzo semaforo, a destra. (*eh doh*-poh eel *tehr*-tsoh seh-*mah*-foh-roh, ah *dehs*-trah.) (*It's after the third light, on the right.*)

Ha sbagliato strada. (ah sbah-*lyah*-toh *strah*-dah.) (*You're on the wrong road.*)

Mapping the quarters and following directions

Four orientations you already know are the cardinal points of the compass: north, south, east, and west. The four directions are especially helpful to know when you use a map. The following are **i quattro punti cardinali** (ee *kwaht*-troh *poohn*-tee kahr-dee-*nah*-lee) (*the four cardinal points*):

- ✔ **nord** (nohrd) (*north*)
- ✔ **sud** (soohd) (*south*)
- ✔ **est** (ehst) (*east*)
- ✔ **ovest** (*oh*-vehst) (*west*)

You may hear the directions used in sentences like the following:

Trieste è a nord-est. (*tryeh*-steh eh ah nohrd-*ehst*.) (*Trieste is to the northeast.*)

Napoli è a sud. (*nah*-poh-lee eh ah soohd.) (*Naples is to the south.*)

Roma è a ovest. (*roh*-mah eh ah *oh*-vehst.) (*Rome is to the west.*)

Bari è a sud-est. (*bah*-ree eh ah soohd-*ehst*.) (*Bari is to the southeast.*)

Some lovely city centers, such as the ones in Verona and Ravenna, are closed off to traffic, so you really need to explore them by foot. You need to know how to orient yourself in relation to people and buildings when following or giving directions. Italians also frequently use meters to describe distances on foot:

- ✔ **davanti a** (dah-*vahn*-tee ah) (*in front of*)
- ✔ **dietro a** (*dyeh*-troh ah) (*behind*)
- ✔ **vicino a** (vee-*chee*-noh ah) (*beside; next to*)
- ✔ **di fronte a** (dee-*frohn*-teh ah) (*opposite*)
- ✔ **dentro** (*dehn*-troh) (*inside*)
- ✔ **fuori** (*fwoh*-ree) (*outside*)
- ✔ **sotto** (*soht*-toh) (*under; below*)
- ✔ **sopra** (*soh*-prah) (*above*)

You also need to know relationships between distance and **la direzione** (lah dee-reh-*tsyoh*-neh) (*the direction*):

- **dritto** (*dreet*-toh) (*straight*)
- **sempre dritto** (*sehm*-preh *dreet*-toh) (*straight ahead*)
- **fino a** (*fee*-noh ah) (*to; up to*)
- **prima** (*pree*-mah) (*before*)
- **dopo** (*doh*-poh) (*after*)
- **a destra** (ah *dehs*-trah) (*on the right*)
- **a sinistra** (ah see-*nees*-trah) (*on the left*)
- **dietro l'angolo** (*dyeh*-troh *lahn*-goh-loh) (*around the corner*)
- **all'angolo** (ahl-*lahn*-goh-loh) (*at the corner*)
- **all'incrocio** (ahl-leen-*kroh*-choh) (*at the intersection*)

Here's more vocabulary you can use for giving and receiving directions:

- **la calle** (lah *kahl*-leh) (*narrow Venetian street* [term found only in Venice])
- **il corso** (eel *kohr*-soh) (*avenue; boulevard*)
- **il largo** (eel *lahr*-goh) (*wide square*)
- **il marciapiede** (eel mahr-chah-*pyeh*-deh) (*sidewalk*)
- **la piazza** (lah *pyahts*-tsah) (*square*)
- **il ponte** (eel *pohn*-teh) (*bridge*)
- **il sottopassaggio** (eel *soht*-toh-pahs-*sahj*-joh) (*underpass*)
- **la strada** (lah *strah*-dah) (*road; street*)
- **la via** (lah *vee*-ah) (*road; street*)
- **la via principale** (lah *vee*-ah preen-chee-*pah*-leh) (*main street*)
- **il viale** (eel *vyah*-leh) (*parkway; avenue*)
- **il vicolo** (eel *vee*-koh-loh) (*alley; lane*)

Talkin' the Talk

Laurie is visiting Florence from Oregon and has just finished a mid-morning coffee break in Piazza della Repubblica. She asks the man standing near her how to get to the post office. (Track 17)

Laurie: **Scusi, dov'è l'ufficio postale?**
skooh-zee, doh-*veh* loohf-*feech*-oh poh-*stah*-leh?
Excuse me, where is the post office?

Enzo: **È dietro l'angolo, là, sotto i portici. L'accompagno?**
eh dyeh-troh *lahn*-goh-loh, lah, *soht*-toh ee *pohr*-tee-chee. lah-kohm-*pah*-nyoh?
It's around the corner, over there, underneath the porticoes. Shall I accompany you?

Laurie: **No grazie, vado da sola.**
noh *grah*-tsyeh, *vah*-doh dah *soh*-lah.
No thank you, I can go by myself.

La strada and la via are synonymous, but you always use **via** when the name is specified:

È una strada molto lunga. (*eh ooh*-nah *strah*-dah *mohl*-toh *loohn*-gah.) (*It's a very long road.*)

Abito in via Merulana. (*ah*-bee-toh een *vee*-ah meh-rooh-*lah*-nah.) (*I live in Via Merulana.*)

Talkin' the Talk

Mary is in **Bologna** (boh-*loh*-nyah) for the first time. She has visited the city and walked a lot, and now she wants to go back to the train station. Because she can't remember the way, she asks a passerby. (Track 18)

Mary: **Scusi?**
skooh-zee?
Excuse me?

Man: **Sì?**
See?
Yes?

Mary: **Dov'è la stazione centrale?**
doh-*veh* lah stah-*tsyoh*-neh chehn-*trah*-leh?
Where is the central station?

Man: **Prenda la prima a destra.**
prehn-dah lah *pree*-mah ah *dehs*-trah.
Take the first right.

Mary:	**Poi?**
	Pohy?
	Then?
Man:	**Poi la terza a sinistra.**
	pohy lah *tehr*-tsah ah see-*nees*-trah.
	Then the third left.
Mary:	**Sì?**
	See?
	Yes?
Man:	**Poi la seconda, no la prima . . .**
	pohy lah seh-*kohn*-dah, noh lah *pree*-mah . . .
	Then the second, no the first . . .
Mary:	**Grazie; prendo un taxi!**
	grah-tsyeh; *prehn*-doh oohn *tahk*-see!
	Thank you; I'll take a taxi!

Expressing verbs on the move

You need to know certain verbs when trying to understand directions. Some of the verbs you'll find handy for finding your way include the following:

- **andare** (ahn-*dah*-reh) (*to go*)
- **girare a destra/a sinistra** (jee-*rah*-reh ah *dehs*-trah/ah see-*nees*-trah) (*to turn right/left*)
- **prendere** (*prehn*-deh-reh) (*to take*)
- **proseguire** (proh-seh-*gwee*-reh) (*to go on*)
- **seguire** (seh-*gwee*-reh) (*to follow*)
- **tornare indietro** (tohr-*nah*-reh een-*dyeh*-troh) (*to go back*)

Imperatives are useful verb forms to know in a variety of situations, including when you're trying to get around in unfamiliar territory. This list shows the informal verb form (**tu**), the formal verb form (**Lei**), the informal plural form (**voi**), and the formal plural form (**Loro**). Check out Book I, Chapter 3, for help on deciding whether to use formal or informal forms.

What to say when you don't understand

Occasionally, maybe frequently, you may not understand the directions someone gives you. For those times, you need some useful polite expressions to ask the other people to repeat their directions:

✔ **Come, scusi?** (*koh*-meh, *skooh*-zee?) (*I beg your pardon?* [formal])

✔ **Come, scusa?** (*koh*-meh, *skooh*-zah?) (*I beg your pardon?* [informal])

✔ **Mi scusi, non ho capito.** (mee *skooh*-zee, nohn oh kah-*pee*-toh.) (*I'm sorry, I didn't understand.*)

✔ **Può ripetere più lentamente, per favore?** (*pwoh* ree-*peh*-teh-reh pyooh lehn-tah-*mehn*-teh, pehr fah-*voh*-reh?) (*Can you please repeat it more slowly?*)

When someone does you a favor — explaining the way or giving you directions — you probably want to thank him or her, and that's the easiest task: **Mille grazie!** (*meel*-leh *grah*-tsyeh!) (*Thank you very much!*)

Here are conjugations of some regular and irregular verbs:

✔ **Va'/Vada/Andate/Vadano!** (*vah*/*vah*-dah/ahn-*dah*-teh/*vah*-dah-noh!) (*Go!*)

✔ **Gira/Giri/Girate/Girino!** (*jee*-rah/*jee*-ree/jee-*rah*-teh/*jee*-ree-noh!) (*Turn!*)

✔ **Prendi/Prenda/Prendete/Prendano!** (*prehn*-dee/*prehn*-dah/prehn-*deh*-teh/*prehn*-dah-noh!) (*Take!*)

✔ **Prosegui/Prosegua/Proseguite/Proseguano!** (proh-*seh*-gwee/proh-*seh*-gwah/ proh-seh-*gwee*-teh/proh-*seh*-gwah-noh!) (*Go on!*)

✔ **Segui/Segua/Seguite/Seguano!** (*seh*-gwee/*seh*-gwah/seh-*gwee*-teh/seh-*gwah*-noh!) (*Follow!*)

✔ **Torna/Torni/Tornate/Tornino!** (*tohr*-nah/*tohr*-nee/tohr-*nah*-teh/*tohr*-nee-noh!) (*Go back!*)

✔ **Attraversa/Attraversi/Attraversate/Attraversino!** (aht-trah-*vehr*-sah/ aht-trah-*vehr*-see/aht-trah-vehr-*sah*-teh/aht-trah-*vehr*-see-noh!) (*Cross!*)

Notice that the endings of these verbs vary, apparently without any consistent pattern. These aren't typing mistakes — they're determined by the ending of the infinitive form of the verb (**-are**, **-ere**, or **-ire**) and also whether the verb is regular or irregular. The easiest way to handle this is to simply memorize the verbs and their endings. You may want to know how near or far you are from your destination. Some typical questions and responses are as follows:

Quant'è lontano? (kwahn-*teh* lohn-*tah*-noh?) (*How far is it?*)

È molto lontano? (*eh mohl*-toh lohn-*tah*-noh?) (*Is it very far?*)

Quanto dista? (*kwahn*-toh *dees*-tah?) (*How far is it?*)

Saranno cinque minuti. (sah-*rahn*-noh *cheen*-kweh mee-*nooh*-tee.) (*About five minutes.*)

Circa un chilometro. (*cheer*-kah oohn kee-*loh*-meh-troh.) (*About one kilometer.*)

Non saranno più di 150 metri. (Nohn sah-*rahn*-noh *pyooh* dee *chehn*-toh-cheen-*qwahn*-tah *meh*-tree.) (*It's no more than 150 meters away.*)

No, un paio di minuti. (noh, oohn *pah*-yoh dee mee-*nooh*-tee.) (*No, a couple of minutes.*)

Posso arrivarci a piedi? (*pohs*-soh ahr-ree-*vahr*-chee ah *pyeh*-dee?) (*Can I walk there?*)

Certo, è molto vicino. (*chehr*-toh, *eh mohl*-toh vee-*chee*-noh.) (*Sure, it's very close.*)

È un po' lontano. (*eh* oohn poh lohn-*tah*-noh.) (*It's a bit far away.*)

È proprio a due passi. (*eh proh*-pryoh ah *dooh*-eh *pahs*-see.) (*It's very close.*) (Literally: *Just a couple of steps away.*)

È all'incirca 20 metri di distanza. (*eh* ahl-leen-*cheer*-kah *vehn*-tee *meh*-tree dee dee-*stahn*-tsah.) (*It's about 20 meters away.*)

Words to Know

numero [m]	*nooh*-meh-roh	number
minuto [m]	mee-*nooh*-toh	minute
lentamente	lehn-tah-*mehn*-teh	slowly
autobus [m]	*ou*-toh-boohs	bus
fermata [f]	fehr-*mah*-tah	bus stop
macchina [f]	*mahk*-kee-nah	car

Exploring Italian Cities and Towns

If you look at a map of an Italian city, you can easily distinguish **il centro storico** (eel *chehn*-troh *stoh*-ree-koh) (*the historic downtown area*) from the rest of the urban space. In the historic area, the roads are often narrow and winding because they were drawn when there were no cars. Here, you also find the city's most important **palazzi e monumenti** (pah-*laht*-tsee eh moh-nooh-*mehn*-tee) (*buildings and monuments*). Moreover, the historic downtown area has a strong appeal for its commercial activities and for the presence of many offices.

The distinction between center and periphery is relatively recent, dating to the late 19th century, when industrial activities grew and led to the growth of cities. In Italian cities, the most recent **quartieri** (kwahr-*tyeh*-ree) (*neighborhoods*) have expanded dramatically and are now larger than the downtown area. Consequently, cities are no longer defined by **mura di cinta** (*mooh*-rah dee *cheen*-tah) walls, as in medieval times, but by the expressways and highways that surround the modern neighborhoods.

Book II

Exploring and Wandering About

La piazza: The heart of the Italian city

In Italy, every city or village has a **piazza** (*pyat*-tsah) (*town square*) — tiny or large, medieval or Renaissance, modern or ancient. In the Italian **piazzas** you find **chiese** (*kyeh*-seh) (*churches*) as well as shops, restaurants, and bars. The **piazza** is the heart of Italy, the hub of city life. It's the place where young and old alike come together, meet, do business, and enjoy each other's company.

Viewing famous sites and architectural styles

To journey into the past, begin by visiting the main **resti preistorici e romani** (*reh*-stee preh-ee-*stoh*-ree-chee eh roh-*mah*-nee) (*prehistoric and Roman ruins*) and the Christian **catacombe** (kah-tah-*kohm*-beh) (*catacombs*) in Rome. Then continue your journey by visiting the great Florentine churches of **Santa Maria Novella** (1279), **Santa Maria del Fiore** (1296), and **Santa Croce** (*Holy Cross*) (1294 to 1295); the **Basilica di San Petronio** in Bologna (1390); and the **Duomo di Milano** (*Cathedral of Milan*) (construction began in 1386 but was completed several centuries later). In Naples, the Angioinis' rule (1265 to 1442 AD) coincided with the construction of several impressive **edifici in stile gotico** (eh-dee-*fee*-chee een *stee*-leh *goh*-tee-koh) (*Gothic buildings*), including the **Basilica of San Lorenzo Maggiore**, the church of **San Domenico Maggiore**, the monastery of **Santa Chiara** (largely rebuilt after World War II), and the **Cathedral.** The Gothic style of architecture was not, however, very popular in Rome. The only Gothic piece in this city is the church of **Santa Maria sopra Minerva** (*Santa Maria over Minerva*).

If you travel to Veneto (one of 20 regions in Italy), don't miss the **Palladian Basilica**, the **Palazzo Chiericati**, and **Villa Capra** in Vicenza, as well as the **Basilica of San Giorgio Maggiore** and the **Chiesa del Redentore** (*Church of the Redeemer*) in Venice. They're all extraordinary examples from the **Rinascimento** (ree-nah-shee-*mehn*-toh) (*Renaissance*). However, if you want to experience full-immersion **nell' arte e nell'architettura barocca** (nehl-*lahr*-teh e nehl-ahr-kee-teht-*tooh*-rah bah-*rohk*-kah) (*Baroque art and architecture*), stay in Rome, where you can visit **Chiesa di Sant'Andrea al Quirinale** (*Church of Saint Andrew at the Quirinal*), **Chiesa dell'Assunzione** (*Church of the Assumption*) at Ariccia, **Chiesa di Sant'Agnese in Agone** (*Church of Saint Agnes in Agone*), **San Carlo alle Quattro Fontane** (*Saint Charles at the Four Fountains*), **Sant'Ivo alla Sapienza** (*Saint Yves at La Sapienza*), and the nave of **San Giovanni in Laterano** (*St. John Lateran*) and civic buildings (**Palazzo Barberini** [Barberini Palace] by Gian Lorenzo Bernini [1598 to 1680] and Francesco Borromini [1599 to 1667], **Palazzo Montecitorio** [Montecitorio Palace], and the **Galleria Spada** [*gallery of the Spada Palace*]). The most famous **fontana** (fohn-*tah*-nah) (*fountain*) and **piazza** (*pyaht*-tsah) (*square*) in the world are also Baroque: **Fontana di Trevi** (*Trevi Fountain*) and **Piazza di Spagna** (*the Spanish Steps*)! If you like walking outdoors, visit the city of Caserta in Campania (a region in central Italy) and admire **la Reggia e i Giardini** (lah *rehj*-jah eh ee jahr-*dee*-nee) (*the Royal Palace and Gardens*), begun in 1752 by Luigi Vanvitelli.

Going farther south, you find examples of the 20th-century, eclectic architectural style in Palermo, a city in the island region of Sicily, including the **Palazzina Cinese** (*Chinese Palace*), the **Ginnasio dell'Orto botanico** (*Gymnasium of the Botanical Garden*), and the late **Teatro Massimo** (*Massimo Theater*). Echoes of this style can be found in North Italy in the Piedmont region, including the **Mole Antonelliana** in Turin and the **Basilica of San Gaudenzio** (*St. Gaudenzio Cathedral*) in Novara. In the region of Lombardy, not too far from Piedmont, you won't want to miss the **Galleria Vittorio Emanuele II** (*Victory Emanuel II Gallery*) in Milan, which, along with **Via Montenapoleone** and **Via della Spiga,** is considered the heart of **acquisti di lusso** (ah-*kwee*-stee dee *loohs*-soh) (*luxury shopping*) in North Italy. In Southern Italy, in the city of San Giovanni Rotondo, be sure to visit the **Convento Santuario di Padre Pio** (*Monastery and Sanctuary of Padre Pio*) by Renzo Piano, who also designed the **Stadio San Nicola** (*St. Nicolas Stadium*) in the city of Bari. Returning to Naples, the **Museo della Stazione Metropolitana** (*Museum Subway Station*) designed by Gae Aulenti is well worth a visit.

Finding the places you're looking for

When you're searching for a specific place, sentences like these can help you ask the right questions:

Mi sa dire dov'è la stazione? (mee sah *dee*-reh doh-*veh* lah stah-*tsyoh*-neh?) (*Can you tell me where the station is?*)

Devo andare all'aeroporto. Quale strada devo prendere? (*deh*-voh ahn-*dah*-reh *ahl*-lah-eh-roh-*pohr*-toh. *kwah*-leh *strah*-dah *deh*-voh *prehn*-deh-reh?) (*I have to go to the airport. What road should I take?*)

Sto cercando il teatro Valle. (stoh chehr-*kahn*-doh eel teh-*ah*-troh *vahl*-leh.) (*I'm looking for the Valle theater.*)

Dov'è il cinema Astoria, per favore? (doh-*veh* eel *chee*-neh-mah ah-*stoh*-ryah, pehr fah-*voh*-reh?) (*Where is the Astoria cinema, please?*)

Come posso arrivare al Museo Etrusco? (*koh*-meh *pohs*-soh ahr-ree-*vah*-reh ahl mooh-*zeh*-oh eh-*trooh*-skoh?) (*How can I get to the Etruscan Museum?*)

La strada migliore per il centro, per favore? (lah *strah*-dah mee-*lyoh*-reh pehr eel *chehn*-troh, pehr fah-*voh*-reh?) (*The best way to downtown, please?*)

Che chiesa è questa? (keh *kyeh*-zah *eh kwehs*-tah?) (*What church is this?*)

Quale autobus va all'ospedale? (*kwah*-leh *ou*-toh-boohs vah ahl-lohs-peh-*dah*-leh?) (*Which bus goes to the hospital?*)

Come faccio ad arrivare all'università? (*koh*-meh *fach*-choh ahd ahr-ree-*vah*-reh ahl-*looh*-nee-vehr-see-*tah?*) (*How can I get to the university?*)

Book II

Exploring and Wandering About

Words to Know

a destra	ah <u>dehs</u>-trah	to the right
a sinistra	ah see-<u>nees</u>-trah	to the left
la rotonda [f]	la roh-<u>tohn</u>-dah	rotary; circle
stazione [f]	stah-<u>tsyoh</u>-neh	station
aeroporto [m]	ah-eh-roh-<u>pohr</u>-toh	airport
teatro [m]	teh-<u>ah</u>-troh	theater
cinema [m]	<u>chee</u>-neh-mah	cinema
chiesa [f]	<u>kyeh</u>-zah	church
ospedale [m]	ohs-peh-<u>dah</u>-leh	hospital
ponte (m)	<u>pohn</u>-teh	bridge

The evolution of Italian architecture

Early Italian **architettura** (ahr-kee-teht-*tooh*-rah) (*architecture*) was strongly influenced by Etruscan and Greek culture. Later, with the advent of the Roman Empire, it began to develop original features, particularly its use of **archi** (*ahr*-kee) (*arches*), **volte** (*vohl*-teh) (*vaults*), and **cupole** (*kooh*-poh-leh) (*domes*). Important examples are **i bagni** (ee *bah*-nyee) (*baths*) (**Terme di Caracalla, Terme di Diocleziano**), **gli anfiteatri** (lyee ahn-fee-teh-*ah*-tree) (*amphitheaters*) (**Colosseum, Arena di Verona**), **i teatri** (ee teh-*ah*-tree) (*theaters*) (**Teatro di Marcello**), **le chiese** (leh *kyeh*-seh) (*churches*) (such as the **Basilica di Massenzio**), and **i templi** (ee *tehm*-plee) (*temples*) (**Pantheon**).

From the Christian and Byzantine era to the **Medioevo** (meh-dyoh-*eh*-voh) (*Middle Ages*), the architectural context was predominantly ecclesiastical and **religioso** (reh-lee-*joh*-soh) (*religious*). In the Middle Ages, **l'architetto** (lahr'kee-*teht*-toh) (*the architect*) was a master craftsman who, after years of experience, supervised the design of the building and the development of the project. In the "Humanist" period that followed the Middle Ages, the architect became more of an artist and less of a craftsman.

During the Renaissance, Italy developed an entirely new way of looking at architecture. Leon Battista Alberti developed the concept of the **città ideale** (cheet-*tah* ee-deh-*ah*-leh) (*ideal city*). Now, for the first time, architecture became concerned with the idea of planning an ideal city with the proper arrangement of its elements.

Lo stile barocco (loh *stee*-leh bah-*rohk*-koh) (*the Baroque style*), linked to the Counter-Reformation, was developed in Rome and exercised its influence throughout the Catholic world. The first examples of this style are found in works (mostly religious) by Carlo Maderno, Gian Lorenzo Bernini, Francesco Borromini, and Pietro da Cortona. They introduced new shapes into architectural design, such as **ellissi** (ehl-*lees*-see) (*ellipses*), **spirali** (spee-*rah*-lee) (*spirals*), and **curve policentriche** (*koohr*-veh poh-lee-*chehn*-tree-keh) (*polycentric curves*), thus elaborating and modifying the concept of space. The Baroque style soon spread beyond the borders of Rome to the rest of Italy.

The 1800s, the "eclectic" century, saw the reemergence of many past architectural styles, including neo-Renaissance, neo-Baroque, neo-Romanesque, and neo-Gothic styles, as well as later echoes of the Imperial style. The 20th century finally brought some novelty: from art nouveau to the completely new language proposed by Antonio di Sant'Elia in his 1914 *Manifesto of Futurist Architecture* and from rationalism to the works of the new, emerging architects — Luigi Moretti, Carlo Scarpa, Franco Albini, Gio Ponti, Tomaso Buzzi, and Pier Luigi Nervi. Currently, the Italian architectural landscape claims Renzo Piano, architect of international fame, as its foremost representative.

Chapter 2

Having Fun Out on the Town

In This Chapter

▶ Enjoying movies, art, theater, and other forms of entertainment

▶ Giving and receiving invitations

Going out on the town is always fun. In general, Italians are sociable people who enjoy having a good time. You see them having espressos together **al bar** (ahl bahr) (*in the bar*) or drinks at night **in piazza** (*een pyaht*-tsah) (*on the public square*). Most Italians love to go out in the evening, crowding the streets until late at night.

Italy is a popular vacation destination, and Italian cities have a great variety of cultural offerings, from the numerous local fairs and **sagre** (*sah*-greh) (*town celebrations relating to harvest, wild boar, or saints, for example*) to open-air festivals and music events to city-wide celebrations. The variety is endless, and fun is guaranteed. The festivals relating to saints are for the **santo patrono** (*sahn*-toh pah-*troh*-noh) (*patron saint*). The **sagre** are to celebrate agricultural products. These two things are different.

In this chapter, I give you a lot of information you need to take in cultural attractions and socialize.

Experiencing Italian Culture

No matter where you live or where you travel, most major cities have a weekly **pubblicazione** (poohb-blee-kah-*tsyoh*-neh) (*publication*), listing information about upcoming events. These publications include dates, descriptions, and time schedules for theaters, exhibitions, festivals, films, and so on. They also provide tips for shopping and restaurants.

In smaller towns without weekly magazines, you may see events announced on posters. You can also find information in the local newspapers.

Of course, newspapers aren't your only source of information about things to do and see. Asking the following questions can get you answers you want.

Cosa c'è da fare di sera? (*koh*-zah cheh dah *fah*-reh dee *seh*-rah?) (*Are there any events in the evenings?*)

Può suggerirmi qualcosa? (pwoh soohj-jeh-*reer*-mee kwahl-*koh*-zah?) (*Can you recommend something to me?*)

C'è un concerto stasera? (cheh oohn kohn-*chehr*-toh stah-*seh*-rah?) (*Is there a concert tonight?*)

Ci sono ancora posti? (chee *soh*-noh ahn-*koh*-rah *pohs*-tee?) (*Are there any seats left?*)

Dove si comprano i biglietti? (*doh*-veh see *kohm*-prah-noh ee bee-*lyeht*-tee?) (*Where can we get tickets?*)

Quanto vengono i biglietti? (*kwahn*-toh *vehn*-goh-noh ee bee-*lyeht*-tee?) (*How much are the tickets?*)

A che ora comincia lo spettacolo? (ah keh *oh*-rah koh-*meen*-chah loh speht-*tah*-koh-loh?) (*What time does the show begin?*)

Non c'è niente di più economico? (nohn cheh *nyehn*-teh dee *pyooh* eh-koh-*noh*-mee-koh?) (*Isn't there anything cheaper?*)

Talkin' the Talk

Arturo works at a theater. He is bombarded with questions from patrons before the show.

Sig. Paoli: **Quando comincia lo spettacolo?**
kwahn-doh koh-*meen*-chah loh speht-*tah*-koh-loh?
When does the show start?

Arturo: **Alle sette e mezza.**
ahl-leh *seht*-teh eh *mehd*-dzah.
At half past seven.

Erika: **A che ora finisce lo spettacolo?**
ah keh *oh*-rah fee-*nee*-sheh loh speht-*tah*-koh-loh?
What time is the show going to end?

Arturo: **Verso le dieci.**
            vehr-soh leh *dyeh*-chee
            About 10 p.m.

Erika: **C'è un intervallo?**
            cheh oohn een-tehr-*vahl*-loh?
            Is there an intermission?

Arturo: **Sì, tra il secondo e il terzo atto.**
            see, trah eel seh-*kohn*-doh eh eel *tehr*-tsoh *aht*-toh.
            Yes, between the second and third acts.

Words to Know

A che ora?	ah keh <u>oh</u>-rah?	What time?
Quando?	<u>kwahn</u>-doh?	When?
Dove?	<u>doh</u>-veh?	Where?
divertente	dee-vehr-<u>tehn</u>-teh	fun
biglietto [m]	bee-<u>lyeht</u>-toh	ticket
spettacolo [m]	speht-<u>tah</u>-koh-loh	show
cominciare	koh-meen-<u>chah</u>-reh	to start
finire	fee-<u>nee</u>-reh	to end

Taking in a movie

Going **al cinema** (ahl *chee*-neh-mah) (*to the movies*) is a popular activity almost everywhere. In Italy, American films usually are **doppiati** (dohp-*pyah*-tee) (*dubbed*) into Italian. On the other hand, why not go to an original Italian film? Doing so provides you with a good opportunity to polish your Italian.

Some special questions for the movies include

- **Andiamo al cinema?** (ahn-*dyah*-moh ahl *chee*-neh-mah?) (*Shall we go to the movies?*)

- **Cosa danno?** (*koh*-zah *dahn*-noh?) (*What's playing?*)

- **Dove lo danno?** (*doh*-veh loh *dahn*-noh) (*Where is [the movie] being shown?*)

- **È in lingua (versione) originale?** (eh in *leen*-gwah [vehr-*syoh*-neh] oh-ree-jee-*nah*-leh?) (*Is the film in the original language?*)

- **Dov'è il cinema Trianon?** (doh-*veh* eel *chee*-neh-mah *tree*-ah-nohn?) (*Where is the Trianon cinema?*)

  Often saying the name of the movie theater is sufficient, for example, **Dov'è il Trianon?** (doh-*veh* eel *tree*-ah-nohn?) (*Where is the Trianon?*)

Italian movie theaters used to be rather small, showing only one movie at a time. Now virtually all large Italian cities have big **multisala** (moohl-tee-*sah*-lah) (*multiplex*) cinemas, with many screens.

Here are a few other terms to help you navigate the experience of going to and discussing a movie in Italian:

- **Chi è il regista?** (kee *eh* eel reh-*jees*-tah?) (*Who is the director?*)

- **Chi sono gli attori?** (kee *soh*-noh lyee aht-*toh*-ree?) (*Who's starring?*)

- **attore** (aht-*toh*-reh) (*actor*)

- **attrice** (aht-*tree*-cheh) (*actress*)

- **regista** (reh-*jees*-tah) (*director*)

- **trama** (*trah*-mah) (*plot*)

- **scena** (*sheh*-nah) (*scene*)

Going to the theater

The languages of the theater and the cinema are very similar. Of course, when you attend a play, opera, or symphony performance, you have a variety of seats. For example, you can sit in the **platea** (plah-*teh*-ah) (*orchestra*), in the **palchi** (*pahl*-kee) (*box seats*), in the **galleria** (gahl-leh-*ryah*) (*balcony*), or in the **loggione** (lohj-*joh*-neh) (*gallery*), which used to be called **la piccionaia** (lah peech-choh-*nah*-yah) (Literally: *the pigeon house*) because it's high up.

Italian films

It's well known that Italy produces a great number of films, and many Italian directors are famous throughout the world, such as Fellini, Rossellini, Bertolucci, De Sica, and Nanni Moretti. Some of their works are considered classics of Italian culture, and I highly recommend them to you. Other contemporary directors to look for include Giuseppe Tornatore, Gabriele Salvatores, Francesca Archibugi, Ferman Ozpetek, Matteo Garrone, and Emanuele Crialese.

La dolce vita and **La strada** are among Fellini's masterpieces. The dramatic and moving **Roma, città aperta** (*Open City*) is one of Rossellini's most significant movies. To complete the image of the Italian cinema between 1948 and 1957, you need to include De Sica's **Ladri di biciclette** (*The Bicycle Thief*). Bertolucci belongs to a subsequent period and is known for his **Il conformista** (*The Conformist*) whereas Moretti's **Caro diario** (*Dear Diary*) and **La stanza del figlio**

(*The Son's Room*) made big contributions to disseminating Italian culture abroad in the 1990s.

Then there's Roberto Benigni, who not only directed one of the most successful films of modern times but also won an Academy Award for acting in **La vita è bella** (*Life Is Beautiful*). Many of the great Italian film directors — among them Gabriele Salvatores, Giuseppe Tornatore, Paolo Sorrentino and Giovanni Veronesi — and beloved actors — Ambra Angiolini, Raoul Bova, Ricky Memphis, Enrico Brignano, Francesco Mandelli, Toni Servillo, Luca Argentero, Carlo Verdone, Elio Germano, Sabrina Ferilli and many others — worked together in films during 2013, making it a memorable year for Italian cinema. The resulting films, **Reality, La miglior offerta** (*The Best Offer*), **Un giorno devi andare** (*There Will Come a Day*), and **La grande bellezza** (*The Great Beauty*), have made audiences laugh, cry and dream — Italian style.

Book II

Exploring and Wandering About

Talkin' the Talk

In the following exchange, Eugenio wants to know whether seats are available for a certain performance of a play he wants to see. He's speaking on the phone with the person at the theater box office.

Ticket Agent:	**Pronto?** *prohn-toh?* *Hello?*
Eugenio:	**Buongiorno. È il Teatro Valle?** bwohn-*johr*-noh. *eh* eel teh-*ah*-tro *vahl*-leh? *Good morning. Is this the Valle Theater?*

Ticket Agent:	**Sì. Mi dica.** see. mee *dee*-kah. *Yes. Can I help you? (Literally: Tell me.)*
Eugenio:	**Vorrei prenotare dei posti.** vohr-*rey* preh-noh-*tah*-reh dey *pohs*-tee. *I'd like to reserve some seats.*
Ticket Agent:	**Per quale spettacolo?** pehr *kwah*-leh speht-*tah*-koh-loh? *For which performance?*
Eugenio:	***Aspettando Godot*, domani sera.** ahs-peht-*tahn*-doh goh-*doh*, doh-*mah*-nee *seh*-rah. *Waiting for Godot, tomorrow evening.*
Ticket Agent:	**Mi dispiace; è tutto esaurito.** mee dee-*spyah*-cheh; eh *tooht*-toh eh-zou-*ree*-toh. *I'm sorry; it's sold out.*
Eugenio:	**Ci sono repliche?** chee *soh*-noh *reh*-plee-keh? *Are there other performances?*
Ticket Agent:	**L'ultima è dopodomani.** *loohl*-tee-mah *eh* doh-poh-doh-*mah*-nee. *The last one is the day after tomorrow.*

Did you notice that the title of the play, *Waiting for Godot,* has no preposition in Italian? In English, you wait for someone, but Italian speakers say *waiting somebody* — **aspettare qualcuno** (ahs-peht-*tah*-reh kwahl-*kooh*-noh). You may also hear **ti aspetto** (tee ahs-*peht*-toh) (*I'm waiting for you*).

Some theaters don't accept telephone reservations; you can only *reserve at the box office* — **prenotazione al botteghino** (preh-noh-tah-*tsyoh*-neh ahl boht-teh-*gee*-noh). You can pay for the tickets and pick them up immediately or before the performance begins.

Exploring a museum

A recent report shows that all the tickets sold in 2012 by the Italian State for access to national museums, monuments, and art galleries produced 25 percent less revenue than the Louvre Museum in Paris, France, alone. Some critics point out that no museum in the world can stand on the sale of tickets alone and that statues and paintings, villas and fountains can't be used with the objective of making money. Unfortunately, the protection and maintenance of the Italian cultural heritage requires considerable funds, for which such revenue would be an important source. Here are some of the most frequented museums with the richest collections: the **Uffizi** (oohf-*fee*-tsee) Gallery in Florence; **La Galleria Borghese** (lah gahl-leh-*ree*-ah bohr-*geh*-seh) and the **Musei Vaticani** (mooh-*zeh*-ee vah-tee-*kah*-nee) in Rome; the Peggy Guggenheim Collection in Venice; and **Il Museo della Scienza e della Tecnica** (eel mooh-*zeh*-oh dehl-lah *shehn*-zah eh *dehl*-lah *tehk*-nee-kah) in Milan. Every two years, there's also the **Biennale di Venezia** (byehn-*nah*-leh dee veh-*neh*-tsyah) where you can view the work of many well-known contemporary international artists.

Book II

Exploring and Wandering About

Experiencing a local festival

This chapter's introduction refers to the many local **sagre** (*sah*-greh) (*fairs; festivals*) and festivals you can find in Italy, especially during the spring, summer, and fall. The themes of these fairs vary, ranging from the ones that are political in origin, such as **La festa dell'Unità** (lah *fehs*-tah dehl-looh-nee-*tah*) (*a left-leaning newspaper*), to the ones that are nature-related — **La sagra del cinghiale** (lah *sah*-grah dehl cheen-*gyah*-leh) (*the wild-boar festival*) and **La sagra del pesce azzurro** (lah *sah*-grah dehl *peh*-sheh adz-*zooh*-roh) (*the Blue Fish Fair*) are two that come to mind. Do drop in if you find one because they're often the perfect venues for experiencing local culture and homemade food.

Talkin' the Talk

Paola tries to convince Martino to go to a festival.

Paola: **Lo sai che oggi c'è la Sagra dell'uva a Bertinoro?**
loh sahy keh *oj*-jee cheh lah *sah*-grah dehl-*looh*-vah ah behr-teen-*oh*-roh?
Did you know that today there is the grape festival in Bertinoro?

Martino: **Divertente! Oh, facciamoci un salto!**
dee-vehr-*tehn*-teh! oh fahch-*chah*-moh-chee oohn *sahl*-toh!
What fun! Oh, let's stop by!

Paola: **Partiamo subito?**
pahr-*tyah*-moh *sooh*-bee-toh?
Shall we leave right away?

Martino:	**Sì, perché no?**
	see, pehr-*keh* noh?
	Yes, why not?
Paola:	**In quel paese fanno anche degli ottimi cappelletti!**
	een kwehl pah-*eh*-zeh *fahn*-noh *ahn*-keh *deh*-lyee
	oht-tee-mee kahp-pehl-*leht*-tee!
	They also make great cappelletti in that town!
Martino:	**Ottimo, così ci fermiamo a cena.**
	oht-tee-moh, koh-*zee* chee fehr-*myah*-moh ah
	cheh-nah.
	Great! This way we can stay for supper.

Taking in the Italian Music Scene

Italy has a rich musical history, from classic operas by Verdi and Puccini to the popular song "Volare" by Domenico Modugno, which became an international hit in the 1950s. Although popular Italian songs use standard language, some contemporary artists incorporate dialect in their lyrics, especially the Neapolitan (heavily used by Pino Daniele), and the Genoese (in Fabrizio De Andre's songs). These musical experiments (increasingly numerous) are in line with the revitalization of dialects by the younger generations and have been encouraged, especially over the last decade, by the growing success of such musical genres as hip-hop, rap, and reggae.

Catching a concert

If you're interested in music, you'll certainly please your ear in Italy, from the **Umbria** (*oohm*-bryah) **Jazz Festival** to the theater **Festival dei due mondi** (*fehs*-tee-vahl dey *dooh*-eh *mohn*-dee) in Spoleto to your favorite Italian **cantautore** (kahn-tou-*toh*-reh) (*singer-songwriter*).

Italy is full of old and beautiful churches and cathedrals where **musicisti** (mooh-zee-*chees*-tee) (*musicians*) often present classical music concerts. You can also hear concerts in other places — sometimes in the center of a city in a piazza.

Talkin' the Talk

La signora and il signor Tiberi are reading the morning paper. Suddenly, la signora Tiberi cries out:

Sig.ra Tiberi: **Guarda qui!**
gwahr-dah kwee!
Look here!

Sig. Tiberi: **Che c'è?**
keh cheh?
What's up?

Sig.ra Tiberi: **Martedì c'è Pollini a Roma!**
mahr-teh-*dee* cheh pohl-*lee*-nee ah *roh*-mah!
Pollini is in Rome on Tuesday!

Sig. Tiberi: **Tiene un concerto?**
tyeh-neh oohn kohn-*chehr*-toh?
Is he going to give a concert?

Sig.ra Tiberi: **Sì, al Conservatorio.**
see, ahl kohn-sehr-vah-*toh*-ryoh.
Yes, at the Conservatory.

Sig. Tiberi: **Sarà tutto esaurito?**
sah-*rah toot*-toh eh-zou-*ree*-toh?
Will it already be sold out?

Sig.ra Tiberi: **Forse no!**
fohr-seh noh!
Maybe not!

Sig. Tiberi: **Vai al botteghino?**
vahy ahl boht-teh-*gee*-noh?
Are you going to the box office?

Sig.ra Tiberi: **Prima telefono.**
pree-mah teh-*leh*-foh-noh.
I'm going to call first.

Maurizio Pollini is an internationally famous Italian pianist. We do hope that signor and signora Tiberi find two tickets for this event. **Buona fortuna!** (*bwoh*-nah fohr-*tooh*-nah!) (*Good luck!*)

Words to Know

musica [f]	<u>mooh</u>-zee-kah	music
concerto [m]	kohn-<u>chehr</u>-toh	concert
esaurito	eh-zou-<u>ree</u>-toh	sold out
piano(forte) [m]	<u>pyah</u>-noh(<u>fohr</u>-teh)	piano
museo [m]	mooh-<u>zeh</u>-oh	museum
insieme	een-<u>syeh</u>-meh	together

Maybe you know a musician or someone who plays an instrument in his or her leisure time. You're probably curious about some things, such as the following:

✔ **Che strumento suoni?** (keh strooh-*mehn*-toh *swoh*-nee?) (*Which instrument do you play?*)

Suono il violino. (*swoh*-noh eel vyoh-*lee*-noh.) (*I play the violin.*)

✔ **Dove suonate stasera?** (*doh*-veh swoh-*nah*-teh stah-*seh*-rah?) (*Where are you playing tonight?*)

Suoniamo al Blu Notte. (swoh-*nyah*-moh ahl blooh *noht*-teh.) (*We play/ We're playing at the Blu Notte.*)

✔ **Chi suona in famiglia?** (kee *swoh*-nah in fah-*mee*-lyah?) (*Who in your family plays?*)

Suonano tutti. (*swoh*-nah-noh *tooht*-tee.) (*All of them play.*)

Exploring the world of Italian opera

If you go to Italy, you can catch an opera by Verdi, Puccini, or Rossini in wonderful theaters, such as Milan's **La Scala** (lah *skah*-lah), Naples's **San Carlo** (sahn *kahr*-loh), Venice's **La Fenice** (lah pheh-*nee*-cheh), and the theaters of Florence and Palermo. In the summer months, try to check out theater festivals (which include a wide variety of repertoires and venues citywide), like the famous Ravenna Festival. You can also see outdoor operas in Verona, at the old **Roman Arena** (*roh*-mahn ah-*reh*-nah). Following are some phrases concerning performances:

- ✔ **la danza classica/moderna/contemporanea** (lah *dahn*-zah *klahs*-see-kah/moh-*dehr*-nah/kohn-tehm-poh-*rah*-neh-ah) (*classical/modern/contemporary dance*)

- ✔ **lo spettacolo** (loh speht-*tah*-koh-loh) (*the show; the performance*)

- ✔ **la prova generale pubblica** (lah *proh*-vah jeh-neh-*rah*-leh *poohb*-blee-kah) (*public dress rehearsal*)

- ✔ **la replica** (lah *reh*-plee-kah) (*repeat performance*)

- ✔ **il matinée** (eel mah-tee-*neh*) (*matinee*)

- ✔ **lo spettacolo pomeridiano** (loh speht-*tah*-koh-loh poh-meh-ree-*dyah*-noh) (*afternoon performance*)

Book II

Exploring and Wandering About

Opera buffa

The **opera buffa** (*oh*-peh-rah *boohf*-fah) (*comic opera*) was developed in the 18th century in Naples, which was then one of the most important musical centers in Europe. Unlike in the **opera seria** (*oh*-peh-rah *seh*-riah) (*serious opera*) (see the next section), the **opera buffa** puts more emphasis on the action **sul palcoscenico** (soohl pahl-koh-*sheh*-nee-koh) (*on the stage*), which requires music to follow the changes of the dramatic action and **cantanti** (kahn-*tahn*-tee) (*singers*), who are also good **attori** (aht-*toh*-ree) (*actors*), to enhance performance. **Libretti** (lee-*breht*-tee) (*librettos*) are inspired by **commedia dell'arte** (kohm-*meh*-dyah dehl-*lahr*-teh) (*comedy of art*) and consist of simple plots, with some characters that use colloquial language — almost slang — with short, snappy sentences, onomatopoeia, and realistic effects, such as yawning, sneezing, and laughing. In the second half of the 18th century, comic opera reached the peak of its success with the collaboration of playwright Carlo Goldoni and composer Baldassare Galuppi.

CULTURAL WISDOM

Master of Italian opera: Giuseppe Verdi

The man who revolutionized opera in the 19th century, Giuseppe Verdi, was born in Roncole, near Parma, on October 10, 1813. His **umili origini** (*ooh*-mee-lee oh-*ree*-jee-nee) (*humble origins*) (his father was an innkeeper and his mother, a spinner) make him an unlikely candidate for musical fame, but he found mentors who believed in his talent and helped him to pursue his passion.

His first opera, *Oberto,* was performed at La Scala in 1839 and proved **un successo** (oohn soohch-*chehs*-soh) (*a success*). It was soon followed by **capolavori** (kah-poh-lah-*voh*-ree) (*masterpieces*) such as **Il Nabucco,** the trilogy **Rigoletto, Trovatore, Traviata,** and the operas of his later years: **La forza del destino, Don Carlos, Aida, Otello,** and **Falstaff.** In the last years of his life, Verdi founded a retirement home in Milan for **musicisti** (mooh-see-*chee*-stee) (*musicians*), which is still active. He died on January 7, 1901.

CULTURAL WISDOM

Master of Italian opera: Giacomo Puccini

Puccini is one of the major figures of the Italian opera in the 19th and 20th centuries, an artist who tried to break away from the cultural and artistic movements of his time. He was born in Lucca on December 22, 1858, and died in November 1924 in Brussels after major throat surgery. During his life, he composed a limited number of works — 12 to be exact — because his main interest was to improve his theatrical skills to create "perfect" works. **Varietà** (vah-ryeh-*tah*) (*variety*), **velocità** (veh-loh-chee-*tah*) (*speed*), and **trovate sceniche** (troh-*vah*-teh *sheh*-nee-keh) (*stage tricks*) are the basic ingredients of his theater. Among Puccini's operas, **La Boheme, Tosca,** and **Madama Butterfly** are still the most frequently performed in the standard repertoire.

The public, although sometimes taken aback by his unique style, always followed and supported Puccini. Music critics, however, remained **ostili** (oh-*stee*-lee) (*hostile*) and suspicious until the last decade of the century, when his work was reevaluated and highly appreciated by the greatest authors of his time, including Stravinsky, Schoenberg, Webern, and Ravel.

Opera seria

During the 18th century, **i poeti** (ee poh-*eh*-tee) (*poets*) who were members of the Academy of Arcadia (a literary academy founded in Rome in 1690) influenced the Italian musical drama. They encouraged the simplification **delle trame** (*dehl*-leh *trah*-meh) (*of the plots*), the elimination of comic subjects, the reduction of the number of arias, and exalted the values of **fedeltà** (feh-dehl-*tah*) (*fidelity*), **amicizia** (ah-mee-*chee*-tsyah) (*friendship*), and **virtù** (veer-*tooh*) (*virtue*) present in the ancient **teatro tragico** (teh-*ah*-troh *trah*-jee-koh) (*tragic theater*) and in the modern French performances.

Popular Italian music

You may sometimes find that **il testo** (eel *teh*-stoh) (*the lyrics*) of many **canzoni popolari italiane** (kahn-*tsoh*-nee poh-poh-*lah*-ree ee-tah-lee-*ah*-neh) (*popular Italian songs*) sound much like **poesia** (poh-eh-*see*-ah) (*poetry*), and for good reason — many of these song lyrics were written by poets. For instance, Pasquale Panella wrote for Lucio Battisti; Roberto Roversi, for Lucio Dalla; Manlio Sgalambro, for Franco Battiato; and Alda Merini, for Milva. Many poets of the past have also inspired contemporary **cantanti** (kahn-*tahn*-tee) (*singers*) and **cantautori** (kahn-tah-ooh-*toh*-ree) (*singer-songwriters*); you can find hints of Edgar Lee Masters's and Yeats's poems, respectively, in **canzoni** (kahn-*tsoh*-nee) (*songs*) by Fabrizio De André and those of Angelo Branduardi.

Sanremo, the most popular Italian song festival, has had a key role in the music world since its inception in 1951. It's a singing contest for Italian performers that serves to gauge the popular trends in Italian music. Typical **Sanremo** songs use simple and catchy **ritornelli** (ree-tohr-*nehl*-lee) (*refrains*), rich in monosyllables, as in the famous song by Domenico Modugno **"Volare . . . oh, oh! / Cantare . . . oh, oh, oh, oh!"** from **Nel blu dipinto di blu** (Nehl blooh d**ee**-*peen*-toh dee blooh) (*In the blue, painted blue*), 1958.

Modugno's style characterized the 1950s. **I critici musicali** (ee *kree*-tee-chee mooh-see-*kah*-lee) (*music critics*) argue that this style, which had several traits in common with the language of opera, brought about musical and linguistic innovations and inspired other singers, such as Mina and Adriano Celentano. The 1960s were marked by the emergence of not one but several popular Italian singer-songwriters, mostly from Genoa (Gino Paoli, Bruno Lauzi, Luigi Tenco, and Fabrizio De André). They, along with Lucio Battisti, Lucio Dalla, Francesco Guccini, and Franco Battiato, bridged the '60s to the '70s, a decade characterized by songs with **temi politici** (*teh*-mee poh-*lee*-tee-chee) (*political themes*).

Since the 1980s, up to the 21st century, Italian songs have seen a gradual increase in the use of foreign languages (mainly English and Spanish), dialects, and **turpiloquio** (toohr-pee-*loh*-kwyoh) (*foul language*). In addition to the frequent use of English and informal, sometimes almost trivial, registers, in the songs of this period, you'll find references to sex, alcohol, and drugs, often presented through the **metafora** (meh-*tah*-foh-rah) (*metaphor*) of the "journey." Cinema, television, and advertising are common themes in the works of famous **contemporanei** (kohn-tehm-poh-*rah*-nehy) (*contemporary*) Italian pop-rock singers, including Vasco Rossi, Ligabue, Gianna Nannini, and Jovanotti, who was on tour in the United States in 2012.

Inviting Fun

Getting or giving **un invito** (oohn een-*vee*-toh) (*an invitation*) is always a pleasurable experience. A party (**una festa**) (*ooh*-nah *fehs*-tah) is a good opportunity to meet new people. In Italian, the verb **invitare** (een-vee-*tah*-reh) frequently means to treat someone to something. For example, if someone says **Posso invitarti a teatro?** (*pohs*-soh een-vee-*tahr*-tee ah teh-*ah*-troh?) (*May I invite you to the theater?*), it means that the person is going to make the arrangements and pay for you.

The following expressions are other ways to suggest an activity:

> **Che ne pensa di andare a Roma?** (keh neh *pehn*-sah dee ahn-*dah*-reh ah *roh*-mah?) (*What do you think of going to Rome?* [formal])

Book II

Exploring and Wandering About

Che ne dici di uscire stasera? (keh neh *dee*-chee dee ooh-*shee*-reh stah-*seh*-rah?) (*What do you say about going out tonight?* [informal])

Andiamo in piscina! (ahn-*dyah*-moh in pee-*shee*-nah!) (*Let's go to the swimming pool!*)

Mangiamo una pizza! (mahn-*jah*-moh *ooh*-nah *peet*-tsah!) (*Let's eat a pizza!*)

Perché non andiamo a teatro? (pehr-*keh* nohn ahn-*dyah*-moh ah teh-*ah*-troh?) (*Why don't we go to the theater?*)

You can see that suggesting an activity in Italian isn't so different from the way you do it in English. You can ask **Perché non . . .** (pehr-*keh* nohn . . .) (*Why don't we . . .*) or **Che ne pensi . . .** (keh neh *pehn*-see . . .) (*What do you think about . . .*).

The word **perché** is special. It's used in this chapter to ask the question *why?* However, it can also mean *because.* A dialogue can go like this:

Perché non mangi? (pehr-*keh* nohn *mahn*-jee?) (*Why aren't you eating?*)

Perché non ho fame. (pehr-*keh* nohn oh *fah*-meh.) (*Because I'm not hungry.*)

Nowadays, you can issue and receive invitations any number of ways. You can receive an invitation by phone or e-mail, or your **ospite** (*oh*-spee-teh) (*host*) may ask you face to face.

Talkin' the Talk

Guido will have a party at his house next Saturday. He calls Sara to invite her. (Track 19)

Sara:	**Ciao Guido, come va?**
	chou *gwee*-doh, *koh*-meh vah?
	Hi Guido, how are you?

Guido:	**Molto bene! Sei libera sabato sera?**
	mohl-toh *beh*-neh! sey *lee*-beh-rah *sah*-bah-toh *seh*-rah?
	Very well! Are you free Saturday night?

Sara:	**È un invito?**
	eh oohn een-*vee*-toh?
	Is this an invitation?

Guido: **Sì, alla mia festa.**
see, *ahl*-lah *mee*-ah *fehs*-tah.
Yes, to my party.

Sara: **Fantastico! A che ora?**
fahn-*tah*-stee-koh! ah keh *oh*-rah?
Great! What time?

Guido: **Verso le nove.**
vehr-soh leh *noh*-veh.
About nine.

Sara: **Cosa posso portare? Il gelato va bene?**
koh-zah *pohs*-soh pohr-*tahr*-eh? eel jeh-*lah*-toh vah
beh-neh?
What can I bring? Is ice cream okay?

Guido: **Ottimo. Quello piace a tutti.**
oht-tee-moh. *qwehl*-loh *pyah*-cheh ah *tooht*-tee.
Great. Everyone likes ice cream.

Sara: **Allora, d'accordo.Grazie!**
ahl-*loh*-rah, dahk-*kohr*-doh. *grah*-tsyeh!
Okay then. Thanks!

Words to Know

invito [m]	een-<u>vee</u>-toh	invitation
festa [f]	<u>fehs</u>-tah	party
suonare	swoh-<u>nah</u>-reh	to play (a musical instrument)
perché	pehr-<u>keh</u>	why; because
bere	<u>beh</u>-reh	to drink
ballare	bahl-<u>lah</u>-reh	to dance

Chapter 3

Exploring the Outdoors, Sports, and Hobbies

*1*n this chapter, we talk about the fun stuff — playing sports, delighting in hobbies, and generally enjoying yourself. Plus we throw in a section about reflexive verbs so you can talk correctly about enjoying yourself.

Maybe you use your **fine settimana** (*fee*-neh *seht*-tee-*mah*-nah) (*weekends*) as a chance to play sports, like **calcio** (*kahl*-choh) (*soccer*), **tennis** (*tehn*-nees) (*tennis*), or **pallavolo** (*pahl*-lah-*voh*-loh) (*volleyball*). Or perhaps you park yourself in front of the TV to watch **pallacanestro** (*pahl*-lah-kah-*nehs*-troh) (*basketball*). In any case, being able to talk about sports and other recreational activities is a plus in any language.

Italy's rich and varied natural attractions are the perfect setting for a holiday. You can be in contact with nature and stay in cozy cottages or fishermen's lodges. You can explore the country and taste authentic food, or choose a cultural itinerary and breathe the atmosphere of history and traditions in quiet villages. If you're brave enough, you can climb six among the ten tallest mountains in Europe: **Monte Bianco** (*mohn*-teh *byahn*-koh) (*white mountain*), **Monte Rosa** (*mohn*-teh *roh*-sah) (*pink mountain*), **Cervino** (cher-*vee*-noh), **Gran Paradiso** (grahn pah-rah-*dee*-soh) (*big paradise*), **Bernina** (behr-*nee*-nah), and **Monviso** (mohn-*vee*-soh), in the **Alpi** (*ahl*-pee) (*alps*). If water is your element, then explore the incredible seabed of **Ponza** (*pohn*-dzah) or **Sardegna** (sahr-*deh*-nyah) (*Sardinia*).

Getting Close to Nature

Maybe you like to go up into the mountains to be close to nature. Even when **ti godi** (tee *goh*-dee) (*you enjoy*) Mother Nature on your own, however, you may want to know some vocabulary to express the wonders you see, such as **Che bel panorama!** (keh behl pah-noh-*rah*-mah!) (*What a great view!*)

- **l'albero** (*lahl*-beh-roh) (*tree*)
- **il bosco** (eel *bohs*-koh) (*wood*)
- **la campagna** (lah kahm-*pah*-nyah) (*countryside*)
- **il fiore** (eel *fyoh*-reh) (*flower*)
- **il fiume** (eel *fyooh*-meh) (*river*)
- **il lago** (eel *lah*-goh) (*lake*)
- **il mare** (eel *mah*-reh) (*sea*)
- **la montagna** (lah mohn-*tah*-nyah) (*mountain*)
- **il panorama** (eel pah-noh-*rah*-mah) (*view*)
- **la pianta** (lah *pyahn*-tah) (*plant*)
- **il pino** (eel *pee*-noh) (*pine*)
- **il prato** (eel *prah*-toh) (*meadow, lawn*)
- **la quercia** (lah *kwehr*-chah) (*oak*)
- **il tramonto** (eel trah-*mohn*-toh) (*sunset*)
- **l'ulivo** (ooh-*lee*-voh) (*olive tree*)

Notice in the following sentences that Italian has appropriated a couple English words — *picnic* and *jog*.

- **Mi piace camminare nel verde.** (mee *pyah*-cheh kahm-mee-*nah*-reh nehl *vehr*-deh.) (*I like to walk in nature.*)
- **Facciamo un picnic sul prato?** (fahch-*chah*-moh oohn peek-*neek* soohl *prah*-toh?) (*Should we have a picnic on the lawn?*)

✔ **Ti piace fare bird-watching?** (tee *pyah*-cheh *fah*-reh *behrd*-ooh-oh-cheen?) (*Do you like bird-watching?*)

✔ **Faccio jogging nel parco.** (*fahch*-choh *johg*-geeng nehl *pahr*-koh.) (*I go jogging in the park.*)

Talkin' the Talk

Animals are always an interesting topic, and knowing the names of some of them in another language can be helpful. Here's an exchange about animals:

Book II

Exploring and Wandering About

Carla:	**Ti piacciono gli animali?** tee *pyach*-choh-noh lyee ah-nee-*mah*-lee? *Do you like animals?*
Alessandra:	**Sì, ho una piccola fattoria.** see, oh *ooh*-nah *peek*-koh-lah faht-toh-*ree*-ah. *Yes, I have a small farm.*
Carla:	**Davvero?** dahv-*veh*-roh? *Really?*
Alessandra:	**Ho un cane, due gatti e un maialino.** oh oohn *kah*-neh, *dooh*-eh *gaht*-tee eh oohn mah-yah-*lee*-noh. *I have a dog, two cats, and a small pig.*
Carla:	**Ti piacciono i cavalli?** tee *pyahch*-choh-noh ee kah-*vahl*-lee? *Do you like horses?*
Alessandra:	**No, preferisco le mucche.** noh, preh-feh-*rees*-koh leh *moohk*-keh. *No, I prefer cows.*

Words to Know

cane [m]	<u>kah</u>-neh	dog
cavallo [m]	kah-<u>vahl</u>-loh	horse
capra [f]	<u>kah</u>-prah	goat
gallo [m]	<u>gahl</u>-loh	rooster
gatto [m]	<u>gaht</u>-toh	cat
gallina [f]	gahl-<u>lee</u>-nah	chicken
maiale [m]	mah-<u>yah</u>-leh	pig
mucca [f]	<u>moohk</u>-kah	cow
uccello [m]	oohch-<u>chehl</u>-loh	bird
lupo [m]	<u>looh</u>-poh	wolf
pecora [f]	<u>peh</u>-koh-rah	sheep
tacchino [m]	tahk-<u>kee</u>-noh	turkey

Playing and Watching Sports

Playing and talking about sports is a favored pastime of people the world over. And whether you travel to Italy, invite your Italian neighbor to play tennis, or just want to practice your Italian with a friend, knowing sports terms is always helpful.

Using the right names and verbs for sports talk

Some sports you *do* in Italian. Therefore, you pair those words with **fare** (*fah-reh*) (*to do, to practice*). With other sports, however, you must use **giocare** (joh-*kah*-reh) (*to play*) or **andare** (ahn-*dah*-reh) (*to go*). Then you have verbs that describe the sport itself, like **pattinare** (paht-tee-*nah*-reh) (*to skate*). Table 3-1 lists the most common sports and the verbs you use with them.

Table 3-1	Sports Verbs	
Italian	*Pronunciation*	*Translation*
fare	*fah*-reh	*to do; to practice*
atletica leggera	ah-*tleh*-tee-kah lehj-*jeh*-rah	*track*
canottaggio	kah-noht-*tahj*-joh	*crew rowing*
ciclismo	chee-*klees*-moh	*cycling*
danza	*dahn*-dsah	*dance*
equitazione	eh-kwee-tah-*tsyoh*-neh	*riding*
ginnastica artistica	jeen-*nah*-stee-kah ahr-*tee*-stee-kah	*gymnastics*
jogging	*johg*-geeng	*jogging*
lotta	*loht*-tah	*wrestling*
nuoto	*nwoh*-toh	*swimming*
palestra	pah-*lehs*-trah	*going to the gym*
scherma	*skehr*-mah	*fencing*
lo sci	loh shee	*skiing*
lo sci nautico	loh shee *nou*-tee-koh	*water skiing*
sollevamento pesi	sohl-leh-vah-*mehn*-toh *peh*-zee	*weight lifting*
lo snowboarding	loh snoh-*borh*-deeng	*snowboarding*

(continued)

Book II

Exploring and Wandering About

Table 3-1 (continued)

Italian	Pronunciation	Translation
giocare a	joh-*kah*-reh ah	*to play*
calcio	*kahl*-choh	*soccer*
pallacanestro/basket	*pahl*-lah-kah-*nehs*-troh/*bahs*-keht	*basketball*
pallavolo/volley	*pahl*-lah-*voh*-loh/*vohl*-ley	*volleyball*
ping pong	peeng-pohng	*Ping-Pong*
tennis	*tehn*-nees	*tennis*
golf	gohlf	*golf*
andare	ahn-*dah*-reh	*to go*
a cavallo	ah kah-*vahl*-loh	*to ride*
in bicicletta	een bee-chee-*kleht*-tah	*to cycle*

Le ragazze (leh rah-*gaht*-tseh) (*girls*) don't play **calcio** in Italy the way they do in other countries, but they do play **pallavolo.** Many **ragazzi** (rah-*gaht*-tsee) (*boys*) play **calcio,** and men play **calcetto** (kahl-*cheht*-toh), also called **calcio a cinque** (*kahl*-choh ah *cheen*-kweh), which is five-against-five soccer, often played indoors on a smaller field. Then there's **bocce** (*bohch*-cheh) (*lawn bowling*). Many towns offer small **bocce** courts where older men usually play.

The following conjugations are for the three important sports verbs: **fare, andare,** and **giocare.**

Conjugation	Pronunciation
Fare	
io faccio	*ee*-oh *fahch*-choh
tu fai	tooh fahy
lui/lei fa	*looh*-ee/ley fah
noi facciamo	nohy fahch-*chah*-moh
voi fate	vohy *fah*-teh
loro fanno	*loh*-roh *fahn*-noh

Conjugation	*Pronunciation*
Andare	
io vado	*ee*-oh *vah*-doh
tu vai	tooh vahy
lui/lei va	*looh*-ee/ley vah
noi andiamo	nohy ahn-*dyah*-moh
voi andate	vohy ahn-*dah*-teh
loro vanno	*loh*-roh *vahn*-noh
Giocare	
io gioco	*ee*-oh *joh*-koh
tu giochi	tooh *joh*-kee
lui/lei gioca	*looh*-ee/ley *joh*-kah
noi giochiamo	nohy joh-*kyah*-moh
voi giocate	vohy joh-*kah*-teh
loro giocano	*loh*-roh *joh*-kah-noh

Here are some examples, using the list of sports from Table 3-1 and the correct verb conjugations:

> **Le ragazze che fanno danza hanno molta grazia ed eleganza.** (leh rah-*gaht*-tseh keh *fahn*-noh *dahn*-dzah *ahn*-noh *mohl*-tah *grah*-tsyah ehd eh-leh-*gahn*-tsah.) (*Girls who dance have a lot of grace and elegance.*)

> **So andare a cavallo, ma non so andare in bicicletta.** (soh ahn-*dah*-reh ah kah-*vahl*-loh, mah nohn soh ahn-*dah*-reh een bee-chee-*kleht*-tah.) (*I can ride a horse, but I can't ride a bike.*)

> **Pochi Italiani giocano a golf, ma moltissimi giocano a calcio.** (*poh*-kee ee-tah-*lyah*-nee *joh*-kah-noh ah gohlf, mah mohl-*tees*-see-mee *joh*-kah-noh ah *kahl*-choh.) (*Few Italians play golf, but many play soccer.*)

Talkin' the Talk

Giulia and Stefano have just met at the university and found out that they live in the same neighborhood. On the way to the bus stop, Stefano strikes up a conversation about his favorite topic — sports. (Track 20)

Stefano:	**Che sport pratichi?** keh sport *prah*-tee-kee? *What sports do you play?*
Giulia:	**Faccio nuoto e vado a cavallo.** *fahch*-choh *nwoh*-toh eh *vah*-doh ah kah-*vahl*-loh. *I swim and ride.*
Stefano:	**Equitazione?** eh-kwee-tah-*tsyoh*-neh? *Riding?*
Giulia:	**È il mio sport preferito.** eh eel *mee*-oh sport preh-feh-*ree*-toh. *It's my favorite sport.*
	Giochi a tennis? *joh*-kee ah *tehn*-nees? *Do you play tennis?*
Stefano:	**No, faccio palestra.** noh, *fahch*-choh pah-*lehs*-trah. *No, I go to the gym.*
Giulia:	**Body building?** *boh*-dee *beel*-deeng? *Body building?*
Stefano:	**Uso le machine come il tapis roulant in inverno e corro in pineta in estate.** *ooh*-zoh leh *mahk*-kee-neh *koh*-meh eel tah-*pee* rooh-*lahn* een een-*vehr*-noh eh *kohr*-roh een pee-neh-tah een eh-*stah*-teh. *I use the machines, like the treadmill in the winter, and I run in the pine forest in the summer.*

Italians use the French word **tapis roulant** for treadmill.

Watching sports

Watching sports on TV is a favorite pastime for any fan; here's a list of Italian favorites more or less by popularity:

- **calcio** (*kahl*-choh) (*soccer*)
- **Formula 1** (*fohr*-mooh-lah *ooh*-noh) (*Formula One car racing*)
- **ciclismo** (chee-*klees*-moh) (*cycling*)
- **moto GP** (*moh*-toh gee-pee) (*motorcycle racing*)
- **pugilato** (pooh-jee-*lah*-toh) (*boxing*)
- **lo sci alpino** (loh shee ahl-*pee*-noh) (*downhill ski racing*)

When you want to catch a sport live at the field or arena, you may find the following sections helpful.

Going to an Italian soccer game

If you like **il calcio italiano** (eel *kahl*-choh ee-tah-lee-*ah*-noh) (*Italian soccer*), **andare allo stadio** (ahn-*dah*-reh *ahl*-loh *stah*-dyoh) (*going to the stadium*) is an unforgettable experience. Here, you share your emotions with a large **pubblico di tifosi** (*poohb*-blee-koh dee tee-*foh*-see) (*audience of supporters*). Being there isn't the same as watching **la partita di calcio** (lah pahr-*tee*-tah dee *kahl*-choh) (*the football game*) on a TV screen! To ensure **la pubblica sicurezza** (lah *poohb*-blee-kah see-kuh-*reht*-tsah) (*public safety*), some **misure di controllo e prevenzione** (mee-*sooh*-reh dee kohn-*trohl*-loh eh preh-vehn-*tsyoh*-neh) (*control and prevention measures*) have been recently introduced in Italian stadiums, such as **la tessera del tifoso** (lah *tehs*-seh-rah dehl tee-*foh*-soh) (*the fan card*), which is issued by **le società di calcio** (leh soh-cheh-*tah* dee *kahl*-choh) (*soccer societies*) to their **soci** (*soh*-chee) (*members*) only after the applicants get police clearance. However, if you're traveling to Italy, you don't need a fan card to attend a game; you can buy a ticket from any authorized agency.

Checking out the car racing circuits

Circuiti cittadini (cheer-*koo*-ee-tee cheet-tah-*dee*-nee) (*road racing circuits*) and race events are historic in Italy. **Coppa Florio** (one of the oldest automobile races) was established in 1900 in Brescia and then transferred to the Madonie circuit in northern Sicily in 1906, to become the renowned **Targa Florio**. The **Targa Florio** competition continued until 1973. In 1927, the first **Mille Miglia** (an open-road endurance race) — *The Thousand Miles* — took place on the route connecting Rome to Brescia and back again. Between 1918 and 1939, the Montenero circuit at Livorno became home of the **Coppa**

Ciano, while in 1939 the first Italian Grand Prix was held in Brescia, and the Garda circuit was used until the 1960s.

You can find road racing circuits in almost every region in Italy: Abruzzo (Pescara circuit), Campania (circuits in Caserta, Salerno, Avellino, and Naples), and Emilia Romagna (Modena circuit). Rome hosted the Grand Prix of Rome from 1925 to 1963, when it was transferred to Vallelunga, while the Mugello circuit in Florence in the 1920s ran from north Florence to Bologna, crossing the Appeninines in the Futa Pass.

If you happen to be a fan of car racing — or even if you're not — here are a few terms to help you talk your way through the victory lap:

- **la coppa** (lah *kohp*-pah) (*cup*)
- **la curva** (lah *koor*-vah) (*curve*)
- **la discesa** (lah dee-*sheh*-sah) (*descent*)
- **il pilota** (eel pee-*loh*-tah) (*pilot*)
- **la pista** (lah *pee*-stah) (*race track*)
- **il podio** (eel *poh*-dyoh) (*podium*)
- **la salita** (lah sah-*lee*-tah) (*climb*)
- **il sorpasso** (eel sohr-*pahs*-soh) (*overtaking*)
- **la vittoria** (lah veet-*toh*-ryah) (*victory*)

CULTURAL WISDOM

The Italian dream: la Ferrari

If you like **motori potenti** (moh-*toh*-ree poh-*tehn*-tee) (*powerful engines*) and elegant designs and have a lot of money at your disposal, you may be interested in Ferrari cars, which have long been objects of desire for many. Prominent designers, such as Giugiaro and Pininfarina, Scaglietti, Bertone, and Vignale, have drawn up many of Ferrari's models. Ferrari's "father" is Enzo Ferrari, who founded the company in Maranello, near Modena, in 1929.

The story goes that the official symbol, historically represented by **un cavallino rampante** (oohn kah-vahl-*lee*-noh rahm-*pahn*-teh) (*a prancing horse*), is attributable to Francesco Baracca, a World War I flying ace. Enzo Ferrari's mother donated it to Enzo Ferrari in 1923, and it has since become the Ferrari mascot. In Shanghai (China), Ferrari recently opened its first **museo** (mooh-*seh*-oh) (*museum*) outside the Italian borders.

Talking about Hobbies and Interests

You can certainly do a lot of other things in your leisure time besides playing or watching sports. Some hobbies are more sedentary, like reading, sewing, or playing musical instruments.

Here are some typical questions (and varied responses) to ask about **il tempo libero** (eel *tehm*-poh *lee*-behr-oh) (*free time*):

✔ **Che cosa ti piace fare nel tempo libero?** (keh *koh*-zah tee *pyah*-che *fah*-reh nehl *tehm*-poh *lee*-beh-roh?) (*What do you like to do in your free time?*)

Mi piace cucinare e fare l'uncinetto. (mee *pyah*-cheh kooh-chee-*nah*-reh eh *fah*-reh loohn-chee-*neht*-toh.) (*I like to cook and crochet.*)

✔ **Qual è il tuo passatempo preferito?** (kwahl *eh* eel *tooh*-oh pahs-sah-*tehm*-poh preh-feh-*ree*-toh?) (*What is your favorite pastime?*)

Il mio passatempo preferito è . . . /i miei passatempi preferiti sono . . . (eel *mee*-oh pahs-sah-*tehm*-poh preh-feh-*ree*-toh eh . . . /ee *myeh*-ee pahs-sah-*tehm*-pee preh-feh-*ree*-tee *soh*-noh . . .) (*My favorite pastime is . . . /My favorite pastimes are . . .*)

. . . **fare i giochi da tavolo o giocare a scacchi.** (. . . *fah*-reh ee *joh*-kee dah *tah*-voh-loh oh joh-*kah*-reh ah *skahk*-kee.) (. . . *playing board games or chess.*)

. . . **stare con gli amici.** (. . . *stah*-reh kohn lyee ah-*mee*-chee.) (. . . *hanging out with friends.*)

Note: You may want to start your sentence with the possessive adjective in this response if you're writing rather than speaking to someone.

✔ **Vai spesso ai concerti?** (*Vahy spehs*-soh *ahy* kohn-*cher*-tee? (*Do you often go to concerts?*)

Vado soltanto a quelli di musica rock. (*vah*-doh sohl-*tahn*-toh ah *kwehl*-lee dee *mooh*-see-kah rohk.) (*I only go to rock music concerts.*)

Many people love music, whether they like to **ascoltare la musica** (ah-skohl-*tah*-reh lah *mooh*-zee-kah) (*listen to music*) or **suonare uno strumento** (swoh-*nah*-reh *ooh*-noh strooh-*mehn*-toh) (*play an instrument*). Of course, there are all kinds of music, from **classica** (*klahs*-see-kah) (*classical*) to **jazz** (*jats*) to **rock** (*rohk*).

Book II

Exploring and Wandering About

Talkin' the Talk

Emilia and Isabel are two classmates getting to know each other a little better.

Emilia: **Mi piace molto ascoltare la musica. E a te?**
mee *pyah*-cheh *mohl*-toh ah-skohl-*tah*-reh lah *mooh*-zee-kah. eh ah teh?
I like to listen to music a lot. And you?

Isabel: **Ho molta musica sul mio iPod.**
oh *mohl*-tah *mooh*-zee-kah soohl *mee*-oh *ahy*-pohd.
I have a lot of music on my iPod.

Emilia: **Tu suoni uno strumento?**
tooh *swoh*-nee *ooh*-noh strooh-*mehn*-toh?
Do you play an instrument?

Isabel: **Suono il violoncello e il pianoforte.**
swoh-noh eel vyoh-lohn-*chehl*-loh eh eel *pyah*-noh-*fohr*-teh.
I play the cello and the piano.

Emilia: **Sei brava?**
sey *brah*-vah?
Are you good?

Isabel: **Si, mi piace molto suonare. E a te?**
see, mee *pyah*-cheh *mohl*-toh swoh-*nah*-reh. eh ah teh?
I guess so. I really like to play music. And you?

Emilia: **Suono il flauto, ma preferisco cantare nel coro.**
swoh-noh eel *flou*-toh, mah preh-feh-*rees*-koh kahn-*tah*-reh nehl *koh*-roh.
I play the flute, but I prefer to sing in the chorus.

Words to Know

ascoltare	ah-skohl-<u>tah</u>-reh	to listen to
batteria	baht-teh-<u>reh</u>-ah	drums
chitarra	kee-<u>tahr</u>-rah	guitar
clarinetto	klah-ree-<u>neht</u>-toh	clarinet
flauto	<u>flou</u>-toh	flute
giocare	joh-<u>kah</u>-reh	to play a sport, cards, game
pianoforte	<u>pyah</u>-noh-<u>fohr</u>-teh	piano
sassofono	sahs-<u>soh</u>-foh-noh	saxophone
suonare	swoh-<u>nah</u>-reh	to play an instrument
tromba	<u>trohm</u>-bah	trumpet
violoncello	vyoh-lohn-<u>chehl</u>-loh	cello
violino	vyoh-<u>lee</u>-noh	violin
voce	<u>voh</u>-cheh	voice

Book II

Exploring and Wandering About

And when you say you like something, use the verb **piacere** (pyah-*cheh*-reh). This verb is a bit different because you usually use it only in the third person singular or the third person plural of any verb tense.

- ✔ **Third person singular:** If what you like is singular or an infinitive:

     Mi piace correre. (mee *pyach*-eh *kohr*-reh-reh.) (*I like to run.*)

     Mi piace il mare. (mee *pyach* eel *mah*-reh.) (*I like the sea.*)

- ✔ **Third person plural:** If what you like is plural:

     Mi piacciono gli sport invernali. (mee *pyach*-choh-noh lyee spohrt een-vehr-*nah*-lee.) (*I like winter sports.*)

Only your pronouns change, which are indirect object pronouns and literally mean "such and such a thing is pleasing to me." These are **mi, ti, gli, le, ci, vi,** and **gli/loro** (mee, tee, lyee, leh, chee, vee, lyee/*loh*-roh) (*me, you, him, her, us, you,* and *them*). You don't use personal pronouns (**io, tu, lui, lei,** and so on) with the verb **piacere.** (Turn to Chapter 4 in Book IV for more on the verb **piacere.**)

Speaking Reflexively

When you say "to enjoy yourself," you use a reflexive verb. That is, you turn the action back to yourself. The same applies in Italian. But not all Italian reflexive verbs are reflexive in English, and vice versa. Some verbs, such as **riposarsi** (ree-poh-*zahr*-see) (*to rest oneself*) and **svegliarsi** (zveh-*lyahr*-see) (*to wake oneself*), are not reflexive in English, although they are in Italian.

In Italian, you can tell whether a verb is reflexive by looking at the infinitive form. If the last syllable of the infinitive is **-si** (*see*), which translates as *oneself,* then the verb is reflexive. When you conjugate a reflexive verb, you must change the last syllable from **-si** to something else. The following conjugation of **divertirsi** (dee-vehr-*teer*-see) (*to enjoy oneself, to have a good time*) demonstrates the conjugation of the verb. The only difference is that you add the reflexive pronoun, which refers to the person concerned (the subject). After you have removed the **-si** at the end of a reflexive verb, you conjugate it just like any other **-are, -ere,** or **-ire** verb. Notice how **divertirsi** becomes a regular present tense **-ire** verb, with the exception that you then need the reflexive pronouns.

Conjugation	*Pronunciation*
mi diverto	mee dee-*vehr*-toh
ti diverti	tee dee-*vehr*-tee
si diverte	see dee-*vehr*-teh
ci divertiamo	chee dee-vehr-*tyah*-moh
vi divertite	vee dee-vehr-*tee*-teh
si divertono	see dee-*vehr*-toh-noh

Here are some more examples:

- ✔ **divertirsi: Mi diverto molto a cantare.** (mee dee-*vehr*-toh *mohl*-toh ah kahn-*tah*-reh.) (*I really enjoy singing.*)

- ✔ **annoiarsi** (ahn-noh-*yahr*-see) (*to be bored*): **Vi annoiate in campagna?** (vee ahn-noh-*yah*-teh een kahm-*pah*-nyah?) (*Do you get bored in the country?*)

- ✔ **svegliarsi** (zveh-*lyahr*-see) (*to wake up*): **A che ora ti svegli?** (ah keh *oh*-rah tee *zveh*-lyee?) (*What time do you wake up?*)

- ✔ **mettersi** (*meht*-tehr-see) (*to put on/to wear*): **Mi metto la giacca nera.** (mee *meht*-toh lah *jahk*-kah *neh*-rah.) (*I'm going to wear my black jacket.*)

- ✔ **lavarsi** (lah-*vahr*-see) (*to wash*): **Ti sei lavata i denti?** (tee sey lah-*vah*-tah ee *dehn*-tee?) (*Did you brush your teeth?*)

Book II

Exploring and Wandering About

Chapter 4

Planning a Trip

*E*verybody likes to get away from the daily grind and check out new environments and activities during their free time. Tourists and Italians alike flock **la spiaggia** (lah *spyahj*-jah) (*to the beach*), head **in montagna** (een mohn-*tah*-nyah) (*to the mountains*), or get away **in campagna** (een kahm-*pay*-nyah) (*to the countryside*). Some Italians take long trips outside of Italy. Whatever you do, **buon viaggio!** (bwohn *vyahj*-joh!) (*have a nice trip!*) or **buone vacanze!** (*bwoh*-neh vah-*kahn*-tzeh!) (*have a nice vacation!*)

Deciding When and Where to Go

Deciding when to take a trip can be just as important as choosing your destination. Italy has many cities that really heat up in the summer. In fact, many Italians living in those cities escape to cooler places in the summer, such as the beaches of Sardegna or the cool Dolomites. On the other hand, summer months are also **l'alta stagione** (*lahl*-tah stah-*joh*-neh) (*high season*) for tourists.

Talkin' the Talk

Enzo is talking to Cristina about their vacation for the summer. He has it all figured out already, but Cristina is skeptical. (Track 21)

Enzo:	**Quest'anno andiamo in montagna!**
	kwehs-tahn-noh ahn-dyah-moh een mohn-tah-nyah!
	This year we're going to the mountains!

Cristina:	**Stai scherzando?**
	stahy skehr-tsahn-doh?
	Are you kidding?

Enzo:	**È rilassante: boschi, aria fresca . . .**
	eh ree-lahs-sahn-teh: bohs-kee, ah-ree-ah frehs-kah . . .
	It's relaxing: woods, fresh air . . .

Cristina:	**È noioso. E non si può nuotare!**
	eh noy-oh-zoh. eh nohn see pwoh nwoh-tah-reh!
	It's boring. And you can't swim!

Enzo:	**Ci sono le piscine, i laghi e i fiumi!**
	chee soh-noh leh pee-shee-neh, ee lah-gee eh ee fyooh-mee!
	There are swimming pools, lakes and rivers!

Cristina:	**Ma dai, pensa al mare, al sole . . .**
	mah dahy, pehn-sah ahl mah-reh, ahl soh-leh . . .
	Come on, think of the sea, the sun . . .

Enzo:	**Facciamo passeggiate, visitiamo i rifugi, mangiamo quel buon cibo di montagna.**
	fach-chah-moh pahs-sehj-jah-teh, vee-see-tyah-moh ee ree-fooh-jee, mahn-jah-moh qwel bwohn chee-boh dee mohn-tah-nyah.
	We can go hiking, visit some retreats, and eat that good mountain food.

Cristina:	**Oh no. Io rimango a casa!**
	oh noh. yoh ree-mahn-goh ah kah-sah!
	Oh no. I'll stay home!

Words to Know

rimanere	ree-mah-<u>neh</u>-reh	to stay
campagna [f]	kahm-<u>pah</u>-nyah	countryside
fiume [m]	<u>fyooh</u>-meh	river
mare [m]	<u>mah</u>-reh	sea
montagna [f]	mohn-<u>tah</u>-nyah	mountain

Book II

Exploring
and
Wandering
About

CULTURAL WISDOM

The Alps and Dolomites offer marvelous terrain for hiking and skiing. A **rifugio** (ree-*fooh*-joh) is a rustic mountain retreat that people hike or ski to, for the most part. You can enjoy a warm, home-cooked meal there, and even spend the night in some **rifugi** (ree-*fooh*-jee) (*retreats*).

Going to agriturismo

Several years ago, a new vacation concept became popular in Italy: **l'agriturismo** (lah-gree-tooh-*reez*-moh) (*the farm holiday*). During these types of vacations, people travel to the country or the mountains where they stay in farmhouses. These accommodations range from Spartan to luxurious and romantic; most are good options for families. Guests can help out on the farm, ride horses, and swim at some **agriturismi.** This type of lodging also enables you to eat the traditional food of the region, and you're miles away from formal, impersonal hotels.

Another popular type of lodging is the bed and breakfast, which you can find throughout the countryside as well as in big cities like Rome and Milan. The concept of B&B in Italy is different than in the U.S. — it's open to families, not only to couples who don't want to be bothered by the sounds of children or other domestic commotions.

You can easily find an abundance of both on the web as you're doing your research for your trip.

Sending letters and postcards

If you're one of those people who still like to send **cartoline** (kahr-toh-*lee*-neh) (*postcards*) and **lettere** (*leht*-teh-reh) (*letters*) while traveling, you're going to need to find an **ufficio postale** (oohf-*fee*-choh pohs-*tah*-leh) (*post office*), a **tabaccaio** (tah-bahk-*kah*-yoh) (*tobacconist*), or a **cartoleria** (kahr-toh-leh-*ree*-ah) (*stationery shop*) where you can purchase **francobolli** (frahn-koh-*bohl*-lee) (*stamps*) and **buste** (*boohs*-teh) (*envelopes*).

Going to the beach and spa

Italy has 7,600 kilometers of coastline, so it's no surprise that Italians and tourists alike flock to Italy's famous beaches, which can be both **sabbia** (*sahb*-byah) (*sand*) or **scoglio** (*skoh*-lyoh) (*rock*), each with its decided advantages (and clientele). Most beaches have that most wonderful of Italian institutions called **il bagno** (eel *bahn*-yoh). This is not a bathroom or a bath, but a combination bar/beach club/restaurant, where you can show up and rent an **ombrellone** (ohm-brehl-*loh*-neh) (*beach umbrella*) and **un lettino** (oohn leht-*tee*-noh) (*a lounge chair*) for the day, week, or month. Here, you and the children can also play **beach volley** (*beach volleyball*) or **racchettoni** (rahk-eht-*toh*-nee) (similar to beach tennis, but without a net), or rent a **pedalò** (peh-dah-*loh*) (*paddle boat*).

Italy also has many wonderful naturally heated **terme** (*tehr*-meh) (*thermal springs*) and spas. Some of these are quite well-equipped, and you pay for their services (like Chianciano, Montecatini, and Fiuggi). Other **terme** can be accessed for free in places like Vulcano, Ischia, and Calabria.

Visiting castles, palaces, and estates

Travel to any remote area of Italy, and you'll find **castelli** (kah-*stehl*-lee) (*castles*), **palazzi** (pah-*laht*-tsee) (*palaces*), and **tenute** (teh-*nooh*-teh) (*estates*). Their presence tells the story of a frontier territory, a crucial place located along strategic routes for commercial traffic. These lands' strategical advantages made them objects of contention between peoples. Castles, palaces, and estates played a crucial role in the defense and control of these disputed territories and are an integral part of the **patrimonio culturale italiano** (pah-tree-*moh*-nee-oh koohl-tooh-*rah*-leh ee-tah-lee-*ah*-noh) (*Italian cultural heritage*), the history of the urban fabric and the countryside. A recent census shows that about 17,000 palaces, villas, castles, and gardens exist in Italy.

CULTURAL WISDOM

Visas and passports

All you need is **un passaporto** (oohn pahs-sah-*pohr*-toh) (*a passport*) to visit Italy if you go for less than six months. If you go for longer, you need **un visto** (oohn *vees*-toh) (*a visa*).

If you fly to Italy, the main airports are **Malpensa** (mahl-*pehn*-sah) in Milan and **Leonardo da Vinci** (leh-oh-*nahr*-doh dah *veen*-chee) in Rome, but you can also fly into Venice, Bologna, Palermo, and Naples, which are other popular (and less hectic) airports.

Taking a Tour

Whether you're in a city or rural area, you can usually find fun and interesting sights to see. Bus tours are organized in great detail for the most part, and the price generally includes the cost of the bus, lunch, dinner, and the services of a tour guide. A guided tour or day-trip, called **una gita organizzata** (*ooh*-nah *jee*-tah ohr-gah-nee-*dzah*-tah) (*an organized tour*), may be the most efficient, cost-effective, and informative way to check out nearby attractions. You can ask these questions to get information about available tours:

Ci sono gite organizzate? (chee *soh*-noh *jee*-teh ohr-gah-need-*dzah*-teh?) (*Are there any organized tours?*)

Quanto costa la gita? (*kwahn*-toh *kohs*-tah lah *jee*-tah?) (*How much does the tour cost?*)

C'è una guida che parla inglese? (cheh *ooh*-nah *gwee*-dah keh *pahr*-lah een-*gleh*-zeh?) (*Is there an English-speaking guide?*)

Dove si comprano i biglietti? (*doh*-veh see *kohm*-prah-noh ee bee-*lyeht*-tee?) (*Where do you buy tickets?*)

Talkin' the Talk

Lucia and Renzo are in a tour office, talking to a tour agent and deciding which trip to go on the next day.

Lucia: **C'è una bella gita sul lago di Como domani.**
cheh *ooh*-nah *behl*-lah *jee*-tah soohl *lah*-goh dee *koh*-moh doh-*mah*-nee.
We can take a nice trip to Lake Como tomorrow.

Renzo: **Vuoi andare, vero?**
vwohi ahn-*dah*-reh, *veh*-roh?
You want to go, don't you?

Lucia: **Sarebbe carino. E tu?**
sah-*rehb*-beh kah-*ree*-noh. eh tooh?
It would be nice. What about you?

Renzo: **Non amo le gite in autobus.**
nohn *ah*-moh leh *jee*-teh een *ou*-toh-boohs.
I don't like bus trips.

Lucia: **Ma è una gita a piedi!**
mah *eh ooh*-nah *jee*-tah ah *pyeh*-dee!
But it's a walking tour!

Renzo: **Ottimo! A che ora inizia la gita?**
oht-tee-moh! ah keh *oh*-rah ee-*nee*-tsyah lah *jee*-tah?
Great! What time does the trip start?

Agent: **Alle sette e trenta.**
ahl-leh *seht*-teh eh *trehn*-tah.
At seven-thirty a.m.

Renzo: **Quanto dura?**
kwahn-toh *dooh*-rah?
How long is it going to last?

Agent: **Circa cinque ore.**
cheer-kah *cheen*-kweh *oh*-reh.
About five hours.

Words to Know

viaggio organizzato [m]	<u>vyahj</u>-joh ohr-gah-nee-<u>dzah</u>-toh	organized trip
gita [f]	<u>jee</u>-tah	trip/tour
guida [f]	<u>gwee</u>-dah	guide
lago [m]	<u>lah</u>-goh	lake

Booking a Trip outside of Italy

You never know — you just may want to book a trip to another country while you're in Italy. When you're ready to book your flight or hotel, you may want to consider using **un'agenzia viaggi** (ooh-nah-jehn-*tsee*-ah *vyahj*-jee) (*a travel agency*). There you can get plane tickets, hotel reservations, or complete tour packages.

As you walk by the travel agency, undoubtedly your eye will be drawn to special, all-inclusive package deals to Malta, Tunisia, and the Canary Islands, to name a few, in ads like this one:

> **INCREDIBILI OFFERTE!! Gran Canaria, La Palma. Euro 616 a persona. Comprende: volo + hotel + tasse e commissioni. Colazione a buffet.**
>
> (een-kreh-*dee*-bee-lee ohf-*fehr*-teh! grahn kah-*nah*-ryah, lah *pahl*-mah. eh-ooh-roh sehy-*chehn*-toh-*seh*-dee-chee ah pehr-*soh*-nah. kohm-*prehn*-deh: *voh*-loh pee-*ooh* oh-*tehl* pee-*ooh* tahs-seh eh kom-mees-*syoh*-neh. koh-lah-*tsyoh*-neh ah booh-*fey*.)
>
> (*Incredible deals! Gran Canaria, La Palma. 616 euros per person. Includes flight, hotel departure fees, and buffet breakfast.*)

Book II

Exploring and Wandering About

Talkin' the Talk

Alessandro has just seen a sign advertising the Canary Islands. He's talking to Giorgio, a travel agent.

Giorgio: **Buongiorno, mi dica.**
bwohn-*johr*-noh, mee *dee*-kah.
Good morning, can I help you? (Literally: *Tell me.*)

Alessandro: **Vorrei fare un viaggio alle Isole Canarie.**
vohr-*rey fah*-reh oohn *vyahj*-joh *ahl*-leh ee-zoh-leh kah-*nah*-ryeh.
I'd like to take a trip to the Canary Islands.

Giorgio: **Dove, esattamente?**
doh-veh, eh-zaht-tah-*mehn*-teh?
Where, exactly?

Alessandro: **Tenerife o La Palma.**
teh-neh-*ree*-feh oh lah *pahl*-ma.
Tenerife or La Palma.

Giorgio: **Un viaggio organizzato?**
oohn *vyahj*-joh ohr-gah-nee-*dzah*-toh?
An organized trip?

Alessandro: **No, vorrei soltanto prenotare il volo.**
noh, vohr-*rey* sohl-*tahn*-toh preh-noh-*tah*-reh eel
voh-loh.
No, I'd like to book just the flight.

Giorgio: **E per gli spostamenti interni?**
eh pehr lyee *spoh*-stah-*mehn*-tee een-*tehr*-nee?
And what about moving around between islands?

Alessandro: **Mi sposterò in autobus e traghetto.**
mee spohs-tehr-*oh* een *ou*-toh-boohs eh
trah-*geht*-toh.
I'll get around by bus and ferry.

Giorgio: **Quando vuole partire?**
kwahn-doh *vwoh*-leh pahr-*tee*-reh?
When do you want to leave?

Alessandro: **La prima settimana di febbraio.**
lah *pree*-mah seht-tee-*mah*-nah dee fehb-*brah*-yoh.
The first week of February.

Giorgio: **E il ritorno?**
eh eel ree-*tohr*-noh?
And return?

Alessandro: **La terza settimana di febbraio.**
lah *tehr*-tsah seht-tee-*mah*-nah dee fehb-*brah*-yoh.
The third week of February.

Words to Know

viaggiare	vee-ahj-<u>jah</u>-reh	to travel
volo [m]	<u>voh</u>-loh	flight
traghetto [m]	trah-<u>geht</u>-toh	ferry
autobus [m]	<u>ou</u>-toh-boohs	bus

Arriving and Leaving with Arrivare and Partire

When you use the verbs **arrivare** (ahr-ree-*vah*-reh) (*to arrive*) and **partire** (pahr-*tee*-reh) (*to leave*) in connection with specific places, certain prepositions accompany them. You always follow **arrivare** with the preposition **a** (ah) (*at/to/in*) when you're in a city; when you arrive in a country, you use the preposition **in** (een) (*in*). You always follow **partire** with the preposition **da** (dah) (*from*) when you're leaving a place behind; when leaving to go to a place, you follow it with the preposition **per** (pehr) (*for*).

You conjugate the verbs **partire** and **arrivare** like other regular **-are** and **-ire** verbs, which you can check out in Chapter 1 of Book IV.

To help you understand how to use these verbs properly, here they are in some simple sentences:

> **Luca parte da Torino alle cinque.** (*looh*-kah *pahr*-teh dah toh-*ree*-noh *ahl*-leh *cheen*-kweh.) (*Luca leaves from Turin at 5 o'clock.*)

> **Arrivo a Taormina nel pomeriggio.** (ahr-*ree*-voh ah tah-ohr-*mee*-nah nehl poh-meh-*reej*-joh.) (*I'm arriving in Taormina in the afternoon.*)

Book II

Exploring and Wandering About

Talkin' the Talk

Filippo and Marzia are spending some time together before Filippo has to catch a plane. (Track 22)

Marzia:	**A che ora parte l'aereo?** ah keh *oh*-rah *pahr*-teh lah-*eh*-reh-oh? *What time does the plane leave?*
Filippo:	**Alle nove di mattina.** *ahl*-leh *noh*-veh dee maht-*tee*-nah. *At nine a.m.*
Marzia:	**A che ora arrivi a Los Angeles?** ah keh *oh*-rah ahr-*ree*-vee ah lohs *ahn*-jeh-lehs? *What time will you arrive in Los Angeles?*
Filippo:	**Alle undici di notte.** *ahl*-leh *oohn*-dee-chee dee *noht*-teh. *At eleven p.m.*

Using the Simple Future Tense

Sometimes you need a verb form that indicates that something will happen in the near future. In Italian, this tense is called **futuro semplice** (foh-*tooh*-roh *sehm*-plee-cheh) (*simple future*). However, you can also use the present tense when referring to a point in the future. The following sentences use the simple future tense:

> **Andrò in Italia.** (ahn-*droh* een ee-*tah*-lee-ah.) (*I will go to Italy.*)
>
> **Quando arriverai a Palermo?** (*kwahn*-doh ahr-ree-veh-*rahy* ah pah-*lehr*-moh?) (*When will you arrive in Palermo?*)
>
> **Non torneremo troppo tardi.** (nohn tohr-neh-*reh*-moh *trohp*-poh *tahr*-dee.) (*We won't be back too late.*)

To form the simple future tense of regular verbs, take the whole infinitive, cut off the final **e**, and add the same set of endings (**ò, ai, à, emo, ete, anno**). For **-are** verbs, you need to change the **a** in the infinitive to an **e**. Note the stem change in Table 4-1, which illustrates the simple future tenses of four common verbs.

Table 4-1		Simple Future Tenses		
Parlare = PARLER	**Prendere = PRENDER**	**Partire = PARTIR**	**Finire = FINIR**	**Translation**
parler**ò**	prender**ò**	partir**ò**	finir**ò**	(*I will talk/have/leave/finish*)
parler**ai**	prender**ai**	partir**ai**	finir**ai**	(*you will talk/have/leave/finish*)
parler**à**	prender**à**	partir**à**	finir**à**	(*he/she/you will talk/have/leave/finish*)
parler**emo**	prender**emo**	partir**emo**	finir**emo**	(*we will speak/have/leave/finish*)
parler**ete**	prender**ete**	partir**ete**	finir**ete**	(*you will speak/have/leave/finish*)
parler**anno**	prender**anno**	partir**anno**	finir**anno**	(*they will speak/have/leave/finish*)

Chapter 5

Money, Money, Money

- -

- -

On the one hand, you can never have enough money; on the other hand, it can cause trouble. This statement is particularly true in situations abroad or when you're dealing with foreign money in general. This chapter covers not only currency — you know how tiresome converting foreign currencies can be — but all the terms you need to know about money.

Going to the Bank

Dealing with banks isn't always fun, but sometimes you can't avoid them. You aren't often in the position of being able to cash a big check; you may have other, more painful, transactions to perform. In this section, we give you some banking terms that can help you manage a dialogue in a bank.

You may need to go to the bank for several reasons. For example, you may want **cambiare valuta** (kahm-*byah*-reh vah-*looh*-tah) (*to change money*), **prelevare contante** (preh-leh-*vah*-reh cohn-*tahn*-tee) (*to withdraw money*), or **versare soldi sul tuo conto** (vehr-*sah*-reh sohl-dee soohl *tooh*-oh *kohn*-toh) (*to deposit money into your account*). Other reasons could be to **aprire un conto** (ah-*pree*-reh oohn *kohn*-toh) (*open an account*) or **riscuotere un assegno** (ree-*skwoh*-teh-reh oohn ahs-*seh*-nyoh) (*to cash a check*).

Other phrases you may find helpful include:

Mi dispiace, il suo conto è scoperto. (mee dees-*pyah*-cheh, eel *sooh*-oh *kohn*-toh eh skoh-*pehr*-toh.) (*I'm sorry, your account is overdrawn.*)

Può girare l'assegno per favore? (*pwoh* jee-*rah*-re lahs-*seh*-nyoh pehr fah-*voh*-reh?) (*Could you endorse the check, please?*)

Quant'è il tasso d'interesse? (kwant-*eh* eel *tahs*-soh deen-teh-*rehs*-seh?) (*What is the interest rate?*)

Vorrei cambiare dei traveler's checks. (vohr-*ray* kahm-*byah*-reh dey traveler's checks.) (*I'd like to change some traveler's checks.*)

When you're in the lucky situation of having money left, you may like to invest it. Here is some of the present tense conjugation for **investire** (een-vehs-*tee*-reh) (*to invest*), which is conjugated like any other regular **-ire** verb without the "isc" (see Chapter 1 in Book IV).

Conjugation	Pronunciation
io investo	*ee*-oh een-*vehs*-toh
tu investi	tooh een-*vehs*-tee
lui/lei investe	*looh*-ee/ley een-*vehs*-teh

To make life easier for you and to help you avoid standing in front of closed doors, we give you the hours of Italian banks: Banks are open Monday through Friday, generally from 8:30 a.m. to 1:30 p.m; then they reopen from 2:30 to 4 p.m. These are general guidelines; the hours differ from city to city. Nowadays it is more common to see banks that are open from 8:30 a.m. to 4 p.m.

Changing Money

You're more likely to need to change money when you're abroad. If you're in Italy and want to change some dollars into **euros** (*eh*-ooh-roh), you go to either a **banca** (*bahn*-kah) (*bank*), an **ufficio di cambio** (oohf-*fee*-choh dee *kahm*-byoh) (*exchange office*), or, more common still, a **bancomat** (*bahn*-koh-maht) (*ATM*). Some places definitely offer better exchange rates, so shop around if you have time.

Words to Know

conto [m] corrente	<u>kohn</u>-toh kohr-<u>rehn</u>-teh	checking account
estratto conto [m]	eh-<u>straht</u>-toh <u>kohn</u>-toh	bank statement
tasso d'interesse [m]	<u>tahs</u>-soh deen-teh-rehs-seh	interest rate
libretto degli assegni [m]	lee-<u>breht</u>-toh <u>deh</u>-lyee ahs-<u>seh</u>-nyee	checkbook
carta di credito [f]	<u>kahr</u>-tah dee <u>kreh</u>-dee-toh	credit card
ricevuta [f]	ree-cheh-<u>vooh</u>-tah	receipt
girare	jee-<u>rah</u>-reh	to endorse

Book II

Exploring and Wandering About

Because Italy is highly frequented by tourists from all over the world, the clerks in exchange offices have experience with people speaking English. Still, you just might want to complete a transaction in an exchange office in Italian.

Talkin' the Talk

Liza Campbell, an American tourist, needs to change some dollars for euros. She goes to the bank and talks to the teller. (Track 23)

Ms. Campbell: **Buongiorno, vorrei cambiare alcuni dollari in euro.**
bwohn-*johr*-noh, vohr-*rey* kahm-*byah*-reh ahl-*kooh*-nee *dohl*-lah-ree een *eh*-ooh-roh.
Hello, I'd like to change some dollars into euros.

Teller:
Benissimo. Quanti dollari?
beh-*nees*-see-moh. *kwahn*-tee *dohl*-lah-ree?
Very well. How many dollars?

Ms. Campbell:
Duecento. Qual è il cambio?
dooh-eh-*chehn*-toh. kwah-*leh* eel *kahm*-byoh?
Two hundred. What's the exchange?

Teller:
Oggi un euro costa un dollaro e venti più cinque euro di commissione.
oh-jee oohn *eh*-ooh-roh *kohs*-tah oohn *dohl*-lah-roh eh *vehn*-tee pyooh *cheen*-kweh *eh*-oohr-oh dee kohm-mees-*syoh*-neh.
Today the euro costs a dollar and twenty cents plus five euros for the service charge.

Ms. Campbell:
Va bene.
vah *beh*-neh.
Okay.

Teller:
Mi serve un documento.
mee *sehr*-veh oohn doh-kooh-*mehn*-toh.
I need some ID.

Ms. Campbell:
Ecco.
ehk-koh.
Here.

Teller:
Sono 175 Euro meno i 5 Euro di commmissione.
soh-noh *chehn*-toh seht-*tahn*-tah *cheen*-kweh *eh*-ooh-roh *meh*-noh ee *cheen*-kweh *eh*-ooh roh dee kom-mee-*syoh*-neh.
It comes to 175 euros less the 5 euro exchange fee.

Ms. Campbell:
Grazie mille!
grah-tsyeh *meel*-leh!
Thanks a million!

Nowadays, changing money is not the most efficient way to get the local currency. In Italy, as in most Western countries, you can find a **bancomat** almost anywhere. Also, depending on where you shop and eat, you can pay directly with a **carta di credito** (*kahr*-tah dee *kreh*-dee-toh) (*credit card*). The following phrases can help you find the cash you need (or at least the cash machine):

Dov'è il bancomat più vicino? (doh-*veh* eel *bahn*-koh-maht pyooh vee-*chee*-noh?) (*Where is the nearest ATM?*)

Posso pagare con la carta di credito? (*pohs*-soh pah-*gah*-reh kohn lah *kahr*-tah dee *kreh*-dee-toh?) (*May I pay with my credit card?*)

Mi scusi, potrebbe cambiarmi una banconota da 100 euro? (mee *skooh*-zee, poh-*trehb*-beh kahm-*byahr*-mee *ooh*-nah bahn-koh-*noh*-tah da *chehn*-toh *eh*-ooh-roh?) (*Excuse me, would you be able to change a 100 euro bill?*)

Mi dispiace, non accettiamo carte di credito. (mee dee-*spyah*-cheh, nohn ahch-cheht-*tyah*-moh *kahr*-teh dee *kreh*-dee-toh.) (*I'm sorry, we don't accept credit cards.*)

Mi dispiace, non ho spiccioli. (mee dees-*pyah*-cheh, nohn oh *speech*-choh-lee.) (*I'm sorry, I don't have any small change.*)

Words to Know

in contanti	een kohn-<u>tahn</u>-tee	in cash
riscuotere	ree-<u>skwoh</u>-teh-reh	to cash
accettare	ahch-cheht-<u>tah</u>-reh	to accept
bancomat [m]	<u>bahn</u>-koh-maht	ATM
cambiare	kahm-<u>byah</u>-reh	to change
spiccioli [m]	<u>speech</u>-choh-lee	small change

Using Credit Cards

In Canada and the United States you can take care of almost all your financial needs without ever handling cash. You can pay for almost everything with your debit or credit card. You can even use your credit card to get cash at ATMs and in some banks. This is the same in Italy, although cash is still the customary form of payment in many parts of Italy.

Talkin' the Talk

Ms. Johnson wants to withdraw some euros with her credit card but discovers that the ATM is out of order. She enters the bank and asks the cashier about the problem.

Ms. Johnson: **Scusi, il bancomat non funziona.**
skooh-zee eel, *bahn*-koh-maht nohn foohn-*tsyoh*-nah.
Excuse me, the ATM isn't working.

Cashier: **Lo so, signora, mi dispiace!**
loh soh, see-*nyoh*-rah, mee dees-*pyah*-cheh!
I know, madam, I'm sorry!

Ms. Johnson: **Ma ho bisogno di contanti.**
mah oh bee-*zoh*-nyoh dee kohn-*tahn*-tee.
But I need cash.

Cashier: **Può prelevarli qui alla cassa.**
pwoh preh-leh-*vahr*-lee kwee *ahl*-lah *kahs*-sah.
You can withdraw it here at the counter.

Ms. Johnson: **D'accordo, grazie.**
dak-*kohr-doh*, *grah*-tsyeh.
Okay, thanks.

Normally, things go easily and you don't have any problems using credit cards. But you may be asked to show your identification for security purposes. The following phrases can help you be prepared for this situation:

Potrei vedere un documento per favore? (poh-*trey* veh-*deh*-reh oohn doh-kooh-*mehn*-toh pehr fah-*voh*-reh?) (*May I please see your identification?*)

Potrebbe darmi il suo passaporto, per favore? (poh-*trehb*-beh *dahr*-mee eel *sooh*-oh pahs-sah-*pohr*-toh, pehr fah-*voh*-reh?) (*Would you please give me your passport?*)

Il suo indirizzo? (eel *sooh*-oh een-dee-*reet*-tsoh?) (*What is your address?*)

You may have to wait to exchange money. The following sentence says all you need to know about this rather formal verb: **attendere** (aht-*tehn*-deh-reh) (*to wait*).

Attenda, per favore. (aht-*tehn*-dah, pehr fah-*voh*-reh.) (*Please wait.*)

Words to Know

Certo!	<u>chehr</u>-toh!	Of course!
digitare	dee-gee-<u>tah</u>-reh	to enter
prelevare	preh-leh-<u>vah</u>-reh	to withdraw
funzionare	foon-tsyoh-<u>nah</u>-reh	to work; to function
Che domanda!	keh doh-<u>mahn</u>-dah	What a question!

Looking at Various Currencies

Along with many other European countries, the Italian monetary unit is the **euro** (*eh*-ooh-roh). There are 1-euro coins and 2-euro coins as well as larger bills (5, 10, 20, 50, 100, and so on). The plural form is **euro** (*eh*-ooh-roh), and the abbreviation is €. (That's right, the singular and the plural forms are exactly the same). Smaller denominations are in **centesimi** (chehn-*teh*-zee-mee) (*cents*) and are coins. (You can check out Chapter 2 in Book I for numbers.)

Talkin' the Talk

Patrizia is planning her vacation to Croatia. She is planning on taking the **aliscafo** (ah-leeh-*skah*-foh) (*high-speed ferry*) from Ancona tomorrow. She talks to her friend, Milena, about exchanging her money. (Track 24)

Patrizia: **Sai qual è il cambio euro in kuna croata?**
sayh kwah-*leh* eel *kahm*-byoh *eh*-ooh-roh een *kooh*-nah kroh-*ah*-tah?
Do you know the exchange rate for euros to Croatian kuna?

Milena: **Non ne ho idea!**
nohn neh oh ee-*deh*-ah!
I have no idea!

Patrizia:	**Domani parto per Zara per un mese.**
	doh-*mah*-nee *pahr*-toh pehr *dsah*-rah perh oohn *meh*-zeh.
	Tomorrow I'm leaving for Zara for a month.

Milena:	**E non hai ancora cambiato!**
	eh nohn ahy ahn-*koh*-rah kahm-*byah*-toh!
	And you haven't changed your money yet!

Patrizia:	**Posso farlo al porto.**
	pohs-soh *fahr*-loh ahl *pohr*-toh.
	I can do it at the port.

Milena:	**Ma no, è più caro!**
	mah *noh*, eh pyooh *kah*-roh!
	No, that's more expensive!

Patrizia:	**Mi accompagni in banca?**
	mee ahk-kohm-*pah*-nyee een *bahn*-kah?
	Will you come with me to the bank?

The **euro** is legal tender in 17 of the 27 countries that belong to the European Union (EU). So, if you travel among EU countries after you have euros in your possession, you don't have to change money in every country you visit. Since 2002, the Italian **lira** has disappeared, and the euro is the only valid currency in Italy.

Table 5-1 shows the currencies of various countries.

Table 5-1	Currencies		
Italian	*Pronunciation*	*Translation (Singular/Plural)*	*Where Used*
dollaro; dollari	*dohl*-lah-roh; *dohl*-lah-ree	*dollar; dollars*	Canada; United States
lira/e; sterlina/e	*lee*-rah/eh; stehr-*lee*-nah/neh	*pound; pounds*	Ireland; United Kingdom
peseta; pesetas	peh-*seh*-tah; peh-*seh*-tahs	*peseta; pesetas*	Mexico

Words to Know

prendere	<u>prehn</u>-deh-reh	to take
viaggio [m]	<u>vyahj</u>-joh	trip
aeroporto [m]	ah-eh-roh-<u>pohr</u>-toh	airport
domani	doh-<u>mah</u>-nee	tomorrow

Chapter 6

Getting Around: Planes, Trains, Taxis, and Buses

● ●

In This Chapter

▶ Traveling by airplane

▶ Declaring your goods to customs

▶ Getting a rental car

▶ Using public transportation

▶ Talking about departures and delays

● ●

*W*hether you're visiting Italy or you just need to explain to an Italian-speaking friend how to get across town, transportation vocabulary comes in handy. This chapter helps you make your way through the airport and also helps you secure transportation to get where you're going once you're on the ground, whether by taxi, bus, car, or train. Further, you discover what to do at customs, how to find missing luggage, and how to rent a car. **Andiamo!** (ahn-*dyah*-moh!) (*Let's go!*)

Getting through the Airport

You're lucky, because it's very likely that you can get by with English when you're at an Italian airport. Both Italian and English are usually spoken there. But, you just may be in a situation where the person next to you in an airport knows only Italian. Just in case, you should know some useful navigational phrases. Besides, you'll probably want a chance to practice the language in which you'll be immersed once you step outside the airport.

Checking in

Italians refer to the moment you finally get rid of your luggage as **accettazione** (ahch-cheht-tah-*tsyoh*-neh) (*check-in*). Sometimes they use the English *check-in* instead of **accettazione.** You pick up your boarding pass at the check-in counter, where speaking is usually inevitable. The following dialogue contains some of the sentences people commonly exchange.

Talkin' the Talk

Ms. Adami is checking in. She shows her ticket and passport to the agent and leaves her suitcases at the counter.

Agent: **Il suo biglietto, per favore.**
eel *sooh*-oh bee-*lyeht*-toh, pehr fah-*voh*-reh.
Your ticket, please.

Sig.ra Adami: **Ecco.**
ehk-koh.
Here it is.

Agent: **Passaporto?**
pahs-sah-*pohr*-toh?
Passport?

Sig.ra Adami: **Prego.**
preh-goh.
Here you are.

Agent: **Quanti bagagli ha?**
kwahn-tee bah-*gah*-lyee ah?
How many suitcases do you have?

Sig.ra Adami: **Due valigie e un bagaglio a mano.**
dooh-eh vah-*lee*-jeh eh oohn bah-*gah*-lyoh ah *mah*-noh.
Two suitcases and one piece of carry-on luggage.

Agent: **Qual è la sua destinazione?**
qwahl *eh* lah *sooh*-ah deh-stee-nah-*tsyoh*-neh?
What is your destination?

Sig.ra Adami:	**New York.** nooh yohrk. *New York.*
Agent:	**Ha fatto Lei le proprie valige?** ah *faht*-toh ley leh *proh*-pryeh vah-*lee*-jeh? *Did you pack your own bags?*
Sig.ra Adami:	**Sì.** see. *Yes.*
Agent:	**Le ha sempre avute sotto mano da quando le ha chiuse?** leh ah *sehm*-preh ah-*vooh*-teh *soht*-toh *mah*-noh dah *qwahn*-doh leh ah *kyooh*-zeh? *Have they been with you the whole time since you closed them?*
Sig. ra Adami:	**Sì; posso avere un posto vicino al finestrino, per favore?** see; *pohs*-soh ah-*veh*-reh oohn *pohs*-toh vee-*chee*-noh ahl fee-neh-*stree*-noh, pehr fah-*voh*-reh? *Yes (I have); may I please have a window seat?*
Agent:	**Un attimo, ora controllo . . . si, glielo do. Ecco la sua carta d'imbarco.** oohn *aht*-tee-moh, *oh*-rah kohn-*trohl*-loh . . . see, *lyeh*-lah doh. *ehk*-koh lah *sooh*-ah *kahr*-tah deem-*bahr*-koh. *One second, I'm going to check now . . . yes, I can. Here is your boarding pass.*
	L'imbarco è alle nove e quindici, uscita tre. Prosegua al controllo di sicurezza. leem-*bahr*-koh eh *ahl*-leh *noh*-veh eh *kween*-dee-chee, ooh-*shee*-tah treh. proh-*seh*-gwah ahl kohn-*trohl*-loh dee see-koohr-*ehts*-tsah. *Boarding is at 9:15, gate 3. You can move on to security now.*

Words to Know

imbarco [m]	eem-<u>bahr</u>-koh	boarding
valigia [f]	vah-<u>lee</u>-jah	suitcase
uscita [f]	ooh-<u>shee</u>-tah	gate
bagaglio [m]	bah-<u>gah</u>-lyoh	baggage
bagaglio a mano [m]	bah-<u>gah</u>-lyoh ah <u>mah</u>-noh	carry-on luggage
passaporto [m]	pahs-sah-<u>pohr</u>-toh	passport

Dealing with excess baggage

Sometimes your suitcases are so heavy that the airline charges an extra fee to transport your luggage. The truth is that you really can't say much; you simply have to pay.

Questa valigia eccede il limite. (*kweh*-stah vah-*lee*-jah ehch-*cheh*-deh eel *lee*-mee-teh.) (*This bag is over the weight limit.*)

Ha un eccesso di bagaglio. (ah oohn ehch-*ches*-soh dee bah-*gah*-lyoh.) (*You have excess luggage.*)

Deve pagare un supplemento. (*deh*-veh pah-*gah*-reh oohn soohp-pleh-*mehn*-toh.) (*You have to pay a surcharge.*)

Questo bagaglio a mano eccede le misure. (*kweh*-stoh bah-*gah*-lyoh ah *mah*-noh ehch-*che*-deh leh mee-*zooh*-reh.) (*This carry-on bag exceeds the size limit.*)

Before you go to the airport, always find out the weight limit of your bags and how much an extra suitcase will cost. Then you can buy an extra suitcase if necessary and avoid having to throw out precious items at check-in.

Waiting to board the plane

Before boarding, you may encounter unforeseen situations, such as delays. If you do, you'll probably want to ask some questions. Read the following dialogue for an example of what you can say when you're dealing with a delay.

Talkin' the Talk

Mr. Campo is in the boarding area. He asks the agent whether his flight is on time. Always be prepared for cryptic answers.

Sig. Campo: **Il volo è in orario?**
eel *voh*-loh eh een oh-*rah*-ryoh?
Is the flight on time?

Agent: **No, è in ritardo.**
noh, eh een ree-*tahr*-doh.
No, there has been a delay.

Sig. Campo: **Di quanto?**
dee *kwahn*-toh?
How much?

Agent: **Non si sa.**
nohn see sah.
No one knows.

Book II

Exploring and Wandering About

Words to Know

in ritardo	een ree-<u>tahr</u>-doh	late/delayed
volo [m]	<u>voh</u>-loh	flight
in orario	een oh-<u>rah</u>-ree-oh	on time

Coping after landing

After you exit a plane in Italy, you're immediately hit by voices speaking a foreign language. You have to take care of necessities, such as finding a bathroom, changing money, looking for the baggage claim area, and securing a luggage cart and a taxi.

Visitors from countries in the European Union need only **la carta d'identità** (lah *kahr*-tah dee-dehn-tee-*tah*) (*the identity card*) to enter Italy. Nationals of all other countries need a valid **passaporto** (pahs-sah-*pohr*-toh) (*passport*), and sometimes also a visa. Usually, at **controllo passaporti** (kohn-*trohl*-loh pahs-sah-*pohr*-tee) (*passport control*), you don't exchange many words, and the ones you do exchange are usually routine.

Here are some words that are likely to come in handy:

- **arrivo** (ahr-*ree*-voh) (*arrival*)
- **cambio** (*kahm*-byoh) (*money exchange*)
- **consegna bagagli** (kohn-*seh*-nyah bah-*gah*-lyee) (*baggage claim*)
- **destinazione** (deh-stee-nah-*tsyoh*-neh) (*destination*)
- **entrata** (ehn-*trah*-tah) (*entrance*)
- **partenza** (pahr-*tehn*-tsah) (*departure*)
- **uscita** (ooh-*shee*-tah) (*exit*)
- **vacanza** (vah-*kahn*-zah) (*vacation*)

Dealing with lost luggage

Losing luggage is always a possibility when flying to Italy, especially if you're changing planes, but don't despair; 80 percent of misplaced luggage turns up within 24 hours, and the other 20 percent usually turns up within three days. The airline will deliver your bags to your hotel or apartment, or you can go back to the airport for them if you need them sooner.

Going through Customs

You can't get into a foreign country without going through customs. When you have something to declare, you do so **alla dogana** (*ahl*-lah doh-*gah*-nah) (*at customs*). These examples should relieve you of any possible worries.

Generally, you can just walk through the line that says "**Niente da dichi-arare**," (nee-*ehn*-teh dah dee-kyah-*rah*-reh) ("*Nothing to declare*") and no one one will say anything to you, but sometimes you may be stopped.

> **Niente da dichiarare?** (nee-*ehn*-teh dah dee-kyah-*rah*-reh?) (*Anything to declare?*)
>
> **No, niente.** (noh, nee-*ehn*-teh.) (*No, nothing.*)
>
> **Per favore, apra questa valigia.** (pehr fah-*voh*-reh, *ah*-prah *kweh*-stah vah-*lee*-jah.) (*Please, open this suitcase.*)
>
> **È nuovo il computer?** (eh *nwoh*-voh eel kohm-*pu*-tehr?) (*Is this computer new?*)
>
> **Sì, ma è per uso personale.** (see, mah eh pehr *ooh*-zoh pehr-soh-*nah*-leh.) (*Yes, but it's for personal use.*)
>
> **Per questo deve pagare il dazio.** (pehr *kwehs*-toh *deh*-veh pah-*gah*-reh eel *dah*-tsyoh.) (*You have to pay duty on this.*)

When you pass through customs, you may have to declare any goods that you purchased that are over a certain dollar/euro amount.

> **Ho questo/queste cose da dichiarare.** (oh *kwehs*-toh/*kweh*-steh *koh*-seh dah dee-kyah-*rah*-reh.) (*I have to declare this/these things.*)

Book II

Exploring and Wandering About

Words to Know

dogana [f]	doh-*gah*-nah	customs
dichiarare	dee-kyah-*rah*-reh	to declare
niente	nee-*ehn*-teh	nothing
pagare	pah-*gah*-reh	to pay
uso personale	*ooh*-zoh pehr-soh-*nah*-leh	personal use
modulo [m]	*moh*-dooh-loh	form
ricevute [f, pl]	ree-cheh-*vooh*-teh	receipts

Renting a Car

Italy is a beautiful country, and if you visit, you may want to consider taking driving tours of the cities and the countryside. If you don't have a car, renting one to visit various places is a good idea, but don't forget that Italian traffic is not very relaxed. Italians don't stay in their own lanes on highways, and finding a place to park can tax your patience — especially in town centers, some of which don't even allow cars. Even medium-sized cars often can't get through narrow streets and make turns where cars are allowed. I don't want to scare you, though; just enjoy the adventure!

To drive a car or motorcycle in Italy, you must be at least 18 years old. Furthermore, you need a valid **patente** (pah-*tehn*-teh) (*driver's license*). A foreign driver's license is good for a maximum of 12 months in Italy. For periods exceeding the year, you need to get an Italian one. Finding a car to rent is easy at all airports.

Whether you rent a car by phone, online, or directly from a rental service, the process is the same: Just tell the rental company what kind of car you want and under what conditions you want to rent it. Research your options before getting to Italy, if possible. This way, you can have a car waiting for you upon your arrival. The following dialogue represents a typical conversation on this topic.

Talkin' the Talk

Mr. Brown is staying in Italy for two weeks and wants to rent a car to visit different cities. He goes to the rental service booth at the airport and talks to **l'impiegato** (leem-pyeh-*gah*-toh) (*the employee*).

Mr. Brown:	**Vorrei noleggiare una macchina.**
	vohr-*rey* noh-lehj-*jah*-reh *ooh*-nah *mahk*-kee-nah.
	I would like to rent a car.

Agent:	**Che tipo?**
	keh *tee*-poh?
	What kind?

Mr. Brown:	**Di media cilindrata col cambio automatico.**
	dee *meh*-dyah chee-leen-*drah*-tah kohl *kahm*-byoh ou-toh-*mah*-tee-koh.
	A mid-size with an automatic transmission.

Agent:	**Per quanto tempo?** pehr *kwahn*-toh *tehm*-poh? *For how long?*
Mr. Brown:	**Una settimana.** *ooh*-nah seht-tee-*mah*-nah. *One week.*
	Quant'è per la settimana? *kwahn-teh* pehr lah seht-tee-*mah*-nah? *What does it cost for a week?*
Agent:	**C'è una tariffa speciale: 18 Euro al giorno.** cheh *ooh*-nah tah-*reef*-fah speh-*chah*-leh: deech-*oht*-toh *eh*-oohr-oh ahl *johr*-noh. *There is a special rate: 18 Euros per day.*
Mr. Brown:	**L'assicurazione è inclusa?** lahs-see-kooh-rah-*tsyoh*-neh eh een-*klooh*-zah? *Is insurance included?*
Agent:	**Sì, con la polizza kasco.** see, kohn lah *poh*-leets-tsah *kahs*-koh. *Yes, a comprehensive policy.*

Other words and expressions that you may need when renting a car or getting fuel at a gas station include the following:

- **l'aria condizionata** (*lah*-ryah kohn-dee-tsyoh-*nah*-tah) (*air conditioning*)
- **la benzina super** (lah behn-*dzee*-nah *sooh*-pehr) (*premium fuel*)
- **la benzina verde** (làh behn-*dzee*-nah *vehr*-deh) (*unleaded fuel*)
- **il cabriolet** (eel *kah*-bryoh-*leh*) (*convertible*)
- **Controlli l'olio.** (kohn-*trohl*-lee *loh*-lyoh.) (*Check the oil.*)
- **Faccia il pieno.** (*fahch*-chah eel *pyeh*-noh.) (*Fill it up.*)
- **fare benzina** (*fah*-reh behn-*dzee*-nah) (*to put in gas*)

A car with an automatic transmission costs significantly more because these are rare in Italy, where everyone drives a car with a manual shift.

Navigating Public Transportation

If you'd rather not drive yourself, you can get around quite comfortably using public transportation, such as taxis, trains, and buses. The following sections tell you how to do so using Italian.

Calling a taxi

The process of hailing a taxi is the same in Italy as it is in the United States — you even use the same word: **Taxi** (*tah*-ksee) has entered the Italian language. The only challenge for you is that you have to communicate in Italian. Here are some phrases to help you on your way:

> **Può chiamarmi un taxi?** (pwoh kyah-*mahr*-mee oohn *tah*-ksee?) (*Can you call me a taxi?*)

> **Vorrei un taxi, per favore.** (vohr-*rey* oohn *tah*-ksee, pehr fah-*voh*-reh.) (*I'd like a taxi, please.*)

In case you're asked **per quando?** (pehr *kwahn*-doh?) (*for when?*), you need to be prepared with an answer. Following are some common ones:

- ✔ **alle due del pomeriggio** (*ahl*-leh *dooh*-eh dehl poh-meh-*reej*-joh) (*at 2:00 p.m.*)

- ✔ **domani mattina alle 5:30** (doh-*mah*-nee maht-*tee*-nah *ahl*-leh *cheen*-qweh eh *trehn*-tah) (*tomorrow morning at 5:30*)

- ✔ **fra un'ora** (frah oohn-*oh*-rah) (*in one hour*)

- ✔ **subito** (*sooh*-bee-toh) (*right now*)

After you seat yourself in a taxi, the driver will ask where to take you. Here are some potential destinations:

- ✔ **all'areoporto** (*ahl*-lah-reh-oh-*pohr*-toh) (*to the airport*)

- ✔ **a questo indirizzo: via Leopardi, numero 3** (ah *kweh*-stoh een-dee-*ree*-tsoh: *vee*-ah leh-oh-*pahr*-dee *nooh*-meh-roh treh) (*to this address: via Leopardi, number 3*)

- ✔ **alla stazione, per favore** (*ahl*-lah stah-*tsyoh*-neh, pehr fah-*voh*-reh) (*to the station, please*)

- ✔ **in via Veneto** (een *vee*-ah *veh*-neh-toh) (*to via Veneto*)

Finally, you have to pay. Simply ask the driver, **Quant'è?** (kwahn-*teh?*) (*How much is it?*) For more information about money, see Chapter 5 in Book II.

Moving by train

You can buy a train ticket **alla stazione** (*ahl*-lah stah-*tsyoh*-neh) (*at the station*) or at **un'agenzia di viaggi** (*ooh*-nah-jehn-*tsee*-ah dee vee-*ahj*-jee) (*a travel agency*). If you want to take a **treno rapido** (*treh*-noh *rah*-pee-doh) (*express train*) that stops only in the main stations, you pay a **supplemento** (soohp-pleh-*mehn*-toh) (*surcharge*). You can travel first class or second class. On some trains it's a good idea to reserve your seat; on others, a reservation is absolutely required. The faster trains in Italy are called **Inter City (IC)** or **Euro City (EC)** if their final destination is outside Italy. The **Euro Star** and the different kinds of **Freccia** (*frehch*-chah) are even faster options (the **Frecciarossa** [*frehch*-chah *rohs*-sah] and **Freccia argento** [*frehch*-chah ahr-*jehn*-toh] being the fastest at 250+ kilometers per hour).

Keep in mind that in Italy you have to validate your ticket before getting on the train at **il binario** (eel bee-*nah*-ryoh) (*the platform; the track*). Therefore, the ticket validation boxes are located, in most cases, on the platforms. If they're out of order (sometimes it happens!), write the date and the time on your ticket. This is considered a proper validation.

You can find out all about trains by checking out the Italian national rail website at www.trenitalia.com. It tells you about duration of the trip and price, and it even lets you purchase your ticket ahead of time. After exploring your options, you have to make a decision and buy a ticket.

Book II

Exploring and Wandering About

Talkin' the Talk

Bianca is at the train station in Rome. She goes to an **ufficio informazioni** (oohf-*feech*-oh een-fohr-mats-*yoh*-neh) (*information counter*) to ask about a connection to Perugia. (Track 25)

Bianca: **Ci sono treni diretti per Perugia?**
chee *soh*-noh *treh*-nee dee-*reht*-tee pehr peh-*rooh*-jah?
Are there direct trains to Perugia?

Agent: **No, deve prendere un treno per Terni.**
noh, *deh*-veh *prehn*-deh-reh oohn *treh*-noh pehr *tehr*-nee.
No, you have to take a train to Terni.

Bianca: **E poi devo cambiare?**
eh pohy *deh*-voh kahm-*byah*-reh?
And then do I have to change [trains]?

Agent: **Sì, prende un locale per Perugia.**
see, *prehn*-deh oohn loh-*kah*-leh pehr peh-*rooh*-jah.
Yes, you take a local (slow) train for Perugia.

Bianca: **A che ora parte il prossimo treno?**
ah keh *oh*-rah *pahr*-teh eel *prohs*-see-moh *treh*-noh?
What time does the next train leave?

Agent: **Alle diciotto e arriva a Terni alle diciannove.**
ahl-leh dee-*choht*-toh eh ahr-*ree*-vah ah *tehr*-nee *ahl*-leh *dee*-chahn-*noh*-veh.
At 18 hours (6 p.m.). It arrives in Terni at 19 hours (7 p.m.).

Bianca: **E per Perugia?**
eh pehr peh-*rooh*-jah?
And to Perugia?

Agent: **C'è subito la coincidenza.**
cheh *sooh*-bee-toh lah koh-een-chee-*dehn*-tsah.
There is an immediate connection.

Words to Know

binario [m]	bee-<u>nah</u>-ryoh	platform; track
biglietto [m]	bee-<u>lyeht</u>-toh	ticket
andata [f]	ahn-<u>dah</u>-tah	one way
ritorno [m]	ree-<u>tohr</u>-noh	return trip
supplemento [m]	soohp-pleh-<u>mehn</u>-toh	surcharge

Going by bus or tram

To get from point A to point B without a car, you most likely walk or take **l'autobus** (*lou*-toh-boohs) (*the bus*), **il tram** (eel trahm) (*the tram; the street-car*), or **la metropolitana** (lah meh-troh-poh-lee-*tah*-nah) (*the subway*) in bigger cities.

Some Italian cities have streetcars, or trams, and most have buses. Little buses are called **il pulmino** (eel poohl-*mee*-noh). Big buses that take you from one city to another are called **il pullman** (eel *poohl*-mahn) or **la corriera** (lah kohr-*ryeh*-rah). There are subways in Milan, Rome, Catania, and Naples.

You can buy bus or tram tickets in Italian bars, **dal giornalaio** (dahl johr-nah-*lah*-yoh) (*at a newspaper stand*), or **dal tabaccaio** (dahl tah-bahk-*kah*-yoh) (*at a tobacco shop*). **Tabaccai** are little shops where you can purchase cigarettes, stamps, newspapers, and so on. You can find them on virtually every street corner in Italy; they're recognizable by either a black-and-white sign or a blue-and-white sign with a big T on it.

Book II

Exploring and Wandering About

Talkin' the Talk

Tom, a Canadian tourist, wants to visit a cathedral downtown. He asks about the bus, but a woman advises him to take the subway because it takes less time. (Track 26)

Tom: **Scusi, quale autobus va al Duomo?**
             skooh-zee, *kwah*-leh ou-toh-boos vah ahl *dwoh*-moh?
             Excuse me, which bus goes to the Cathedral?

Woman: **Perché non prende la metropolitana?**
             pehr-*keh* nohn *prehn*-deh lah
             meh-troh-poh-lee-*tah*-nah?
             Why don't you take the subway?

Tom: **È meglio?**
             eh *meh*-lyoh?
             Is it better?

Woman: **Sì, ci mette cinque minuti!**
             see, chee *meht*-teh *cheen*-kweh mee-*nooh*-tee!
             Yes, it takes five minutes!

Tom: **Dov'è la fermata della metropolitana?**
             doh-*veh* lah fehr-*mah*-tah *dehl*-lah
             meh-troh-poh-lee-*tah*-nah?
             Where is the subway station?

Woman: **Dietro l'angolo.**
             dyeh-troh *lahn*-goh-loh.
             Around the corner.

On the subway, Tom asks the young woman sitting next to him where he should get off. Note that he uses **tu,** the informal form of *you,* now.

Tom: **Scusa, sai qual è la fermata per il Duomo?**
skooh-zah, sahy kwahl *eh* lah fehr-*mah*-tah pehr eel *dwoh*-moh?
Excuse me, do you know which is the stop for the Cathedral?

Woman: **La prossima fermata.**
lah *pros*-see-mah fehr-*mah*-tah.
The next stop.

Tom: **Grazie!**
grah-tsyeh!
Thanks!

Woman: **Prego.**
preh-goh.
You're welcome.

Reading maps and schedules

You don't need to know much about reading maps except for the little bit of vocabulary written on them. Reading a schedule can be more difficult for travelers because the schedules are usually written only in Italian. You frequently find the following words on schedules:

- **l'orario** (loh-*rah*-ryoh) (*the timetable*)
- **partenze** (pahr-*tehn*-tseh) (*departures*)
- **arrivi** (ahr-*ree*-vee) (*arrivals*)
- **giorni feriali** (*johr*-nee feh-*ryah*-lee) (*weekdays*)
- **giorni festivi** (*johr*-nee feh-*stee*-vee) (*Sundays and holidays*)
- **il binario** (eel bee-*nah*-ryoh) (*the track; the platform*)

The schedule shown in Figure 6-1 shows you train names, the lengths of trips, and the differences in price between first and second class.

DEPARTURE STATION: BOLOGNA (TUTTE LE STAZIONI)	ARRIVAL STATION: ROMA (TUTTE LE STAZIONI)				DATE: 19/1/2011	

DEPARTURE	ARRIVAL	LENGTH OF JOURNEY	TRAIN NO.	TRAIN CATEGORY	1ST CLASS*	2ND CLASS*	SELECT
10:53 BOLOGNA	13:13 ROMA TE	02:20	9413 FRECCIARGENTO	➤2	80,00€	58,00€	⬤
10:23 BOLOGNA	12:45 ROMA TE	02:22	9519 FRECCIAROSSA	➤2	80,00€	58,00€	⬤
10:38 BOLOGNA	12:55 ROMA TE	02:17	9415 FRECCIARGENTO	➤2	80,00€	58,00€	⬤
11:18 BOLOGNA	15:24 ROMA TE	04:06	589	IC	52,00€	38,50€	⬤
13:00 BOLOGNA	15:22 ROMA TE	02:22	9521 FRECCIAROSSA	➤2	80,00€	58,00€	⬤

Figure 6-1:
A typical
Italian train
schedule.

Illustration by Elizabeth Kurtzman

Keep in mind that Europeans don't write *a.m.* or *p.m.;* they count the hours from 0.00 to 24.00, otherwise known as military time. Therefore, 1.00 is the hour after midnight, and 13.00 is 1:00 p.m.

Being Early or Late

You don't always arrive on time, and you may have to communicate that you'll be late or early, or apologize to someone for being delayed. The following list contains important terms that you can use to do so:

- ✔ **essere in anticipo** (*ehs*-seh-reh een ahn-*tee*-chee-poh) (*to be early*)
- ✔ **essere puntuale** (*ehs*-seh-reh poohn-*twah*-leh) (*to be on time*)
- ✔ **essere in ritardo** (*ehs*-seh-reh een ree-*tahr*-doh) (*to be late*)

These examples use the preceding phrases in sentences:

Probabilmente sarò in anticipo. (proh-bah-beel-*mehn*-teh sah-*roh* een ahn *tee*-chee-poh.) (*[I'll] probably be early.*)

L'autobus non è mai puntuale. (*lou*-toh-boohs nohn *eh* mahy *poohn*-*twah*-leh.) (*The bus is never on time.*)

L'aereo è in ritardo. (lah-*eh*-reh-oh *eh* een ree-*tahr*-doh.) (*The plane is late.*)

Mi scusi, sono arrivata in ritardo. (mee *skooh*-zee, *soh*-noh ahr-ree-*vah*-tah een ree-*tahr*-doh.) (*I'm sorry, I arrived late.*)

Meno male che sei puntuale. (*meh*-noh *mah*-leh keh sey poohn-*twah*-leh.) (*It's a good thing you're on time.*)

When talking about lateness, you probably can't avoid the verb **aspettare** (ahs-peht-*tah*-reh) (*to wait*). Following are a few examples using this verb:

Aspetto l'autobus da un'ora. (ahs-*peht*-toh *lou*-toh-boohs dah ooh-*noh*-rah.) (*I've been waiting for the bus for an hour.*)

Aspetta anche lei il ventitré? (ahs-*peht*-tah *ahn*-keh ley eel vehn-tee-*treh?*) (*Are you also waiting for the number 23 bus?*)

Aspetto mia madre. (ahs-*peht*-toh *mee*-ah *mah*-dreh.) (*I'm waiting for my mother.*)

Note that the verb **aspettare** takes no preposition, whereas the English *to wait (for)* does.

Chapter 7

Finding a Place to Stay

In This Chapter
▶ Researching and reserving a place
▶ Arriving at your hotel

To really get to know Italians and the Italian language, and to enjoy the Italian lifestyle, you need to travel to Italy. If you're not lucky enough to have Italian friends who can offer you a place to stay, you have to find a hotel, of which many creative varieties exist. This chapter shows you how to make yourself understood when you ask for a room or check in to a hotel.

Choosing a Place to Stay

Research the different places you can stay while you're in Italy, and try to find options with an authentic flair to them. You'll likely find a broad range of places to suit everyone. At the top, you have conventional three-to-five-star **alberghi** (ahl-*behr*-gee) (*hotels*) and **villaggi turistici** (veel-*laj*-jee tooh-*rees*-tee-chee) (*resorts*) — usually in hot spots — that offer either **mezza pensione** (*medz*-ah pehn-*syoh*-neh) (*breakfast plus one other meal*) or **pensione completa** (pehn-*syoh*-neh kohm-*pleh*-tah) (*breakfast, lunch, and dinner included in the price*). The smaller, more personal lodgings include family-run **bed and breakfasts** (pronounced just the same as in English but with the rolled **r**), **pensioni** (pehn-*syoh*-neh) (*small hotels or part of someone's house where breakfast is usually served*), mountain **rifugi** (ree-*fooh*-jee) (*mountain huts that range from spartan to spa quality*), and the increasingly popular **agriturismo** (ah-gree-tooh-*reez*-moh) (*farm stay*). And don't forget all those former monasteries and convents!

Reserving a Room

When you reserve a room in a hotel, you use the same terms as you do **prenotare/fare una prenotazione** (preh-noh-*tah*-reh/*fah*-reh *ooh*-nah preh-noh-*tsyoh*-neh) (*to make a reservation*) in a restaurant. Use either of the synonyms **la camera** (lah *kah*-meh-rah) or **la stanza** (lah *stahn*-zah) (*the room*).

La camera singola (lah *kah*-meh-rah *seen*-goh-lah) is a room with one twin bed. **La camera doppia** (lah *kah*-meh-rah *dohp*-pyah) is a room with two twin beds, whereas **la camera matrimoniale** (lah *kah*-meh-rah *mah*-tree-moh-*nyah*-leh) has one big bed for two persons. In Italy, people commonly refer to rooms simply as **una doppia**, **una matrimoniale**, and **una singola.** Everyone understands that you're talking about hotel rooms.

As you probably already know, making reservations in advance is important, especially for the **alta stagione** (*ahl*-tah stah-*joh*-neh) (*peak season*) — in Italy, it's the summer months and from December to early February for ski resorts.

When you're making reservations or staying at a hotel, you may have a few questions about the room and the amenities. You'll probably encounter and use some of these common Italian sentences and phrases.

- **La stanza è con bagno?** (lah *stahn*-zah *eh* kohn *bah*-nyoh?) (*Does the room have a bathroom?*) (Very rarely, even fabulous five-star hotels still have some single rooms without bathrooms, but when you're in a nice hotel, ask this question only if you're asking for an inexpensive single.)

- **Posso avere una stanza con doccia?** (*pohs*-soh ah-*veh*-reh *ooh*-nah *stahn*-zah kohn *dohch*-chah?) (*May I have a room with a shower?*)

- **Non avete stanze con la vasca?** (nohn ah-*veh*-teh *stahn*-zeh kohn lah *vahs*-kah?) (*Don't you have rooms with bathtubs?*)

- **Avete una doppia al primo piano?** (ah-*veh*-teh *ooh*-nah *dohp*-pyah ahl *pree*-moh *pyah*-noh?) (*Do you have a double room on the first floor?*) Note that this would be the second floor for Americans.

- **È una stanza tranquillissima e dà sul giardino.** (eh *ooh*-nah *stahn*-tsah trahn-kweel-*lees*-see-mah eh dah soohl jahr-*dee*-noh.) (*The room is very quiet and looks out onto the garden.*)

- **La doppia viene duecento Euro a notte.** (lah *dohp*-pee-ah *vyeh*-neh dooh-eh-*chehn*-toh *eh*-ooh-roh ah *noht*-teh.) (*A double room costs 200 euros per night.*)

- **Può darmi una camera con aria condizionata?** (pwoh *dahr*-mee *ooh*-nah *kah*-meh-rah kohn *ah*-ryah kohn-dee-tsyoh-*nah*-tah?) (*Can you give me a room with air conditioning?*)

✔ **Dove sono i suoi bagagli?** (*doh*-veh *soh*-noh ee swohy bah-*gah*-lyee?) (*Where is your baggage?*)

✔ **Può far portare le mie valige in camera, per favore?** (pwoh fahr pohr-*tah*-reh leh *mee*-eh vah-*lee*-jeh *een kah*-meh-rah, pehr fah-*voh*-reh?) (*Would you please have my bags brought to my room?*)

Most hotels include breakfast with your reservation, but you should ask just to be certain: **La colazione è compresa?** (lah koh-lah-*tsyoh*-neh *eh* kohm-*preh*-sah?) (*Is breakfast included?*)

Talkin' the Talk

Donatella is making reservations for five people. The receptionist says that only two double rooms are left, so Donatella has to figure out how to accommodate all five people.

Donatella: **Buonasera.**
              bwoh-nah-*seh*-rah.
              Good evening.

Receptionist: **Buonasera, prego?**
              bwoh-nah-seh-*rah preh*-goh?
              Good evening, can I help you?

Donatella: **Avete stanze libere?**
              ah-*veh*-teh *stahn*-tseh lee-beh-reh?
              Do you have any vacant rooms?

Receptionist: **Non ha la prenotazione?**
              nohn *ah* lah preh-noh-tah-*tsyoh*-neh?
              You don't have a reservation?

Donatella: **Eh, no . . .**
              eh, *noh* . . .
              Well, no . . .

Receptionist: **Abbiamo soltanto due doppie.**
              ahb-*byah*-moh sohl-*tahn*-toh *dooh*-eh *dohp*-pyeh.
              We have just two double rooms.

Donatella: **Non c'è una stanza con tre letti?**
              nohn cheh *ooh*-nah *stahn*-zah kohn treh *leht*-tee?
              Isn't there a room with three beds?

Receptionist: **Possiamo aggiungere un letto.**
pohs-*syah*-moh ahj-*joohn*-jeh-reh oohn *leht*-toh.
We can add a bed.

Donatella: **Benissimo, grazie.**
beh-*nees*-see-moh, *grah*-tsee-eh.
Very well, thank you.

Words to Know

aria condizionata [f]	*ah*-ree-ah kohn-dee-tsee-oh-*nah*-tah	air conditioning
camera [f]; stanza [f]	*kah*-meh-rah; *stahn*-zah	room
camera singola [f]	*kah*-meh-rah *seen*-goh-lah	single room
camera doppia [f]	*kah*-meh-rah *dohp*-pee-ah	room with two twin beds
camera matrimoniale [f]	*kah*-meh-rah mah-tree-moh-nee-*ah*-leh	room with a queen- or king-size bed
colazione [f]	koh-lah-*tsyoh*-neh	breakfast
culla [f]	*koohl*-lah	crib
letto supplementare [m]	*leht*-toh soohp-pleh-mehn-*tah*-reh	extra bed
servizio in camera [m]	sehr-*vee*-tsee-oh een *kah*-meh-rah	room service
mezza pensione [f]	*medz*-ah pehn-*syoh*-neh	half board
pensione completa [f]	pehn-*syoh*-neh kohm-*pleh*-tah	full board
servizio sveglia [m]	sehr-*vee*-tsee-oh *sveh*-lyah	wake-up call

Checking In

Registering at an Italian hotel isn't as difficult as you may imagine, but do expect the person at the front desk to ask for **un documento** (oohn doh-kooh-*mehn*-toh) (*ID*), such as a passport. The hotel manager may even want to hang on to it for a few hours, but don't worry; you'll get it back!

After you're in your room, you may find that you forgot to bring something you need or discover that you need something in addition to all you brought. Many rooms come with items like **una cassaforte** (*ooh*-nah *kahs*-sah-*fohr*-teh) (*a safe*) for your valuables and **un frigorifero** (oohn free-goh-*ree*-feh-roh) (*a refrigerator*), but you may need help in figuring out how they work. You may also need a **phon** (fohn) (*blow dryer*). In these instances, you can ask the receptionist, the doorman, or the maid for what you need. The following phrases can help you ask for the things you need. Don't forget to say **scusi** (*skooh*-zee) (*excuse me*) and **per favore** (pehr-fah-*voh*-reh) (*please*)!

- ✔ **Non trovo l'asciugacapelli/il fon.** (nohn *troh*-voh lah-*shooh*-gah-kah-*pehl*-lee/il fohn.) (*I can't find the hair dryer.*)

- ✔ **Manca la carta igenica.** (*mahn*-kah lah *kahr*-tah ee-*jeh*-nee-kah.) (*There is no toilet paper.*)

- ✔ **È ancora aperto il bar?** (*eh* ahn-*koh*-rah ah-*pehr*-toh eel bahr?) (*Is the coffee place still open?*)

- ✔ **Vorrei un'altra coperta per favore.** (vohr-*rey* oohn-*ahl*-trah koh-*pehr*-tah pehr fah-*voh*-reh.) (*I'd like one more blanket please.*)

- ✔ **Dov'è la farmacia più vicina?** (doh-*veh* lah fahr-mah-*chee*-ah pyooh vee-*chee*-nah?) (*Where is the closest pharmacy?*)

- ✔ **Vorrei la sveglia domattina.** (vohr-*rey* lah *sveh*-lyah doh-maht-*tee*-nah.) (*I'd like to get an early wake-up call tomorrow morning.*)

- ✔ **C'è il telefono nella mia stanza?** (cheh eel teh-*leh*-foh-noh *nehl*-lah *mee*-ah *stahn*-tsah?) (*Is there a telephone in my room?*)

If you want another something, notice that you write the feminine form **un'altra** (oohn-*ahl*-trah) differently from the masculine **un altro** (oohn *ahl*-troh). Feminine words require an apostrophe; masculine words don't. This construction is also valid for all other words that begin with a vowel.

The following list contains more words you may find useful during a hotel stay:

- ✔ **fazzolettino di carta** (faht-tsoh-leht-*tee*-noh dee *kahr*-tah) (*tissue*)

- ✔ **lettino** (leht-*tee*-noh) (*cot*)

✔ **negozio di regali** (neh-*goh*-tsyoh dee reh-*gah*-lee) (*gift shop*)

✔ **parrucchiere** (pahr-roohk-*kyeh*-reh) (*hairdresser*)

✔ **portacenere** (pohr-tah-*cheh*-neh-reh) (*ashtray*)

✔ **piscina** (pee-*shee*-nah) (*swimming pool*)

Talkin' the Talk

Mr. Baricco arrives at the hotel where he made reservations two weeks ago. He walks up to the receptionist. (Track 27)

Sig. Baricco: **Buonasera, ho una stanza prenotata.**
bwoh-nah-*seh*-rah, oh *ooh*-nah *stahn*-tsah preh-noh-*tah*-tah.
Good evening, I have a reservation.

Receptionist: **Il suo nome, prego?**
eel *sooh*-oh *noh*-meh, *preh*-goh?
Your name, please?

Sig. Baricco: **Baricco.**
bah-*reek*-koh.
Baricco.

Receptionist: **Sì, una singola per due notti.**
see, *ooh*-nah *seen*-goh-lah pehr *dooh*-eh *noht*-tee.
Yes, a single (room) for two nights.

Può compilare la scheda, per favore?
pwoh kohm-pee-*lah*-reh lah *skeh*-dah, pehr fah-*voh*-reh?
Could you fill out the form, please?

Sig. Baricco: **Certo. Vuole un documento?**
chehr-toh. *vwoh*-leh oohn doh-kooh-*mehn*-toh?
Sure. Do you want identification?

Receptionist: **Sì, grazie . . . Bene . . . ecco la sua chiave. Stanza numero quarantadue, al quarto piano.**
see, *grah*-tsyeh . . . *beh*-neh . . . *ehk*-koh lah *sooh*-ah *kyah*-veh. *stahn*-zah *nooh*-meh-roh kwah-*rahn*-tah-*dooh*-eh ahl *kwahr*-toh *pyah*-noh.
Yes, thanks . . . Well . . . Here is your key to room number 42, fourth floor.

Sig. Baricco:	**Grazie. A che ora è la colazione?**
	grah-tsee-eh. ah keh oh-rah eh lah
	koh-lah-tsyoh-neh?
	Thank you. What time is breakfast?
Receptionist:	**Dalle sette alle nove.**
	dahl-leh seht-teh ahl-leh noh-veh.
	From seven until nine.
Sig. Baricco:	**Grazie. Buonanotte.**
	grah-tsyeh. bwoh-nah-noht-teh.
	Thank you. Good night.
Receptionist:	**Buonanotte.**
	bwoh-nah-noht-teh
	Good night.

Words to Know

avete...?	ah-*veh*-teh...?	do you (plural) have...?
dov'è...?	doh-*veh*...?	where is...?
dove sono...?	*doh*-veh *soh*-noh...?	where are...?
saldare il conto	sahl-*dah*-reh eel *kohn*-toh	to check out
indirizzo [m]	een-dee-*reet*-tsoh	address
Può ripetere per favore?	pwoh ree-*peh*-teh-reh pehr fah-*voh*-reh?	Could you repeat that please?

Table 7-1 shows the singular and plural form of several hotel-related words with their proper articles. For more on forming singular and plural articles and nouns, see Chapter 2 in Book III.

Table 7-1	Making Plurals	
Singular, Plural	*Pronunciation*	*Translation*
la cameriera, le cameriere	lah kah-meh-*ryeh*-rah, leh kah-meh-*ryeh*-reh	*chambermaid, chambermaids, waitress, waitresses*
il bagno, i bagni	eel *bah*-nyoh, ee *bah*-nyee	*bathroom, bathrooms*
la chiave, le chiavi	lah *kyah*-veh, leh *kyah*-vee	*key, keys*
il cameriere, i camerieri	eel kah-meh-*ryeh*-reh, ee kah-meh-*ryeh*-ree	*waiter, waiters*
lo specchio, gli specchi	loh *spehk*-kyoh, lyee *spehk*-kyee	*mirror, mirrors*
l'albergo, gli alberghi	lahl-*behr*-goh, lyee ahl-*behr*-gee	*hotel, hotels*
la stanza, le stanze	lah *stahn*-tsah, leh *stahn*-tseh	*room, rooms*
la camera, le camere	lah *kah*-meh-rah, leh *kah*-meh-reh	*room, rooms*
la persona, le persone	lah pehr-*soh*-nah, leh pehr-*soh*-neh	*person, persons*
il letto, i letti	eel *leht*-toh, ee *leht*-tee	*bed, beds*
la notte, le notti	lah *noht*-teh, leh *noht*-tee	*night, nights*
l'entrata, le entrate	lehn-*trah*-tah, leh ehn-*trah*-teh	*entrance, entrances*

Chapter 8

Handling Emergencies

In This Chapter

▶ Asking for help
▶ Going to the doctor, pharmacy, and dentist
▶ Communicating with legal authorities
▶ Describing car troubles

A sking for help is never fun, because you need help only when you're in a jam. For the purposes of this chapter, think about what unfortunate things could happen to you and in what difficulties you may find yourself. Some of these situations are minor, and others are much more serious. We give you the language tools you need to communicate your woes to the people who can help.

Getting Help Fast

 If you're in Italy and you have an emergency, call 113, the Italian national police, who will also send you an ambulance if you need one. This number is valid for all of Italy.

Here is a general sampling of asking-for-help sentences. The first two are important for real emergencies:

▶ **Aiuto!** (ah-*yooh*-toh!) (*Help!*)

▶ **Aiutami!** (ah-*yooh*-tah-mee!) (*Help me!* [informal])

▶ **Mi aiuti, per favore.** (mee ah-*yooh*-tee, pehr fah-*voh*-reh.) (*Help me, please.* [formal])

▶ **Chiamate la polizia!** (kyah-*mah*-teh lah poh-lee-*tsee*-ah!) (*Call the police!*)

▶ **Ho bisogno di un medico.** (*oh* bee-*zoh*-nyoh dee oohn *meh*-dee-koh.) (*I need a doctor.*)

> ✔ **Dov'è il pronto soccorso?** (doh-*veh* eel *prohn*-toh sohk-*kohr-soh?*) (*Where's the emergency room?*)
>
> ✔ **Chiamate un'ambulanza!** (kyah-*mah*-teh ooh-nahm-booh-*lahn*-tsah!) (*Call an ambulance!*)

As you may have noticed, you conjugate sentences directed at a group of people in the plural **voi** form, **chiamate.** In an emergency situation, you can use this form with anyone who may be listening to you.

In some situations, you must ask for a competent authority who speaks English. Do so by asking the following:

> ✔ **Mi scusi, parla inglese?** (mee *skooh*-zee, *pahr*-lah een-*gleh*-zeh?) (*Excuse me, do you speak English?*)
>
> ✔ **C'è un medico che parli inglese?** (cheh oohn *meh*-dee-koh keh *pahr*-lee een-*gleh*-zeh?) (*Is there a doctor who speaks English?*)
>
> ✔ **Dove posso trovare un avvocato che parli inglese?** (*doh*-veh *pohs*-soh troh-*vah*-reh oohn ahv-voh-*kah*-toh keh *pahr*-lee een-*gleh*-zeh?) (*Where can I find a lawyer who speaks English?*)

If you can't find a professional who speaks English, you may be able to find **un interprete** (oohn een-*tehr*-preh-teh) (*an interpreter*) to help you.

Receiving Medical Attention

When you're in **l'ospedale** (loh-speh-*dah*-leh) (*the hospital*) or at **il medico** (eel *meh*-dee-koh) (*the doctor*), you must explain where you hurt or what the problem is. This task isn't always easy because pointing to a spot may not be sufficient. This section shows you how to refer to your body parts in Italian and what to say in a medical emergency.

Describing what ails you

Before you can get relief for what hurts or feels uncomfortable, you have to be able to note which body part is the problem:

> ✔ **il braccio** (eel *brahch*-choh) (*arm*)
>
> ✔ **il collo** (eel *kohl*-loh) (*neck*)
>
> ✔ **la gamba** (lah *gahm*-bah) (*leg*)
>
> ✔ **la mano** (lah *mah*-noh) (*hand*)

- **l'occhio** (*lohk*-kyoh) (*eye*)

- **la pancia** (lah *pahn*-chah) (*belly*)

- **il petto** (eel *peht*-toh) (*chest*)

- **il piede** (eel *pyeh*-deh) (*foot*)

- **lo stomaco** (loh *stoh*-mah-koh) (*stomach*)

- **la testa** (lah *tehs*-tah) (*head*)

When you want to indicate the left or right body part, you must know that body part's gender. For a masculine part, you say **destro** (*dehs*-troh) (*right*) and **sinistro** (see-*nees*-troh) (*left*), whereas for a feminine part, you change the ending: **destra** (*dehs*-trah) and **sinistra** (see-*nees*-trah).

Book II

Exploring and Wandering About

The following phrases indicate how to say something hurts. You can say what hurts in two ways: The first takes the construction **fare male** (*fah*-reh *mah*-leh) (*to hurt*). Use **fa** (fah) for body parts in the singular that hurt. Follow these examples:

Mi fa male la gamba. (mee fah *mah*-leh lah *gahm*-bah.) (*My leg hurts.*)

Mi fa male lo stomaco. (mee fah *mah*-leh loh *stoh*-mah-koh.) (*My stomach hurts.*)

Mi fa male tutto il corpo. (mee fah *mah*-leh *tooht*-toh eel *kohr*-poh.) (*My whole body aches.*)

Use **fanno** (*fahn*-noh) for things in the plural that hurt.

Mi fanno male gli occhi. (mee *fahn*-noh *mah*-leh lyee *ohk*-kee.) (*My eyes hurt.*)

The other way to say something hurts is **avere mal di . . .** (ah-*veh*-reh mahl dee) (*my . . . hurts/hurt*), but you need to conjugate the verb **avere** (ah-*veh*-reh) (*to have*), depending on who has the pain. Here are some examples:

Ho mal di schiena. (oh mahl dee *skyeh*-nah.) (*I have a backache.*)

Ho mal di testa. (oh mahl dee *tehs*-tah.) (*I have a headache.*)

Mia figlia ha mal di denti. (*mee*-ah *fee*-lyah ah mahl dee *dehn*-tee.) (*My daughter has a toothache.*)

Here are even more ways to describe what ails you and explain your symptoms.

- **Mi sono rotto/rotta una gamba.** (mee *soh*-noh *roht*-toh/*rot*-tah *ooh*-nah *gahm*-bah.) (*I broke my leg.*) (Use the feminine participle if you're a woman.)

- ✔ **Ho la gola arrossata.** (oh lah *goh*-lah ahr-rohs-*sah*-tah.) (*I have a sore throat.*)

- ✔ **Ho la pelle irritata.** (oh lah *pehl*-leh eer-ee-*tah*-tah.) (*My skin is irritated.*)

- ✔ **Mi sono storto/storta il piede/la caviglia.** (mee *soh*-noh *stohr*-toh/*stohr*-tah eel *pyeh*-deh/lah cah-*vee*-lyah.) (*I sprained my foot/ankle.*)

- ✔ **Ho disturbi al cuore.** (oh dee-*stoohr*-bee ahl *kwoh*-reh.) (*I have heart problems.*)

- ✔ **Mi bruciano gli occhi.** (mee *brooh*-chah-noh lyee *ohk*-kee.) (*My eyes burn.*)

- ✔ **Mi sono slogata la spalla.** (mee *soh*-noh zloh-*gah*-tah lah *spahl*-lah.) (*I've dislocated my shoulder.*)

- ✔ **Mi sono fatta/o male alla mano.** (mee *soh*-noh *faht*-tah/toh *mah*-leh *ahl*-lah *mah*-noh.) (*I've hurt my hand.*)

- ✔ **Sono caduta/o.** (*soh*-noh cah-*dooh*-tah/toh.) (*I fell.*)

- ✔ **Mia figlia ha questa brutta orticaria.** (*mee*-ah *fee*-lyah ah *kweh*-stah *brooht*-tah ohr-tee-*kah*-ryah.) (*My daughter has this terrible rash.*)

- ✔ **Mio figlio ha la febbre a 40.** (*mee*-oh *fee*-lyoh ah lah *fehb*-breh ah qwah-*rahn*-tah.) (*My son's temperature is 40 degrees [or 104 degrees Fahrenheit].*)

Talkin' the Talk

Gloria goes to the doctor because her leg is swollen. Without further examination, however, the doctor can't determine the problem. (Track 28)

Gloria: **Mi fa molto male questa gamba.**
mee fah *mohl*-toh *mah*-leh *kweh*-stah *gahm*-bah.
This leg hurts very much.

Doctor: **Vedo che è gonfia.**
veh-doh keh *eh gohn*-fyah.
Yes, I can see it's swollen.

Gloria: **Devo andare all'ospedale?**
deh-voh ahn-*dah*-reh alloh-speh-*dah*-leh?
Do I have to go to the hospital?

Doctor: **Sì, bisogna fare le lastre.**
see, bee-*zoh*-nyah *fah*-reh le *lahs*-treh.
Yes, you need to have some X-rays.

Words to Know

aiuto [m]	ah-<u>yooh</u>-toh	help
pronto soccorso [m]	<u>prohn</u>-toh sohk-<u>kohr</u>-soh	emergency room
un'ambulanza [f]	oohn ahm-booh-<u>lahn</u>-tsah	an ambulance
chiamata [f]	kyah-<u>mah</u>-teh	call
fare male	<u>fah</u>-reh <u>mah</u>-leh	to hurt
ospedale [m]	ohs-peh-<u>dah</u>-leh	hospital
lastre [f, pl]	<u>lahs</u>-treh	X-rays
sinistra/o [f/m]	see-<u>nees</u>-trah/troh	left
stomaco [m]	<u>stoh</u>-mah-koh	stomach
febbre [f]	<u>fehb</u>-breh	fever
gonfia/o [f/m]	<u>gohn</u>-fyah/oh	swollen
muscolo [m]	<u>mooh</u>-skoh-loh	muscle
tendine [m]	<u>tehn</u>-dee-neh	tendon
mi gira la testa	mee <u>gee</u>-rah lah <u>tehs</u>-tah	I'm dizzy
mi sento svenire	mee <u>sehn</u>-toh zveh-<u>nee</u>-reh	I'm about to faint
avere mal di	ah-<u>veh</u>-reh mahl dee	to have a _____ache

Understanding professional medical vocabulary

Various professional people can offer you medical help. They include the following:

- **il medico** [f/m] (eel *meh*-dee-koh) (*doctor*)
- **il dottore** [f/m] (eel doht-*toh*-reh) (*doctor*)
- **la dottoressa** (lah doht-toh-*rehs*-sah) (*female doctor*)
- **la/lo specialista** [f/m] (lah/loh speh-chah-*lees*-tah) (*specialist*)
- **la/il dentista** [f/m] (lah/eel dehn-*tees*-tah) (*dentist*)
- **il chirurgo** [f/m] (eel kee-*roohr*-goh) (*the surgeon*)
- **l'infermiera** (leen-fehr-*myeh*-rah) (*female nurse*)
- **l'infermiere** (leen-fehr-*myeh*-reh) (*male nurse*)

Here's a question that you may need to ask in a doctor's office, with typical replies:

> **Devo prendere qualcosa?** (*deh*-voh *prehn*-deh-reh kwahl-*koh*-zah?) (*Do I have to take anything?*)

> **No, si riposi e beva molta acqua.** (noh, see ree-*poh*-zee eh *beh*-vah *mohl*-tah *ah*-kwah.) (*No, rest and drink a lot of water.*)

> **Ecco la ricetta.** (*ehk*-koh lah ree-*cheht*-tah.) (*Here is your prescription.*)

Getting what you need at the pharmacy

If you need **una medicina** (*ooh*-nah meh-dee-*chee*-nah) (*a medicine*), you'll probably look for the closest **farmacia** (fahr-mah-*chee*-ah) (*pharmacy*). Usual pharmacy hours are from 8:30 a.m. to 8 p.m., generally with a lunch break from 1 to 4 p.m. But a pharmacy is always open in case of an emergency! You can find the address and phone number of the **farmacia di turno** (fahr-mah-*chee*-ah dee *toohr*-noh) (*open pharmacy*) written on all pharmacy doors.

Italy is one of those places where pharmacists still give medical advice. These places are true pharmacies without all the non-drug items for sale like you find in your typical big drug store in the United States, where you can get everything from canned food to beach chairs. Furthermore, you generally don't walk in, browse, and help yourself to even simple things like aspirin. This is the same for many other types of stores in Italy, the **profumeria** (proh-fooh-meh-*ryah*) (*toiletries shop*), shoe stores, and small clothing shops in particular. Many items are kept behind the counter. So if you or a loved one has a slight ailment and it's not an emergency, you can go into the pharmacy for help.

Here are some items you may go to a pharmacy for:

- ✔ **le lenti a contatto** [f, pl] (leh *lenhn*-tee ah kohn-*taht*-toh) (*contact lenses*)
- ✔ **soluzione** (soh-looh-*tsyoh*-neh) (*solution*)
- ✔ **pomata** (poh-*mah*-tah) (*cream; lotion*)
- ✔ **ricetta** (ree-*cheht*-tah) (*prescription*)

Braving the dentist

You may need some emergency dental work while you're in Italy. The first thing to ask the concierge at your hotel, the pharmacist, or the friendly **barista** where you've been having breakfast every morning is **Scusi, mi può consigliare un dentista di fiducia?** (*skooh*-zee, mee pwoh *kohn*-see-*lyah*-reh oohn dehn-*tees*-tah dee fee-*dooh*-chah?) (*Excuse me, would you please recommend a good dentist?*)

Handling Legal Matters

When traveling in Italy, you may find yourself in a bind, requiring help from the police or a lawyer. This section guides you through vocabulary that you hope you never have to use, but it's best to be prepared in case the need arises.

Reporting an accident

In addition to medical emergencies, other types of emergencies may require you to call the police to report something you've witnessed.

Talkin' the Talk

Elena has just seen an elderly woman on her bicycle hit by a scooter. She calls the police. (Track 29)

Officer: **Polizia.**
                poh-lee-*tsee*-ah.
                Police.

Elena: **C'è stato un incidente!**
                cheh *stah*-toh oohn een-chee-*dehn*-teh!
                There's been an accident!

Officer:	**Dove?**
	doh-veh?
	Where?
Elena:	**In Piazza Mattei.**
	een *pyaht*-tsah maht-*tehy*.
	In Piazza Mattei.
Officer:	**Ci sono feriti?**
	chee *soh*-noh feh-*ree*-tee?
	Is anyone injured?
Elena:	**C'è una persona ferita e incosciente.**
	cheh *ooh*-na pehr-*soh*-nah feh-*ree*-tah eh
	in-ko-*shehn*-teh.
	Someone is injured and unconscious.
Officer:	**Mandiamo subito un'ambulanza.**
	mahn-*dyah*-moh *sooh*-bee-toh
	ooh-nahm-booh-*lahn*-tsah.
	We'll send an ambulance right away.

Words to Know

ambulanza [f]	ahm-booh-<u>lahn</u>-tsah	ambulance
Che è successo?	keh eh sooh-<u>chehs</u>-soh?	What happened?
emergenza [f]	eh-mehr-<u>jehn</u>-tsah	emergency
incidente [m]	in-chee-<u>dehn</u>-teh	accident
ferito [m]	feh-<u>ree</u>-toh	injured (person)

Reporting a robbery

No one ever wants to be the target of a robbery, but if you are, you should be prepared with these important phrases when the police arrive.

Sono stata/o derubata/o. (*soh*-noh *stah*-tah/toh deh-rooh-*bah*-tah/toh.)
(*I've been robbed.*)

C'è stato un furto nel mio appartamento. (*cheh stah*-toh oohn *foohr*-toh nehl *mee*-oh ahp-pahr-tah-*mehn*-toh.) (*There was a burglary in my apartment.*)

Sono entrati dei ladri in casa nostra. (*soh*-noh ehn-*trah*-tee dey *lah*-dree een *kah*-sah *nohs*-trah.) (*Thieves broke into our house.*)

Mi hanno rubato la macchina. (mee *ahn*-noh rooh-*bah*-toh lah *mahk*-kee-nah.) (*My car has been stolen.*)

Mi hanno scippata. (mee *ahn*-noh sheep-*pah*-tah.) (*My handbag was snatched.*)

Talkin' the Talk

A moped driver just stole Anna's **borsa** (*bohr*-sah) (*handbag*). Distraught, she calls 113 for the police to **denunciare** (deh-noohn-*chah*-reh) (*report*) **il furto** (eel *foohr*-toh) (*the theft*).

Officer: **Polizia.**
poh-lee-*tsee*-ah.
Police.

Anna: **Mi hanno appena scippata!**
mee *ahn*-noh ahp-*peh*-nah sheep-*pah*-tah!
They just snatched my handbag!

Officer: **Si calmi e venga in questura.**
see *kahl*-mee eh *vehn*-gah een kwehs-*tooh*-rah.
Calm down and come to police headquarters.

Anna: **È stato un uomo in motorino.**
eh *stah*-toh oohn *woh*-moh een moh-toh-*ree*-noh.
It was a man on a moped.

Officer: **Ho capito, ma deve venire qui.**
oh kah-*pee*-toh, mah *deh*-veh veh-*nee*-reh *kwee.*
I got it, but you have to come here.

Anna: **Dov'è la questura?**
doh-*veh* lah kweh-*stooh*-rah?
Where is police headquarters?

Officer: **Dietro la posta centrale.**
dyeh-troh lah *pohs*-tah chehn-*trah*-leh.
Behind the main post office.

Anna: **Vengo subito.**
vehn-goh *sooh*-bee-toh.
I'm coming at once.

Words to Know

borsa [f]	<u>bohr</u>-sah	handbag
furto [m]	<u>foohr</u>-toh	theft
denunciare	deh-noohn-<u>chah</u>-reh	to report
motorino [m]	moh-toh-<u>ree</u>-noh	moped
questura [f]	kweh-<u>stooh</u>-rah	police headquarters
scippare	sheep-<u>pah</u>-reh	to snatch a handbag
scippo [m]	<u>sheep</u>-poh	theft of a handbag

When you have to report someone and describe the thief, you must know some essential words, such as hair color, height, and so on. Many of these adjectives also come in handy when describing other people — friends, family members, classmates — not just thieves! You can form descriptive sentences like this:

✔ **La persona era . . .** (lah pehr-*soh*-nah *eh*-rah . . .) (*The person was . . .*)

- **alta** (*ahl*-tah) (*tall*)

- **bassa** (*bahs*-sah) (*short*)

- **di media statura** (dee *meh*-dyah stah-*tooh*-rah) (*of medium build*)

- **grassa** (*grahs*-sah) (*fat*)

- **magra** (*mah*-grah) (*thin*)

Note: The preceding adjectives end in **-a** because they refer to the noun **la persona,** which is feminine.

✔ **I capelli erano . . .** (ee kah-*pehl*-lee *eh*-rah-noh . . .) (*The hair was . . .*)

- **castani** (kahs-*tah*-nee) (*brown*)

- **biondi** (*byohn*-dee) (*blond*)

- **neri** (*neh*-ree) (*black*)

- **rossi** (*rohs*-see) (*red*)

- **scuri** (*skooh*-ree) (*dark*)
- **chiari** (*kyah*-ree) (*fair*)
- **lisci** (*lee*-shee) (*straight*)
- **ondulati** (ohn-dooh-*lah*-tee) (*wavy*)
- **ricci** (*reech*-chee) (*curly*)
- **corti** (*kohr*-tee) (*short*)
- **lunghi** (*loohn*-gee) (*long*)

✔ **Aveva gli occhi . . .** (ah-*veh*-vah lyee *ohk*-kee . . .) (*His/Her eyes were . . .*)

- **azzurri** (ahdz-*zooh*-ree) (*blue*)
- **grigi** (*gree*-jee) (*gray*)
- **marroni** (mahr-*roh*-nee) (*brown*)
- **neri** (*neh*-ree) (*black; dark*)
- **verdi** (*vehr*-dee) (*green*)

✔ **Era . . .** (*eh*-rah . . .) (*He/she was . . .*)

- **calvo** (*kahl*-voh) (*bald*)
- **rasato** (rah-*zah*-toh) (*clean-shaven*)

✔ **Aveva . . .** (ah-*veh*-vah . . .) (*He/She had . . .*)

- **la barba** (lah *bahr*-bah) (*a beard*)
- **i baffi** (ee *bahf*-fee) (*a moustache*)
- **la bocca larga** (lah *bohk*-kah *lahr*-gah) (*a wide mouth*)
- **la bocca stretta** (lah *bohk*-kah *streht*-tah) (*thin lips*)
- **la bocca carnosa** (lah *bohk*-kah kahr-*noh*-zah) (*a plump mouth*)
- **il naso lungo** (eel *nah*-zoh *loohn*-go) (*a long nose*)
- **il naso corto** (eel *nah*-zoh *kohr*-toh) (*a short nose*)

Reporting a lost or stolen passport

Imagine you lose your passport, or it gets stolen while you're napping on the train. (These things happen!) The conversation that follows will help you get a new one.

Talkin' the Talk

When Diane gets off the train in Florence, she realizes that she no longer has her passport. She goes immediately to the police station.

Diane: **Ho perso il passaporto! Non so cosa fare!**
oh *pehr*-soh eel pahs-sah-*pohr*-toh! nohn *soh koh*-zah *fah*-reh!
I've lost my passport! I don't know what to do!

Police: **Sa dirmi dove, come, quando?**
sah *deer*-mee *doh*-veh, *koh*-meh, *kwahn*-doh?
Can you tell me where, when, and how?

Diane: **Penso di averlo perso in treno.**
pehn-soh dee ah-*vehr*-loh *pehr*-soh een *treh*-noh.
I think I lost it on the train.

Police: **Ora facciamo la denuncia.**
oh-rah fach-*chah*-moh lah deh-*noohn*-chah.
We'll file a report now.

Con questa denuncia, deve rivolgersi alla sua ambasciata o consolato.
kohn *kweh*-stah deh-*noohn*-chah, *deh*-veh ree-*vohl*-jehr-see *ahl*-lah *sooh*-ah ahm-bah-*shah*-tah oh kohn-soh-*lah*-toh.
You're going to need this report when you go to your Embassy or Consulate to apply for a new one.

Diane: **Grazie.**
grah-tsyeh.
Thank you.

(at the Embassy or Consulate)

Consulate Agent: **Dica?**
dee-kah?
How can I help you?

Diane: (agitated) **Mi serve un nuovo passaporto! Subito!**
mee *sehr*-veh oohn *nwoh*-voh pahs-sah-*pohr*-toh! *sooh*-bee-toh!
I need a new passport! Right away!

Consulate Agent:	**Si calmi. Occorrono due foto tessera . . .**
	see *kahl*-mee. ohk-*khor*-roh-noh *dooh*-eh *foh*-toh *tehs*-seh-rah . . .
	Calm down. You're going to need two ID-size photos . . .
	. . . la denuncia della polizia, una copia del passaporto originale. . .
	. . . lah deh-*noohn*-chah *dehl*-lah poh-lee-*tsee*-ah, *ooh*-nah *koh*-pyah dehl pahs-sah-*pohr*-toh oh-ree-jee-*nah*-leh . . .
	. . . official police report, a copy of your original passport (your hotel should have a copy of this) . . .
	. . . e un altro documento.
	. . . eh oohn *ahl*-troh doh-kooh-*mehn*-toh.
	. . . and another form of ID.

Getting legal help

Many unpleasant moments in life require that you seek the help of an authorized person. Often, this person is a lawyer who can help you in complicated situations. Therefore, knowing how to contact a lawyer is rather important. You can use the following general questions and sentences to request legal help in Italian.

> **Mi serve l'aiuto di un avvocato.** (mee *sehr*-veh lah-*yooh*-toh dee oohn ahv-voh-*kah*-toh.) (*I need the help of a lawyer.*)

> **Ho bisogno di assistenza legale.** (oh bee-*zoh*-nyoh dee ahs-see-*stehn*-tsah leh-*gah*-leh.) (*I need legal assistance.*)

> **Vorrei consultare il mio avvocato.** (vohr-*rey* kohn-soohl-*tah*-reh eel *mee*-oh ahv-voh-*kah*-toh.) (*I'd like to consult my lawyer.*)

> **Chiamate il mio avvocato, per favore.** (kyah-*mah*-teh eel *mee*-oh ahv-voh-*kah*-toh, pehr fah-*voh*-reh.) (*Call my lawyer, please.*)

After you find a lawyer, you can speak to him or her about your situation. Here are some examples of what you may need to say:

> **Sono stato truffato/a.** (*soh*-noh *stah*-toh troohf-*fah*-toh/tah.) (*I was cheated.*)

> **Voglio denunciare un furto.** (*voh*-lyoh deh-noohn-*chah*-reh oohn *foohr*-toh.) (*I want to report a theft.*)

Devo stipulare un contratto. (*deh*-voh stee-pooh-*lah*-reh oohn kohn-*traht*-toh.) (*I have to negotiate a contract.*)

Ho avuto un incidente stradale. (oh ah-*vooh*-toh oohn een-chee-*dehn*-teh strah-*dah*-leh.) (*I've had a traffic accident.*)

Voglio che mi vengano risarciti i danni. (*voh*-lyoh keh mee *vehn*-gah-noh ree-sahr-*chee*-tee ee *dahn*-nee.) (*I want to be compensated for the damages.*)

Sono stato/a arrestato/a. (*soh*-noh *stah*-toh/ah ahr-reh-*stah*-toh/tah.) (*I've been arrested.*)

Words to Know

danno [m]	<u>dahn</u>-noh	damage
denunciare	deh-noohn-<u>chah</u>-reh	to report
denuncia [f]	deh-<u>noohn</u>-chah	report
incidente stradale [m]	een-chee-<u>dehn</u>-teh strah-<u>dah</u>-leh	traffic accident
targa [f]	<u>tahr</u>-gah	license plate
patente [f]	pah-<u>tehn</u>-teh	license
libretto [m]	lee-<u>breht</u>-toh	registration
assicurazione [f]	ahs-see-kooh-rah-<u>tsyoh</u>-neh	insurance

Dealing with Car Trouble

You don't have to be involved in a car crash to experience car trouble. Perhaps some sort of mechanical problem makes your car break down. In such cases, you need to call an auto mechanic who can help you out of this situation. Here are some terms that may help:

- **fermare** (fehr-*mah*-reh) (*to stop*)

- **macchina** (*mahk*-kee-nah) (*car*)

- **il più presto possibile** (eel pyooh *prehs*-toh pohs-*see*-bee-leh) (*as soon as possible*)

- **soccorso stradale** (sohk-*kohr*-soh strah-*dah*-leh) (*roadside assistance*)

- **corsia di emergenza** (kohr-*see*-ah dee eh-mehr-*jehn*-tsah) (*emergency lane*)

- **traffico** (*trahf*-fee-koh) (*traffic*)

- **meccanico** (mehk-*kah*-nee-koh) (*mechanic*)

- **una gomma a terra** (*ooh*-nah *gohm*-mah ah *tehr*-rah) (*a flat tire*)

- **carro attrezzi** (*kahr*-roh aht-*treht*-tsee) (*tow truck*)

Book II

Exploring and Wandering About

Book III

Grasping Basic Grammar Essentials for Communication

Common Italian Pronouns

Pronoun as . . .	Singular	Plural
Personal subject	**io** (*I*) **tu** (*you* [familiar]) **lui, lei, esso Lei** (*he, she, it, you* [formal])	**noi** (*we*) **voi** (*you* [familiar], *you guys, y'all*) **loro, Loro** (*they, you* [formal])
Direct object	**mi** (*me*) **ti** (*you*) **lo** (*him*) **la** (*her*) **La** (*you* [formal])	**ci** (*us*) **vi** (*you*) **li** (*them* [masculine]) **le** (*them* [feminine]) **Le** (*you* [formal])
Indirect object	**mi** (*to/for me*) **ti** (*to/for you*) **gli** (*to/for him*) **le** (*to/for her*) **Le** (*to/for you* [formal])	**ci** (*to/for us*) **vi** (*to/for you*) **loro, gli** (*to/for them* [masculine, feminine]) **loro, gli** (*to/for them*) **Loro, Gli** (*to/for you* [formal])

Italians are known to be passionate people, and their language is appropriately descriptive. You can use color words not just as adjectives but also as idioms to express your feelings. Check out the free article about using colorful adjectives appropriately at www.dummies.com/extras/italianaio.

Contents at a Glance

Chapter 1

What Do You Know? Parts of Speech

*I*talian grammar is both complex and logical, or as logical as any language's grammar may be. It has a lot of rules — and a lot of exceptions to those rules. This chapter provides an overview of all that's involved with Italian grammar before diving into the more specific aspects of grammar throughout the rest of this book.

Grammar consists of the parts of speech and their interrelationships and is the basis of the Italian (and any) language. Understanding grammar lets you expand your knowledge and control of the language.

Fortunately, Italian grammar is a lot like English grammar, and the two languages share the same parts of speech. Working from what you already know, you can use this chapter to begin building or to reinforce your command of Italian.

Recognizing the Parts of Speech

Learning another language involves starting with the basics — in this case, the parts of speech — and then putting those basics together. The parts of speech serve as a foundation for content to come and allow you to create and support content.

This section provides an overview of the parts of speech (which you probably haven't seen since elementary school) and shows their purpose and relation to each other.

English has eight parts of speech, and Italian has nine, as listed in Table 1-1.

Table 1-1	Parts of Speech		
Part of Speech	*Definition*	*Examples*	*Notes*
articolo (*article*)	A special qualifier that modifies a noun by "determining" it	**il, lo, la, l'** (*the* [singular]); **i, gli, le** (*the* [plural]); **un, un', uno, una** (*a; an*)	When referring to a specific object, you use a definite article. To point to an object among many like objects, you use an indefinite article. The article and the noun it refers to share the same gender and number.
nome (*noun*)	A word that indicates a person, animal, thing, or idea; it can be accompanied by an article	**uomo** (*man*), **cane** (*dog*), **penisola** (peninsula), **amore** (*love*)	In Italian, all nouns are either masculine, such as **il tavolo** (*table*), or feminine, such as **la sedia** (*chair*).
aggettivo (*adjective*)	A word that describes a noun, a name, or a pronoun	**piccolo** (small), **grande** (large)	Adjectives must match the word they refer to in gender and number.

Part of Speech	Definition	Examples	Notes
pronome (*pro-noun*)	A word that substitutes for a noun, name, or a phrase already mentioned; the replaced word or phrase is the *antecedent* of the pronoun; the pronouns **io** (*I*), **tu** (*you*), **noi** (*we*), and **voi** (*you*) are not replacements but rather identify speakers/listeners	**io** (*I*), **tu** (*you* [singular]), **lui** (*he*), **lei** (*she*), **esso, essa** (*it*), **noi** (*we*), **voi** (*you* [plural]), **loro, essi, esse** (*they*)	In the preceding column I list the subject pronouns. Italian is so rich in pronouns that it's not possible to list them all here.
verbo (*verb*)	A word that shows an action, an event, or a state of being	**andare** (*to go*), **brillare** (*to shine*), **soffrire** (*to suffer*)	In Italian, verbs take different endings for each of the six subjects.
avverbio (*adverb*)	A word that qualifies a verb, adjective, another adverb, or a sentence	**velocemente** (*quickly*), **bene** (*well*), **male** (*badly*)	Adverbs are invariable. Some are original words, but many others can be derived from adjectives by adding the ending **-mente,** which corresponds to the ending *-ly* in English.

(continued)

Book III

Grasping Basic Grammar Essentials for Communication

Table 1-1 *(continued)*

Part of Speech	Definition	Examples	Notes
preposizione (*preposition*)	A word that identifies a prepositional phrase or introduces nouns, names, and pronouns, linking them to the rest of the sentence	**di** (*of; from*), **a** (*at; to*), **da** (*from; by*), **in** (*in*), **su** (*on*), **con** (*with*), **per** (*for*), **fra/tra** (*between; among*)	Prepositions are invariable. Italian has eight basic prepositions that are often combined with the definite article.
congiunzione (*conjunction*)	A word that connects two words, phrases, or clauses	**e** (*and*), **ma** (*but*), **o** (*or*), **che** (*that*), **quando** (*when*), **perché** (*because; why*)	Conjunctions are invariable. You use coordinating conjunctions to link independent clauses together; you use subordinating conjunctions to tie a dependent clause to an independent clause.
interiezione (*interjection*)	A word used to express strong feeling or sudden emotion; generally placed at the beginning of the sentence and followed by an exclamation point	**ahah!** (*ah!*), **ahi!** (*ouch!*), **uau!** (*wow!*)	Besides words that are only interjections (which are invariable), in both Italian and English you can use a lot of words to the same effect, as in **Bene!** (*Well!*) or **Davvero?** (*Indeed?, Really?*).

Nouns

A *noun* (**sostantivo**) names a person, place, or thing. In Italian, a noun can be singular or plural, collective, concrete or abstract, common or proper, and even masculine or feminine. A noun functions as any of the following:

- ✔ **Subject:** The person, place, or thing performing an action or simply existing — that is, in a state of being, if that's not too existential

- ✔ **Direct object:** The person, place, or thing receiving the action transmitted by the verb from the subject

- ✔ **Indirect object:** To or for whom or what the action is directed

- ✔ **Object of a prepositional phrase:** The person, place, or thing that follows any of the prepositions

For example, in the sentence **Mario dà il regalo a Fausta** (*Mario is giving the gift to Fausta*), **Mario**, the subject, performs an action with the verb **dà** (*is giving*); **il regalo** (*the gift*) is the direct object, or what was given, so it receives the action; and **Fausta**, the indirect object, is the person to whom the action was directed. Technically, **a Fausta** is also a prepositional phrase serving as the indirect object, with **Fausta**, the person, following **a** (*to*), a preposition.

Just as nouns have different roles in a sentence, they also have different characteristics. A noun can be proper, common, abstract, or concrete. A name of a person, city, or country is a *proper noun* (in English, proper nouns are usually capitalized): Mario, Fausta, Roma, and Italia. (In Italian, days of the week and months of the year aren't capitalized.)

Common nouns are objects, such as a cat, dog, car, or school. Common nouns aren't capitalized in Italian or in English. An *abstract noun* may be something intangible, like your thoughts or desires; a *concrete noun* is anything you can touch, see, or taste.

Collective nouns, like *family* or *people*, are singular in Italian. For example: **La famiglia è molto tradizionale** (*The family is very traditional*); and **La gente è proprio simpatica** (*The people are really nice*) — note the plural verb in English.

Pronouns

Pronouns take the place of nouns and add variation to a sentence. They have the same jobs as nouns but are simply a little more vague. Table 1-2 lists the most commonly used pronouns in Italian.

Table 1-2	Common Italian Pronouns	
Pronoun as . . .	**Singular**	**Plural**
Personal subject	**io** (*I*)	**noi** (*we*)
	tu (*you,* familiar)	**voi** (*you* [familiar], *you guys, y'all*)
	lui, lei, esso, Lei (*he, she, it, you* [formal])	**loro, Loro** (*they, you* [formal])
Direct object	**mi** (*me*)	**ci** (*us*)
	ti (*you*)	**vi** (*you*)
	lo (*him*)	**li** (*them* [masculine])
	la (*her*)	**le** (*them* [feminine])
	La (*you* [formal])	**Le** (*you* [formal])
Indirect object	**mi** (*to/for me*)	**ci** (*to/for us*)
	ti (*to/for you*)	**vi** (*to/for you*)
	gli (*to/for him*)	**loro, gli** (*to/for them* [masculine and feminine])
	le (*to/for her*)	
	Le (*to/for you* [formal])	**loro, gli** (*to/for them*)
		Loro, Gli (*to/for you* [formal])

In general, **loro,** which follows the verb, has been replaced by **gli,** which precedes the verb.

Articles

Articles are the small words that precede nouns and can be specific, or definite, meaning *the,* such as *the* book; or they can be indefinite, or vague, meaning *a* or *an,* such as *a* book.

✔ Definite articles: **il, l', lo** (singular masculine); **la, l'** (singular feminine); **i, gli** (plural masculine); **le** (plural feminine)

✔ Indefinite articles: **un, uno** (singular masculine); **una, un'** (singular feminine)

Articles must agree in number and gender with the nouns they accompany. When using articles, you also need to consider the beginning letters of the words following the article. That's why so many articles exists: masculine singular, feminine singular, feminine plural, and masculine plural.

Verbs

Verbs bring a language to life. You use verbs to show action and states of being, to comment and to question, to contemplate and to create. Language really doesn't exist without verbs, at least not sentient and sophisticated language.

For example: **Giovanni scrive canzoni ed è molto felice** (*John writes songs and is very happy*). **Scrive** (*he writes*) shows action; **è** (*is*) tells you how John is feeling.

Verbs change shape — must change shape — to show who's doing something or what's happening. Italian verbs characterize themselves by their *infinitives,* the unconjugated verb form that translates into the English *to* form (*to eat, to play,* and so on). After you understand the appropriate forms of conjugation for different verbs, you can use those same forms for hundreds of other verbs in the same category.

Besides the subject of the verb, you need to keep in mind verb tense (when an action is taking place), mood (the mood or point of view of the subject), and voice (active or passive). Verbs come in 22 tenses (past, present, and future, to name a few) and 7 moods (indicative, subjunctive, conditional, imperative, infinitive, gerund, and participle); and they have two voices (active and passive). They follow a strict set of sequencing rules, as do English verbs.

Verbs are both complex and central to mastering the Italian language, but discovering verbs in all their forms will expand your vocabulary exponentially.

Adjectives

Adjectives add flavor, dimension, interest, and opinion. They let you describe in detail people, places, and things. They make self-expression possible.

Adjectives accompany nouns and pronouns. To say someone is happy or something is new, you use adjectives. Adjectives agree in number and gender with whatever they modify. For example **rosso** (*red*) has masculine singular, masculine plural (**rossi**), feminine singular (**rossa**), and feminine plural (**rosse**) forms.

Here are a couple more facts about Italian adjectives:

- ✔ Some adjectives end in the letter **e** and have only two forms: singular, ending in **e**, and plural, ending in **i**: **Importante** (*important*) in the feminine and masculine singular becomes **importanti** in the feminine and masculine plural, as in **una donna importante** (*an important lady*), **due donne importanti** (*two important ladies*), **un ragazzo importante** (*an important boy*), and **due ragazzi importanti** (*two important boys*).

- ✔ Adjectives of nationality often end in **e**: **inglese** (*English*), **francese** (*French*), and **svedese** (*Swedish*); there are some exceptions, such as **americano/a, italiano/a,** and **spagnolo/a.**

Adverbs

Similar to adjectives, adverbs add detail and description but to actions rather than things. Adverbs can exaggerate, and they can understate. How much did you study? *A lot.* When? *Constantly.* Where? *Nearby.* For how long? *Endlessly.* How exactly did you go about studying? *Obsessively.* Really? *Absolutely.* Adverbs tell you the place, time, quantity, and quality of what's happening.

The good news about adverbs is that they're invariable. As the very name says, **a** (*to*) **verbi** (*verbs*), adverbs generally accompany verbs and, thus, don't have number and gender agreement issues. Even when they qualify adjectives and other adverbs, they remain unchanged. For example:

Le Smart sono incredibilmente piccole. (*Smart [cars] are incredibly small.*)

I grattacieli sono incredibilmente alti. (*Skyscrapers are incredibly tall.*)

The most common adverb, in almost any language, is *very* (**molto**). For example: **La ragazza è molto bella** (*The girl is very pretty*); **I cani sono molto docili** (*The dogs are very tame*); and **Le macchine sono molto veloci** (*The cars are very fast*).

Prepositions

Prepositions are the unruly children of Italian. They are ever present, unpredictable, and idiosyncratic. They vary widely (and wildly) in meaning, depending on context.

The preposition **a**, for example, can mean *to, at,* or *in:*

> **Vado a Roma.** (*I'm going to Rome.*)
>
> **Sto a casa.** (*I'm at home.*)
>
> **Abito a Firenze.** (*I live in Florence.*)

Likewise, **in** can mean *to, at,* or *in:*

> **Vado in Italia.** (*I'm going to Italy.*)
>
> **Sono in ufficio.** (*I'm at the office.*)
>
> **Lavoro in giardino.** (*I'm working in the yard.*)

Prepositions are small words with big impact. They connect nouns and pronouns to each other or to other phrases. They show the relationship among individual words, phrases, actions, places, and times.

Although prepositions are always first and foremost prepositions, they can function as adverbs, objects, or adjectives (usually as part of a phrase). They announce themselves by being prepositioned, or coming before a phrase: The girl *with* the pearl earring. The hordes are *at* the gates.

Book III

Grasping Basic Grammar Essentials for Communication

Conjunctions

Conjunctions, as their name indicates, (con)join words, phrases, or sentence clauses. They make compound and complex sentences possible. The most common forms of conjunctions are **e** (*and*), **ma** (*but*), **perché** (*because*), and **come** (*as*). For example: **Il cane è enorme perché mangia molto** (*The dog is huge because he eats a lot*).

Some conjunctions foreshadow the subjunctive mood, which you can find more about in Chapter 6 of Book IV.

Interjections

Interjections are individual words or short phrases that express emotions. They're exclamatory, and Italian is peppered with them. You use interjections to say hello and goodbye (**ciao**), and you use them to be polite (**grazie**). Interjections can be mild or heated, sincere or sarcastic.

Interjections aren't only verbal. Hand gestures and whole body poses can be as expressive as words. Leave gestural language alone until you're completely comfortable speaking Italian, though. All too often foreign speakers of Italian misinterpret gestures they pick up from stereotypes in B-grade movies or television.

Hundreds of interjections exist, making up some of the most basic expressions. For example, did you know that **ciao** (*hi; bye*) is an interjection? These words often change, just as they do in English, to reflect current usages.

Conjugating Verbs in the Present Tense

When using and conjugating verbs, you not only have to know the meaning, and thus be able to choose which verbs to use, but you also have to keep in mind a bunch of other considerations, such as the following:

✔ The verb has to reflect and agree in number with the subject (be first, second, or third person singular or plural).

✔ The verb has to tell when something is happening (present, past, future, and so on).

✔ The verb has to reveal the attitude or *mood* of the subject (indicative or factual, subjunctive or subjective, conditional or what if, imperative or commanding).

✔ The verb has a voice (active or passive).

All these elements allow you to conjugate a verb to make it useful and pertinent. To begin, you choose the infinitive and change endings that show tense, mood, and voice.

Identifying infinitives

The infinitive form of a verb is raw — it shows no tense and voice. It has no subject. It reveals no action. An English infinitive uses *to* as an indicator that the verb hasn't been put into action; for example, *to eat, to sing, to sleep,* and *to travel* are infinitives. In Italian, most infinitives end in **-are, -ere,** or **-ire,** such as **parlare** (*to speak*), **scrivere** (*to write*), and **dormire** (*to sleep*).

To conjugate a verb, you drop the characteristic ending and add new endings that show the subject, tense, and mood.

Establishing subject-verb agreement

To conjugate a verb, you need to know who or what is doing the action of the sentence. The verb must agree with the subject in person (for example, *I, we, you, they, he,* and *it*) and number (*I* is singular, and *we* is plural, for example).

After you establish the subject, you choose the correct ending to the verb.

In the present tense, you first remove the infinitive's ending (**-are, -ere,** or **-ire**), leaving the verb stem. **Parlare** (*to speak*), for example, drops the **-are** and leaves you with **parl.** You then add the indicative's present tense endings. Present tense endings are letters that indicate who is doing the action of the verb.

The following table shows a simple conjugation of the **-are** verb **parlare** in the present tense. Notice that the subject pronoun and the verb endings both tell who's doing the action. Because the verb endings are so different, the conjugated verb alone often suffices to name the subject. So instead of saying **io parlo,** you can say simply **parlo** (*I speak*). However, because the third person singular and plural forms have conjugations for multiple subjects, you may want to keep the specific subject named in those cases.

parlare (*to speak*)	
io **parlo**	noi **parliamo**
tu **parli**	voi **parlate**
lui, lei, Lei **parla**	loro, Loro **parlano**

Moving on to Other Verb Tenses

Italian has 22 verb tenses, and 9 are compound, meaning they take a helping verb to form. Books IV and V focus on the tenses you use most often: present, past, and future.

That sounds deceptively simple, but each tense has its own endings and peculiarities and combined with mood — conditional, what if; imperative, commanding; subjunctive, subjective; indicative, factual — makes speaking Italian both rewarding and challenging. Throughout this book, you find out how to combine tense and mood, and occasionally voice, to express yourself precisely and even elegantly.

Composing a Simple Sentence

In Italian, composing a sentence can be remarkably easy. You need a subject, a verb that agrees with that subject, and a tense, mood, and voice to tell you when and how something happened.

Taking a simple sentence like **io parlo** or **parlo** (*I speak*), you can embellish what you're saying by adding adjectives, adverbs, prepositions, or objects. And you can use conjunctions to make the sentence more complex. For example, here's a building process that makes a sentence more interesting:

> **Io parlo.** (*I speak.*)
>
> **Io parlo italiano.** (*I speak Italian.*)
>
> **Io parlo bene italiano.** (*I speak Italian well.*)
>
> **Io parlo bene italiano perché lo parlo con degli amici italiani.** (*I speak Italian well because I speak it with some Italian friends.*)

To ask questions in Italian, you can invert subjects and verbs, or you can simply change your intonation. To invert a subject and verb, you can change **Carlo parla italiano** (*Carlo speaks Italian*) to something like **Parla italiano Carlo?** (*Does Carlo speak Italian?*)

Intonation makes the first sentence a statement by changing the high and low pitch of your sentence, much as you do when speaking English. The words *he speaks Italian* can be either a statement (*He speaks Italian.*) or a question (*He speaks Italian?*), depending on the tone and pitch of your voice.

To ask and respond to questions with more than a simple **sì** (*yes*) or **no** (*no*), you need interrogative words like **chi** (*who*), **che, che cosa** (*what*), **quanto** (*how much*), **dove** (*where*), and so on. Usually, these words come at the very beginning of a sentence: **Chi è?** (*Who is it/he/she?*)

Chapter 2

Noun and Article Basics: Gender and Number

In This Chapter

▶ Sorting out definite and indefinite articles

▶ Drawing the line between masculine and feminine nouns

▶ Working with plural nouns and articles

*N*ouns serve similar purposes in English and Italian, but in English, nouns don't have a gender, whereas in Italian, they can be masculine or feminine. When Italian nouns refer to things or abstractions, their grammatical gender is merely a product of convention and usage: **sole** (*sun*) is masculine, but **luna** (*moon*) is feminine. At times, nouns are masculine or feminine because they refer to a male or female person or animal. This chapter shows you how to distinguish between feminine and masculine nouns and how to move from the masculine to the feminine (and vice versa when changing gender is possible).

In many cases, you can make out the gender of a noun from its ending. But in a lot of cases, you can't. You have to know a noun's gender by memorizing it or by looking at clues in other words that accompany the noun. Because the clearest indicator of gender is the definite article (corresponding to the English *the*), this chapter starts with articles and then introduces nouns.

As in English, Italian nouns can be singular or plural. Most follow regular patterns, but some behave irregularly or come only in the singular or the plural. In this chapter, you find out how to form the plural and how to reconstruct the singular masculine form of a noun. Because the masculine is usually the default gender in Italian, you find words listed in that gender in dictionaries.

A Primer on Articles

Looking at nouns out of context helps you understand the general rules that govern grammar, but because you need to know each noun's gender and because the most reliable indicator of a noun's gender is the definite article, this first section is devoted to articles.

English has a definite and an indefinite article — *the* and *a/an,* respectively — as does Italian. With the definite article, you point to a specific item, as in **Il bambino è caduto dall'altalena** (*The child fell off the swing*). With the indefinite article, you point to one thing among many like things, as in **Leggi un libro?** (*Are you reading a book?*)

Memorize new nouns with their articles to make sure you know their gender as well.

Definite articles: Dealing with "the"

In Italian, articles vary in gender, number, and spelling. English and Italian use the *definite article* to point to a specific thing or person, as in these examples:

> **Il libro è sul tavolo.** (*The book [we are/were talking about] is on the table.*)

> **I bambini stanno giocando in giardino.** (*The children are playing in the garden.*)

Table 2-1 provides the three forms of the singular definite article, **il, lo,** and **l',** which you use with singular masculine nouns. It also presents the two forms of the masculine plural definite article, **i** and **gli,** which you use with plural masculine nouns.

Table 2-1	Masculine Definite Articles			
Placement	*Singular*	*Singular Examples*	*Plural*	*Plural Examples*
Before most single consonants	il	**il gioco** (*the game*), **il senatore** (*the senator*), **il treno** (*the train*)	i	**i giochi** (*the games*), **i senatori** (*the senators*), **i treni** (*the trains*)

Placement	Singular	Singular Examples	Plural	Plural Examples
Before **gn-**, **pn-**, **ps-**, **s** + another consonant, **x-**, **y-**, and **z-**	**lo**	**lo gnocco** (*the dumpling*), **lo pneumatico** (*the car tire*), **lo psicologo** (*the psychologist*), **lo spettro** (*the ghost*), **lo yogurt** (*the yogurt*), **lo zaino** (*the backpack*)	**gli**	**gli gnocchi** (*the dumplings*), **gli pneumatici** (*the car tires*), **gli psicologi** (*the psychologists*), **gli spettri** (*the ghosts*), **gli yogurt** (*the yogurts*), **gli zaini** (*the backpacks*)
Before any vowel	**l'**	**l'uomo** (*the man*), **l'ufficio** (*the office*)	**gli**	**gli uomini** (*the men/human beings*), **gli uffici** (*the offices*)

Table 2-2 lists the two forms of the definite article used with singular feminine nouns, **la** and **l'**, as well as the plural feminine article, which has only one form: **le.**

Table 2-2   **Feminine Definite Articles**

Placement	Singular	Singular Examples	Plural	Plural Examples
Before any consonant or group of consonants	**la**	**la casa** (*the house*), **la trappola** (*the trap*)	**le**	**le case** (*the houses*), **le trappole** (*the traps*)
Before any vowel	**l'**	**l'anima** (*the soul*), **l'ora** (*the hour*)	**le**	**le anime** (*the souls*), **le ore** (*the hours*)

Book III

Grasping Basic Grammar Essentials for Communication

The feminine **l'** is the same as **la** but with the **-a** replaced by an apostrophe. Likewise, the masculine **l'** is the same as **lo** but with the **-o** replaced by an apostrophe.

In Italian, the definite article can play the role the possessive adjective plays in English, as in **Cerco la borsa** (*I'm looking for my handbag*).

Indefinite articles: Saying "a" or "an"

Besides the definite article, Italian uses the indefinite articles **un, un', una,** and **uno,** which correspond to the English *a* or *an*. Because **un** means *one,* you can use it only with singular nouns, as in **una villa** (*a villa*) or **un paese** (*a village*). Table 2-3 lays out the forms of the indefinite article used with singular masculine nouns, and Table 2-4 does the same for the feminine article.

Table 2-3	Masculine Indefinite Articles	
Article	*Placement*	*Examples*
un	Before any vowel or consonant and most groups of consonants	**un ufficio** (*an office*), **un uomo** (*a man*), **un treno** (*a train*)
uno	Before **gn-, pn-, ps-, s** + another consonant, **x-, y-,** and **z-**	**uno gnocco** (*a dumpling*), **uno pneumatico** (*a car tire*), **uno psicologo** (*a psychologist*), **uno studente** (*a student*), **uno xilofono** (*a xylophone*), **uno yogurt** (*a yogurt*), **uno zaino** (*a backpack*)

Table 2-4	Feminine Indefinite Articles	
Article	*Placement*	*Examples*
una	Before any consonant or group of consonants	**una casa** (*a house*), **una trappola** (*a trap*), **una strega** (*a witch*)
un'	Before any vowel	**un'amica** (*a girlfriend*), **un'ora** (*an hour*)

Distinguishing between Masculine and Feminine Nouns

In most Indo-European languages (the family to which both Italian and English belong), nouns have a gender. In Italian, you deal with only two genders: masculine and feminine. Other parts of speech have a gender as well, and as you progress through this book, you discover how to match these other words to the gender of the noun.

This section focuses on nouns, discussing what word endings tell you about gender and which words can and should undergo a gender change.

Recognizing common noun endings

In Italian, most nouns are masculine or feminine. Grammatically, their endings in the singular help you figure out to which gender they belong. Masculine nouns often end in **-o** or a consonant, if it's a foreign word, as in these examples:

- **-o:** **letto** (*bed*), **libro** (*book*), **giorno** (*day*), **gatto** (*male cat*), **buco** (*hole*)
- A consonant: **autobus** (*bus*), **sport** (*sport*), **bar** (*bar*), **chef** (*chef; cook*), **zar** (*czar*)

However, some nouns ending in **-o** are feminine, such as **auto** (*automobile*), **radio** (*radio*), **mano** (*hand*), and **moto** (*motorbike*). So are some foreign words, especially when they translate an Italian word that has the same meaning, such as **star dello spettacolo** (*show business star*).

Feminine nouns often end in

- **-a:** **barca** (*boat*), **ora** (*hour*), **pianta** (*plant, tree*)
- **-i:** **analisi** (*analysis*), **crisi** (*crisis*), **tesi** (*thesis*), **diagnosi** (*diagnosis*)
- **-tà** or **-tù:** **bontà** (*goodness*), **virtù** (*virtue*), **verità** (*truth*)

Some nouns ending in **-a** are masculine because they derive from classical Greek, such as **problema** (*problem*), **tema** (*theme*), and **programma** (*program*).

Book III

Grasping Basic Grammar Essentials for Communication

Some words have a masculine and a feminine version, with different meanings. For example, **il buco** (*hole*), **la buca** (*pit; hole in golf*); **il foglio** (*sheet of paper*), **la foglia** (*leaf*); **il fine** (*aim; goal*), **la fine** (*end*); **il capitale** (*financial capital*), **la capitale** (*capital city*).

Both masculine and feminine nouns can end in **-e;** the only general rule is that usually words ending in **-ione** are feminine, as in **direzione** (*direction*) or **spiegazione** (*explanation*), while words ending in **-ore** are masculine, as in **direttore** (*director*) or **produttore** (*producer*). For the rest, no specific rule exists — for example, **sole** (*sun*) is masculine, but **notte** (*night*) is feminine — so just have a dictionary on hand until you're more familiar with noun gender.

Sorting nouns into classes

When it comes to gender, you find three classes of nouns in Italian:

- **Nouns that are gender-specific:** If the individual in question is male, you use one word — **il padre** (*father*) — if it's female, use another word — **la madre** (*mother*).

- **Nouns that can move from masculine to feminine:** The masculine is the default gender, so you tend to look up a noun in the masculine and then see whether you make a feminine noun out of it — for example, **lo zio** (*uncle*) becomes **la zia** (*aunt*). In real life, of course, you may encounter a noun in the feminine first and then wonder whether it has a masculine version. It usually does, but the masculine may be really different from the feminine; for example, **la dottoressa** (*female doctor/graduate*) doesn't become il dottoresso but rather **il dottore** (*male doctor/graduate*).

- **Nouns that are used for males and females but don't change:** La guida (*guide*) is feminine, but it's used for men, too; **il soprano** (*soprano*) is masculine, but it's used for women.

Gender-specific nouns

Some nouns are gender-specific — that is, you use different words to refer to masculine and feminine variations of the noun. See Table 2-5 for a sampling of these nouns.

Table 2-5   Nouns that Indicate the Gender of the Individual

Masculine Noun	Feminine Noun
il padre (*father*)	**la madre** (*mother*)
il papà (*dad*)	**la mamma** (*mom*)
il fratello (*brother*)	**la sorella** (*sister*)

Masculine Noun	Feminine Noun
il marito (*husband*)	**la moglie** (*wife*)
il genero (*son-in-law*)	**la nuora** (*daughter-in-law*)
l'uomo (*man*)	**la donna** (*woman*)
il porco (*pig; boar*)	**la scrofa** (*sow*)
il toro (*bull*)	**la mucca** (*cow*)

Universal nouns that switch gender

For nouns that aren't gender-specific, you take the masculine noun and change either the article alone or the article and the ending to make the noun feminine. This change can play out in several ways, depending on the spelling of the masculine noun. Table 2-6 breaks down the possibilities.

Table 2-6	Making Masculine Nouns Feminine		
Masculine	**Ending Change**	**Masculine Noun**	**Feminine Noun**
-o	Change **-o** to **-a**	**l'amico** (*friend*), **il figlio** (*son*), **lo zio** (*uncle*), **il lupo** (*male wolf*)	**l'amica** (*friend*), **la figlia** (*daughter*), **la zia** (*aunt*), **la lupa** (*female wolf*)
-ista, -cida, sometimes **-e**	None; only article changes	**il giornalista** (*male journalist*), **l'omicida** (*male killer*), **il nipote** (*grandson; nephew*)	**la giornalista** (*female journalist*), **l'omicida** (*female killer*), **la nipote** (*granddaughter; niece*)
-tore	Change **-tore** to **-trice**	**l'imperatore** (*emperor*), **l'attore** (*actor*), **il pittore** (*male painter*)	**l'imperatrice** (*empress*), **l'attrice** (*actress*), **la pittrice** (*female painter*)
-e (many professions; animals)	Change **-e** to **-essa**	**il principe** (*prince*), **lo studente** (*male student*), **il leone** (*lion*), **l'elefante** (*male elephant*)	**la principessa** (*princess*), **la studentessa** (*female student*), **la leonessa** (*lioness*), **l'elefantessa** (*female elephant*)

Book III

Grasping Basic Grammar Essentials for Communication

Some names of professions or people's titles change the final **-e** to **-a,** such as **il cameriere** (*waiter*), **la cameriera** (*waitress*), **il signore** (*gentleman; Sir*), and **la signora** (*lady; Madam; Ms.*). There's neither rhyme nor reason to why these nouns take **-a** instead of **-essa,** except, perhaps, ease of pronunciation — camerieressa sounds horrible.

And newly invented words take either **-essa** or **-a,** like **l'avvocato** (*male lawyer*), **l'avvocatessa** (*female lawyer*), **l'architetto** (*male architect*), and **l'architetta** (*female architect*). How do you know whether a word is new? Practice and a dictionary.

Nouns used for both males and females

Some masculine nouns can refer to females, and some feminine nouns can refer to males. Nouns that are always masculine, regardless of the gender of the animal or person described include **il pavone** (*peacock*), **il serpente** (*snake*), and **il cicerone** (*tour guide*).

Some nouns that are always feminine, regardless of the gender of the animal or person described, are **la tigre** (*tiger*), **la volpe** (*fox*), and **la spia** (*spy*).

To distinguish between male and female animals, add the words **maschio** (*male*) and **femmina** (*female*) to the basic noun:

- **la volpe maschio** (*male fox*)
- **la volpe femmina** (*female fox*)
- **il serpente maschio** (*male snake*)
- **il serpente femmina** (*female snake*)

Moving from Singular to Plural: Basic Rules

As in English, Italian nouns can become plural by changing the ending, and the plural of nouns varies depending on the ending of the singular. Table 2-7 illustrates the regular patterns.

Table 2-7	Regular Plural Noun Endings		
Masculine Singular	**Masculine Plural**	**Feminine Singular**	**Feminine Plural**
-o: gatto (*cat*)	**-i: gatti** (*cats*)	**-a: casa** (*house; home*)	**-e: case** (*houses; homes*)
-e: pesce (*fish*)	**-i: pesci** (*fish[es]*)	**-e: chiave** (*key*)	**-i: chiavi** (*keys*)
-a: problema (*problem*)	**-i: problemi** (*problems*)		

Plural and singular nouns share some of the same endings, so it may be difficult to tell the number and gender of a noun such as **sere;** after all, **-e** is an ending for feminine plural nouns, masculine singular nouns, and feminine singular nouns. If the noun comes with the article, you know at once: **Le sere** is the feminine plural of **la sera** (*evening*). If the context doesn't help you, consult a dictionary (check out Appendix B for an Italian-English mini-dictionary). Dictionaries list nouns in their default form, usually the masculine singular form. You can use trial and error until you find the right noun.

Some nouns have both a masculine and a feminine plural, but there's no rule establishing which meaning is associated with which gender. You pick up on these variations as you encounter them in context. Here are some examples:

Singular	*Masculine Plural*	*Feminine Plural*
il braccio	**i bracci** (*wings; branches*)	**le braccia** (*body arms*)
il membro	**i membri** (*members*)	**le membra** (*limbs*)
l'osso	**gli ossi** (*animal bones*)	**le ossa** (*human bones*)

Book III

Grasping Basic Grammar Essentials for Communication

Making Exceptions to the Basic Rules on Number

With language, nothing's ever quite as simple as it may seem. When you get a rule or pattern, you have to accept the fact that languages can't be rationalized beyond a certain point. This section contains the many exceptions to those rules related to nouns and number.

Changing more than just the ending

Some groups of nouns don't change only the last vowel when you turn them into the plural but rather the entire last syllable. Other nouns switch genders. Check out the following rules:

- Nouns ending in **-co, -go, -ca,** and **-ga,** which have a hard sound in the singular, add an **h** before the suffix of the plural to preserve it. See these examples:

cuoco (*cook*)	**cuochi** (*cooks*)
fungo (*mushroom*)	**funghi** (*mushrooms*)
barca (*boat*)	**barche** (*boats*)
strega (*witch*)	**streghe** (*witches*)

  The most important words that are exceptions to this rule are **medico** (*physician*), **medici** (*physicians*); **amico** (*friend*), **amici** (*friends*); and **nemico** (*enemy*), **nemici** (*enemies*). However, the feminine versions — **amica** (*girlfriend*) and **nemica** (*female enemy*) — do become **amiche** (*girlfriends*) and **nemiche** (*female enemies*). Other words, such as **chirurgo** (*surgeon*), **chirurghi/chirurgi** (*surgeons*) and **stomaco** (*stomach*), **stomachi/stomaci** (*stomachs*), can have either ending.

- Nouns ending in **-cia** or **-gia** accented on a syllable that isn't the last one add **-e** if the last syllable is preceded by a consonant, and they add **-ie** if the last syllable is preceded by a vowel. For example:

provincia (*province*)	**province** (*provinces*)
spiaggia (*beach*)	**spiagge** (*beaches*)
camicia (*shirt*)	**camicie** (*shirts*)
valigia (*suitcase*)	**valigie** (*suitcases*)

  Nouns that end in **-cìa** or **-gìa,** accented on the **ì,** form the plural by adding **-ie,** for example **allergia** (*allergy*) becomes **allergie** (*allergies*). However, be aware that the accent isn't marked in Italian, so you have to figure out which nouns are accented on the **i** as you go along.

- Nouns ending in **-io** take **-ii** in the plural if the accent falls on the **ì** and take only **-i** if the accent falls on a preceding syllable (the accent isn't marked). Here are a couple examples:

pendio (*slope*)	**pendii** (*slopes*)
viaggio (*trip*)	**viaggi** (*trips*)

  If nouns end in **-ia,** the plural is regular; for example, **biglia** (*pinball*) becomes **biglie** (*pinballs*).

✔ Some nouns change gender from the singular to the plural. The following words are among the most frequently used:

il dito (*finger; toe*)	**le dita** (*fingers; toes*)
l'uovo (*egg*)	**le uova** (*eggs*)
il ginocchio (*knee*)	**le ginocchia** (*knees*)
il braccio (*arm*)	**le braccia** (*arms*)

Changing only the article

Some nouns are *invariable,* so you need to check the article to find out whether they're used in the singular or in the plural form. Some common examples include the following:

✔ Masculine nouns: **cinema, brindisi, caffè, film, re**

✔ Feminine nouns: **radio, metropoli, città, serie, gru, virtù, novità, possibilità**

Using nouns only in the singular or the plural

Book III

Grasping Basic Grammar Essentials for Communication

You can use some nouns only in the singular or only in the plural. Following are some categories of singular nouns, along with some examples:

✔ Abstractions: **il coraggio** (*courage*), **la fede** (*faith*)

✔ Chemical elements and metals: **l'oro** (*gold*), **il rame** (*copper*)

✔ Some festivities: **il Natale** (*Christmas*), **la Pasqua** (*Easter*)

✔ Foods: **il grano** (*wheat*), **il vino** (*wine*), **l'acqua** (*water*), **il latte** (*milk*)

✔ Nouns such as **la fame** (*hunger*), **la sete** (*thirst*), **il sangue** (*blood*)

When used in the plural, nouns such as **i vini** and **le acque minerali** mean *kinds of wine* and *kinds of mineral water,* respectively; **le fedi** means *confessions.*

Following are some categories of nouns used in the plural, along with some examples:

✔ Objects that come in pairs (often preceded by **un paio di . . .** [*a pair of . . .*]): **i pantaloni/un paio di pantaloni** (*trousers/a pair of trousers*), **gli occhiali/un paio di occhiali** (*eyeglasses/a pair of eyeglasses*), **le forbici/ un paio di forbici** (*scissors/a pair of scissors*)

✔ Sets: **i piatti** (*dishes*), **gli spiccioli** (*coins; change*), **le dimissioni** (*resignation*)

✔ Nouns that come in the plural from Latin: **le nozze** (*nuptials*), **le ferie** (*paid vacation days*), **le tenebre** (*darkness*)

Deciding When to Include an Article

When you're confident in your knowledge of nouns as they relate to gender and number, you can move on to when and how to use articles and nouns together. Deciding when to use the indefinite article is easier because people use it in similar ways in English and Italian. Also, all you need to know is that you're singling out one item among many; for example, **Un cane abbaia** (*A dog is barking*).

Becoming confident in using the definite article is more challenging than choosing when to use the indefinite. The following sections indicate the instances when the use of each type of article is correct and the few when it's definitely incorrect.

When (and when not) to use a definite article

Deciding when and when not to use the definite article is a tricky topic in both Italian and English. One rule of thumb is that Italian uses the definite article much more than English. For example, Italian uses articles before foods (**il pane** [*bread*], **la mela** [*apple*]), before body parts (**il braccio** [*arm*] **le dita** [*finger*]), before dates (**il 25 aprile** [*April 25*]), before titles (**il professor Baldini** [*Professor Baldini*]), and before abstract nouns (**la forza** [*strength*]). It also uses the article before possessive adjectives (**la mia borsa** [*my handbag*]) and family members when referred to in the plural (**le mie sorelle** [*my sisters*]).

People

You use Italian articles when referring to a professional (**il dott. Cecconi**) or before a female name to express affection and familiarity (**la Elena**), but not when addressing someone directly. For example, you use the article when you say **Ho visto il dott. Cecconi martedì sera** (*I saw Dr. Cecconi on Tuesday evening*), but you don't use it when you say **Buon giorno, dott. Cecconi** (*Good morning, Dr. Cecconi*).

Places

You use the Italian definite article with the following geographical features:

- ✔ Mountains, rivers, and lakes: **le Alpi** (*the Alps*), **il Monte Bianco** (*Mont Blanc*), **il Po** (*the Po River*), **il (lago di) Garda** (*Lake Garda*), **il lago Michigan** (*Lake Michigan*)

- ✔ Many large islands and archipelagos: **la Sicilia** (*Sicily*), **l'Inghilterra** (*England*), **le Bahamas** (*the Bahamas*); but skip the article for **Long Island** (*Long Island*) and **Cuba** (*Cuba*)

- ✔ Regions and states: **il Lazio** (*the Lazio region*), **la Puglia** (*Apulia*), **la California** (*California*)

- ✔ Nations (singular or plural) and continents: **l'Italia** (*Italy*), **gli Stati Uniti** (*the United States*), **l'Asia** (*Asia*)

Italian doesn't use the definite article before names of cities and most small islands: **Bologna, Roma** (*Rome*), **New York, Capri, Malta.**

The rules for articles change when using prepositions and idiomatic expressions. With idiomatic usage, you don't use an article with a preposition unless the object of the preposition is modified and the preposition is contracted. For example, you don't use an article when you say **Vado in Italia** (*I'm going to Italy*), but you do use an article when you say **Vado nell'Italia centrale** (*I'm going to central Italy*).

Things

Use the definite article with the following things:

- ✔ Countable plural nouns: **Le scimmie e le mucche sono mammiferi** (Literally: *Monkeys and cows are mammals*).

- ✔ Uncountable nouns: **il sale** (*salt*), **lo zucchero** (*sugar*), **l'acqua** (*water*).

  In English, uncountable nouns take the definite article only when you mean a type of or a portion of something, as in **Mi passi il sale, per favore?** (*Can I have the salt, please?*); but when you talk (in English) about salt, sugar, water, and so on in general, you use neither the definite nor the indefinite article. In Italian, you have to use the definite article.

- ✔ Possessive adjectives and pronouns: **La nostra macchina è rossa** (*Our car is red*); **La macchina rossa è la nostra** (*The red car is ours*).

- ✔ Firms, institutions, and clubs: **la General Motors** (*General Motors*), **la Chiesa** (*the Church*), **la Roma** (*Roma Football Club*).

- ✔ Abstractions: **La tolleranza è fondamentale in democrazia** (*Toleration is fundamental in democracies*).

Book III

Grasping Basic Grammar Essentials for Communication

When (and when not) to use an indefinite article

Although Italian uses the indefinite article much the same as English does, in some situations where an indefinite article is appropriate in English, Italian leaves it out. Consider the following situations where you'd leave out the indefinite article:

✔ When using a noun as a qualifier of the subject after the verbs **essere** (*to be*): **Mia madre è vedova** (*My mother is a widow*); **Suo fratello è medico** (*Her brother is a physician*).

✔ In exclamations introduced by **che** and **quanto** (*how*): **Che uomo coraggioso!** (*What a courageous man!*)

Chapter 3

All about Pronouns

*I*talian has many types of pronouns, each with a special function. Most pronouns replace people, places, concepts, and quantities that have already been mentioned. *Subject pronouns* don't replace anything but rather convey who's performing the action. Italian uses pronouns often because they allow you to avoid repetition and shorten sentences.

Understanding and using Italian pronouns is challenging because they vary so much in form, position, and function, but they're indispensable, so you need to work through the tough stuff. This chapter presents the various pronouns and the functions they perform. They can be

✔ Subject pronouns, as in **<u>Io</u> ho telefonato a Giovanna** (*I called Giovanna*)

✔ Stressed pronouns, as in **Non credo di andare al cinema con <u>lei</u>** (*I don't think I'll go to the movies with her*)

✔ Direct object pronouns, as in **<u>Li</u> ha già ordinati** (*She already ordered them*)

✔ Indirect objects pronouns, as in **<u>Le</u> ho detto che ero stanca** (*I told her that I was tired*)

This chapter also covers two other pronouns that perform a lot of functions in Italian: **ci** (*here; there; about this/that; of this/that; on this/that*) and **ne** (*of/ about it/him/her/them/this/that*). You also may use another set of pronouns, called *reflexive pronouns,* when the object of the sentence is the same as the subject. In English, it's translated with *myself, yourself,* and so on. Reflexive pronouns don't substitute already mentioned concepts, but they're conjugated directly with the verbs.

In most cases, Italian and English use pronouns in similar ways, but they also have some differences:

- **Italian uses subject pronouns much less than English.** In Italian, you can omit subject pronouns because the verb conjugation indicates the person performing the action.

- **Italian has several sets of pronouns.** Even when they perform the same function, the object pronouns may change in form, depending on where they're placed in the sentence.

- **Italian conveys a direct object or the pronoun <u>ne</u> and an indirect object together by forming double pronouns.** The indirect object pronoun always precedes the direct object pronoun or **ne.** Remember to change the indirect object pronouns **mi, ti, ci,** and **vi** into **me, te, ce,** and **ve.**

Meeting the Subject Pronouns

Grammatically speaking, six persons can perform an action: the first, second, and third persons, singular and plural. But there are more pronouns than persons because the third person differentiates among masculine, feminine, and neuter (it) forms.

Table 3-1 lists the subject pronouns. *Note:* In Italian, when animals are seen as possessing feelings and even a personality, you use pronouns once reserved for human beings: **lui** (*he*), **lei** (*she*), and **loro** (*they*).

Table 3-1	Subject Pronouns	
Person	*Singular*	*Plural*
First	**io** (*I*)	**noi** (*we*)
Second	**tu** (*you*)	**voi** (*you*)
Third	**lui** (*he*), **lei** (*she*)	**loro** (*they*)
Third (used to address people formally)	**Lei** (*you*)	**Loro** (*you*)

The traditional subject pronouns for people are **egli** (*he*), **ella** (*she*), and **essi/esse** (*they*). You may find them used in older writings and formal settings. Today, the third person pronouns **lui, lei,** and **loro** are used as pronouns.

The following sections show you when to use subject pronouns and how to use them informally and formally.

Knowing when to use subject pronouns

Most of the time, you don't use subject pronouns in Italian because the verb conjugations indicate the subject. In the sentence **Guardano la televisione tutte le sere** (*They watch TV every night*), you know the subject is **loro** (*they*) because **guardano** is conjugated in the third person plural form. (See verb conjugation details in Book IV.)

At times, you do need subject pronouns, such as when you're

- Emphasizing what a particular person is doing: **Io darò le dimissioni** (*I'm going to resign*).

- Emphasizing one subject over another (often inverting the word order): **Decido io, non tu, a che ora devi tornare a casa!** (*I'm the one who decides what time you must come home, not you!*)

- Forming a sentence that may generate confusion about the subject: **Lui capisce cose che io non capisco** (*He understands things that I don't understand*).

Adapting subject pronouns for informal and formal usage

You can address people informally or formally in Italian, altering your pronoun and verb choice accordingly:

- Informally, you address people with the following pronoun-verb combinations:
  - **tu** (*you* [singular]) + the verb in the second person singular: **[Tu] vieni alla partita, Andrea?** (*Are you coming to the game, Andrea?*)
  - **voi** (*you* [plural]) + the verb in the second person plural: **[Voi] venite alla partita, Andrea e Giacomo?** (*Are you coming to the game, Andrea and Giacomo?*)

- Formally, you address people with the following pronoun-verb combinations:

- **Lei** (*you*) with either a man or a woman + the verb in the third person singular: **[Lei] viene alla partita, Signore/Signora?** (*Are you coming to the game, Sir/Madam?*)

- **Loro** (*you*) + the verb in third person plural: **[Loro] vengono alla partita, Signori/Signore/Signori e Signore?** (*Are you coming to the game, Ladies/Gentlemen/Ladies and Gentlemen?*)

✔ Nowadays you can use **voi** (*you* [plural]) to address more than one person informally or formally, as in **[Voi] venite alla partita, Signori/Signore/Signori e Signore?** (*Are you coming to the soccer game, Ladies/Gentlemen/Ladies and Gentlemen?*)

When you address someone formally, you use his or her last name preceded by **Signor** (*Mr.*), **Signora** (*Mrs., Ms.*), **Signorina** (*Miss, Ms.*), **Dottor/Dottoressa** (*Dr.* for all those with a **laurea** or *university degree*), **Ingegner** (*Engineer*), **Avvocato** (*Counselor*), and so on with specific professional titles.

Emphasizing Stressed Pronouns

Stressed pronouns are most often placed after a preposition, as in **Vieni con me al mercato!** (*Come to the market with me!*) But you also can use them directly after a verb without a preposition for emphasis, as in **La mamma vuole te!** (*Mom wants you!*) At this stage, to make your life simpler, use the stressed pronoun only when you have a preposition. For example, **Qualcuno ha lasciato un messaggio per te** (*Someone left a message for you*).

Table 3-2 demonstrates the forms of the stressed pronouns. As you can see, the only forms that change from the subject pronouns listed earlier in this chapter are the forms for **io** (**me**) and **tu** (**te**). Although only four prepositions are shown here, you can combine any preposition with a stressed pronoun.

Table 3-2	Stressed Pronouns
Pronouns	*Translation*
me (*me*)	**a/con/di/per me** (*to/with/about/for me*)
te (*you* [singular, informal])	**a/con/di/per te** (*to/with/about/for you*)
lui (*him*), **lei** (*her*)	**a/con/di/per lui/lei** (*to/with/about/for him/her/it*)
Lei (*you* [singular, formal])	**a/con/di/per Lei** (*to/with/about/for you*)
noi (*us*)	**a/con/di/per noi** (*to/with/about/for us*)
voi (*you* [plural, informal])	**a/con/di/per voi** (*to/with/about/for you*)
loro (*them*)	**a/con/di/per loro** (*to/with/about/for them*)
Loro (*you* [plural, formal])	**a/con/di/per Loro** (*to/with/about/for you*)

Digging into Direct Object Pronouns

Whereas subject pronouns are sometimes optional, object pronouns aren't. You rely on object pronouns to replace objects or people who are recipients of that action — nice and straightforward. The following sections tell you more.

What direct object pronouns are and what they do

Here are a few key points about direct objects and direct object pronouns:

✔ Direct objects follow transitive verbs and are called such because the action affects the object directly, as in **Vedo Angela** (*I see Angela*). If you replace **Angela** with a pronoun, the sentence becomes **La vedo** (*I see her*).

✔ Direct object pronouns usually answer the questions *who?* or *what?* When you can answer those questions, you can replace the answer (the direct object) with a pronoun. For example, **Leggo il giornale la domenica** (*I read the paper on Sunday*): What do I read? The paper. **Lo leggo** (*I read it*).

Here's another example: **Ho invitato i nostri amici a cena** (*I invited our friends to dinner*). Who? Our friends. **Li ho invitati a cena** (*I invited them to dinner*).

✔ Direct object pronouns can replace people, animals, things, and abstractions. For example, **Il ragazzo accarezza il cucciolo** (*The boy is petting the puppy*); **[Lo] L'accarezza** (*He is petting it*). **Quell'uomo ha perso la libertà** (*That man lost his freedom*); **L'ha persa** (*He lost it*).

Table 3-3 shows the direct object pronouns.

Table 3-3	Direct Object Pronouns
Singular	*Plural*
mi (*me*)	**ci** (*us*)
ti (*you* [informal])	**vi** (*you* [informal])
lo (*him*)	**li/le** (*them*)
la (*her*)	**Li/Le** (*you* [formal])
lo/la (*it*)	
La (*you* [formal])	

__Book III__

__Grasping Basic Grammar Essentials for Communication__

When you address someone formally in speech or writing, you use the direct object pronouns **La** (*you* [singular]) for a man or a woman, **Li** (*you* [plural]) for a group of men, **Le** for a group of women, or **Li** for a group of men and women:

> **Signore/Signora, La ringrazio di essere venuto/a.** (*Sir/Madam, thank you for coming.*)

> **Signori/Signore e Signori, Li ringrazio di essere venuti/e.** (*Gentlemen/ Ladies and Gentlemen, thank you for coming.*)

> **Signore, Le ringrazio di essere venute.** (*Ladies, thank you for coming.*)

In everyday life, the **voi** (*you* [plural]) form is much more commonly used (formally or informally), which simplifies things considerably. For example, **Signore e Signori, Vi ringrazio di essere venuti** (*Ladies and Gentlemen, thank you for coming*).

Where to place direct object pronouns

Placement of the direct object pronoun varies according to the verb form:

✔ The direct object pronoun often precedes the conjugated verb: **Quel ragazzo non dice mai la verità** (*That boy doesn't ever tell the truth*); **Non la dice mai** (*He never tells it*).

✔ If the verb is in the infinitive, imperative, or gerund form, you attach the pronoun to the verb. When attached to the infinitive, the final **-e** is dropped.

  • Infinitive: **Ti piacerebbe comprare la borsa? Sì, mi piacerebbe comprarla** (*Would you like to buy the purse? Yes, I would like to buy it*).

  • Imperative: **Porta i bambini al mare!** (*Take the children to the beach!*) **Portali al mare!** (*Take them to the beach!*)

  • Gerund: **Avendoli preparati (i panini), li ho portati al mare** (*Having made the sandwiches, I took them to the beach*).

✔ When using the direct object pronouns **lo** and **la** before a verb that begins with a vowel, you can drop **-o** or **-a** and replace it with an apostrophe (**l'**), or you can keep them as they are, as in **Bianca lo/l'aspetta** (*Bianca's waiting for him*).

When using a direct object pronoun with a compound tense (see Book V for details), the past participle agrees in gender and number with the pronoun. Here are some examples:

> **Hanno ricevuto la lettera? No, non (la) l'hanno ancora ricevuta.** (*Did they receive the letter? No, they didn't receive it yet.*)

> **Avete fatto i compiti? Li abbiamo fatti!** (*Did you do your homework? We did [it]!*)

Investigating Indirect Object Pronouns

Indirect object pronouns refer to living beings. They're used with transitive verbs and answer the question **a chi?** (*to whom?*) Prepositions used with indirect objects can include **a/per/con** (*to/for/with*) + a person or animal; see these examples:

> **Scrivo a mia madre ogni giorno** (*I write to my mother every day*) becomes **Le scrivo ogni giorno** (*I write to her every day*).

> **Telefono a Luigi una volta alla settimana** (*I call Luigi once a week*) becomes **Gli telefono una volta alla settimana** (*I call him once a week*).

Table 3-4 lists the indirect object pronouns that you generally place before the verb or attach to it when the verb is an infinitive, an imperative, or a gerund. *Note:* The **loro** form always follows the verb, as in **Ho detto loro quello che pensavo** (*I told them what I was thinking*).

Table 3-4	Indirect Object Pronouns
Singular	*Plural*
mi (*to/for me*)	**ci** (*to/for us*)
ti (*to/for you* [informal])	**vi** (*to/for you* [informal])
gli (*to/for him*)	**gli** (or **loro** after the verb with or without a preposition) (*to/for them*)
le (*to/for her*)	**gli** (or **Loro** after the verb with or without a preposition) (*you* [formal])
Le (*to/for you* [formal])	

Note the following nuances of the indirect object pronouns:

✔ In the third person plural form, you use **gli** for both masculine and feminine forms. **Compro un regalo per le mie figlie** (*I'm buying a gift for my daughters*) becomes **Gli compro un regalo** (*I'm buying a gift for them*). You also can use **gli** for only males or male and female combined, as in **Cosa regali ai nonni per Natale? Gli regalo una radio** (*What are you giving our grandparents for Christmas? I'm giving them a radio*).

✔ When you address people formally, you use the **Le** form in the third person singular for both male and female, as in **Signore/Signora, Le apro io la porta** (*Sir/Madam, I'll open the door for you*).

✔ Note that the third person plural form has two options that mean the same thing. The **gli** form is used more frequently in modern spoken Italian, although the **loro** form is still acceptable. In the plural, you may use the pronoun **Loro** after the verb with or without a preposition, as in **Signori/Signore/Signore e Signori, apro Loro la porta/apro la porta per Loro** (*Gentlemen/Ladies/Ladies and Gentlemen, I'll open the door for you*).

Contrary to the rules of direct object pronouns earlier in this chapter, the past participle in compound tenses doesn't agree in gender and number with the indirect object pronoun. Rather, the past participle remains unchanged; see this example:

Avete telefonato ad Adriana? No, non le abbiamo telefonato. (*Did you call Adriana? No, we didn't call her.*)

Forming Double Pronouns

Italians say things quickly and take for granted that the listener understands what they're talking about after they've mentioned something once. The language accommodates this through double pronouns, which, like the other pronouns covered in this chapter, are placed either before the verb or attached to the infinitive, imperative, or gerund. You form double pronouns by combining the indirect object pronouns (**mi, ti, gli, le, ci, vi,** and **gli**) with the direct object pronouns, usually in the third person singular and plural (**lo, la, li,** and **le**). You use double pronouns when you want to convey both a direct object and an indirect object together.

When combining **gli** + **lo, la, li** or **le,** you connect them with an **e: glielo, gliela, glieli, gliele.**

The following sections show you how to replace direct and indirect object pronouns and provide some common double pronouns.

Figuring out how to replace direct and indirect object pronouns

The following examples show how to replace the direct object and the indirect object with pronouns. In the sentence **Regalo un libro al bambino** (*I give a book to the little boy*), **un libro** (*a book*) is the direct object, and **al bambino** (*to the little boy*) is the indirect object. Here's how to recast this sentence, combining the direct and indirect object pronouns:

- ✓ Replace **al bambino** with the indirect object pronoun **gli: Gli regalo un libro** (*I give him a book*).

- ✓ Replace **un libro** with the direct object pronoun **lo: Lo regalo al bambino** (*I give it to the little boy*).

- ✓ Combine the two object pronouns, starting with the indirect object pronoun followed by the direct object pronoun: **Glielo** is the combination of **gli** meaning *to him* and **lo** meaning *the book,* so you get **Glielo regalo** (*I give it to him*).

REMEMBER

When combining the two object pronouns in the third person, the indirect object pronoun is always **gli** even if the translation is *to her.* You know that the pronoun **le** means *to her,* but when combining pronouns, the indirect object pronoun will always be **gli.** In the same example **Regalo un libro al bambino,** substitute **al bambino** with **alla bambina.** Watch the transformation: Replace **alla bambina** with the indirect object pronoun **gli** (not **le**), and replace the direct object pronoun with **lo.** The combination is the same: **Glielo regalo.**

When using the combined pronouns and a compound tense, the past participle agrees in gender and number with the direct object pronoun. For example, **Ho regalato una bicicletta alla bambina** (*I gave a bicycle to the little girl*) becomes **Gliel'ho regalata** (*I gave it to her*). When **lo** and **la** precede the verb **avere** (*to have*), you can drop the vowel and replace it with an apostrophe, or you can keep them as they are.

When using double pronouns with the imperative, one-syllable commands (**da', fa', sta', di',** and **va'**) followed by a direct, indirect, or combined pronoun, double the initial consonant of the pronoun attached. For example, **Da' il conto a me!** becomes **Dammelo!** (*Give the bill to me!*)

Checking out common double pronouns

Table 3-5 lists pronoun combinations. **Mi, ti, ci,** and **vi** change to **me, te, ce,** and **ve** to ease pronunciation, and the third person singular and plural becomes one word.

Table 3-5	Double Pronouns: Indirect + Direct Object Pronouns
Double Pronouns	*Translation*
me lo/la/li/le	*him/her/it/them/ to me*
te lo/la/li/le	*him/her/it/them to you* (singular, informal)
glielo/gliela/glieli/gliele	*him/her/it/them to him/her*
Glielo/Gliela/Glieli/Gliele	*him/her/it/them to you* (singular, formal)
ce lo/la/li/le	*him/her/it/them to us*
ve lo/la/li/le	*him/her/it/them to you* (plural, informal)
glielo/gliela/glieli/gliele	*him/her/it/them to them*
Glielo/Gliela/Glieli/Gliele	*him/her/it/them to you* (plural, formal)

Note that in the third person plural, you can replace **glielo** (in its various forms) with **loro** after the verb. For example, **Lo compro loro** (*I'll buy it for you/them*).

But Wait, There's More! Special Italian Pronouns

Italian has two special pronouns: **ci** (*here; there*) and **ne** (*of this/that/him/ her/them*). They're considered pronouns because they replace prepositional phrases. The pronoun **ci** generally replaces the prepositions **a, in,** and **su** + a place or a thing. **Ne** generally replaces the prepositions **di** and **da** + a person or thing. When used idiomatically, both pronouns can refer to entire sentences or ideas. The following sections give details on each pronoun.

The adverbial pronoun ci

All languages have *homonyms* — that is, words that look and sound alike but have different meanings. For example, *sound* may mean "noise" or "stretch of water." In Italian, the pronoun **ci** is similar: It can mean *us/to us,* but it's also an adverbial pronoun that can mean *here, there.*

For example, if someone says **Sei andato agli Uffizi quest'estate?** (*Did you go to the Uffizi Museum this summer?*), you answer **No, ci sono andato l'estate scorsa** (*No, I went there last summer*). The **ci** stands for **agli Uffizi.**

You can also use **ci** with the verb **essere** (*to be*) to mean *there is/there was* and *there are/there were.* You use the present indicative **c'è** (*there is*), or the imperfect indicative **c'era**, with a noun or name in the singular, and the present indicative **ci sono** (*there are*), or the imperfect indicative **c'erano**, with a noun or name in the plural.

C'è/ci sono also can take the spelling **vi è/vi sono,** although you see that more in literature than in spoken language. However, if you do see **vi è/vi sono,** be careful not to confuse **vi** with the pronoun *you.*

Here are some examples of the adverbial pronouns at work:

> **C'è molta neve in montagna.** (*There's a lot of snow in the mountains.*)

> **C'era una volta una bellissima principessa. . . .** (*Once upon a time, there was a beautiful princess. . . .*)

You also can use **ci** as a pronoun referring to

- ✔ Places already mentioned, with phrases such as **qui/lì** (*here*), **là**, **in quel posto** (*there; in/to that place*), **da/per/attraverso quel posto** (*through there/that place*)

  > **Vieni spesso a Firenze? Sì, ci vengo ogni estate.** (*Do you come to Florence often? Yes, I come here every summer.*)

- ✔ With special verbs having idiomatic meaning, such as **pensarci** (*to think about*), **vederci** (*to see*), **volerci** (*to take; to need*), and **crederci** (*to believe*)

  > **Hai pensato al tuo dilemma? Ci ho pensato.** (*Did you think about your dilemma? I thought about it.*)

Book III

Grasping Basic Grammar Essentials for Communication

The verb **volerci** is conjugated in the third person singular and plural forms, depending on the subject of the sentence. For example, **Ci vogliono tre ore per andare a Roma da qui** (*It takes three hours to get to Rome from here [three hours are needed]*), but **Ci vuole un uovo per questa ricetta** (*You need one egg for this recipe [one egg is necessary]*).

✔ Things or situations already mentioned, with such phrases as **a questo, a quello, a ciò** (*of/about this/that*):

> **Tu credi a quello che ha detto? No, non ci credo.** (*Do you believe what he said? No, I don't believe it.*)

It may help you to think about **ci** like this: When you have a place introduced by the prepositions **a** (*at; to*), **in** (*in*), or **per** (*through*), you can use **ci** to refer to the preposition + noun combination in the sentence that follows. Some examples include the verbs **andare a/in** (*to go to*), **entrare a/in** (*to enter*), **passare per** (and also **di/da**) (*to go through*), **stare a/in** (*to stay at/in*), and others. For example, **Sei mai stato in Croazia? No, non ci sono mai stato** (*Have you ever been to Croatia? No, I've never been there*).

The pronoun ne

Ne (*of this/that/him/them, from this/that place*) is a useful pronoun. It can refer to people, animals, things, individual objects, or entire sentences that have already been mentioned. You place **ne** before the verb or attach it to the verb if it's an infinitive, imperative, or gerund.

Ne means *of this, of them,* and *from there* because it's used with verbs that are always followed by either **di** (*of; about*) or **da** (*by; from*). For example, if someone asks you **Avete fatto delle foto?** (*Did you take some pictures?*), you can answer **Ne abbiamo fatte molte** (*We took many of them*). If someone asks you **Ritorni adesso dal mercato?** (*Are you just now coming back from the market?*), you can answer **Ne ritorno adesso** (*I've just come back [from it]*), although this is unusual, because the verb **ritornare** (*to return; to come back*) can be followed by the preposition **da.** Therefore, when you have a thing or a place introduced by the preposition **di** or **da,** you can use **ne** to refer to the preposition + noun combination.

The following examples further illustrate the use of **ne** with a verb that takes **di** and one that takes **da:**

> **Hai parlato di tua figlia con il medico? Gliene ho parlato.** (*Did you speak to the doctor about your daughter? I spoke to him about her.*)

Quando sei arrivato da Pisa? Ne sono arrivato mezz'ora fa. (*When did you get in from Pisa? I just got here half an hour ago.*)

Verbs with which you commonly see **ne** include **andare via da** (*to go away from; to leave*), **pensare bene/male di** (*to think well/badly of someone*), and **venire da** (*to come from*). For example, **Dov'è Massimo? Si è arrabbiato e se n'è andato** (*Where's Massimo? He got mad and left*).

Ne can replace the following phrases:

- ✔ **di lui** (*of/about him*), **di lei** (*of/about her*), **di loro** (*of/about them*)

- ✔ **da lui** (*by/from him*), **da lei** (*by/from her*), **da loro** (*by/from them*)

- ✔ **di ciò** (*of/about this*), **di questo, da quello** (*of/about this/that*)

- ✔ **da qui** (*from here*), **da lì/da là** (*from there*), **da questo/da quel posto** (*from this/that place*)

A few other uses of **ne** include the following:

- ✔ You can pair **ne** with indirect object pronouns (**mi, ti, le, gli, ci, vi, gli**) to form double pronouns (**me ne, te ne, gliene, ce ne, ve ne, gliene, ne . . . loro**). A sentence such as **Ha parlato a te di quel problema?** (*Did he talk to you about that problem?*) can become **Te ne ha parlato?** (*Did he talk to you about it?*)

- ✔ **Ne** can substitute for words that indicate quantity, such as **molto, parecchio, tanto** (all which mean *a lot*), and **un po' di** (*a little; some*). For example, **Vorresti un po' d'acqua? Ne vorrei proprio un po', grazie** (*Would you like a little water? I'd like just a little, thanks*).

- ✔ **Ne** is used idiomatically when asking the date: **Quanti ne abbiamo oggi?** (*What day of the month is today?*)

When you address someone directly, you don't use **ne** but rather repeat the preposition + personal pronoun construction:

Hai sentito parlare di me? Ho sentito parlare di te. (*Have you heard anything about me? Yes, I have [heard something about you].*)

When **ne** substitutes for a partitive, the past participle agrees in number and gender with the object it replaces, as in **Hanno bevuto tanta birra? Sì, ne hanno bevuta tanta** (*Did they drink a lot of beer? Yes, they drank a lot [of it]*).

Book III

Grasping Basic Grammar Essentials for Communication

When the Subject Is Also the Object: Reflexive Pronouns

Reflexive pronouns convey that the subject is also the recipient of the action, as in **Mi lavo ogni mattina** (*I wash myself every morning*). You use these pronouns with reflexive verbs (see Chapter 3 in Book IV for details). Table 3-6 lists the pronouns.

Table 3-6	Reflexive Pronouns
Singular	*Plural*
mi (*myself*)	**ci** (*ourselves*)
ti (*yourself*)	**vi** (*yourselves* [informal])
si (*himself, herself, itself*)	**si** (*themselves*)
Si (*yourself* [formal])	**Si** (*yourselves*, [formal])

When conjugating a reflexive verb, conjugate it exactly as you would a verb that's not reflexive, but place the reflexive pronoun in front of the conjugated verb:

> **Marco si sveglia ogni mattina alle 6:00 ma non si alza fino alle 6:30. Io mi sveglio alle 6:00 ma mi alzo subito.** (*Marco wakes up every morning at 6:00, but he doesn't get out of bed until 6:30. I wake up every morning at 6:00, but I get up immediately.*)

Chapter 4

Adjectives, Adverbs, and Comparisons

. . . .

In This Chapter

▶ Coordinating nouns and adjectives

▶ Locating the best spots in a sentence for adjectives

▶ Creating adverbs and putting them in the proper spot

▶ Establishing comparisons and rankings

. . . .

If you say **Marina ha una casa grande** (*Marina has a big house*) or **Marina ha una casa piccola** (*Marina has a small house*), all that changes is one word, but you're saying two very different things. **Grande** (*big*) and **piccola** (*small*) are adjectives that convey qualities of people, animals, objects, and situations. In Italian, as in English, you employ adjectives with nouns, names, and pronouns.

Adverbs are a part of speech that helps you describe actions. In both Italian and English, adverbs are invariable, which means that you don't need to match them to the words they modify. You can add an adverb to qualify a verb, an adjective, a noun, a sentence, and even another adverb. For example, if you say **È molto presto** (*It's very early*), you're using two adverbs — **molto** and **presto** — together.

In using adjectives and adverbs, you may want to establish comparisons and rankings between two or more things or people. Consider these examples: **Gianni è alto come Umberto** (*Gianni is as tall as Umberto*); **Pino è il più alto della classe** (*Pino is the tallest in his class*); and **È arrivata più tardi del solito** (*She arrived later than usual*).

This chapter explains the various endings adjectives can have as well as the differences between masculine and feminine, singular and plural adjectives and how to match them to the words they refer to. It also talks about where to place adjectives in the sentence. As for adverbs, this chapter explains the difference between original and derived adverbs and how to form the latter.

It also gives you suggestions for their placement in sentences. The chapter wraps up with coverage of comparatives and superlatives, helping you figure out how to use them to best express yourself.

Matching Adjectives to Nouns in Gender and Number

In Italian, you must match adjectives in gender and number to the nouns they modify. You need a masculine singular adjective with a masculine singular noun, a feminine singular adjective with a feminine singular noun, and so forth. For example, **Maria + bello** → **Maria è bella** (*Maria is beautiful*).

Note: A few adjectives are invariable; they have only one form. See the most important ones in the later section "Invariable adjectives."

When you match an adjective and a noun, you may end up with two words with the same ending, as in **Il cavallo è piccolo** (*The horse is small*), or you may not, as in **Il cavallo è intelligente** (*The horse is smart*). If you check the possible endings of nouns listed in Chapter 2 in Book III and look at the possible endings of adjectives listed in this chapter, you can come up with several combinations. (This is a good exercise for you to practice your mastery of noun-adjective endings and combinations.)

To come up with the right match, you must consider the gender of the noun and then choose the gender of the adjective. For example, if you choose the feminine noun **penna** (*pen*) and the adjective **verde** (*green*), the right combination is **penna verde** (*green pen*); if you choose the noun **quaderno** (*notebook*), which ends in **-o**, and the adjective **verde** (*green*), which ends in **-e**, the right combination is **quaderno verde** (*green notebook*) because the adjective **verde** has one ending for both the masculine and feminine genders.

Adjectives fit into one of three categories, depending on how they change to match a noun's gender and number.

- ✔ **Regular adjectives** vary in their endings depending on gender (masculine or feminine) and/or number (singular or plural). Regular adjectives are clustered in three broad categories:

  - **Those with four endings** (masculine and feminine, singular and plural)

  - **Those with two endings** (singular and plural)

  - **Those with three endings,** one for the singular (masculine and feminine) and two for the plural

✔ **Irregular adjectives** change the spelling of several letters, not just the last one, especially when going from singular to plural.

✔ **Invariable adjectives** are few and far between; you don't need to change their ending when you match them to the words they describe.

The following sections are organized according to the categories in the preceding list. When you finish them, you should be able to take an adjective you've never seen before and place it in the proper group just by looking at its ending. When in doubt, as usual, consult a dictionary.

Regular adjectives

Regular adjectives are those that modify only the last letter to change either gender and number or only number. Table 4-1 shows the possible variations and some example adjectives.

Table 4-1	Variations of Regular Adjective Endings		
Type of Noun	Four Endings: -o, -a, -i, -e	Two Endings: -e, -i	Three Endings: -a, -i, -e
Masculine singular (MS)	piccolo (small; short)	intelligente (intelligent)	egoista (selfish)
Feminine singular (FS)	piccola	intelligente	egoista
Masculine plural (MP)	piccoli	intelligenti	egoisti
Feminine plural (FP)	piccole	intelligenti	egoiste

Book III

Grasping Basic Grammar Essentials for Communication

When used after a noun, **bello** (*beautiful*) and **buono** (*good*) are regular adjectives with four possible endings. When used before a noun, though, they don't take the same endings as all other adjectives ending in **-o**. Instead, they follow these rules:

✔ **Bello** follows the rules of the definite article:

- Use **bel** before a singular masculine noun that starts with one or more consonants (exceptions follow): **bel treno** (*beautiful train*); use **bei** with the same kinds of nouns in the plural: **bei treni** (*beautiful trains*).

- Use **bello** before a singular masculine noun starting with **gn-**, **pn-**, **ps-**, **s** + consonant, **z-**, **x-**, or **y-**: **bello spazio** (*beautiful space*); use **begli** with the same kinds of nouns in the plural: **begli spazi** (*beautiful spaces*).

- Use **bell'** before a singular masculine noun starting with a vowel: **bell'orologio** (*beautiful watch*); use **begli** with the same kinds of nouns in the plural: **begli orologi** (*beautiful watches*).

- Before a singular or plural feminine noun, use **bella** and **belle**: **bella ragazza** (*beautiful girl*), **belle ragazze** (*beautiful girls*).

✔ **Buon** follows the rules of

- The indefinite article when used with singular nouns: For example, before a singular masculine noun that starts with a vowel or consonant, use **buon**: **buon anno** (*good year*), **buono sconto** (*good discount*), **buona fortuna** (*good luck*), and **buon'amica** (*good friend*).

- The definite article when used with plural nouns: Used with plural nouns, it works as a four-ending adjective, so you'd say: **buoni zii** (*good uncles*), **buone famiglie** (*good families*).

See Chapter 2 of Book III for details on the rules of definite and indefinite articles. The later section "Putting adjectives in their place" explains where to use adjectives properly.

Irregular adjectives

When forming plurals, irregular adjectives modify more letters than just the last one, usually to preserve the soft or hard sound of the singular masculine, as in **bianco, bianca, bianchi, bianche** (*white*). But many times, the variations from the norm are accidents of history, for which the reasons are unknown. Table 4-2 breaks down the ending changes for irregular adjectives, with examples.

Table 4-2	Variations of Irregular Adjective Endings	
Type of Singular Adjective to Start	*What the Plural Ending Changes to*	*Examples*
Two-syllable adjective ending in **-co**, **-go**, **-ca**, or **-ga**	**-chi**, **-che**, **-ghi**, **-ghe**	bianco (*white*) → bianchi bianca → bianche lungo (*long*) → lunghi lunga → lunghe

Type of Singular Adjective to Start	What the Plural Ending Changes to	Examples
Multi-syllable adjective with the accent on the second-to-last syllable and ending in **-co** or **-ca**	-ci, -che	**simpatico** (*nice*) → **simpatici** **simpatica** → **simpatiche**
Multi-syllable adjective ending in **-io** or **-ia**	-i, -ie	**necessario** (*necessary*) → **necessari** **necessaria** → **necessarie**
Two-syllable or multi-syllable adjective preceded by a vowel and ending in **-cio, -gio, -cia,** or **-gia**	-ci, -gi, -cie/-ce, -gie/-ge	**sudicio** (*dirty; filthy*) → **sudici** **sudicia** → **sudicie** (or **sudice**) **grigio** (*gray*) → **grigi** **grigia** → **grigie** (or **grige**)
Two-syllable or multi-syllable adjective preceded by a consonant and ending in **-cio, -cia, -gio,** or **-gia**	-i, -e	**liscio** (*smooth*) → **lisci** **liscia** → **lisce** **saggio** (*wise*) → **saggi** **saggia** → **sagge**

Book III

Grasping Basic Grammar Essentials for Communication

Invariable adjectives

A few adjectives are *invariable,* meaning that the ending remains the same regardless of how the noun changes in gender or number. Key invariable adjectives include the following:

✔ Some adjectives for color: **blu** (*blue*), **beige** (*beige*), **lilla/lillà** (*lilac*), **rosa** (*pink*), **turchese** (*turquoise*), and **viola** (*violet; mauve*)

✔ The word **arrosto** (*roasted*)

✔ The mathematical qualifiers **pari** (*even*) and **dispari** (*odd*)

✔ Adjectives taken from other languages: **snob** (*snobbish*), **chic** (*chic*), **trendy** (*trendy*), and **bordeaux** (*burgundy*)

Associating One Adjective with More Than One Noun

An adjective may refer to more than one person or thing, in three ways:

- ✔ With a plural noun (or name or pronoun), as in **Le suore sono silenziose** (*The nuns are quiet*)

- ✔ With two separate nouns of different genders, as in **Le piante e gli animali sono utili** (*Plants and animals are useful*)

- ✔ With one adjective referring to two different things that are singular and share the same gender, as in **Il professore parla di letteratura e storia tedesca** (*The professor is talking about German literature and history*)

You need to decide the adjective's gender and number so it matches the noun. Follow these guidelines:

- ✔ If you have one plural subject, the adjective should be in the plural and match the noun in gender (as explained earlier in this chapter). For example, **I miei fratelli sono bassi** (*My brothers are short*); **Le mie sorelle sono basse** (*My sisters are short*).

- ✔ If you have a masculine noun and a feminine noun, you choose the masculine plural adjective. For example, **Pietro e Luciana sono bassi** (*Pietro and Luciana are short*).

- ✔ If you don't know the gender, use the masculine. For example, [**Loro**] **Sono giovani** (*They are young*).

- ✔ If you have one adjective referring to two singular nouns of the same gender, choose the singular form of the adjective in the gender that matches the nouns. For example, in the following sentence, **romana** (*Roman*) matches the gender of the nouns **pittura** (*painting*) and **scultura** (*sculpture*): **Bianca è un'esperta di pittura e scultura romana** (*Bianca is an expert of Roman painting and sculpture*).

Putting Adjectives in Their Place

In English, you place adjectives after verbs that indicate a status or a condition, such as *to be* or *to feel,* as you do in Italian; for example, **Gina è contenta** (*Gina is happy*). When you attach an adjective to a noun, though, in English you place it before the noun to which it refers, as in *a blue sky.* In Italian, you usually do the opposite, as in **Hanno scritto dei libri importanti** (*They've written important books*).

However, you place some commonly used adjectives before the noun. For example, you say **Hanno una bella casa** (*They have a beautiful house*), even though everyone will understand you if you say **Hanno una casa bella.** The next section provides a list of the most important adjectives that take this placement.

In a few cases, the adjective changes meaning depending on whether you place it before or after the noun. For example, if you say **È un grand'uomo** (*He's a great man*), you mean something very different from **È un uomo grande** (*He's a big man*). You can find more on these adjectives in the later section "Using placement to change an adjective's meaning."

Recognizing the adjectives that come before nouns

Italian has some basic adjectives that you place before nouns, such as the following:

- **bello** (*beautiful*)
- **brutto** (*ugly*)
- **buono** (*good*)
- **cattivo** (*nasty; evil*)
- **breve** (*short; brief*)
- **lungo** (*long*)

Book III

Grasping Basic Grammar Essentials for Communication

Using placement to change an adjective's meaning

Some adjectives change meaning depending on whether you place them before or after the nouns they qualify. For example, if you say **Ho rivisto un caro amico** (*I saw a dear friend again*), **caro** means *dear to your heart;* but if you say **È un negozio caro** (*It's an expensive store*), **caro** means *expensive.* Here's another example: **Solo** means *lonely* in **Un uomo solo è spesso triste** (*A lonely man is often sad*), and it means *only* in **Sono le sole pesche che abbiamo** (*These are the only peaches we have*). Table 4-3 lists the most commonly used adjectives of this sort.

Table 4-3	Common Adjectives That Change Meaning Depending on Placement	
Adjective	Translation When Placed before the Noun	Translation When Placed after the Noun
caro	dear to one's heart	expensive
grande	great in spirit or deeds	big
piccolo	not important; minor	small
povero	pitiable	poor
solo	the only one	lonely
vecchio	of many years	old
nuovo	another	new

Forming Adverbs the Italian Way

In Italian, adverbs add details and nuances by modifying verbs, adjectives, nouns, entire sentences, and other adverbs. Adverbs can radically change the meaning of what you're saying; for example, **Lia si comporta bene** (*Lia behaves well*) as opposed to **Lia si comporta male** (*Lia behaves badly*). Adverbs are invariable in the sense that they have neither gender nor number, so you don't have to worry about coordinating them to the words they modify.

In Italian, adverbs fall into two categories:

- **Original:** These adverbs aren't derived from other words, and they vary widely.
- **Derived:** These adverbs are derived from adjectives.

Original adverbs

Original adverbs don't have a fixed form, so you're forced to simply learn them as you go. Here are some important adverbs to remember:

- **abbastanza** (*enough*)
- **adesso/ora** (*now*)

- ✔ **anche** (*also*)
- ✔ **ancora** (*still; yet*)
- ✔ **bene** (*well*)
- ✔ **davvero** (*really*)
- ✔ **domani** (*tomorrow*)
- ✔ **fa** (*ago*)
- ✔ **già** (*already*)
- ✔ **ieri** (*yesterday*)
- ✔ **mai/non . . . mai** (*ever; never*)
- ✔ **male** (*badly*)
- ✔ **no** (*no*)
- ✔ **non** (*not*)
- ✔ **oggi** (*today*)
- ✔ **presto** (*soon; early*)
- ✔ **purtroppo** (*unfortunately*)
- ✔ **sempre** (*always*)
- ✔ **sì** (*yes*)
- ✔ **spesso** (*often*)
- ✔ **subito** (*at once; right away*)
- ✔ **tardi** (*late*)

Book III

Grasping Basic Grammar Essentials for Communication

Some adjectives play the role of adverbs. To use them as adverbs, you always use the masculine singular form. For example, **Sandro e Marco corrono piano** (*Sandro and Marco run slowly*). These adverbs can only qualify verbs, adjectives, and other adverbs (or sentences) because when you apply them to nouns, names, and pronouns, their "nature" as adjectives takes over and you need to coordinate them with the words they refer to. So you'd say **Sandro e Marco sono corridori veloci** (*Marco and Sandro are fast runners*).

Key adjectives that you can use as adverbs include:

- ✔ **chiaro** (*clear; light in color*)
- ✔ **comodo** (*comfortable*)
- ✔ **duro** (*hard; tough*)
- ✔ **forte** (*strong*)

- ✔ **giusto** (*right*)
- ✔ **leggero** (*light*)
- ✔ **molto** (*very; much*)
- ✔ **parecchio** (*a lot*)
- ✔ **poco** (*little*)
- ✔ **quanto** (*how; how much*)
- ✔ **sicuro** (*sure*)
- ✔ **solo** (*alone; only*)
- ✔ **tanto** (*so; so much*)
- ✔ **troppo** (*too*)
- ✔ **veloce** (*fast*)
- ✔ **vicino** (*near*)

Derived adverbs

You form most derived adverbs by taking the singular form of an adjective and adding **-mente** (the equivalent of *-ly* in English) to it. Here are the basic rules for forming these adverbs, followed by some examples:

- ✔ If the adjective ends in **-o,** you add **-mente** to the feminine singular form of the adjective. For example, **curioso** (*curious*) → **curiosamente** (*curiously*).

- ✔ If the adjective ends in **-e,** you add **-mente** to that adjective. For example, **dolce** (*sweet*) → **dolcemente** (*sweetly*).

- ✔ If the adjective ends in **-e** but the **-e** is preceded by **-l** or **-r,** you drop the **-e** before adding **-mente.** For example, **normale** (*normal*) → **normalmente** (*normally*); **celere** (*rapid*) → **celermente** (*rapidly*).

Finding a Place for Adverbs

In general, you place most adverbs close to the words they modify — that is, before the adjective and the noun and after the verb (in both its simple and compound forms). Here are a few examples (note that the adverbs are **spesso** and **molto**):

> **Roberto gioca spesso a golf.** (*Roberto plays golf often.*)
>
> **Mi è piaciuto molto il concerto.** (*I liked the concert a lot.*)

Exceptions to the general rule are the simple adverbs **appena** (*just*), **ancora** (*yet; still*), **già** (*already*), and **mai** (*ever*), and the compound adverbs **non . . . mai** (*ever; never*), **non . . . ancora** (*not yet*), and **non . . . più** (*no more; no longer*). The following guidelines explain where to place them:

✔ With a compound verb composed of an auxiliary and a past participle, you place the simple adverbs listed previously between the auxiliary and the past participle, as in **Il film è già finito** (*The film has ended already*). For more about compound verbs, see Book V.

> If you have a verbal form consisting of a modal auxiliary and a verb in the infinitive, you place the adverb between the two verbs, as in **Volete ancora venire?** (*Do you still want to come?*).

✔ With compound adverbs, **non** precedes the verb, and **mai/ancora/più** follows it. For example, **Non mangio più il sushi** (*I don't eat sushi anymore*).

> If the verb is in a compound form or is accompanied by a modal auxiliary, you place the second word of the adverb between the two verbs, as in **Non ho ancora mangiato il dolce** (*I haven't eaten dessert yet*).

Ancora means *yet* or *still,* but it also means *some more* or *again.* Regardless of meaning, its placement in the sentence remains the same. Here are a few examples:

> **È ancora presto per telefonargli.** (*It's still too early to call him.*)
>
> **Vuoi ancora del gelato?** (*Do you want some more ice cream?*)

The adverb **sempre,** however, can go either between or after components of a compound tense or verbal form, without any change in meaning. For example, **Ha sempre giocato con lei** and **Ha giocato sempre con lei** both mean *He's always played with her.*

You have more freedom in placing all other adverbs, depending on what you want to emphasize. You can say **Improvvisamente, se ne andarono** (*Suddenly, they left*) or **Se ne andarono improvvisamente** (*They left suddenly*). As usual, when it's a matter of emphasis and style, no precise rules exist. Notice where they're placed when reading and try different options when writing.

Making Comparisons

In general, you make three kinds of comparisons in Italian:

- Those of equality (*as pretty as her mother*)

- Those of inequality (*more rich than smart; less tall than his father*)

- Those called comparatives, and relative or absolute superlatives (*better, worse, the best, the very worst*).

Each sort of comparison uses specific adverbs and forms in its own idiosyncratic way.

Comparisons of equality

Comparisons of equality use adverbs to say that two (or more) things or verbs being compared are equal. You use **così . . . come** (*as . . . as*) or **tanto . . . quanto** (*as much . . . as*) to make such comparisons. These constructs, however, are becoming uncommon, and you frequently leave out **così** and **tanto** because they're understood rather than voiced.

- The **così . . . come** construction puts **così** often before an adjective or a verb; an adjective, a pronoun, or a noun follow **come**.

  Quel ragazzo è [così] bello come suo padre. (*That boy is as handsome as his father.*)

  Questa nuova casa non è [così] comoda come quella vecchia. (*This new house isn't as comfortable as that old one.*)

  Lei è [così] vecchia come lui. (*She is as old as him.*)

  Lui è [così] dotato come Leonardo. (*He is as gifted as Leonardo.*)

  Mi piace [così] mangiare come dormire. (*I like eating as much as sleeping.*)

  È importante [così] studiare come divertirsi. (*It is as important to study as to have fun.*)

- **Tanto**, from the **tanto . . . quanto** way of stating comparison, also must precede an adjective or a verb. You can also leave out **tanto**.

  Laura è [tanto] simpatica quanto sua sorella. (*Laura is as nice as her sister.*)

> **La nostra casa è [tanto] vecchia quanto la vostra.** (*Our house is as old as yours.*)
>
> **Il liceo è [tanto] famoso quanto l'università.** (*The high school is as famous as the university.*)
>
> **Woody Allen può [tanto] dirigere un film quanto recitare.** (*Woody Allen can direct a movie as well as he can act.*)

Comparisons of inequality

With comparisons of inequality, you say that something is **più** (*more*) or **meno** (*less*) big, small, numerous, whatever, than something else: **più grande** (*more grand*), **meno simpatico** (*less nice*), **più case** (*more houses*), **meno ponti** (*fewer bridges*).

You can also use *than* when making comparisons of inequality; for example, **Lei è più alta di suo fratello** (*She is taller than her brother*) and **Ci sono più bambini che adulti** (*There are more children than adults*). *Than* is translated as **di** or **che,** depending on what you're comparing.

✔ If you're comparing two distinct things or people, you use **di.**

> **Il gatto è più giovane del cane.** (*The cat is younger than the dog.*) Here you're comparing two things, a cat and a dog, so you use **di.**
>
> **Le tue ricette sono più buone di quelle nel libro.** (*Your recipes are better than those in the book.*) You're comparing your recipes to those in the book — two things — so you use **di** to mean *than.*
>
> **L'italiano è più bello dell'inglese.** (*Italian is prettier than English.*) Again, you're comparing two things — Italian and English — so you use **di** to mean *than.*

✔ To comment on one thing and compare two characteristics or properties of that one thing, you use **che** to mean *than.*

> **Firenze ha meno abitanti che turisti.** (*Florence has fewer inhabitants than tourists.*)
>
> **È più bello che intelligente.** (*He is more handsome than [he is] smart.*)
>
> **Mi piace più leggere che guardare la televisione.** (*I like reading more than [I like] watching television.*)

All three sentences have single subjects: **Firenze** (*Florence*), **lui** (*he*), and **io** (*I*). In each case, you're discussing one thing or person, and comparing things about that person or thing.

You can follow *than* with a conjugated verb as well. If you want to say, for example, that Venice is cleaner than you thought, that is, following *than* with a conjugated verb (*I thought*), then you say **Venezia è più pulita di quel che credevo.** Here are a couple of additional examples:

> **I gatti sono più simpatici di quel che mi hai detto.** (*The cats are nicer than you told me.*)

> **Il museo è meno vicino di quel che sembrava.** (*The museum is less near than it seemed.*)

The best and the worst: Superlatives

Just as in English, in Italian you can rank objects to establish which one is the highest or the lowest in a series or group. And you can declare that one object is excellent at something even if you don't compare it with anything else.

To rank objects as the highest or lowest when the second term is a noun or pronoun, you use **il più/il meno . . . di/in** (*the most/least . . . of/in*). You match the adjective with the noun that it refers to.

> **Luciano è il più alto dei figli.** (*Luciano is the tallest of the children.*)

> **Marta è la meno agile della squadra.** (*Marta is the least agile on the team.*)

The absolute superlative expresses the greatest degree of an adjective or an adverb, as in **I ragazzi sono lentissimi** (*The boys are very slow*). In English, you convey it by adding *very, much, by far, incredibly, amazingly,* and so on to an adjective or an adverb.

To express the absolute superlative in Italian, you modify adjectives by dropping the final vowel and adding **-issimo, -issima, -issimi,** or **-issime;** for example, **gentile → gentilissimo** (*very kind*) and **alto → altissimo** (*very tall*). When the adjective or adverb ends in **-i,** you add only **-ssimo.** For example, **tardi → tardissimo** (*very late*). As usual, you coordinate the adjective to the noun in gender and number.

> **Quei vestiti sono carissimi.** (*Those dresses are very expensive.*)

> **Torno a casa prestissimo.** (*I'll be coming home very early.*)

When you want to convey a superlative less emphatically, in Italian you can add **molto** or **assai** (*very*). Despite the fact that **molto** and **assai** mean *very,* the phrase **molto grande** means *large, big,* or *rather big* instead of *very large,* which translates to **grandissimo.**

For some emphasis, you also have the option of repeating a short adjective or adverb, like **grande grande** or **presto presto** (with no comma between them). For example, **Le diede un abbraccio forte forte** (*She gave her a really strong hug*). You typically don't do this with long words because it doesn't sound good.

Special comparatives and superlatives

In Italian you have two ways of saying that someone has **più** (*more*) or **meno** (*less*) of the qualities expressed by the adjectives **buono** (*good*), **cattivo** (*bad*), **grande** (*big*), and **piccolo** (*small; little*). You can add **più** or **meno** to the adjective, or use special words, as listed in Table 4-4.

Table 4-4	Comparatives and Superlatives of Adjectives with Special Forms		
Adjective	*Comparatives*	*Relative Superlatives*	*Absolute Superlatives*
buono (*good*)	**più buono, migliore** (*better*)	**il più buono, il migliore** (*the best*)	**buonissimo/ ottimo** (*very good*)
cattivo (*bad*)	**più cattivo, peggiore** (*worse*)	**il più cattivo, il peggiore** (*the worst*)	**cattivissimo/ pessimo** (*very bad*)
grande (*great; big*)	**più grande, maggiore** (*greater; bigger; major; older*)	**il più grande, il maggiore** (*the greatest; the biggest; the maximum; the oldest*)	**grandissimo/ massimo** (*very big; maximum*)
piccolo (*small*)	**più piccolo, minore** (*smaller; lesser; younger*)	**il più piccolo, il minore** (*the smallest; the least; the youngest*)	**piccolissimo/ minimo** (*very small*)

With the adverbs **bene** (*well*), **male** (*badly*), **molto** (*much*), and **poco** (*little*), you only have special forms to express the comparatives and superlatives of these qualities, listed in Table 4-5.

Book III

Grasping Basic Grammar Essentials for Communication

Table 4-5	Comparatives and Superlatives of Adverbs with Special Forms	
Adverb	*Comparative*	*Absolute Superlative*
bene (*well*)	**meglio** (*better*)	**benissimo** (*very well*)
male (*badly*)	**peggio** (*worse*)	**malissimo** (*very badly*)
molto (*very; much*)	**più** (*more*)	**moltissimo** (*mostly*)
poco (*too little*)	**meno** (*less*)	**pochissimo** (*very little*)

In all other respects, you use these special forms as you use the other comparatives.

Umberto è il più grande dei fratelli or **Umberto è il fratello maggiore.** (*Umberto is the oldest of the siblings.*)

Penso che il parmigiano sia migliore della fontina or **Penso che il parmigiano sia più buono della fontina.** (*I think that parmesan is better than fontina.*)

Chapter 5

Meeting the Challenge of Prepositions

· ·

In This Chapter

▶ Sorting out articles combined with basic prepositions

▶ Creating complements with prepositions and nouns, names, or pronouns

· ·

*P*repositions are invariable words you need to link other words in a sentence when adding a name, pronoun, or noun by itself isn't enough. For example, *I'm going school* isn't a complete sentence; you need to say, *I'm going to school.*

Choosing one preposition over another leads you to say different things, such as *I'm speaking to you* or *I'm speaking about you.* One preposition can also play different functions. In the sentence *I'm at home,* the word *at* conveys place. In the sentence *He's at ease,* it conveys someone's feelings. On the other hand, different prepositions can convey similar meanings, as with *in the evening* or *at night.*

Prepositions are difficult to master in any language because their use is idiomatic in many cases. The basic rule, therefore, is practice, practice, and more practice. This chapter guides you through the main Italian prepositions (called **preposizioni semplici** [*simple prepositions*]) and how to combine them with articles. You discover how to choose the preposition that corresponds to the one you'd use in English in the same situation, because literal translation won't do. For example, the preposition **di** usually translates to *of,* but in the expression *to think of someone,* you use **a,** which usually means *at* or *to:* **pensare a qualcuno.**

Combining Basic Prepositions with Articles

Italian has eight basic prepositions, corresponding to the basic prepositions used in English. They're listed here in order of most-frequently used. You find the translation that reflects their meanings in the two languages, but keep in mind that you can't assume that you'll use the same preposition in Italian and English every time.

- **di** (*of; about*)
- **a** (*at; to*)
- **da** (*from; by*)
- **in** (*in; into*)
- **con** (*with*)
- **su** (*on; onto*)
- **per** (*for; through*)
- **fra/tra** (*between; among*)

REMEMBER

With prepositions, the word order is strict: A preposition precedes and is never separated from the word with which it forms a unit of meaning; for example, **a me** (*to me*) and **con coraggio** (*with courage*). *The girl whom I was thinking of* can be translated only as **La ragazza a cui pensavo** (*The girl of whom I was thinking*).

When you have a definite article between a preposition and a noun, you fuse six of the eight prepositions with the articles to form one word. Table 5-1 lists the simple prepositions in their combined forms.

Table 5-1		**Prepositions Combined with Articles**				
Definite Article	**di**	**a**	**da**	**in**	**con**	**su**
il	del	al	dal	nel	con il	sul
lo, l'	dello, dell'	allo, all'	dallo, dall'	nello, nell'	con lo **coll'** (found sometimes in literary texts)	sullo, sull'

Definite Article	di	a	da	in	con	su
la, l'	della, dell'	alla, all'	dalla, dall'	nella, nell'	con la **coll'** (found sometimes in literary texts)	sulla, sull'
i	dei	ai	dai	nei	con i	sui
gli	degli	agli	dagli	negli	con gli	sugli
le	delle	alle	dalle	nelle	con le	sulle

Forming Complements (Preposition + Noun, Name, or Pronoun)

You can form short phrases by putting together a preposition and a noun, a name, or a pronoun. These combinations are called **complementi** (*complements*) because they complete the meaning of a sentence. Italian has a vast array of complements, as you see if you check an Italian grammar book.

You use certain prepositions in a given context: place, for example. If you want to say, *I'm going from Florence to Palermo,* you need two prepositions that have to do with place (*from* and *to*). As you get familiar with prepositions, you'll realize that you can use the same preposition in different contexts, as happens in English with *in,* for example, which works with both *place* and *time* (as happens in Italian, too). The following sections provide the main contexts and the prepositions you use to talk about each of them.

Book III

Grasping Basic Grammar Essentials for Communication

Possession and specification

If you say that something belongs to someone, or if you convey information about someone or something, you use **di** (*of; about*), as in these examples: **il succo di mele** (*apple juice*); **le foto del matrimonio** (*the photos of the wedding*); **la paura della fame** (*the fear of hunger*).

In English, you attribute characteristics to people or other things by inverting the word order or placing *of* between an object and another noun representing a feature that object possesses (*the brilliance of diamonds*). You also may add an apostrophe and *s* to a noun or a name or use a possessive adjective, such as *his* or *her*. Here's how Italian works:

- ✔ Use **di** to link a feature to a person or thing that has that feature, as in **il piano del tavolo** (*the table top*).

- ✔ To convey ownership, use possessive adjectives and pronouns (see Chapter 6 in Book III for details) or **di** followed by the thing owned, as in **il gatto di Marta** (*Marta's cat*) or **il suo gatto [di Marta]** (*her cat*).

Qualities and functions

You can talk about features of things by emphasizing a characteristic that makes them what they are, as in **la scollatura a V** (*a V-neck*), or by indicating their function, as in **le carte da gioco** (*playing cards*). In English, you invert the word order or add an adjective to a noun. So when you have those two constructions in English, you have to decide whether to use **di** (*of*), **a** (*at; in*), or **da** (*by; from*) in Italian.

You can test which preposition works by performing the following experiment. If you say *the table top,* can you change that phrase to *the top of the table?* The answer is yes. In Italian, you use **di,** writing **il piano del tavolo.** But if you say *a motor boat,* can you turn it into *the boat of a motor?* Unlikely. You're talking about *a boat with a motor.* In Italian, it's **la barca a motore.** And if you say, *a pleated skirt,* can you turn it into *the skirt's pleated?* Obviously not. It's *a skirt with pleats.* In Italian, it becomes **la gonna a pieghe.** And what about *a golf ball?* Are you talking about *a ball's golf, a golf's ball,* or *a ball you use to play golf?* Clearly, the latter. When you describe what something is used for, you choose **da** in Italian: **la pallina da golf.** Here are the general rules:

- ✔ To indicate a feature of an object, you use noun + **a** + another noun: **la barca a vela** (*sailing boat*).

- ✔ To indicate a feature that explains the function of an object, you use noun + **da** + noun: **la palla da tennis** (*tennis ball*).

You also use **da** + number to convey value, as in **Vuoi un anello da 10.000 euro?!** (*You want a ring that costs 10,000 euro?!*), but you use **di** for numbers to count things, such as **Legge un libro di cinquecento pagine** (*She's reading a 500-page book*).

Place

Place is a label that refers to activities ranging from staying still to going through, both physically and metaphorically. English uses only *to* (and *into* or *onto*) to convey motion toward something, whereas Italian uses **in** (*in*), **a** (*at; to*), **da** (*by*, as in *by the window*), and **su** (*on*). Italian chooses the preposition on the basis of various features of place.

In, into, on, over, above, and behind

You use the following prepositions regarding place, depending on what you're discussing:

- For a point in space, use **a: a Genova** (*in/to Genoa*); **all'angolo** (*at/to the corner*); **al Colosseo** (*at/to the Coliseum*); **al primo piano** (*on the first floor*).

- To indicate geographical position and distance, use **a: Siamo a nord-ovest di Trieste** (*We are northwest of Trieste*); **Siamo a 50 chilometri da Siena** (*We're 50 kilometers away from Siena*).

- For states, countries, and big islands, use **in** (*in*): **in Italia** (*in/to Italy*); **negli Stati Uniti** (*in/to the United States*).

- When you say you're *in* or are getting *on* a means of transportation, use **in** (*in; into*) + noun (with or without the article) or **su** (*on; onto*): **in macchina** (*in/inside/into the car*); **nel treno** (*in/into the train*); **sull'aereo** (*on/onto the plane*); **sul treno** (*on/onto the train*).

- For volumes, use **in** (*in; into*) + noun followed by the article or not: **nel cielo** (*in the sky*); **in aria** (*in the air*).

- For small islands, which can also be countries, use **a** (*in; to; on*): **a Capri** (*in/to Capri; on the Isle of Capri*); **a Long Island** (*on/to Long Island*); **all'isola d'Elba** (*on Elba Island*).

- For large islands, use **in** (*in; to*): **in Sicilia** (*in/to Sicily*); **in Gran Bretagna** (*in/to Great Britain*).

- For physical place, use **in** + article: **nell'ufficio del dottore** (*in/into the doctor's office*); **nella mia cartella** (*in/into my briefcase*).

- For expressing *above/over* and *under,* use **su/sopra** and **sotto** + article: **su/sopra il tavolo** (*on/over the table*); **sotto il tavolo** (*under the table*); **sottoterra** (*underground*).

  Whether there's physical contact isn't important when choosing between **su** and **sopra,** for example, **L'aereo vola sulla/sopra la città** (*The plane is flying over the city*).

- For expressing *in front of* and *behind,* use **davanti/davanti a** (you can use them interchangeably, however, **davanti a** is the correct standard Italian) and **dietro/dietro a/di** (use **dietro a** for figurative meaning and **dietro di** before disjunctive pronouns): **Siamo davanti a San Pietro** (*We're standing in front of St. Peter's*); **Il melo è dietro la casa** (*The apple tree is behind the house*); **Va dietro a ogni moda** (*She/he goes after any fashion*); **La macchina è dietro di te** (*The car is behind you*).

Book III

Grasping Basic Grammar Essentials for Communication

From, through, across, and among

To convey origin, motion through, and separation, you use the following prepositions, depending on what you're discussing:

- ✔ For conveying someone's origin and being born into a certain family, use **essere** + **di** (*to be from*): **Sono di Venezia** (*They're from Venice*); **Maria è di buona famiglia** (*Maria comes from a well-to-do family*).

- ✔ For motion from, origin, distance, and movement out of containers/elements, use **da** (*from; out of*): **La neve cade dal cielo** (*The snow falls from the sky*); **Ha tolto il cellulare dalla borsa** (*She took the mobile phone out of her bag*).

    With verbs of motion, such as **andare** (*to go*), **venire** (*to come*), and **viaggiare** (*to travel*), you use **da** (*from*) or **a** (*to*). But the verb **partire** (*to leave*) requires the preposition **per** (*for; to*) to indicate the destination, so you say, **Vanno da Roma ad Atene** (*They'll go from Rome to Athens*) but **Partiamo per Nairobi** (*We're leaving for Nairobi*).

- ✔ For expressing *through,* use **da** and **per: Passate da/per Oslo?** (*Are you going/driving/flying through Oslo?*); **Non passate per il bosco!** (*Don't go through the woods!*)

- ✔ For expressing *across,* use **dall'altra parte di: Il tabaccaio è dall'altra parte della strada** (*The tobacconist is across the street*).

- ✔ For expressing *between/among,* use **fra/tra: Tra le case c'è una staccionata** (*There is a fence between the houses*). Italian doesn't distinguish whether you're choosing *between* two things or *among* several things.

Place and function

If you say *I'm going to the doctor's,* you can convey two ideas at once: a physical movement (going to your doctor's office) and the service provided there (you're seeing a doctor because you aren't feeling well). In Italian, you can use the following prepositions to express place and function at the same time:

- ✔ **in** + (no article) noun (neither names nor pronouns): **in chiesa** (*at/to church*); **in ospedale** (*at/to the hospital*); **in casa** (*home; at home*); **in giardino** (*in/to/into the garden*); **in latteria** (*at/to the dairy store*); **in ufficio** (*at the office*)

- ✔ **a** + noun/name of a city: **a casa** (*at/to home*); **a teatro** (*at/to the theater*); **a scuola** (*at/to school*); **a Palermo** (*in Palermo*)

- ✔ **a** + definite article + noun (neither names nor pronouns): **all'asilo** (*at/to kindergarten*); **al negozio di . . .** (*at/to the . . . store*); **all'ospedale** (*in/to the hospital*); **al cinema** (*at/to the movie theater*)

✔ **da** + noun, name, or pronoun of a person's profession or role: **dal macellaio** (*at/to the butcher's*); **dal dottore** (*at/to the doctor's*); **da zia Lilla** (*at/to Aunt Lilla's*); **da noi** (*at/to our place*)

Time

With prepositions, time behaves somewhat like space: Things can happen at a specific moment, as in **a Natale** (*at Christmas*), or during a period of time, as in **nel 1975** (*in 1975*). Or they can take a chunk of time, as in **per tre mesi** (*for three months*).

Often you can express time without prepositions, as you can do in English. Examples of such situations include

✔ When something happens on a day of the week, as in **Lo vedo domenica** (*I'll see him this Sunday*)

✔ When you talk about duration, as in **Stanno in Svezia tre mesi** (*They'll stay/be in Sweden for three months*)

✔ With words that express time, such as **oggi** (*today*), **domani** (*tomorrow*), and **l'anno prossimo** (*next year*)

✔ With dates, as in **È nato il 15 agosto 1960** (*He was born [on] August 15, 1960*)

Specific points in time

When you need prepositions to talk about a specific point in time, follow these guidelines:

✔ For days of the week, to indicate habits and repetition in such time frames, use **di** (*on*), as in **di domenica** (*on Sundays*); for moments of the day, use **di** (*in*), as in **di mattina** (*mornings*); and for seasons, use **in** or **di** (*in*), as in **d'estate** or **in estate** (*in summer*).

If you do something every week on a certain day of the week, in Italian you can use the name of that day with the article, without a preposition, as in **Giochiamo a tennis il sabato** (*We play tennis every Saturday*), or with **di** plus the day of the week, as in **Giochiamo a tennis di sabato** (*We play tennis on Saturdays*). If you're talking about doing something on a certain day in the coming week, you use the name of the day alone, as you do in English: **Giochi a tennis sabato?** (*Will you play tennis Saturday?*)

✔ For holidays or named days and months, use **a** (*at; in*), as in **a Pasqua** (*at Easter*), **a Ferragosto** (*at Ferragosto [on August 15]*), and **a maggio** (*in May*).

Book III

Grasping Basic Grammar Essentials for Communication

✔ For telling the time, use **a** + article, as in **alle 9 di mattina** (*at 9 a.m.*), **alle [ore] 21:40** (*at 9:40 p.m.*), and **a mezzogiorno** (*at 12 noon/midday*).

✔ For expressing that something will happen by a certain time, use **tra/fra** (*in*), as in **tra dieci giorni** (*in ten days*) or **tra due settimane** (*in two weeks*). Or use **per** (*by*), as in **per la settimana prossima** (*by next week*).

✔ For expressing origin in time and continuing action, use **da** (*since; from*), as in **da gennaio** (*since/from January*), **dalle sette di mattina** (*since/from 7 in the morning*), **da ieri** (*since/from yesterday*), and **dal 15 luglio** (*since/from July 15*).

✔ For expressing the end of a period of time in the future, use **entro** (*by*), as in **entro lunedì** (*by Monday*), and **entro la fine dell'anno** (*by the end of the year*).

✔ For expressing the onset of something, use **con** (*with; by; at*), as in **con l'arrivo della primavera** (*with the arrival of spring/by springtime*) or **su** (*with; by; around*) if you want to show approximation, as in **sul far del mattino** (*toward/around dawn*).

Periods of time

When something lasts over a period of time, you use the following prepositions:

✔ For unspecified moments during the day, parts of the day, months, seasons, and years, use **in** or **in** + article (*at; in*): **in mattinata** (*in the morning*); **nel pomeriggio** (*in the afternoon*); **in aprile** (*in April*); **in estate/nell'estate** (*during the summer/in summer*); **nel 2005** (*in 2005*). Use **durante** (*in; during*) to emphasize the effects of duration over time, as in **durante il regno di Vittorio Emanuele** (*during Victor Emanuel's reign*).

✔ For a specified amount of time and continuing action, use **da** (*for*) when referring to the past: **da tre mesi** (*for three months*) or **dal 20 luglio** (*since July 20*). Use **per** (*for*) when referring to the future and a definite amount of time: **per tre mesi** (*for three months*).

Prima di/del means *before*. It takes **di** before names and pronouns, and it takes **di** + article before nouns. Here are some examples:

Marisa arriva prima di Silvia/lei. (*Marisa arrives before Silvia/her.*)

Il treno parte prima dell'autobus. (*The train is leaving before the bus.*)

Dopo means *after*. It takes **di** before pronouns and names, but it stands alone when followed by nouns with articles. Here are some examples:

È nato dopo di te. (*He was born after you.*)

Mario parte dopo la mamma. (*Mario is leaving after Mother.*)

Purpose and agent of action

Are you giving someone a present? Are you doing a favor to or for someone? Because Italian looks at these actions as conveying metaphorical movement, you use prepositions indicating motion: **a** (*to*) and **per** (*for*). **A** and **per** are often interchangeable, as they are in English. For example, **Compri i regali per i/ai bambini?** (*Are you buying presents for the kids?*)

When you write about body parts, in Italian you often use verbs that require the preposition **a** (*to*) afterward, such as **farsi male a** (*to hurt one's*), **aver male a** (*for something to hurt*), and **operare a** (*to perform surgery on/to*). Therefore, you have no choice but to use that preposition, as in **Lo operano al piede sinistro** (*They'll do surgery to his left foot*).

If you use a verb that doesn't require a preposition, such as **rompersi qualcosa** (*to break something*), you add the noun of the organ without any preposition, as in **Maria si è rotta un polso** (*Maria broke a wrist*).

If you consider somebody responsible for something, or the *agent* of the action, you use **da** (*by*), as in **La *Nona Sinfonia* è stata composta da Beethoven** (*The* Ninth Symphony *was composed by Beethoven*).

Tools, reasons, and causes

In everyday life, you do a lot of things with, well, things. These objects can be means of transportation or tools you use to do something; or maybe they're causes of events or reasons for your actions.

For means of transportation, you use the following prepositions:

- ✔ **in** (*by*) (without the definite article) followed by a noun in the singular (except for objects like **sci** [*skis*], which are used in pairs): **Verranno in macchina** (*They'll come by car*); **Vanno in paese in sci** (*They're going to town by skis*).

- ✔ **con** + article + noun to convey how one has reached one's destination (rather than the means used): The distinction is meaningful in English, too, as in this example: **Arriva con l'aereo delle 20** (*She'll arrive on the 8 p.m. flight*). You also use **con** if you add any qualification to the means used, as in **Va in giro con la moto di suo fratello** (*He drives around with his brother's motorbike*).

- ✔ **per** to convey *by/via*: **L'ho mandato per posta** (*I sent it by mail*).

Book III

Grasping Basic Grammar Essentials for Communication

✔ **con** + article + noun to talk about the object used to achieve a result: **Mio padre lucida l'automobile con un prodotto speciale** (*My father polishes the car with a special product*).

✔ **da** to express a cause with the verb in the passive form: **La casa è stata distrutta dall'incendio** (*The house was destroyed by the fire*).

The most common prepositions conveying causes and reasons are **da, di,** and **per** (*for; out of; with; because of*). As you can see, you have a lot of options in English as well, showing how difficult it is to give specific rules about how to choose among the various options. If possible, memorize expressions by heart when you encounter them. Here are a few:

✔ **gridare per la rabbia** (*to shout in anger*)

✔ **morire di fame/sete** (*to die from hunger/thirst*)

✔ **piangere di gioia/di dolore; piangere per la gioia/per il dolore** (*to cry for joy/in pain*)

✔ **ridere dalla/per la gioia** (*to laugh for joy*)

✔ **soffrire di/per la nostalgia** (*to suffer from nostalgia; to feel homesick*)

✔ **tremare di/per il freddo** (*to shiver with cold*)

Chapter 6

Demonstrative, Indefinite, and Possessive Qualifiers

In This Chapter

▶ Indicating people and things with "this" and "that"

▶ Using indefinite words as adjectives or pronouns

▶ Expressing who something belongs to with possessive qualifiers

When you want to point to someone or something because you want to make sure that you and your listener or reader are on the same wavelength, you can use a special set of words that help you be specific: words such as *this, some,* and *my.* You can add them to names, nouns, and pronouns, as in **Quel corso di filosofia è difficile** (*That philosophy course is difficult*). Or you can use them by themselves as pronouns, as in **Il nostro viaggio è stato magnifico. E il vostro?** (*Our trip was great. And yours?*)

You have at your disposal different kinds of "pointers," which are the topic of this chapter:

✔ Demonstrative qualifiers, such as **questo** (*this*) and **quello** (*that*), as in **Questa è una bella bambola** (*This is a beautiful doll*)

✔ Indefinite words, such as **alcuni** (*some*) and **nessuno** (*anyone*), as in **Non ho parlato con nessuno** (*I didn't talk to anyone*)

✔ Possessive pronouns and adjectives, such as **mia** and **la mia** (*my; mine*), as in **Questa borsetta è mia!** (*This purse is mine!*) and **Hai visto la mia gatta?** (*Did you see my cat?*)

This chapter points out similarities and differences between Italian and English in the use of these qualifiers, tells you how to match them to the words they refer to, and explains how to express that you're talking about part of a larger set, as in **Molti dei miei studenti sono ammalati** (*Many of my students are sick*).

Pointing to Something with Questo and Quello

The demonstrative qualifiers **questo** (*this*) and **quello** (*that*) are words you use to point to people, things, and situations. You can use them as adjectives or pronouns. They function as adjectives when you add a noun afterward. They function as pronouns when they refer to a noun, name, or pronoun you've already mentioned.

When you use either **questo** or **quello,** you coordinate it in gender and number with the person or thing to which it refers. **Questo** follows the role of the "four ending adjectives" (**-o** for masculine singular, **-i** for masculine plural, **-a** for feminine singular, and **-e** for feminine plural) while **quello** follows the definite article, as in the following examples:

questo libro (*this book*)

questa casa (*this house*)

questi turisti (*these tourists*)

queste montagne (*these mountains*)

quel tappeto [il tappeto] (*that rug*)

quella cornice [la cornice] (*that frame*)

quello specchio [lo specchio] (*that mirror*)

quei ragazzi [i ragazzi] (*those boys/young men*)

quelle attrici [le attrici] (*those actresses*)

quegli orologi [gli orologi] (*those watches*)

When you use either as an adjective followed by a noun, besides gender and number you need to choose the spelling of its ending depending on the vowel or consonant of the word that follows, as you do with the definite article. So, for example, you say **quell'alta torre** (*that high tower*), but **quella torre alta** (*that high tower*). See Chapter 2 in Book I for details.

Demonstrative qualifiers mean exactly the same in Italian and English, with the following exceptions when it comes to using **questo** and **quello** as pronouns:

✔ You use the form **quelli** (*those ones*) only as a pronoun:

> **Quelli non vogliono pagare il conto.** (*Those [people] don't want to pay the bill.*)

When you refer to a group of females only, you use **quelle** (*those ones*), which is the regular plural of **quella.**

✔ You can use **questo** or **quello** reinforced with the adverbs of place **qui/qua** (*here*) for **questo** or **lì/là** (*there*) for **quello.** You can point to a thing:

> **Questo qui è il mio quaderno.** (*This [one] is my notebook.*)

When you employ them to point to a person, you often do it to convey a negative nuance:

> **Non ti fidare di questa qui.** (*Don't trust this one.*)

> **Non parlare a quello là.** (*Don't talk to that one.*)

✔ You can add an adjective to **questo** or **quello** instead of repeating a noun and an adjective, as shown in this question and answer:

> **Vuoi la giacca blu o quella verde?** (*Do you want the blue or the green jacket?*)

> **Quella verde.** (*The green one.*)

Conveying Something Indefinite

This section shows you indefinite words that you can use as adjectives or as pronouns and indefinite words that you can use only as pronouns. Here, you also see how indefinite words can help you indicate a part of a larger whole, as in the following example: **Molti di noi non gli hanno creduto** (*Many of us didn't believe him*). **Molti** (*many*) is the part, and the larger whole is **noi** (*us*).

Mind that in Italian indefinite adjectives and pronouns are often singular even though they may convey either a singular or a plural meaning. An example is the adjective **qualche** (*some*) (which never changes its ending), as in the phrase **Abbiamo ancora qualche dubbio** (*We still have some doubts*). Another example is the pronoun **chiunque** (*anyone*): **Sono disposto a discutere della questione con chiunque!** (*I'm willing to discuss that issue with anyone!*)

Indefinite words used as adjectives or pronouns

Table 6-1 lists indefinite words that can be used as adjectives or pronouns and indicates which ones

- ✔ You can employ only in the singular, the plural, or both.

- ✔ Are invariable, which means that they come in only one form no matter the gender and number of the person or thing to which they refer. If they're singular (which is almost always the case), you conjugate the verb in the third person singular. If the verb is in a compound form, which includes the past participle, you use the past participle in the masculine singular — unless you're sure that the indefinite adjective or pronoun refers to a group of females.

- ✔ Vary in gender and number, ending in **-o, -a, -i** or **-e;** or only in number, ending in **-e** or **-i.** You match variable indefinites with the nouns to which they refer, as you do with describing adjectives.

Table 6-1			Indefinite Adjectives/Pronouns				
Masculine Singular (Default)	**Meaning as an Adjective**	**Meaning as a Pronoun**	**Use**	**Feminine Singular**	**Plural (M/F)**	**Examples**	**Notes**
del, dello, dell'	*some; any; a few*	N/A	It's an indefinite article made of the preposition **di** (*of*) + the definite article. In the singular, it accompanies uncountable nouns.	**della, dell'**	**dei, degli/ delle**	Singular: **Vorrei del pane.** (*I'd like some bread.*) Plural: **Vorrei delle pesche.** (*I'd like some peaches.*)	Not to be confused with the same word meaning *of the*: **Mi piace molto la crosta del pane.** (*I like the crust of the bread a lot.*)
alcuno	*not any*	*some; any; a few*	In the plural it means *some, a few,* as in **Sono venuti alcuni amici** (*Some friends came*). In negative sentences, if you say **Alcuni amici non sono venuti** (*Some friends didn't come*), you mean that some came and others didn't. You use **nessuno** (*no one*) to say that no one came.	**alcuna**	**alcuni/ alcune**	**Alcuni arrivano sempre tardi.** (*Some are always late.*)	In the singular, it's used instead of **nessuno, nessuna** (*no, no one*) in writing negative sentences: **Non ho alcun bisogno di aiuto.** (*I don't need any help.*)

(continued)

Table 6-1 (continued)

Masculine Singular (Default)	Meaning as an Adjective	Meaning as a Pronoun	Use	Feminine Singular	Plural (M/F)	Examples	Notes
qualche	a; some kind of; a few; any	N/A	It's invariable and used with countable nouns. When referring to "something" singular, it means uno, una (one; a; some kind of); when referring to "something" plural, it means some.	qualche	N/A	**Troverò qualche soluzione.** (*I'll find a solution/some kind of solution.*) **Qualche ragazzo si è offeso.** (*Some/A few boys were offended.*)	
ciascuno	each	each	It's used with countable nouns or to refer to them as a pronoun. It's used only in the singular form.	ciascuna	N/A	**Ciascuna proposta verrà esaminata.** (*Each proposal will be examined.*) **Ciascuno può esprimere la propria opinione.** (*Everyone can express their opinion.*)	
ogni	every; each	N/A	It's used with countable nouns and only in the singular form.	ogni	N/A	**Ogni medaglia ha il suo rovescio.** (*Every coin has a flip side.*)	

Masculine Singular (Default)	Meaning as an Adjective	Meaning as a Pronoun	Use	Feminine Singular	Plural (M/F)	Examples	Notes
qualunque	*any*	N/A	It's used with countable nouns and only in the singular form. It means *any one you want/prefer.*	qualunque	N/A	**Telefona a qualunque ora.** (*You can call any time.*)	
un certo	*a; a certain*	N/A	It's used with countable nouns. In the singular, you add the article **un** (MS) or **una** (FS); as a pronoun in the plural, it means *those unspecified items or people.*	una certa	certi/ certe	**Devo finire certi lavori.** (*I need to finish certain jobs.*) **Ha telefonato una certa Signora Rossi.** (*A Mrs. Rossi called.*) **Certi sostengono che non c'è il surriscaldamento globale.** (*Some people maintain that there is no global warming.*)	Used without the article when followed by collective singular words, such as **gente** (*people*)

(continued)

Book III

Grasping Basic Grammar Essentials for Communication

Table 6-1 (continued)

Masculine Singular (Default)	Meaning as an Adjective	Meaning as a Pronoun	Use	Feminine Singular	Plural (M/F)	Examples	Notes
[l', un] altro	[the; an] other	[the] other(s)	It's used also with the definite or indefinite article.	[l', un'] altra	[gli] altri [le] altre	**L'altro giorno pioveva.** (*It was raining the other day.*) **È passato un altro ragazzo a cercarti.** (*Another boy came looking for you.*)	Used in various combinations: **l'un, l'altro** (*each other; one another*), **l'uno … l'altro** (*one … the other*), **gli uni … gli altri** (*some … others; the ones … the others*)
nessuno	no	no one; nobody	It's used only in the singular form.	nessuna	N/A	**Non vidi nessuna bambina.** (*I saw no little girl.*)(*I didn't see any little girl.*)	If used at the beginning of a negative sentence, **non** (*not*) is omitted: **Nessuno ha telefonato.** (*No one called.*)
molto	much; a lot	much; a lot	It's used with uncountable nouns in the singular and countable nouns in the plural.	molta	molti/ molte	**Ha bisogno di molto zucchero?** (*Do you need a lot of sugar?*) **Hanno perso molte partite.** (*They lost a lot of games.*)	

Masculine Singular (Default)	Meaning as an Adjective	Meaning as a Pronoun	Use	Feminine Singular	Plural (M/F)	Examples	Notes
tanto	*so much; so many*	*so much; so many*	It's used with uncountable nouns in the singular and countable nouns in the plural.	tanta	tanti/ tante	**Ha fatto tanta fatica!** (*She made such a big effort!*) **Abbiamo visto tante farfalle!** (*We saw [so] many butterflies!*)	
troppo	*too much; too many*	*too much; too many*	It's used with uncountable nouns in the singular and countable nouns in the plural.	troppa	troppi/ troppe	**C'è troppo zucchero.** (*There's too much sugar.*) **Abbiamo troppe barche.** (*We have too many boats.*)	
poco	*too little; few*	*few*	When it means *too little*, it's used with singular, uncountable nouns; in the plural, it means *few* with plural, countable nouns.	poca	pochi/ poche	**Ho poco vino.** (*I have too little wine.*) **Poche persone gli credono.** (*Only a few people believe him.*)	

(continued)

Book III

Grasping Basic Grammar Essentials for Communication

Table 6-1 *(continued)*

Masculine Singular (Default)	Meaning as an Adjective	Meaning as a Pronoun	Use	Feminine Singular	Plural (M/F)	Examples	Notes
parecchio	*a lot of, several*	*several*	It's used with uncountable nouns in the singular and countable nouns in the plural.	**parecchia**	**parecchi/ parecchie**	**Ho ancora parecchio tempo.** (*I still have a lot of time.*) **Hai ancora parecchi compiti da fare?** (*Do you still have several assignments to do?*)	
qualsiasi	*whatever; whichever*	N/A	It's used with countable nouns and only in the singular form.	**qualsiasi**	N/A	**Qualsiasi cosa dica, non gli credo.** (*Whatever he says, I don't believe him.*)	
tutto il	*entire; whole; all*	N/A	It's used with countable and uncountable nouns. In the singular, it means *the entire, the whole*; in the plural, it means *all*.	**tutta la**	**tutti i/ tutte le**	**Hanno consumato tutta la benzina!** (*They used the entire tank of gas!*) **Hai visto tutti i suoi film?** (*Have you seen all his/her movies?*)	

In Italian, as in English, the indefinite adjectives/pronouns *both* and *either* are used only with plural, countable nouns. The most common phrase is **tutti e due** (masculine)/**tutte e due** (feminine), but you also see **ambedue** (masculine/feminine) and **entrambi** (masculine)/**entrambe** (feminine), especially in writing.

Indefinite words used solely as pronouns

Table 6-2 lists some indefinite words that you can use only as pronouns. Most of these indefinite pronouns are singular and invariable, but they do convey a generic, singular or plural meaning. Look at the following example:

Hai visto qualcuno? (*Did you see someone?*)

Sì, ho contattato tre dottori. (*Yes, I saw three doctors.*)

Table 6-2		Indefinite Pronouns		
Masculine Singular (Default)	**Feminine**	**Translation**	**Example**	**Notes**
uno	una	*one; someone*	**Ha telefonato una.** (*Someone/A woman called.*)	
ognuno	ognuna	*everyone; each; each one*	**Ognuno è contento.** (*Everyone is happy.*)	It takes the verb in the singular but refers to a generic, singular or plural subject. Use the feminine when you refer to women only.
qualcuno	qualcuna	*someone; somebody*	**Hai contattato qualcuno?** (*Did you contact someone?*) **Sì, ho contattato tre avvocati.** (*Yes, I contacted three lawyers.*)	It takes the verb in the singular but refers to a generic, singular or plural subject. Use the feminine when you refer to women only.

Book III

Grasping Basic Grammar Essentials for Communication

(continued)

Table 6-2 *(continued)*

Masculine Singular (Default)	Feminine	Translation	Example	Notes
chiunque		*anyone; anybody*	**Chiunque avrebbe fatto ciò che hai fatto tu.** (*Anyone would've done what you did.*)	It takes the verb in the singular but refers to a generic, singular or plural subject.
qualcosa		*something; anything*	**Posso fare qualcosa per te?** (*Can I do something for you?*)	Add **altro** (*else*) to **qualcuno** or **qualcosa** to translate *someone else, something else:* **Chiediamo a qualcun altro** (*Let's ask someone else*).
tutto		*everything*	**Ada ha capito tutto.** (*Ada understood everything.*) **Hanno parlato di tutto.** (*They spoke about everything.*)	It's used as the direct object of a sentence. When you use it as a subject, you need to add **ciò**: **Tutto ciò è falso** (*All this is false*).
niente, nulla		*nothing*	**Niente serve quanto essere pazienti.** (*Nothing helps so much as being patient.*)	Skip the adverb **non** (*not*) when you begin a sentence with **niente/nulla.**

In English nowadays, you use *everyone* to mean *all people.* You add third person plural possessive adjectives and personal pronouns, as in *Everyone thinks that his/her team is better.* In Italian, you can't use **ognuno** that way. You use **tutti** (masculine, plural), as in **Tutti pensano che la loro squadra sia la migliore** or **tutte** (feminine, plural) if you know the group includes only women.

To convey *whoever, whatever,* and *whichever,* you can use

- **chiunque** + verb in the subjunctive, as in **Chiunque sia stato, lo scopriranno** (*Whoever did it, they'll find them*)

- **chiunque** + **di** + noun/pronoun to refer to people, as in **Chiunque sia stato di loro, lo scopriranno** (*Whoever did it, they'll find them*)

- **qualunque** or **qualsiasi** + noun, as in **Qualunque regalo tu le faccia, non sarà contenta** (*Whatever present you give her, she won't be happy*); **Puoi scegliere il gusto che vuoi** (*You may choose whichever flavor you want*)

Note: **Chiunque, qualunque,** and **qualsiasi** often require the verb in the subjunctive as shown in the preceding examples. See Chapter 6 in Book IV for details about the subjunctive.

Indefinite words that express a part of a set

When you employ an indefinite pronoun, it often refers to part of a set. For example, in the sentence **Alcuni di loro non verranno alla festa** (*Some of them won't come to the party*), **alcuni** (*some*) is the indefinite pronoun and **loro** (*of them*) is the set. You can employ the following formulas using pronouns and other words to convey a part of a larger whole:

- **ognuno/ciascuno** (*each*), **chiunque** (*any*), **nessuno** (*none*), **qualcuno** (*any; some*), or **uno** (*one*) + the preposition **di** (*of*) or **tra** (*among*) + the verb in the third person singular

  If there's a past participle, you leave it in the masculine, as in **Qualcuno di voi ha scritto al giornale** (*Some of you wrote to the paper*), unless you know that the group consists of only females. For example, **Una delle ragazze si è fatta male** (*One of the girls got hurt*).

- **alcuni** (*some; a few*), **molti** (*many; a lot of*), **parecchi** (*several*), **pochi** (*few*), **tanti** (*so many*), or **troppi** (*too many*) + **di** or **tra** + the verb in the third person plural

    Alcuni di voi hanno chiesto un rinvio. (*Some of you have asked for a postponement.*)

- The indefinite article **del, dello, della, dell'** (*some*) in the singular + nouns that are uncountable or indicate things in bulk, such as **acqua** (*water*), **vino** (*wine*), or **pioggia** (*rain*)

    Vuoi del vino? (*Do you want some wine?*)

Book III

Grasping Basic Grammar Essentials for Communication

✔ The adverbial phrase **un po' di** (*a little of*) + uncountable concrete nouns or abstractions

>**Sì, vorrei un po' di vino, grazie.** (*Yes, I'd like some wine, thank you.*)

>**Ci vuole un po' di costanza.** (*You need a little perseverance.*)

You use **di** after an indefinite pronoun when an adjective follows:

>**Hai visto qualcosa di interessante alla mostra?** (*Did you see something/ anything interesting at the exhibit?*)

When you don't want to repeat the noun or pronoun representing a set already mentioned in a sentence with an indefinite pronoun, you can replace the set with the pronoun **ne** (*of those; them*), either placed before the verb or attached to the infinitive or the gerund. If you use a past participle or another adjective, you coordinate it with the word **ne** refers to:

>**Hai comprato delle banane?** (*Did you buy some bananas?*)

>**Sì, ma forse ne ho comprate troppe!** (*Yes, but maybe I bought too many [of those]!*)

If you use **uno/nessuno** (*one/none*), the past participle takes the singular, coordinated in gender with the item you're talking about:

>**Hai visto i tuoi amici?** (*Did you see your friends?*)

>**No, non ne ho visto nessuno.** (*No, I didn't see any [of them].*)

You can employ any quantifier, not just indefinites, to express a part of a set. For example:

>**Hai comprato dieci borse?!** (*Did you buy ten handbags?!*)

>**No! Ne ho comprate due!** (*No! I bought two!*)

Assigning Ownership with Possessive Qualifiers

To assign ownership in English, you add a possessive adjective (*my* or *our*) to the object owned by referring to that object through a possessive pronoun (*mine* or *ours*) or by adding *'s* (or just the apostrophe) to the noun or name that conveys the owner. In Italian, you have three options: Add a possessive adjective to the owner, introduce the owner with the preposition **di** (*of*), or employ the idiomatic expression **essere di** + the owner's name, which means something like *to belong to*.

Unlike in English, in the third person singular Italian, the possessive adjective or pronoun doesn't convey whether the owner is male or female. That information is clarified only by the context of the sentence; for example, **la sua gatta** can mean *his/her cat.*

Table 6-3 lists possessive adjectives and pronouns, which are identical in Italian, along with the corresponding definite articles.

Table 6-3	Possessive Qualifiers and Pronouns			
Translation	*Masculine Singular*	*Masculine Plural*	*Feminine Singular*	*Feminine Plural*
my; mine	**mio, il mio**	**miei, i miei**	**mia, la mia**	**mie, le mie**
your; yours	**tuo, il tuo**	**tuoi, i tuoi**	**tua, la tua**	**tue, le tue**
his; hers; its	**suo, il suo**	**suoi, i suoi**	**sua, la sua**	**sue, le sue**
our; ours	**nostro, il nostro**	**nostri, i nostri**	**nostra, la nostra**	**nostre, le nostre**
your; yours	**vostro, il vostro**	**vostri, i vostri**	**vostra, la vostra**	**vostre, le vostre**
their; theirs	**loro, il loro**	**loro, i loro**	**loro, la loro**	**loro, le loro**

In Italian you use the definite article with possessive adjectives and pronouns, except in two cases:

- You don't use the article with the names of close relatives in the singular form, but you do with the modified version of these nouns (for example: **mia sorella/la mia sorellina, mia madre/la mia matrigna**) except for the use with **loro.** So you say: **mio marito** (*my husband*); **vostra nonna** (*your grandmother*); **i loro genitori** (*their parents*); **la loro famiglia** (*their family*).

- When you use a possessive word after the verb **essere** (*to be*), you can use the article or skip it, whichever comes easier, as when you say **Quell'automobile è la mia** (*That car is mine*) or **Quell'automobile è mia** (*That car is mine*).

  Note, however, that the presence or absence of the article conveys a slightly different meaning: **Quell'automobile è la mia** (pronoun) means *That car is mine* (as opposed to being *yours* or *hers,* and so forth). **Quell'automobile è mia** (adjective), on the other hand, means simply *That car belongs to me* (as in, *I bought it; I didn't rent it*).

Book III

Grasping Basic Grammar Essentials for Communication

If you select one or more items out of a group of things owned, in Italian you can use

- Any quantifier (a number or an indefinite pronoun) followed by **dei, degli,** or **delle** + a possessive qualifier + a noun in the plural:

    Sono tre dei miei amici. (*They're three of my friends.*)

- **uno** or **dei** + a possessive adjective + a noun:

    È un mio amico. (*He's a friend of mine.*)

    Sono dei miei amici. (*They're friends of mine.*)

Note, however, that **È un amico dei miei** means *He's a friend of my parents.*

Chapter 7

Making Connections with Conjunctions and Relative Pronouns

In This Chapter

▶ Joining thoughts thanks to conjunctions and prepositions

▶ Linking clauses with relative pronouns

*I*n speech and writing, you use many sentences, not just one. You can string them out one after another, separating them with periods. But you often need to link together thoughts expressed in different sentences. This chapter shows you how to do that with coordinating or subordinating conjunctions or with relative pronouns.

Linking Words and Clauses with Conjunctions and Prepositions

As you know, a clause is a grouping of words that includes a verb, which sometimes is all you need: **Entrate!** (*Come in!*) But in most situations, you need a subject, an object, adjectives and other qualifiers, other nouns introduced by a preposition, and so forth to express your meaning. When you're on a roll with sentence construction and want to keep going, you can link full sentences together using conjunctions and prepositions.

When you rely on conjunctions, you employ invariable words whose only purpose in life is to join clauses. In both Italian and English, you encounter coordinating and subordinating conjunctions. Here's a rundown of both:

✔ You use coordinating conjunctions — such as **e** (*and*), **o/oppure** (*or*), or **ma** (*but*) — when you link together clauses that are (grammatically) of equal standing.

> **Vai in crociera o stai sul lago?** (*Are you going on a cruise or are you staying at the lake?*)

✔ You use subordinating conjunctions — such as **perché** (*because*), **quando** (*when*), or **finché** (*in so far as, as long as*) — when you link together dependent and independent clauses.

> **Quando torni dobbiamo parlare.** (*When you come back, we need to talk.*)

Connecting words or sentences with coordinating conjunctions

You can use coordinating conjunctions in various ways:

✔ To link names, nouns, pronouns, adjectives, and adverbs in the same sentence.

> **Mi piacciono i romanzi e i resoconti di viaggio.** (*I like novels and travel books.*)

> **Vorrei un vestito elegante, ma comodo.** (*I'd like an elegant but comfortable dress.*)

✔ To coordinate verbs in the infinitive, such as when they follow a modal auxiliary.

> **No so né sciare né arrampicarmi/scalare.** (*I can neither ski nor climb.*)

✔ To link together two (or more) sentences that remain meaningful even if you take the conjunction away.

> **Lia scrive poesie e Ugo suona il piano.** (*Lia writes poems, and Ugo plays the piano.*)

Table 7-1 lists coordinating conjunctions you can use to link words or sentences.

Table 7-1	Coordinating Conjunctions		
Coordinating Conjunction	*Translation*	*Coordinating Conjunction*	*Translation*
allora, poi	*then*	**ma, però, tuttavia**	*but; however*

Coordinating Conjunction	Translation	Coordinating Conjunction	Translation
anzi, piuttosto	rather	né . . . né	neither . . . nor (di + infinitive)
cioè	that is	non solo . . . ma anche	not only . . . but also
comunque	however	o, oppure	or
e	and	o . . . o	either . . . or
e . . . e, sia . . . sia	both . . . and	perciò, dunque	therefore
infatti	in fact; indeed	quindi	so; therefore; thus

When you use the conjunction **e**, you can invert the order of the sentences. Think of them in mathematical terms: In multiplication or addition, the product or sum doesn't change if you move numbers around. This is also the case with **o** (*or*), **o . . . o** (*either . . . or*), **né . . . né** (*neither . . . nor*), and **sia . . . sia** (*either . . . or*). But with other conjunctions (as with division and subtraction), order matters. You can't swap the sentence order if you

✔ Establish a contrast with **ma** (*but*) or **tuttavia** (*however*).

✔ Point to a conclusion or a consequence with **quindi** (*thus*) or **perciò** (*therefore*).

✔ Convey a temporal sequence with **allora, poi** (*then*).

Consider the following example:

Mia le fa un regalo, ma non dirglielo. (*Mia will give her a present, but don't tell her.*)

Book III

Grasping Basic Grammar Essentials for Communication

Joining a dependent clause with an independent one

If you subordinate one sentence to another, you establish a relationship of dependence between a main or independent clause and a subordinate or dependent one. With subordination, the meaning of the combined sentences is very different from their meanings if left independent of one another. Consider this example:

Mangio la verdura perché fa bene. (*I eat vegetables because they're good for me.*)

This sentence means that you eat vegetables because they're healthy food. Now take a look at the following:

> **Mangio la verdura. La verdura fa bene.** (*I eat vegetables. Vegetables are good for one's health.*)

In this instance, you may eat vegetables because you like them, because you have nothing else in the refrigerator, or for any other reason. The fact that you eat veggies isn't necessarily tied to their health benefits.

You can subordinate a dependent clause to a dependent one in two ways:

- ✔ With a subordinating conjunction
- ✔ With a preposition or prepositional phrase that does the work of a conjunction

With a subordinating conjunction

Subordinating conjunctions tie one or more dependent clauses to an independent one, as in **Gioco con te se mi presti la tua bici** (*I'll play with you if you lend me your bike*). This process is called *subordination*.

Table 7-2 lists the most common subordinating conjunctions.

Table 7-2	Subordinating Conjunctions		
Subordinating Conjunction	*Translation*	*Subordinating Conjunction*	*Translation*
affinché	*in order to*	**nonostante**	*although*
[non] appena	*as soon as*	**perché**	*because; why; so that; in order that*
che	*that*	**più ... di quanto/a/e/i** **più ... che** **più ... di quello/a/i/e che**	*more ... than* *more ... than* *what*
come	*as; how*	**poiché, dal momento che, dato che**	*as; for; since; given that*
così ... come **tanto ... quanto** **tale ... quale**	*as ... as* *as much ... as* *such ... as*	**prima che**	*before*
da quando	*ever since*	**purché**	*as long as; provided that*

Subordinating Conjunction	Translation	Subordinating Conjunction	Translation
dopo che	*after*	quando	*when; as*
dove	*where*	quanto/i/a/e	*how much; how many*
finché	*until*	se	*if; whether*
finché non	*until*	sebbene, benché	*although; even though*
meno . . . di quanto/a/i/e meno . . . che meno . . . di quello/i/a/e che	*less . . . than* *less . . . than* *what*	senza che	*without +* subjunctive
mentre	*whereas; while*	tanto/a/i/e che	*so [much so]; that; to the point that*

Conjunctions are invariable, with the exception of words you use to convey comparisons, such as **tante . . . quante** (*as many . . . as*).

When you link sentences through subordination, the main clause and the conjunction you choose determine the mood and tense of the verb in the dependent clause. You can link sentences with the declarative and the *if . . . then* constructions, which often use the subjunctive. Other constructions require the conjunction in the dependent clause, including **affinché** (*in order to*), **perché** (when it means *in order to*), **a meno che** (*unless; except if*), **non-ostante/nonostante che** (*although*), **prima che** (*before*), **purché** (*as long as; provided that*), **sebbene/benché** (*although; even though*), and **senza che** (*without*). Here's an example:

> **Mi spiegate cosa sta succedendo sui mercati affinché non perda tutti i miei soldi?** (*Can you explain to me what's happening in the markets so I won't lose all my money?*)

With a preposition or prepositional phrase

As long as the subject of both clauses is the same, you can introduce a dependent clause with a preposition, or with phrases that include a preposition, followed by an infinitive. In the sentence **Ho deciso di andare a pescare** (*I've decided to go fishing*), the preposition **di** (*to*) introduces a dependent clause. In fact, you can replace the preposition with the declarative conjunction **che** (*that*): **Ho deciso che vado a pescare** (*I've decided that I'll go fishing*). Table 7-3 lists prepositions and phrases with prepositions that can introduce verbs in the infinitive.

Book III

Grasping Basic Grammar Essentials for Communication

When you use the preposition **da,** the infinitive can refer to the object of the sentence, as in **Dammi un libro da leggere** (*Give me a book to read/that I can read/for me to read*). And you can have two different subjects when you use **su** + article, as in **Partimmo sul sorgere del sole** (*We left while the sun was rising*).

Table 7-3	Prepositions Working as Conjunctions		
Preposition	*Translation*	*Preposition*	*Translation*
a	*to* + infinitive (or gerund)	**in modo da**	*in such a way to* + infinitive; *so as to* + infinitive
a tal punto da	*to the point of* + gerund	**invece di**	*instead of* + gerund
da	*to* + infinitive	**oltre a**	*besides* + gerund
di	*of* + gerund	**per**	*to* + infinitive; *for* + gerund
dopo + past	*after* + gerund	**prima di**	*before* + gerund infinitive
fino a	*to the point of* + gerund	**senza**	*without* + gerund
in + article + infinitive	*in* + gerund	**su** + article + infinitive	*on* + gerund; *while* + finite verb

Joining Clauses That Belong Together

You may need a full sentence to point to a person or a thing already mentioned. Consider this example:

>**L'attrice ha vinto l'Oscar. L'attrice è francese.** (*The actress won the Oscar. The actress is French.*)

You can link the two sentences by using a relative pronoun, which introduces a relative clause. The two sentences become one:

>**L'attrice che ha vinto l'Oscar è francese.** (*The actress who won the Oscar is French.*)

In this sentence, **che** (*who*) is the relative pronoun that introduces the relative clause, **ha vinto l'Oscar** (*won the Oscar*).

There's a special set of combined demonstrative + relative pronouns that do double duty: The (implied) demonstrative pronoun belongs to the independent clause while the relative component introduces the dependent clause, as in **Hai visto chi ha mandato questo pacco?** (*Did you see who sent this package?*) In this example, **chi** combines **la persona che** (*the person who*) and **quello che** (*the one who*). (You can also use the non-combined form if you prefer, but the combined form is handy.)

In English, you often can skip the relative pronoun unless it's the subject of the relative clause. In Italian, you may not. For example, in English, you may say *Did you like the wine that we drank last night?* or *Did you like the wine we drank last night?* Either is correct. In Italian, though, you must include **che** (*that*): **Ti è piaciuto il vino che abbiamo bevuto ieri sera?** (*Did you like the wine that we drank last night?*)

Italian has a set of relative pronouns that have counterparts in English, such as **che/il quale/la quale** (*who; whom*) or **i quali/le quali** (*who; whom* [plural]). But Italian also has a set of combined relative pronouns. They convey (but don't spell out) a demonstrative pronoun, such as **quello** (*that*) or **colui** (*the one*), and a relative pronoun, such as **che** (*who*), to form the combined pronoun **chi** (*who*), which means **colui che** (*the one who*). Turn to the later section, "Economy of speech: Combined pronouns" to see more on this subject.

Book III

Grasping Basic Grammar Essentials for Communication

Dealing with your average relative pronouns

Italian has two sets of (non-combined) relative pronouns: invariable and variable.

- Invariable relative pronouns don't change their endings to match the words they replace in gender and number (for once!). An example is **che** (*who; whom*), which can refer to a singular, plural, masculine, or feminine person or thing, as in **Le bambine che hai visto al parco sono le mie sorelle** (*The little girls you saw in the park are my sisters*).

- Variable relative pronouns are formed of two words: the relative word **quale** and the definite article. **Quale** changes in number, but not in gender: **quale, quali.** It always takes the definite article, which conveys both gender and number — **il, la, i, le** (*the*) — to form the pronoun **il quale** (and its variations) meaning *who, whom, which*. For example, **La bambine le quali hai visto al parco sono le mie sorelle** (*The little girls you saw in the park are my sisters*).

When you use the variable set, you coordinate the pronoun with the word in the preceding clause that the pronoun replaces. You change the ending of the pronoun in number and the article in both gender and number. For example, in the sentence **La gatta della quale ti avevo parlato è morta** (*The female cat about whom I talked to you died*), **la gatta** is feminine singular, as is the relative pronoun **della quale.**

You also have to contend with the pronoun **cui,** which never changes and can't be used as a subject or a direct object. You can use it in only two ways:

✔ Accompanied by the definite **il, la, i, le** (*the*), which conveys both gender and number to form the pronoun **il cui** (and its variations). In this form, **il cui** means *whose.*

> **Hai visto quel film il cui titolo ora non ricordo?** (*Did you see that movie whose title I can't remember right now?*)

✔ Accompanied by a preposition but without an article, as in **da cui** (*by/ from whom*).

Table 7-4 illustrates the functions of the variable and invariable relative pronouns.

Table 7-4			Relative Pronouns			
Translation	*Invariable*	*Masculine Singular*	*Feminine Singular*	*Masculine Plural*	*Feminine Plural*	*Use*
who; whom; that; which	**che**	**il quale**	**la quale**	**i quali**	**le quali**	Subject or direct object
of; about; which/ whom		**del quale**	**della quale**	**dei quali**	**delle quali**	Indicates specification or possession
of; about; which/ whom	**di cui**					Indicates specification
whose		**il cui**	**la cui**	**i cui**	**le cui**	Indicates specification or possession
whose		**del quale**	**della quale**	**dei quali**	**delle quali**	Indicates specification or possession

Translation	Invariable	Masculine Singular	Feminine Singular	Masculine Plural	Feminine Plural	Use
to/for whom	[a] cui	al quale	alla quale	ai quali	alle quali	Indicates aim or purpose
from; whom/ which; by whom/ which; to whom/ which; or any other preposition	da cui, a cui, or any other preposition	dal quale, al quale	dalla quale, alla quale	dai quali, ai quali	dalle quali, alle quali	Other complements

When it comes to deciding which pronoun to use, if you use a relative pronoun as a subject or a direct object, you can choose between the invariable form **che** or the variable form **il quale.**

✔ Choose the word **che** when it's very clear to whom you're referring, as in **Ho visto Giovanna che andava in palestra** (*I saw Giovanna, who was going to the gym*).

✔ Choose the variable form **il quale** (or one of its forms) when you want to avoid ambiguity. If you say **Ho incontrato il figlio della signora Maria, che ti manda tanti saluti** (*I met Maria's son, who sends you his greetings*), in Italian nothing makes you really certain who sent you greetings, whether **Maria** or **il figlio.** But if you say **Ho incontrato il figlio della signora Maria, il quale ti manda i saluti,** you know for sure that you're talking about **il figlio,** which is masculine singular, because **il quale** is masculine singular as well.

Book III

Grasping Basic Grammar Essentials for Communication

When you use a preposition with the relative pronoun because you want to convey an indirect object, you can choose between **cui** (plus article *or* preposition) or **quale** (plus preposition *and* article). When in English

✔ You use *of* or *about* before a relative pronoun, use **di + cui** in Italian.

> **Non possiamo fare la vacanza di cui ti ho parlato.** (*We can't take the vacation which I spoke to you about.*)

(But remember that the formula **Non possiamo fare la vacanza della quale ti ho parlato** is perfectly correct and used all the time.)

✔ You use the pronoun *whose,* meaning that someone already mentioned possesses a certain trait or that something already mentioned has a certain characteristic, in Italian use **il cui (la cui, i cui, le cui).**

> **Ho visto una ragazza la cui bellezza mi ha colpito.** (*I saw a girl whose beauty struck me.*)

> **Abbiamo fatto una riunione il cui scopo non mi era chiaro.** (*We had a meeting whose purpose wasn't clear to me.*)

✔ You need any other preposition before the relative pronoun, you can use indifferently **cui** or **il quale.** You add only the preposition to **cui: con cui** (*with whom/which*), **da cui** (*by whom/which*), or **su cui** (*on whom/ which*). You add a combined article to **quale: con il quale** (*with whom/ which*), **dal quale** (*by whom/which*), or **sul quale** (*on whom/which*).

> **La persona sulla quale avevamo contato non ci può aiutare** or **La persona su cui avevamo contato non ci può aiutare** (*The person on whom we had counted can't help us*).

If you need a preposition with the relative pronoun (either **il quale** or **cui**), you may not skip it. However, with **cui** only, you may (but don't have to) skip the preposition **a** (*to*) or **per** (*for*) to indicate aim or purpose (not motion), and leave **cui** all by itself, as in **La faccenda cui ti riferisci è stata sistemata** (*The problem you're referring to has been solved*).

Following are some examples of relative pronouns at work combining two sentences:

> **Ho conosciuto un cantante famoso. Questo cantante famoso una volta ha vinto il Festivalbar.** (*I met a famous singer. This famous singer once won Festivalbar.*)

> **Ho conosciuto un cantante famoso che una volta ha vinto il Festivalbar.** (*I met a famous singer who once won the Festivalbar.*)

> **Compro caramelle ogni giorno. Ogni giorno compro caramelle alla liquirizia.** (*I buy candies every day. Every day I buy licorice candies.*)

> **Le caramelle che compro ogni giorno sono alla liquirizia.** (*The candies that I buy every day are licorice.*)

> **Vedo che ti piace dipingere. Dipingi soprattutto quadri astratti.** (*I [can] see that you like to paint. You especially paint abstract paintings.*)

> **I quadri che ti piace dipingere di più sono quelli astratti.** (*The paintings that you mostly prefer to paint are abstract paintings.*)

> **Roma è una città affascinante. Provengo da Roma.** (*Rome is a fascinating city. I come from Rome.*)

Roma, la città da cui provengo, è affascinante. (*Rome, the city I come from, is fascinating.*)

Hai parlato di un problema col tuo capo. È un problema di stipendio? (*You discussed a problem with your boss. Is it a salary-related problem?*)

Il problema di cui hai parlato col tuo capo è di stipendio? (*Is the problem that you discussed with your boss salary-related?*)

Siamo partiti dall'aeroporto JFK di New York. Siamo tornati all'aeroporto JFK di New York. (*We left from New York's JFK airport. We returned to New York's JFK airport.*)

Siamo tornati all'aeroporto JFK di New York, da cui eravamo partiti. (*We returned to New York's JFK airport, from which we had left.*)

Si crede agli UFO. Si crede alle favole. (*You can believe in UFOs. You can believe in fairy tales.*)

C'è chi crede agli UFO e alle favole. (*There are some [people] who believe in UFOs and in fairy tales.*)

Economy of speech: Combined pronouns

In addition to relative pronouns, Italian has combined relative pronouns. A combined pronoun is a single word that conveys two meanings: a demonstrative word and a relative pronoun. For example, the pronoun **quanto** (*what; all that; which*) contains both the demonstrative **quello** (*that*), **tutto quello** (*all that*), and the relative pronoun **che** (*which*). For example, **Farò quanto mi è possibile/Farò tutto quello che mi è possibile** (*I'll do what I can*).

You can use the combined or non-combined form of the relative pronouns — it's your choice. The combined forms are very convenient, just as the pronoun *what* is in English.

If you use a non-combined form, you can see that each of the two components of the pronoun plays a different function. Consider this example: **Non faccio favori a coloro che non lo meritano** (*I don't do favors to those who don't deserve them*). With the demonstrative component **a coloro** (*to those*), you convey aim or purpose; in fact, you need the preposition **a** (*to*). The relative component **che** (*who*) is the subject of the relative clause. And because in this case the demonstrative **coloro** is plural, the verb of the relative clause is plural, too.

Book III

Grasping Basic Grammar Essentials for Communication

If you collapse the two components in a combined form, you're also collapsing the two grammatical functions. So, in keeping with the preceding example, **a coloro che** becomes **a chi** (*those who*): The pronoun takes the preposition **a** to convey aim or purpose, but it's a singular pronoun, so you need the verb in the singular in the relative clause, as in **Non faccio favori a chi non lo merita** (*I don't do favors to those who don't deserve them*).

Remember that the combined pronouns can convey

✔ A direct object and a subject, as in **Lisa ringrazia chi le ha mandato i fiori/ Lisa ringrazia coloro che le hanno mandato i fiori** (*Lisa thanks those who sent her flowers*) or **Lisa ringrazia colei/colui che le ha mandato i fiori** (*Lisa thanks the person who sent her flowers*). (Given the context at your disposal, the pronoun **chi** can refer to all the persons mentioned.)

✔ Two direct objects, as in **Invito quanti ne voglio** or **Invito tutti coloro che voglio** (*I'm inviting all those I want to invite*).

✔ An indirect object and a subject, as in **Siamo riconoscenti per quanto hanno fatto per noi** or **Siamo riconoscenti per quello che hanno fatto per noi** (*We're thankful for what they did for us*).

Table 7-5 presents the combined pronouns and their non-combined counterparts along with some examples.

Table 7-5   Combined Demonstrative + Relative Pronouns

Combined Pronoun	Demonstrative + Relative Pronoun	Translation	Example
chi	colui che (MS); colei che (FS); coloro che (M/F)	the one; those who	Chi è uscito per ultimo non ha chiuso la porta. (*The person who went out last didn't lock the door.*)
quanto	tutto quello che (refers to situations only)	what; all that; which	Farò quanto mi è possibile. (*I'll do what I can.*)
quanti, quante, quelli che, quelle che	tutti coloro che (MP); tutte coloro che (FP)	all those who; people who	La festa è riservata a quanti hanno ricevuto l'invito. (*The party is reserved for those who have received the invitation.*)

Chapter 8

Asking and Answering Questions

*W*ho? What? When? Where? Why? How? These basic questions, and variations on them, allow you to get the information you need in any language. Knowing how to ask questions is essential in the Italian world (and beyond). Here are some simple questions that can be answered with *yes, no,* or one or two words.

> **Vieni con noi?** (*Are you coming with us?*) **Sì.** (*Yes.*)
>
> **È già arrivata?** (*Has she already arrived?*) **No.** (*No.*)
>
> **Come stai?** (*How are you?*) **Bene, grazie.** (*Fine, thanks.*)
>
> **Chi parla?** (*Who's speaking?*) **Elisabetta.** (*Elizabeth.*)

But questions become more open-ended as you dig deeper and want more details and as you gain confidence and build your vocabulary. You also become more skilled at understanding and answering questions asked of you. This chapter assists you in asking and answering questions, which leads to conversation, discussion, even disagreement — all forms of your ultimate linguistic goal: communication.

Looking at Ways of Asking Questions in Italian

"Curiouser and curiouser" is the language-learner's motto. To satisfy your curiosity and to understand both a different language and a different culture, you need to be able to ask questions. You have relatively easy ways to do this: You can change your tone (or pitch) of voice, you can add a word like *right?* to the end of a sentence, or you can move the subject from the beginning to the end of a sentence.

Adjusting your intonation

Language is musical, and nowhere do you hear that better than in crafting sentences to make a statement, to exclaim, or to ask a question.

With a statement, you keep your voice pretty level. For example: **Carlo parla italiano** (*Carlo speaks Italian*) has a level tone with a slight drop at the end. To make this statement into a question, you raise your tone (think of it as going up a couple of notes on the musical scale) on the next-to-last syllable and then drop back a note on the very last syllable: **Carlo parla ital /ia \no?** (*Does Carlo speak Italian?*) Listen to yourself ask that question in both English and Italian; you discover that you make this same tone change in English.

Another option is to leave the sentence as a statement but finish it off with words like **no? non è vero?** or just **vero?** All translate, more or less, into *right?* or *isn't that so?* You can also say **ok?** or **va bene?** both of which mean *okay?* When you use these words, your intonation again goes up a note or two on the musical scale. Here are some examples:

> **Ho comprato i biglietti, va bene?** (*I've bought the tickets, okay?*)
>
> **Andiamo al cinema domani, no?** (*We're going to the movies tomorrow, aren't we?*)
>
> **Tuo padre lavora sempre a Milano, vero?** (*Your father still works in Milan, doesn't he?*)

Inverting the word order

Another way to turn a statement into a question is to move the subject from the beginning to the end of the sentence. **Carlo parla italiano** (*Carlo speaks Italian*) is a statement; **Parla italiano, Carlo?** (*Does Carlo speak Italian?*) is a question.

This technique works only if you have a stated subject. Here's another example:

Il gatto ha mangiato tutto il cibo. (*The cat has eaten all the food.*) **Ha mangiato tutto il cibo, il gatto?** (*Has the cat eaten all the food?*)

Asking some common questions

The following standard questions will get you into the practice of asking about things. Some are more open-ended (like those that ask where something is) and may elicit a longer response than you can understand at first. You can anticipate an answer to a *where* question by using props — a street map, for example, allows someone to show you what they're talking about.

- ✔ **Come sta?** (*How are you?* [formal])
- ✔ **Come stai?** (*How are you?* [familiar])
- ✔ **Come va?** (*How are things going?*)
- ✔ **Come si chiama?** (*What is your name?* [formal])
- ✔ **Come ti chiami?** (*What is your name?* [familiar])
- ✔ **Chi è?** (*Who is it?*)
- ✔ **Che tempo fa?** (*What's the weather like?*)
- ✔ **Come si dice _____?** (*How do you say_____ [in Italian]?*)
- ✔ **Cosa vuol dire _____?** (*What does _____ mean?*)
- ✔ **Dove/dov'è/dove sono _____?** (*Where/where is/where are _____?*)
- ✔ **Quanto costa?** (*How much is it?*)
- ✔ **Come?** (*Huh?*) (*What did you say?*)
- ✔ **Perché?** (*Why?*)
- ✔ **Pronto?** (*Hello?* [used to answer the phone])

Book III

Grasping Basic Grammar Essentials for Communication

Digging Deeper: Asking More Complex Questions

To ask more complicated questions, beyond the most basic ones that require only a *yes, no,* or brief one- or two-word response, you need the interrogative adjectives, adverbs, and pronouns that lead to more profound conversations.

Here are some examples:

Chi è quel bell'uomo? (_Who_ is that handsome man?)

Cosa ne sai? (_What_ do you know about her/him/it?)

Quando è successo l'incidente e dove? (_When_ did the accident happen, and _where?_)

Perché non sei andato alla festa? (_Why_ didn't you go to the party?)

Quanti figli hanno? (_How many_ children do they have?)

Quale formaggio preferisci? (_Which_ cheese do you prefer?)

Employing interrogative adjectives

You use two adjectives to ask questions: **quanto/a** (_how much_), **quanti/e** _how many_), and **quale** (_which_).

Adjectives modify a noun or pronoun; because **quanto** and **quale** are adjectives, you need to make them agree in number (singular, plural) and gender (masculine, feminine) with the words they modify.

Finding how much or how many with quanto

Quanto (_how much; how many_) has four forms:

- ✔ **quanto** (masculine, singular)
- ✔ **quanti** (masculine, plural)
- ✔ **quanta** (feminine, singular)
- ✔ **quante** (feminine, plural)

These words allow you to find out how much or how many of something you're asking about. Here are some examples, using the four forms of **quanto:**

Quanto denaro hai con te? (_How much money do you have with you?_)

Quanto tempo sarà necessario? (_How much time will be needed?_)

Quanti libri hai letto quest'anno? (_How many books have you read this year?_)

Quanti studenti ci sono in classe? (_How many students are there in class?_)

Quanta carne mangi? (_How much meat do you eat?_)

Quanta gente c'è? (_How many people are there?_)

Quante ragazze sanno ballare? (*How many girls know how to dance?*)

Quante macchine sono nuove? (*How many cars are new?*)

Determining which one with quale

Quale (*which*) has only two forms:

- ✔ **quale** (masculine/feminine, singular)
- ✔ **quali** (masculine/feminine, plural)

It means *which* and, like **quanto,** agrees in number with the thing you're asking about. Here are a few examples:

Quale libro preferisci? (*Which book do you prefer?*)

Quale casa è la più moderna? (*Which house is the most modern?*)

Dei documenti, qual è più importante? (*Of the documents, which is more important?*)

When **quale** precedes the verb **è** (*is*), you drop the final **e** from **quale.** You do not, however, write **qual** and **è** together with an apostrophe; you write **Qual è la risposta giusta?** (*Which is the correct response?*) You can find more details about using **quale** as a pronoun in the later section "Inquiring about who, what, which one, and how many: Interrogative pronouns." The following examples show the plural form of **quale:**

Quali studenti vanno alla partita? (*Which students are going to the game?*)

Quali sedie sono comode? (*Which chairs are comfortable?*)

Book III

Grasping Basic Grammar Essentials for Communication

Requesting the location and time: Interrogative adverbs

Where (**dove**) and *when* (**quando**) do you use interrogative adverbs? Evidently, here and now. These interrogative adverbs keep you up-to-date on events. For example:

Dove andiamo? (*Where are we going?*)

Quando partiamo? (*When are we leaving?*)

Come andiamo, in treno o in macchina? (*How are we going, by train or by car?*)

You put all interrogative adverbs right next to the verb in your question.

Because **dove, quando,** and **come** are adverbs, they're invariable. You don't have to think about number and gender.

Determining where with dove

With **dove** (*where*), you often use **è** (*is*) or **sono** (*are*). To produce the singular form (*where is*), you drop the final **e** from **dove** and use an apostrophe to connect it to the verb **è**. For example:

> **Dov'è la stazione?** (*Where is the station?*)
>
> **Dov'è il ristorante?** (*Where's the restaurant?*)

The plural is simply **dove sono** (*where are*):

> **Dove sono le chiavi?** (*Where are the keys?*)
>
> **Dove sono i turisti?** (*Where are the tourists?*)

Finding out when with quando

Quando (*when*) stays the same whether you use it with a singular or a plural verb. See the following examples:

> **Quando arrivano gli ospiti?** (*When are the guests arriving?*)
>
> **Quando parte il treno?** (*When does the train leave?*)
>
> **Quando vieni a trovarmi?** (*When are you coming to see me?*) (Literally: *When are you coming to find me?*)

Knowing how and what with come

The third interrogative adverb, **come,** has two meanings: *how* and *what*. If you don't catch what someone is saying, you ask **Come?** (a nicer form than the English *Huh?* but with the same meaning). It also means *what* when used with **essere** (*to be*). When used with **è** (*is*), you drop the final **e** and use an apostrophe to form **com'è** (*what is something or someone like?* [permanently]).

> **Com'è Elena?** (*What is Elena like?*) **È bionda con gli occhi azzurri.** (*She's blond with blue eyes.*)
>
> **Come sono gli studenti?** (*What are the students like?*) **Sono intelligenti.** (*They're bright.*)

You use **come** as *how* most frequently to ask about someone's health, a temporary condition.

> **Come sta, Signorina?** (*How are you, Miss?*)
>
> **Come stai, Cinzia?** (*How are you, Cinzia?*)

You always put **come** right next to a verb.

> **Come hanno giocato?** (*How did they play?*)
>
> **Come ti senti oggi?** (*How are you feeling today?*)

Inquiring about who, what, which one, and how many: Interrogative pronouns

When question words can stand alone, or aren't necessarily tied to a verb, they're called *interrogative pronouns.* They replace nouns and must agree in number (singular/plural) and gender (masculine/feminine) with those nouns. They don't stand alone exclusively, but they can. Also, not all interrogative pronouns change. **Chi** (*who*) and **che, che cosa, cosa** (*what*) are invariable; **quale** (*which one*) and **quanto/a/i/e** (*how much; how many*) aren't. Here are some example questions with these interrogative pronouns:

> **Chi mi ha telefonato?** (*Who called me?*)
>
> **Chi è?** (*Who is it?*)
>
> **Chi sarà?** (*Who could it be?*) (*Who will it be?*)
>
> **Che fai?** (*What are you doing?*)
>
> **Che cosa studi?** (*What are you studying?*)
>
> **Cosa è/Cos'è?** (*What is it?*)
>
> **A che ora mangiamo?** (*What time are we eating?*)

Quale (*which one*) uses only two forms: **quale** (*which one?* [masculine/ feminine, singular]) and **quali** (*which ones?* [masculine/feminine, plural]).

> **Quale preferisci?** (*Which one do you prefer?*)
>
> **Quali compri?** (*Which ones are you buying?*)
>
> **Qual è [il] tuo?** (*Which one is yours?*)

When you use **quale** with **è**, you drop its final **e.** You do not, however, connect **qual** with **è** by adding an apostrophe.

Only **quanto** (*how much; how many*) has four forms: **quanto** (masculine, singular), **quanti** (masculine, plural), **quanta** (feminine, singular), and **quante** (feminine, plural).

> **Quanti libri compri?** (*How many books are you buying?*)
>
> **Quante portano uno zaino?** (*How many [girls] are carrying a backpack?*)

Quanto costa un telefonino? (*How much does a cellphone cost?*)

Quanta bistecca vuoi? (*How much steak do you want?*)

Providing Detailed Answers to Questions

To answer information questions (as opposed to yes/no questions), you need to listen very carefully. You have the vocabulary you need for your answer in the question. Keep in mind that the question word (*who, what, when, where, why, how*) is likely to begin the sentence; the content of the question (whose vocabulary you can appropriate) follows. Here's a sample information question with steps to answer it.

1. **Listen carefully to the question:**

    Quando partiamo domani? (*When are we leaving tomorrow?*)

2. **Break the question into two parts:**

    Quando (question word: *when*) **partiamo domani** (content: *are we leaving tomorrow*)**?**

3. **Start your answer with the vocabulary from the content.**

    Partiamo domani . . . (*We are leaving . . .*)

4. **Fill in your answer to the question quando (*when*).**

    Partiamo domani sera. (*We are leaving tomorrow night.*)

    You can answer this question in several ways; here are a couple of examples:

    Non partiamo domani. Partiamo dopodomani. (*We're not leaving tomorrow. We're leaving day after tomorrow.*)

    Partiamo domani a mezzogiorno. (*We're leaving tomorrow at noon.*)

    You can even answer with a question of your own:

    Partiamo domani? (*We're leaving tomorrow?*)

Sometimes, you need to reverse the word order so that the subject precedes the verb in your answer.

Dovè il museo? (*Where's the museum?*) **Il museo è all'angolo.** (*It's on the corner.*)

Quando partono loro? (*When are they leaving?*) **Loro partono domani.** (*They are leaving tomorrow.*)

To answer a question involving quantities, you replace the question word with an amount or a number, as in these examples:

> **Quante persone vanno alla spiaggia?** (*How many people are going to the beach?*) **Tre persone vanno alla spiaggia.** (*Three people are going to the beach.*)

> **Quanti ponti ci sono a Firenze?** (*How many bridges are there in Florence?*) **Ci sono cinque ponti a Firenze.** (*There are five bridges in Florence.*)

 For questions designed to elicit specific answers from you (about you), you need to change the verb in the question before using it in the answer. In English, when someone asks *Are you a student?* you answer with a different form of the verb, *I am a student.*

Answering Questions Negatively

In Italian, you can use two, even three, negative words in the same sentence without incurring funny looks from native speakers. Double negatives are the norm, not a broken rule. For example:

> **Non ho mai fatto nulla di cattivo.** (*I've never done anything bad.*) (Literally: *I have not never done nothing bad.*)

The following lists some of the most common negative adverbs. The spaces indicate that a verb is needed for the adverb to cozy up to.

- ✔ **non _____ mai** (*never*)
- ✔ **non _____ nessuno** (*no one*)
- ✔ **non _____ niente, nulla** (*nothing*)
- ✔ **non _____ più** (*no more; no longer*)
- ✔ **non _____ neache, nemmeno, neppure** (*not even*)
- ✔ **non _____ né . . . né . . .** (*neither . . . nor . . .*)
- ✔ **non _____ mica** (*not really*)
- ✔ **non _____ affatto, per nulla, per niente** (*not at all*)

You can also put the adverb (without **non**) at the beginning of a sentence, making your meaning more emphatic.

Book III

Grasping Basic Grammar Essentials for Communication

Here are some examples using the negative adverbs.

Non sono mai andato in Italia. (*I've never gone to Italy.*)

Non c'è nessuno. (*No one is there.*)

Non c'è niente da fare. (*There's nothing you can do about it.*)

Non abito più in quella città. (*I don't live in that city any longer.*)

Non è neanche italiano. (*He's not even Italian.*)

Non è né pesce né carne. (*It's neither fish nor fowl.*)

Lei non è mica magra. (*She's not really thin.*)

Non è affatto grasso. (*He's not fat at all.*)

Non mi piace affatto. (*I don't like it at all.*)

Mai ci vado. (*I never go there.*)

Mica male. (*Not bad.*)

Neanche lui lo farebbe. (*Not even he would do it.*)

Book IV
Mastering Italian Verbs and Tenses

Using Avere as To Be

Italian	English
avere fame	to be hungry
avere sete	to be thirsty
avere sonno	to be sleepy
avere caldo	to be hot
avere freddo	to be cold
avere fretta	to be in a hurry
avere ragione	to be right
avere torto	to be wrong
avere bisogno (di)	to need
avere voglia (di)	to feel like
avere paura (di)	to be afraid of
avere vergogna	to be ashamed
avere . . . anni	to be . . . years old

If you like the Trevi Fountain, master the future indicative tense, because chances are that you'll go to Rome to see it! Head to www.dummies.com/extras/italianaio for a free article about *La Fontana di Trevi* and how it relates to the future tense.

Contents at a Glance

Chapter 1

Jumping into Action with Italian Regular Verbs

*V*erbs bring language to life. Without them, you can't tell, question, evaluate, or comment. You can't share how you *enjoy learning* Italian. Verbs reflect actions, whether they're immediate, ongoing, or habitual. You use verbs to talk about what you've done, what you hope to do, and where you've been. Verbs let you state facts — and opinions, for that matter. In short, without using verbs, you can't fully express yourself in Italian or in any other language.

Verbs have many forms; you have to know how to say a verb, such as *eat,* in the present tense (*I eat*), the past tense (*I ate*), and the future tense (*I will eat*). Expressing a verb in various tenses is called *conjugation.* With some verbs, the rules for conjugation are always the same. For example, in English you simply add *-ed* to the end of many verbs to express them in the past tense. Verbs that follow these rules are called *regular* verbs. Verbs that don't follow these rules are called *irregular* verbs, which are discussed in Chapter 2 of Book IV.

This chapter looks at Italian regular verbs and how to conjugate them so you can avoid being "all words and no action" in the past, present, and future. Here, you discover that Italian and English are remarkably similar in their use of verbs and that, thankfully, Italian has more regular verbs than English does.

Conjugating Regular Verbs in Italian

Italian verbs are categorized by type, according to their *infinitive* form — a verb's most basic form. In English, an infinitive is always preceded by *to* (*to be, to do,* and *to read*). In its infinitive form, a verb has no subject and isn't conjugated. When you discover a new verb in Italian, you realize this "raw" form. To use the verb effectively, you need to understand the rules of conjugation.

To start, look at some infinitives. The three major types of Italian infinitives end in **-are, -ere,** and **-ire,** with the majority ending in **-are,** followed by **-ere** then **-ire.** Here are some examples:

> **parlare** (*to speak*)
>
> **scrivere** (*to write*)
>
> **dormire** (*to sleep*)

A small number of verbs end in **-orre, -urre,** and **-arre,** such as **proporre** (*to propose*), **tradurre** (*to translate*), and **attrarre** (*to attract*). See Chapter 2 in Book IV for an overview of the **-orre, -urre,** and **-arre** verbs.

To conjugate verbs, you need to know who or what the subject is. The subject tells you what to add to the verb *stem,* which you get by removing the identifying **-are, -ere,** or **-ire.** For example, the stem of **parlare** is **parl-**.

To this stem, you add endings based on the subject. Each subject, or subject pronoun, calls for a specific ending. For example, **io** (*I*) means that you add an **-o** to the verb stem: **io parlo,** or *I am speaking.* **Noi** (*we*) gets the ending **-iamo,** as in **Noi mangiamo** (*We eat*). Although in English you can't say just *speaking* or *eating* without naming the subject, in Italian, the endings **-o** and **-iamo** tell you what the subject is. In a sense, the subject pronouns are redundant in Italian.

English also has a different verb ending depending on the subject. For example, *I eat, you eat, he/she/it eats* — but you must state the subject. Here's a list of Italian subject pronouns with their English equivalents. (See the later sections on individual types of verbs for more on Italian subject pronouns.)

- **io** (*I*)
- **tu** (*you* [singular, informal])
- **lui** (*he, it*)
- **lei** (*she, it*)

> ✔ **Lei** (*you* [singular, formal])
>
> ✔ **noi** (*we, you* [plural, informal])
>
> ✔ **loro** (*they* [plural, masculine/feminine])
>
> ✔ **Loro** (*you* [plural, formal])

The following sections explain how to conjugate each verb type according to the subject pronoun that accompanies it.

Conjugating -are verbs

This largest category of Italian verbs is wonderfully dependable — and mostly regular in conjugation. A few **-are** verbs have pronunciations that are a bit different; they have the so-called **accento sdrucciolo** (*slippery accent*), explained later in this section.

To conjugate or use an **-are** verb, first you remove the letters **-are** from the infinitive, which leaves you with the stem:

> infinitive: **parlare**
>
> stem: **parl-**

To the stem, you add the ending (**-o, -i, -a, -iamo, -ate,** or **-ano**) that reflects the subject (**io, tu, lui, lei, Lei, noi, voi, loro,** and **Loro**). The following table shows a sample conjugation.

parlare (*to speak*)	
io **parlo**	noi **parliamo**
tu **parli**	voi **parlate**
lui, lei, Lei **parla**	loro, Loro **parlano**

All regular **-are** verbs (in other words, the vast majority of them) follow this pattern of conjugation in the present tense. The subject pronouns and corresponding endings, then, are as follows: **io = -o; tu = -i; lui/lei/Lei = -a; noi = -iamo; voi = -ate; loro/Loro = -ano.**

Here are some of the more commonly used **-are** verbs, which you'll see throughout this book. Each of these verbs follows the conjugation pattern for regular **-are** verbs.

Book IV

Mastering Italian Verbs and Tenses

- abbracciare (*to hug*)
- abitare (*to live*)
- ascoltare (*to listen*)
- aspettare (*to wait for*)
- baciare (*to kiss*)
- ballare (*to dance*)
- cercare (*to look for*)
- cominciare (*to begin; to start*)
- comprare (*to buy*)
- comunicare (*to communicate*)
- frequentare (*to attend*)
- giocare (a) (*to play a sport or a game*)
- guardare (*to look at*)
- guidare (*to drive*)
- imparare (*to learn*)
- incontrare (*to meet; to encounter; to run into*)
- indicare (*to indicate*)
- insegnare (*to teach*)
- inviare (*to send*)
- lavorare (*to work*)
- mangiare (*to eat*)
- negare (*to deny*)
- pagare (*to pay for*)
- parlare (*to talk; to speak*)
- pensare (*to think*)
- portare (*to wear; to carry; to bring*)
- ritornare (*to return; to go back*)
- salutare (*to greet*)
- sciare (*to ski*)
- spiegare (*to explain*)
- studiare (*to study*)
- suonare (*to play a musical instrument*)
- telefonare (a) (*to call on the phone*)
- visitare (*to visit*)

Several verbs have built-in prepositions. **Pagare,** for example, means *to pay for,* without having to add an additional preposition to the verb. **Aspettare** (*to wait for*), likewise, needs no additional preposition: **Io aspetto la posta** (*I'm waiting for the mail*). **Cercare** (*to look for*) follows the same pattern: **Lui cerca le chiavi** (*He is looking for the keys*).

Verbs ending in -care and -gare

To maintain the sound of the **-are** infinitives in their conjugated forms, you find a few verbs, specifically, those ending in **-care** and **-gare,** that require some spelling changes.

Instead of simply adding subject endings to the stems of the **tu** and **noi** forms, you need to insert the letter **h** to keep the hard *c* or *g* sound. The following tables show conjugations of **-care** and **-gare** verbs that have spelling changes.

cercare (*to look for*)	
io **cerco**	noi **cerchiamo**
tu **cerchi**	voi **cercate**
lui, lei, Lei **cerca**	loro, Loro **cercano**

pagare (*to pay for*)	
io **pago**	noi **paghiamo**
tu **paghi**	voi **pagate**
lui, lei, Lei **paga**	loro, Loro **pagano**

Other verbs with the **-care** and **-gare** endings include **comunicare** (*to communicate*), **giocare** (*to play a game or sport*), **indicare** (*to indicate; to point out*), **criticare** (*to criticize*), **negare** (*to deny*), and **spiegare** (*to explain*).

Verbs ending in -iare

As with **-care** and **-gare** verbs, you make some spelling changes to verbs that end in **-iare**. These changes make the conjugated forms sound the way the infinitive does.

Some of the more common verbs ending in **-iare** include **cominciare** (*to begin*), **mangiare** (*to eat*), **abbracciare** (*to hug*), **baciare** (*to kiss*), and **studiare** (*to study*).

Dropping the **-are** from the infinitive leaves you with the letter **i** on the end of the stem. You don't want a double **i** in your conjugation, so the **tu** and **voi** forms drop the **i** from the stem. All the other forms keep it.

The following tables show the conjugated forms of **-iare** verbs.

cominciare (*to begin*)	
io **comincio**	noi **cominciamo**
tu **cominci**	voi **cominciate**
lui, lei, Lei **comincia**	loro, Loro **cominciano**

mangiare (*to eat*)	
io **mangio**	noi **mangiamo**
tu **mangi**	voi **mangiate**
lui, lei, Lei **mangia**	loro, Loro **mangiano**

studiare (*to study*)	
io **studio**	noi **studiamo**
tu **studi**	voi **studiate**
lui, lei, Lei **studia**	loro, Loro **studiano**

Although you usually drop the **i** from the **tu** and **noi** stems of **-iare** verbs, in some cases, you keep it when the **i** in the **io** form is stressed: For example, **[io] invío** and **[io] scío** become **[tu] invìi** and **[tu] scìi.** But for the **noi** form of these verbs, you drop the **i** because the stress is on **inviàmo** and **sciàmo.**

Along these same lines, some **-are** verbs undergo a pronunciation change and use the **accento sdrucciolo.** So instead of stressing the second-to-last syllable on the singular conjugations, or the third-to-last syllable on the third person plural, you back the stress up by one syllable. Thus, **abito** has a stressed **a.** Following is a sample conjugation of such a verb, with the stressed syllable in bold. The **noi** and **voi** forms follow regular rules of pronunciation and stress the second-to-last syllable.

io **à**bito

tu **à**biti

lui, lei, Lei **à**bita

noi abi**tià**mo

voi abi**tà**te

loro, Loro **à**bitano

Common verbs that carry this particular stress include **telefonare** (*to call*), **terminare** (*to end*), **preoccupare** (*to worry*), **partecipare** (*to participate*), **desiderare** (*to want*), **significare** (*to mean*), and **ordinare** (*to order*). You can't predict which verbs use this stress — it's something you pick up as you go.

Conjugating -ere verbs

The second largest category of Italian verb conjugations is as dependable as the first. The **-ere** verbs strictly follow the path of removing **-ere** from the infinitive and adding the subject endings specific to the conjugation. You have no spelling changes to remember here because only the **-are** verbs maintain the pronunciation of the infinitive. The following tables show the various endings for **-ere** verbs.

scrivere (*to write*)	
io **scrivo**	noi **scriviamo**
tu **scrivi**	voi **scrivete**
lui, lei, Lei **scrive**	loro, Loro **scrivono**

leggere (*to read*)	
io **leggo**	noi **leggiamo**
tu **leggi**	voi **leggete**
lui, lei, Lei **legge**	loro, Loro **leggono**

Notice that **leggere** in its conjugations has different sounds, some of which are *not* true to the sound of the infinitive. The **io** and **loro** forms both have a hard *g* sound, while all the other forms keep the soft *g* of the infinitive. Because **-ere** verbs derive from two Latin conjugations, the infinitives may not follow the general Italian rule of placing stress on the next-to-last syllable. Compare the following infinitives' pronunciations. Accents indicate where the stress falls. Many **-ere** verbs use the **accento sdrucciolo**, so the accent falls on the third-to-last syllable.

- **chièdere** (*to ask*)
- **chiùdere** (*to close*)
- **conóscere** (*to know a person or place; to be acquainted with*)
- **crédere** (*to believe*)

Book IV

Mastering Italian Verbs and Tenses

- **lèggere** (*to read*)
- **prèndere** (*to take; to eat; to drink*)
- **ripètere** (*to repeat*)
- **rispóndere** (*to reply*)
- **scrìvere** (*to write*)
- **véndere** (*to sell*)
- **vìvere** (*to live*)

Conjugating -ire verbs

Although **-ire** verbs follow pronunciation rules reliably, they have a different surprise in store — they come in two types. The first is a regular, normal Italian verb, such as **dormire** (*to sleep*); the second is known as an **isc** verb because all the conjugated forms, except for **noi** and **voi,** insert the letters **isc** between the stem and the endings.

Compare the following conjugations.

dormire (*to sleep*)	
io **dormo**	noi **dormiamo**
tu **dormi**	voi **dormite**
lui, lei, Lei **dorme**	loro, Loro **dormono**

capire (isc) (*to understand*)	
io **capisco**	noi **capiamo**
tu **capisci**	voi **capite**
lui, lei, Lei **capisce**	loro, Loro **capiscono**

How do you know which verbs take **isc** in their conjugation? You don't. You have to refer to the dictionary, which shows the conjugation right after the infinitive. In this book, you see **isc** after those infinitives that use it. The best thing is to memorize the most commonly used **isc** verbs from the get-go. Only a few will be useful at this point, including the following:

Multiplying your vocabulary with conjugations

After you figure out how to conjugate each of the three infinitive types, you immediately multiply your vocabulary by a factor of six — and that's just in the present tense.

Another element that multiplies your vocabulary exponentially comes with meanings in the present tense.

Parlo, for example, means *I speak, I do speak,* and *I am speaking.* You can use it to make statements or to ask questions. Still using **parlare,** the **tu** form, **parli,** can mean many things. **Parli italiano** is a statement: *You speak Italian. You are speaking Italian. You do speak Italian.* It can also be a question: *Do you speak Italian? Are you speaking Italian? You speak Italian?* All of that comes in one five-letter word.

- ✔ **capire (isc)** (*to understand*)
- ✔ **finire (isc)** (*to finish*)
- ✔ **preferire (isc)** (*to prefer*)
- ✔ **guarire (isc)** (*to heal*)
- ✔ **garantire (isc)** (*to guarantee*)
- ✔ **punire (isc)** (*to punish*)
- ✔ **pulire (isc)** (*to clean*)

Spedire (*to send*) is an **isc** verb, but you can use the regular **-are** verbs **mandare** or **inviare** to mean the same thing.

Here are the most common **-ire** verbs (without **isc**):

- ✔ **dormire** (*to sleep*)
- ✔ **aprire** (*to open*)
- ✔ **partire** (*to leave; to depart*)
- ✔ **seguire** (*to follow*)
- ✔ **sentire** (*to hear; to feel*)
- ✔ **mentire** (*to lie*)
- ✔ **coprire** (*to cover*)

Book IV

Mastering Italian Verbs and Tenses

Moving Past the Present Tense

You can "get by" in a language by sticking to the present tense. With it, you can discuss what's actually happening: **Ora i bambini dormono** (*Right now, the kids are sleeping*). You can describe a permanent or continuing situation: **La mamma lavora senza sosta** (*Mom works without stopping*). To express something that's a given, you can say **Il ristorante chiude il mercoledì** (*The restaurant closes on Wednesdays*).

You can even discuss the future, so long as it's the not-too-distant future and what you're talking about is a sure thing:

>**Questa settimana lavoro ogni giorno.** (*This week I'm working every day.*)

>**Domani preparo il pollo.** (*Tomorrow, I'm fixing the chicken.*)

>**Ci vediamo domani.** (*We'll see each other tomorrow.*) (*See you tomorrow.*)

Finally, you use the present after the preposition **da** (*from; since; by*) to express the English present progressive tense:

>**Abito qui da dieci anni.** (*I've been living here for ten years.*)

>**Marco studia l'inglese dal 2000.** (*Marco has been studying English since 2000.*)

Some conversational clues tell you that you can use the present tense, such as the following common words and phrases:

- ✔ **a mezzogiorno** (*at noon*, or at any other specific time)
- ✔ **ogni giorno** (*every day*)
- ✔ **oggi** (*today*)
- ✔ **domani** (*tomorrow*)
- ✔ **stasera** (*this evening*)
- ✔ **mai** (*never*)
- ✔ **mai più** (*never again*)
- ✔ **sempre** (*always*)
- ✔ **il lunedì, il martedì . . .** (*Mondays, Tuesdays,* and so on)

When you tire of sounding like a precocious 4-year-old and are comfortable with the present tense, you can add in other tenses.

Communicating Quickly with Verbs

No doubt you want to communicate in Italian, but maybe you feel that you don't yet have an adequate vocabulary. There's so much to remember. And verbs, the lifeline of any language, take work, practice, and patience.

Here are some verbs you can use to express yourself quickly and easily. As in English, they're followed by an infinitive. Rather than learning all the conjugations immediately, try these verbs — all of which are in the **io** conjugation, but not all of which are in the present tense — and attach infinitives that express your daily wants, needs, and actions. Because they're all in the **io** form, you can choose to use the subject pronoun or not.

- **preferisco** (*I prefer to*)
- **vorrei** (*I would like to*)

    Note: This is in the present conditional tense because it is much more polite than the present indicative "I want."

- **mi piacerebbe** (*I would like to*)

    Note: This is in the present conditional tense because it is much more polite than the present indicative "I want."

- **devo** (*I must; I have to*)
- **posso** (*I am able to; I can*)
- **so, non so** (*I know how to; I don't know how to*)
- **ho bisogno di** (*I need to*)
- **ho voglia di** (*I feel like*)
- **sto per** (*I'm about to*)

Consider your daily movements. Which infinitives would you attach to these expressions? (If you need to, review the verbs already presented in this chapter.) Here are some examples:

> **Devo studiare. Mi piacerebbe guardare la televisione. Ma non posso.** (*I have to study. I would like to watch television. But I can't.*)

> **So parlare italiano. Vorrei parlare italiano molto bene. Sto per studiare. Ma prima, vorrei mangiare e prendere un caffè.** (*I know how to speak Italian. I would like to speak Italian really well. I'm about to study. But first, I'd like to eat and have a cup of coffee.*)

Book IV

Mastering Italian Verbs and Tenses

Posso ballare? No. Non so ballare. Posso cantare? No. Posso suonare uno strumento musicale? No. Ma posso scrivere belle poesie. (*Can I dance? No. I don't know how to dance. Can I sing? No. Can I play a musical instrument? No. But I can write nice poetry.*)

Ho voglia di andare al cinema. Vorrei vedere quel nuovo film di Benigni. Invece, devo lavorare. (*I feel like going to the movies. I'd like to see that new Benigni film. Instead, I have to work.*)

Sto per uscire. Posso telefonare dopo? (*I'm about to leave. Can I call later?*)

Looking More Closely at Personal Subject Pronouns

Personal subject pronouns tell you who the subject of a verb is or who is completing an action. They also determine which form of a conjugated verb to use.

Italian formal *you* forms of address include the plural **Loro.** But when addressing people, you often use **voi** instead.

In an attempt to make Italian more egalitarian, during the 1940s, the government abolished the distinction between the formal and informal singular forms and used **voi** instead. If someone addresses you (just you, one of you) as **voi,** it probably means that he or she is of an advanced age or is speaking "opera," where use of **voi** is ubiquitous.

Because verb endings always indicate the subject, personal subject pronouns aren't required in the present tense. However, if you want to be really clear, you should still use them. For example, the verb endings for *he, she, it,* and *you* (formal) are the same. **Giorgio e Mirella? Lui canta e lei balla.** (*George and Mirella? He sings and she dances.*) The pronouns make it clear that Giorgio is singing and Mirella is dancing.

Sometimes, to be particularly emphatic, you use a pronoun: **Oggi pago io** (*Today, I'm paying*). Another variation is to use **anche** (*too; also*): **Anche Lei?** (*You, too?*) or **Anch'io** (*Me, too*).

To express more complicated thoughts and actions, you need a few basic *conjunctions* — words that join two or more parts of a sentence. To begin, you can use the most prevalent Italian conjunctions shown here.

- **e** (*and*)
- **ed** (*and;* used before a vowel)
- **ma** (*but*)
- **o** (*or*)
- **perché** (*because*)

Combining pronouns takes practice. If you're referring to yourself and someone else, **Mario ed io** (*Mario and I*), but don't want to name names, you may use **noi** (*we*). Remember that the verb conjugation must agree with this double subject. **Mario ed io mangiamo insieme ogni giorno** (*Mario and I eat together every day*) is the same as **Noi mangiamo insieme ogni giorno** (*We eat together every day*).

Here are some other examples of double or compound subjects:

> **tu e Giuseppe cantate** (*you and Giuseppe* = **voi**)
>
> **voi ed io parliamo** (*you and I* = **noi**)
>
> **Marco, Beppe, e Margherita scrivono** (*Marco, Beppe, and Margherita* = **loro**)

When you see double or compound subjects, the verb needs a plural ending.

Until you're comfortable with the conjugations, you may want to use the personal subject pronouns. You'll notice, however, that you use them less and less frequently as your command of Italian grows.

Book IV

Mastering Italian Verbs and Tenses

Chapter 2

Talking in the Present Tense with Irregular Verbs

In This Chapter

▶ Understanding how irregular verbs work

▶ Conjugating common irregular verbs in the present tense

▶ Using irregular verbs in idiomatic expressions

*I*rregular verbs work the same way regular verbs do: You use them to tell, question, evaluate, and comment. They reflect actions (immediate, ongoing, or habitual). They enable you to state facts and opinions. In short, you need them to communicate.

Like all verbs, you conjugate irregular verbs so that the subject and verb agree in number. The difference is, irregular verbs aren't particularly straightforward about their conjugations, as are their regular verb counterparts (see Chapter 1 in Book IV). Although you can often trace the linguistic genealogy of irregular verbs, you frequently can't assign any logic to their formations. You could say that irregular verbs aren't entirely user-friendly, but they can be conquered with practice, repetition, and memorization.

Moreover, in Italian, irregular verbs frequently show up in idiomatic expressions. *Idiomatic expressions* are those language constructions that make little to no sense if translated word for word but that collectively convey an idea or make an allusion. For example, the English idiom "having a long face" means nothing if translated literally to another language, but English speakers know it means someone looks unhappy.

Idiomatic expressions are as common in Italian as they are in most languages. Recognizing them allows you to sound more Italian and, perhaps more important, to understand what's being said to you. Idioms can also provide witty insights into the culture.

This chapter explores common irregular verbs and shows you how to conjugate them. You pick up some idiomatic expressions that contain irregular verbs (as well as a dash of Italian culture) and get to know the most commonly used irregular verbs and how they team up with phrases and other words to make idiomatic speech possible.

To Be or Not to Be: Conjugating Essere

The most fundamental of verbs, **essere** (*to be*), is always irregular, across languages and across tenses. And, along with several other irregular verbs introduced later in this chapter, **essere** allows you to say almost anything. It will prove a mainstay in your linguistic wardrobe.

The following table shows the conjugation of **essere** in the present tense.

essere (*to be*)	
io **sono**	noi **siamo**
tu **sei**	voi **siete**
lui, lei, Lei **è**	loro, Loro **sono**

The verb **essere** is a good example of why you don't need personal subject pronouns all the time. The only duplicate form in the conjugated **essere** is **sono** (*I am; they are*), but context often makes its meaning clear.

You use **essere** to form compound verb tenses, of which there are seven in Italian.

No separate word for the English subject *it* exists in Italian. **È** means *it is,* the *it* being understood. *It,* however, does have a gender in Italian. For example: **È bello. È bella.** The first refers to a masculine subject; the second, to a feminine subject.

> **È lunedì.** (*It is Monday.*)
>
> **È una giornata splendida.** (*It's a gorgeous day.*)

Other basic expressions that include the invisible *it* are **Quanto è?** (*How much is it?*); **Dov'è?** (*Where is it?*); and **Chi è?** (*Who is it?*).

Essere appears in many idiomatic expressions in Italian. See the section "Using Irregular Verbs in Idiomatic Expressions," later in this chapter, for examples.

To Have and to Hold: Conjugating Avere

Avere (*to have*) rivals **essere** (*to be*) for being ubiquitous. In fact, it's used in many expressions that allow it to do double duty because it can also mean *to be*. Find out more about that later in this section. First, have a look at the conjugation of **avere.**

avere (*to have*)	
io **ho**	noi **abbiamo**
tu **hai**	voi **avete**
lui, lei, Lei **ha**	loro, Loro **hanno**

Also, as with **essere,** *it* is included in the verb. For example: **Ha un aspetto meraviglloso** (*It has a great look to it*). This expression is frequently used to comment on a dish being served at table.

When accompanied by certain specific nouns, **avere** forms part of little units that, taken in their entirety, change its meaning from *to have* to *to be*. Table 2-1 shows some of these expressions.

Table 2-1	Using Avere as to Be
Italian	*English*
avere fame	*to be hungry*
avere sete	*to be thirsty*
avere sonno	*to be sleepy*
avere caldo	*to be hot, personally*
avere freddo	*to be cold, personally*
avere fretta	*to be in a hurry*
avere ragione	*to be right*
avere torto	*to be wrong*
avere bisogno (di)	*to need*
avere voglia (di)	*to feel like*
avere paura (di)	*to be afraid of*
avere vergogna (di)	*to be ashamed of*
avere . . . anni	*to be . . . years old*

Book IV

Mastering Italian Verbs and Tenses

One rule for knowing whether to use **essere** or **avere** to mean *to be* is that **essere** generally accompanies permanent states of being: **sono carini** (*they are nice*); **è alta** (*she is tall*); **siamo americani** (*we are American*). **Avere** tends to refer to temporary situations: **ho fame e sete** (*I'm hungry and thirsty*); **ha fretta** (*she is in a hurry*); **abbiamo freddo** (*we're cold*).

To Make or to Do: Conjugating Fare

In its most basic form, **fare** means *to make* or *to do*. With **essere** (*to be*) and **avere** (*to have*), it's one of the most versatile and useful Italian verbs.

Fare is also one of the most idiomatic verbs. Dozens of idiomatic expressions use **fare** as their base; you can find a useful list of **fare** expressions in the later section "Using Irregular Verbs in Idiomatic Expressions." See the following table for the conjugation of **fare**.

fare (*to make* or *to do*)	
io **faccio**	noi **facciamo**
tu **fai**	voi **fate**
lui, lei, Lei **fa**	loro, Loro **fanno**

Fare can stand alone in its irregular state. For example: **Io non faccio nulla di interessante** (*I'm not doing anything interesting*). A common question used by a parent speaking to a child is **Cosa fai?** (*What are you doing?*), though friends also use it to ask *What are you doing? What are you up to?*

To Give: Dare

Dare (*to give*) isn't terribly irregular. It follows the conjugation pattern of the **-are** regular verbs, with the exception of the **loro** forms, which double the consonant **n.**

dare (to give)	
io **do**	noi **diamo**
tu **dai**	voi **date**
lui, lei, Lei **dà**	loro, Loro **danno**

Dai (*you give/are giving*) can also mean *come on!* in Italian and is pronounced like the English *die*.

The third person singular form of **dare, dà** (*he/she/it, gives* or *you* [formal] *give*), carries an accent to distinguish it from the preposition **da** (*from; by*), without an accent.

To Ask How Others Are: Stare

You use **stare** to ask how someone is: **Come stai?** ([familiar] *How are you?*) or **come sta?** ([formal] *How are you?*) It can also mean *to stay,* physically, somewhere. **Sto all'Albergo Magnifico** (*I'm staying at the Magnifico Hotel*); **Sto a casa** (*I'm staying home*). Accompanied by the preposition **per,** it means *to be about to.* **Sto per mangiare** (*I'm about to eat*).

Like **dare, stare** isn't as irregular as some verbs in that it follows the conjugation pattern of the **-are** verbs, with the exception of the **loro** forms, which double the consonant **n.**

stare (to be)	
io **sto**	noi **stiamo**
tu **stai**	voi **state**
lui, lei, Lei **sta**	loro, Loro **stanno**

Stare has one other extremely important use. It combines with a verb's present participle (*-ing* form, like *eating, sleeping,* or *reading*) to make up the *present progressive verb tense.* As serious and confusing as that sounds, it's pretty much still the present tense; it's simply a little more immediate. For example, if someone calls and asks whether he's interrupting, you may say **Sto mangiando** (*I'm eating [right now]*).

Book IV

Mastering Italian Verbs and Tenses

You form the participles of verbs by dropping a verb's traditional or identifying ending and substituting **-ando** for **-are** and **-endo** for **-ere** and **-ire**. Here are some examples:

> **Sto mangiando.** (*I am eating.*)
>
> **Stiamo parlando.** (*We are talking.*)
>
> **Stai leggendo.** (*You are reading.*)
>
> **State partendo.** (*You are leaving.*)
>
> **Sta pulendo.** (*He/she/it is cleaning.*) (*You* [formal] *are cleaning.*)
>
> **Stanno vivendo.** (*They are living.*) (*You* [formal] *are living.*)

To Come and to Go: Venire and Andare

"What is all this coming and going?" asks a worried Rodolfo from the opera *La Bohème*. Coming and going are so much a part of daily activity that the verbs **venire** (*to come*) and **andare** (*to go*) are terrifically useful. And, grammatically speaking, it's safe to say that figuring out how to use both verbs is pretty straightforward — but still irregular.

Venire (*to come*) is the opposite of **andare. Vieni alla festa?** (*Are you coming to the party?*); **Vengono** (*They are coming*). Other verbs also mean *to go,* such as **partire** (*to go,* as in *to leave for a trip*) and **uscire** (*to go out*). **Uscire** has its own section later in this chapter.

Andare refers to going to a particular destination or to leaving. For example, you can say **Vado via** (*I am going away*) or the emphatic, and slightly petulant, **Me ne vado** (*I'm getting out of here*). You can also say, simply, **Vanno a teatro** (*They are going to the theater*); **Vai in ufficio?** (*Are you going to the office?*); or **Non vado a scuola oggi** (*I'm not going to school today*).

A useful expression that takes **andare** is **andare di male in peggio** (*to go from bad to worse*). For example: **La situazione va di male in peggio** (*The situation is going from bad to worse*).

Check out the following conjugations for **venire** and **andare.**

venire (to come)	
io **vengo**	noi **veniamo**
tu **vieni**	voi **venite**
lui, lei, Lei **viene**	loro, Loro **vengono**

andare (to go)	
io **vado**	noi **andiamo**
tu **vai**	voi **andate**
lui, lei, Lei **va**	loro, Loro **vanno**

Venire has the added attraction of serving as a base verb; that is, when altered by the addition of prefixes, it noticeably expands your vocabulary — and you have only one irregular conjugation to remember. For example, **svenire** adds the letter **s**, which often changes a word into its opposite. In this case, **svenire** means *to come undone* or *to faint*.

Declaring Needs, Wants, and Abilities: Dovere, Volere, and Potere

You use the verbs **dovere** (*to have to*), **volere** (*to want*), and **potere** (*to be able to*) to express your needs, desires, and abilities. They're very personal verbs in that you use them to communicate intimate or personal ideas.

These verbs are also called *semi-auxiliary* or "sort of" helping verbs. You can use them with infinitives, and you often will. For example: **Devo andare** (*I have to go*); **Non posso** (*I can't*); and **Vorrei mangiare** (*I would like to eat*).

The following tables show the conjugations of **dovere, volere,** and **potere.**

Book IV

Mastering Italian Verbs and Tenses

dovere (*to have to*)	
io **devo**	noi **dobbiamo**
tu **devi**	voi **dovete**
lui, lei, Lei **deve**	loro, Loro **devono**

volere (*to want*)	
io **voglio**	noi **vogliamo**
tu **vuoi**	voi **volete**
lui, lei, Lei **vuole**	loro, Loro **vogliono**

potere (*to be able to*)	
io **posso**	noi **possiamo**
tu **puoi**	voi **potete**
lui, lei, Lei **può**	loro, Loro **possono**

The first person singular, or *I* form, of **volere** isn't terribly polite. Consider the difference between *I want* (**voglio**) and *I would like* (**vorrei**). It's not that you never use **voglio,** but **vorrei** is much more polite and the form you may want to use in public (in a restaurant, for example).

In moods other than the indicative (the condition is the mood of **vorrei**), these verbs change their basic meaning and allow you to use *should, might, could,* and *ought to.* In other words, they add nuance, and occasionally sarcasm, to your Italian.

Do Tell: Dire

Dire (*to say; to tell*) is another verb that serves as the base for other common verb forms. After you know the conjugation of **dire,** you can add prefixes to change its meaning. **Disdire,** for example, means *to take back* or *to cancel (an appointment),* while **maledire** becomes *to curse.*

dire (*to say; to tell*)	
io **dico**	noi **diciamo**
tu **dici**	voi **dite**
lui, lei, Lei **dice**	loro, Loro **dicono**

Dire gives you the chance to use conversational fillers. For example, after interrupting your flow of thought, you can return to your point by saying **dicevo** (*as I was saying*). You can sum something up by saying **detto questo** (*this having been said*), a form, the ablative absolute, taken directly from that most economical of languages, Latin. Or you can use (sparingly, and only with a close friend or relative) the phrase **non te l'avevo detto?** (*didn't I tell you?*)

Stepping Out: Uscire

To go has shades of meaning, even in English. In Italian, more than one verb means *to go,* each with a particular sense.

Uscire means *to go out or exit a room/location.* For example: **Esco con degli amici** (*I am going out with some friends*) and **Lui non esce mai** (*He never goes out*). **Andare,** mentioned earlier in this chapter, means *to undertake the physical act of going somewhere,* such as **Vado in giardino** (*I'm going to the garden*) or **Vanno a Napoli** (*They are going to Naples*). **Partire** means *to leave* or *to depart.* It has a regular **-ire** conjugation: **Noi partiamo per l'Italia domani mattina** (*We are leaving for Italy tomorrow morning*).

Here's the irregular conjugation for **uscire.** (See the earlier section "To Come and to Go: Venire and Andare" for the conjugation of **andare.**)

uscire (*to go out*)	
io **esco**	noi **usciamo**
tu **esci**	voi **uscite**
lui, lei, Lei **esce**	loro, Loro **escono**

Uscire shows up with the prefix **ri-** (literally: *again*) and is a type of synonym to **potere** (*to be able to*) that means *to succeed.* Should someone say to you **Non riesco a farlo,** it doesn't mean he or she isn't going out again; it means he or she is unable to do something or *doesn't succeed in doing something.*

Bottom's Up: Bere

Bere (*to drink*) is another commonly used irregular verb, and its conjugation is shown in the following table.

bere (*to drink*)	
io **bevo**	noi **beviamo**
tu **bevi**	voi **bevete**
lui, lei, Lei **beve**	loro, Loro **bevono**

You can use **bere** to **bere alla salute** (*drink to someone's health*), but for having a cup of coffee or tea or a glass of wine, you can just as easily use **prendere**, a regular **-ere** verb. For example: **Io bevo thè** and **Io prendo thè** mean *I'm drinking tea.* The difference in meaning is very slight. **Bevo** (*I'm drinking*) is perhaps more immediate. **Prendo** (*I'm drinking*) carries the sense of ordering, as in *I'm having tea.*

The -orre, -urre, and -arre Verbs

The **-orre**, **-urre**, and **-arre** verbs are most useful as base verbs from which you can construct other verbs with expanded meanings. See the following tables for their conjugations.

porre (*to put*)	
io **pongo**	noi **poniamo**
tu **poni**	voi **ponete**
lui, lei, Lei **pone**	loro, Loro **pongono**

tradurre (*to translate*)	
io **traduco**	noi **traduciamo**
tu **traduci**	voi **traducete**
lui, lei, Lei **traduce**	loro, Loro **traducono**

trarre (*to pull; to lead; to drag; to get out*)	
io **traggo**	noi **traiamo**
tu **trai**	voi **traete**
lui, lei, Lei **trae**	loro, Loro **traggono**

Other incarnations of these kinds of verbs are dependent on the addition of prefixes, as in the following:

- **Porre** by itself means *to put;* add **pro-,** and it becomes *to propose;* add **com-,** and it becomes *to compose.*

- **Tradurre** means *to translate;* change the prefix from **tra-** to **de-,** and you have *to deduce.*

- **Trarre** means *to draw conclusions or consequences;* **trarre [fuori] da** means *to draw or pull out of* (troubles or a mess, for example). but enhanced forms are more useful: **attrarre** (*to attract*), **contrarre** (*to contract a disease*), and **distrarre** (*to distract*).

Using Irregular Verbs in Idiomatic Expressions

While an English speaker may be born with a silver spoon in his mouth, a similarly endowed Italian is born wearing a shirt. In English, it rains cats and dogs; in Italian, basins full of water. Cultural bias or proclivity also shows up in idiomatic expressions: In English, something can be ugly as sin; in Italian, something truly ugly is **brutto come la fame** (*as ugly as hunger*). In a similar vein, something or someone really good is **buono come il pane** (*as good as bread*).

Both idiomatic expressions and allusions make use of **essere.** When you follow **essere** with the preposition **di,** you indicate possession. For example: **È il libro di Giulio** (*It's Giulio's book*) and **La macchina? È di Luigi** (*The car? It's Luigi's*). You can also use **essere** with **di** to say where you're from, such as **Io sono di Firenze; lui è di Roma** (*I'm from Florence; he's from Rome*).

When you learn a foreign language, it's important not only to understand the literal meaning but also the metaphorical, symbolic, and cultural value of phrases and expressions. Practice this skill with **essere, fare, dare,** and **stare** idiomatic expressions.

Idiomatic expressions with essere

If you want to show off your Italian, use the following **essere** idiomatic expressions:

- ✔ **essere in gamba** (*to be on top of things; to be clever*)
- ✔ **essere al verde** (*to be broke*)
- ✔ **essere in vena** (*to be in the mood*)
- ✔ **essere un Cincinnato** (*to be an honest, simple, humble person*)
- ✔ **essere una Cassandra** (*to predict disaster and not be believed*)

Idiomatic expressions with fare

Idiomatic expressions also come in handy when your speech still lacks some verbs. Look at what **fare** + a noun can do for you:

- ✔ **fare una foto** instead of **fotografare** (*to take a picture*)
- ✔ **fare un viaggio** instead of **viaggiare** (*to take a trip*)
- ✔ **fare la conoscenza di** instead of **conoscere** (*to make the acquaintance of*)
- ✔ **fare una domanda a** instead of **chiedere/interrogare** (*to ask someone a question*)
- ✔ **fare una telefonata** instead of **telefonare** (*to make a phone call*)
- ✔ **fare una passeggiata** instead of **passeggiare** (*to take a walk*)

Here are some other of the most common **fare** idiomatic expressions:

- ✔ **fare lo spiritoso** (*to be funny*)
- ✔ **fare le valigie** (*to pack the suitcases*)
- ✔ **fare un bagno/una doccia** (*to take a bath/shower*)
- ✔ **fare finta di** (*to pretend*)
- ✔ **fare una bella figura** (*to make a good impression*)
- ✔ **fare una brutta figura** (*to make a bad impression*)

- ✔ **fare colazione** (*to eat breakfast*)

- ✔ **Ci fa il conto?** (*Could you get us the check?*)

- ✔ **Non si fa.** (*One doesn't do that.*)

- ✔ **Fa bene/male.** (*It's good for you/bad for you.*)

- ✔ **Fallo pure!** (*Just do it!*)

- ✔ **Fa bel/brutto tempo.** (*It's nice weather/nasty weather.*)

Idiomatic expressions with dare and stare

As is the case with many irregular verbs, **dare** and **stare** both create idiomatic speech. For example, **dare noia a** and **dare fastidio a** both mean *to annoy or bother:* **Il fratellino mi dà fastidio!** (*My little brother annoys me!*) When you meet someone **tu dai la mano a lui** (*you shake hands with him*).

You may begin conversations with new acquaintances, using the formal form of address (a wise move when dealing with anyone in a position of authority). One of you may say, probably sooner rather than later, **Ma ci diamo del tu** (*Let's use the informal*). To feed your pet, **Gli dai da mangiare** (*You are giving him food*). Perhaps you want a mechanic to look over your car's engine or a friend to look over something you've done. In both cases, that person **dà un'occhiata** (*looks over*) whatever you need evaluated. In a moment, that's probably counterintuitive to English speakers, to *take* an exam is, in Italian, to *give* an exam: **Loro danno un esame oggi.** (*They are taking an exam today*).

Other idiomatic phrases or expressions with **stare** include the following:

- ✔ **stare fresco** (*to be in trouble*)

- ✔ **stare sulle spine** (*to be on pins and needles*)

- ✔ **stare attento a** (*to be careful; to watch out for*)

- ✔ **Ci sto!** (*I'm game!*)

Book IV

Mastering Italian Verbs and Tenses

Chapter 3

Using Reflexive Forms and the Imperative Mood

In This Chapter
▶ Understanding reflexive verbs
▶ Using commands formally and informally

*V*erbs come in a variety of tenses (such as past, present, and future), moods (imperative and indicative), and voices (passive or active). They tell you who is doing something and what is happening.

Sometimes verbs reflect the action right back onto the subject, by way of a pronoun. These verbs are called *reflexive* verbs. They're more common in Italian than in English, and you'll find yourself using them frequently to describe everyday actions.

This chapter focuses on how reflexive verbs are used throughout the day in Italian. It also covers another type of common verbs, conjugated in the imperative mood. You use imperative verbs to issue commands, give orders, or deliver instructions.

Reflecting on Reflexive Verbs

Reflexive verbs are introverted. They direct the action characteristic of verbs back on their subjects by way of a pronoun. That means that the subject both gives and receives the action of the verb. In English, it's like saying, "I call myself Mary," instead of the more linear, "My name is Mary."

Reflexive verbs appear much more frequently in Italian than in English. From waking up (**svegliarsi**) to falling asleep (**addormentarsi**), in Italian, you use reflexive verbs all through the day.

These verbs are easy to recognize in the infinitive form because the standard **-are, -ere,** and **-ire** endings drop the final **e** and finish with **si.** For example, **chiamarsi** (*to be called*), **alzarsi** (*to get up*), and **domandarsi** (*to wonder*) (literally: *to ask oneself*). The conjugations of reflexive verbs follow the normal pattern for all tenses of **-are, -ere,** and **-ire** verbs, but they're preceded by reflexive pronouns.

The following sections show you how to use reflexive pronouns and verbs, including how to pair them together, and guide you through the reciprocal form and the impersonal **si.**

Pairing reflexive pronouns with reflexive verbs

To use a reflexive verb, you need the reflexive pronouns. Table 3-1 lists the Italian reflexive pronouns and their English equivalents.

Table 3-1	Reflexive Pronouns
Singular	*Plural*
mi (*me, myself*)	**ci** (*us, ourselves*)
ti (*you, yourself* [informal])	**vi** (*you, yourselves* [informal])
si (*himself, herself, itself, yourself* [formal])	**si** (*themselves, yourselves* [formal])

When you're building a sentence with reflexive pronouns, you put the reflexive pronoun after the personal subject pronoun (if used, which you usually don't in this case) and before the conjugated verb form. For example, **io mi alzo** uses the subject pronoun **io** (*I*) and follows it with the reflexive pronoun **mi** (*myself*) and the conjugated verb **alzo** (*get up*). The reflexive pronoun is part of the appropriate verb conjugation.

The following table shows the conjugation of the reflexive verb **chiamarsi** (*to call oneself*). This verb is the most common of reflexive verbs and is probably the first one you'll use when introducing yourself to strangers in Italian.

chiamarsi (*to call oneself; to be named*)	
io mi **chiamo**	noi ci **chiamiamo**
tu ti **chiami**	voi vi **chiamate**
lui, lei, Lei si **chiama**	loro, Loro si **chiamano**

For example: Use **Come si chiama?** (*What is your name?* [formal]) and **Come ti chiami?** (*What's your name?* [familiar]) to begin conversations. And after you ask someone else's name, it's nice to be able to offer your own: **Mi chiamo . . .** (*My name is . . .*).

Come si chiama also means *What is his/her/its/your* [formal] *name?* For example:

> **Come si chiama quella signora?** (*What is that woman's name?*)
>
> **Che bel gatto! Come si chiama?** (*What a beautiful cat! What's its name?*)
>
> **Come si chiama quella trattoria?** (*What's the name of that restaurant?*)

The importance of reflexive pronouns becomes clear if you consider that almost all reflexive verbs have nonreflexive forms and functions. Compare the use of the following verbs in their reflexive and nonreflexive forms:

> **Io mi sveglio alle sei, poi sveglio i bambini.** (*I wake up at six, and then I wake up the children.*)
>
> **Mi vesto, poi vesto i bambini perché i bambini sono piccoli e non sanno vestirsi.** (*I dress myself, and then I dress the children because the children are little and don't know how to dress themselves.*)
>
> **Mi diverto quando diverto i bambini.** (*I have fun when I amuse the children.*)

Using reflexive verbs throughout the day

Reflexive verbs carry you through the day. Although they may be introverted, they're also responsible. All the actions they portray carry right back to the subject.

To begin the day, you can use these verbs:

- ✔ **alzarsi** (*to get up*)
- ✔ **farsi il bagno/la doccia** (*to take a bath/shower*)
- ✔ **lavarsi** (*to wash up*)
- ✔ **lavarsi i denti** (*to brush one's teeth*)
- ✔ **mettersi** (*to put on; to wear*)
- ✔ **pettinarsi** (*to comb one's hair*)
- ✔ **radersi** (*to shave*)
- ✔ **svegliarsi** (*to wake up*)
- ✔ **vestirsi** (*to get dressed*)

Book IV

Mastering Italian Verbs and Tenses

During the day, you may do any of the following things:

- **accorgersi (di)** (*to realize*)
- **affrettarsi** (*to hurry*)
- **arrabbiarsi** (*to get angry*)
- **avvicinarsi** (*to get near*)
- **divertirsi** (*to have a good time*)
- **domandarsi** (*to wonder*)
- **fermarsi** (*to stop by; to stop from doing something; to stop when in motion*)
- **innamorarsi (di)** (*to fall in love with*)
- **lamentarsi (di)** (*to complain*)
- **laurearsi** (*to graduate from college*)
- **diplomarsi** (*to graduate from high school*)
- **muoversi** (*to move [bodily]*)
- **preoccuparsi** (*to worry*)
- **prepararsi** (*to prepare*)
- **ricordarsi (di)** (*to remember*)
- **trasferirsi (isc)** (*to move [from one city to another, for example]*)

And, finally, you can finish your day by doing the following:

- **addormentarsi** (*to go to sleep*)
- **coprirsi** (*to cover up*)
- **spogliarsi** (*to undress*)

Another extremely important reflexive verb is **trovarsi.** It's a synonym for both **essere** and **stare,** another way to say *to be.* For example:

> **Mi trovo molto bene.** (*I'm very well.*)
>
> **Dove ti trovi?** (*Where are you?*)
>
> **Si trovano in Italia.** (*They are in Italy.*)

Altering the position of reflexive pronouns

Sometimes you can attach the reflexive pronoun (**mi, ti, si, ci, vi,** and **si**) to the verb but only to infinitives and present participles. **Non voglio alzarmi** presto (*I don't want to get [myself] up early*), for example, attaches the reflexive pronoun **mi** to the infinitive **alzare,** after dropping the final **e** from the infinitive. You can also say **Sto alzandomi presto** (*I'm getting [myself] up early*) by using the present participle *getting* and attaching the reflexive pronoun **mi** to that participle (see Chapter 1 in Book V for more on participle mood). Using the semi-auxiliaries, or a kind of helping verb, **dovere** (*to have to; must*), **potere** (*to be able to; can*), and **volere** (*to want*), you can construct sentences that are truly idiomatic.

Attaching to infinitives

In the present tense, you don't want two conjugated verb forms next to one another, though a conjugated form followed by an infinitive works. For example, you say

> **Io devo svegliarmi alle sette.** (*I have to wake up at 7:00.*)
>
> **Non puoi svegliarti alle otto perché la classe comincia alle 8.05.** (*You can't wake up at 8:00 because class starts at 8:05.*)
>
> **Vuole svegliarsi alle nove per andare al parco.** (*He wants to wake up at 9:00 to go to the park.*)
>
> **Io devo studiare ma preferisco divertirmi.** (*I have to study, but I prefer to have a good time.*)

Notice two things about this construction:

- First, infinitives follow **devo, puoi, vuole,** and **preferisco.** English does the same.
- Second, the pronoun attached to **divertirmi** is the pronoun that reflects the implied subject **io.**

Joining up with present participles

You can also attach pronouns to the present participles, as shown in the following examples.

> **Io sto divertendomi.** (*I'm having a good time.*)
>
> **Tu stai divertendoti.** (*You* [singular, informal] *are having a good time.*)
>
> **Lui/lei/Lei sta divertendosi.** (*He/She/It/You* [singular, formal] *is/are having a good time.*)
>
> **Noi stiamo divertendoci.** (*We are having a good time.*)
>
> **Voi state divertendovi.** (*You* [plural, informal] *are having a good time.*)
>
> **Loro stanno divertendosi.** (*They are having a good time.*) (*You* [plural, formal] *are having a good time.*)

Book IV

Mastering Italian Verbs and Tenses

Notice that the subjects (**io, tu, lui, lei, noi, voi,** and **loro**) are reflected in the attached reflexive pronouns (**mi, ti, si, ci, vi,** and **si**) and that both are in agreement with the verb conjugations (**sto, stai, sta, stiamo, state,** and **stanno**).

Giving and taking with the reciprocal form

Almost any verb can be reflexive. Reciprocal reflexives take the process one step further. They use everyday verbs and show how people interact. In other words, they throw the action back on more than one subject and state things people do to each other. In the following examples, *each other* is the key phrase:

Paolo e Francesca si parlano. (*Paolo and Francesca talk to each other.*)

Ci vediamo. (*We'll see each other.*)

Cristina e Piero già si conoscono. (*Cristina and Piero already know each other.*)

Parlare (*to speak*), **vedere** (*to see*), and **conoscere** (*to know*) aren't normally reflexive verbs, but when they become reciprocal reflexives, they show people interacting with each other.

Reciprocal verbs mostly work in plural forms (in other words, with the pronouns **ci, vi,** and **si**). If the form is singular (with the pronouns **mi, ti, si**) it is often followed by a preposition that expresses reciprocity. For example:

Vi conoscete, vero? (*You know each other, right?*)

Non vi ricordate? (*You don't remember each other?*)

Non ti ricordi [di . . .]? (*You don't remember. . . ?*)

Si innamorano. (*They are falling in love with each other.*)

Mi innamoro [di . . .] (*I am falling in love with . . .*)

Si sposano. (*They are marrying each other.*) (*They are getting married.*)

Si sposa [con . . .] (*She/He is marrying . . .*)

Ci sentiamo. (Literally: *We'll hear from each other.*) This phrase is often used on the phone to mean that *we'll talk to each other again, perhaps tomorrow.*

Using the impersonal si

The impersonal construction with the reflexive pronoun **si** comes across in English as passive. And although situations occur in which the passive voice actually works better than an active form, in general, you don't want to use passive. In English, you use active voice to say, "She bought the car." But if you say, "The car was bought by her," you're using passive construction. Which do you think sounds better?

A more useful remark in the passive would be something like **Qui si parla inglese** (*English is spoken here*). Notice that the subject follows the verb. Here's another example: **si servono biscotti** (*cookies are served*). You have to keep track of the subject and make sure the verb agrees in number with it. Consider the following examples:

> **Si vendono francobolli.** (*Stamps are sold.*)
>
> **Si vende caffè.** (*Coffee is sold.*)
>
> **Si parlano italiano, francese, giapponese, e inglese.** (*Italian, French, Japanese, and English are spoken.*)

Giving a Commanding Performance with the Imperative

Nowhere is the divide between familiar and formal forms of address more evident than when you use the imperative. The very distinction between familiar and formal tells you something important about manners. If you wouldn't use a command (often a demand) in English, then you certainly wouldn't use it in Italian.

The imperative isn't a tense; it's a mood. Italian has four moods:

- ✔ Indicative (used to indicate something; see Chapters 1 and 2 in Book IV)

- ✔ Subjunctive (subjective; see Chapter 6 in Book IV)

- ✔ Conditional (used when something is dependent on certain conditions, such as "what if . . ."; see Chapter 5 in Book IV)

- ✔ Imperative (used with a sense of immediacy, though it's often made to sound like a request)

Book IV

Mastering Italian Verbs and Tenses

You can buffer your commands by including yourself in them. For example, in English, you may say, "Let's do that," which is more gentle than saying, "Do that." Most commands, however, are directed at other people. So you need to be familiar or formal, and you need to know how many people you're addressing. Because you'll probably use familiar commands more often than formal ones, surprisingly often in fact, the first part of this section focuses on those "friendly" forms. The rest covers irregular imperative forms, formal commands, where to put pronouns that you use with commands, and commonly used commands.

Constructing commands (of the tu, noi, and voi variety)

Mangia! (*Eat!*) says the proverbial Italian restaurant advertisement. This command is directed specifically at you in an informal way. To create the **tu** form of a positive or affirmative command, you first need to figure out whether the infinitive belongs to the **-are, -ere,** or **-ire** family of conjugations. Check out some affirmative **tu** commands in Table 3-2.

Table 3-2	Tu Commands in the Affirmative	
Infinitive	*Present Indicative Tu Form*	*Imperative Tu Form*
mangiare	mangi (*you eat/are eating*)	mangia! (*eat!*)
parlare	parli (*you speak/are speaking*)	parla! (*speak!*)
ascoltare	ascolti (*you listen/are listening*)	ascolta! (*listen!*)
abitare	abiti (*you live/are living*)	abita! (*live!*)
scrivere	scrivi (*you write/are writing*)	scrivi! (*write!*)
leggere	leggi (*you read/are reading*)	leggi! (*read!*)
dormire	dormi (*you sleep/are sleeping*)	dormi! (*sleep!*)
capire (isc)	capisci (*you understand/are understanding*)	capisci! (*understand!*)
finire (isc)	finisci (*you finish/are finishing*)	finisci! (*finish!*)
servire	servi (*you serve/are serving*)	servi! (*serve!*)

Notice anything in Table 3-2? The only **tu** form that changes belongs to **-are** verbs. And you don't use the personal subject pronouns. As for **-ere** and **-ire** verbs (including **isc** verbs), the indicative **tu** and the imperative **tu** forms are the same. **Scrivi una lettera** can mean *you are writing a letter,* or it can mean *write a letter.* **Leggi un libro** can indicate that *you are reading a book,* or it can be a command, probably from a teacher: *Read a book.*

More good news as far as the familiar commands go: The **noi** and **voi** present indicative and imperative forms are also identical for the standard and regular **-are, -ere,** and **-ire** verbs. The **noi** form comes across as more of a suggestion. For example: **Mangiamo!** (*Let's eat!*) **Andiamo!** (*Let's go!*) **Finiamo!** (*Let's finish!*) You use the **voi** form to address friends because it can have a stronger edge to it — **Andate!** (*Go!*) — but it also retains its present indicative conjugated form.

To make these commands negative, you simply put **non** before them, though only with **noi** and **voi**. For example: **Non mangiate** (*don't eat*) and **non finite** (*don't finish*). To make a **tu** command negative, you start with **non** (*don't*), but then you follow it with the original infinitive, such as these examples.

> **Non mangiamo più carne!** (*Let's not eat meat anymore!* [*we* (**noi**)])
>
> **Non mangiate più grassi!** (*Don't eat fats anymore!* [*you,* plural (**voi**)])
>
> **Non mangiare caramelle.** (*Don't eat candies.* [*you,* singular (**tu**)])
>
> **Non parlare con loro.** (*Don't talk to them.* [*you,* singular (**tu**)])

Use **tu, noi,** and **voi** forms only with people whom you're familiar with, such as family, friends, peers, children, and pets.

Dealing with irregular imperatives for tu, noi, and voi

To create commands with irregular verbs, the same rules apply as for regular forms (see the preceding section). **Noi** and **voi** commands are the same as the present indicative tense conjugations, though perhaps said in a different tone of voice. The **tu** forms are different enough that they deserve a little more attention. Table 3-3 lists the familiar **tu** commands, both positive and negative, of some irregular verbs. The apostrophes show that some commands are simply shortened versions of the **tu** form in the present indicative tense.

Book IV

Mastering Italian Verbs and Tenses

Table 3-3	Singular Familiar (Tu) Commands in Irregular Verbs	
Infinitive	*Affirmative Command*	*Negative Command*
essere (*to be*)	**sii** (*be*)	**non essere** (*don't be*)
avere (*to have*)	**abbi** (*have*)	**non avere** (*don't have*)
fare (*to make; to do*)	**fa'** (*make; do*)	**non fare** (*don't make; don't do*)
dare (*to give*)	**da'** (*give*)	**non dare** (*don't give*)
dire (*to tell; to say*)	**di'** (*tell; say*)	**non dire** (*don't tell; don't say*)
stare (*to be; to stay*)	**sta'** (*be; stay*)	**non stare** (*don't be; don't stay*)
andare (*to go*)	**va'** (*go*)	**non andare** (*don't go*)

Occasionally, you'll hear someone say **Dai!** This isn't a comment on your mortality but a way to say *Come on!* It's actually a form of encouragement. It's also used to mean *Really?* in the sense of *Oh, come on,* or *You're kidding, right?* In English, a similar phrase may be *Come off it!*

Commanding politely: Forming the Lei and Loro forms of the imperative

Regular and irregular forms of the polite (formal) imperative change the characteristic vowel of the infinitive. **A** becomes **i**, and **e** and **ono** change to **a** and **ano**. So if you want to say **Lei parl<u>a</u>** (*you* [singular, formal] *are speaking*) as a command, you'd say **parl<u>i</u>** (*speak*); **Lei chied<u>e</u>** (*you* [singular, formal] *ask*) becomes **chied<u>a</u>** (*ask*); **Loro finisc<u>ono</u>** (*you* [plural, formal] *are finishing*) becomes **finisc<u>ano</u>** (*finish*).

As a general rule, the **Lei** command for irregular verbs takes its stem from the first person singular of the verb's present indicative. You can see examples in Table 3-4.

Table 3-4	Lei Commands of Irregular Verbs	
Infinitive	*First Person Singular Present Indicative*	*Lei Command*
venire (*to come*)	**io vengo** (*I come*)	**venga** (*come*)
andare (*to go*)	**io vado** (*I go*)	**vada** (*go*)
dire (*to tell; to say*)	**io dico** (*I tell*)	**dica** (*tell*)
fare (*to make; to do*)	**io faccio** (*I make*)	**faccia** (*make*)
porre (*to put; to place*)	**io pongo** (*I put*)	**ponga** (*put*)
tradurre (*to translate*)	**io traduco** (*I translate*)	**traduca** (*translate*)

Naturally, **avere** (*to have*) and **essere** (*to be*) continue to do their own idiosyncratic thing. The **Lei** command for **essere** is **sia;** for **avere**, it's **abbia.**

These days, people don't use the formal plural command **Loro** often. If you're speaking to a group of people, formally, chances are you're going to use the **voi** form instead of **Loro.** Instead of saying **Parlino** (*Speak*), you'd say **Parlate.** Instead of saying **Ripetano** (*Repeat*), say **Ripetete.** This increasingly common practice will simplify your linguistic life to no end.

When in doubt — such as when you're talking to someone you met at a conference, or to a bureaucrat — use the formal, just as you do in speaking English.

In some instances, you never use the familiar. For example, you'll probably always be formal with the butcher you've gone to for 20 years; likewise, you'll be formal with your doctor or a teacher. Every now and again, you can avoid the use of a command completely. When asking a waiter for the bill, you say **Ci fa il conto per favore?** (*Would you bring the bill please?*) This isn't a direct translation, but you get the idea. It's polite without being demanding.

Adding pronouns to imperatives

Some general — even dependable — rules exist for adding pronouns to the imperative.

- Affirmative familiar commands attach pronouns to the end of the command. The indirect object always precedes the direct object pronoun. For example: **Alzati** (*Get up*) and **Leggimelo** (*Read it to me*).

- When using the one-syllable commands (refer to Table 3-3 for examples), you double the initial letter of the direct object pronoun, except when the pronoun is **gli.** For example: **Dammelo** (*Give it to me*), **Fammi vedere** (*Show me*), and **Diglielo** (*Tell it to him*).

- With negative familiar commands, you have a choice: You can either attach the pronouns to the ends of the commands (dropping the final **e** from the infinitive in the case of the **tu** form) or put the pronouns in front of the command, like this: **Non lo fare** (*Don't do it*), **Non mi parlare** (*Don't talk to me*), and **Non me lo dare** (*Don't give it to me*). You can also say **Non farlo, Non parlarmi,** and **Non darmelo.**

- Formal commands, both affirmative and negative, always place the pronoun before the command itself. Therefore, you say **Non lo faccia** (*Don't do it*) or **Mi dica** (*Tell me*).

To visualize and compare all these forms, check out Table 3-5.

Book IV

Mastering Italian Verbs and Tenses

Table 3-5	Familiar and Formal Commands	
Person	*Affirmative Command*	*Negative Command*
tu	**mangia** (*eat*)	**non mangiare** (*don't eat*)
	scrivi (*write*)	**non scrivere** (*don't write*)
	scriviglielo (*write it to him/her/them*)	**non scriverglielo** (*don't write it to him/her/them*)
	dormi (*sleep*)	**non dormire** (*don't sleep*)
	fa' (*do; make*)	**non fare** (*don't do; don't make*)
	fallo (*do it*)	**non lo fare** (*don't do it*)
Lei (formal)	**mangi** (*eat*)	**non mangi** (*don't eat*)
	scriva (*write*)	**non scriva** (*don't write*)
	glielo scriva (*write it to him/her/them*)	**non glielo scriva** (*don't write it to him/her/them*)
	dorma (*sleep*)	**non dorma** (*don't sleep*)
	faccia (*do*)	**non faccia** (*don't do*)
noi	**mangiamo** (*let's eat*)	**non mangiamo** (*let's not eat*)
	scriviamo (*let's write*)	**non scriviamo** (*let's not write*)
	scriviamoglielo (*let's write it to him/her/them*)	**non scriviamoglielo** (*let's not write it to him/her/them*)
	dormiamo (*let's sleep*)	**non dormiamo** (*let's not sleep*)
	facciamo (*let's do*)	**non facciamo** (*let's not do*)
voi	**mangiate** (*eat*)	**non mangiate** (*don't eat*)
	scrivete (*write*)	**non scrivete** (*don't write*)
	scriveteglielo (*write it to him/her/them*)	**non scriveteglielo** (*don't write it to him/her/them*)
	dormite (*sleep*)	**non dormite** (*don't sleep*)
	fate (*do*)	**non fate** (*don't do*)
Loro (formal)	**mangino** (*eat*)	**non mangino** (*don't eat*)
	scrivano (*write*)	**non scrivano** (*don't write*)
	Glielo scrivano (*write it to him/her/them*)	**non glielo scrivano** (*don't write it to him/her/them*)
	dormano (*sleep*)	**non dormano** (*don't sleep*)
	facciano (*do*)	**non facciano** (*don't do*)

Checking out commonly used commands

As you're going about your day and practicing Italian, you may find yourself using some of the more commonly used commands, such as the following expressions.

✔ In formal situations:

- **Scusi** (*Excuse me*). This word is often the only one tourists know, and it's greatly overused. To get through a crowd, you can also say **Permesso** (*Permission*). To get someone's attention (a ticket vendor, for example), you can use **Senta** (*Listen*).

- **Mi dica** (*Tell me*). If you're asking for information, this expression is especially useful.

- **Si accomodi** (*Make yourself comfortable*) (*Take a seat*). You hear this often in an office, where you're waiting to meet with someone.

✔ In more familiar surroundings:

- **Figurati** (*Thanks, don't mention it*). It also appears as **figuriamoci** ([between two friends] *don't think anything of it*).

- **Fallo pure** (*Just do it*) (*Go ahead*). If a friend is dithering about whether to do something, this is the common piece of advice.

- **Fammi sapere** (Literally: *Make me know*). Another way to say *Tell me everything* or *Let me know*.

- **Fammi vedere** (Literally: *Make me see*). Another way to say *Show me*.

- **Ma dai** (*Oh, come on*).

- **Non facciamo complimenti** (*Let's be frank with each other*).

Book IV

Mastering Italian Verbs and Tenses

Chapter 4

Declaring Your Likes (And Dislikes) with Piacere

•••

In This Chapter

▶ Combining indirect object pronouns with **piacere** to express likes and dislikes

▶ Using **piacere** in different tenses

▶ Familiarizing yourself with other verbs that work like **piacere**

•••

The key to expressing yourself in any language is being able to share what you enjoy and what you don't care for. Getting to know people without understanding what hobbies they enjoy or what activities they really don't like can be difficult. A waiter will be better able to recommend a dish for you if you can let him know you don't care for anchovies or that you're crazy about a particular type of cheese.

This chapter explains how to express likes and dislikes across the verb tenses with **piacere** (*to please*) and shows you other verbs that work in a similar fashion. To use **piacere,** you need to construct sentences backward — at least to begin with. In English, if you want to say that you like something, you simply say *I like coffee,* for example; in Italian, this phrase takes the form *Coffee is pleasing to me.* You build your sentence so it reads, literally, *To me* (**mi**) *is pleasing* (**piace**) *coffee* (**il caffè**).

Using **piacere** also requires indirect object pronouns (**mi** [*to/for me*], **ti** [*to/ for you*], and so on), which you find out about in this chapter. You use either the singular **piace** (*it is pleasing*) or the plural **piacciono** (*they are pleasing*) and the object(s) (one or many) of your desire.

Understanding How to Use Piacere

To say you like something in English, you use a direct manner, such as *I like to read.* In Italian, you explain that something pleases you: **Mi piace leggere** (Literally: *Reading is pleasing to me*). In other words, Italian reverses the subject and object; the English direct object (*to read*) becomes an Italian subject (*reading*). The English subject (*I*) turns into an Italian indirect object pronoun (*me*). Whatever is liked becomes the subject. Whoever is doing the liking becomes the object.

With **piacere,** indirect object pronouns reveal who is pleased by (or who likes) something, so this section starts with a discussion on indirect object pronouns; then it goes on to talk about conjugating **piacere** in the present tense and shows you how to combine it with indirect object pronouns.

Working with indirect object pronouns

In general, pronouns replace nouns in sentences and help to avoid monotonous repetition. For example: *Enrico gives the old car to the twins. He gives it to them.* In the second sentence, *Enrico,* the subject, is replaced by the pronoun *he.* The direct object (or what is being given), *the car,* is replaced by the direct object pronoun *it.* And the indirect object (or who receives the gift), *the twins,* is replaced by the indirect object pronoun *them.* Here's another example:

> **[Io] Mando molte cartoline agli amici**. (*I send friends a lot of postcards.*)
>
> **Gli mando molte cartoline.** (*I send them a lot of postcards.*)

Here, you replace **agli amici** (*to friends*) with **Gli** (*to them*).

In the same way, **piacere** uses indirect object pronouns to tell who likes something or to whom something is pleasing. For example:

> **Mi piacciono i fiori.** (*I like flowers.*) (Literally: *Flowers are pleasing to me.*)
>
> **Ti piacciono i fiori?** (*Do you like flowers?*) (Literally: *Do flowers please you?*)

Indirect objects are recognizable (and distinguished from direct objects) by the questions they answer: *To or for whom?* and *to or for what?* Indirect objects are preceded by a preposition (*to, for,* and so on). In English, this preposition is often understood rather than expressed, as in *Giuseppe gives [to] them the car.* In Italian, the preposition is built into the indirect object pronoun (**Giuseppe gli dà la macchina**).

Table 4-1 lists the indirect object pronouns in Italian and their English equivalents.

Table 4-1	Indirect Object Pronouns
Singular	*Plural*
mi (*to/for me*)	**ci** (*to/for us*)
ti (*to/for you* [informal])	**vi** (*to/for you* [informal])
gli (*to/for him*)	**loro, gli** (*to/for them* [masculine, feminine])
le (*to/for her*)	**Loro, Gli** (*to/for you* [formal])
Le (*to/for you* [formal])	

Loro has largely given way to **gli,** which can mean *to/for him, to/for them,* and *to/for you* (formal). If it's combined with a direct object pronoun (**lo, la, li,** or **le**), it becomes **glielo, gliela, glieli,** or **gliele** and can also mean *to/for her.* So **Mario glielo dà** can mean *Mario gives it to her/him/it/you/them,* depending on context.

Conjugating piacere in the present tense

The verb **piacere** conjugates irregularly. It doesn't use subject pronouns, so in the tables throughout this chapter, when the subject pronouns are included for reference, they're placed in brackets. You can see the basic present tense conjugation of **piacere** in the following table.

Book IV

Mastering Italian Verbs and Tenses

piacere (*to please*)	
io **piaccio**	noi **piacciamo**
tu **piaci**	voi **piacete**
lui, lei, Lei **piace**	loro, Loro **piacciono**

The forms you'll use almost exclusively in the present tense are **piace** and **piacciono.** If you like one thing, you use the singular **piace. Mi piace leggere,** for example, is *I like to read.* An infinitive is singular, and even when you add more than one infinitive, **piace** is the form to use: **Mi piace leggere, scrivere e mangiare** (*I like to read, write, and eat*).

When you're talking about two or more things that you like, you use **piacciono.** Here are a couple of examples:

> **Mi piacciono i gatti.** (*I like cats.*)
>
> **Gli piacciono gli sport.** (*He likes sports.*)

Notice that the second **gli** is an article, not an indirect object pronoun. In Italian, you use the article before the thing that is liked.

Use **non piacere** to express dislikes, as in **Non gli piacciono i balli moderni** (*He/She doesn't like modern dances*) and **Perché non ti piace la cioccolata?** (*How come you don't like chocolate?*). Note that **dispiacere** means *to be sorry, to mind*: **Mi dispiace sapere che parti** (*I am sorry to learn that you are leaving*); **Ti dispiace** (the conditional **ti dispiacerebbe** is even more polite) **passarmi del pane?** (*Would you mind passing some bread?*).

Combining piacere with indirect object pronouns

How do **piacere** and indirect object pronouns combine to tell who likes something? You or someone likes one thing (**piace**) or more than one thing (**piacciono**); the indirect object pronoun specifies who does the liking, and it always appears at the start of the sentence. Table 4-2 shows how to use **piace/piacciono** with the indirect object pronouns. When combined with the indirect object pronouns, **piacere's** meaning becomes *to like.*

Table 4-2	Piacere and Indirect Object Pronouns	
Singular	*Plural*
mi piace/piacciono (*I like*)	**ci piace/piacciono** (*we like*)
ti piace/piacciono (*you like*)	**vi piace/piacciono** (*you like*)
gli piace/piacciono (*he likes*)	**gli piace/piacciono** (*they like*)
le piace/piacciono (*she likes*)	**Gli piace/piacciono** (*you* [formal] *like*)
Le piace/piacciono (*you* [formal] *like*)	

Most of the time, people use only the third person singular and plural forms of **piacere.** However, occasionally, you'll hear someone say **le piaccio** (*she likes me*) (Literally: *I am pleasing to her*); **so che piaccio di più con i capelli corti** (Literally: *I please to them more when I have short hair*). If someone says to you **mi piaci,** he or she is saying *I like you* (Literally: *You are pleasing to me*). Keep in mind that you're building sentences backward (placing the indirect object *before* the subject).

Another oddity, if you will, about using **piacere** is that you don't have to state the Italian subject or what in English would be the direct object if you can infer it from the context. Here are some examples:

> **I bambini? Sì, mi piacciono.** (*Children? Yes, I like [them].*) *Them* is understood, though not expressed in Italian.

> **Ti piace viaggiare? Sì, mi piace.** (*Do you like to travel? Yes, I like [it].*)

> **Le piace cucinare? No, non le piace.** (*Does she like to cook? No, she doesn't like [it].*)

Finally, what if you want to say that a specific person, such as Rodolfo, likes something? That is, you specifically want to name whoever is doing the liking. Simply keep in mind that **piace/piacciono** means *is/are pleasing,* and you need to indicate that something is pleasing *to* someone. Adding the preposition **a** before a person or a pronoun gives you that *to;* this construction replaces the indirect object pronoun (refer to Table 4-2). For example:

> **A Rodolfo piace scrivere/gli piace scrivere.** (*Rodolfo likes to write.*)
> (Literally: *Writing is pleasing to Rodolfo/to him.*)

> **A Laura piacciono i fiori/le piacciono i fiori.** (*Laura likes flowers.*)
> (Literally: *Flowers are pleasing to Laura/to her.*)

Book IV

Mastering Italian Verbs and Tenses

If you're using pronouns that are a little more emphatic, you may say **A lui piacciono i fiori** rather than **Gli piacciono i fiori** (*He likes flowers*). Some of the subject pronouns change form when preceded by a preposition, such as the following:

Subject Pronoun	Changes to . . .	Example
io	mi/a me	**Mi/A me piacciono le mele.** (*I like apples.*)
tu	ti/a te	**Ti/A te piacciono le mele.** (*You* [informal, singular] *like apples.*)
lui	gli/a lui	**Gli/A lui piacciono le mele.** (*He likes apples.*)
lei, Lei	le/a lei, Le/a Lei	**Le/A lei piacciono le mele.** (*She likes apples.*) **Le/A Lei piacciono le mele.** (*You* [formal, singular] *like apples.*)
noi	ci/a noi	**Ci/A noi piacciono le mele.** (*We like apples.*)
voi	vi/a voi	**Vi/A voi piacciono le mele.** (*You* [informal, plural] *like apples.*)
loro, Loro	gli/a loro, Gli/a Loro	**Gli/A loro piacciono le mele.** (*They like apples.*) **Gli/A Loro piacciono le mele.** (*You* [formal, plural] *like apples.*)

Never use both the regular indirect object pronouns and the form that follows **a** together (such as **a me mi piace**).

Using piacere as a noun

Piacere does double linguistic duty. It isn't just a verb (although that would be noteworthy enough); it's also a noun. You use it as a noun most frequently when you meet someone. Upon being introduced, you say **Piacere** (*It's a pleasure*). The person you've just met may respond with **Il piacere è tutto mio** (*The pleasure is all mine*).

At its most basic, the noun **piacere** means *a pleasure.* You can make something into a great pleasure by adding the suffix **-one. Un piacerone** refers to something that is **un vero piacere** (*a true pleasure*).

Expressing Likes (And Dislikes) in Any Tense

You can conjugate all verbs in all indicative and subjunctive moods across the tenses. **Piacere** and **dispiacere** are no exception. Did you notice the verb **dispiacere** (*to dislike; to displease; to hate; to be sorry; to mind*)? To express these feelings in Italian, simply add the prefix **dis-** before **piacere,** as you do in English with *like* and *dislike*. For example: **Se non vi piacciono/se odiate/ se vi dispiaccono le regole di grammatica complicate, il verbo dispiacere è perfetto per voi!** (*If you dislike/displease/hate complicated grammar rules, the verb to dislike is perfect for you!*) The present indicative tense, the present subjunctive mood, and the past absolute tense are irregular, but **piacere** and **dispiacere** turn regular for all other conjugated forms. Check out these conjugations in the following sections.

Dispiacere can also mean *to be sorry*. You bump into someone and say **Mi dispiace** (*I'm sorry*). You lose your passport, and a friend says **Mi dispiace tanto** (*I'm so sorry*).

Conjugating piacere and dispiacere in the subjunctive and past absolute

The earlier section "Conjugating **piacere** in the present tense" provides the present indicative tense conjugation of **piacere.** This section shows you how to conjugate **piacere** and **dispiacere** in the present subjunctive and the past absolute; these conjugations are irregular. (In other tenses and in the conditional mood, **piacere** and **dispiacere** follow regular rules of conjugation; for details, see the later section "Checking out more conjugations for piacere and dispiacere.")

Subjunctive

The subjunctive mood (see Chapter 6 in Book IV) lets you express possibility, doubt, fear, emotions; it's ultimately subjective.

Nowhere is sound as important as in the subjunctive because one difference in the pronunciation lets you know that a different verb mood is being used. Because the subjunctive lets you express nuance, doubt, and emotion (among other things), pronunciation is important. Flip to Chapter 1 in Book I for an introduction to pronunciation.

Ti piace/dispiace (*You like/dislike it*) indicates that you definitely like/dislike something. **Credo che ti piaccia/dispiaccia** (*I think you like/dislike it*) means that you're not entirely sure. To say that you don't like something, you can also simply say **No, non mi piace.** The word **non** makes the sentiment negative.

Past absolute

You use the past absolute (see Chapter 1 in Book V) to describe things that happened long ago and far away.

Use of the past absolute, or the **passato remoto,** varies depending on where you are. Some regions of Italy hardly ever use it; in other regions, especially Sicily, people use it more often.

The past absolute shows up most frequently in literature and opera. To read Dante's *Inferno,* or any of the classics for that matter, you need to be able to recognize the past absolute. For example, **com'altrui piacque** (*as pleased another*) achieves almost formulaic status in the *Inferno.* The past absolute is notoriously irregular, so much so that when you look at conjugated forms, you sometimes can't figure out what the source infinitive is.

Being able to recognize the past absolute and understanding the most irregular forms are generally all you need to get by. You probably don't need to study the past absolute too much or memorize its conjugations. Here are the past absolute forms of **piacere** and **dispiacere.**

piacere (*to like; to please*)/ dispiacere (*to dislike; to displease; to hate; to be sorry; to mind*)	
io **piacqui/dispiacqui**	noi **piacemmo/dispiacemmo**
tu **piacesti/dispiacesti**	voi **piaceste/dispiaceste**
lui, lei, Lei **piacque/dispiacque**	loro, Loro **piàcquero/dispiàcquero**

Checking out more conjugations for piacere and dispiacere

Piacere has different conjugations for the future, the conditional, the present perfect, and the imperfect. This section covers all of them. *Note:* In the interests of giving you workable (read: useful) grammar, this section uses only the third person forms of these various tenses and moods.

Future

The future tense of **piacere/dispiacere** is **piacerà/dispiacerà** (singular) and **piaceranno/dispiaceranno** (plural). If, for example, you're telling a friend about a movie you just saw that you think she'll like, you use the future tense and say **Ti piacerà** (*You'll like it*). You can also use this tense to introduce someone to friends who you think that person will like: **Ti piaceranno** (*You'll like them*). Check out the following examples:

> **I miei amici italiani ti piaceranno di sicuro**. (*You will certainly like my Italian friends.*)

> **Ti dispiacerà sapere che il volo è stato cancellato.** (*You will be sorry to know that the flight has been canceled.*)

You can use the future tense to indicate probability. So **ti piacerà** can also mean *you will probably like it*. Check out Chapter 5 in Book IV for more about the future tense.

Conditional

You use the conditional (**piacerebbe/dispiacerebbe** [singular] or **piacerebbero/dispiacerebbero** [plural]) to express something that may be. For example, say you're expressing reservations about something, so you say **Non mi dispiacerebbe ma . . .** (*I wouldn't mind it, but . . .*). Or you think someone would like something: **Ti piacerebbero** (*You would like them*).

Frequently, this construction includes a follow-up clause, explaining just why you like or don't like something. The conditional is often part of a complex sentence that uses the subjunctive for its second half. Flip to Chapter 5 in Book IV for more about the conditional.

Present perfect and imperfect

Knowing when to use either the present perfect or the imperfect takes practice. You can simplify this decision by considering the following questions each tense answers.

- ✔ **The present perfect** (**è piaciuto/a, è dispiaciuto/a** [singular] or **sono piaciuti/e, sono dispiaciuti/e** [plural]) answers the questions, "What happened? What did you (or someone else) do?" In the case of **piacere**, it's often paired with the question, "Did you like it/them?"

  The present perfect refers to a completed past action, something you started and finished, something that's over.

Book IV

Mastering Italian Verbs and Tenses

✔ The **imperfect** (**piaceva** [singular] or **piacevano** [plural]) answers different questions: "What was something like? What was going on? What used to (habitually) go on? What did you used to do, regularly?"

The imperfect is the ultimate descriptive tense. The reason fairy tales begin with **C'era una volta . . .** (*Once upon a time, there was . . .*) is because they're opening up a story about the past that isn't completed, that isn't yet perfected — that's imperfect. See Chapter 1 in Book V for more on past tenses.

For example, you give someone a book to read and want to know whether she liked it: **Ti è piaciuto il libro?** (*Did you like the book?*) Or you show a friend a house you're thinking of renting or buying and want to get his opinion: **Gli è piaciuta la casa** (*He liked the house*). In both cases, you're talking about something that has happened, so you use the present perfect: She liked the book. He liked the house. End of story.

The thing liked determines the gender of **piaciuto**. A book, being masculine, takes **piaciuto**. A house, being feminine, takes **piaciuta**. The plural forms follow this suit, too.

> **Ti sono piaciuti i libri?** (*Did you like the books?*)
>
> **Gli sono piaciute le case.** (*He liked the houses.*)

Verbal clues that tell you an action is recent and completed include **ieri** (*yesterday*), **due settimane fa** (*two weeks ago*), and other phrases that fix a time.

On the other hand, the very meaning of **piacere**, *liking*, lends itself to the imperfect because liking tends to be ongoing, unconfined by time. Rarely do you like something only between 2 and 4 p.m. when it wasn't raining, for example. Once again, context is everything.

Take this example: **Da bambino, gli piaceva andare al cinema il sabato** (*As a child, he liked going to the movies on Saturdays*). This sentence has two clues that you want to use the imperfect: *As a child* indicates an ongoing time, and *Saturdays* indicates that this action was a habitual one.

Other words that indicate habitual action are **ogni** (*every*), **spesso** (*often*), **qualche volta** (*sometimes*), **sempre** (*always*), and **non . . . mai** (*never*). For example: **Ci piaceva guardare la televisione ogni giorno** (*Every day, we liked to watch TV*).

Here are a couple of additional examples of the imperfect:

Ci piacevano gli animali. (*We liked animals.*) (*We have always liked animals.*) Here, the speaker is talking about something they've always liked, as opposed to the animals they saw at the zoo this afternoon.

Le piaceva nuotare. (*She liked swimming.*) Again, you're saying that this is something she has always liked.

Recent pluperfect

The recent pluperfect (to distinguish it from the remote pluperfect, or preterite perfect), or past perfect (**era piaciuto/a, era dispiaciuto/a** [singular] or **erano piaciuti/e, erano dispiaciuti/e** [plural]), follows the same rules as the present perfect in the preceding section. The only difference is in the helping verb, which you use in the imperfect rather than the present (**era** instead of **è**, and **erano** instead of **sono**). The pluperfect refers to something that had happened, often before another event being discussed. In English, you may say, *He had finished the first book before he began the second.* The first verb, *had finished,* is in the pluperfect; the second, *began,* is in the present perfect.

Likewise, you distinguish the pluperfect from the imperfect by asking the same questions: "What had happened? What had he done?" In the case of **piacere,** "What had he liked?" It refers, in other words, to something that occurred and is over.

For example: **Non gli era piaciuto il libro** (*He hadn't liked the book*). A further elaboration may include the phrase *when he read it the first time.* **Non gli erano piaciute le poesie di quello scrittore** (*He hadn't liked that writer's poetry*). If you are eager for more on past tenses, check out Chapter 1 in Book V.

Looking at Other Verbs that Work Backward

Several Italian verbs work the same way as **piacere** — that is, backward and with accompanying indirect object pronouns. Some of them make more sense than others, as you find out in the following sections.

A few other verbs similar to **piacere** that aren't included in the next sections include **dare fastidio** (*to bother; to annoy*), **disturbare** (*to bother*), and **servire** (*to serve*). These verbs work similarly to **piacere** when used to speak or write.

Verbs that carry the indirect object in their constructions

Those that make the most sense are **bastare** (*to be enough*), **sembrare** (*to seem*), **importare** (*to be important*), and **interessare** (*to be of interest*). All these verbs in English carry the stated or unstated indirect object in their constructions. For example: *Two are enough for me. It seems to me. It's not important to me. It's of no interest to me.*

Here are the most used forms of these verbs:

- ✔ **basta** (*it's enough*)/**bastano** (*they're enough*)
- ✔ **sembra** (*it seems*)/**sembrano** (*they seem*)
- ✔ **importa** (*it's important*)/**importano** (*they're important*)
- ✔ **interessa** (*it's of interest*)/**interessano** (*they're of interest*)

The indirect object pronoun is *always* stated with these verbs. As with **piacere,** it precedes the conjugated forms. The following examples show how they work. They really aren't so different from their English counterparts; the main difference is that, in English, you don't usually add the indirect object.

Mi basta un esempio. (*One example is enough for me.*)

Ti bastano dieci giorni? (*Are ten days enough for you?*)

Mi sembra sincero. (*He seems honest to me.*)

Non mi sembrano veri. (*They don't seem real to me.*)

Non mi importa. (*It's not important to me.*) (*It doesn't matter.*)

Non mi importano le regole. (*The rules don't matter to me.*)

Non gli interessa. (*He isn't interested in it.*) (*It's of no interest to him.*)

Ci interessano. (*We're interested in them.*) (*They're of interest to us.*)

The verb mancare

One other fairly common verb that works backward is **mancare** (*to miss*). For example: *I may miss my friends; you may miss your family; the cat misses his owner.* The conjugation of the basic verb **mancare** is regular, as you can see in the following table. But the translation includes the added prepositions *to* or *by,* as in *I am missing to* or *I am missed by.*

mancare (*to miss*)	
io **manco**	noi **manchiamo**
tu **manchi**	voi **mancate**
lui, lei, Lei **manca**	loro, Loro **mancano**

In other words, you, they, I, he, and we, for example, are missing *to* someone. To put it more idiomatically, they're missed *by* someone. If I miss my friends **Mi mancano** (*I miss them*) or (*They are missed by me*). If you say to someone **Ti manco,** you may sound more coy than you want because it means *You miss me* or *I am missed by you.*

To know who is doing the actual missing, you plug in the appropriate indirect object pronoun. For example:

> **Mi mancate.** (*I miss you* [plural].)
>
> **Mi manchi.** (*I miss you.*)
>
> **Gli mancano i bambini.** (*He misses the kids.*)
>
> **Ci manca la spiaggia; ti mancano le montagne.** (*We miss the beach; you miss the mountains.*)

Admittedly, this verb takes some getting used to. Just keep in mind that the indirect object pronoun, which precedes the verb, reveals who the subject is.

Chapter 5

The Future Tense and the Conditional Mood

In This Chapter

▶ Using regular and irregular forms of the future tense

▶ Checking out the conditional

*I*n this chapter, you discover two verb forms — the future tense and the conditional mood — to help you speak about what's in the near future as well as in the far future. You'll be able to make plans for next weekend or dream about the rest of your life.

Focusing on the Future

The Italian future tense in its current form is not a direct legacy of classical Latin, as other Italian tenses are. In fact, Latin used a variant of the future completely different from what's used today. This form resembled the forms of the indicative imperfect tense and with time has fallen into disuse.

Only the imperative and indicative moods have this tense. The future indicates present situations and present and future events that are somewhat uncertain. This section shows you how to form the regular future tense and spells out -**are** exceptions; then, you work with irregular roots and find out how to talk about the future with some handy expressions.

Forming the regular future tense

The regular future tense is one of the easiest tenses to form. (Later in this chapter, you can see how to form some irregular future tense stems.) To form the regular future tense, follow these simple steps:

1. Take the infinitive of an **-are, -ere,** or **-ire** verb.

2. Drop the final **e** only to form the future tense stem.

3. Add the future tense ending.

Okay, you have to pay attention to one exception: **-are** verbs require a slight modification — you change the **a** in the stem to an **e**. (The next section presents greater detail on the spelling changes for **-are** verbs.) The following list provides a few examples of the modified future tense stems:

- **-are:** The stem for **parlare** (*to speak*) is **parler-** (because you change the **a** to an **e**).
- **-ere:** The stem for **prendere** (*to have; to take*) is **prender-**.
- **-ire:** The stem for **partire** (*to leave*) is **partir-**.

Note: The stems you create are the same stems you use for the conditional mood, discussed later in this chapter.

The following list shows the endings that you attach to these stems. The future tense endings are the same for **-are, -ere,** and **-ire** verbs.

- **io: -ò**
- **tu: -ai**
- **lui, lei, Lei: -à**
- **noi: -emo**
- **voi: -ete**
- **loro, Loro: -anno**

The following tables show examples of regular **-are, -ere,** and **-ire** verbs conjugated in the future tense.

parlare (*to speak*)	
io **parlerò**	noi **parleremo**
tu **parlerai**	voi **parlerete**
lui, lei, Lei **parlerà**	loro, Loro **parleranno**
Parlerò col professore dopodomani. (*I'll talk with the professor the day after tomorrow.*)	

prendere (*to have; to take*)	
io **prenderò**	noi **prenderemo**
tu **prenderai**	voi **prenderete**
lui, lei, Lei **prenderà**	loro, Loro **prenderanno**
Prenderemo una bella bistecca alla fiorentina! (*We're going to have a nice steak Florentine style!*)	

partire (*to leave*)	
io **partirò**	noi **partiremo**
tu **partirai**	voi **partirete**
lui, lei, Lei **partirà**	loro, Loro **partiranno**
Maria partirà per gli Stati Uniti domenica. (*Mary will leave/will be leaving for the United States on Sunday.*)	

Spelling out -are exceptions in the future tense

Okay, the previous section gets all the really simple stuff out of the way. As with all languages, you have to jump through a few hoops here and there (but you can't be too upset . . . not many languages have more hoops than English!). The following sections cover the spelling changes you need to make with **-are** verbs.

Verbs that end in -care and -gare

With verbs ending in **-care** (for example, **cercare** [*to look for*] and **dimenticare** [*to forget*]) and **-gare** (**pagare** [*to pay*]), you add an **h** after the **c** or **g** in their future stems. This change allows the verbs to keep their hard *c* and hard *g* sounds. For example, with **pagare,** you add the **h** to the stem **pag-** and then add the ending **erò**. The following tables provide examples of the change.

Book IV

Mastering Italian Verbs and Tenses

cercare (*to look for*)	
io **cercherò**	noi **cercheremo**
tu **cercherai**	voi **cercherete**
lui, lei, Lei **cercherà**	loro, Loro **cercheranno**
Cercheranno un albergo quando arriveranno a Roma. (*They'll look for a hotel when they get to Rome.*)	

pagare (*to pay*)	
io **pagherò**	noi **pagheremo**
tu **pagherai**	voi **pagherete**
lui, lei, Lei **pagherà**	loro, Loro **pagheranno**
Pagherà (Lei) in contanti o con la carta di credito? (*Will you* [formal] *be paying with cash or a credit card?*)	

Verbs that end in -ciare and -giare

When conjugating verbs that end in **-ciare** and **-giare,** like **cominciare** (*to begin*) and **mangiare** (*to eat*), you drop the **i** in the future tense stem because you don't pronounce the **i;** it's there only to maintain the soft *g* and *c* sounds. You can see these future tense forms at work in the following tables.

cominciare (*to begin*)	
io **comincerò**	noi **cominceremo**
tu **comincerai**	voi **comincerete**
lui, lei, Lei **comincerà**	loro, Loro **cominceranno**
Da domani cominceremo una dieta molto rigida. (*Starting tomorrow, we will start a very strict diet.*)	

mangiare (*to eat*)	
io **mangerò**	noi **mangeremo**
tu **mangerai**	voi **mangerete**
lui, lei, Lei **mangerà**	loro, Loro **mangeranno**
Mangeremo soltanto frutta e verdura. (*We will eat only fruit and vegetables.*)	

Working with irregular roots

Some verbs have irregular roots in the future tense, meaning that their stems change with regard to the regular future tense stems in the previous sections (where you keep most of the infinitives). But don't worry: After you change the stems of the verbs in the following sections, you use the same future tense endings (**-ò, -ai, -à, -emo, -ete,** and **-anno**) as you do with regular verb roots.

Losing the second-to-last vowel

Some common verbs change their stems in the future tense by dropping the second-to-last vowel in the infinitives, as you can see in Table 5-1.

Table 5-1   Common Verbs with Future Stems That Drop a Vowel

Infinitive	Future Tense Stem
andare (*to go*)	**andr-**
avere (*to have*)	**avr-**
cadere (*to fall*)	**cadr-**
dovere (*must; to have to; to need to*)	**dovr-**
potere (*to be able to*)	**potr-**
sapere (*to know*)	**sapr-**
vedere (*to see*)	**vedr-**
vivere (*to live*)	**vivr-**

Adding a double r

Other future tense stems of verbs take on a double **r**, as you can see in Table 5-2.

Table 5-2   Common Verbs with Future Stems That Have Double Rs

Infinitive	Future Stem
bere (*to drink*)	**berr-**
mantenere (*to maintain*)	**manterr-**
ottenere (*to obtain*)	**otterr-**
rimanere (*to stay*)	**rimarr-**

(continued)

Table 5-2 *(continued)*

Infinitive	Future Stem
sostenere (*to sustain; to support*)	sosterr-
tenere (*to hold*)	terr-
venire (*to come*)	verr-
volere (*to want*)	vorr-

Keeping the a

You can group the verbs **dare, fare,** and **stare** together because even though they're **-are** verbs, they drop only the final **e** of **-are** and then take the endings **-ò, -ai, -à, -emo, -ete,** and **-anno** to form the future (see Table 5-3).

Table 5-3   The Future Forms of Dare, Fare, and Stare

Infinitive	Future Stem
dare (*to give*)	dar-
fare (*to do; to make*)	far-
stare (*to be; to stay*)	star-

All alone: The verb essere

The verb **essere** (*to be*) is in a category all by itself! Its future tense stem becomes **sar-,** upon which you add the future endings. The following table shows you the full conjugation.

essere (*to be*)	
io **sarò**	noi **saremo**
tu **sarai**	voi **sarete**
lui, lei, Lei **sarà**	loro, Loro **saranno**
Sarò contenta quando avrò finito questo lavoro. (*I'll be happy when I finish this job.*)	

Talking about the future with some handy expressions

TIP

"Let's forget about **domani,** let's forget about **domani,** let's forget about **domani,** 'cause **domani** never comes." Although this popular tune encourages you to forget about **domani** (*tomorrow*) and the future, the elements of the future are important frames of reference for your daily existence. You can use the phrases in Table 5-4 to speak in precise terms about the future.

Table 5-4	Common Expressions That Often Take the Future		
Phrase	*Translation*	*Phrase*	*Translation*
domani	tomorrow	fra qualche giorno	in a few days
domani mattina	tomorrow morning	fra qualche mese	in a few months
domani sera	tomorrow evening	fra qualche anno	in a few years
dopodomani	the day after tomorrow	fra tre giorni	in three days
sabato prossimo	next Saturday	quando	when
domenica prossima	next Sunday	appena	as soon as
la settimana prossima	next week	se	if
il mese prossimo	next month	più tardi	later
l'anno prossimo	next year	entro giugno	by June
quest'estate	this summer	entro la fine del mese	by the end of the month
stasera	this evening		

Could-ing and Would-ing: The Conditional Mood

The Italian conditional mood corresponds to saying *could, would,* or *should* in English. For example, the conditional mood allows you to focus on the finer, most important things in life, like "I could never get tired of eating ice cream"; "I would go to Italy in a heartbeat"; and "I should buy a Ferrari." The conditional is also the perfect mood for telling people what to do: "You should marry George," or "You could be a little nicer!" In the following sections, you practice using and conjugating the conditional.

Covering the uses of the conditional

The conditional mood has a couple specific uses:

✔ **Asking a question:** When asking a question, the conditional is the polite way to go.

> **<u>Potrei</u> <u>provare</u> questi stivali?** (*Would I be able to try on these boots?*)

> **<u>Sarebbe</u> possibile <u>avere</u> un po' d'acqua, per favore?** (*Would it be possible to have some water, please?*)

✔ **Noting that one event is dependent upon (conditional to) another event occurring:** In this usage, the conditional often appears in the same sentence with the imperfect subjunctive and with "if" sentences. See Chapters 4 and 5 in Book V for more on the subjunctive mood.

But in this chapter, the conditional either exists by itself or is tied to another condition in the present tense or **passato prossimo,** as in this example:

> **Claudio <u>si</u> <u>sposerebbe</u> ma non <u>ha</u> <u>trovato</u> la donna giusta.**
> (*Claudio would get married, but he hasn't found the right woman.*)

Forming the regular conditional

If you enjoy forming the regular future tense in Italian (covered earlier in this chapter), you'll love forming the regular conditional mood because the two use the exact same infinitive stems. (Note that the **a** in the stem of **-are** verbs becomes an **e.**) And you add the same set of conditional endings for all three verb conjugations (**-are, -ere,** and **-ire** verbs) to the conditional stems.

The following list shows the conditional endings for the three verb conjugations.

- ✔ **io: -ei**
- ✔ **tu: -esti**
- ✔ **lui, lei, Lei: -ebbe**
- ✔ **noi: -emmo**
- ✔ **voi: -este**
- ✔ **loro, Loro: -ebbero**

The following tables show some examples of regular **-are, -ere,** and **-ire** verbs conjugated in the conditional mood.

lavorare (*to work*)	
io **lavorerei**	noi **lavoreremmo**
tu **lavoreresti**	voi **lavorereste**
lui, lei, Lei **lavorerebbe**	loro, Loro **lavorerebbero**
Lavorereste con me su questo progetto? (*Would you [all] work with me on this project?*)	

prendere (*to take; to have*)	
io **prenderei**	noi **prenderemmo**
tu **prenderesti**	voi **prendereste**
lui, lei, Lei, **prenderebbe**	loro, Loro **prenderebbero**
Prenderebbero il gelato tutti i giorni! (*They would have ice cream every day!*)	

aprire (*to open*)	
io **aprirei**	noi **apriremmo**
tu **apriresti**	voi **aprireste**
lui, lei, Lei **aprirebbe**	loro, Loro **aprirebbero**
Apriresti la finestra, per piacere? (*Would you open the window, please?*)	

Book IV

Mastering Italian Verbs and Tenses

Creating the irregular conditional

The irregular conditional mood and the spelling exceptions in the conditional mood use the same irregular stems as the irregular future tense verbs covered earlier in this chapter. These stems appear again in Table 5-5 for your conjugating pleasure. ***Note:*** You use the conditional endings **-ei, -esti, -ebbe, -emmo, -este,** and **-ebbero.**

Table 5-5	Forming Irregular Conditional Verbs		
Infinitive	*Conditional Stem*	*Infinitive*	*Conditional Stem*
andare	andr-	ottenere	otterr-
avere	avr-	pagare	pagher-
bere	berr-	potere	potr-
cadere	cadr-	rimanere	rimarr-
cercare	cercher-	sapere	sapr-
cominciare	comincer-	sostenere	sosterr-
dare	dar-	stare	star-
dovere	dovr-	tenere	terr-
essere	sar-	vedere	vedr-
fare	far-	venire	verr-
mangiare	manger-	vivere	vivr-
mantenere	manterr-	volere	vorr-

Using dovere, potere, and volere in the conditional

The irregular verbs **dovere** (*to have to; must*), **potere** (*to be able to; can*), and **volere** (*to want; wish*) always enrich a sentence (check out Table 5-5 for their conditional stems), and their use in the conditional mood is no exception. These verbs translate as *should* (**dovere**), *could* (**potere**), and *would like to* (**volere**).

Dovere, potere, and volere are often followed in the conditional by a second verb in the infinitive form:

Dovrei studiare. (*I should study.*)

Potrei dormire tutto il giorno. (*I could sleep all day.*)

Vorrei sapere chi ti credi di essere. (*I'd like to know who you think you are.*)

The conditional is considered the polite mood, especially when combined with **dovere, potere,** and **volere.** Note the following three examples:

Dovremmo spostarci? Diamo fastidio? (*Should we move [our spot]? Are we in the way?*)

Potresti darmi una mano, per piacere? (*Would you please give me a hand?*)

Vorrei un cappuccino, per favore. (*I'd like a cappuccino, please.*)

Chapter 6

Getting into the Subjunctive Mood

*P*rior to this chapter, most of this book has dealt with the *indicative mood,* which has present, past, imperfect, and past perfect tenses. You use the indicative mood when expressing certainty and objectivity (for example, **mangio con Anna oggi** [*I'm eating with Anna today*] and **so che sei arrabbiato** [*I know that you're angry*]). But now the time has come to introduce a little uncertainty into your life with the *subjunctive mood.* The subjunctive expresses doubt, uncertainty, opinion, emotions — generally, all things *subjective* (for example, **non so se Anna mangi con me oggi** [*I don't know if Anna is eating with me today*] and **penso che tu sia arrabbiato** [*I think that you're angry*]).

In this chapter, you discover how to form and use the present and imperfect subjunctive conjugations for a variety of Italian verbs.

Forming the Present Subjunctive Mood

The formation of the subjunctive mood usually calls for a dependent clause, which you introduce with the word **che** (*that*). (See the later section "Making the Present Subjunctive a Valuable Tool" for different uses of the subjunctive and the verbs that usually require it.) Notice the position of the subjunctive in the following sentence and the kind of verb used in the main clause:

<u>**Credo**</u> che Emilia <u>**dorma**</u> poco. (*I think that Emilia sleeps little.*)

In this sentence, **credo** is in the present indicative tense, and **dorma** is in the present subjunctive tense. Note, also, that the subject in the main clause (**io** [*I*]) is different from the subject in the dependent clause (**Emilia**).

In English, you may say *I think Emilia sleeps little;* you sometimes omit the *that* in English, but you never omit it in Italian.

The following similarities can help you remember your subjunctive conjugations:

- ✔ The verb ending for **-are** verbs is the same for the first three persons (first, second, and third person singular): **-i.**

- ✔ The verb ending for both **-ere** and **-ire** verbs in the first three persons is the same: **-a.**

- ✔ The verb endings for first person plural (**noi**) and second person plural (**voi**) verbs are the same for **-are, -ere,** and **-ire** verbs: **-iamo** and **-iate.**

- ✔ The verb ending for an **-are** verb in the third person plural (**loro**) is **-ino,** and the ending for **-ere** and **-ire** verbs is **-ano.**

So you can think that many present subjunctive endings are almost the *opposites* of the present indicative endings. (See Chapter 1 in Book IV for an introduction to present indicative endings.)

Here are some examples of the verb endings in action:

> **È importante che il nostro presidente <u>parli</u> con il vostro.** (*It's important that our president speaks with yours.*)

> **La scuola <u>esige</u> che tutti gli studenti <u>vengano</u> alla riunione.** (*The school mandates that all the students come to the meeting.*)

The personal pronoun is often superfluous and unnecessary in Italian because the person is inherent in the verb form. But in the present subjunctive, you use the same verb for all three first persons. Therefore, you should use the personal pronoun (**io, tu, lui, lei, Lei**) or subject (Gianni, for example) with the present subjunctive to avoid confusing your reader/listener.

> **È essenziale che <u>io capisca</u> questo congiuntivo.** (*It's essential that I understand this subjunctive.*)

> **È bene che <u>lei capisca</u> sua nipote.** (*It's a good thing that she understands her niece.*)

The following table shows the present subjunctive -**are** verb endings: -**i**, -**iamo**, -**iate**, and -**ino**. The word **che** precedes the verb in these constructions and the rest in this section.

parlare (to speak)	
che io **parli**	che noi **parliamo**
che tu **parli**	che voi **parliate**
che lui, lei, Lei **parli**	che loro, Loro **parlino**
Penso che voi **parliate** molto bene l'italiano! (*I think that you all speak Italian well!*)	

The following two tables show the present subjunctive -**ere** and -**ire** verb endings: -**a**, -**iamo**, -**iate**, and -**ano**.

vedere (to see)	
che io **veda**	che noi **vediamo**
che tu **veda**	che voi **vediate**
che lui, lei, Lei **veda**	che loro, Loro **vedano**
Speriamo che **vediate** questo film. (*We hope that you see this film.*)	

partire (to leave; to depart)	
che io **parta**	che noi **partiamo**
che tu **parta**	che voi **partiate**
che lui, lei, Lei **parta**	che loro, Loro **partano**
I miei amici **sono** tristi che io **parta**. (*My friends are sad that I'm leaving.*)	

The following table shows the endings for -**ire (isc)** verbs in the present subjunctive: -**isca**, -**iamo**, -**iate**, and -**iscano**.

The -**ire** verbs come in two types. The first is a regular, normal Italian verb, such as **dormire** (*to sleep*); the second is known as an **isc** verb because all the conjugated forms, except for **noi** and **voi**, insert the letters **isc** between the stem and the endings. Chapter 1 in Book IV includes a thorough discussion of these verbs.

Book IV

Mastering Italian Verbs and Tenses

capire (*to understand*)	
che io **capisca**	che noi **capiamo**
che tu **capisca**	che voi **capiate**
che lui, lei, Lei **capisca**	che loro, Loro **capiscano**
È importante che lui <u>mi capisca</u>. (*It's important that he understand me.*)	

You conjugate reflexive verbs, such as **divertirsi** (*to have fun; to enjoy oneself; to have a good time*), just as you do any of the previous **-are, -ere, -ire,** and **-ire (isc)** verbs in the present subjunctive. The only difference is that you need to add the reflexive pronouns (**mi, ti, si, ci, vi,** and **si**).

divertirsi (*to have fun; to enjoy oneself; to have a good time*)	
che io mi **diverta**	che noi ci **divertiamo**
che tu ti **diverta**	che voi vi **divertiate**
che lui, lei, Lei si **diverta**	che loro, Loro si **divertano**
Quanto <u>sono</u> contenta che <u>vi divertiate</u>! (*I'm so happy that you're having a good time!*)	

Mastering the Present Subjunctive

As with the indicative mood, the present subjunctive mood features verbs that undergo spelling changes and irregular verbs. Spelling exceptions are common, but the good news is that the first three persons in the subjunctive (first, second, and third person singular) are exactly the same. Irregular verbs become easy to handle, too, after you understand their stems and structures. And the good thing about remembering the various exceptions to the present subjunctive? The **io, tu, lei, Lei,** and **loro** forms are the same as the **Lei** and **Loro** command (or imperative) forms described in Chapter 3 of Book IV.

Spelling exceptions

One spelling exception calls for you to add an **h** to the end of the stems of
-care and **-gare** verbs — such as **dimenticare** (*to forget*) and **pagare** (*to pay*) —
before you add their subjunctive endings (see the previous section for regular
endings). Doing so allows you to keep the hard *c* and *g* sounds throughout,
similar to the spelling exception you see in the present indicative tense. In the
indicative, however, the spelling change occurs only in the **tu** and **noi** persons;
in the subjunctive, you add the **h** to all six persons.

> **È probabile che io <u>dimentichi</u> questo congiuntivo.** (*It's probable that I'm
> going to forget this subjunctive.*)

> **È probabile che il nonno <u>paghi</u> la cena.** (*It's probable that Grandpa is
> paying for dinner.*)

Other verbs in the present subjunctive, like **cominciare** (*to begin*), **mangiare**
(*to eat*), **lasciare** (*to leave*), and **svegliare** (*to wake*) — in other words, verbs
that end in **-iare** — drop the **i** before you add the subjunctive endings. This
is a functional change so you don't have to double up on the **i.** The following
table shows the structure of **-iare** verbs, using **cominciare** as an example.

cominciare (*to begin*)	
che io **cominci**	che noi **cominciamo**
che tu **cominci**	che voi **cominciate**
che lui, lei, Lei **cominci**	che loro, Loro **comincino**
È ora che io <u>cominci</u> a <u>studiare</u>. (*It's time that I begin to study.*)	

Irregular forms

The conjugations of the **lei** and **loro** imperative forms are very similar to the
conjugations of irregular verbs in the present subjunctive. In fact, the conjugations are essentially the same. Table 6-1 lists the main irregular forms.

Book IV

**Mastering
Italian
Verbs and
Tenses**

Note: The three singular forms of each verb are the same, meaning that **io, tu, lui, lei, Lei** are all included in the first conjugation you see. For example, **Pensa** che io <u>abbia</u> <u>fame</u> (*He thinks that I have hunger*); **Pensa** che tu <u>abbia</u> <u>fame</u> (*He thinks that you have hunger*); **Pensa** che Lei <u>abbia</u> <u>fame</u> (*He thinks that you* [formal] *have hunger*).

Table 6-1	Irregular Present Tense Subjunctive Verbs	
Infinitive	*Conjugation*	*Example*
andare (*to go*)	vada, andiamo, andiate, vadano	**È bene che vadano via.** (*It's a good thing that they're going away.*)
avere (*to have*)	abbia, abbiamo, abbiate, abbiano	**Non so chi abbia il mio libro.** (*I don't know who has my book.*)
bere (*to drink*)	beva, beviamo, beviate, bevano	**Si dice che lui beva troppo.** (*They say that he drinks too much.*)
dare (*to give*)	dia, diamo, diate, diano	**Vuoi che gli dia una mano?** (*Do you want me to give him a hand?*)
dire (*to say*)	dica, diciamo, diciate, dicano	**Sembra che dicano la verità.** (*It seems that they're telling the truth.*)
dovere (*to have to*)	debba (deva), dobbiamo, dobbiate, debbano (devano)	**Peccato che dobbiate partire così presto.** (*It's too bad you have to leave so early.*)
essere (*to be*)	sia, siamo, siate, siano	**Voglio che tu sia felice.** (*I want for you to be happy.*)
fare (*to do; to make*)	faccia, facciamo, facciate, facciano	**È ora che io faccia il footing.** (*It's time for me to go jogging.*)
potere (*to be able to*)	possa, possiamo, possiate, possano	**È strano che i miei amici possano stare fuori fino alle 3 di notte, e io no.** (*It's strange that my friends can stay out until 3 in the morning, and I can't.*)
proporre (*to propose*)	proponga, proponiamo, proponiate, propongano	**Cosa vuoi che io ti proponga?** (*What would you like me to suggest to you?*)
rimanere (*to stay*)	rimanga, rimaniamo, rimaniate, rimangano	**Sperano che io rimanga vicino a casa.** (*They hope I'm going to stay close to home.*)
sapere (*to know*)	sappia, sappiamo, sappiate, sappiano	**Bisogna che tu sappia.** (*You need to know.*)

Infinitive	Conjugation	Example
scegliere (*to choose*)	scelga, scegliamo, scegliate, scelgano	**Mi dispiace che tu scelga un'università così lontana.** (*I'm sorry that you're choosing a university so far away.*)
stare (*to be*)	stia, stiamo, stiate, stiano	**Immagino che stiano ancora insieme.** (*I guess they're still together.*)
uscire (*to go out*)	esca, usciamo, usciate, escano	**Non voglio che tu esca senza il cappotto.** (*I don't want you to go out without a coat.*)
venire (*to come*)	venga, veniamo, veniate, vengano	**Può darsi che veniamo in Italia.** (*It's possible that we're coming to Italy.*)
volere (*to want*)	voglia, vogliamo, vogliate, vogliano	**Spero che Emilia voglia andare alla splaggia oggi.** (*I hope that Emilia wants to go to the beach today.*)

Making the Present Subjunctive a Valuable Tool

You have some options when it comes to using the present subjunctive. You can use it in different ways and in different expressions, all of which are presented in the following sections.

Expressing desires, wishes, commands, emotions, doubts, and beliefs

A subjunctive verb almost always appears in the dependent clause, generally introduced by the word **che** (*that*). The verb in the main clause, on the other hand, has to be a verb or expression that requires the subjunctive. Also note that the main and the dependent clause have to have two different subjects: **[Io] desidero che tu vada agli allenamenti** versus **[Io] desidero andare agli allenamenti,** where the second verb is an infinitive and no **che** is required.

Book IV

Mastering Italian Verbs and Tenses

Even though the word **che** separates the dependent and independent clauses in the following setences, the indicative always appears with the verb **sapere** (*to know*), and the subjunctive always goes with the verb **dubitare** (*to doubt*). *Remember:* You use the indicative mood when expressing certainty and objectivity and the subjunctive mood when expressing doubt, uncertainty, opinion, or emotions. **Sapere** is certainty; **dubitare** is uncertainty.

> <u>So</u> che <u>sei</u> intelligente. (*I know that you are intelligent.*)

> <u>Dubito</u> che tu <u>sia</u> intelligente. (*I doubt that you are intelligent.*)

The verbs in Table 6-2 all require that their accompanying verbs be in the subjunctive, because they express desires, wishes, commands, emotions, doubts, or disbeliefs. All these expressions should be followed by **che** and, in this chapter, the present subjunctive.

Table 6-2   Verbs Indicating a Desire, Wish, Command, Emotion, Doubt, or Belief

Verb or Expression	Translation	Verb or Expression	Translation
augurarsi	*to hope*	**non essere certo/a/i/e**	*to not be certain*
avere l'impressione che	*to have the impression/ feeling/idea*	**non essere sicuro/a/i/e**	*to not be certain*
avere paura che	*to be afraid*	**non sapere**	*to not know*
chiedere	*to ask for*	**pensare**	*to think*
credere	*to believe*	**permettere**	*to allow; to permit*
desiderare	*to desire; to wish*	**preferire**	*to prefer*
dispiacere	*to be sorry*	**pretendere**	*to demand; to expect*
esigere	*to demand*	**proibire (isc)**	*to forbid*
essere contenta/o/i/e	*to be happy*	**sperare**	*to hope*
essere triste/i	*to be sad*	**temere**	*to fear; to worry*
immaginare	*to imagine*	**volere**	*to want*

Working with impersonal expressions

Ready for Round Two? Another instance when you use the subjunctive is when a verb in the main clause is an impersonal expression and the subject of the dependent clause is articulated:

> **È importante <u>studiare</u>.** (*It's important to study.*) In this example, no subject is articulated.

> **È importante che io <u>studi</u>.** (*It's important that I study.*) In this example, the subject in the dependent clause is specified, so you use the subjunctive.

An *impersonal expression* has no specific subject and often translates as *one*, *you*, or *it*. Table 6-3 provides you with a list of common impersonal expressions. These impersonal expressions usually start with the third person singular of the verb **essere** (*to be*): **È** (**È bene che . . .** [*It's a good thing that . . .*]). Not all impersonal expressions, however, require the subjunctive. For example, **È certo che . . .** (*It's certain that . . .*) accepts both the subjunctive and the indicative because it expresses a certainty: **È certo che lui <u>viene</u>** (*It's certain that he's going to come*) is as correct as **È certo che lui <u>venga</u>** (*It's certain that he's going to come*). So to recognize the need for impersonal expressions in the subjunctive, familiarize yourself with Table 6-3.

All the impersonal expressions you see in Table 6-3 can go before the second part (the part after **che**) of the following sample sentence:

> **È essenziale che lo <u>facciate</u>.** (*It's essential that you* [plural] *do it.*)

Table 6-3	Impersonal Expressions in Main Clauses
Expression	*Translation*
bisogna che	*it's necessary that; to have to; should*
è bene che	*it's good that*
è importante che	*it's important that*
è incredibile che	*it's incredible that*
è inutile che	*it's useless that; it's pointless that*
è male che	*it's bad that*
è meglio che	*it's better that*
è ora che	*it's time that*

(continued)

Table 6-3 *(continued)*

Expression	Translation
è (im)possibile che	it's (im)possible that
è (im)probabile che	it's (im)probable that; it's (un)likely that
è strano che	it's strange that
pare che	it seems that
peccato che	it's too bad that
può darsi che	it's possible that
sembra che	it seems that

Handling conjunctions and words that end in -unque

Now you get to review a couple more categories of words and conditions that require the subjunctive tense! (Quite a useful tense, aye?) These areas include *conjunctions* (words connecting two different clauses) and indefinite forms ending in **-unque**. You don't use these constructions as frequently as the impersonal expressions (refer to Table 6-3) and the verbs and expressions in Table 6-2, but you should acquaint yourself with them anyway. Check out Table 6-4 for some conjunctions and Table 6-5 for some **-unque** words.

You attach the present subjunctive tense to the conjunctions and indefinite expressions, which will be in dependent clauses. Main clauses here should appear in the present indicative for the most part, but they can also be in the future tense (see Chapter 5 in Book IV for details on this tense). The order of the clauses doesn't matter, provided that you keep the subjunctive with its conjunction or **-unque** word.

Here's an example, using a **-unque** word, that illustrates that the clause position doesn't matter:

> **Dovunque tu vada, ti amerò.** (*Wherever you go, I shall love you.*)
>
> **Ti amerò, dovunque tu vada.** (*I shall love you, wherever you go.*)
>
> **Vi telefoneremo, a condizione che [voi] ce lo ricordiate.** (*We will call you, provided that you remind us.*)

A condizione che [voi] ce lo ricordiate, vi telefoneremo. (*Provided that you remind us, we will call you.*)

Prima che si noti il disastro, voglio pulire tutto. (*Before the disaster is evident, I want to clean everything.*)

Voglio pulire tutto prima che si noti il disastro. (*I want to clean everything, before the disaster is evident.*)

Table 6-4	Common Conjunctions
Conjunction	*Translation*
a meno che . . . non	*unless*
affinchè	*so that*
perchè	*so that; because*
di/in modo che	*so that*
benchè	*although*
sebbene	*although*
prima che	*before*
senza che	*without*
purchè	*provided that; on the condition that*
a patto che	*provided that; on the condition that*
a condizione che	*provided that; on the condition that*

Table 6-5	Common -unque Words
-unque Word	*Translation*
chiunque	*whoever*
comunque	*however*
in qualunque modo	*however*
dovunque	*wherever*
qualunque cosa	*whatever*

Book IV

Mastering Italian Verbs and Tenses

Checking out a few other uses of the present subjunctive

You should acknowledge a few less common but still important uses of the subjunctive, such as the following:

- ✔ In a relative clause (a clause introduced by a relative pronoun):

    il/la/i/le più + adjective + **che** + subjunctive:

    Mary è la donna più gentile che io conosca. (*Mary is the nicest woman that I know.*)

    il/la/i/le meno + adjective + **che** + subjunctive:

    Questo sarà l'esercizio meno difficile che facciate. (*This is going to be the least difficult exercise that you do.*)

- ✔ With the adjectives **unico/a/i che** (*only*), **solo/a/i/e** (*only*), **ultimo/a/i/e** (*last*), and **primo/a/i/e** (*first*):

    Laura è l'unica donna che capisca Francesco. (*Laura is the only woman who understands Francesco.*)

- ✔ With a negative expression, such as **niente** (*nothing*) or **nessuno** (*no one*):

    Non c'è niente che io ti possa fare. (*There's nothing that I can do for you.*)

    Non c'è nessuno che parli cinese in questo aereo? (*Isn't there anyone who speaks Chinese on this plane?*)

- ✔ In exclamations and blessings:

    Che Dio ti benedica! (*May God bless you!*)

    Dio ci guardi! (*Lord help us!*)

    Che ti possa venire un colpo! (*May you be struck by lightning!*)

Understanding the Imperfect Subjunctive

The imperfect subjunctive is a construction that tries to hide in subordinate or dependent clauses. It lets all the terms that require the subjunctive make the introductions (*I was hoping that you/he/she/we/they . . .* ; *we were wishing that . . .* ; *I would like that you . . .* — the imperfect subjunctive would follow the ellipsis in each case). The main caveat of the imperfect subjunctive? The verb in the main clause has to be in the conditional or imperfect (in most cases).

The following sections help you get a feel for the imperfect subjunctive by comparing it to the present subjunctive. Here, you find out when to use the imperfect subjunctive, how to conjugate it and form sentences around it, and how to incorporate irregular verbs into the mix.

It's a very good idea to get comfortable with the present indicative, the present subjunctive and the terms that require it, the conditional tense, and the imperfect tense before you go any further in this chapter. Respectively, see Chapter 1 in Book IV, the preceding sections in this chapter, Chapter 5 in Book IV, and Chapter 1 in Book V.

Conjugating the imperfect subjunctive

Before you can jump into forming sentences with the imperfect subjunctive, you first have to find out how to conjugate it. The first, second, and third person singular and plural conjugations for **-are, -ere,** and **-ire** verbs look very similar:

- ✔ **-are** endings: **-assi, -assi, -asse, -assimo, -aste, -assero**
- ✔ **-ere** endings: **-essi, -essi, -esse, -essimo, -este, -essero**
- ✔ **-ire** endings: **-issi, -issi, -isse, -issimo, -iste, -issero**

Repeat these endings a few times to yourself, using a quick pace or a tune, so you begin to memorize them!

Here are some examples that show the different endings in action:

> **Vorrebbero** che **mangiassimo** da loro. (*They'd like us to eat at their place.*)
>
> **Pensavo** che tu **avessi** fame. (*I thought that you were hungry.*)
>
> **Ero** felice che Fabio **venisse** in Italia. (*I was happy that Fabio was coming to Italy.*)
>
> **Era** bene che **studiaste**. (*It was good that you* [plural] *studied.*) ***Note:*** This example is an *impersonal construction,* which means that it doesn't specify a subject.

The following tables show you the conjugations of the **-are, -ere,** and **-ire** verbs in the imperfect subjunctive tense. You'll notice the word **che** (*that; like*), which precedes the verb in the imperfect subjunctive in these constructions.

Book IV

Mastering Italian Verbs and Tenses

parlare (to speak)	
che io **parlassi**	che noi **parlassimo**
che tu **parlassi**	che voi **parlaste**
che lui, lei, Lei **parlasse**	che loro, Loro **parlassero**
<u>Vorrei</u> che tu <u>parlassi</u> con tuo padre. (*I would like you to speak to your father.*)	

leggere (to read)	
che io **leggessi**	che noi **leggessimo**
che tu **leggessi**	che voi **leggeste**
che lui, lei, Lei **leggesse**	che loro, Loro **leggessero**
Rudi <u>era</u> contento che <u>leggessimo</u> il suo libro. (*Rudi was happy that we were reading his book.*)	

capire (to understand)	
che io **capissi**	che noi **capissimo**
che tu **capissi**	che voi **capiste**
che lui, lei, Lei **capisse**	che loro, Loro **capissero**
<u>Sembrava</u> che tu <u>capissi</u> quello che <u>diceva</u> quel signore. (*It seemed that you understood what that man was saying.*)	

Forming the imperfect subjunctive to express doubts, desires, and wants

Finding out how to form the imperfect subjunctive is important if you want to express doubts, desires, and wants. The verbs and constructions that require the present subjunctive also associate with the imperfect subjunctive. The tense of the verb in the main clause determines whether you use the present subjunctive or the imperfect subjunctive in the dependent clause. For example, if the verb in the main clause requires the subjunctive and is in the present tense, you use the present subjunctive or the past subjunctive in the dependent clause (flip to Chapter 4 in Book V for details on the past subjunctive). If the verb in the main clause requires the subjunctive and is in the conditional, the imperfect, or the past subjunctive, you need to use the imperfect subjunctive in the dependent clause.

You usually use the imperfect subjunctive in dependent or subordinate clauses, introduced by the conjunction **che** (*that; like*). The verbs in the main clauses of these constructions are usually in one of two tenses:

- **The conditional:** In the sentence <u>Vorrei</u> **che tu** <u>stessi</u> **zitto** (*I'd like you to be quiet*), **vorrei** is in the conditional, and **stessi** is in the imperfect subjunctive.

- **The imperfect:** In the sentence <u>Speravo</u> **che** <u>arrivassero</u> **in tempo** (*I was hoping that they'd arrive in time*), **speravo** is in the imperfect, and **arrivassero** is in the imperfect subjunctive.

The following examples show the difference between using the present subjunctive and the imperfect subjunctive:

> <u>Credo</u> **che lui** <u>sia</u> **intelligente.** (*I believe that he's intelligent.*)

> <u>Credevo</u> **che lui** <u>fosse</u> **intelligente.** (*I believed that he was intelligent.*)

Here's an easy-to-access formula for the construction of the imperfect subjunctive:

> subject + verb in conditional or imperfect + **che** + imperfect subjunctive

In the previous section on the present subjunctive tense, you see all the different uses of this tense. Table 6-2 gives you a working list of verbs and expressions appearing in the main clause of a sentence that require the present subjunctive in the dependent clause. Such a list will come in handy when working on the imperfect subjunctive. The same verbs and expressions in the main clause of a sentence tell you that the imperfect subjunctive is necessary, so you can refer to this table as necessary.

You can compare the tenses and the inner workings of the imperfect subjunctive in Table 6-6.

Book IV

Mastering Italian Verbs and Tenses

Table 6-6   Using the Correct Subjunctive Dependent Clause

Independent Clause	Dependent Clause	Example
Present indicative	Present subjunctive	<u>Penso</u> **che lui** <u>sia</u> **onesto.** (*I think that he is honest.*)
Present indicative	Past subjunctive	<u>Penso</u> **che lui** <u>sia</u> **stato onesto.** (*I think that he was honest.*)

(continued)

Table 6-6 *(continued)*

Independent Clause	Dependent Clause	Example
Future imperative	Present subjunctive	**Vorrai** che lui **sia** onesto! (*You're going to want him to be honest!*)
Present imperative	Present subjunctive	**Digli** che **sia** onesto! (*Tell him to be honest!*)
Imperfect indicative	Imperfect subjunctive	**Pensavo** che lui **fosse** onesto. (*I thought that he was honest.*)
Present conditional	Imperfect subjunctive	**Penserei** che lui **fosse** onesto. (*I would think that he was honest.*)
Past conditional	Imperfect subjunctive	**Avrei pensato** che lui **fosse** onesto. (*I would've thought that he was honest.*)
Present perfect indicative	Imperfect subjunctive	**Ho pensato** che lui **fosse** onesto. (*I thought that he was honest.*)
Past absolute indicative	Imperfect subjunctive	**Pensai** che lui **fosse** onesto. (*I thought that he was honest.*)

Getting a grip on irregular imperfect subjunctives

Okay, so not every part of the imperfect subjunctive is as simple and beautiful as it seems, judging from the earlier sections of this chapter! You have to deal with some irregular verbs in the imperfect subjunctive. What this means is that you need to change the stems of the verbs before you add the imperfect subjunctive endings. The good news is that you have only a few irregular verbs to worry about. The following are some of the most frequently used irregular verbs, along with their irregular stems:

- **bere** (*to drink*) → **bevessi, bevessi, bevesse, bevessimo, beveste, bevessero**
- **dare** (*to give*) → **dessi, dessi, desse, dessimo, deste, dessero**
- **dire** (*to say; to tell*) → **dicessi, dicessi, dicesse, dicessimo, diceste, dicessero**
- **essere** (*to be*) → **fossi, fossi, fosse, fossimo, foste, fossero**
- **fare** (*to do; to make*) → **facessi, facessi, facesse, facessimo, faceste, facessero**
- **stare** (*to be; to stay*) → **stessi, stessi, stesse, stessimo, steste, stessero**

✔ **tradurre** (*to translate*) → **traducessi, traducessi, traducesse, traducessimo, traduceste, traducessero**

✔ **proporre** (*to propose*) → **proponessi, proponessi, proponesse, proponessimo, proponeste, proponessero**

TIP

Many of these forms share the same irregular stem with the imperfect indicative tense.

The following tables contain the conjugations of **bere** and **tradurre.** You can flip to Appendix A to see how the others conjugate — in the imperfect subjunctive and all the other tenses.

bere (*to drink*)	
che io **bevessi**	che noi **bevessimo**
che tu **bevessi**	che voi **beveste**
che lui, lei, Lei **bevesse**	che loro, Loro **bevessero**
Non <u>sapevo</u> che cosa <u>bevessero</u>. (*I didn't know what they were drinking.*)	

tradurre (*to translate*)	
che io **traducessi**	che noi **traducessimo**
che tu **traducessi**	che voi **traduceste**
che lui, lei, Lei **traducesse**	che loro, Loro **traducessero**
Il professore <u>voleva</u> che noi <u>traducessimo</u> la poesia. (*The professor wanted us to translate the poem.*)	

Bere, dare, dire, fare, stare, tradurre, and **proporre** all follow the **-essi, -essi, -esse, -essimo, -este, -essero** ending pattern. **Essere** goes by **-ossi, -ossi, -osse, -ossimo, -oste, -ossero.**

Book V

Building Compound Tenses

Forming the Regular Past Participle

Infinitive	Past Participle
cercare (*to look for*)	**cercato** (*looked for*)
guardare (*to look at*)	**guardato** (*looked at*)
mangiare (*to eat*)	**mangiato** (*eaten*)
parlare (*to speak*)	**parlato** (*spoken*)
credere (*to believe; to think*)	**creduto** (*believed; thought*)
potere (*to be able*)	**potuto** (*to have been able*)
ricevere (*to receive*)	**ricevuto** (*received*)
volere (*to want*)	**voluto** (*wanted*)
capire (*to understand*)	**capito** (*understood*)
dormire (*to sleep*)	**dormito** (*slept*)
partire (*to leave*)	**partito** (*left*)
sentire (*to hear; to feel*)	**sentito** (*heard; felt*)

Italian culture and language come together with **La Bocca della Verità** (*Mouth of Truth*) in Rome. This symbol of the city raises questions about truth-telling and provides you with an opportunity to practice conjugating the present perfect indicative of **essere sincero/a** (*to be sincere/honest/truthful*) and **mentire** (*to lie*). Go to www.dummies.com/extras/italianaio to find a free article that connects the Roman monument with your language practice.

Contents at a Glance

Chapter 1

Been There, Done That: Talking in the Past Tense

No matter how much you live in the present, you spend a lot of time talking about the past. You tell people where you're from, where you've been, and how long you've been doing something. Whether something occurred in the last ten minutes or the last ten years, understanding how to express events in the past tense is key to communicating in any language.

The past tenses in English are easy to use, if often irregular in form. In Italian, the past tenses are also frequently irregular. But in Italian, it gets a little more complicated: Past tense constructions require a knowledge of *conditions* that English doesn't. For example, in English, you may say *The kids went to school in Chicago.* In Italian, the verb you use for *went* depends on when the kids went to school in Chicago. Did they always go there? Did they go for a summer program? More than once? Was it a hundred years ago?

In English, you supply this information with elaboration. *The kids went to school in Chicago during the 2012 to 2013 school year.* Or during their child-hood. Or around the turn of the last century. Or for summer programs in general. Or for specific summer programs. In Italian, if this information isn't directly stated, you imply it by the tense of the verb you use.

This chapter shows you how to be this specific as you express events in the past tense. This chapter walks you through constructing the present perfect (**passato prossimo,** or the near past), the past absolute (**passato remoto,** or the distant past), and the imperfect (**imperfetto,** or the habitual, repeated, or ongoing past) and helps you understand when to use each one. (Check out Chapter 2 in Book V for specifics on using reflexive verbs in these tenses.)

Forming the Present Perfect Tense

Use the *present perfect* to talk about completed actions in the past. The present perfect is a compound verb, so it takes two words. One is the past participle, such as **guardato** (*looked*), **cotto** (*baked*), **comprato** (*bought*), **domandato** (*asked*), and **detto** (*said*); the other is a helping verb — **essere** (*to be*) or **avere** (*to have*) — conjugated in the present tense.

Past participles

To form a regular past participle, remove the characteristic **-are, -ere,** and **-ire** endings from infinitives (unconjugated verbs) and replace them with **-ato, -uto,** or **-ito,** as shown with some examples in Table 1-1.

Table 1-1	Forming the Regular Past Participle
Infinitive	*Past Participle*
cercare (*to look for*)	**cercato** (*looked for*)
guardare (*to look at*)	**guardato** (*looked at*)
mangiare (*to eat*)	**mangiato** (*eaten*)
parlare (*to speak*)	**parlato** (*spoken*)
credere (*to believe; to think*)	**creduto** (*believed; thought*)
potere (*to be able*)	**potuto** (*to have been able*)
ricevere (*to receive*)	**ricevuto** (*received*)
volere (*to want*)	**voluto** (*wanted*)
capire (*to understand*)	**capito** (*understood*)
dormire (*to sleep*)	**dormito** (*slept*)
partire (*to leave*)	**partito** (*left*)
sentire (*to hear*)	**sentito** (*heard*)

Italian past participles correspond to their English counterparts, which often end in *-ed* such as *looked*. However, many irregular English past participles don't end in *-ed,* such as *bought, saw,* and *read.* Italian, too, has many irregular past participles. Some verbs even have two forms to choose from, such as **perdere** and **vedere** in Table 1-2.

Table 1-2	Forming the Irregular Past Participle for Verbs That Conjugate with Avere
Infinitive	*Past Participle*
fare (*to make; to do*)	**fatto** (*made; done*)
accendere (*to light; to turn on*)	**acceso** (*lit; turned on*)
chiedere (*to ask*)	**chiesto** (*asked*)
chiudere (*to close*)	**chiuso** (*closed*)
decidere (*to decide*)	**deciso** (*decided*)
leggere (*to read*)	**letto** (*read*)
mettere (*to put; to place*)	**messo** (*put; placed*)
perdere (*to lose*)	**perduto, perso** (*lost*)
prendere (*to take*)	**preso** (*taken*)
rispondere (*to reply*)	**risposto** (*replied*)
scrivere (*to write*)	**scritto** (*written*)
spegnere (*to turn off*)	**spento** (*turned off*)
spendere (*to spend*)	**speso** (*spent*)
vedere (*to see*)	**veduto, visto** (*seen*)
vincere (*to win*)	**vinto** (*won*)
vivere (*to live*)	**vissuto** (*lived*)
aprire (*to open*)	**aperto** (*opened*)
dire (*to say; to tell*)	**detto** (*said; told*)
offrire (*to offer*)	**offerto** (*offered*)

Table 1-3 lists some irregular verbs that take **essere** in the past. For more on when to use which auxiliary, or helper, verb, see the following section.

Table 1-3	Irregular Past Tense Verbs That Take Essere
Infinitive	*Past Participle*
nascere (*to be born*)	**nato** (*born*)
rimanere (*to remain*)	**rimasto** (*remained*)
scendere (*to come; to go down*)	**sceso** (*fell*)

(continued)

Table 1-3 *(continued)*

Infinitive	Past Participle
morire (*to die*)	**morto** (*died*)
sopravvivere (*to survive*)	**sopravvissuto** (*survived*)
venire (*to come*)	**venuto** (*came*)
vivere (*to live*)	**vissuto** (*lived*)

You may have noticed that **vivere** appears in both Tables 1-2 and 1-3. Well, that's no mistake. You can use **vivere** with both **avere** and **essere**. You use **avere** when **vivere** is followed by a direct object, as in **Matusalemme ha vissuto una lunga vita** (*Methuselah has lived a long life*); you use **essere** when you specify space, location, or duration, such as **È vissuto a Milano e a Torino** (*He has lived in Milan and Turin*) or **È vissuta fino a 95 anni** (*She has lived 95 years*).

You can also use past participles as adjectives, as long as they agree in number and gender with what they're describing. For example, **la casa preferita** (*the favorite house*) is feminine and singular, so **preferita** is as well. **Il libro preferito** (*the favorite book*) is masculine and singular, so **preferito** reflects that. Speaking of an enthusiastic audience at a concert, the late Luciano Pavarotti urged the conductor to give an encore, and said **Si sono proprio riscaldati** (*They're really warmed up*). **Riscaldati** (from **riscaldare** [*to warm up*]) refers to members of the audience and is masculine and plural.

Auxiliary verbs: Avere and essere

To activate the past participles discussed in the preceding section, you need an auxiliary or helping verb, either **avere** (*to have*) or **essere** (*to be*) conjugated in the present tense.

- ✔ You use **avere** with *transitive verbs* — verbs that can (though don't always) take a direct object; they "transit" action from the subject to a direct object.

- ✔ You use **essere** with verbs that can't take a direct object, called *intransitive verbs,* which are frequently verbs of motion, of coming and going, of leaving and returning.

Transiting action with avere

Direct objects answer questions that ask *who* or *what.* For example:

> **Ho trovato la chiave** (*I found the key*). What did I find? *The key.*
>
> **Lui ha scritto una lettera d'amore** (*He wrote a love letter*). What did he write? *A love letter.*
>
> **Ho visto gli studenti** (*I saw the students*). Who did I see? *The students.*

Think literally for a moment, and the conjugation with **avere** will make perfect sense. **Ho** (*I have*) + **trovato** (*found*); *I have found.* What did I find? **La chiave. Lui ha** (*he has*) + **scritto** (*written*); *he has written.* What has he written? **Una lettera d'amore. Ho** (*I have*) + **visto** (*seen*); *I have seen.* Who have I seen? **Gli studenti.** These three verbs answer the question *what* or *who* and direct the subjects' actions through the verbs to direct objects.

Note: Sometimes the direct object isn't stated but is understood. In this case, you still use **avere** to form the present perfect. The most commonly used verbs with unstated direct objects are **parlare** (*to speak*) because you speak speech, **dormire** (*to sleep*) because you sleep sleep, **sognare** (*to dream*) because you dream dreams, and **camminare** (*to walk*) because you, well, walk the walk.

Verbs with built-in prepositions in English, such as **cercare** (*to look for*), **aspettare** (*to wait for*), and **pagare** (*to pay for*), take direct object pronouns in Italian (though in English they usually take indirect object pronouns).

Moving with essere

Verbs of motion (going, coming, arriving, leaving, becoming) or of stopping motion (staying) don't take direct objects. They conjugate with **essere** rather than **avere,** and the subject and past participle agree in number and gender. Again, think literally for a moment. **Lui è** (*he is*) + **andato** (*gone*) **al cinema.** (*He went to the cinema.*) Or **lei è** (*she is*) + **andata** (*gone*) **al cinema.** (*She went to the cinema.*)

Note: All reflexive verbs conjugate in the present perfect with **essere.** See Chapter 2 in Book V for more about reflexive verbs in the present perfect.

Recognizing that some verbs use both avere and essere

Some verbs "cross-conjugate," meaning they can use either **essere** or **avere** as a helper. Their meanings tell you which helper to use. For example, take **cambiare** (*to change*). It means one thing to say **ho cambiato casa** (*I changed houses*) (*I moved*) and quite another to say **sono cambiato** (*I have changed*) (Literally: *I am changed*).

Here's another example with **finire** (*to finish*). **Ho finito il libro** means *I finished/have finished the book,* but **la commedia è finita** means *the play is over* and **lui è finito in prigione** translates to *he ended up in prison.* The helping verb changes the meaning and function of the verb's past tense.

You don't really want to say **sono finito** because it doesn't mean *I'm finished/ I'm done in.* Instead, it means *there is no hope for me,* or, by extension, *I'm dead.*

Conjugating verbs in the present perfect with avere

Putting a verb into the present perfect when the helper is **avere** involves three steps.

1. **Form a past participle from the infinitive (for example, <u>mangiare</u> becomes <u>mangiato</u> and <u>preferire</u> becomes <u>preferito</u>).**

2. **Conjugate <u>avere</u> in the present indicative tense (see Chapter 2 in Book IV) so that it reflects the subject (<u>io ho</u>, <u>tu hai</u>, and so on).**

3. **Combine the two forms, and you've arrived in the present perfect.**

The following table shows you how to conjugate **trovare** (*to find*) in the present perfect by using the helping verb **avere**.

trovare (*to find*)	
io **ho trovato**	noi **abbiamo trovato**
tu **hai trovato**	voi **avete trovato**
lui, lei, Lei **ha trovato**	loro, Loro **hanno trovato**

Here are some examples of the present perfect tense using **avere:**

Io ho mangiato tutti i biscotti. (*I ate all the cookies.*)

Hai scritto molte lettere oggi. (*You wrote many letters today.*)

Paolo ha letto due libri durante il fine settimana. (*Paolo read two books over the weekend.*)

Abbiamo ricevuto una bella lettera dalla zia. (*We received a lovely letter from our aunt.*)

Avete capito? (*Have you understood?*)

Hanno detto una bugia. (*They told a lie.*)

Avere verbs don't require you to make the participle agree with the subject. They do require agreement, however, if you use a direct object pronoun (see Chapter 3 in Book III). As with most pronouns, direct object pronouns precede the verb. They agree in number and gender with the noun they replace.

When direct object pronouns precede the conjugated **avere** verbs, they look like this:

> **Hanno visitato il museo. L'hanno visitato.** (*They visited the museum. They visited it.*)

Lo (*it*) substitutes for **il museo,** but because it already agrees in number and gender with the participle, **visitato,** nothing changes. **Lo** does contract with **hanno,** in the interests of flow. Now compare these sentences:

> **Hanno visitato la chiesa. L'hanno visitata.** (*They visited the church. They visited it.*)

La (*it*) substitutes for **la chiesa,** so the past participle, **visitata,** takes on a feminine, singular ending. Here are a couple more examples:

> **Ho comprato le scarpe. Le ho comprate.** (*I bought the shoes. I bought them.*)

> **Hai visto gli amici? Li hai visti?** (*Have you seen your friends? Have you seen them?*)

In the first example, **scarpe** are feminine plural, so the pronoun and the participle's ending are also feminine plural. In the second example, **gli amici,** masculine plural, requires the corresponding masculine plural ending on the participle.

The direct object pronouns **mi, ti, ci,** and **vi** don't require agreement between themselves and the past participle. Such agreement does still occur — **Lui ci ha chiamati** (*He called us*) — but it's entirely optional.

Note: **Avere** always conjugates with itself to form the present perfect. Thus, **ho avuto** means *I have had/I had.* The following table shows **avere** conjugated in its entirety.

avere (*to have*)	
io **ho avuto**	noi **abbiamo avuto**
tu **hai avuto**	voi **avete avuto**
lui, lei, Lei **ha avuto**	loro, Loro **hanno avuto**

Conjugating verbs in the present perfect with essere

To conjugate a verb in the present perfect, using **essere** as its helper, you need to take three steps.

1. **Form a past participle.**

    For example, **andare** becomes **andato**, and **partire** becomes **partito**.

2. **Conjugate <u>essere</u> in the present tense so it reflects the subject.**

    For example, **io sono, tu sei, lei è,** and so on. (Flip to Chapter 2 in Book IV for details.)

3. **Put the conjugated form of <u>essere</u> before the past participle, and make the subject and the past participle agree in number and gender.**

    Lui è andato (*he went*) but **lei è andata** (*she went*). **Noi** (*we* — a mixed group, thus masculine plural) **siamo andati** (*went*). **Noi** (*we* — a group of women) **siamo andate** (*went*).

The following table shows a verb of motion, **andare** (*to go*), conjugated in the present perfect with **essere.**

andare (*to go*)	
io **sono andato/andata**	noi **siamo andati/andate**
tu **sei andato/andata**	voi **siete andati/andate**
lui, lei, Lei **è andato/andata**	loro, Loro **sono andati/andate**

The conjugated form of **essere** reveals the subject and that determines the gender and number of the past participle. Here are some examples:

È stato a casa. (*He was at home.*)

È partita stamattina. (*She left this morning.*)

Siamo andate a teatro insieme. (*We went to the theater together.*)

Franco e Chiara sono arrivati tardi. (*Franco and Chiara arrived late.*)

The participles' endings tell you that the first subject was a man; the second was a woman; the third, all women; and the fourth, a mixed gender group. For this last example, keep in mind that if you have a mixed group (even one man and 17 women, for example), you use the masculine.

The peculiarities of avere and essere

Both **avere** and **essere** have their own peculiarities. **Avere** wants agreement between participles and direct object pronouns. (If there were ever a reason to be specific, that would be it!) **Essere** wants agreements between participles and subjects. Something the two helping verbs share, however, is the ability to accept a word inserted between the helping verb and the past participle. This makes English speakers who were taught never to split an infinitive (such as *to already know*) nervous. For Italian speakers, the equivalent reaction is evoked when verbs are separated, generally **non posso lo leggere**. This is a mistake that makes Italian speakers cringe!

In this case, though, in a compound tense, you can insert a few little words: **già** (*already*), **appena** (*just*), and **ancora** (*yet*). The following constructions, then, are both normal and acceptable in Italian.

> **La signora è già partita.** (*The lady has already left.*)
>
> **Sono appena arrivati.** (*They have already arrived.*)
>
> **Non hanno ancora parlato con il direttore.** (*They haven't yet spoken with the director.*)

Note: **Essere** always conjugates with itself to form the present perfect. Thus, **sono stato/sono stata** means *I was* (masculine and feminine speakers). The following table shows **essere** conjugated in its entirety.

essere (*to be*)	
io **sono stato/stata**	noi **siamo stati/state**
tu **sei stato/stata**	voi **siete stati/state**
lui, lei, Lei **è stato/stata**	loro, Loro **sono stati/state**

Over and Done with: The Past Absolute

You use the present perfect (discussed earlier in this chapter) to talk about past (completed) actions. For example:

> **Giuseppe è arrivato.** (*Giuseppe arrived.*)
>
> **Maria ha dato dei bei regali.** (*Maria gave some beautiful presents.*)
>
> **Non sono andati.** (*They didn't go.*)

On a related note, you use the past absolute to discuss a completed action from long ago and far away.

> **Giuseppe arrivò negli Stati Uniti molti anni fa.** (*Giuseppe arrived in the United States many years ago.*)
>
> **Maria diede dei bei regali.** (*Maria gave beautiful presents.*)
>
> **Non andarono a scuola.** (*They didn't go to school.*)

As you see, the past absolute consists of just one conjugated verb; it's not compound like the present perfect. You conjugate it by adding the appropriate endings to the verb stem (what's left of the verb after you remove the infinitive's ending). For the three types of infinitives, the endings are as shown in Table 1-4.

Table 1-4 — Conjugations in the Past Absolute Tense

-are Verbs	-ere Verbs	-ire Verbs
parlare (*to talk*)	**ripetere** (*to repeat*)	**dormire** (*to sleep*)
io **parlai**	io **ripetei**	io **dormii**
tu **parlasti**	tu **ripetesti**	tu **dormisti**
lui, lei, Lei **parlò**	lui, lei, Lei **ripetè**	lui, lei, Lei **dormì**
noi **parlammo**	noi **ripetemmo**	noi **dormimmo**
voi **parlaste**	voi **ripeteste**	voi **dormiste**
loro, Loro **parlarono**	loro, Loro **ripeterono**	loro, Loro **dormirono**

The past absolute stem for some verbs is highly irregular. Table 1-5 shows you some of the most common forms.

Table 1-5 — Conjugations of Irregular Stems in the Past Absolute

Verb Infinitive	Stem	Conjugation
avere (*to have*)	ebb-	**ebbi, avesti, ebbe, avemmo, aveste, ebbero**
conoscere (*to know*)	conobb-	**conobbi, conoscesti, conobbe, conoscemmo, conosceste, conobbero**
dare (*to give*)	died-	**diedi, desti, diede, demmo, deste, dettero (diedero)**

Verb Infinitive	Stem	Conjugation
dire (*to say; to tell*)	diss-	dissi, dicesti, disse, dicemmo, diceste, dissero
essere (*to be*)	fu-	fui, fosti, fu, fummo, foste, furono
fare (*to make; to do*)	fec-	feci, facesti, fece, facemmo, faceste, fecero
nascere (*to be born*)	nacqu-	nacqui, nascesti, nacque, nascemmo, nasceste, nacquero
piacere (*to like*)	piacqu-	piacqui, piacesti, piacque, piacemmo, piaceste, piacquero
rompere (*to break*)	rupp-	ruppi, rompesti, ruppe, rompemmo, rompeste, ruppero
sapere (*to know*)	sepp-	seppi, sapesti, seppe, sapemmo, sapeste, seppero
scrivere (*to write*)	scriss-	scrissi, scrivesti, scrisse, scrivemmo, scriveste, scrissero
stare (*to stay*)	stett-	stetti, stesti, stette, stemmo, steste, stettero
vedere (*to see*)	vid-	vidi, vedesti, vide, vedemmo, vedeste, videro
venire (*to come*)	venn-	venni, venisti, venne, venimmo, veniste, vennero
vivere (*to live*)	viss-	vissi, vivesti, visse, vivemmo, viveste, vissero
volere (*to want*)	voll- (the meaning changes in the past absolute from *wants* to *insists*)	volli, volesti, volle, volemmo, voleste, vollero

The past absolute is the literary past, and you're going to find it useful to recognize, if not produce. As for use in everyday speech, the past absolute often gets used in parts of Tuscany and the south of Italy to refer to the not-so-distant past. If you want to see these forms in action, look at the titles of operatic arias: **donna non vidi mai** (*I never saw such a woman*), **vissi d'arte** (*I lived for art*), and **nacqui all'affanno** (*I was born to worry*). Or look at a biography: **Rossini nacque il 29 febbraio nel 1792** (*Rossini was born February 29, 1792*); **morì nel 1868** (*He died in 1868*).

Once Upon a Time: The Imperfect Tense

The imperfect tense is just that — imperfect. In other words, the actions of imperfect verbs aren't perfected, not finished. The imperfect tense sets the stage for what's to come and frequently answers questions like, "What was something or someone like? What did you used to do (habitually, regularly)? What was happening?"

The imperfect tense allows you to use verbs to describe physical and mental states. If someone was rich, poor, tall, short, hungry, thirsty, sleepy, sad, or happy, then you use the imperfect tense to express these conditions.

The imperfect also tells you about things that used to be or that used to happen. For example: *I used to cut school every day. It was a beautiful time. The weather was glorious. Every Sunday they came to dinner. Every Monday we had leftovers.*

You can combine the imperfect with the present perfect to indicate that while one thing was going on (in the imperfect tense), something else happened (in the present perfect). *While I was eating* (imperfect), *the phone rang* (present perfect).

Other uses of the imperfect include telling what time it was (*it was 3:00 in the morning*), discussing weather conditions (*it was a dark and stormy night*), and reporting indirect discourse (what someone said): *My friend told me* (present perfect) *that he was* (imperfect) *unhappy.*

The following sections explain how to form the imperfect and when to use it.

Forming the imperfect

The imperfect tense is the most regular of any of the Italian verb tenses. To form it, you drop only the final two letters (**-re**) from any infinitive, leaving the stem to which you attach subject-specific endings.

Here's the good news: The endings are the same for all the different conjugations. Nothing in Italian could (or ever will) be simpler. See the examples in Table 1-6.

Table 1-6	Conjugations in the Imperfect Tense	
-are Verbs	*-ere Verbs*	*-ire (including isc) Verbs*
parlare (*to talk; to speak*)	**scrivere** (*to write*)	**dormire** (*to sleep*)
io **parlavo**	io **scrivevo**	io **dormivo**
tu **parlavi**	tu **scrivevi**	tu **dormivi**
lui, lei, Lei **parlava**	lui, lei, Lei **scriveva**	lui, lei, Lei **dormiva**
noi **parlavamo**	noi **scrivevamo**	noi **dormivamo**
voi **parlavate**	voi **scrivevate**	voi **dormivate**
loro, Loro **parlavano**	loro, Loro **scrivevano**	loro, Loro **dormivano**

You can also translate these forms as, for example, *I used to sleep,* or simply, *I slept.*

Of all the Italian verbs, only three are irregular in the imperfect tense. **Essere** (*to be*) is irregular because it's always irregular. Irregularity is in its nature and, no doubt, part of its charm. (**Avere,** which means *to have,* is regular in the imperfect, for a change.) The following table shows you how **essere** conjugates in the imperfect.

essere (*to be*)	
io **ero**	noi **eravamo**
tu **eri**	voi **eravate**
lui, lei, Lei **era**	loro, Loro **erano**

The other two verbs that are irregular in the imperfect are **dire** (*to tell; to say*) and **fare** (*to make; to do*). Their Latin roots show; their stems, respectively, are **dice** and **face** (from the Latin verbs **dicere** and **facere**). See the following tables for these verb conjugations.

dire (*to tell; to say*)	
io **dicevo**	noi **dicevamo**
tu **dicevi**	voi **dicevate**
lui, lei, Lei **diceva**	loro, Loro **dicevano**

fare (*to make; to do*)	
io **facevo**	noi **facevamo**
tu **facevi**	voi **facevate**
lui, lei, Lei **faceva**	loro, Loro **facevano**

Perfecting the use of the imperfect

Certain clues tell you to use the imperfect tense. For example: Adverbial expressions (saying when or how often something happened) include the following:

- **a volte** (*sometimes*)
- **di quando in quando** (*sometimes; from time to time*)
- **ogni giorno** (*every day*)
- **ogni** (*every*)
- **mentre** (*while*)
- **senza sosta** (*without stopping*)
- **spesso** (*often*)
- **di solito** (*usually*)

Here are a few sample sentences:

Lui lavorava senza sosta. (*He worked without stopping.*)

Ogni giorno leggevo un po'. (*Every day I read a little bit.*)

Mentre mangiavamo, ascoltavamo l'opera. (*While we were eating, we were listening to the opera.*)

Certain verbs, if you think about their meaning (Did you feel a certain way? What were you thinking, fearing, loving?), also predominantly use the imperfect in the past. They all indicate an ongoing state of mind. A few of these follow:

- **amare** (*to love*)
- **credere** (*to believe; to think*)

- ✔ **desiderare** (*to want*)
- ✔ **odiare** (*to hate*)
- ✔ **pensare** (*to think*)
- ✔ **temere** (*to fear*)
- ✔ **volere** (*to want*)

Your meaning determines the tense. If, for example, you say that someone *gave a party,* or in a fairy tale, *gave a ball,* you use the present perfect: **lui ha organizzato un ballo.** But if he *gave parties (for beneficence; to raise funds)* for some purpose, then use the imperfect: **lui organizzava balli [di beneficenza; per raccogliere fondi].** However, all the physical and emotional states of being introduced with **avere** and **essere** are likely to appear in the imperfect tense (as opposed to the present perfect).

Adding Nuance to Meaning with Verb Tense

La sfumatura (*nuance*) is an art historical term that refers to shading. Choice of verb tenses allows you to add nuance to your Italian. Not all verbs undergo changes in meaning, but those that do can lend precision to your language.

Pensare (*to think*) doesn't change meaning. **Ho pensato** (*I had a thought*), in the present perfect, and **pensavo** (*I was thinking*), in the imperfect, essentially mean the same thing.

The prepositions that follow **pensare,** however, do modify the meaning to some degree. **Pensare a** means *to think about,* and you can express it as **ci penso** (*I'm thinking about it*); this phrase can be useful when confronted with an overzealous store clerk. **Pensare di,** on the other hand, means *to intend to.* **Non pensavo di interrompere** (*I didn't intend to interrupt*).

Five other verbs have more definite changes in meaning, depending on the tense you use. See Table 1-7 for these verbs' subtleties of meaning.

Table 1-7	Verbal Nuance with Tenses		
Infinitive	**Present Indicative**	**Imperfect**	**Present Perfect**
conoscere (*to know; to know someone; to be acquainted with someone or with a place*)	**conosco** (*I know*)	**conoscevo** (*I knew; I was acquainted with*)	**ho conosciuto** (*I met [someone]*)
sapere (*to know; to have know-how; to be aware of something*)	**so** (*I know*)	**sapevo** (*I knew [how to]; I was aware of*)	**ho saputo** (*I found out*)
dovere (*to have to*)	**devo** (*I have to*)	**dovevo** (*I was supposed to*)	**ho dovuto** (*I had to*)
potere (*to be able to; can*)	**posso** (*I can*)	**potevo** (*I was able to*)	**ho potuto** (*I managed*)
volere (*to want*)	**voglio** (*I want/ would like*)	**volevo** (*I wanted; I intended to; I meant to*)	**ho voluto** (*I wanted [and more or less insisted]*)

Some of these changes are slight, but they allow you to achieve a certain specificity of language. Probably the most important changes are in **conoscere, sapere,** and **dovere.**

> **La madre di Marco? Non la conoscevo ma l'ho conosciuta ieri.** (*Marco's mother? I didn't know her but met her yesterday.*)

> **Sapeva usare il cambio manuale.** (*She/he knew how to use manual transmissions.*)

> **Dovevo studiare, ma non ne avevo voglia.** (*I was supposed to study, but I didn't feel like it.*) Compare this with **Ho dovuto studiare per l'esame.** (*I had to study for the exam.*)

A side effect of using the imperfect involves manners. It's simply more polite to say that you wanted to see someone (**volevo vedere il dottore**) than to say that you want to see someone. Consider the English counterparts. *I want to see the doctor. I wanted to see the doctor.* The second sentence is less brusque. The same holds true for the Italian.

Chapter 2

Reflexive Verbs in the Past

*Y*ou use reflexive verbs in Italian throughout the day, from when you wake to when you fall asleep. Reflexive verbs often express personal actions, such as ways you care for yourself. For example, to say that you brushed your teeth, you use the verb **lavarsi i denti.** You also use reflexive verbs to communicate ways you interact with others, for example, **innamorarsi** (*to fall in love*).

The reflexive part of a reflexive verb refers to the pronouns that you use to accompany them. For example, you say **mi chiamo** to indicate *my name is* (literally: *I call myself*) because **mi** indicates where you're directing the action of **chiamo** (*I call*). **Si innamorano** means *they fall in love with each other;* **innamorano** means *they fall in love,* and the pronoun **si** means *with each other*.

The reflexive infinitive is a variation of the **-are, -ere,** and **-ire** infinitives. It drops the **-e** from all three and replaces it with **-si.** This conjugation tells you that the verb reflects action back onto the subject through an added pronoun, called, appropriately enough, the *reflexive pronoun.*

Reciprocal verbs are a type of reflexive verb; they're verbs that indicate that an action is being performed on two or more subjects equally and at the same time. Reciprocal verbs are a combination of a verb and a reciprocal pronoun: **mi, ti, si, ci, vi,** or **si.**

This chapter shows you how reflexive and reciprocal verbs work in the present perfect tense, walks you through using these verbs in the imperfect tense, and explains how to choose between the present perfect and the imperfect. Check out Chapter 3 in Book IV for a list of commonly used reflexive verbs and pronouns; Chapter 1 in Book V introduces the present perfect and imperfect tenses.

Forming the Present Perfect of Reflexive Verbs

The present perfect lets you talk about the past in specific terms. It answers the question *What happened?* or *What did you do?* It refers to a completed past action or event.

The present perfect is a compound tense, consisting of a past participle (such as *saw, went, bought, looked,* or *asked*) and a conjugated helping verb — in this case, **essere** (*to be*). All reflexive verbs conjugate with **essere.** Always. Without exception.

To discuss the past with a reflexive verb, you need three words:

- ✔ **The reflexive pronoun:** This pronoun reflects the action of the verb back onto the subject: **mi** (*myself*), **ti** (*yourself*), **si** (*himself, herself, itself, yourself* [formal]), **ci** (*ourselves*), **vi** (*yourselves*), and **si** (*themselves, yourselves* [formal]).

- ✔ **The helping verb:** This is the conjugated form of **essere** that's appropriate to the subject.

- ✔ **The past participle of the verb you're using:** For example, **Mi sono svegliato/svegliata** (*I woke [myself] up*). In English, you don't usually state the *self* being addressed by the verb. The past participle reflects the gender and number of both the giver and the receiver of the action. If you're a woman, you say **svegliata,** ending the past participle with the feminine singular **-a.** A man says **svegliato,** using the masculine singular ending, **-o.** (Flip to Chapter 1 in Book V to review how to form the present perfect tense and how to form past participles.)

Table 2-1 shows you how these three words fit together and how the pronoun and participle reflect the subject. The table demonstrates these concepts using the verb **alzarsi** (*to get [oneself] up*).

Table 2-1	Conjugation of the Reflexive Verb Alzarsi in the Present Perfect Tense	
[Subject] and Reflexive Pronoun	**Helping Verb Essere**	**Past Participle**
[io] mi	sono	**alzato** ([m, sing.] *I got up*)
[io] mi	sono	**alzata** ([f, sing.] *I got up*)
[tu] ti	sei	**alzato** ([m, sing.] *you got up*)
[tu] ti	sei	**alzata** ([f, sing.] *you got up*)
[lui] si	è	**alzato** (*he got up*)
[lei] si	è	**alzata** (*she got up*)
[Lei] si	è	**alzato/alzata** ([m/f, sing., formal] *you got up*)
[noi] ci	siamo	**alzati** ([m, pl. or mixed group] *we got up*)
[noi] ci	siamo	**alzate** ([f, pl.] *we got up*)
[voi] vi	siete	**alzati** ([m, pl. or mixed group] *you got up*)
[voi] vi	siete	**alzate** ([f, pl.] *you got up*)
[loro] si	sono	**alzati** ([m, pl. or mixed group] *they got up*)
[loro] si	sono	**alzate** ([f, pl.] *they got up*)
[Loro] si	sono	**alzati/alzate** ([m/f, pl., formal] *you got up*)

Consider this use of reflexive verbs in your (imaginary and admittedly extravagantly full) day, for example:

Mi sono svegliato/svegliata alle 5.00. (*I woke up at 5:00.*)

Mi sono alzato/alzata immediatamente. (*I got up immediately.*)

Mi sono lavato/lavata i denti. (*I brushed my teeth.*)

Mi sono fatto/fatta la doccia. (*I took a shower.*)

Mi sono pettinato/pettinata. (*I did my hair.*)

In ufficio, mi sono arrabbiato/arrabbiata perché i clienti si sono lamentati. (*In the office, I got angry because the clients complained.*)

Mi sono ricordato/ricordata di un appuntamento all'università. (*I remembered an appointment at the university.*)

Mi sono laureato/laureato. (*I graduated.*)

Mi sono divertito/divertita con degli amici. (*I had fun with some friends.*)

Mi sono innamorato/innamorata. (*I fell in love.*)

Mi sono sposato/sposata. (*I got married.*)

Mi sono domandato/domandata: è possibile tutto questo? (*I asked myself: Is all this possible?*)

A casa, finalmente, ci siamo addormentati. (*At home, finally, we fell asleep.*)

Using Reciprocal Verbs in the Present Perfect

Reciprocal verbs in the present perfect show how people interacted, as in these examples:

Si sono parlati. (*They talked to each other.*)

Si sono visti. (*They saw each other.*)

Si sono incontrati. (*They met each other for dinner or coffee.*)

Obviously, it takes more than one person to do these things, so you use only plural verb forms.

To use the reciprocal reflexive in the present perfect, you need the following three components:

✔ **A reflexive pronoun to indicate interaction:** You have only three to choose from: **ci** (*we interact*), **vi** (*you* [plural] *interact*), and **si** (*they interact*).

✔ **The conjugated helping verb (essere):** For example, **ci siamo, vi siete,** or **si sono.**

✔ **A past participle:** For example, **incontrati/incontrate** or **abbracciati/abbracciate,** in either the masculine plural or the feminine plural form.

Here are some example sentences:

Quando vi siete incontrate per la prima volta? (*When did you meet [each other] for the first time?*)

Vi siete abbracciate? (*Did you hug [each other]?*)

Dove si sono conosciuti i genitori? (*Where did your parents meet [each other]?*)

You can make many verbs reciprocal. All you need to keep in mind is that the action of the verb goes between two or more people. **Parlare** (*to speak*), for example, isn't normally a reflexive verb. If you want to say *We spoke to each other on the phone,* however, you can turn it into a reciprocal reflexive that uses the present perfect: **Ci siamo parlati al telefono.**

Just as you can make many verbs reciprocal by adding pronouns that change their meaning to include a reference to "each other," you can also make many reflexive verbs nonreflexive. Consider the changes in the following sentences. In the present perfect tense, you say **Mi sono divertita** (*I had a good time*) (*I amused myself*). But to make this verb nonreflexive, you say **La sua barzelletta mi ha divertito/a** (*Her/his joke amused me*). To carry this example a step further, the verb can become reciprocal in meaning (as well as a regular present perfect) if you change it to **Ci siamo divertiti <u>a vicenda/l'un l'altro/gli uni con gli altri</u>** (*We had a good time*) (*We amused each other*).

You can see this same progression of meanings in this set of examples:

Mi sono svegliata. (*I woke [myself] up.*)

Ho svegliato i bambini. (*I woke the kids.*)

Ci siamo svegliati <u>a vicenda/l'un l'altro/gli uni con gli altri</u>. (*We woke each other up.*)

Forming the Imperfect of Reflexive Verbs

The imperfect is the simplest of all verb tenses in Italian. Most conjugations are regular, and the endings are the same for **-are, -ere,** and **-ire** (including **isc**) verbs.

The imperfect tense answers these questions: *What was going on? What did you used to do?* (in English, this question is sometimes rendered as *What would you do in those days?*) and *What was something or someone like?* You use the imperfect to

✔ **Describe physical, mental, and emotional states of being:** *I was happy* (or *sad, tall, short, poor, rich,* or whatever the case may be).

✔ **Talk about time and weather:** *It was midnight* or *It was freezing,* for example.

✔ **Reminisce:** *Remember when we used to . . .*

With reflexive verbs, you often use the imperfect to describe habits and customs. Here are a couple examples:

Il gatto si lamentava quando aveva fame. (*The cat complained when it was hungry.*)

Lui si metteva una cravatta diversa ogni giorno. (*He used to put on a different tie every day.*)

Certain verbal clues tell you to use the imperfect. Keep in mind that you're not under time constraints with the imperfect. You're not talking about something that happened just once, between, say, 2:00 and 2:30 in the afternoon, when you received a phone call from your insurance agent. You're talking about things that were habitual and ongoing. The key phrase in English that triggers the imperfect is *used to,* as in *I used to go to the museum every Thursday afternoon. We used to eat fish all the time. She used to shop early in the day.* (For details, see the later section "Picking the Present Perfect or the Imperfect for Reflexive Verbs.")

The following tables show you just how regular reflexive verbs are conjugated in the imperfect tense; just follow the guidelines on forming the imperfect in Chapter 1 of Book V, and then add the correct reflexive pronoun.

alzarsi (*to get up*)	
io mi **alzavo** (*I used to get up*)	noi ci **alzavamo** (*we used to get up*)
tu ti **alzavi** (*you used to get up*)	voi vi **alzavate** (*you used to get up*)
lui, lei, Lei si **alzava** (*he, she, it, you* [formal] *used to get up*)	loro, Loro si **alzavano** (*they, you* [formal] *used to get up*)

mettersi (*to wear; to put on*)	
io mi **mettevo**	noi ci **mettevamo**
tu ti **mettevi**	voi vi **mettevate**
lui, lei, Lei si **metteva**	loro, Loro si **mettevano**

divertirsi (*to have a good time*)	
io mi **divertivo**	noi ci **divertivamo**
tu ti **divertivi**	voi vi **divertivate**
lui, lei, Lei si **divertiva**	loro, Loro si **divertivano**

Checking Out Reciprocal Verbs in the Imperfect

The imperfect of reciprocal verbs follows the same rules as the imperfect of reflexive verbs.

As mentioned in the earlier section "Using Reciprocal Verbs in the Present Perfect," you can make many verbs reciprocal in other tenses as well, the imperfect tense included. Consider these examples:

>**Si parlavano ogni giorno.** (*They talked to each other every day.*)
>
>**Vi vedevate spesso.** (*You saw each other often.*)
>
>**Ci visitavamo ogni estate.** (*We visited each other every summer.*)

In the imperfect, reciprocal verbs are not just descriptive; they have an almost gossipy quality.

>**Si amavano tanto.** (*They loved each other so much.*)
>
>**Si vedevano ogni giorno.** (*They saw each other every day.*)

Picking the Present Perfect or the Imperfect for Reflexive Verbs

The easiest way to remember whether to use the present perfect or the imperfect is to keep in mind clues dealing with time and emotional or physical states. Present perfect clues that tell you that you're talking about a completed past action include

- **ieri** (*yesterday*)
- **ieri sera** (*yesterday evening; last night*)
- **la settimana scorsa** (*last week*)
- **lunedì, martedì, . . .** (*Monday, Tuesday, . . .*)

Here are some example sentences that use present perfect reflexive verbs:

Ieri ci siamo divertiti moltissimo. (*Yesterday, we had a great time.*)

La settimana scorsa vi siete sposati, vero? (*Last week, you got married, right?*)

Lunedì mi sono trasferita. (*Monday, I moved.*)

Clues that you should use the imperfect, on the other hand, indicate emotional or physical states of being, or habitual or ongoing actions or events, and are often accompanied by these words or phrases:

- **ogni . . .** (*every . . .*)
- **ogni giorno, ogni anno, ogni inverno** (*every day, every year, every winter*)
- **qualche volta** (*sometimes*)
- **frequentemente** (*frequently; often*)
- **spesso** (*often*)
- **mentre** (*while*)
- **sempre** (*always; all the time*)
- **da bambino/da bambina** (*as a child*)

Thus, you may say some of the following expressions, which use imperfect reflexive verbs:

> **Ogni giorno ci divertivamo.** (*Every day, we had fun.*)
>
> **Il lunedì si parlavano.** (*Every Monday, they talked to each other.*)
>
> **Si pensavano sempre.** (*They thought about each other all the time.*)

Verbs that lend themselves to the imperfect (though they can also appear in the present perfect) include those listed here. Remember that they can be reciprocal or not reciprocal.

Here are some examples of these verbs in action:

> **Paolo e Francesca si desideravano.** (*Paolo and Francesca desired/wanted each other.*)
>
> **Si volevano bene.** (*They loved/were fond of each other.*) (*They wanted each other's company.*)
>
> **Si pensavano ogni giorno.** (*They were thinking of each other every day.*)
>
> **Si amavano tanto.** (*They loved each other so much.*)
>
> **Ci odiavamo.** (*We hated each other.*)

Recognizing Reciprocal Verbs in the Past Absolute

Reciprocal verbs in the past absolute discuss a completed, reciprocal action from long ago and far away:

> **Si salutarono.** (*They greeted each other.*)
>
> **Si baciarono.** (*They kissed each other.*)
>
> **Si promisero di rivedersi.** (*They promised each other to meet again.*)

For more details on the past absolute, see Chapter 1 in Book V.

Chapter 3

Second-Guessing Actions with the Past Conditional and Past Perfect

*I*n Italian, you use the past conditional tense (**condizionale passato**) to indicate what you would, could, or should have done, said, eaten, and so on. Unlike the present conditional tense, which implies the possibility that action could still take place, the past conditional generally forecloses possibility, implying that "it's too late now!"

You very often see the past conditional in conjunction with the past perfect subjunctive (**trapassato congiuntivo;** see Chapter 4 in Book V) and with "if" sentences (**frasi ipotetiche;** see Chapter 5 in Book V) — for example, **Se io avessi saputo, avrei telefonato** (*If I had known, I would've called*). The past conditional, however, can stand on its own and sometimes with the present perfect tense (**passato prossimo;** see Chapter 1 in Book V), the imperfect tense (**imperfetto;** see Chapter 1 in Book V), and gerunds (see Chapter 6 in Book V).

The **trapassato prossimo** (*past perfect*) tense corresponds to this English construction: had + a past participle. For example, you often say *had eaten, had left, had finished, had married,* and *had enjoyed.*

You often use the past perfect tense to describe an activity done prior to another activity that also has taken place — **Siccome non avevo studiato, ho fatto finta di essere malata** (*Since I hadn't studied, I pretended I was sick*). You often find past perfect verbs accompanied by the adverbs **già** (*already*), **non . . . ancora** (*not yet*), and **appena** (*just*). Some other common uses of **the trapassato prossimo** include use with the imperfect subjunctive (see Chapter 6 in Book IV), with the past perfect subjunctive (see Chapter 4 in Book V), and in fairy tales and literature.

This chapter provides you with examples of all the past conditional and past perfect possibilities.

Forming the Past Conditional

The past conditional tense is easy to form in Italian. Like most compound tenses, you precede the verb in question with the auxiliary verb **essere** (*to be*) or **avere** (*to have*). To form the past conditional, you put the auxiliary verb into the present conditional tense (see Chapter 5 in Book IV) and add the past participle (see Chapter 1 in Book V).

Here are a couple examples of this construction:

> **Cosa avresti** (auxiliary verb) **fatto** (past participle) **tu?** (*What would you have done?*)

> **Sarei** (auxiliary verb) **andata** (past participle) **via.** (*I would've gone away.*)

The following tables show example conjugations for the verbs **parlare** (which uses **avere**), **uscire** (which uses **essere**), and **fermarsi** (a reflexive verb, hence it uses **essere**).

parlare (*to speak*)	
io **avrei parlato**	noi **avremmo parlato**
tu **avresti parlato**	voi **avreste parlato**
lui, lei, Lei **avrebbe parlato**	loro, Loro **avrebbero parlato**
Io avrei parlato con lui, ma avevo paura. (*I would've spoken with him, but I was afraid.*)	

uscire (*to go out*)	
io **sarei uscita/o**	noi **saremmo uscite/i**
tu **saresti uscita/o**	voi **sareste uscite/i**
lui, lei, Lei **sarebbe uscita/o**	loro, Loro **sarebbero uscite/i**
Tu saresti uscita con lui? (*Would you have gone out with him?*)	

Note: The past participles of verbs conjugated with **essere** must always agree in gender (masculine or feminine) and number (singular or plural) with the subjects of the sentences — hence the four possibilities of past participle endings.

fermarsi (*to stop*)	
mi **sarei fermata/o**	ci **saremmo fermate/i**
ti **saresti fermata/o**	vi **sareste fermate/i**
si **sarebbe fermata/o**	si **sarebbero fermate/i**
Abbiamo detto che ci saremmo fermati tornando da Venezia. (*We said that we would stop by on the way back from Venice.*)	

Note: **Fermarsi** is a reflexive verb, so it takes the reflexive pronouns that you see in the previous table. For more on conjugating reflexive verbs, check out Chapter 3 in Book IV.

The verb **avere** takes **avere** as its auxiliary verb in the past conditional, and the verb **essere** takes **essere** as its auxiliary verb in the past conditional.

Using the Past Conditional to Play "Woulda, Coulda, Shoulda"

You use the past conditional in Italian in many of the same situations when you'd use it in English (heck, "you'd use it" is in the present conditional, so the conditional is all over the place).

The following is a list of the past conditional's common uses:

- ✔ You can use the past conditional to identify what you would/could/ should have done if something hadn't prevented you from doing it. You use the word **ma** (*but*) to indicate that something stood in your way. For example:

    Avrei studiato, ma ero stanca. (*I would've studied, but I was tired.*)

    Saremmo andati al cinema, ma non avevamo soldi. (*We would've gone to the movies, but we didn't have any money.*)

- ✔ You can use the past conditional tense to ask for or offer an opinion. For example:

    Che cosa avresti fatto al posto mio? (*What would you have done in my place?*)

- ✔ The past conditional appears with verbs and expressions of knowing, believing, and saying, such as **sapere** (*to know*), **capire** (*to understand*), **dire** (*to say; to tell*), **promettere** (*to promise*), and **scrivere** (*to write*), to name a few. These uses of the past conditional translate into the present conditional in English. Here are some examples:

    Era chiaro che non sarebbero andati d'accordo. (*It was clear that they wouldn't get along.*)

    Hai detto che avresti studiato! (*You said that you would study!*)

    Ho detto che avrei chiamato, e invece non ho chiamato. (*I said that I would call, and instead I didn't call.*)

Expressing Responsibilities, Desires, and Abilities in the Past Conditional

You often use the verbs **dovere** (*to have to*), **volere** (*to want to*), and **potere** (*to be able to*) in the past conditional tense to express the following, respectively:

- ✔ *I (you/he/we/they) should've . . .*
- ✔ *I would've liked to . . .*
- ✔ *I could've . . .*

You can also express negative connotations such as **non avrei/sarei dovuto . . .** (*I shouldn't have . . .*) and **non avrei/sarei potuto . . . ?** (*Couldn't I have . . . ?*).

To use **dovere**, **volere**, and **potere** in the past conditional, you first decide whether you should use the conditional of the auxiliary verb **essere** or **avere**, and then you add the past participle — **dovuto, voluto,** or **potuto** — to the auxiliary verb. Both of these forms precede the action verb in the sentence:

> **Avrei dovuto prendere gli spiedini di seppia!** (*I should've gotten the squid kebobs!*)
>
> **Sarei dovuta partire prima.** (*I should've left earlier.*)

Use the **avere** conditional when the infinitive that follows the past participle (**dovuto, voluto,** or **potuto**) generally takes **avere**, and use **essere** when the infinitive that follows the past participle is an intransitive verb (in other words, a verb that takes **essere**). See more on transitive and intransitive verbs in Chapter 1 in Book V.

Note the following examples of **avere**:

> **Avresti dovuto provare di più.** (*You should've tried harder/rehearsed more.*)
>
> **Avrei voluto studiare sociologia.** (*I would've rather studied sociology.*)
>
> **Il babbo avrebbe potuto telefonare.** (*Dad could've called.*)

Note the following examples of **essere**:

> **Saresti dovuto/a partire prima!** (*You should've left earlier.*)
>
> **Sarei voluto/a diventare veterinario/a.** (*I would've liked to become a veterinarian.*)
>
> **Il babbo si sarebbe potuto divertire di più** or **Il babbo avrebbe potuto divertirsi di più.** (*Dad could've had more fun.*)

Note that if you prefer attaching the **si** to the infinitive of the verb, you need to use the auxiliary **avere**.

Forming and Implementing the Past Perfect Tense

You form the **trapassato prossimo** (*past perfect*) like the other compound tenses in Italian: You combine the imperfect of **avere** (*to have*) or **essere** (*to be*) with the past participle of the verb in question. A brief recap may suffice: When you have a transitive verb, your auxiliary verb will be **avere**; when you have an intransitive verb or any reflexive verb, your auxiliary verb will be **essere** — and keep in mind that when you have a reflexive verb, you need to add a reflexive pronoun.

Here are some examples of the past perfect in action:

A 6 anni, Daniel non aveva ancora cominciato a nuotare. (*When he was 6, Daniel hadn't yet begun to swim.*)

A 6 anni, Daniel era già stato in Italia. (*When he was 6, Daniel had already been to Italy.*)

A 6 anni, Daniel si era già abituato a fare i compiti da solo. (*When he was 6, Daniel had already gotten used to doing his homework by himself.*)

When forming the past perfect in Italian, you often need to use the adverb **già** (*already*), which should be placed between the auxiliary verb and the past participle.

La mamma aveva già preparato tutto quando siamo arrivati. (*Mom had already prepared everything when we arrived.*)

The adverb **non . . . ancora** (*not . . . yet*) works in the same way — **Luisa non aveva ancora capito che doveva studiare** (*Luisa hadn't yet understood that she needed to study*) — as do the adverbs **non . . . mai** (*never*) — **Non si era mai sposato, Donald** (*Donald hadn't ever gotten married*) — and **appena** (*just*) — **Mi ero appena alzata . . .** (*I had just gotten up . . .*).

The following tables show examples of a transitive verb (which takes **avere**), an intransitive verb (which takes **essere**), and a reflexive verb in the **trapassato prossimo** tense.

mangiare (*to eat*)	
io **avevo mangiato**	noi **avevamo mangiato**
tu **avevi mangiato**	voi **avevate mangiato**
lui, lei, Lei **aveva mangiato**	loro, Loro **avevano mangiato**
Abbiamo detto di no perchè avevamo mangiato a casa. (*We said no because we had eaten at home.*)	

partire (*to leave; to depart*)	
io **ero partito/a**	noi **eravamo partiti/e**
tu **eri partito/a**	voi **eravate partiti/e**
lui, lei, Lei **era partito/a**	loro, Loro **erano partiti/e**
Quando sono arrivata, tu eri già partita. (*When I got there, you had already left.*)	

Note: The past participles of verbs conjugated with **essere** (in any compound tense) must agree in number and gender with their subjects.

alzarsi (*to get up*)	
mi **ero alzato/a**	ci **eravamo alzati/e**
ti **eri alzato/a**	vi **eravate alzati/e**
si **era alzato/a**	si **erano alzati/e**
Quando è suonata la sveglia, Nicole e Mark si erano già alzati. (*When the alarm rang, Nicole and Mark had already gotten up.*)	

Chapter 4

I Hope That You've Had Fun! The Subjunctive Mood in the Past

- -

- -

The subjunctive mood expresses doubt, uncertainty, opinion, emotion — all the things required for *subjective* thoughts (you know, things like, *I'm happy that you love Italian food, I don't think that pasta is sitting too well,* or *I think this book is great!*). Sometimes you want or need to express doubt or uncertainty in the past tense, which is the job of the past subjunctive (for example, *It's probable that I loved Italian food before I ate that pasta and read this book*).

Sometimes you may also need the past perfect subjunctive tense, which refers to a specific time and generally translates as *had eaten* or *had jumped*. Like the other three tenses in the subjunctive (the present subjunctive, the imperfect subjunctive, and the past subjunctive), it's most often used in subordinate clauses, introduced by the conjunction **che** (*that*).

This chapter provides you with some stellar past subjunctive explanations, shows you how to form the past perfect subjunctive, and provides you with a handy refresher on how to form sentences by using all four subjunctive tenses. Enjoy!

Forming the Past Subjunctive

If you have a handle on using the present subjunctive tense (see Chapter 6 in Book IV), you should find the past subjunctive to be a breeze. You follow the same format, except you express doubt, uncertainty, and so on about an action that occurred in the past.

The past subjunctive (or **congiuntivo passato**) is a compound tense. In most cases, you form the past subjunctive with the following parts:

> Main clause + **che** (*that*) + present subjunctive of **avere** (*to have*) or **essere** (*to be*) + past participle

Just like with the present subjunctive, the past subjunctive appears in the dependent clause, usually introduced by **che.** The verb in the main clause needs to be a verb that denotes uncertainty, emotion, and so on.

> **Present subjunctive:** <u>Dubito</u> che loro <u>vengano</u>. (*I doubt that they're coming.*)

> **Past subjunctive:** <u>Dubito</u> che loro <u>siano venuti</u>. (*I doubt that they came.*)

You use the past subjunctive when the action in the dependent clause (the verb in the past subjunctive) happened before the action in the main clause. The verb in the main clause appears in the present tense (generally) or in the future or imperative tense (less frequently); see the later section "Sequencing Your Tenses in the Subjunctive" for more details.

The following tables show three examples of the past subjunctive: a transitive verb (one that takes **avere**), an intransitive verb (one that takes **essere**), and a reflexive verb (which takes **essere**), respectively.

mangiare (*to eat*)	
che io **abbia mangiato**	che noi **abbiamo mangiato**
che tu **abbia mangiato**	che voi **abbiate mangiato**
che lui, lei, Lei **abbia mangiato**	che loro, Loro **abbiano mangiato**
Siamo contenti che abbiate mangiato bene! (*We're pleased that you ate well!*)	

arrivare (*to arrive*)	
che io **sia arrivato/a**	che noi **siamo arrivati/e**
che tu **sia arrivato/a**	che voi **siate arrivati/e**
che lui, lei, Lei **sia arrivato/a**	che loro, Loro **siano arrivati/e**
Benchè io sia arrivata ultima al traguardo, adoro le competizioni come queste! (*Even though I arrived last at the finish line, I love competitions like this one!*)	

vestirsi (*to get dressed*)	
che io mi **sia vestito/a**	che noi ci **siamo vestiti/e**
che tu ti **sia vestito/a**	che voi vi **siate vestiti/e**
che lui, lei, Lei si **sia vestito/a**	che loro, Loro si **siano vestiti/e**
Come si è vestito Rudi per la festa? (*How did Rudi dress for the party?*) **Non so come si sia vestito.** (*I don't know what he wore.*)	

The adverbs of time — **già** (*already*), **mai** (*never; ever*), and **ancora** (*still; yet*) — go between the auxiliary verb and the past participle.

Composing the Past Perfect Subjunctive

The **trapassato congiuntivo** (*past perfect subjunctive*), typically shortened to **trapassato,** is a compound tense that you form by combining these parts:

> **Che** (*that*) + the imperfect subjunctive of **avere** (*to have*) or **essere** (*to be*) + the past participle of the verb in question

If you guessed that from the start, congratulations! You may have guessed it because you form the **trapassato** just like you form the other compound tenses in Book V. (If you need the scoop on the imperfect subjunctive, check out Chapter 6 in Book IV.)

The following tables give you three examples: a transitive verb (one that takes **avere**), an intransitive verb (one that takes **essere**), and a reflexive verb (which takes **essere**) in the **trapassato,** respectively. *Note:* For the reflexive verb, you must add the proper reflexive pronoun during conjugation (**mi, ti, si, ci, vi,** or **si**).

mangiare (*to eat*)	
che io **avessi mangiato**	che noi **avessimo mangiato**
che tu **avessi mangiato**	che voi **aveste mangiato**
che lui, lei, Lei **avesse mangiato**	che loro, Loro **avessero mangiato**
Scusate! Pensavo che aveste già mangiato! (*I'm sorry! I thought that you had already eaten!*)	

uscire (*to go out*)	
che io **fossi uscito/a**	che noi **fossimo usciti/e**
che tu **fossi uscito/a**	che voi **foste usciti/e**
che lui, lei, Lei **fosse uscito/a**	che loro, Loro **fossero usciti/e**
Tina e Gina avrebbero voluto che Lisa fosse uscita con loro. (*Tina and Gina would have liked Lisa to go out with them.*)	

comportarsi (*to behave*)	
che io mi **fossi comportato/a**	che noi ci **fossimo comportati/e**
che tu ti **fossi comportato/a**	che voi vi **foste comportati/e**
che lui, lei, Lei si **fosse comportato/a**	che loro, Loro si **fossero comportati/e**
Chi avrebbe mai creduto che Janine si fosse comportata in quel modo? (*Who would have ever believed that Janine behaved/had behaved in that way?*)	

The **trapassato** usually occurs in a dependent clause, introduced most often by the word **che** (*that*) when the verb in the main clause is a present or a past perfect conditional (see Table 4-1, later in this chapter). You use it to express an action that has been completed before the action in the main clause. For example:

> **<u>Avrei preferito</u> che tu <u>ti fossi sposata</u> con Gino.** (*I would've preferred that you marry Gino.*)

The verb in the main clause must be in some specific tense:

✔ The past conditional or the past perfect (see Chapter 3 in Book V):

> Past conditional: **<u>Sarebbe stato</u> meglio che tu non <u>avessi detto</u> nulla.** (*It would've been better had you said nothing.*)

✔ The imperfect (see Chapter 1 in Book V):

> **Mia madre <u>credeva</u> che io <u>fossi diventata</u> importante.** (*My mom believed that I had become important.*)

✔ The **passato prossimo** (*present perfect;* see Chapter 1 in Book V):

> **Ci <u>è parso</u> che <u>fossero</u> già <u>partiti</u>.** (*It seemed to us that they had already left./We thought they'd already left.*)

✔ The **trapassato prossimo** (*past perfect;* see Chapter 3 of Book V):

> **Non avevamo creduto nemmeno per un momento che Claudia avesse scritto il tema da sola.** (*We didn't believe for a moment that Claudia had written the essay by herself.*)

You also use the **trapassato** frequently in "if" clauses, which are discussed in Chapter 5 of Book V.

Students always worry about knowing when to put what tense where. A good rule of thumb, at least with the **trapassato,** is that when you have a compound tense in the main or independent clause, you place the **trapassato** in the dependent clause. Of course, this rule of thumb isn't set in stone, as evidenced in the previous verb table showing the conjugation of **mangiare:** <u>Pensavo</u> **che** <u>aveste</u> **già** <u>mangiato</u>! (*I thought that you had already eaten!*) Let practice, repetition, and context be your guide!

Sequencing Your Tenses in the Subjunctive

Italian has four subjunctive tenses: the present subjunctive, the imperfect subjunctive, the past subjunctive, and the past perfect subjunctive (the first two are covered in Chapter 6 of Book IV; the other two are discussed earlier in this chapter). The best way to sequence verb tenses in the subjunctive is to consider the relationship between the verb in the main clause and the verb in the dependent clause and determine the time frame of the two "actions": whether the two verbs are contemporaneous (happening in the same period of time), or whether the one in the dependent clause is antecedent (occurring prior to) or subsequent to (occurring later than) the verb in the main clause. Table 4-1 presents all the different variations to keep in mind while you're in the subjunctive mood.

Table 4-1	Sequencing the Subjunctive		
Main Clause	*+ Dependent Clause*	*Time Frame*	*Examples*
Present indicative	+ present subjunctive ...	... if the verbs in the two clauses are contemporaneous (happening in the same period of time)	**Credi che quelle scarpe costino troppo?** (*Do you believe that those shoes cost too much?*)
Future indicative			**Non crederai che quelle scarpe costino troppo!** (*You will not believe that those shoes cost too much!*)
Present imperative			**Non credere che quelle scarpe costino troppo.** (*Do not believe that those shoes cost too much.*)

(continued)

Table 4-1 *(continued)*

Main Clause	+ Dependent Clause	Time Frame	Examples
Present indicative	+ past subjunctive . . .	. . . if the verb in the dependent clause is prior, or antecedent, to the one in the main clause	**Credi che quelle scarpe siano costate troppo?** (*Do you believe that those shoes have cost too much?*)
Future indicative			**Non crederai che quelle scarpe siano costate troppo!** (*You will not believe that those shoes have cost too much!*)
Present imperative			**Non credere che quelle scarpe siano costate troppo.** (*Don't believe that those shoes have cost too much.*)
Present indicative	+ present subjunctive (but future indicative is also acceptable) . . .	. . . if the verb in the dependent clause is later than, or subsequent to, the one in the main clause	**Credi che quelle scarpe costino/costeranno troppo?** (*You believe that those shoes cost/will cost too much?*)
Future indicative			**Non crederai che quelle scarpe costino/costeranno troppo!** (*You will not believe that those shoes cost/will cost too much!*)
Present imperative			**Non credere che quelle scarpe costino/costeranno troppo.** (*Do not believe that those shoes cost/will cost too much.*)

Main Clause	+ Dependent Clause	Time Frame	Examples
Present perfect indicative	+ imperfect subjunctive . . .	. . . if the verbs in the two clauses are contemporaneous (happening in the same period of time)	**Non hai mai creduto che quelle scarpe costassero troppo.** (*You have never believed that those shoes cost too much.*)
Past absolute indicative			**Non credesti per un momento che quelle scarpe costassero troppo.** (*You never believed [not even] for a moment that those shoes cost too much.*)
Imperfect indicative			**Credevi che quelle scarpe costassero troppo.** (*You believed that those shoes cost too much.*)
Past perfect indicative			**Avevi creduto che quelle scarpe costassero troppo.** (*You had believed that those shoes cost too much.*)
Present perfect indicative	+ past perfect indicative . . .	. . . if the verb in the dependent clause is prior, or antecedent, to the one in the main clause	**Hai creduto che quelle scarpe fossero costate troppo.** (*You have believed that those shoes had cost too much.*)
Past absolute indicative			**Non credesti per un momento che quelle scarpe fossero costate troppo.** (*You didn't believe that those shoes had cost too much.*)
Imperfect indicative			**Credevi che quelle scarpe fossero costate troppo.** (*You believed that those shoes had cost too much.*)
Past perfect indicative			**Avevi creduto che quelle scarpe fossero costate troppo.** (*You had believed that those shoes had cost too much.*)

(continued)

Table 4-1 *(continued)*

Main Clause	+ Dependent Clause	Time Frame	Examples
Present perfect indicative	+ present perfect conditional . . .	. . . if the verb in the dependent clause is later than, or subsequent to, the one in the main clause	**Hai creduto che quelle scarpe sarebbero costate troppo.** (*You have believed that those shoes would have cost too much.*)
Past absolute indicative			**Credesti che quelle scarpe sarebbero costate troppo.** (*You believed that those shoes would have cost too much.*)
Imperfect indicative			**Credevi che quelle scarpe sarebbero costate troppo.** (*You believed that those shoes would have cost too much.*)
Past perfect indicative			**Avevi creduto che quelle scarpe sarebbero costate troppo.** (*You had believed that those shoes had cost too much.*)
Present conditional	+ imperfect subjunctive . . .	. . . if the verbs in the two clauses are contemporaneous (happening at the same time)	**Crederesti che quelle scarpe costassero troppo.** (*You would believe that those shoes cost too much.*)
Present perfect conditional			**Avresti creduto che quelle scarpe costassero troppo.** (*You would have believed that those shoes cost too much.*)
Present conditional	+ past perfect subjunctive . . .	. . . if the verb in the dependent clause is prior, or antecedent, to the one in the main clause	**Crederesti che quelle scarpe fossero costate troppo.** (*You would believe that those shoes had cost too much.*)
Present perfect conditional			**Avresti creduto che quelle scarpe fossero costate troppo.** (*You would have believed that those shoes had cost too much.*)

Chapter 5

"If" Clauses, the Impersonal, and the Passive

. . . .

In This Chapter

▶ Checking out "if" clauses

▶ Investigating the impersonal and the passive

. . . .

Sentences transmit messages and are composed of clauses. Verbs and subjects are essential to understanding clauses and consequently comprehending the message of a sentence. This chapter shows you how to use "if" clauses in hypothetical constructions, how to use impersonal forms to express actions that don't have a clearly identified subject, and how to recognize actions that are performed by an indirect object on a receiving subject (passive form).

Hypothetically Speaking: "If" Clauses throughout the Tenses

Hypothetical sentences, known in Italian as **frasi ipotetiche con se**, translate into English as *If . . .* sentences. They cover a wide range of speech and include many of the tenses covered in this book. Hypothetical constructions always have two parts: a dependent clause introduced by the word **se** (*if*), and the main or independent clause that refers to the result of whatever you postulate or hypothesize in the "if" clause. The verb tenses you use in both clauses depend on the type of hypothetical sentence you want to construct.

Italian features three types of hypothetical constructions: expressions of reality, probability, and impossibility. Each type uses specific verb tenses. And guess what? All three are covered in the following sections, and so is the phrase *as if*.

Expressing conditions within the realm of reality

One type of hypothetical construction lies within the realm of fact, reality, or actuality. If you say, for example, **Se <u>mangio</u> il gelato, <u>ingrasso</u>** (*If I eat ice cream, I gain weight*), you express a fact or a reality in your life. Notice the use of the present tense in both the dependent clause (**mangio**) and independent clause (**ingrasso**). You gain weight if you eat ice cream — period!

As in English, the order of your clauses doesn't matter; you can also say **<u>Ingrasso</u> se <u>mangio</u> il gelato** (*I gain weight if I eat ice cream*). What matters is that you attach the word **se** to the dependent clause (the "if" statement that implies the condition, not the result).

The verb tenses you use for the fact/reality hypothetical construction are precisely those tenses that allow you to speak with certainty, as outlined in Table 5-1.

Table 5-1	Hypothetical Constructions in Reality	
Se + Dependent Clause	*Independent Clause*	*Example*
Present indicative*	Present indicative*	**Se <u>studi</u>, <u>impari</u>.** (*If you study, you learn.*)
Present reflexive	Present	**Se <u>ti alzi</u> presto domani, <u>ti porto</u> a scuola.** (*If you get up early tomorrow, I bring you to school.*)
Present indicative*	Imperative	**Se <u>hai</u> fame, <u>mangia</u>!** (*If you're hungry, eat!*)
Present indicative*	Future	**Se <u>ti innamori</u>, te ne <u>pentirai</u>.**** (*If you fall in love, you will regret it.*)
Future	Future	**Se <u>arriveranno</u> a luglio, <u>potremo andare</u> in Sardegna insieme.** (*If they arrive in July, we can go to Sardegna together.*)
Present perfect	Present indicative*	**Se Maria <u>ha telefonato</u>, significa che <u>ha</u> notizie.** (*If Maria called, it means that she has news.*)
Present perfect	Present perfect	**Se <u>hai studiato</u>, perchè non <u>hai passato</u> l'esame?** (*If you studied, why did you fail the exam?*)

Se + Dependent Clause	Independent Clause	Example
Imperfect	Imperfect	**Se <u>avevamo</u> sete, <u>prendevamo</u> un'aranciata.** (*If we were thirsty, we would get an orange soda.*)
Imperfect	Present perfect	**Se Maria <u>voleva venire</u> alla festa, perchè non è venuta?** (*If Maria wanted to come to the party, why didn't she come?*)

*Present indicative listings also include reflexive verbs
Both of these verbs are reflexive: **innamorarsi** and **pentirsi

All the examples in Table 5-1 denote, in some way or another, the certainty of something that's happening, that happened, that didn't happen, or that will happen. You see no doubt implied in any of the examples.

You don't always combine the verb tenses from the dependent clause in the left column in Table 5-1 with the verb tenses directly opposite them in the right-hand column denoting the main (independent) clause. You can mix and match your possibilities of hypothetical constructions in the realm of reality, as in the following examples. It all depends on what you want to say!

> **Present perfect + future: Se <u>hai fatto</u> tutto, non <u>dovrai preoccuparti</u>.** (*If you've done everything, you'll not have to worry.*)

> **Present indicative + imperative: Se <u>vuole sedersi</u>, <u>si sieda, prego</u>!** (*If you wish to sit, please have a seat!*)

Examining hypothetical constructions of probability and possibility

The hypothetical condition of probability and possibility implies that an action is conditional. In other words, this type of sentence always translates into, roughly, "If such and such were to happen, this and that would happen." Probability constructions are much more straightforward and simple than reality constructions (see the previous section). They usually require two different tenses: the imperfect subjunctive (see Chapter 6 in Book IV) and the conditional (see Chapter 5 in Book IV):

> **Se** + **congiuntivo imperfetto** (*imperfect subjunctive*) + **il condizionale** (*present conditional*): **Se io <u>studiassi</u>** (imperfect subjunctive), **<u>andrei bene</u>** (present conditional) **<u>a scuola</u>.** (*If I were to study [If I studied], I would do well in school.*)

You can also reverse the order of the clauses, placing the independent one first — it doesn't matter as long as the imperfect subjunctive is in the dependent or subordinate clause:

> <u>Uscirei</u> (present conditional) **se non <u>dovessi studiare</u>** (imperfect subjunctive) **questi verbi!** (*I'd go out if I didn't have to study these verbs!*)

You may also use a second, less-common verb tense combination for probability constructions. This combination comes in handy when you want to express regret, after the fact. You're speaking from a present standpoint about the past (even though you use the imperfect subjunctive). For example, **Se io <u>fossi</u> intelligente, <u>avrei studiato</u> ieri invece di <u>andare</u> a <u>ballare</u>** (*If I were smart, I would have studied yesterday instead of going dancing*). Here's the structure:

> **Se** + **congiuntivo imperfetto** (*imperfect subjunctive*) + **condizionale passato** (*conditional perfect*): **Se io <u>fossi</u>** (imperfect subjunctive) **in te, <u>sarei rimasta</u>** (conditional perfect) **a Tucson.** (*If I were you, I would have stayed in Tucson.*)

What-iffing the impossible

The hypothetical construction that denotes impossibility suggests that whatever action you would've done in the past is no longer possible now, no matter your desires. You can demonstrate this by saying, for example, **Se io <u>avessi saputo</u> che <u>venivi</u>, <u>avrei cotto</u> una bistecca in più** (*If I had known you were coming, I would've made an extra steak*). In other words, it's now too late for you to have made the extra steak while you were cooking. Nothing keeps you from making a steak now, of course, but if you want to convey that, you don't need an if clause!

As you can see from the preceding example, the hypothetical construction denoting impossibility is composed of two compound tenses. You form it by rendering the structure of the construction of probability into the past: **trapassato congiuntivo** (*the past perfect subjunctive;* see Chapter 4 in Book V) and **condizionale passato** (*the past conditional;* see Chapter 3 in Book V).

Se + **trapassato congiuntivo** (*past perfect subjunctive*) + **condizionale passato** (*past conditional*): **Se Toby <u>avesse riconosciuto i visitatori</u>** (present perfect subjunctive), **non <u>avrebbe abbaiato</u>** (conditional perfect). (*If Toby had recognized the visitors, he would not have barked.*)

Alternatively, but less commonly, you may have the following structure:

Se + present perfect subjunctive + conditional

It comes in handy with recriminations. For example:

Se tu non <u>avessi speso</u> tutti i tuoi soldi per <u>divertirti</u>, adesso non <u>ti trovaresti</u> in questa situazione. (*If you hadn't spent all your money having a good time, you wouldn't find yourself in this situation now.*)

Se <u>mi avessi ascoltato</u> (present perfect subjunctive), **non <u>saresti</u>** (conditional) **in questi guai ora.** (*If you had listened to me, you wouldn't be in this trouble now.*)

Se <u>avessi sposato</u> (present perfect subjunctive) **Enzo, ora <u>abiterei</u>** (conditional) **a Cortona.** (*If I had married Enzo, I'd be living in Cortona now.*)

Come se: In a category of its own

The phrase **come se** means *as if,* and it works somewhat differently from the other hypothetical constructions you see in previous sections in this chapter.

The **imperfetto congiuntivo** (*imperfect subjunctive*) and the **trapassato congiuntivo** (*present perfect subjunctive*) always follow the expression **come se,** regardless of the tense in the main clause (see Chapter 4 in Book V for details on these tenses). Here's the structure:

Any tense that makes sense + **come se** + imperfect subjunctive or present perfect subjunctive

Here are a couple examples:

Lui <u>tratta</u> la moglie come se <u>fosse</u> una bambina. (*He treats his wife as if she were a child.*)

<u>Mi sono comportata</u> come se non <u>fosse successo</u> niente. (*I acted as if nothing had happened.*)

Putting a Personal Touch on the Impersonal and the Passive

Come <u>si forma</u> il si impersonale? (*How do you form the impersonal?*) **Quando è usata la forma passiva?** (*When is the passive voice used?*) Did you just notice the use of the **si impersonale** (*impersonal you*) in the first sentence and the **costruzione passiva** (*passive construction*) in the second? **Bravo/ Brava!** (*Good job!*) These constructions **sono usate** (*are used*) — another example! — all the time in everyday language.

In the following sections, you discover how to form and use the impersonal *you* across many tenses, and you find out how to recognize and use the passive voice when appropriate.

Forming the impersonal in the present

How do you form the **si impersonale,** and what does it mean? It translates as the impersonal *you/we/they/people*. The form is synonymous with the less common *one* — as in, how does one form the **si impersonale?** And, as you can see, the subject is indefinite. More than in American English, however, people often use the impersonal *you* in Italian to talk about their everyday activities. For example, you often hear the question **Quando <u>si parte</u>?** (*When are we leaving?*)

To form the **si impersonale** in the present tense, you take the word **si** (*one/ you/we/they/people*) and add either of the following:

✔ The third person singular form of a verb (and a singular direct object, if you have one)

✔ The third person plural form of a verb (with a plural direct object)

Here are some examples that use **si** + third person singular of a verb:

Come <u>si dice</u> "hi" in italiano? (*How do you say "hi" in Italian?*)

Cosa <u>si mangia</u> stasera? (*What are we eating tonight?*)

<u>Si mangia</u> la pasta (singular direct object). (*We're eating pasta.*)

Here are some examples that use **si** + third person plural of a verb:

Cosa <u>si mangia</u> stasera? (*What are we eating tonight?*) <u>**Si mangiano**</u> **gli gnocchi** (plural direct object). (*We're eating gnocchi.*)

Dove <u>si comprano</u> i francobolli (plural direct object) **in Italia?** (*Where can you buy stamps in Italy?*)

When you have to deal with reflexive verbs and the reciprocal form (see Chapter 3 in Book IV), you start with the impersonal pronoun **si,** but you transform it miraculously into the word **ci** (**ci** doesn't translate, except as the impersonal *you*). At that point, you *add* the third person reflexive pronoun **si** and then include the third person singular. (You can't very well have one **si** right after the other, can you?)

Here's this construction broken down and compared with a sentence in the present indicative that has a specified subject:

<u>**Ci**</u> + <u>**si**</u> + <u>**sveglia**</u> **presto in vacanza.** (*You/they/people get up early on vacation.*) This is the impersonal *you* without a specified subject.

I ragazzi <u>si svegliano</u> presto in vacanza. (*The kids get up early on vacation.*) This is the present indicative with a specified subject (**i ragazzi** — *the kids*).

Here are some examples of the reflexive construction in the **si impersonale:**

<u>**Ci si alza**</u> **presto in campagna.** (*They/people get up early in the country.*)

<u>**Ci si vede**</u> (from the reciprocal verb **vedersi**). (*See you around.*)

<u>**Ci si diverte**</u> **in Italia; <u>ci si diverte</u> a sciare.** (*People have fun in Italy; skiing is fun.*)

Applying the impersonal in other tenses

Technically, you can apply the **si impersonale** to any verb tense — and certainly any of the tenses covered in this book. You simply take the word **si** + the verb in the tense you need, be it third person singular or plural. (The only exception to this construction is the present perfect impersonal, discussed in a moment.) But, for the sake of brevity, you can look at the impersonal in only a few of the more common tenses in Table 5-2.

Table 5-2	Forming the Impersonal in Common Tenses		
Tense	Infinitive	Example	Translation
Imperfect	**parlare** (*to speak; to talk*)	**Si parlava spesso al telefono.**	*We used to speak often on the phone.*
		Si parlavano l'inglese e l'italiano a casa.	*We used to speak English and Italian at home.*
Future	**visitare** (*to visit*)	**Si visiterà una vetreria.**	*We're going to visit a glass-blowing factory.*
		Si visiteranno le vetrerie a Murano.	*We're going to visit the glass-blowing factories in Murano.*
Subjunctive	**dire** (*to say; to tell*)	**Non so come si dica "earnest."**	*I don't know how to say "earnest."*
		È bene che si dicano le regole.	*It's a good thing that they articulate the rules.*

The present perfect (covered in Chapter 1 of Book V) is similar to the normal construction of the impersonal, but it has its own set of quirky rules. For the present perfect, always use the verb **essere** (*to be*) as your auxiliary verb, regardless of whether you're working with an **essere** verb (intransitive and reflexive) or an **avere** (*to have;* transitive) verb. Nonetheless, you still distinguish between the transitive and intransitive verbs!

Verbs that take **essere** have the following structure:

> **Si** + past participle ending in **-i**

Here are some examples:

> **Si è andati a letto presto.** (*Everyone went to bed early.*) (**Andare** is an intransitive verb that takes **essere**.)

> **Ci si è divertiti alla festa!** (*We had fun at the party!*) (**Divertirsi** is a reflexive verb that takes **essere**.)

Verbs that take **avere** have a past participle that ends in **-o** if the sentence identifies no object. If the sentence specifies a direct object, the past participle agrees with the direct object (**-o, -a, -i, -e**):

<u>Si è parlato</u> del più e del meno. (*We talked about this and that.*)

<u>Si è preparata</u> la cena. (*The dinner was prepared.*)

<u>Si sono comprati</u> gli stivali a Venezia. (*Boots were bought in Venice.*) (*We/they bought boots in Venice.*)

<u>Si sono dette</u> delle brutte cose. (*Ugly things were said.*) (*They said ugly things.*)

No subject is really specified with the **si impersonale.** And when you see the pronoun **ci** placed before the pronoun **si,** you know that the verb is reflexive.

Getting proactive about the passive voice

The passive voice takes the action out of a sentence. For example, you can change the sentence **La bambina <u>apparecchia</u> la tavola** (*The little girl is setting the table*) to the passive form: **La tavola <u>è apparecchiata</u> dalla bambina** (*The table is set by the little girl*).

The passive voice is very similar in meaning to the impersonal *you* (see the previous sections). For example, when you ask the question **Scusi, <u>si parla</u> inglese?** (*Excuse me, is English spoken here?*) by using the impersonal *you,* you may also say, **Scusi, l'inglese <u>è parlato</u> qui?** (*Excuse me, is English spoken here?*) In this particular case, the impersonal is the more common of the two, but many other cases call for the passive voice as the more common construction. For example, if you don't want to assign blame, you can use the passive voice as a tool. Science and medicine often use the passive voice in writings. After you understand how to form it — which is quite simple — you'll find yourself using it quite often in conversation (much to your English teacher's chagrin).

To form the passive voice in any tense — present, present perfect, past absolute, imperfect, future, conditional, present subjunctive, imperfect subjunctive, past subjunctive, and so on — you take the verb **essere** (*to be*) (in that particular tense) + the past participle of the verb. The past participle always agrees with the subject in number and gender. You can use only transitive verbs (verbs that usually take **avere** [*to have*] in compound tenses) in the passive voice. However, as part of the passive construction, transitive verbs take **essere.** Don't worry, this only sounds confusing! Consider these examples:

Le poesie <u>sono pubblicate</u> da una casa editrice italiana. (*The poems are published by an Italian publisher.*)

La cena <u>è preparata</u> dal babbo. (*Dinner is being prepared by Dad.*)

With the passive voice, you reverse the order of a sentence in the indicative or subjunctive: The direct object becomes the subject, and the subject (person or thing doing the action), if articulated, is introduced by the preposition **da** (*by*) by itself or contracted with a definite article. Table 5-3 gives you a listing of definite articles and where they appear in passive constructions.

Table 5-3	Definite Articles That Introduce Subjects		
Singular Article	*Position in Sentence*	*Plural Article*	*Position in Sentence*
dal	In front of masculine, singular nouns beginning with most consonants	**dai**	In front of masculine, plural nouns beginning with most consonants
dallo	In front of masculine, singular nouns beginning with **z-, st-, sp-, gn-**	**dagli**	In front of masculine, plural nouns beginning with **z-, st-, sp-, gn-,** and also vowels
dall'	In front of masculine or feminine, singular nouns beginning with a vowel		
dalla	In front of feminine, singular nouns beginning with a consonant	**dalle**	In front of feminine, plural nouns

Here are some examples of the passive voice across the tenses:

> **Present: Le pesche <u>sono vendute</u> solo a luglio e agosto.** (*Peaches are sold only in July and August.*)

> **Past: Questo libro <u>fu scritto</u> nel 1906.** (*This book was written in 1906.*)

> **Future: Emilia <u>sarà ricevuta</u> alla stazione dalla sua famiglia-ospite.** (*Emilia will be welcomed at the station by her host family.*)

Chapter 6

Progressing through Gerunds in Italian

. . . .

In This Chapter

▶ Creating gerunds in the present tense

▶ Incorporating irregular gerunds into your constructions

▶ Taking on the past gerund form

▶ Concentrating on the now with the present progressive

▶ Utilizing the imperfect progressive form

. . . .

Gerunds (words ending in *-ing* in English) are common in spoken and written Italian, much as they are in English. They give immediacy to a sentence or phrase and can express action. For example, you're *reading* this book, and you're really *enjoying* it! The Italian gerund (in the present) corresponds roughly to the English present participle ending in *-ing:* eating (**mangiando**), waking up (**svegliandosi**), going out (**uscendo**), and so on.

When you combine the verb **stare** (*to be*) + a gerund, you form what's called the *progressive,* which you use to describe things that are going on right at this moment or to describe things that were going on at a precise moment in the past. For example: **Cosa stai facendo?** (*What are you doing?*) **Sto scrivendo questa frase** (*I'm writing this sentence*).

In this chapter, you discover how to use Italian gerunds and form them in the present and past tenses. You also get to work with the irregular forms of gerunds. From there, you move on to the present and imperfect progressive forms.

Forming Gerunds in the Present Tense

In many cases, you may need to use a gerund by itself, as with *present gerunds.* In this case, the subject is the same in both parts of your sentence. Notice that the gerunds in the following examples are in the subordinate clauses (the part of a sentence that can't stand on its own two legs):

> **Tornando a casa, mi fermo al mercato.** (*On the way home/While returning home [Literally: Returning home], I'm going to stop at the market.*)

> **Essendo stanco, Josh ha dormito tutto il giorno.** (*Being tired [or Because he was tired], Josh slept all day.*)

Gerunds that appear in the present tense are quite easy to form. You take the stem of **-are** verbs and add **-ando,** the stem of **-ere** verbs and add **-endo,** and the stem of **-ire** verbs and add **-endo.** The gerunds of reflexive verbs become **-andosi** (for **-arsi** verbs), **-endosi** (for **-ersi** verbs), and **-endosi** (for **-irsi** verbs). Here are some examples:

- **-are: parlare → parlando** (*speaking, talking*): **Parlando con te, ho perso il treno** (*While I was talking to you, I missed the train*).

- **-ere: mettere → mettendo** (*putting*): **Ci sono rimasti duecento dollari, mettendone 300 da parte per l'albergo** (*We have 200 dollars left, putting aside 300 for the hotel*).

- **-ire: partire → partendo** (*leaving*): **Partendo in orario, sarò da te alle 10.00** (*If I leave/Leaving on time, I'll be there at 10:00*).

- **-arsi: alzarsi → alzandosi** (*getting up*): **Alzandomi presto, riesco a produrre di più** (*Getting up early, I can accomplish more*).

- **-ersi: sedersi → sedendosi** (*sitting*): **Sedendoci in prima fila, possiamo seguire meglio lo spettacolo.** (*[By] sitting in the first row, we can follow the show better.*)

- **-irsi: dimenticarsi → dimenticandosi** (*forgetting*): **Dimenticandoti sempre tutto, prima o poi ti troverai nei guai** (*By always forgetting everything, sooner or later you will find yourself in troubles*).

When you have a reflexive, direct object, or indirect object pronoun (see Chapter 3 in Book III for details on these pronouns), you attach it to the end of the gerund (again, the subject in the main and dependent clauses is the same), as in these examples:

> **Vedendomi** così in contemplazione, Angelina mi chiese . . . (*Seeing me that way in contemplation, Angelina asked me . . .*)
>
> **Essendosi** alzati presto, i ragazzi hanno fatto una colazione abbondante. (*Having woken up early, the kids had an abundant breakfast.*)
>
> **Parlandogli** a quattro occhi, mi sono resa conto che era un idiota. (*Speaking to him face to face, I realized he was an idiot.*)

Working with Irregular Gerund Forms

Not every gerund construction is as easy as you see in the previous section, of course! You have to deal with some irregular gerund forms when writing and speaking in Italian. But even the irregular forms will come easily if you can master the irregular stems of the **imperfetto** (*imperfect tense;* see Chapter 1 of Book V for details).

Verbs that have irregular stems in the imperfect tense — such as **bere** (*to drink*), **dire** (*to say; to tell*), **fare** (*to do; to make*), **porre** (*to pose*), and so on — also have irregular stems when forming a gerund. However, after you isolate the irregular stem, you add the appropriate gerund ending from the preceding section. This formation goes for all gerunds, period (whether they're in the present or past or combined with **stare**).

- ✔ Bere: Stai **bevendo** troppo! (*You're drinking too much!*)
- ✔ Dire: Sto **dicendo** la verità! (*I'm telling the truth!*)
- ✔ Fare: La mamma sta **facendo** la spesa. (*Mom's buying groceries.*)
- ✔ Porre (like **imporre** and **supporre**): **Ponendo** il problema del giorno, il professore inizia la lezione. (*Posing the problem of the day, the professor begins the class.*)

Creating Gerunds in the Past Tense

The past gerund is a compound tense that you form by using the gerund of **essere** (**essendo** [*having*]) or **avere** (**avendo** [*having*]) plus the past participle (see Chapter 1 in Book V). Both past gerunds translate as *having . . . .* It's understood that the subject in both the dependent and main clauses is the same.

Because reflexive verbs take **essere** in compound tenses, you use **essendosi** + the past participle (see the previous sections to find out how to combine gerund endings and reflexive pronouns).

You can see from the following examples that there's no single way to translate the past gerund:

> **Avendo ballato** tutta la notte, i ragazzi erano stanchi. (*Since they danced all night/Because they danced all night/Having danced all night, the boys and girls were tired.*)

> **Essendo partiti** presto, siamo arrivati in anticipo. (*Having left early, we arrived early.*) This sentence can also mean *Because we left early/Given that we left early . . .*

> **Essendosi innamorati** all'improvviso, i due erano confusi. (*Because they fell in love quickly/Having fallen suddenly in love, both were confused.*)

Putting Gerunds in the Present Progressive

Il progressivo presente (*present progressive*) is a wonderful tense that you use to talk about something that's going on at the same time you're talking about it. In this way, the present progressive corresponds somewhat in meaning to the present indicative, but the gerunds in the present progressive allow you to more specifically refer to an action in progress. For example, when you say **Sto studiando** in the present progressive, it means *I'm studying* (right now, at this moment); **studio** in the present indicative can mean one of several things, including *I do study, I am studying, I study*.

To form the present progressive, you use the present form of **stare** (*to be*) + the present gerund form of the verb in question. The following table shows the conjugation of a verb in the present progressive and an example.

mangiare (*to eat*)	
io **sto mangiando**	noi **stiamo mangiando**
tu **stai mangiando**	voi **state mangiando**
lui, lei, Lei **sta mangiando**	loro, Loro **stanno mangiando**
Cosa state mangiando? (*What are you* [plural] *eating?*)	

What Were You Thinking? The Imperfect Progressive

You use the **imperfetto progressivo** (*imperfect progressive*) to refer to an action or event that *was* in the process of happening. For example, you can say **Cosa <u>stavi facendo</u>?** (*What were you doing?*) when you want to query a guilty-looking child. You may also want to use the imperfect progressive to discuss an action or event that was in the process of happening when something else happened. For example, you can get more specific by saying **Cosa <u>stavi facendo</u> quando ho telefonato?** (*What were you doing when I called?*)

You form the imperfect progressive with the imperfect form of the verb **stare** (*to be*) + the present gerund of the verb in question. The following table shows the imperfect progressive conjugation of the verb **dormire** and an example.

dormire (*to sleep*)	
io **stavo dormendo**	noi **stavamo dormendo**
tu **stavi dormendo**	voi **stavate dormendo**
lui, lei, Lei **stava dormendo**	loro **stavano dormendo**
Stavo dormendo quando ho sentito suonare il telefono. (*I was sleeping when I heard the phone ring.*)	

Book VI
Appendixes

the
appendixes

Contents at a Glance

Appendix A

Verb Tables

. . . .

*V*erbs have a fundamental role in the construction of a sentence. Italian philosopher and writer Niccolò Machiavelli said that the verb was "the chain and nerve of the language." The verb is the center around which you organize the different elements that compose any sentence.

This appendix provides the conjugations of commonly used verbs in various tenses of the infinitive, indicative, participle, and gerund moods. You first find the present infinitive, the past participle, and the present gerund of a verb and then the conjugations of the verb in the present **io scrivo/sto scrivendo** (*I write/I am writing*), present perfect (also simple past in English) **io ho scritto** (*I have written/I wrote*), future **io scriverò** (*I shall write*), and imperfect **io scrivevo** (*I wrote/used to write*) indicative forms. You need to know the past participle form of the verb to form compound tenses; the verb tables provide a notation with the correct (auxiliary) helping verb **essere** (*to be*) or **avere** (*to have*) to use with the past participle in the compound tenses, so your Italian sentences are flawless!

The first verbs presented are the helping verbs **avere** (*to have*), **essere** (*to be*), **dovere** (*ought to; to have to; must*), **potere** (*can; to be able to*), and **volere** (*to want*). Then there's a section that shows how to conjugate all regular **-are, -ere, -ire,** and **isc** verbs. Continue reading to find the patterns you need to conjugate verbs with a reflexive pronoun. You use these patterns for reflexive and reciprocal verbs (see Chapter 3 in Book IV for more on these forms). The appendix wraps up with a section on irregular verbs — how boring Italian would be without them! But don't worry: In here, you'll find the most commonly used irregular verbs and how to conjugate them.

If you don't get quite enough on verbs in this appendix, refer to Books IV and V.

Italian Helping Verbs

The verbs **avere** and **essere** help form compound tenses, as in **ho scritto** (*I have written*) and **ero andata** (*I had gone*). The verbs **dovere, potere,** and **volere** help convey the idea of obligation, possibility/ability, or willingness implied by the verb that follows. For example, **devono studiare** (*they must study*) and **vogliono studiare** (*they want to study*) explain student attitudes toward books and schoolwork. For their function in the sentence, **avere, essere, dovere, potere,** and **volere** are called *helping verbs* (auxiliary verbs in Italian.)

avere (to have)
Past Participle: avuto (had) (with avere);
Present Gerund: avendo (having)

	Present	Present Perfect	Future	Imperfect
io (I)	ho	ho avuto	avrò	avevo
tu (you, inf.)	hai	hai avuto	avrai	avevi
lui/lei/Lei (he/she/you, form.)	ha	ha avuto	avrà	aveva
noi (we)	abbiamo	abbiamo avuto	avremo	avevamo
voi (you)	avete	avete avuto	avrete	avevate
loro/Loro (they/you, form. pl.)	hanno	hanno avuto	avranno	avevano

essere (to be)
Past Participle: stato (been) (with essere);
Present Gerund: essendo (being)

	Present	Present Perfect	Future	Imperfect
io (I)	sono	sono stato/a	sarò	ero
tu (you, inf.)	sei	sei stato/a	sarai	eri
lui/lei/Lei (he/she/you, form.)	è	è stato/a	sarà	era
noi (we)	siamo	siamo stati/e	saremo	eravamo
voi (you)	siete	siete stati/e	sarete	eravate
loro/Loro (they/you, form. pl.)	sono	sono stati/e	saranno	erano

dovere (ought to; to have to; must)
Past Participle: dovuto (had to) (with avere);
Present Gerund: dovendo (having to)

	Present	Present Perfect	Future	Imperfect
io (I)	devo (debbo)	ho dovuto	dovrò	dovevo
tu (you, inf.)	devi	hai dovuto	dovrai	dovevi
lui/lei/Lei (he/she/you, form.)	deve	ha dovuto	dovrà	doveva
noi (we)	dobbiamo	abbiamo dovuto	dovremo	dovevamo
voi (you)	dovete	avete dovuto	dovrete	dovevate
loro/Loro (they/you, form. pl.)	devono (debbono)	hanno dovuto	dovranno	dovevano

potere (can; to be able to)
Past Participle: potuto (been able to) (with avere);
Present Gerund: potendo (being able to)

	Present	Present Perfect	Future	Imperfect
io (I)	posso	ho potuto	potrò	potevo
tu (you, inf.)	puoi	hai potuto	potrai	potevi
lui/lei/Lei (he/she/you, form.)	può	ha potuto	potrà	poteva
noi (we)	possiamo	abbiamo potuto	potremo	potevamo
voi (you)	potete	avete potuto	potrete	potevate
loro/Loro (they/you, form. pl.)	possono	hanno potuto	potranno	potevano

volere (to want)
Past Participle: voluto (wanted) (with avere);
Present Gerund: volendo (wanting)

	Present	Present Perfect	Future	Imperfect
io (I)	voglio	ho voluto	vorrò	volevo
tu (you, inf.)	vuoi	hai voluto	vorrai	volevi
lui/lei/Lei (he/ she/you, form.)	vuole	ha voluto	vorrà	voleva
noi (we)	vogliamo	abbiamo voluto	vorremo	volevamo
voi (you)	volete	avete voluto	vorrete	volevate
loro/Loro (they/ you, form. pl.)	vogliono	hanno voluto	vorranno	volevano

Regular Italian Verbs

Regular verbs are those verbs that keep the stem in all its forms and take the normal conjugation endings.

Regular Verbs Ending with -are
Example: cucinare (to cook)

Past Participle: cucinato (cooked) (with avere);
Present Gerund: cucinando (cooking)

	Present	Present Perfect	Future	Imperfect
io (I)	cucino	ho cucinato	cucinerò	cucinavo
tu (you, inf.)	cucini	hai cucinato	cucinerai	cucinavi
lui/lei/Lei (he/ she/you, form.)	cucina	ha cucinato	cucinerà	cucinava
noi (we)	cuciniamo	abbiamo cucinato	cucineremo	cucinavamo
voi (you)	cucinate	avete cucinato	cucinerete	cucinavate
loro/Loro (they/ you, form. pl.)	cucinano	hanno cucinato	cucineranno	cucinavano

Example: disegnare (to draw)
Past Participle: disegnato (drawn) (with avere);
Present Gerund: disegnando (drawing)

	Present	Present Perfect	Future	Imperfect
io (I)	disegno	ho disegnato	disegnerò	disegnavo
tu (you, inf.)	disegni	hai disegnato	disegnerai	disegnavi
lui/lei/Lei (he/ she/you, form.)	disegna	ha disegnato	disegnerà	disegnava
noi (we)	disegniamo	abbiamo disegnato	disegneremo	disegnavamo
voi (you)	disegnate	avete disegnato	disegnerete	disegnavate
loro/Loro (they/ you, form. pl.)	disegnano	hanno disegnato	disegne-ranno	disegnavano

Example: giocare (to play a game, a sport)
Past Participle: giocato (played) (with avere);
Present Gerund: giocando (playing)

	Present	Present Perfect	Future	Imperfect
io (I)	gioco	ho giocato	giocherò	giocavo
tu (you, inf.)	giochi	hai giocato	giocherai	giocavi
lui/lei/Lei (he/ she/you, form.)	gioca	ha giocato	giocherà	giocava
noi (we)	giochiamo	abbiamo giocato	giocheremo	giocavamo
voi (you)	giocate	avete giocato	giocherete	giocavate
loro/Loro (they/ you, form. pl.)	giocano	hanno giocato	giocheranno	giocavano

Example: imparare (to learn)
Past Participle: imparato (learned/learnt) (with avere);
Present Gerund: imparando (learning)

	Present	Present Perfect	Future	Imperfect
io (I)	imparo	ho imparato	imparerò	imparavo
tu (you, inf.)	impari	hai imparato	imparerai	imparavi
lui/lei/Lei (he/she/you, form.)	impara	ha imparato	imparerà	imparava
noi (we)	impariamo	abbiamo imparato	impareremo	imparavamo
voi (you)	imparate	avete imparato	imparerete	imparavate
loro/Loro (they/you, form. pl.)	imparano	hanno imparato	impareranno	imparavano

Example: insegnare (to teach)
Past Participle: insegnato (taught) (with avere);
Present Gerund: insegnando (teaching)

	Present	Present Perfect	Future	Imperfect
io (I)	insegno	ho insegnato	insegnerò	insegnavo
tu (you, inf.)	insegni	hai insegnato	insegnerai	insegnavi
lui/lei/Lei (he/she/you, form.)	insegna	ha insegnato	insegnerà	insegnava
noi (we)	insegnamo	abbiamo insegnato	insegneremo	insegnavamo
voi (you)	insegnate	avete insegnato	insegnerete	insegnavate
loro/Loro (they/you, form. pl.)	insegnano	hanno insegnato	insegneranno	insegnavano

Example: lavorare (to work)
Past Participle: lavorato (worked) (with avere);
Present Gerund: lavorando (working)

	Present	Present Perfect	Future	Imperfect
io (I)	lavoro	ho lavorato	lavorerò	lavoravo
tu (you, inf.)	lavori	hai lavorato	lavorerai	lavoravi
lui/lei/Lei (he/ she/you, form.)	lavora	ha lavorato	lavorerà	lavorava
noi (we)	lavoriamo	abbiamo lavorato	lavoreremo	lavoravamo
voi (you)	lavorate	avete lavorato	lavorerete	lavoravate
loro/Loro (they/ you, form. pl.)	lavorano	hanno lavorato	lavoreranno	lavoravano

Book VI

Appendixes

Example: mangiare (to eat)
Past Participle: mangiato (eaten) (with avere);
Present Gerund: mangiando (eating)

	Present	Present Perfect	Future	Imperfect
io (I)	mangio	ho mangiato	mangerò	mangiavo
tu (you, inf.)	mangi	hai mangiato	mangerai	mangiavi
lui/lei/Lei (he/ she/you, form.)	mangia	ha mangiato	mangerà	mangiava
noi (we)	mangiamo	abbiamo mangiato	mangeremo	mangiavamo
voi (you)	mangiate	avete mangiato	mangerete	mangiavate
loro/Loro (they/ you, form. pl.)	mangiano	hanno mangiato	mangeranno	mangiavano

Example: parlare (to speak; to talk)
Past Participle: parlato (spoken; talked) (with avere);
Present Gerund: parlando (speaking; talking)

	Present	Present Perfect	Future	Imperfect
io (I)	parlo	ho parlato	parlerò	parlavo
tu (you, inf.)	parli	hai parlato	parlerai	parlavi
lui/lei/Lei (he/ she/you, form.)	parla	ha parlato	parlerà	parlava
noi (we)	parliamo	abbiamo parlato	parleremo	parlavamo
voi (you)	parlate	avete parlato	parlerete	parlavate
loro/Loro (they/ you, form. pl.)	parlano	hanno parlato	parleranno	parlavano

Example: studiare (to study)
Past Participle: studiato (studied) (with avere);
Present Gerund: studiando (studying)

	Present	Present Perfect	Future	Imperfect
io (I)	studio	ho studiato	studierò	studiavo
tu (you, inf.)	studi	hai studiato	studierai	studiavi
lui/lei/Lei (he/ she/you, form.)	studia	ha studiato	studierà	studiava
noi (we)	studiamo	abbiamo studiato	studieremo	studiavamo
voi (you)	studiate	avete studiato	studierete	studiavate
loro/Loro (they/ you, form. pl.)	studiano	hanno studiato	studieranno	studiavano

Example: suonare (to play an instrument)
Past Participle: suonato (played) (with avere);
Present Gerund: suonando (playing)

	Present	Present Perfect	Future	Imperfect
_io (I)_	suono	ho suonato	suonerò	suonavo
tu (you, inf.)	suoni	hai suonato	suonerai	suonavi
lui/lei/Lei (he/ she/you, form.)	suona	ha suonato	suonerà	suonava
noi (we)	suoniamo	abbiamo suonato	suoneremo	suonavamo
voi (you)	suonate	avete suonato	suonerete	suonavate
loro/Loro (they/ you, form. pl.)	suonano	hanno suonato	suoneranno	suonavano

Regular Verbs Ending with -ere
Example: chiudere (to close)

Past Participle: chiuso (closed) (with avere);
Present Gerund: chiudendo (closing)

	Present	Present Perfect	Future	Imperfect
_io (I)_	chiudo	ho chiuso	chiuderò	chiudevo
tu (you, inf.)	chiudi	hai chiuso	chiuderai	chiudevi
lui/lei/Lei (he/ she/you, form.)	chiude	ha chiuso	chiuderà	chiudeva
noi (we)	chiudiamo	abbiamo chiuso	chiuderemo	chiudevamo
voi (you)	chiudete	avete chiuso	chiuderete	chiudevate
loro/Loro (they/ you, form. pl.)	chiudono	hanno chiuso	chiuderanno	chiudevano

Example: leggere (to read)
Past Participle: letto (read) (with avere);
Present Gerund: leggendo (reading)

	Present	Present Perfect	Future	Imperfect
io (I)	leggo	ho letto	leggerò	leggevo
tu (you, inf.)	leggi	hai letto	leggerai	leggevi
lui/lei/Lei (he/she/you, form.)	legge	ha letto	leggerà	leggeva
noi (we)	leggiamo	abbiamo letto	leggeremo	leggevamo
voi (you)	leggete	avete letto	leggerete	leggevate
loro/Loro (they/you, form. pl.)	leggono	hanno letto	leggeranno	leggevano

Example: mettere (to put)
Past Participle: messo (put) (with avere);
Present Gerund: mettendo (putting)

	Present	Present Perfect	Future	Imperfect
io (I)	metto	ho messo	metterò	mettevo
tu (you, inf.)	metti	hai messo	metterai	mettevi
lui/lei/Lei (he/she/you, form.)	mette	ha messo	metterà	metteva
noi (we)	mettiamo	abbiamo messo	metteremo	mettevamo
voi (you)	mettete	avete messo	metterete	mettevate
loro/Loro (they/you, form. pl.)	mettono	hanno messo	metteranno	mettevano

Example: prendere (to take; to have)
Past Participle: preso (taken; had) (with avere);
Present Gerund: prendendo (taking; having)

	Present	Present Perfect	Future	Imperfect
io (I)	prendo	ho preso	prenderò	prendevo
tu (you, inf.)	prendi	hai preso	prenderai	prendevi
lui/lei/Lei (he/she/you, form.)	prende	ha preso	prenderà	prendeva
noi (we)	prendiamo	abbiamo preso	prenderemo	prendevamo
voi (you)	prendete	avete preso	prenderete	prendevate
loro/Loro (they/you, form. pl.)	prendono	hanno preso	prenderanno	prendevano

Book VI

Appendixes

Example: ripetere (to repeat)
Past Participle: ripetuto (repeated) (with avere);
Present Gerund: ripetendo (repeating)

	Present	Present Perfect	Future	Imperfect
io (I)	ripeto	ho ripetuto	ripeterò	ripetevo
tu (you, inf.)	ripeti	hai ripetuto	ripeterai	ripetevi
lui/lei/Lei (he/she/you, form.)	ripete	ha ripetuto	ripeterà	ripeteva
noi (we)	ripetiamo	abbiamo ripetuto	ripeteremo	ripetevamo
voi (you)	ripetete	avete ripetuto	ripeterete	ripetevate
loro/Loro (they/you, form. pl.)	ripetono	hanno ripetuto	ripeteranno	ripetevano

Example: scrivere (to write)
Past Participle: scritto (written) (with avere);
Present Gerund: scrivendo (writing)

	Present	Present Perfect	Future	Imperfect
io (I)	scrivo	ho scritto	scriverò	scrivevo
tu (you, inf.)	scrivi	hai scritto	scriverai	scrivevi
lui/lei/Lei (he/she/you, form.)	scrive	ha scritto	scriverà	scriveva
noi (we)	scriviamo	abbiamo scritto	scriveremo	scrivevamo
voi (you)	scrivete	avete scritto	scriverete	scrivevate
loro/Loro (they/you, form. pl.)	scrivono	hanno scritto	scriveranno	scrivevano

Example: vedere (to see)
Past Participle: visto, veduto (seen) (with avere);
Present Gerund: vedendo (seeing)

	Present	Present Perfect	Future	Imperfect
io (I)	vedo	ho visto/veduto	vedrò	vedevo
tu (you, inf.)	vedi	hai visto/veduto	vedrai	vedevi
lui/lei/Lei (he/she/you, form.)	vede	ha visto/veduto	vedrà	vedeva
noi (we)	vediamo	abbiamo visto/veduto	vedremo	vedevamo
voi (you)	vedete	avete visto/veduto	vedrete	vedevate
loro/Loro (they/you, form. pl.)	vedono	hanno visto/veduto	vedranno	vedevano

Example: vendere (to sell)
Past Participle: venduto (sold) (with avere);
Present Gerund: vendendo (selling)

	Present	Present Perfect	Future	Imperfect
io (I)	vendo	ho venduto	venderò	vendevo
tu (you, inf.)	vendi	hai venduto	venderai	vendevi
lui/lei/Lei (he/ she/you, form.)	vende	ha venduto	venderà	vendeva
noi (we)	vendiamo	abbiamo venduto	venderemo	vendevamo
voi (you)	vendete	avete venduto	venderete	vendevate
loro/Loro (they/ you, form. pl.)	vendono	hanno venduto	venderanno	vendevano

Example: vivere (to live)
Past Participle: vissuto (lived);
Present Gerund: vivendo (living)

(with avere) (transitive; + direct object)

	Present	Present Perfect	Future	Imperfect
io (I)	vivo	ho vissuto	vivrò	vivevo
tu (you, inf.)	vivi	hai vissuto	vivrai	vivevi
lui/lei/Lei (he/ she/you, form.)	vive	ha vissuto	vivrà	viveva
noi (we)	viviamo	abbiamo vissuto	vivremo	vivevamo
voi (you)	vivete	avete vissuto	vivrete	vivevate
loro/Loro (they/ you, form. pl.)	vivono	hanno vissuto	vivranno	vivevano

(with essere) (intransitive; + indirect object)

	Present	Present Perfect	Future	Imperfect
io (I)	vivo	sono vissuto/a	vivrò	vivevo
tu (you, inf.)	vivi	sei vissuto/a	vivrai	vivevi
lui/lei/Lei (he/ she/you, form.)	vive	è vissuto/a	vivrà	viveva
noi (we)	viviamo	siamo vissuti/e	vivremo	vivevamo
voi (you)	vivete	siete vissuti/e	vivrete	vivevate
loro/Loro (they/ you, form. pl.)	vivono	sono vissuti/e	vivranno	vivevano

Regular Verbs Ending with -ire
Example: aprire (to open)

**Past participle: aperto (opened);
Present Gerund: aprendo (opening)**

	Present	Present Perfect	Future	Imperfect
io (I)	apro	ho aperto	aprirò	aprivo
tu (you, inf.)	apri	hai aperto	aprirai	aprivi
lui/lei/Lei (he/ she/you, form.)	apre	ha aperto	aprirà	apriva
noi (we)	apriamo	abbiamo aperto	apriremo	aprivamo
voi (you)	aprite	avete aperto	aprirete	aprivate
loro/Loro (they/ you, form. pl.)	aprono	hanno aperto	apriranno	aprivano

Example: coprire (to cover)
Past Participle: coperto (covered) (with avere);
Present Gerund: coprendo (covering)

	Present	Present Perfect	Future	Imperfect
io (I)	copro	ho coperto	coprirò	coprivo
tu (you, inf.)	copri	hai coperto	coprirai	coprivi
lui/lei/Lei (he/she/you, form.)	copre	ha coperto	coprirà	copriva
noi (we)	copriamo	abbiamo coperto	copriremo	coprivamo
voi (you)	coprite	avete coperto	coprirete	coprivate
loro/Loro (they/you, form. pl.)	coprono	hanno coperto	copriranno	coprivano

Example: dormire (to sleep)
Past Participle: dormito (slept) (with avere);
Present Gerund: dormendo (sleeping)

	Present	Present Perfect	Future	Imperfect
io (I)	dormo	ho dormito	dormirò	dormivo
tu (you, inf.)	dormi	hai dormito	dormirai	dormivi
lui/lei/Lei (he/she/you, form.)	dorme	ha dormito	dormirà	dormiva
noi (we)	dormiamo	abbiamo dormito	dormiremo	dormivamo
voi (you)	dormite	avete dormito	dormirete	dormivate
loro/Loro (they/you, form. pl.)	dormono	hanno dormito	dormiranno	dormivano

Example: partire (to leave; to go on a trip)
Past Participle: partito (left; went) (with essere);
Present Gerund: partendo (leaving; going)

	Present	**Present Perfect**	**Future**	**Imperfect**
io (I)	parto	sono partito/a	partirò	partivo
tu (you, inf.)	parti	sei partito/a	partirai	partivi
lui/lei/Lei (he/ she/you, form.)	parte	è partito/a	partirà	partiva
noi (we)	partiamo	siamo partiti/e	partiremo	partivamo
voi (you)	partite	siete partiti/e	partirete	partivate
loro/Loro (they/ you, form. pl.)	partono	sono partiti/e	partiranno	partivano

Example: sentire (to hear/listen/feel/taste/touch)
Past Participle: sentito (heard; listened; felt; tasted; touched)
(with avere);
Present Gerund: sentendo (hearing; listening; feeling; tasting; touching)

	Present	**Present Perfect**	**Future**	**Imperfect**
io (I)	sento	ho sentito	sentirò	sentivo
tu (you, inf.)	senti	hai sentito	sentirai	sentivi
lui/lei/Lei (he/ she/you, form.)	sente	ha sentito	sentirà	sentiva
noi (we)	sentiamo	abbiamo sentito	sentiremo	sentivamo
voi (you)	sentite	avete sentito	sentirete	sentivate
loro/Loro (they/ you, form. pl.)	sentono	hanno sentito	sentiranno	sentivano

Regular -ire Verbs with isc
Example: capire (to understand)

Past Participle: capito (understood) (with avere);
Present Gerund: capendo (understanding)

	Present	Present Perfect	Future	Imperfect
io (I)	capisco	ho capito	capirò	capivo
tu (you, inf.)	capisci	hai capito	capirai	capivi
lui/lei/Lei (he/ she/you, form.)	capisce	ha capito	capirà	capiva
noi (we)	capiamo	abbiamo capito	capiremo	capivamo
voi (you)	capite	avete capito	capirete	capivate
loro/Loro (they/ you, form. pl.)	capiscono	hanno capito	capiranno	capivano

Example: costruire (to build)
Past Participle: costruito (built) (with avere);
Present Gerund: costruendo (building)

	Present	Present Perfect	Future	Imperfect
io (I)	costruisco	ho costruito	costruirò	costruivo
tu (you, inf.)	costruisci	hai costruito	costruirai	costruivi
lui/lei/Lei (he/ she/you, form.)	costruisce	ha costruito	costruirà	costruiva
noi (we)	costruiamo	abbiamo costruito	costruiremo	costruivamo
voi (you)	costruite	avete costruito	costruirete	costruivate
loro/Loro (they/ you, form. pl.)	costruiscono	hanno costruito	costruiranno	costruivano

Book VI

Appendixes

Example: finire (to finish)
Past Participle: finito (finished) (with avere);
Present Gerund: finendo (finishing)

	Present	Present Perfect	Future	Imperfect
io (I)	finisco	ho finito	finirò	finivo
tu (you, inf.)	finisci	hai finito	finirai	finivi
lui/lei/Lei (he/she/you, form.)	finisce	ha finito	finirà	finiva
noi (we)	finiamo	abbiamo finito	finiremo	finivamo
voi (you)	finite	avete finito	finirete	finivate
loro/Loro (they/you, form. pl.)	finiscono	hanno finito	finiranno	finivano

Example: interferire (to interfere)
Past Participle: interferito (interfered) (with avere);
Present Gerund: interferendo (interfering)

	Present	Present Perfect	Future	Imperfect
io (I)	interferisco	ho interferito	interferirò	interferivo
tu (you, inf.)	interferisci	hai interferito	interferirai	interferivi
lui/lei/Lei (he/she/you, form.)	interferisce	ha interferito	interferirà	interferiva
noi (we)	interferiamo	abbiamo interferito	interferiremo	interferivamo
voi (you)	interferite	avete interferito	interferirete	interferivate
loro/Loro (they/you, form. pl.)	interferiscono	hanno interferito	interferiranno	interferivano

Example: preferire (to prefer)
Past Participle: preferito (preferred) (with avere);
Present Gerund: preferendo (preferring)

	Present	Present Perfect	Future	Imperfect
io (I)	preferisco	ho preferito	preferirò	preferivo
tu (you, inf.)	preferisci	hai preferito	preferirai	preferivi
lui/lei/Lei (he/ she/you, form.)	preferisce	ha preferito	preferirà	preferiva
noi (we)	preferiamo	abbiamo preferito	preferiremo	preferivamo
voi (you)	preferite	avete preferito	preferirete	preferivate
loro/Loro (they/ you, form. pl.)	preferiscono	hanno preferito	preferiranno	preferivano

Example: pulire (to clean)
Past Participle: pulito (cleaned) (with avere);
Present Gerund: pulendo (cleaning)

	Present	Present Perfect	Future	Imperfect
io (I)	pulisco	ho pulito	pulirò	pulivo
tu (you, inf.)	pulisci	hai pulito	pulirai	pulivi
lui/lei/Lei (he/ she/you, form.)	pulisce	ha pulito	pulirà	puliva
noi (we)	puliamo	abbiamo pulito	puliremo	pulivamo
voi (you)	pulite	avete pulito	pulirete	pulivate
loro/Loro (they/ you, form. pl.)	puliscono	hanno pulito	puliranno	pulivano

Book VI

Appendixes

Reflexive Verbs
Example: addormentarsi (to fall asleep)

Past Participle: addormentato (fallen asleep) (with essere);
Present Gerund: addormentandosi (falling asleep)

	Present	Present Perfect	Future	Imperfect
io (I)	mi addormento	mi sono addormentato/a	mi addormenterò	mi addormentavo
tu (you, inf.)	ti addormenti	ti sei addormentato/a	ti addormenterai	ti addormentavi
lui/lei/Lei (he/she/you, form.)	si addormenta	si è addormentato/a	si addormenterà	si addormentava
noi (we)	ci addormentiamo	ci siamo addormentati/e	ci addormenteremo	ci addormentavamo
voi (you)	vi addormentate	vi siete addormentati/e	vi addormenterete	vi addormentavate
loro/Loro (they/you, form. pl.)	si addormentano	si sono addormentati/e	si addormenteranno	si addormentavano

Example: alzarsi (to get up)
Past Participle: alzato (got up) (with essere);
Present Gerund: alzandosi (getting up)

	Present	Present Perfect	Future	Imperfect
io (I)	mi alzo	mi sono alzato/a	mi alzerò	mi alzavo
tu (you, inf.)	ti alzi	ti sei alzato/a	ti alzerai	ti alzavi
lui/lei/Lei (he/she/you, form.)	si alza	si è alzato/a	si alzerà	si alzava
noi (we)	ci alziamo	ci siamo alzati/e	ci alzeremo	ci alzavamo
voi (you)	vi alzate	vi siete alzati/e	vi alzerete	vi alzavate
loro/Loro (they/you, form. pl.)	si alzano	si sono alzati/e	si alzeranno	si alzavano

Example: divertirsi (to have fun)
Past Participle: divertito (had fun) (with essere);
Present Gerund: divertendosi (having fun)

	Present	Present Perfect	Future	Imperfect
io (I)	mi diverto	mi sono divertito/a	mi divertirò	mi divertivo
tu (you, inf.)	ti diverti	ti sei divertito/a	ti divertirai	ti divertivi
lui/lei/Lei (he/she/you, form.)	si diverte	si è divertito/a	si divertirà	si divertiva
noi (we)	ci divertiamo	ci siamo divertiti/e	ci divertiremo	ci divertivamo
voi (you)	vi divertite	vi siete divertiti/e	vi divertirete	vi divertivate
loro/Loro (they/you, form. pl.)	si divertono	si sono divertiti/e	si divertiranno	si divertivano

Book VI

Appendixes

Example: innamorarsi (to fall in love)
Past Participle: innamorato (fallen in love) (with essere);
Present Gerund: innamorandosi (falling in love)

	Present	Present Perfect	Future	Imperfect
io (I)	mi innamoro	mi sono innamorato/a	mi innamorerò	mi innamoravo
tu (you, inf.)	ti innamori	ti sei innamorato/a	ti innamorerai	ti innamoravi
lui/lei/Lei (he/she/you, form.)	si innamora	si è innamorato/a	si innamorerà	si innamorava
noi (we)	ci innamoriamo	ci siamo innamorati/e	ci innamoreremo	ci innamoravamo
voi (you)	vi innamorate	vi siete innamorati/e	vi innamorerete	vi innamoravate
loro/Loro (they/you, form. pl.)	si innamorano	si sono innamorati/e	si innamoreranno	si innamoravano

Example: lavarsi (to wash oneself)
Past Participle: lavato (washed) (with essere);
Present Gerund: lavandosi (washing)

	Present	Present Perfect	Future	Imperfect
io (I)	mi lavo	mi sono lavato/a	mi laverò	mi lavavo
tu (you, inf.)	ti lavi	ti sei lavato/a	ti laverai	ti lavavi
lui/lei/Lei (he/she/you, form.)	si lava	si è lavato/a	si laverà	si lavava
noi (we)	ci laviamo	ci siamo lavati/e	ci laveremo	ci lavavamo
voi (you)	vi lavate	vi siete lavati/e	vi laverete	vi lavavate
loro/Loro (they/you, form. pl.)	si lavano	si sono lavati/e	si laveranno	si lavavano

Example: mettersi (to put [something] on)
Past Participle: messo (put on) (with essere);
Present Gerund: mettendosi (putting on)

	Present	Present Perfect	Future	Imperfect
io (I)	mi metto	mi sono messo/a	mi metterò	mi mettevo
tu (you, inf.)	ti metti	ti sei messo/a	ti metterai	ti mettevi
lui/lei/Lei (he/she/you, form.)	si mette	si è messo/a	si metterà	si metteva
noi (we)	ci mettiamo	ci siamo messi/e	ci metteremo	ci mettevamo
voi (you)	vi mettete	vi siete messi/e	vi metterete	vi mettevate
loro/Loro (they/you, form. pl.)	si mettono	si sono messi/e	si metteranno	si mettevano

Example: permettersi (to afford)
Past Participle: permesso (afforded) (with essere);
Present Gerund: permettendosi (affording)

	Present	Present Perfect	Future	Imperfect
io (I)	mi permetto	mi sono permesso/a	mi permetterò	mi permettevo
tu (you, inf.)	ti permetti	ti sei permesso/a	ti permetterai	ti permettevi
lui/lei/Lei (he/she/you, form.)	si permette	si è permesso/a	si permetterà	si permetteva
noi (we)	ci permettiamo	ci siamo permessi/e	ci permetteremo	ci permettevamo
voi (you)	vi permettete	vi siete permessi/e	vi permetterete	vi permettevate
loro/Loro (they/you, form. pl.)	si permettono	si sono permessi/e	si permetteranno	si permettevano

Book VI

Appendixes

Example: sentirsi (to feel)
Past Participle: sentito (felt) (with essere);
Present Gerund: sentendosi (feeling)

	Present	Present Perfect	Future	Imperfect
io (I)	mi sento	mi sono sentito/a	mi sentirò	mi sentivo
tu (you, inf.)	ti senti	ti sei sentito/a	ti sentirai	ti sentivi
lui/lei/Lei (he/she/you, form.)	si sente	si è sentito/a	si sentirà	si sentiva
noi (we)	ci sentiamo	ci siamo sentiti/e	ci sentiremo	ci sentivamo
voi (you)	vi sentite	vi siete sentiti/e	vi sentirete	vi sentivate
loro/Loro (they/you, form. pl.)	si sentono	si sono sentiti/e	si sentiranno	si sentivano

Irregular Italian Verbs

Irregular verbs don't follow the typical **-are, -ere,** and **-ire** conjugations. The irregularities may consist in changing the stem and/or the endings.

andare (to go)
Past Participle: andato (went) (with essere);
Present Gerund: andando (going)

	Present	Present Perfect	Future	Imperfect
io (I)	vado	sono andato/a	andrò	andavo
tu (you, inf.)	vai	sei andato/a	andrai	andavi
lui/lei/Lei (he/ she/you, form.)	va	è andato/a	andrà	andava
noi (we)	andiamo	siamo andati/e	andremo	andavamo
voi (you)	andate	siete andati/e	andrete	andavate
loro/Loro (they/ you, form. pl.)	vanno	sono andati/e	andranno	andavano

bere (to drink)
Past Participle: bevuto (drunk) (with avere);
Present Gerund: bevendo (drinking)

	Present	Present Perfect	Future	Imperfect
io (I)	bevo	ho bevuto	berrò	bevevo
tu (you, inf.)	bevi	hai bevuto	berrai	bevevi
lui/lei/Lei (he/ she/you, form.)	beve	ha bevuto	berrà	beveva
noi (we)	beviamo	abbiamo bevuto	berremo	bevevamo
voi (you)	bevete	avete bevuto	berrete	bevevate
loro/Loro (they/ you, form. pl.)	bevono	hanno bevuto	berranno	bevevano

dare (to give)
Past Participle: dato (given) (with avere);
Present Gerund: dando (giving)

	Present	Present Perfect	Future	Imperfect
io (I)	do	ho dato	darò	davo
tu (you, inf.)	dai	hai dato	darai	davi
lui/lei/Lei (he/she/you, form.)	dà	ha dato	darà	dava
noi (we)	diamo	abbiamo dato	daremo	davamo
voi (you)	date	avete dato	darete	davate
loro/Loro (they/you, form. pl.)	danno	hanno dato	daranno	davano

Book VI

Appendixes

dire (to say; to tell)
Past Participle: detto (said; told) (with avere);
Present Gerund: dicendo (saying; telling)

	Present	Present Perfect	Future	Imperfect
io (I)	dico	ho detto	dirò	dicevo
tu (you, inf.)	dici	hai detto	dirai	dicevi
lui/lei/Lei (he/she/you, form.)	dice	ha detto	dirà	diceva
noi (we)	diciamo	abbiamo detto	diremo	dicevamo
voi (you)	dite	avete detto	direte	dicevate
loro/Loro (they/you, form. pl.)	dicono	hanno detto	diranno	dicevano

fare (to do; to make)
Past Participle: fatto (done; made) (with avere);
Present Gerund: facendo (doing; making)

	Present	Present Perfect	Future	Imperfect
io (I)	faccio	ho fatto	farò	facevo
tu (you, inf.)	fai	hai fatto	farai	facevi
lui/lei/Lei (he/ she/you, form.)	fa	ha fatto	farà	faceva
noi (we)	facciamo	abbiamo fatto	faremo	facevamo
voi (you)	fate	avete fatto	farete	facevate
loro/Loro (they/ you, form. pl.)	fanno	hanno fatto	faranno	facevano

imporre (to impose)
Past Participle: imposto (imposed) (with avere);
Present Gerund: imponendo (imposing)

	Present	Present Perfect	Future	Imperfect
io (I)	ho impongo	ho imposto/a	ho imporrò	imponevo
tu (you, inf.)	hai imponi	hai imposto/a	hai imporrai	imponevi
lui/lei/Lei (he/ she/you, form.)	ha impone	ha imposto/a	ha imporrà	imponeva
noi (we)	abbiamo imponiamo	abbiamo imposto	abbiamo imporremo	imponevamo
voi (you)	aveta imponete	aveta imposto	aveta imporrete	imponevate
loro/Loro (they/ you, form. pl.)	hanno impongono	hanno imposto	hanno imporranno	imponevano

morire (to die)
Past Participle: morto (died) (with essere);
Present Gerund: morendo (dying)

	Present	Present Perfect	Future	Imperfect
io (I)	muoio	sono morto/a	morirò	morivo
tu (you, inf.)	muori	sei morto/a	morirai	morivi
lui/lei/Lei (he/she/you, form.)	muore	è morto/a	morirà	moriva
noi (we)	moriamo	siamo morti/e	moriremo	morivamo
voi (you)	morite	siete morti/e	morirete	morivate
loro/Loro (they/you, form. pl.)	muoiono	sono morti/e	moriranno	morivano

opporsi (to oppose)
Past Participle: opposto (opposed) (with essere);
Present Gerund: opponendosi (opposing)

	Present	Present Perfect	Future	Imperfect
io (I)	mi oppongo	mi sono opposto/a	mi opporrò	mi opponevo
tu (you, inf.)	ti opponi	ti sei opposto/a	ti opporrai	ti opponevi
lui/lei/Lei (he/she/you, form.)	si oppone	si è opposto/a	si opporrà	si opponeva
noi (we)	ci opponiamo	ci siamo opposti/e	ci opporremo	ci opponevamo
voi (you)	vi opponete	vi siete opposti/e	vi opporrete	vi opponevate
loro/Loro (they/you, form. pl.)	si oppongono	si sono opposti/e	si opporranno	si opponevano

piacere (to like)
Past Participle: piaciuto (liked) (with essere);
Present Gerund: piacendo (liking)

	Present	Present Perfect	Future	Imperfect
io (I)	piaccio	sono piaciuto/a	piacerò	piacevo
tu (you, inf.)	piaci	sei piaciuto/a	piacerai	piacevi
lui/lei/Lei (he/she/you, form.)	piace	è piaciuto/a	piacerà	piaceva
noi (we)	piacciamo	siamo piaciuti/e	piaceremo	piacevamo
voi (you)	piacete	siete piaciuti/e	piacerete	piacevate
loro/Loro (they/you, form. pl.)	piacciono	sono piaciuti/e	piaceranno	piacevano

porre (to put)
Past Participle: posto (put) (with avere);
Present Gerund: ponendo (putting)

	Present	Present Perfect	Future	Imperfect
io (I)	pongo	ho posto	porrò	ponevo
tu (you, inf.)	poni	hai posto	porrai	ponevi
lui/lei/Lei (he/she/you, form.)	pone	ha posto	porrà	poneva
noi (we)	poniamo	abbiamo posto	porremo	ponevamo
voi (you)	ponete	avete posto	porrete	ponevate
loro/Loro (they/you, form. pl.)	pongono	hanno posto	porranno	ponevano

proporsi (to propose)
Past Participle: proposto (proposed) (with essere);
Present Gerund: proponendosi (proposing)

	Present	Present Perfect	Future	Imperfect
io (I)	mi propongo	mi sono proposto/a	mi proporrò	mi proponevo
tu (you, inf.)	ti proponi	ti sei proposto/a	ti proporrai	ti proponevi
lui/lei/Lei (he/ she/you, form.)	si propone	si è proposto/a	si proporrà	si proponeva
noi (we)	ci proponiamo	ci siamo proposti/e	ci proporremo	ci proponevamo
voi (you)	vi proponete	vi siete proposti/e	vi proporrete	vi proponevate
loro/Loro (they/ you, form. pl.)	si propongono	si sono proposti/e	si proporranno	si proponevano

rimanere (to stay; to remain)
Past Participle: rimasto (stayed; remained) (with essere);
Present Gerund: rimanendo (staying; remaining)

	Present	Present Perfect	Future	Imperfect
io (I)	rimango	sono rimasto/a	rimarrò	rimanevo
tu (you, inf.)	rimani	sei rimasto/a	rimarrai	rimanevi
lui/lei/Lei (he/ she/you, form.)	rimane	è rimasto/a	rimarrà	rimaneva
noi (we)	rimaniamo	siamo rimasti/e	rimarremo	rimanevamo
voi (you)	rimanete	siete rimasti/e	rimarrete	rimanevate
loro/Loro (they/ you, form. pl.)	rimangono	sono rimasti/e	rimarranno	rimanevano

salire (to go up)
Past Participle: salito (went up) (with essere);
Present Gerund: salendo (going up)

	Present	Present Perfect	Future	Imperfect
io (I)	salgo	sono salito/a	salirò	salivo
tu (you, inf.)	sali	sei salito/a	salirai	salivi
lui/lei/Lei (he/ she/you, form.)	sale	è salito/a	salirà	saliva
noi (we)	saliamo	siamo saliti/e	saliremo	salivamo
voi (you)	salite	siete saliti/e	salirete	salivate
loro/Loro (they/ you, form. pl.)	salgono	sono saliti/e	saliranno	salivano

sapere (to know)
Past Participle: saputo (known) (with avere);
Present Gerund: sapendo (knowing)

	Present	Present Perfect	Future	Imperfect
io (I)	so	ho saputo	saprò	sapevo
tu (you, inf.)	sai	hai saputo	saprai	sapevi
lui/lei/Lei (he/ she/you, form.)	sa	ha saputo	saprà	sapeva
noi (we)	sappiamo	abbiamo saputo	sapremo	sapevamo
voi (you)	sapete	avete saputo	saprete	sapevate
loro/Loro (they/ you, form. pl.)	sanno	hanno saputo	sapranno	sapevano

scegliere (to choose)
Past Participle: scelto (chosen) (with avere);
Present Gerund: scegliendo (choosing)

	Present	Present Perfect	Future	Imperfect
io (I)	scelgo	ho scelto	sceglierò	sceglievo
tu (you, inf.)	scegli	hai scelto	sceglierai	sceglievi
lui/lei/Lei (he/she/you, form.)	sceglie	ha scelto	sceglierà	sceglieva
noi (we)	scegliamo	abbiamo scelto	sceglieremo	sceglievamo
voi (you)	scegliete	avete scelto	sceglierete	sceglievate
loro/Loro (they/you, form. pl.)	scelgono	hanno scelto	sceglieranno	sceglievano

sedersi (to sit)
Past Participle: seduto (sat) (with essere);
Present Gerund: sedendosi (sitting)

	Present	Present Perfect	Future	Imperfect
io (I)	mi siedo/seggo	mi sono seduto/a	mi sederò/siederò	mi sedevo
tu (you, inf.)	ti siedi	ti sei seduto/a	ti sederai/siederai	ti sedevi
lui/lei/Lei (he/she/you, form.)	si siede	si è seduto/a	si sederà/siederà	si sedeva
noi (we)	ci sediamo	ci siamo seduti/e	ci sederemo/siederemo	ci sedevamo
voi (you)	vi sedete	vi siete seduti/e	vi sederete/siederete	vi sedevate
loro/Loro (they/you, form. pl.)	si siedono/seggono	si sono seduti/e	si sederanno/siederanno	si sedevano

stare (to stay; to be)
Past Participle: stato (stayed; been) (with essere);
Present Gerund: stando (staying; being)

	Present	Present Perfect	Future	Imperfect
io (I)	sto	sono stato/a	starò	stavo
tu (you, inf.)	stai	sei stato/a	starai	stavi
lui/lei/Lei (he/she/you, form.)	sta	è stato/a	starà	stava
noi (we)	stiamo	siamo stati/e	staremo	stavamo
voi (you)	state	siete stati/e	starete	stavate
loro/Loro (they/you, form. pl.)	stanno	sono stati/e	staranno	stavano

tacere (to be silent)
Past Participle: taciuto (been silent) (with avere);
Present Gerund: tacendo (being silent)

	Present	Present Perfect	Future	Imperfect
io (I)	taccio	ho taciuto	tacerò	tacevo
tu (you, inf.)	taci	hai taciuto	tacerai	tacevi
lui/lei/Lei (he/she/you, form.)	tace	ha taciuto	tacerà	taceva
noi (we)	tacciamo	abbiamo taciuto	taceremo	tacevamo
voi (you)	tacete	avete taciuto	tacerete	tacevate
loro/Loro (they/you, form. pl.)	tacciono	hanno taciuto	taceranno	tacevano

tenere (to hold)
**Past Participle: tenuto (held) (with avere);
Present Gerund: tenendo (holding)**

	Present	Present Perfect	Future	Imperfect
io (I)	tengo	ho tenuto	terrò	tenevo
tu (you, inf.)	tieni	hai tenuto	terrai	tenevi
lui/lei/Lei (he/ she/you, form.)	tiene	ha tenuto	terrà	teneva
noi (we)	teniamo	abbiamo tenuto	terremo	tenevamo
voi (you)	tenete	avete tenuto	terrete	tenevate
loro/Loro (they/ you, form. pl.)	tengono	hanno tenuto	terranno	tenevano

togliere (to take away)
**Past Participle: tolto (taken away) (with avere);
Present Gerund: togliendo (taking away)**

	Present	Present Perfect	Future	Imperfect
io (I)	tolgo	ho tolto	toglierò	toglievo
tu (you, inf.)	togli	hai tolto	toglierai	toglievi
lui/lei/Lei (he/ she/you, form.)	toglie	ha tolto	toglierà	toglieva
noi (we)	togliamo	abbiamo tolto	toglieremo	toglievamo
voi (you)	togliete	avete tolto	toglierete	toglievate
loro/Loro (they/ you, form. pl.)	tolgono	hanno tolto	toglieranno	toglievano

uscire (to go out)
Past Participle: uscito (went out) (with essere);
Present Gerund: uscendo (going out)

	Present	Present Perfect	Future	Imperfect
io (I)	esco	sono uscito/a	uscirò	uscivo
tu (you, inf.)	esci	sei uscito/a	uscirai	uscivi
lui/lei/Lei (he/ she/you, form.)	esce	è uscito/a	uscirà	usciva
noi (we)	usciamo	siamo usciti/e	usciremo	uscivamo
voi (you)	uscite	siete usciti/e	uscirete	uscivate
loro/Loro (they/ you, form. pl.)	escono	sono usciti/e	usciranno	uscivano

venire (to come)
Past Participle: venuto (come) (with essere);
Present Gerund: venendo (coming)

	Present	Present Perfect	Future	Imperfect
io (I)	vengo	sono venuto/a	verrò	venivo
tu (you, inf.)	vieni	sei venuto/a	verrai	venivi
lui/lei/Lei (he/ she/you, form.)	viene	è venuto/a	verrà	veniva
noi (we)	veniamo	siamo venuti/e	verremo	venivamo
voi (you)	venite	siete venuti/e	verrete	venivate
loro/Loro (they/ you, form. pl.)	vengono	sono venuti/e	verranno	venivano

Appendix B

Italian-English Mini-Dictionary

Key: m = masculine, f = feminine, s = singular, pl = plural

A

a (ah): at, in, to

a buon mercato (ah *bwohn* mehr-*kah*-toh): cheap

a destra (ah *dehs*-trah): (on the) right

a domani (ah doh-*mah*-nee): see you tomorrow

a dopo (ah *doh*-poh): see you later

a meno che (ah *meh*-noh keh): unless

a meno di (ah *meh*-noh dee): unless

a sinistra (ah see-*nees*-trah): (on the) left

abbastanza (ahb-bah-*stahn*-tsah): enough

abbigliamento (ahb-bee-lyah-*mehn*-toh) m: clothing

abitare (ah-bee-*tah*-reh): to live

abito (*ah*-bee-toh) m: suit

accessorio (ahch-chehs-*soh*-ryoh) m: accessory

acqua (*ahk*-kwah) f: water

acquistare (ah-kwee-*stah*-reh): to buy

acrilica (ah-*kree*-lee-kah) f; **acrilico** (ah-*kree*-lee-koh) m: acrylic

adesso (ah-*dehs*-soh): now

aereo (ah-*eh*-reh-oh) m: airplane

aeroporto (ah-eh-roh-*pohr*-toh) m: airport

affittare (un appartamento) (ahf-feet-*tah*-reh [oohn ahp-pahr-tah-*mehn*-toh]): to rent (an apartment)

agosto (ah-*gohs*-toh): August

aiuto (ah-*yooh*-toh): help

albergo (ahl-*behr*-goh) m: hotel

alcuno (ahl-*kooh*-noh) m, s; **alcuni** (ahl-*kooh*-nee) m, pl: a few; any; some

allevare (ahl-leh-*vah*-reh): to raise

allora (ahl-*loh*-rah): then

alta (*ahl*-tah) f; **alto** (*ahl*-toh) m: high; tall

amare (ah-*mah*-reh): to love

amaro (ah-*mah*-roh) m: bitter

ambiente (ahm-*byehn*-teh) m: environment

americana (ah-meh-ree-*kah*-nah) f; **americano** (ah-meh-ree-*kah*-noh) m: American

amica (ah-*mee*-kah) f; **amico** (ah-*mee*-koh) m: friend

amicizia (ah-mee-*chee*-tsyah) f: friendship

amore (ah-*moh*-reh) m: love

anche (*ahn*-keh): also

ancora (ahn-*koh*-rah): still; yet; more

andare (ahn-*dah*-reh): to go

andata (ahn-*dah*-tah) f: one-way (ticket)

andata e ritorno (ahn-*dah*-tah eh ree-*tohr*-noh) m: round trip

anno (*ahn*-noh) m: year

annoiare (ahn-noh-*yah*-reh): to bore

annuale (ahn-nooh-*ah*-leh): annual

annullare (ahn-noohl-*lah*-reh): to cancel

antica (ahn-*tee*-kah) f; **antico** (ahn-*tee*-koh) m: ancient

antipasti (ahn-tee-*pahs*-tee) m: appetizers

anziana (ahn-tsee-*ah*-nah) f; **anziano** (ahn-tsee-*ah*-noh) m: old (for persons)

appartamento (ahp-pahr-tah-*mehn*-toh) m: apartment

aprile (ah-*pree*-leh): April

aprire (ah-*pree*-reh): to open

architetto (ahr-kee-*teht*-toh) m: architect

arredamento (ahr-reh-dah-*mehn*-toh) m: furniture

arrivare (ahr-ree-*vah*-reh): to arrive

arrivederci (ahr-ree-veh-*dehr*-chee): see you; good-bye

arte (*ahr*-teh) f: art

articolo (ahr-*tee*-koh-loh) m: article

artigianale (ahr-tee-jah-*nah*-leh): handcrafted

artigianato (ahr-tee-jah-*nah*-toh) m: artisan craft

artistica (ahr-*tee*-stee-kah) f; **artistico** (ahr-*tee*-stee-koh) m: artistic

ascoltare (ah-skohl-*tah*-reh): to listen to

aspettare (ah-speht-*tah*-reh): to wait

assegno (ahs-*seh*-nyoh) m: check

attività (aht-tee-veeh-*tah*) f: activity

attore (aht-*toh*-reh) m: actor

attraente (aht-trah-*ehn*-teh): attractive

attraverso (aht-trah-*vehr*-soh): through

attrazione (aht-trah-*tsyoh*-neh) f: attraction

attrezzatura (aht-trehts-ah-*tooh*-rah) f: equipment

attrice (aht-*tree*-cheh) f: actress

attualità (aht-twah-lee-*tah*) f: current events

attualmente (aht-twahl-*mehn*-teh): currently; now

autista (ah-ooh-*tee*-stah) m: driver

autobus (*ou*-toh-boohs) m: bus

automobile (ou-toh-*moh*-bee-leh) f: car

avere (ah-*veh*-reh): to have

avere bisogno di (ah-*veh*-reh bee-*soh*-nyoh dee): to need

avvocato (ahv-voh-*kah*-toh) m: lawyer

B

bambina (bahm-*bee*-nah) f; **bambino** (bahm-*bee*-noh) m: child

banca (*bahn*-kah) f: bank

basso (*bahs*-soh) m: short; low

bella (*behl*-lah) f; **bello** (*behl*-loh) m: beautiful

bellezza (behl-*lehts*-tsah) f: beauty

bene (*beh*-neh): well; good

bere (*beh*-reh): to drink

bianca (*byahn*-kah) f; **bianco** (*byahn*-koh) m: white

bicchiere (beek-*kyeh*-reh) m: glass

bicicletta (bee-chee-*kleht*-tah) f: bicycle

biglietto (bee-*lyeht*-toh) m: ticket

birra (*beer*-rah) f: beer

blu (blooh) f/m: blue

borsa (*bohr*-sah) f: bag; handbag

bottiglia (boht-*tee*-lyah) f: bottle

braccio (*brahch*-choh) m: arm

brutto (*brooht*-toh) m: ugly

buffa (*boohf*-fah) f; **buffo** (*boohf*-foh) m: comic

buona (*bwoh*-nah) f; **buono** (*bwoh*-noh) m: good

buonanotte (*bwoh*-nah-*noht*-teh): good-night

buonasera (*bwoh*-nah-*seh*-rah): good evening

buongiorno (bwohn-*johr*-noh): good morning; good day

C

cadere (kah-*deh*-reh): to fall

caffè (kahf-*feh*) m: coffee

calcio (*kahl*-choh) m: soccer

calda (*kahl*-dah) f; **caldo** (*kahl*-doh) m: warm; hot

cambiare (kahm-bee-*ah*-reh): to change

cambio (*kahm*-byoh) m: conversion rate

cameriera (kah-meh-*ryeh*-rah) f: waitress

cameriere (kah-meh-*ryeh*-reh) m: waiter

camicia (kah-*mee*-chah) f: shirt

camminare (kahm-mee-*nah*-reh): to walk

campagna (kahm-*pah*-nyah) f: country; countryside

canadese (kah-nah-*deh*-zeh) f/m: Canadian

cancellare (kahn-chehl-*lah*-reh): to cancel

cancelleria (kahn-chel-leh-*ree*-ah) f: stationery

candidato (kahn-deeh-*dah*-toh) m: candidate

cane (*kah*-neh) m: dog

cantante (kahn-*tahn*-teh) m: singer

cantare (kahn-*tah*-reh): to sing

cantautore (kahn-tah-ooh-*toh*-reh) m: singer-songwriter

canzone (kahn-*tsoh*-neh) f: song

capelli (kah-*pehl*-lee) m, pl: hair

capolavoro (kah-poh-lah-*voh*-roh) m: masterpiece

cappello (kahp-*pehl*-loh) m: hat

cappotto (kahp-*poht*-toh) m: coat

cara (*kah*-rah) f; **caro** (*kah*-roh) m: dear; expensive

carina (kah-*ree*-nah) f; **carino** (kah-*ree*-noh) m: nice; pretty

carriera (kahr-*ryeh*-rah) f: career

carta (*kahr*-tah) f: paper; card

carta di credito (*kahr*-tah dee *kreh*-dee-toh) f: credit card

cattiva (kaht-*tee*-vah) f; **cattivo** (kaht-*tee*-voh) m: bad

casa (*kah*-zah) f: house; home

cassa (*kahs*-sah) f: cash register

cassetto (kahs-*seht*-toh) m: drawer

castello (kah-*stehl*-loh) m: castle

cavallino (kah-vahl-*lee*-noh) m: little horse

cavallo (kah-*vahl*-loh) m: horse

c'è (cheh): there is

cena (*cheh*-nah) f: dinner

censura (chehn-*sooh*-rah) f: censorship

cento (*chehn*-toh): hundred

ceramica (cheh-*rah*-mee-kah) f: ceramics

cercare (chehr-*kah*-reh): to look for; to try

cesto (*cheh*-stoh) m: basket

che (keh): that; who; whom; which; what

che cosa (keh *koh*-sah): what

che fai? (keh fahy?): what do you do?

chi (kee): who; those who

chiamare (kyah-*mah*-reh): to call

chiamarsi (kyah-*mahr*-see): for one's name to be

chiara (*kyah*-rah) f; **chiaro** (*kyah*-roh) m: light-colored; clear

chiudere (*kyooh*-deh-reh): to close; to shut

chiunque (*kyoohn*-qweh): anyone; whoever

ci (chee): here; there; us

ci sono (chee *soh*-noh): there are

ciao (chou): hello; good-bye

ciascuno (chah-*skooh*-noh) m: everyone

cinema (*chee*-neh-mah) m: cinema

cinquanta (cheen-*kwahn*-tah): fifty

cinque (*cheen*-kweh): five

cinta (*cheen*-tah) f: belt

cioccolata (choh-koh-*lah*-tah) f; **cioccolato** (chohk-koh-*lah*-toh) m: chocolate

circuito (cheer-*kooh*-ee-toh) m: circuit

città (cheet-*tah*) f: city; town

cittadina (cheet-tah-*dee*-nah) f; **cittadino** (cheet-tah-*dee*-noh) m: citizen

cliente (*klyehn*-teh) f/m: customer

codice postale (*koh*-dee-cheh pohs-*tah*-leh) m: zip code

colazione (koh-lah-*tsyoh*-neh) f: breakfast

collega (kohl-*leh*-ghah): co-worker

collo (*kohl*-loh) m: neck

colloquio (kohl-*loh*-kweeh-oh) m: interview

colore (koh-*loh*-reh) m: color

come (*koh*-meh): how

commedia (kohm-*meh*-dyah) f: comedy

commessa (kohm-*mehs*-sah) f; **commesso** (kohm-*mehs*-soh) m: sales clerk

comoda (*koh*-moh-dah) f; **comodo** (*koh*-moh-doh) m: comfortable

comportamento (kohm-pohr-tah-*mehn*-toh) m: behavior

comprare (kohm-*prah*-reh): to buy

con (kohn): with

condivisa (kohn-dee-*vee*-sah) f; **condiviso** (kohn-dee-*vee*-soh) m: shared

conoscere (koh-*noh*-sheh-reh): to be acquainted with; to know

contemporanea (kohn-tehm-poh-*rah*-neh-ah) f; **contemporaneo** (kohn-tehm-poh-*rah*-neh-oh) m: contemporary

contratto (kohn-*traht*-toh) m: contract

contro (*kohn*-troh): against

controllo (kohn-*trohl*-loh) f: control

coppa (*kohp*-pah) f: cup

correggere (kohr-*rehj*-jeh-reh): to correct

cosa (*koh*-sah): what

così (koh-*see*): so

costosa (koh-*stoh*-sah) f; **costoso** (koh-*stoh*-soh) m: expensive

costruire (koh-strooh-*ee*-reh): to build

costume da bagno (kohs-*tooh*-meh dah *bah*-nyoh) m: bathing suit

cotone (koh-*toh*-neh) m: cotton

cravatta (krah-*vaht*-tah) f: tie

credere (*kreh*-deh-reh): to believe

crema (*kreh*-mah) f: custard

crescere (*kreh*-sheh-reh): to grow

crescita (*kreh*-shee-tah) f: growth

critico (*kree*-tee-koh) m: critic

cultura (koohl-*too*-rah) f: culture

culturale (koohl-too-*rah*-leh): cultural

cuoio (*kwoh*-ee-oh) m: leather

cura (*kooh*-rah) f: care

curva (*koohr*-vah) f: curve

D

da (dah): by; from; through

da nessuna parte (dah nehs-*sooh*-nah *pahr*-teh): nowhere

da qualche parte (dah *kwahl*-keh *pahr*-teh): somewhere

da quando (dah *kwahn*-doh): ever since

d'accordo (dahk-*kohr*-doh): all right; okay

dai (dahy): come on

dappertutto (dahp-pehr-*tooht*-toh): everywhere

dare (*dah*-reh): to give

dare in prestito (*dah*-reh een *preh*-stee-toh): to loan

del (dehl) m; **dello** (*dehl*-loh) m; **della** (*dehl*-lah) f; **dei** (dehy) m, pl; **degli** (*deh*-lyee), m, pl; **delle** (*dehl*-leh) f, pl; **dell'** (dehl) m/f: a little; some of the

dentista (dehn-*tees*-tah) f/m: dentist

dentro (*dehn*-troh): inside

desiderare (deh-see-deh-*rah*-reh): to wish

dettaglio (deht-*tah*-lyoh) m: detail

di (dee): about; of; from

di fronte [a] (dee *frohn*-teh [ah]): in front of; before

di meno (dee *meh*-noh): less

di nuovo (dee *nwoh*-voh): again

di più (dee pyooh): more

di sotto (dee *soht*-toh): below

dialetto (dyah-*leht*-toh) m: dialect

dicembre (dee-*chehm*-breh): December

diciannove (dee-chahn-*noh*-veh): nineteen

diciassette (dee-chahs-*seht*-teh): seventeen

diciotto (dee-*choht*-toh): eighteen

dieci (*dyeh*-chee): ten

dietro a (*dyeh*-troh ah): behind

difendere (dee-*fehn*-deh-reh): to defend

difficile (deef-*fee*-chee-leh): difficult

dimenticare (dee-mehn-tee-*kah*-reh): to forget

dimenticarsi (dee-mehn-tee-*kahr*-see): to forget

dire (*dee*-reh): to say; to tell

discesa (dee-*sheh*-sah) f: descent

dito (*dee*-toh) m: finger

divorziare (dee-vohr-*tsyah*-reh): to divorce

dodici (*doh*-dee-chee): twelve

dolce (*dohl*-cheh) f/m: sweet

domani (doh-*mah*-nee): tomorrow

donare (doh-*nah*-reh): to give

donna (*dohn*-nah) f: woman

dopo (*doh*-poh): after

dormire (dohr-*mee*-reh): to sleep

dottore (doht-*toh*-reh) m: doctor

dove (*doh*-veh): where

dovere (doh-*veh*-reh): must; shall; to have to; to be obliged to

due (*dooh*-eh): two

E

e (eh): and

effettivamente (ehf-feht-tee-vah-*mehn*-teh): actually

eleganza (eh-leh-*gahn*-tsah) f: elegance

emergenza (eh-mehr-*jehn*-tsah) f: emergency

emittente radiofonica (eh-meet-*tehn*-teh rah-dyoh-*foh*-nee-kah) f: radio broadcaster

emittente televisiva (eh-meet-*tehn*-teh teh-leh-vee-*see*-vah) f: TV; broadcasting station; TV channel

entrare (ehn-*trah*-reh): to enter

entrata (ehn-*trah*-tah) f: entrance

essere (*ehs*-seh-reh): to be

essere abituato a (*ehs*-seh-reh ah-bee-*twah*-toh ah): to be used to

essere nato (*ehs*-seh-reh *nah*-toh): to be born

est (ehst) m: east

estetica (eh-*steh*-tee-kah) f: aesthetics

etichetta (eh-tee-*keht*-tah) f: etiquette

evento (eh-*vehn*-toh) m: event

F

faccia (*fahch*-chah) f: face

facile (*fah*-chee-leh): easy

fame (*fah*-meh) f: hunger

fare (*fah*-reh): to do; to make

febbraio (fehb-*brah*-yoh): February

fedeltà (feh-dehl-*tah*) f: fidelity

felice (feh-*lee*-cheh): happy

ferie (*feh*-ryeh) f: holidays

fermare (fehr-*mah*-reh): to stop

fermarsi (fehr-*mahr*-see): to stop

festa (*fehs*-tah) f: party; holiday

figlia (*fee*-lyah) f: daughter

figlio (*fee*-lyoh) m: son

figura (fee-*gooh*-rah) f: figure

fila (*fee*-lah) f: line

finché (feen-*keh*): until

fine (*fee*-neh) f: end

finestra (fee-*nehs*-trah) f: window

finire (fee-*nee*-reh): to end; to finish

fino a quando (*fee*-noh ah *kwahn*-doh): until

fiore (*fyoh*-reh) m: flower

firma (*feer*-mah) f: brand product

folla (*fohl*-lah) f: crowd

fonte (*fohn*-teh) m: source

forbici (*fohr*-bee-chee) f: scissors

formaggio (fohr-*mahj*-joh) m: cheese

forte (*fohr*-teh): strong; fast

fra (frah): among; between

fragola (*frah*-goh-lah) f: strawberry

fratello (frah-*tehl*-loh) m: brother

fredda (*frehd*-dah) f; **freddo** (*frehd*-doh) m: cold

fresca (*freh*-skah) f; **fresco** (*freh*-skoh) m: fresh; cool

frutta (*frooht*-tah) f: fruit

funzionalità (foohn-tsyo-nah-lee-*tah*) f: functionality

fuori (*fwoh*-ree): out; outside

G

gatto (*gaht*-toh) m: cat

gelato (jeh-*lah*-toh) m: ice cream

gennaio (jehn-*nah*-yoh): January

gente (*jehn*-teh) f: people

gentile (jehn-*tee*-leh) m: kind

ghiaccio (*gyahch*-choh) m: ice

già (jah) already

giacca (*jahk*-kah) f: jacket; blazer

gialla (*jahl*-lah) f; **giallo** (*jahl*-loh) m: yellow

giardino (jahr-*dee*-noh) m: garden

ginocchio (jee-*nohk*-kyoh) m: knee

giocare (joh-*kah*-reh): to play

gioco (*joh*-koh) m: game

gioiello (joh-*yehl*-loh) m: jewel

giornale (johr-*nah*-leh) m: newspaper

giorno (*johr*-noh) m: day

giovane (*joh*-vah-neh) f/m: young

giù (jooh) down

giugno (*jooh*-nyoh): June

giusta (*jooh*-stah) f; **giusto** (*jooh*-stoh) m: right; correct

gli (lyee): the

gonna (*gohn*-nah) f: skirt

grande (*grahn*-deh) f/m: great; big; large; tall

grande magazzino (*grahn*-deh mah-gaht-*tsee*-noh) m: department store

grassa (*grahs*-sah) f; **grasso** (*grahs*-soh) m: fat

grazie (*grah*-tsyeh): thank you

grigia (*gree*-jah) f; **grigio** (*gree*-joh) m: gray

grossa (*groh*-sah) f; **grosso** (*grohs*-soh) m: big

guanto (*gwahn*-toh) m: glove

guardare (gwahr-*dah*-reh): to watch; to look at

guidare (gwee-*dah*-reh): to drive

I

i (ee) m: the

ieri (*yeh*-ree): yesterday

il (eel) m: the

impermeabile (eem-pehr-meh-*ah*-bee-leh) m: raincoat

impiegata (eem-pyeh-*gah*-tah) f; **impiegato** (eem-pyeh-*gah*-toh) m: employee

imprenditorialità (eem-prehn-dee-toh-ree-ah-lee-*tah*) f: entrepreneurship

in, in (+ means of transportation) (een): in; at; to; by

in modo da (een *moh*-doh dah); **in modo che** (een *moh*-doh keh): so as

in fretta (een *freht*-tah): fast; quickly

in ritardo (een ree-*tahr*-doh): late

incominciare (een-koh-meehn-*chah*-reh) to begin; to start

incontrare (een-kohn-*trah*-reh): to meet

indirizzo (een-dee-*reet*-tsoh) m: address

indossare (een-dohs-*sah*-reh): to wear

infermiera (een-fehr-*myeh*-rah) f: nurse

informazione (een-fohr-mah-*tzyo*-neh) f: information

ingegnere (een-jeh-*nyeh*-reh) m: engineer

insalata (een-sah-*lah*-tah) f: salad

intelligente (een-tehl-lee-*jehn*-teh): intelligent

interessante (een-teh-rehs-*sahn*-teh): interesting

intervista (een-tehr-*vee*-stah): interview

intorno (een-*tohr*-noh): around

inventore (een-vehn-*toh*-reh) m: inventor

invito (een-*vee*-toh) m: invitation

io (*ee*-oh): I

italiana (ee-tah-lee-*ah*-nah) f; **italiano** (ee-tah-lee-*ah*-noh) m: Italian

J

jeans (jeenz) m: jeans

L

l' (l-) f/m: the

la (lah): the

là (lah): there

lago (*lah*-goh) m: lake

lana (*lah*-nah) f: wool

larga (*lahr*-gah) f; **largo** (*lahr*-goh) m: wide; large

lasciare (lah-*shah*-reh): to leave; to let

latte (*laht*-teh) m: milk

lavorare (lah-voh-*rah*-reh): to work

lavoratore (lah-voh-rah-*toh*-reh) m: worker

lavoratrice (lah-voh-rah-*tree*-cheh) f: worker

lavoro (lah-*voh*-roh) m: work; job

le (leh): the

lei (lehy) f: she; her; you (formal)

lentamente (lehn-tah-*mehn*-teh): slowly

lettino (leht-*teeh*-noh) m: cot

lì (lee): there

libretto (lee-*breht*-toh) m: opera libretto

libro (*lee*-broh) m: book

lingua (*leen*-gwah) f: language; tongue

lino (*lee*-noh) m: linen

lo (loh) m: the

lontano (lohn-*tah*-noh) m: far

loro (*loh*-roh) m: they; them; their; **[il] loro** ([eel] *loh*-roh) m: theirs

luglio (*looh*-lyoh): July

lui (*looh*-ee) m: he; him

M

ma (mah): but

macchina (*mahk*-kee-nah) f: car

madre (*mah*-dreh) f: mother

maggio (*mahj*-joh): May

magra (*mah*-grah) f; **magro** (*mah*-groh) m: thin; skinny

mai (mahy): ever; never

malata (mah-*lah*-tah) f; **malato** (mah-*lah*-toh) m: ill

male (*mah*-leh) badly

malvolentieri (mahl-voh-lehn-*tyeh*-ree): unwillingly

mamma (*mahm*-mah) f: mom

mandare (mahn-*dah*-reh): to send

mangiare (mahn-*jah*-reh): to eat

maniere (mah-nee-*eh*-reh) f, pl: behavior; manners

mano (*mah*-noh) f: hand

marca (*mahr*-kah) f: brand of product

mare (*mah*-reh) m: sea

marito (mah-*ree*-toh) m: husband

marrone (mahr-*roh*-neh) f/m: brown

marzo (*mahr*-tsoh): March

massimo (*mahs*-see-moh) most

materiale (mah-teh-*ryah*-leh) m: material

matita (mah-*tee*-tah) f: pencil

me (meh): me

medicina (meh-dee-*chee*-nah) f: medicine

medico (*meh*-dee-koh) m: physician

meglio (*meh*-lyoh): better

meno (*meh*-noh): less

meno che (*meh*-noh keh): less than

meno di (*meh*-noh dee): less than

mensile (mehn-*see*-leh) m: monthly; monthly magazine

mentre (*mehn*-treh): while; whereas

menzionare (mehn-tsyoh-*nah*-reh): to bring up

mercatino (mehr-kah-*tee*-noh) m: small outdoor market

mercato (mehr-*kah*-toh) m: market

merce (*mehr*-cheh) f: goods

merletto (mehr-*leht*-toh) m: lace

mese (*meh*-zeh) m: month

metafora (meh-*tah*-foh-rah) f: metaphor

metropolitana (meh-troh-poh-lee-*tah*-nah) f: subway

mettere (*meht*-teh-reh): to put

mettersi (*meht*-tehr-see): to wear

mezzi di comunicazione di massa (*meht*-tsee dee koh-mooh-nee-kah-*tsyoh*-neh dee *mahs*-sah) m: media

mia (myah) f; **[la] mia** ([lah] myah) f; **mie** (myeh) f, pl; **[le] mie** ([leh] myeh) f, pl; **miei** (*myehy*) m, pl; **[i] miei** ([ee] myehy), m, pl; **mio** (myoh) m; **[Il] mio** ([eel] myoh) m: my; mine

migliore (mee-*lyoh*-reh): better

mille (*meel*-leh): thousand

minima (*meeh*-neeh-mah) f; **minimo** (*meeh*-neeh-moh) m: minimum; least

misura (mee-*sooh*-rah) f: measurement

moda (*moh*-dah) f: fashion

modernizzazione (moh-dehr-neet-tsah-*tsyoh*-neh) f: modernization

moglie (*moh*-lyeh) f: wife

molta (*mohl*-tah) f; **molte** (*mohl*-teh) f; **molti** (*mohl*-tee) m; **molto** (*mohl*-toh) m: very; much; many; a lot

montagna (mohn-*tah*-nyah) f: mountain

morire (moh-*ree*-reh): to die

motore (moh-*toh*-reh) m: engine

mucchio (*moohk*-kyoh) m: pile

muovere (*mwoh*-veh-reh); **muoversi** (*mwoh*-vehr-see): to move

museo (mooh-*seh*-oh) m: museum

musica (*mooh*-see-kah) f: music

musicale (mooh-see-*kah*-leh): musical

musicista (mooh-see-*chee*-stah) m: musician

N

nascere (*nah*-sheh-reh): to be born

naso (*nah*-zoh) m: nose

naturale (nah-tooh-*rah*-leh): natural

nazionale (nah-tsyoh-*nah*-leh): national

ne (neh): of this; of that; of him; of them

né . . . né (neh . . . neh): neither . . . nor

nebbia (*nehb*-byah) f: fog

negozio (neh-*goh*-tsyoh) m: shop

negozio di scarpe (neh-*goh*-tsyoh dee *skahr*-peh): shoe store

nera (*neh*-rah) f; **nero** (*neh*-roh) m: black

nessuna (nehs-*sooh*-nah) f; **nessuno** (nehs-*sooh*-noh) m: no one; nobody; none

neve (*neh*-veh) f: snow

niente (*nyehn*-teh): nothing

no (noh): no

noi (nohy): we; us

noiosa (no-*yoh*-zah) f; **noioso** (no-*yoh*-zoh) m: boring

noleggiare (un'automobile) (noh-lej-*jah*-reh [oohn ou-toh-*moh*-bee-leh]): to rent (a car)

nome (*noh*-meh) m: name

non (nohn): not

non ancora (nohn ahn-*koh*-rah): not yet

non appena (nohn ahp-*peh*-nah): as soon as

non . . . mai (nohn mahy): never

nord (nohrd) m: north

nostra (*noh*-strah) f; **[la] nostra** ([lah] *noh*-strah) f; **nostre** (*noh*-streh) f, pl; **[le] nostre** [leh] *noh*-streh) f, pl; **nostri** (*noh*-stree) m, pl; **[i] nostri** ([ee] *noh*-stree) m, pl; **nostro** (*noh*-stroh) m; **[il] nostro** ([eel] *noh*-stroh) m: our; ours

Book VI

Appendixes

notizie (noh-*tee*-tsyeh) f: news

notizie d'attualità (noh-*tee*-tsyeh daht-tooh-ah-lee-*tah*) f: current events

notizie economiche (noh-*tee*-tsyeh eh-koh-*noh*-mee-keh) f: economic news

notizie sportive (noh-*tee*-tsyeh spohr-*tee*-veh) f: sports news

notte (*noht*-teh) f: night

nove (*noh*-veh): nine

novembre (noh-*vehm*-breh): November

nulla (*noohl*-lah): nothing

numero (*nooh*-meh-roh) m: number

nuoto (*nwoh*-toh) m: swimming

nuova (*nwoh*-vah) f; **nuovo** (*nwoh*-voh) m: new

O

o (oh): or

o . . . o (oh . . . oh): either . . . or

occhio (*ohk*-kyoh) m: eye

odiare (oh-*dyah*-reh): to hate

offrire (ohf-*free*-reh): to offer

oggetto (ohj-*jeht*-toh) m: object

opera (*oh*-peh-rah) f: opera

opportunità (ohp-pohr-tooh-nee-*tah*) f: opportunity

ora (*oh*-rah) f: hour; now

orecchio (oh-*rehk*-kyoh) m: ear

origine (oh-*ree*-jee-neh) f: origin

ospedale (ohs-peh-*dah*-leh) m: hospital

ostile (oh-*stee*-leh): hostile

ottenere (oht-teh-*neh*-reh): to get

ottima (*oht*-tee-mah) f; **ottimo** (*oht*-tee-moh) m: best

otto (*oht*-toh): eight

ottobre (oht-*toh*-breh): October

ovest (*oh*-vehst) m: west

P

padre (*pah*-dreh) m: father

pagamento (pah-gah-*mehn*-toh) m: payment

palazzo (pah-*laht*-tsoh) m: palace

palcoscenico (pahl-koh-*sheh*-nee-koh) m: stage

panca (*pahn*-kah) f: bench

pane (*pah*-neh) m: bread

panna (*pahn*-nah) f: cream

pantaloni (pahn-tah-*loh*-nee) m, pl: pants; trousers

parecchia (pah-*rehk*-kyah) f; **parecchio** (pah-*rehk*-kyoh) m: a lot; several

parete (pah-*reh*-teh) f: wall

parlare (pahr-*lah*-reh): to talk; to speak

partire (pahr-*tee*-reh): to leave; to go on a trip

partita (pahr-*tee*-tah) f: game

passante (pahs-*sahn*-teh) m: passerby

passaporto (pahs-sah-*pohr*-toh) m: passport

passare (pahs-*sah*-reh): to pass

pasticceria (pahs-teech-cheh-*ree*-ah) f: pastry shop

patrimonio (pah-tree-*mohn*-yoh) m: heritage

pausa (*pah*-ooh-sah) f: break

peggio (*pehj*-joh): worse

peggiore (pehj-*joh*-reh): worse

penna (*pehn*-nah) f: pen

pensare (pehn-*sah*-reh): to think

per (pehr): for; through

per favore (pehr fah-*voh*-reh): please

perché (pehr-*keh*): because; why

perdere (*pehr*-deh-reh): to lose

perdonare (pehr-doh-*nah*-reh): to forgive

periodico (peh-*ryoh*-dee-koh) m: periodical publication

pesce (*peh*-sheh) m: fish

pessima (*pehs*-see-mah) f; **pessimo** (*pehs*-see-moh) m: worst

piacere (pyah-*cheh*-reh): to like; nice to meet you; pleasure

piano (*pyah*-noh): slowly

piazza (*pyaht*-tsah) f: square

piccola (*peek*-koh-lah) f; **piccolo** (*peek*-koh-loh) m: small; short

pilota (pee-*loh*-tah) m: pilot

pioggia (*pyohj*-jah) f: rain

piove (*pyoh*-veh): it's raining

pista (*pee*-stah) f: race track

pittore (peet-*toh*-reh) f: painter

più (pyooh): more

più che (pyooh keh): more than

più di (pyooh dee): more than

poca (*poh*-kah) f; **poco** (*poh*-koh) m: too little; small

poche (*poh*-keh) f; **pochi** (*poh*-kee) m: few

podio (*poh*-dee-oh) m: podium

poesia (poh-eh-*see*-ah) f: poetry

poeta (poh-*eh*-tah) m: poet

poi (*poh*-ee): then

poiché (poh-ee-*keh*): since; as

politica (poh-*lee*-tee-kah) f: politics; political

politico (poh-*lee*-tee-koh) m: political

polizia (poh-lee-*tsee*-ah) f: police

popolare (poh-poh-*lah*-reh): popular

portafoglio (pohr-tah-*foh*-lyoh) m: wallet

portare (pohr-*tah*-reh): to bring; to take; to wear

possedere (pohs-seh-*deh*-reh): to own

potere (poh-*teh*-reh): can; may

pranzare (prahn-*tsah*-reh): to eat lunch

pranzo (*prahn*-tsoh) m: lunch

preferire (preh-feh-*ree*-reh): to prefer

prego (*preh*-goh): you're welcome

prendere (*prehn*-deh-reh): to take; to order (such as in a bar or restaurant)

prendere a prestito (*prehn*-deh-reh ah *preh*-stee-toh): to borrow; to loan

prenotare (preh-noh-*tah*-reh): to reserve; to book

presentare (preh-zehn-*tah*-reh): to introduce

presto (*preh*-stoh): early; soon

prevenzione (preh-vehn-*tsyoh*-neh) f: prevention

prima (*pree*-mah) f: before

primo (*pree*-moh) m: first

prodotto (proh-*doht*-toh) m: product

professionale (proh-fehs-see-oh-*nah*-leh) professional

profumeria (proh-fooh-meh-*ree*-ah) f: beauty shop

programma (proh-*grahm*-mah) m: program; TV show

programma radiofonici (proh-*grahm*-mah rah-dee-oh-*foh*-nee-chee) f: radio program

prossimo (*prohs*-see-moh): next

provare (proh-*vah*-reh): to try

pubblica (*poohb*-blee-kah) f: public

pubblico (*poohb*-blee-koh) m: audience; public

pulire (pooh-*lee*-reh): to clean

punti di vista (*poohn*-teeh dee *veehs*-tah): points of view

Q

qualcosa (kwahl-*koh*-sah): anything; something

qualcuno (kwahl-*kooh*-noh): someone; somebody

quale (*kwah*-leh) f/m; **[il] quale** ([eel] *kwah*-leh) m; **[la] quale** ([lah] *kwah*-leh) f; **[i] quali** ([ee] *kwah*-lee) m; **[le] quali** ([leh] *kwah*-lee) f: which; what; who; that

qualità (kwah-lee-*tah*) f: quality

qualsiasi cosa (kwahl-*see*-ah-see *koh*-sah): anything

quando (*kwahn*-doh): when

quanta (*kwahn*-tah) f; **quante** (*kwahn*-teh) f; **quanti** (*kwahn*-tee) m; **quanto** (*kwahn*-toh) m: how much; how many; as much; as many

quante (*kwahn*-teh) f; **quanti** (*kwahn*-tee) m: all those who

quartiere (kwar-*tyeh*-reh) m: neighborhood

quattordici (kwaht-*tohr*-dee-chee) m: fourteen

quattro (*kwaht*-troh) m: four

quella (*kwehl*-lah) f; **quello** (*kwehl*-loh) m: that

questa (*kweh*-stah) f; **questo** (*kweh*-stoh) m: this

qui (kwee): here

quindici (*kween*-dee-chee): fifteen

quotidiano (kwoh-tee-*dyah*-noh) m: daily newspaper

R

raccontare (rahk-kohn-*tah*-reh): to tell

radio (*rah*-dyoh) f: radio

ragazza (rah-*gaht*-tsah) f: girl

ragazzo (rah-*gaht*-tsoh) m: boy

rampante (rahm-*pahn*-teh): prancing

rapidamente (rah-pee-dah-*mehn*-teh): quickly; fast

rapporto (rahp-*pohr*-toh) m: relationship

raso (*rah*-soh) m: satin

regista (reh-*jee*-stah) m: movie director

regola (*reh*-goh-lah) f: rule

restituire (reh-stee-tooh-*ee*-reh): to give back; to return

retaggio (reh-*tahj*-joh) m: heritage

ricevere (ree-*cheh*-veh-reh): to receive; to get

richiamare (ree-*kyah*-mah-reh): to call back; recall

ricordare (ree-kohr-*dah*-reh): to remember

ricordare qualcosa a qualcuno (ree-kohr-*dah*-reh kwahl-*koh*-sah ah kwahl-*kooh*-noh): to remind someone of something

ricordarsi (ree-kohr-*dahr*-see): to remember

ridere (*ree*-deh-reh): to laugh

ringraziare (reen-grah-*tsyah*-reh): to thank

ripetere (ree-*peh*-teh-reh): to repeat

ripetitiva (reeh-peh-teeh-*teeh*-vah) f; **ripetitivo** (reeh-peh-teeh-*teeh*-voh): repetitive

riposo (reeh-*poh*-soh) m: rest

riso (*ree*-zoh) m: rice; laughter

rispondere (ree-*spohn*-deh-reh): to answer

ritornare (ree-tohr-*nah*-reh): to return

ritornello (ree-tohr-*nehl*-loh) m: refrain

riunione (ree-ooh-*nyoh*-neh) f: meeting

riuscire (ree-ooh-*shee*-reh): to succeed

rivista (ree-*vee*-stah) f: magazine

rossa (*rohs*-sah) f; **rosso** (*rohs*-soh) m: red

S

saldi (*sahl*-dee) m, pl: sales

sale (*sah*-leh) m: salt

salita (sah-*lee*-tah) f: climb

sapere (sah-*peh*-reh): to know

scarpa (*skahr*-pah) f: shoe

scegliere (sheh-*lyeh*-reh): to choose

scenica (*sheh*-nee-kah) f; **scenico** (*sheh*-nee-koh) m: related to stage

schedario (skeh-*dah*-ree-oh) m: file cabinet

scienziato (shehn-*zyah*-toh) m: scientist

scrivania (skree-vah-*nee*-ah) f: desk

scultore (skoohl-*toh*-reh) m: sculptor

scura (*skooh*-rah) f; **scuro** (*skooh*-roh) m: dark

se (seh): if; whether

sebbene (sehb-*beh*-neh): although; even though

sedia (*seh*-dyah) f: chair

sedici (*seh*-dee-chee): sixteen

segretaria (seh-greh-*tah*-ree-ah) f; **segretario** (seh-greh-*tah*-ree-oh) m: secretary

sei (sey): six

sempre (*sehm*-preh): always

sentire (sehn-*tee*-reh): to hear

senza (*sehn*-tsah): without

seria (*seh*-ryah) f; **serio** (*seh*-ryoh) m: serious

seta (*seh*-tah) f: silk

sete (*seh*-teh) f: thirst

sette (*seht*-teh): seven

settembre (seht-*tehm*-breh): September

settimana (seht-tee-*mah*-nah) f: week

settimanale (seht-tee-mah-*nah*-leh) m: weekly; weekly magazine

si (see): one; we; they

sì (see): yes

sia . . . sia (syah . . . syah): both . . . and

sicurezza (see-kuh-*reht*-tsah) f: safety

signora (see-*nyoh*-rah) f: Mrs.; Ms.; woman

signore (see-*nyoh*-reh) m: Mr.; gentleman

sintetica (seehn-*teh*-tee-kah) f; **sintetico** (seehn-*teh*-tee-koh) m: synthetic

sociale (soh-*chah*-leh): social

società (soh-cheh-*tah*) f: society

socio (*soh*-choh) m: member

soldi (*sohl*-dee) m, pl: money

sole (*soh*-leh) m: sun

solo (*soh*-loh): only; just

sopra (*soh*-prah): over

sorella (soh-*rehl*-lah) f: sister

sorpasso (sohr-*pahs*-soh) m: overtaking

sotto (*soht*-toh): below

spalla (*spahl*-lah) f: shoulder

spaventare (spah-vehn-*tah*-reh): to frighten

spedire (speh-*dee*-reh): to send; to ship

spendere (*spehn*-deh-reh): to spend

sperare (speh-*rah*-reh): to hope

spesso (*spehs*-soh): often

spillatrice (speel-lah-*tree*-cheh) f: stapler

sposare (spoh-*sah*-reh): to marry

sposarsi (spoh-*sahr*-see): to get married

stadio (*stah*-dee-oh) m: stadium

stanca (*stahn*-kah) f; **stanco** (*stahn*-koh) m: tired

Book VI

Appendixes

stanza (*stahn*-tsah) f: room

stare (*stah*-reh): to stay

stazione (stah-*tsyoh*-neh) f: station

stessa (*stehs*-sah) f; **stesso** (*stehs*-soh) m: same

stilista (stee-*lee*-stah) m: fashion designer

stipendio (steeh-*pehn*-dyoh) m: salary

stoffa (*stohf*-fah) f: fabric

storica (*stoh*-ree-kah) f; **storico** (*stoh*-ree-koh) m: historic

strada (*strah*-dah) f: street; road

stretta (*streht*-tah) f; **stretto** (*streht*-toh) m: tight; narrow

studente (stooh-*dehn*-teh) m: student

studentessa (stooh-dehn-*tehs*-sah) f: student

studio (*stooh*-dee-oh) m: office; study room

stupida (*stooh*-pee-dah) f; **stupido** (*stooh*-pee-doh) m: stupid

su (sooh): on; up; over

sua (swah) f; **[la] sua** ([lah] swah) f; **sue** (sweh) f, pl; **[le] sue** ([leh] sweh) f, pl; **suo** (swoh) m; **[il] suo** ([eel] swoh) m; **suoi** (swohy) m, pl; **[i] suoi** ([ee] swohy) m, pl: his; her; hers; its

successo (sooch-*chehs*-soh) m: success

sud (soohd): south

sughero (*sooh*-gheh-roh) m: cork

suonare (swoh-*nah*-reh): to play; to ring

supermercato (*sooh*-pehr-mehr-*kah*-toh) m: supermarket

T

tanta (*tahn*-tah) f; **tante** (*tahn*-teh) f; **tanti** (*tahn*-tee) m; **tanto** (*tahn*-toh) m: as much, so much, as many, so many

tardi (*tahr*-dee): late

tassa (*tahs*-sah) f: tax

tavolo (*tah*-voh-loh) m: table

tazza (*taht*-tsah) f: cup

te (teh): you

teatro (teh-*ah*-troh) m: theater

telefonare (teh-leh-foh-*nah*-reh): to call; to telephone

telefono (teh-*leh*-foh-noh) m: phone

televisiva (teh-leh-vee-*see*-vah) f; **televisivo** (teh-leh-vee-*see*-voh) m: TV

tema (*teh*-mah) m: theme

tempo (*tehm*-poh) m: time; weather

tenere (teh-*neh*-reh): to hold; to keep

tenuta (teh-*nooh*-tah) f: estate

territorio (tehr-ree-*toh*-ree-oh) m: territory

testo (*teh*-stoh) m: lyrics

tifosa (tee-*foh*-sah) f; **tifoso** (tee-*foh*-soh) m: supporter

tirare su (tee-*rah*-reh sooh): to bring up; to pull; to throw

titolo (*tee*-toh-loh) m: title

tra (trah): among; between

tradizione (trah-dee-*tsyoh*-neh) f: tradition

tragica (*trah*-jee-kah) f; **tragico** (*trah*-jee-koh) m: tragic

trama (*trah*-mah) f: plot

tre (treh): three

tredici (*treh*-dee-chee): thirteen

treno (*treh*-noh) m: train

triste (*tree*-steh): sad

troppo (*trohp*-poh): too much

trovare (troh-*vah*-reh): to find

trovata (troh-*vah*-tah) f: trick

trucco (*troohk*-koh) m: trick

tu (tooh): you

tua (twah) f; **[la] tua** ([lah] twah) f; **tue** (tweh) f, pl; **[le] tue** ([leh] tweh) f, pl; **tuo** (twoh) m; **[il] tuo** ([eel] twoh) m; **tuoi** (twohy) m, pl; **[i] tuoi** ([ee] twohy) m, pl: your; yours

turista (tooh-*ree*-stah) m: tourist

turistica (tooh-*ree*-stee-kah) f; **turistico** (tooh-*ree*-stee-koh) m: touristic

turpiloquio (toohr-pee-*loh*-kwyoh) m: foul language

tutta (*tooht*-tah) f; **tutto** (*tooht*-toh) m: everything; all

tutte (*tooht*-teh) f; **tutti** (*tooht*-tee) m: everyone; all

U

ufficio (oohf-*fee*-choh) m: office

ultima (*oohl*-tee-mah) f; **ultimo** (*oohl*-tee-moh) m: last; latest

umile (*ooh*-mee-leh): humble

un (oohn) m; **una** (*ooh*-nah) f; **uno** (*ooh*-noh) m: a; an; one

un po' (oohn poh): a little

un po' di (oohn poh dee): a little of

uomo (*woh*-moh) m: man

usare (ooh-*sah*-reh): to use

uscire (ooh-*shee*-reh): to exit; to go out

uscita (ooh-*shee*-tah) f: exit

V

vacanza (vah-*kahn*-tsah) f: vacation

valigia (vah-*lee*-jah) f: suitcase

varietà (vah-ryeh-*tah*) f: variety

vecchia (*vehk*-kyah) f; **vecchio** (*vehk*-kyoh) m: old

vedere (veh-*deh*-reh): to see

velluto (vehl-*looh*-toh) m: velvet

veloce (veh-*loh*-cheh): fast; quick

velocemente (veh-loh-cheh-*mehn*-teh): fast; quickly

velocità (veh-loh-chee-*tah*) f: speed

vendere (*vehn*-deh-reh): to sell

venire (veh-*nee*-reh): to come

venti (*vehn*-tee): twenty

verde (*vehr*-deh) f/m: green

verdura (vehr-*dooh*-rah) f: vegetables

verso (*vehr*-soh): toward

vestito (vehs-*tee*-toh) m: dress

vetrina (veh-*tree*-nah) f: shop window

vetro (*veh*-troh) m: glass

via (*vee*-ah) f: street; road

viaggiare (vyahj-*jah*-reh): to travel

viaggio (*vyahj*-joh) m: travel

viale (vee-*ah*-leh) m: avenue

vicino (vee-*chee*-noh): near; close

vino (*vee*-noh) m: wine

virtù (veer-*tooh*) f: virtue

vittoria (veet-*toh*-ree-ah) f: victory

vivere (*vee*-veh-reh): to live

voi (*voh*-ee): you

volare (voh-*lah*-reh): to fly

volentieri (voh-lehn-*tyeh*-ree): gladly

volere (voh-*leh*-reh): to want; will

vostra (*voh*-strah) f; **[la] vostra** ([lah] *voh*-strah) f; **vostro** (*voh*-stroh) m; **[il] vostro** ([eel] *voh*-stroh) m: your; yours

Z

zero (*dzeh*-roh): zero

zia (*dzee*-ah) f: ant

zio (*dzee*-oh) m: uncle

zona (*dzoh*-nah) f: area

zucchero (*dzoohk*-keh-roh) m: sugar

Appendix C

English-Italian Mini-Dictionary

Key: m = masculine, f = feminine, s = singular, pl = plural

A

a: **un** (oohn) m; **una** (*ooh*-nah) f; **uno** (*ooh*-noh) m

about: **di** (deeh)

above: **sopra** (*soh*-prah); **di sopra** (dee *soh*-prah)

accessory: **accessorio** (ahch-chehs-*soh*-ree-oh) m

acrylic: **acrilica** (ah-*kree*-lee-kah) f; **acrilico** (ah-*kree*-lee-koh) m

actor: **attore** (aht-*toh*-reh) m

actress: **attrice** (aht-*tree*-cheh) f

actually: **effettivamente** (ehf-feht-tee-vah-*mehn*-teh)

address: **indirizzo** (een-dee-*reet*-tsoh) m

aesthetics: **estetica** (eh-*steh*-tee-kah) f

after: **dopo** (*doh*-poh)

again: **di nuovo** (dee nooh-*oh*-voh)

against: **contro** (*kohn*-troh)

airplane: **aereo** (ah-*eh*-reh-oh) m

airport: **aeroporto** (ah-eh-roh-*pohr*-toh) m

all: **tutto** (*tooht*-toh) m; **tutti** (*tooht*-tee) m, pl

all right: **d'accordo** (dahk-*kohr*-doh)

already: **già** (*jah*)

also: **anche** (*ahn*-keh)

although: **sebbene** (sehb-*beh*-neh)

always: **sempre** (*sehm*-preh)

American: **americana** (ah-meh-ree-*kah*-nah) f; **americano** (ah-meh-ree-*kah*-noh) m

among: **tra** (trah); **fra** (frah)

an: **un** (oohn) m; **una** (*ooh*-nah) f; **uno** (*ooh*-noh) m

ancient: **antica** (ahn-*tee*-kah) f; **antico** (ahn-*tee*-koh) m

and: **e** (eh)

to answer: **rispondere** (ree-*spohn*-deh-reh)

any: **alcuno** (ahl-*kooh*-noh) m; **alcuni** (ahl-*kooh*-nee) m, pl

anyone: **chiunque** (kee-*oohn*-qweh)

anything: **qualcosa** (qwahl-*koh*-sah); **qualsiasi cosa** (qwahl-*see*-ah-see *koh*-sah)

apartment: **appartamento** (ahp-pahr-tah-*mehn*-toh) m

appetizers: **antipasti** (ahn-tee-*pahs*-tee) m

April: **aprile** (ah-*pree*-leh)

architect: **architetto** (ahr-kee-*teht*-toh) m

area: **zona** (*dzoh*-nah) f

arm: **braccio** (*brahch*-choh) m

around: **intorno** (eehn-*tohr*-noh)

to arrive: **arrivare** (ahr-ree-*vah*-reh)

art: **arte** (*ahr*-teh) f

artisancraft: **artigianato** (ahr-tee-jah-*nah*-toh) m

artistic: **artistica** (ahr-*tee*-stee-kah) f; **artistico** (ahr-*tee*-stee-koh) m

as many: **quanto** (*qwahn*-toh) m; **quanti** (*qwahn*-tee) m, pl; **tanto** (*tahn*-toh) m; **tanti** (*tahn*-tee) m, pl

as much: **quanto** (*qwahn*-toh) m; **quanti** (*qwahn*-tee) m, pl; **tanto** (*tahn*-toh) m; **tanti** (*tahn*-tee) m, pl

as soon as: **non appena** (nohn ahp-*peh*-nah)

at: **a** (ah); **in** (een)

attraction: **attrazione** (aht-trah-*tsyoh*-neh) f

attractive: **attraente** (aht-trah-*ehn*-teh)

audience: **pubblico** (*poohb*-blee-koh) m

August: **agosto** (ah-*gohs*-toh)

aunt: **zia** (*dzee*-ah) f

avenue: **viale** (vee-*ah*-leh) m

B

bad: **cattiva** (kaht-*tee*-vah) f; **cattivo** (kaht-*tee*-voh) m

badly: **male** (*mah*-leh)

bag: **borsa** (*bohr*-sah) f

bakery: **pasticceria** (pahs-teech-cheh-*ree*-ah) f; panificio (pah-nee-*fee*-choh) f

bank: **banca** (*bahn*-kah) f

basket: **cesto** (*cheh*-stoh) m

bathing suit: **costume da bagno** (kohs-*tooh*-meh dah *bah*-nyoh) m

to be: **essere** (*ehs*-seh-reh)

to be able to: **potere** (poh-*teh*-reh)

to be born: **nascere** (*nah*-sheh-reh); **essere nato** (*eh*-seh-reh *nah*-toh)

to be used to: **essere abituato a** (*ehs*-seh-reh ah-bee-*twah*-toh ah)

beach: **spiaggia** (*spyahj*-jah) f

beautiful: **bella** (*behl*-lah) f; **bello** (*behl*-loh) m

beauty: **bellezza** (behl-*lehts*-tsah) f

beauty shop: **profumeria** (proh-foo-meh-*ree*-ah) f

because: **perché** (pehr-*keh*)

beer: **birra** (*beer*-rah) f

before: **prima** (*pree*-mah); **di fronte [a]** (dee *frohn*-teh [ah])

to begin: **incominciare** (eehn-koh-meehn-*chah*-reh)

behavior: **comportamento** (kohm-pohr-tah-*mehn*-toh) m; **maniere** (mah-*nyeh*-reh) f, pl

behind: **dietro a** (*dyeh*-troh ah)

to believe: **credere** (*kreh*-deh-reh)

below: **sotto** (*soht*-toh); **di sotto** (dee *soht*-toh)

belt: **cinta** (*cheen*-tah) f; **cintura** (cheen-*tooh*-rah) f

bench: **panca** (*pahn*-kah)

best: **ottimo** (*oht*-tee-moh)

better: **meglio** (*meh*-lyoh), **migliore** (mee-*lyoh*-reh)

between: **tra** (trah); **fra** (frah)

bicycle: **bicicletta** (bee-chee-*kleht*-tah) f

big: **grossa** (*groh*-sah) f; **grosso** (*grohs*-soh) m; **grande** (*grahn*-deh) f/m

bitter: **amara** (ah-*mah*-rah) f; **amaro** (ah-*mah*-roh) m

black: **nera** (*neh*-rah) f; **nero** (*neh*-roh) m

blazer: **giacca** (*jahk*-kah) f

blue: **blu** (blooh) f/m

book: **libro** (*lee*-broh) m

to bore: **annoiare** (ahn-noh-*yah*-reh)

boring: **noiosa** (noh-*yoh*-sah) f; **noioso** (noh-*yoh*-soh) m

to borrow: **prendere in prestito** (*prehn*-deh-reh een *preh*-stee-toh)

both . . . and . . .: **sia . . . sia . . .** (syah . . . syah . . .)

bottle: **bottiglia** (boht-*tee*-lyah) f

boy: **ragazzo** (rah-*gaht*-tsoh) m

brand of luxury merchandise: **sartoria** (sahr-toh-*ree*-ah)

brand of product: **firma** (*feer*-mah) f; **marca** (*mahr*-kah) f

bread: **pane** (*pah*-neh) m

break: **pausa** (*pah*-ooh-sah) f

breakfast: **colazione** (koh-lah-*tsyoh*-neh) f

to bring: **portare** (pohr-*tah*-reh)

to bring up: **tirare su** (tee-*rah*-reh sooh); **menzionare** (mehn-tsyoh-*nah*-reh)

brother: **fratello** (frah-*tehl*-loh) m

brown: **marrone** (mahr-*roh*-neh) f/m

to build: **costruire** (koh-strooh-*ee*-reh)

bus: **autobus** (*ou*-toh-boohs) m

but: **ma** (mah)

to buy: **comprare** (kohm-*prah*-reh); **acquistare** (ah-kwee-*stah*-reh)

by: **da** (dah); **in** (+ means of transportation) (een)

C

to call: **chiamare** (kyah-*mah*-reh); **telefonare** (teh-leh-foh-*nah*-reh)

to call back: **richiamare** (ree-kyah-*mah*-reh)

can: **potere** (poh-*teh*-reh)

Canadian: **canadese** (kah-nah-*deh*-zeh) f/m

to cancel: **annullare** (ahn-noohl-*lah*-reh); **cancellare** (kahn-chehl-*lah*-reh); **disdire** (dees-*dee*-reh)

candidate: **candidato** (kahn-deeh-*dah*-toh) m

car: **automobile** (ou-toh-*moh*-bee-leh) f; **macchina** (*mahk*-kee-nah) f

card: **carta** (*kahr*-tah) f

career: **carriera** (kahr-*ryeh*-rah) f

cash register: **cassa** (*kahs*-sah) f

castle: **castello** (kah-*stehl*-loh) m

cat: **gatto** (*gaht*-toh) m

censorship: **censura** (chehn-*sooh*-rah) f

ceramics: **oggetti in ceramica** (ohj-*jeht*-tee een cheh-*rah*-mee-kah) m

chair: **sedia** (*seh*-dyah) f

to change: **cambiare** (kahm-bee-*ah*-reh)

cheap: **a buon mercato** (ah bwohn mehr-*kah*-toh)

check: **assegno** (ahs-*seh*-nyoh) m

checkout counter: **cassa** (*kahs*-sah) f

cheese: **formaggio** (fohr-*mahj*-joh) m

child (female): **bambina** (bahm-*bee*-nah) f

child (male): **bambino** (bahm-*bee*-noh) m

chocolate: **cioccolata** (chohk-koh-*lah*-tah) f; **cioccolato** (chohk-koh-*lah*-toh) m

to choose: **scegliere** (*sheh*-lyeh-reh)

cinema: **cinema** (*chee*-neh-mah) m

city: **città** (cheet-*tah*) f

to clean: **pulire** (pooh-*lee*-reh)

climb: **salita** (sah-*lee*-tah)

close: **vicina** (vee-*chee*-nah) f; **vicino** (vee-*chee*-noh) m

to close: **chiudere** (*kyooh*-deh-reh)

clothing store: **negozio di abbigliamento** (neh-*goh*-tsyoh dee ahb-bee-lyah-*mehn*-toh) m

coat: **cappotto** (kahp-*poht*-toh) m

coffee: **caffè** (kahf-*feh*) m

cold: **fredda** (*frehd*-dah) f; **freddo** (*frehd*-doh)

color: **colore** (koh-*loh*-reh)

to come: **venire** (veh-*nee*-reh)

come on: **dai** (dahy)

comedy: **commedia** (kohm-*meh*-dyah) f

comfortable: **comoda** (*koh*-moh-dah) f; **comodo** (*koh*-moh-doh) m contemporary: **contemporanea** (kohn-tehm-poh-*rah*-neh-ah) f; **contemporaneo** (kohn-tehm-poh-*rah*-neh-oh) m

contract: **contratto** (kohn-*traht*-toh) m

control: **controllo** (kohn-*trohl*-loh) m

conversion rate: **cambio** (*kahm*-byoh) m

cork: **sughero** (s*ooh*-gheh-roh) m

to correct: **correggere** (kohr-*rehj*-jeh-reh)

cot: **lettino** (leht-*teeh*-noh) m

cotton: **cotone** (koh-*toh*-neh) m

country: **campagna** (kahm-*pah*-nyah) f

co-worker: **collega** (kohl-*leh*-gah) f/m

craft: **prodotto artigianale** (proh-*doht*-toh ahr-tee-jah-*nah*-leh) m

cream: **panna** (*pah*-nah) f

credit card: **carta di credito** (*kahr*-tah dee *kreh*-dee-toh) f

critic: **critic** (*kree*-tee-koh) m

crowds: **folla** (*fohl*-lah) f

cultural: **culturale** (kooh-tooh-*rah*-leh)

culture: **cultura** (kooh-*tooh*-rah) f

cup: **tazza** (*taht*-tsah) f; **coppa** (*kohp*-pah) f

current events: **notizie d'attualità** (noh-*tee*-tsyeh daht-tooh-ah-lee-*tah*) f

currently: **attualmente** (aht-twahl-*mehn*-teh)

curve: **curva** (*koor*-vah) f

custard: **crema** (*kreh*-mah) f

customer: **cliente** (*klyehn*-teh) f/m

D

daily newspaper: **quotidiano** (kwoh-tee-*dyah*-noh) m

dark: **scura** (*skooh*-rah) f; **scuro** (*skooh*-roh) m

daughter: **figlia** (*fee*-lyah) f

day: **giorno** (*johr*-noh) m

dear: **cara** (*kah*-rah) f; **caro** (*kah*-roh) m

December: **dicembre** (dee-*chehm*-breh)

to defend: **difendere** (dee-*fehn*-deh-reh)

dentist: **dentista** (dehn-*tees*-tah) f/m

department store: **grande magazzino** (*grahn*-deh mah-gaht-*tsee*-noh) m

descent: **discesa** (dee-*sheh*-sah) f

designer: **stilista** (stee-*lee*-stah) m

desk: **scrivania** (skree-vah-*nee*-ah) f

dessert (sweet): **dolce** (*dohl*-cheh) m

dialect: **dialetto** (dyah-*leht*-toh) m

to die: **morire** (moh-*ree*-reh)

difficult: **difficile** (deef-*fee*-chee-leh)

to divorce: **divorziare** (dee-vohr-*tzyah*-reh)

dinner: **cena** (*cheh*-nah) f

director: **regista** (reh-*jee*-stah) m

to do: **fare** (*fah*-reh)

doctor: **dottore** (doht-*toh*-reh) m

doctor's office: **studio medico** (*stooh*-dee-oh *meh*-dee-koh) m

dog: **cane** (*kah*-neh) m

down: **giù** (jooh)

drawer: **cassette** (kahs-*seht*-toh) m

dress: **vestito** (vehs-*tee*-toh) m

to drink: **bere** (*beh*-reh)

to drive: **guidare** (gwee-*dah*-reh)

driver: **autista** (au-*tee*-stah) f/m

E

ear: **orecchio** (oh-*rehk*-kyoh) m

early: **presto** (*preh*-stoh)

east: **est** (ehst)

easy: **facile** (*fah*-chee-leh) f/m

to eat: **mangiare** (mahn-*jah*-reh)

economic news: **notizie economiche** (noh-*tee*-tsye eh-koh-*noh*-mee-keh) f eight: **otto** (*oht*-toh)

eighteen: **diciotto** (dee-*choht*-toh)

either . . . or: **o . . . o** (oh . . . oh)

elegance: **eleganza** (eh-leh-*gahn*-tsah) f

eleven: **undici** (*oohn*-dee-chee)

emergency: **emergenza** (eh-mehr-*jehn*-tsah) f

employee: **impiegata** (eem-pyeh-*gah*-tah) f; **impiegato** (eem-pyeh-*gah*-toh) m

end: **fine** (*fee*-neh) f

to end: **finire** (fee-*nee*-reh)

engine: **motore** (moh-*toh*-ree) m

engineer: **ingegnere** (een-jeh-*nyeh*-reh) m

enough: **abbastanza** (ahb-bah-*stahn*-tsah)

to enter **entrare** (ehn-*trah*-reh)

entrance: **entrata** (ehn-*trah*-tah) f

entrepreneurship: **imprenditorialità** (eem-prehn-dee-toh-ree-ah-lee-*tah*) f

environment: **ambiente** (ahm-*byehn*-teh) m

equipment: **attrezzattura** (aht-trehts-ah-*tooh*-rah) f

estate: **tenuta** (teh-*nooh*-tah) f

etiquette: **etichetta** (eh-tee-*keht*-tah) f

even though: **sebbene** (sehb-*beh*-neh)

event: **evento** (eh-*vehn*-toh) m

ever: **mai** (mahy)

everybody: **tutti** (*tooht*-tee)

everyone: **ciascuno** (chah-*skooh*-noh); **tutti** (*tooht*-tee)

everything: **tutto** (*tooht*-toh)

everywhere: **dappertutto** (dahp-pehr-*tooht*-toh)

exit: **uscita** (ooh-*shee*-tah) f

to exit: **uscire** (ooh-*shee*-reh)

expensive: **cara** (*kah*-rah) f; **caro** (*kah*-roh) m; **costosa** (koh-*stoh*-sah) f; **costoso** (koh-*stoh*-soh) m

eye: **occhio** (*ohk*-kyoh) m

F

face: **faccia** (*fahch*-chah) f

to fall: **cadere** (kah-*deh*-reh)

fan: **tifoso** (tee-*foh*-soh) m

far: **lontano** (lohn-*tah*-noh)

fashion: **moda** (*moh*-dah) f

fast: **veloce** (veh-*loh*-cheh); **velocemente** (veh-loh-cheh-*mehn*-teh); **in fretta** (een *freht*-tah)

fat: **grassa** (*grahs*-sah) f; **grasso** (*grahs*-soh) m

father: **padre** (*pah*-dreh) m

February: **febbraio** (fehb-*brah*-yoh)

a few: **alcuni** (ahl-*kooh*-nee)

few: **poche** (*poh*-keh) f, pl; **pochi** (*poh*-kee) m, pl

fidelity: **fedeltà** (feh-dehl-*tah*) f

fifteen: **quindici** (*kween*-dee-chee)

fifty: **cinquanta** (cheen-*kwahn*-tah)

figure: **figura** (fee-*goo*-rah) f

file cabinet: **schedario** (skeh-*dah*-ryoh) m

finally: **finalmente** (fee-nahl-*mehn*-teh)

to find: **trovare** (troh-*vah*-reh)

finger: **dito** (*dee*-toh) m

to finish: **finire** (fee-*nee*-reh)

fish: **pesce** (*peh*-sheh) m

five: **cinque** (*cheen*-kweh)

to fly: **volare** (voh-*lah*-reh)

flower: **fiore** (*fyoh*-reh) m

fog: **nebbia** (*nehb*-byah) f

for: **per** (pehr)

to forget: **dimenticare** (dee-mehn-tee-*kah*-reh); **dimenticarsi** (dee-mehn-tee-*kahr*-see)

to forgive: **perdonare** (pehr-doh-*nah*-reh)

foul language: **turpiloquio** (toohr-pee-*loh*-kwyoh) m

Book VI

Appendixes

four: **quattro** (*kwaht*-troh)

fourteen: **quattordici** (kwaht-*tohr*-dee-chee)

fresh: **fresca** (*freh*-skah) f; **fresco** (*freh*-skoh) m

friend: **amica** (ah-*mee*-kah) f; **amico** (ah-*mee*-koh) m

friendship: **amicizia** (ah-mee-*chee*-tsyah) f

to frighten: **spaventare** (spah-vehn-*tah*-reh)

from: **da** (dah); **di** (origin) (dee)

fruit: **frutta** (*frooht*-tah) f

functionality: **funzionalità** (foohn-tsyo-nah-lee-*tah*) f

furniture: **arredamento** (ahr-reh-dah-*mehn*-toh) m

G

game: **partita** (pahr-*tee*-tah) f

garden: **giardino** (jahr-*dee*-noh) m

to get: **ottenere** (oht-teh-*neh*-eh); **ricevere** (ree-*cheh*-veh-reh)

to get married: **sposarsi** (spoh-*sahr*-see)

girl: **ragazza** (rah-*gaht*-tsah) f

to give: **dare** (*dah*-reh); **donare** (doh-*nah*-reh)

to give back: **restituire** (reh-stee-*twee*-reh)

gladly: **volentieri** (voh-lehn-*tyeh*-ree)

glass (drinking cup): **bicchiere** (beek-*kyeh*-reh) m

glass (material): **in vetro** (een *veh*-troh) m

gloves: **guanti** (*gwahn*-tee) m

to go: **andare** (ahn-*dah*-reh)

to go out: **uscire** (ooh-*shee*-reh)

good (adjective): **buona** (*bwoh*-nah) f; **buono** (*bwoh*-noh) m

good (noun, such as merchandise; commodity): **merce** (*mehr*-cheh) f

good evening: **buonasera** (*bwoh*-nah-*seh*-rah)

good morning, good day: **buongiorno** (bwohn-*johr*-noh)

good-bye: **arrivederci** (ahr-ree-veh-*dehr*-chee); **ciao** (chou)

good-night: **buonanotte** (*bwoh*-nah-*noht*-teh)

gray: **grigia** (*gree*-jah) f; **grigio** (*gree*-joh) m

great: **grande** (*grahn*-deh)

green: **verde** (*vehr*-deh) f/m

to grow: **crescere** (*kreh*-sheh-reh)

growth: **crescita** (*kreh*-shee-tah) f

H

hair: **capelli** (kah-*pehl*-lee) m, pl

hand: **mano** (*mah*-noh) f

happy: **felice** (feh-*lee*-cheh)

hat: **cappello** (kahp-*pehl*-loh) m

to hate: **odiare** (oh-*dyah*-reh)

to have: **avere** (ah-*veh*-reh)

to have (at a bar, restaurant): **prendere** (*prehn*-deh-reh)

to have to: **dovere** (doh-*veh*-reh)

he: **lui** (*looh*-ee) m

to hear: **sentire** (sehn-*tee*-reh)

hello: **ciao** (chou)

help: **aiuto** (ah-*yooh*-toh)

her: **lei** (lehy) f; **sua** (*sooh*-ah) f; **[la] sua** ([lah] *sooh*-ah) f; **sue** (*sooh*-eh) f, pl; **[le] sue** ([leh] *sooh*-eh) f, pl; **suo** (*sooh*-oh) m; **[il] suo** ([eel] *sooh*-oh) m; **suoi** (*swoh*-ee) m, pl; **[i] suoi** ([ee] *swoh*-ee) m, pl here: **qui** (kwee); **lì** (lee)

heritage: **patrimonio** (pah-tree-*mohn*-yoh) m

hers: **sua** (*sooh*-ah) f; **[la] sua** ([lah] *sooh*-ah) f; **sue** (*sooh*-eh) f, pl; **[le] sue** ([leh] *sooh*-eh) f, pl; **suo** (*sooh*-oh) m; **[il] suo** ([eel] *sooh*-oh) m; **suoi** (*swoh*-ee) m, pl; **[i] suoi** ([ee] *swoh*-ee) m, pl

high: **alta** (*ahl*-tah) f; **alto** (*ahl*-toh) m

him: **lui** (*looh*-ee) m

his: **sua** (*sooh*-ah) f; **[la] sua** ([lah] *sooh*-ah) f; **sue** (*sooh*-eh) f, pl; **[le] sue** ([leh] *sooh*-eh) f, pl; **suo** (*sooh*-oh) m; **[il] suo** ([eel] *sooh*-oh) m; **suoi** (*swoh*-ee) m, pl; **[i] suoi** ([ee] *swoh*-ee) m, pl

historical: **storica** (*stoh*-ree-kah) f; **storico** (*stoh*-ree-koh) m

to hold: **tenere** (teh-*neh*-reh)

holiday: **ferie** (*feh*-ryeh) f

home: **casa** (*kah*-sah) f

to hope: **sperare** (speh-*rah*-reh)

horse: **cavallo** (kah-*vahl*-loh) m

hospital: **ospedale** (ohs-peh-*dah*-leh) m

hostile: **ostile** (oh-*stee*-leh)

hot: **calda** (*kahl*-dah) f; **caldo** (*kahl*-doh) m

hotel: **albergo** (ahl-*behr*-goh) m

hour: **ora** (*oh*-rah) f

house: **casa** (*kah*-sah) f

how: **come** (*koh*-meh)

how many: **quanti** (*kwahn*-tee)

how much: **quanto** (*kwahn*-toh)

hundred: **cento** (*chehn*-toh)

hunger: **fame** (*fah*-meh) f

husband: **marito** (mah-*ree*-toh) m

I

I: **io** (*ee*-oh)

ice: **ghiaccio** (*gyahch*-choh) m

ice cream: **gelato** (jeh-*lah*-toh) m

if: **se** (seh)

ill: **malata** (mah-*lah*-tah) f; **malato** (mah-*lah*-toh) m

in: **in** (een); **a** (ah)

in front of: **di fronte [a]** (dee *frohn*-teh [ah])

inside: **dentro** (*dehn*-troh)

intelligent: **intelligente** (een-tehl-lee-*jehn*-teh)

interesting: **interessante** (een-teh-rehs-*sahn*-teh)

interview: **colloquio** (kohl-*loh*-kweeh-oh) m; **intervista** (een-tehr-*vee*-stah) f

to introduce: **presentare** (preh-zehn-*tah*-reh)

inventor: **inventore** (een-vehn-*toh*-reh) m

invitation: **invito** (een-*vee*-toh) m

it: **essa** (*ehs*-sah) f; **esso** (*ehs*-soh) m

Italian: **italiana** (ee-tah-lee-*ah*-nah) f; **italiano** (ee-tah-lee-*ah*-noh) m

its: **sua** (*sooh*-ah) f; **[la] sua** ([lah] *sooh*-ah) f; **sue** (*sooh*-eh) f, pl; **[le] sue** ([leh] *sooh*-eh) f, pl; **suo** (*sooh*-oh) m; **[il] suo** ([eel] *sooh*-oh) m; **suoi** (*swoh*-ee) m, pl; **[i] suoi** ([ee] *swoh*-ee) m, pl

J

jacket: **giacca** (*jahk*-kah) f

January: **gennaio** (jehn-*nah*-yoh)

jeans: **jeans** (jeenz) m

jewelry: **gioielli** (joh-*yehl*-lee) m

job: **lavoro** (lah-*voh*-roh) m

July: **luglio** (*looh*-lyoh)

June: **giugno** (*jooh*-nyoh)

just: **solo** (*soh*-loh)

K

to keep: **tenere** (teh-*neh*-reh)

kind: **gentile** (jehn-*tee*-leh)

knee: **ginocchio** (jee-*nohk*-kyoh) m

knife: **coltello** (kohl-*tehl*-loh) m

to know: **sapere** (sah-*peh*-reh);
   conoscere (koh-*noh*-sheh-reh)

L

labor: **lavoro** (lah-*voh*-roh) m

lace: **merletto** (mehr-*leht*-toh) m

lake: **lago** (*lah*-goh) m

language: **lingua** (*leen*-gwah) f

large: **larga** (*lahr*-gah) f; **largo** (*lahr*-goh)
   m; **grande** (*grahn*-deh) f/m

late: **in ritardo** (een ree-*tahr*-doh)

to laugh: **ridere** (*ree*-deh-reh)

lawyer: **avvocato** (ahv-voh-*kah*-toh) m

least: **minima** (*mee*-nee-mah) f; **minimo**
   (*mee*-nee-moh) m

leather: **cuoio** (*kwoh*-yoh) m; **pelle**
   (*pehl*-leh) f

to leave: **lasciare** (lah-*shah*-reh); **partire**
   (pahr-*tee*-reh)

(on the) left: **a sinistra** (ah
   see-*nees*-trah)

to lend: **prestare** (preh-*stah*-reh)

less (*meh*-noh): **meno**

less than: **meno che** (*meh*-noh keh);
   meno di (*meh*-noh dee)

to let: **lasciare** (lah-*shah*-reh);
   permettere (pehr-*meht*-teh-reh)

light-colored: **chiara** (*kyah*-rah) f;
   chiaro (*kyah*-roh) m

to like: **piacere** (pyah-*cheh*-reh)

line: **fila** (*fee*-lah) f

linen: **lino** (*lee*-noh) m

to listen to: **ascoltare** (ah-skohl-*tah*-reh)

little: **piccola** (*peek*-koh-lah) f; **piccolo**
   (*peek*-koh-loh) m

a little, **un po'** (oohn poh)

little horse: **cavallino** (kah-vahl-*lee*-noh) m

a little of: **un po' di** (oohn poh dee)

to live: **abitare** (ah-bee-*tah*-reh); **vivere**
   (*vee*-veh-reh)

to loan: **dare in prestito** (*dah*-reh een
   preh-stee-toh)

to look at: **guardare** (gwahr-*dah*-reh)

to look for: **cercare** (chehr-*kah*-reh)

to lose: **perdere** (*pehr*-deh-reh)

a lot: **molti** (*mohl*-tee) m; **molto** (*mohl*-
   toh) m; **parecchia** (pah-*rehk*-kyah) f;
   parecchio (pah-*rehk*-kyoh) m

to love: **amare** (ah-*mah*-reh)

love: **amore** (ah-*moh*-reh) m

lunch: **pranzo** (*prahn*-tsoh) m

lyrics: **testo** (*teh*-stoh) m

M

magazine: **rivista** (ree-*vee*-stah) f

to make: **fare** (*fah*-reh)

man: **uomo** (*woh*-moh) m

March: **marzo** (*mahr*-tsoh)

market: **mercato** (mehr-*kah*-toh) m

to marry: **sposare** (spoh-*sah*-reh)

masterpiece: **capolavoro** (kah-poh-lah-
   voh-roh) m

material: **material** (mah-teh-*ryah*-leh) m

May: **maggio** (*mahj*-joh)

may: **potere** (poh-*teh*-reh) f

me: **me** (meh)

measure: **misura** (mee-*suh*-rah) f

meat: **carne** (*kahr*-neh) f

media: **mezzi di comunicazione di massa** (*meht*-tsee dee koh-mooh-nee-kah-*tsyoh*-neh di *mahs*-sah) m

medicine: **medicina** (meh-dee-*chee*-nah) f

to meet: **incontrare** (een-kohn-*trah*-reh)

meeting: **riunione** (ree-ooh-*nyoh*-neh) f

member: **socio** (*soh*-choh)

metaphor: **metafora** (meh-*tah*-foh-rah) f

meticulous: **meticolosa** (meh-tee-koh-*loh*-sah) f; **meticoloso** (meh-tee-koh-*loh*-soh) m

milk: **latte** (*laht*-teh) m

mine: **mia** (myah) f; **[la] mia** ([lah] myah) f; **mie** (myeh) f, pl; **[le] mie** ([leh] myeh) f, pl; **miei** (myehy) m, pl; **[i] miei** ([ee] myehy), m, pl; **mio** (myoh) m; **[il] mio** ([eel] myoh) m

minimum: **minima** (*mee*-nee-mah) f; **minimo** (*mee*-neeh-moh) m

modernization: **modernizzazione** (moh-dehr-neet-tsah-*tsyoh*-neh) f

mom: **mamma** (*mahm*-mah) f

money: **soldi** (*sohl*-dee) m

month: **mese** (*meh*-zeh) m

monthly: **mensile** (mehn-*see*-leh)

monthly magazine: **mensile** (mehn-*see*-leh) m

more: **più** (pyooh)

more than: **più che** (pyooh keh); **più di** (pyooh dee)

most: **massimo** (*mahs*-see-moh)

mother: **madre** (*mah*-dreh) f

mountain: **montagna** (mohn-*tah*-nyah) f

to move: **muovere** (*mwoh*-veh-reh); **muoversi** (*mwoh*-vehr-see)

Mr.: **signore** (see-*nyoh*-reh) m

Mrs.: **signora** (see-*nyoh*-rah) f

museum: **museo** (mooh-*seh*-oh) m

music: **musica** (*mooh*-see-kah) f

music critic: **critici musicali** (*kree*-tee-chee mooh-see-*kah*-lee) m

musical: **musicale** (mooh-see-*kah*-leh)

musician: **musicista** (mooh-see-*chee*-stah) m

must: **dovere** (doh-*veh*-reh)

my: **mia** (myah) f; **[la] mia** ([lah] myah) f; **mie** (myeh) f, pl; **[le] mie** ([leh] myeh) f, pl; **miei** (myehy) m, pl; **[i] miei** ([ee] myehy), m, pl; **mio** (myoh) m; **[il] mio** ([eel] myoh) m

N

name: **nome** (*noh*-meh) m

narrow: **stretta** (*streht*-tah) f; **stretto** (*streht*-toh) m

natural: **naturale** (nah-tooh-*rah*-leh)

near: **vicina** (vee-*chee*-nah) f; **vicino** (vee-*chee*-noh) m

neck: **collo** (*kohl*-loh) m

to need: **avere bisogno di** (ah-*veh*-reh bee-*soh*-nyoh dee)

neither . . . nor: **né . . . né** (neh . . . neh)

never (don't ever): **non . . . mai** (nohn . . . mahy)

never (never): **mai** (mahy)

new: **nuova** (*nwoh*-vah) f; **nuovo** (*nwoh*-voh) m

news: **notizie** (noh-*tee*-tsyeh) f

newspaper: **giornale** (johr-*nah*-leh) m

nice: **carina** (kah-*ree*-nah) f; **carino** (kah-*ree*-noh) m

Book VI

Appendixes

nice to meet you: **piacere** (pyah-*cheh*-reh)

night: **notte** (*noht*-teh) f

nine: **nove** (*noh*-veh)

nineteen: **diciannove** (dee-chahn-*noh*-veh)

no: **no** (noh)

no one: **nessuna** (nehs-*sooh*-nah) f; **nessuno** (nehs-*sooh*-noh) m

nobody: **nessuna** (nehs-*sooh*-nah) f; **nessuno** (nehs-*sooh*-noh) m

none: **nessuna** (nehs-*sooh*-nah) f; **nessuno** (nehs-*sooh*-noh) m

north: **nord** (nohrd) m

nose: **naso** (*nah*-zoh) m

not: **non** (nohn)

not yet: **non ancora** (nohn ahn-*koh*-rah)

nothing: **niente** (*nyehn*-teh); **nulla** (*noohl*-lah)

November: **novembre** (noh-*vehm*-breh)

now: **ora** (*oh*-rah); **adesso** (ah-*dehs*-soh)

nowhere: **da nessuna parte** (dah nehs-*sooh*-nah *pahr*-teh)

number: **numero** (*nooh*-meh-roh) m

nurse: **infermiera** (een-fehr-*myeh*-rah) f

old: **vecchia** (*vehk*-kyah) f; **vecchio** (*vehk*-kyoh) m

on: **su** (sooh); **sopra** (*soh*-prah)

one: **si** (see); **una** (*ooh*-nah) f; **uno** (*ooh*-noh) m

one-way (ticket): **andata** (ahn-*dah*-tah) f

only: **solo** (*soh*-loh); **soltanto** (sohl-*tahn*-toh)

to open: **aprire** (ah-*pree*-reh)

opera: **opera** (*oh*-peh-rah) f

opportunity: **opportunità** (ohp-pohr-tooh-nee-*tah*) f

or: **o** (oh)

our, ours: **nostra** (*noh*-strah) f; **[la] nostra** ([lah] *noh*-strah) f; **nostre** (*noh*-streh) f, pl; **[le] nostre** [leh] *noh*-streh) f, pl; **nostri** (*noh*-stree) m, pl; **[i] nostri** ([ee] *noh*-stree) m, pl; **nostro** (*noh*-stroh) m; **[il] nostro** ([eel] *noh*-stroh) m

outdoor market: **mercato** (mehr-*kah*-toh) m

outside: **fuori** (*fwoh*-ree)

over: **sopra** (*soh*-prah)

overtaking: **sorpasso** (sohr-*pahs*-soh) m

to own: **possedere** (pohs-seh-*deh*-reh)

O

October: **ottobre** (oht-*toh*-breh)

of: **di** (dee)

of the: **del** (dehl) m; **dello** (*dehl*-loh) m; **della** (*dehl*-lah) f; **dei** (dehy) m, pl; **degli** (*deh*-lyee), m, pl; **delle** (*dehl*-leh) f, pl; **dell'** (dehl) m/f

to offer: **offrire** (ohf-*free*-reh)

office: **ufficio** (oohf-*fee*-choh) m

often: **spesso** (*spehs*-soh)

okay: **d'accordo** (dahk-*kohr*-doh)

old (for persons): **anziana** (ahn-tsee-*ah*-nah) f; **anziano** (ahn-tsee-*ah*-noh) m

P

painter: **pittore** (peet-*toh*-reh) m

palace: **palazzo** (pah-*laht*-tsoh) m

paper: **carta** (*kahr*-tah) f

party: **festa** (*fehs*-tah) f

to pass: **passare** (pahs-*sah*-reh)

passersby: **passante** (pahs-*sahn*-teh) m

passport: **passaporto** (pahs-sah-*pohr*-toh) m

to pay: **pagare** (pah-*gah*-reh)

payment: **pagamento** (pah-gah-*mehn*-toh) m

pen: **penna** (*pehn*-nah) f

pencil: **matita** (mah-*tee*-tah) f

people: **gente** (*jehn*-teh) f

periodical publication: **periodico** (peh-*ryoh*-dee-koh) m

phone: **telefono** (teh-*leh*-foh-noh) f

physician: **medico** (*meh*-dee-koh) m

pile: **mucchio** (*moohk*-kyoh) m

pilot: **pilota** (pee-*loh*-tah) m

play: **gioco** (*joh*-koh) m

to play (a sport): **giocare** (joh-*kah*-reh)

to play (an instrument): **suonare (uno strumento)** (swoh-*nah*-reh [ooh-noh struh-*mehn*-toh])

please: **per favore** (pehr fah-*voh*-reh)

plot: **trama** (*trah*-mah) f

plurality: **pluralità** (ploo-rah-lee-*tah*) f

podium: **podio** (*poh*-dee-oh) m

poet: **poeta** (poh-*eh*-tah) m

poetry: **poesia** (poh-eh-*see*-ah) f

point of view: **punto di vista** (*poohn*-toh dee *veehs*-tah) m

police: **polizia** (poh-lee-*tsee*-ah) f

political: **politica** (poh-*lee*-tee-kah) f; **politico** (poh-*lee*-tee-koh) m

politics: **politica** (poh-*lee*-tee-kah) f

popular: **popolare** (poh-poh-*lah*-ree)

prancing: **rampante** (rahm-*pahn*-teh)

to prefer: **preferire** (preh-feh-*ree*-reh)

pretty: **carina** (kah-*ree*-nah) f; **carino** (kah-*ree*-noh) m

prevention: **prevenzione** (preh-vehn-*tsyoh*-neh) f

professional: **professionale** (proh-fehs-syoh-*nah*-leh)

proper behavior: **belle maniere** (*behl*-leh mah-*nyeh*-reh) f

public: **pubblica** (*poohb*-blee-kah) f; **pubblico** (*poohb*-blee-koh) m

public safety: **pubblica sicurezza** (*poohb*-blee-kah see-kuh-*reht*-tsah) f

purse: **borsetta** (bohr-*seht*-tah) f

to put: **mettere** (*meht*-teh-reh)

Q

quality: **qualità** (kwah-lee-*tah*) f

quickly: **rapidamente** (rah-pee-dah-*mehn*-teh); **in fretta** (een *freht*-tah)

R

race track: **pista** (*pee*-stah) f

radio: **radio** (*rah*-dyoh) f

radio broadcaster: **emittente radiofonica** (eh-meet-*tehn*-teh rah-dyoh-*foh*-nee-kah) f

radio program: **programma radiofonici** (proh-*grahm*-mah rah-dyoh-*foh*-nee-chee) f

rain: **pioggia** (*pyohj*-jah) f

raincoat: **impermeabile** (eem-pehr-meh-*ah*-bee-leh) m

to raise: **allevare** (ahl-leh-*vah*-reh); **aumentare** (aw-mehn-*tah*-reh)

to recall: **richiamare** (ree-kyah-*mah*-reh)

to receive: **ricevere** (ree-*che*-veh-reh)

red: **rossa** (*rohs*-sah) f; **rosso** (*rohs*-soh) m

refrain: **ritornello** (ree-tohr-*nehl*-loh) m

to remember: **ricordare** (ree-kohr-*dah*-reh); **ricordarsi** (ree-kohr-*dahr*-see)

to remind someone of something: **ricordare qualcosa a qualcuno** (ree-kohr-*dah*-reh kwahl-*koh*-sah ah kwahl-*koo*-noh)

to rent (an apartment): **affittare (un appartamento)** (ahf-feet-*tah*-reh [oohn ahp-pahrt-tah-*mehn*-toh]) to rent (a car): **noleggiare (un'automobile)** (noh-lej-*jah*-reh [oohn ou-toh-*moh*-bee-leh])

to repeat: **ripetere** (ree-*peh*-teh-reh)

repetitive task: **attività ripetitiva** (aht-tee-vee-*tah* reeh-peh-teeh-*teeh*-vah) f

to reserve: **prenotare** (preh-noh-*tah*-reh)

résumé: **curriculum** (koohr-ree-kooh-*loohm*) m

rest: **riposo** (reeh-*poh*-soh) m

to rest: **riposare** (reeh-poh-*sah*-reh)

to return (to a place): **ritornare** (ree-tohr-*nah*-reh)

to return (something): **restituire** (reh-stee-*toohy*-reh)

rice: **riso** (*ree*-zoh) m

[on the] right: **[a] destra** ([ah] dehs-trah)

right: **giusto** (*jooh*-stoh) m; **giusta** (*jooh*-stah) f

road: **strada** (*strah*-dah) f; **via** (*vee*-ah) f

road racing circuit: **circuito** (cheer-*koo*-ee-toh) m; **cittadino** (cheet-tah-*dee*-noh) m

room: **stanza** (*stahn*-tsah) f

round trip: **andata** (ahn-*dah*-tah) f; **e ritorno** (eh ree-*tohr*-noh) m

rule: **regola** (*reh*-goh-lah) f

S

sad: **triste** (*tree*-steh)

salad: **insalata** (een-sah-*lah*-tah) f

salary: **stipendio** (steeh-*pehn*-dyoh) m

sales: **saldi** (*sahl*-dee) m, pl

sales clerk: **commessa** (kohm-*mehs*-sah) f; **commesso** (kohm-*mehs*-soh) m

salt: **sale** (*sah*-leh) m

same: **stessa** (*stehs*-sah) f; **stesso** (*stehs*-soh) m

satin: **raso** (*rah*-soh) m

to say: **dire** (*dee*-reh)

scientist: **scienziato** (shehn-*zyah*-toh) m

scissors: **forbici** (*fohr*-bee-chee) f

sculptor: **scultore** (skoohl-*toh*-reh) m

sea: **mare** (*mah*-reh) m

secretary: **segretaria** (seh-greh-*tah*-ree-ah) f; **segretario** (seh-greh-*tah*-ree-oh) m

to see: **vedere** (veh-*deh*-reh)

see you: **arrivederci** (ahr-ree-veh-*dehr*-chee)

see you later: **a dopo** (ah *doh*-poh)

see you tomorrow: **a domani** (ah doh-*mah*-nee)

to sell: **vendere** (*vehn*-deh-reh)

to send: **mandare** (mahn-*dah*-reh)

September: **settembre** (seht-*tehm*-breh)

serious: **seria** (*seh*-ryah) f; **serio** (*seh*-ryoh) m

seven: **sette** (*seht*-teh)

seventeen: **diciassette** (dee-chahs-*seht*-teh)

shall: **dovere** (doh-*veh*-reh)

shared: **condivisa** (kohn-dee-*vee*-sah) f; **condiviso** (kohn-dee-*vee*-soh) m

she: **lei** (lehy) f

to ship: **spedire** (speh-*dee*-reh)

shirt: **camicia** (kah-*mee*-chah) f

shoe: **scarpa** (*skahr*-pah) f

shoe store: **negozio di scarpe** (neh-*goh*-tsee dee *skahr*-peh) m

shop: **negozio** (neh-*goh*-tsee-oh) m

shop window: **vetrina** (veh-*tree*-nah) f

short: **bassa** (*bahs*-sah) f; **basso** (*bahs*-soh) m; **piccola** (*peek*-koh-lah) f; **piccolo** (*peek*-koh-loh) m shoulder: **spalla** (*spahl*-lah) f

to shut: **chiudere** (*kyooh*-deh-reh)

silk: **seta** (*seh*-tah) f

since: **da quando** (dah *kwahn*-doh);
poiché (poh-ee-*keh*)

to sing: **cantare** (kahn-*tah*-reh)

singer: **cantante** (kahn-*tahn*-teh) m

singer-songwriter: **cantautore** (kahn-tah-ooh-*toh*-reh) m

sister: **sorella** (soh-*rehl*-lah) f

six: **sei** (sey)

sixteen: **sedici** (*seh*-dee-chee)

skirt: **gonna** (*gohn*-nah) f

to sleep: **dormire** (dohr-*mee*-reh)

slowly: **lentamente** (lehn-tah-*mehn*-teh);
piano (*pyah*-noh)

small: **piccola** (*peek*-koh-lah) f; **piccolo**
(*peek*-koh-loh) m

small outdoor market: **mercatino**
(mehr-kah-*tee*-noh) m

snow: **neve** (*neh*-veh) f

so: **così** (koh-*see*)

so as: **in modo da** (een *moh*-doh dah);
in modo che (een *moh*-doh keh)

soccer: **calcio** (*kahl*-choh) m

soccer society: **società di calcio** (soh-cheh-*tah* dee *kahl*-choh) f

social: **sociale** (soh-*chah*-leh) f

some: **un po' di** (oohn *poh* dee); **un po'
del** (oohn *poh* dehl); **alcuni**
(ahl-*kooh*-nee)

something: **qualcosa** (kwahl-*koh*-zah)

somewhere: **da qualche parte** (dah
kwahl-keh *pahr*-teh)

son: **figlio** (*fee*-lyoh) m

song: **canzone** (kahn-*tsoh*-nee) f

soon: **presto** (*preh*-stoh)

sorry: **mi dispiace** (mee
dee-*spyah*-cheh)

source: **fonte** (*fohn*-teh) f

south: **sud** (soohd) m

to speak: **parlare** (pahr-*lah*-reh)

speed: **velocità** (veh-loh-chee-*tah*) f

to spend: **spendere** (*spehn*-deh-reh)

sports news: **notizie sportive** (noh-*tee*-tsyeh spohr-*tee*-veh) f

sportswear: **negozio di articoli sportivi**
(neh-*goh*-tsyoh dee ahr-*tee*-koh-lee
spohr-*tee*-vee) m

square: **piazza** (*pyaht*-tsah) f

stadium: **stadio** (*stah*-dyoh) m

stage: **palcoscenico** (pahl-koh-*sheh*-nee-koh) m

stapler: **spillatrice** (speel-lah-*tree*-cheh) f

station: **stazione** (stah-tsee-*oh*-neh) f

stationery: **cancelleria** (kahn-chehl-leh-*ree*-ah) f

to stay: **stare** (*stah*-reh)

still: **ancora** (ahn-*koh*-rah)

to stop: **fermare** (fehr-*mah*-reh);
fermarsi (fehr-*mahr*-see)

store: **negozio** (neh-*goh*-tsyoh) m

strawberry: **fragola** (frah-*goh*-lah) f

street: **strada** (*strah*-dah) f; **via** (*vee*-ah) f

student: **studente** (stoo-*dehn*-teh) m

stupid: **stupida** (*stooh*-pee-dah) f;
stupido (*stooh*-pee-doh) m

subway: **metropolitana** (meh-troh-poh-lee-*tah*-nah) f

to succeed: **riuscire** (ryooh-*shee*-reh);
succedere (soohch-*cheh*-deh-reh)

success: **successo** (soohch-*chehs*-soh) m

sugar: **zucchero** (*dzook*-keh-roh) m

suit: **abito** (*ah*-bee-toh) m

suitcase: **valigia** (vah-*lee*-jah) f

sun: **sole** (*soh*-leh) m

supermarket: **supermercato** (sooh-pehr-mehr-*kah*-toh) m

supporter: **tifoso** (tee-*foh*-soh) m

sweet: **dolce** (*dohl*-cheh) f/m

swimming: **nuoto** (*nwoh*-toh) m

synthetic: **sintetica** (seehn-*teh*-tee-kah) f; **sintentico** (seehn-*teh*-tee-koh) m

T

table: **tavolo** (*tah*-voh-loh) m

to take: **prendere** (*prehn*-deh-reh); **portare** (pohr-*tah*-reh)

to talk: **parlare** (pahr-*lah*-reh)

tall: **alta** (*ahl*-tah) f; **alto** (*ahl*-toh) m; **grande** (*grahn*-deh) f/m

task: **attività** (aht-tee-veeh-*tah*) f

tax: **dazio** (*dah*-tsee-oh) m; **tassa** (*tahs*-sah) f

telephone: **telefono** (teh-*leh*-foh-noh) m

television broadcaster: **emittente televisiva** (eh-meet-*tehn*-teh teh-leh-vee-*see*-vah) f

television program: **programma televisivo** (proh-*grahm*-mah teh-leh-vee-*see*-voh) m

to tell: **dire** (*dee*-reh); **raccontare** (rahk-kohn-*tah*-reh)

ten: **dieci** (*dyeh*-chee)

territory: **territorio** (tehr-ree-*toh*-ryoh) m

to thank: **ringraziare** (reen-grah-*tsyah*-reh)

thank you: **grazie** (*grah*-tsyah)

that: **che** (keh) f/m; **il quale** (eel *kwah*-leh) m; **la quale** (lah *kwah*-leh) f; **quelle** (*kwehl*-lah) f; **quello** (*kwehl*-loh) m

the: **il** (eel) m; **lo** (loh) m; **la** (lah) f; **i** (ee) m, pl; **gli** (lyee) m, pl; **le** (leh) f, pl; **l'** (l-) m/f

theater: **teatro** (teh-*ah*-troh) m

their: **[il] loro** ([eel] *loh*-roh) m; **[i] loro** ([ee] *loh*-roh) m; **[la] loro** ([lah] *loh*-roh) f; **[le] loro** ([leh] *loh*-roh) f

theirs: **[il] loro** ([eel] *loh*-roh) m; **[i] loro** ([ee] *loh*-roh) m; **[la] loro** ([lah] *loh*-roh) f; **[le] loro** ([leh] *loh*-roh) f

them: **loro** (*loh*-roh)

theme: **tema** (*teh*-mah) m

then: **allora** (ahl-*loh*-rah); **poi** (*poh*-ee)

there: **là** (lah); **ci** (chee)

there are: **ci sono** (chee *soh*-noh)

there is: **c'è** (cheh)

they: **loro** (*loh*-roh)

thin: **magra** (*mah*-grah) f; **magro** (*mah*-groh) m

to think: **pensare** (pehn-*sah*-reh)

thirst: **sete** (*seh*-teh) f

thirteen: **tredici** (*treh*-dee-chee)

this: **questo** (*kweh*-stoh)

thousand: **mille** (*meel*-leh)

three: **tre** (treh)

through: **attraverso** (aht-trah-*vehr*-soh); **per** (pehr); **da** (dah)

ticket: **biglietto** (bee-*lyeht*-toh) m

tie: **cravatta** (krah-*vaht*-tah) f

tight: **stretta** (*streht*-tah) f; **stretto** (*streht*-toh) m

time: **tempo** (*tehm*-poh) m

tired: **stanca** (*stahn*-kah) f; **stanco** (*stahn*-koh) m

title: **titolo** (*tee*-toh-loh) m

to: **a** (ah); **in** (een); **da** (dah)

today: **oggi** (*ohj*-jee)

tomorrow: **domani** (doh-*mah*-nee)

too many: **troppo** (*trohp*-poh); **troppi** (*trohp*-pee)

too much: **troppo** (*trohp*-poh); **troppi** (*trohp*-pee)

tourist: **turista** (tooh-*ree*-stah) m

touristic: **turistica** (tooh-*ree*-stee-kah) f; **turistico** (tooh-*ree*-stee-koh) m

toward: **verso** (*vehr*-soh)

town: **città** (cheet-*tah*) f

tradition: **tradizione** (trah-dee-*tsyoh*-neh) f

tragic: **tragica** (*trah*-jee-kah) f; **tragico** (*trah*-jee-koh) m

train: **treno** (*treh*-noh) m

travel: **viaggio** (vee-*ahj*-joh) m

to travel: **viaggiare** (vyahj-*jah*-reh)

trick: **trovata** (troh-*vah*-tah) f; **trucco** (*troohk*-koh) m

trousers: **pantaloni** (pahn-tah-*loh*-nee) m, pl

to try: **cercare** (chehr-*kah*-reh); **provare** (proh-*vah*-reh)

twelve: **dodici** (*doh*-dee-chee)

twenty: **venti** (*vehn*-teh)

two: **due** (*dooh*-eh)

U

ugly: **brutta** (*brooht*-tah) f; **brutto** (*brooht*-toh) m

uncle: **zio** (*dzee*-oh) m

unless: **a meno che** (ah *meh*-noh keh); **a meno di** (ah *meh*-noh dee)

until: **finché** (feen-*keh*); **finché non** (feen-*keh* nohn)

up: **su** (sooh)

us: **noi** (nohy)

to use: **usare** (ooh-*sah*-reh)

V

vacation: **vacanza** (vah-*kahn*-tsah) f

variety: **varietà** (vah-ryeh-*tah*) f

vegetables: **verdura** (vehr-*dooh*-rah) f

velvet: **velluto** (vehl-*looh*-toh) m

very: **molto** (*mohl*-toh)

victory: **vittoria** (veet-*toh*-ryah) f

virtue: **virtù** (veer-*tooh*) f

W

wage: **stipendio** (stee-*pehn*-dee-oh) m

waiter: **cameriere** (kah-meh-*ryeh*-reh) m

waitress: **cameriera** (kah-meh-*ryeh*-rah) f

wall: **parete** (pah-*reh*-teh) f

wallet: **portafoglio** (pohr-tah-*foh*-lyoh) m

to want: **volere** (voh-*leh*-reh)

warm: **calda** (*kahl*-dah) f; **caldo** (*kahl*-doh) m

water: **acqua** (*ah*-kwah) f

we: **noi** (nohy)

to wear: **mettersi** (*meht*-tehr-see); **indossare** (een-dohs-*sah*-reh); **portare** (pohr-*tah*-reh)

weather: **tempo** (*tehm*-poh) m

week: **settimana** (seht-tee-*mah*-nah) f

weekly: **settimanale** (seht-tee-mah-*nah*-leh)

weekly magazine: **settimanale** (seht-tee-mah-*nah*-leh) m

well (adverb): **bene** (*beh*-neh)

west: **ovest** (*oh*-vehst) m

what: **cosa** (*koh*-sah); **che cosa** (keh *koh*-sah)

what do you do?: **che fai?** (keh fahy?)

when: **quando** (*kwahn*-doh)

where: **dove** (*doh*-veh)

which: **quale** (*kwah*-leh) f/m

white: **bianca** (*byahn*-kah) f; **bianco** (*byahn*-koh) m

who: **chi** (kee)

why: **perché** (pehr-*keh*)

wife: **moglie** (*moh*-lyeh) f

window: **finestra** (fee-*nehs*-trah) f

window shopping: **guardare le vetrine** (gwahr-*dah*-reh leh veh-*tree*-neh)

wine: **vino** (*vee*-noh) m

woman: **donna** (*dohn*-nah) f

Book VI

Appendixes

woodwork: **articolo in legno** (ahr-*tee*-koh-loh een *leh*-nyoh) m

wool: **lana** (*lah*-nah) f

work: **lavoro** (lah-*voh*-roh) m

worker: **lavoratore** (lah-voh-rah-*toh*-reh) m

Y

year: **anno** (*ahn*-noh) m

yellow: **gialla** (*jahl*-lah) f; **giallo** (*jahl*-loh) m

yes: **sì** (see)

yesterday: **ieri** (*yeh*-ree)

yet: **ancora** (ahn-*koh*-rah)

you: **lei** (ley) (formal) s; **tu** (tooh) (informal) s; **voi** (*voh*-ee) (informal/formal) pl

young: **giovane** (*joh*-vah-neh) f/m

your, yours: **tua** (twah) f; **[la] tua** ([lah] twah) f; **tue** (tweh) f, pl; **[le] tue** ([leh] tweh) f, pl; **tuo** (twoh) m; **[il] tuo** ([eel] twoh) m; **tuoi** (twohy) m, pl; **[i] tuoi** ([ee] twohy) m, pl

you're welcome: **prego** (*preh*-goh)

Z

zero: **zero** (*dzeh*-roh)

zip code: **codice postale** (*koh*-dee-cheh pohs-*tah*-leh) m

Appendix D

Fun & Games

• •

This appendix gives you the opportunity to challenge yourself and see how much you've taken away from each chapter. These activities are entertaining and can help you assess your skill with the Italian language. You can find translations and correct answers at the end of the appendix.

Book 1, Chapter 1: Exploring Pronunciations and Italian You May Already Know

Read the following passage, saying the words aloud. Consider the possible meanings of words and see what you can understand of the passage, and then check the translation in the answer key.

Sono americana, ma mi considero cittadina del mondo. Parlo tre lingue, inglese, spagnolo e italiano, e adoro viaggiare. Sono di Chicago e studio storia dell'arte all'università. Adoro l'arte contemporanea, così anche quest'estate andrò a Venezia, per la Biennale. La conoscete? È un'esposizione internazionale di arte contemporanea, famosa in tutto il mondo. Quando partecipo a eventi come questi, incontro tanti giovani che, come me, amano l'arte. Vengono da ogni parte del mondo. Poter comunicare con loro senza barriere di lingua è emozionante. È vero, molti parlano inglese, ma non tutti. Così, la mia conoscenza delle lingue straniere si rivela utilissima.

Quando sono a Chicago, resto in contatto con i miei amici attraverso il mio blog "VagabondA," dove ci scambiamo informazioni sugli eventi culturali dei nostri paesi. Devo dire che quando voglio parlare di una mostra o di un concerto, l'italiano mi aiuta moltissimo. È incredibile il numero di parole che questa lingua ha prestato al vocabolario delle arti! Adesso sto organizzando una mostra d'arte contemporanea nella mia università, a cui ho invitato i molti artisti amici incontrati durante i miei viaggi. Se passate da queste parti, fate un salto. Ne vale la pena!

Book 1, Chapter 2: Dealing with Numbers, Dates, and Time

Take a look at this picture and name the four seasons in Italian. For a more challenging task, name the months that comprise each of the seasons.

Illustration by Elizabeth Kurtzman

A. _____

B. _____

C. _____

D. _____

Book 1, Chapter 3: Buongiorno! Salutations!

A chance meeting leads to a quick introduction in the short dialogue. Fill in the blanks in Italian, using these phrases: **le presento, il piacere, e lei, come sta, conoscerla.**

Gayle: **Buonasera, signora Frederick.** (1) _____?
(*Good afternoon, Ms. Frederick. How are you?*)

Ms. Frederick: **Benissimo, grazie,** (2) _____? (*Very well, thank you, and you?*)

Gayle: **Bene, grazie.** (3) _____ **il mio amico, George.** (*Fine, thanks. I'd like to introduce my friend, George.*)

George: **Lieta di** (4) _____, **signora.** (*Pleased to meet you, Ma'am.*)

Ms. Frederick: (5) _____ **è mio.** (*The pleasure is mine.*)

Book 1, Chapter 4: Making Small Talk

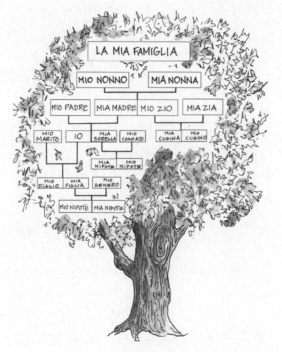

Illustration by Elizabeth Kurtzman

Here are ten fill-in-the-blank questions. Pick words and terms from the family tree to complete each statement. You may need the plural for some of the possessive adjectives and relatives.

1. **I miei genitori sono** _____ **e** _____.

2. **Il figlio di mia madre è** _____.

   3. **I figli di mio fratello sono** _____.

   4. **La madre della mia mamma è** _____.

   5. **La sorella di mia madre è** _____.

   6. **Il marito di mia sorella è** _____.

   7. **La moglie di mio figlio è** _____.

   8. **La sorella di mio figlio è** _____.

   9. **I figli di mia zia sono** _____.

  10. **La mamma di mio marito è** _____.

Book 1, Chapter 5: Casa Dolce Casa: Home Sweet Home

This is an easy one! Identify the various marked rooms and items with their Italian names. For extra credit, name as many items as you can!

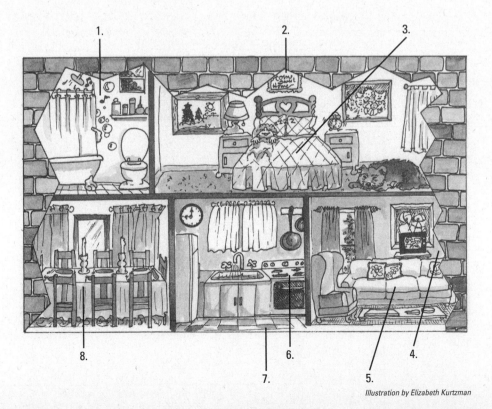

Illustration by Elizabeth Kurtzman

1. _____
2. _____
3. _____
4. _____
5. _____
6. _____
7. _____
8. _____

Book 1, Chapter 6: Using the Phone and Talking Business

You're Mario's guest, but he's gone out for a moment. The telephone rings, and you have to answer it. Fill the gaps in this incomplete phone conversation.

You: (1) _____! (*Hello!*)

Caller: **Ciao, sono Chiara. Con chi** (2) _____? (*Hello, I'm Chiara. Who am I talking to?*)

You: **Sono un** (3) _____ **di Mario.** (*I'm a friend of Mario's.*)

Caller: (4) _____ **Mario?** (*Is Mario in?*)

You: **No, è** (5) _____ **uscito.** (*No, he's just gone out.*)

Caller: **Gli posso** (6) _____? (*Can I leave him a message?*)

You: **Certo.** (7) _____. (*Of course. Please.*)

Mario returns and asks:

Mario: **Ha** (8) _____ **qualcuno per me?** (*Has anybody called for me?*)

Book I, Chapter 7: Food, Glorious Food, and Drink

Chapter 7 of Book I talks a lot about food. To reward yourself for all your hard work, you allow yourself a really good fruit shake. Fill in the Italian for the following various fruits.

1. *pineapple* _____
2. *cherry* _____
3. *grape* _____
4. *pear* _____
5. *watermelon* _____
6. *strawberry* _____

Book I, Chapter 8: Shopping, Italian-Style

Chapter 8 in Book I gives you a lot of information and vocabulary about clothes shopping. See how many articles of clothing you can identify on this couple.

8.

7.

6.

1.

2.

3.

4.

5.

Illustration by Elizabeth Kurtzman

1. _____
2. _____
3. _____
4. _____
5. _____
6. _____
7. _____
8. _____

Book 11, Chapter 1: Where Is the Colosseum? Asking Directions

Take a look at the map of Florence's city center and provide the following information.

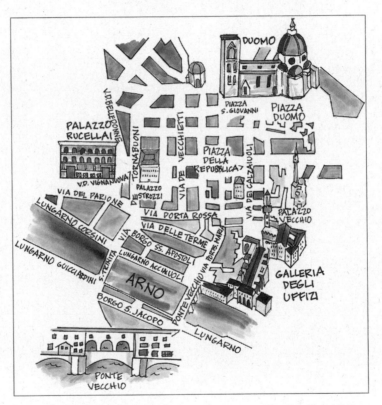

Illustration by Elizabeth Kurtzman

1. Palazzo Rucellai is in via _____.

2. Two bridges on this map are the _____ and the _____.

3. The river that runs through Florence is called the _____.

4. A building that's attached to the Galleria degli Uffizi is the _____.

5. The Duomo sits on what two piazzas? _____.

6. The roads running alongside the Arno have what word in common in their names? _____

7. _____ looks like the main piazza in Florence's center.

Book 11, Chapter 2: Having Fun Out on the Town

It's your turn to invite an Italian friend to your party. Use the following words to fill in the blanks in this invitation: **aspetto, dove, festa, invitato/a, ora, perché, sabato, verso.**

C'è una (1) _____ e tu sei (2) _____.
(*There's a party and you're invited.*)

Quando? (3) _____ 24 luglio. (*When? Saturday, July 24.*)

A che (4) _____? (5) _____ le 9. (*What time? About 9 o'clock.*)

(6) _____? A casa mia. (*Where? At my place.*)

(7) _____? Per festeggiare insieme! (*Why? To celebrate together!*)

Ti (8) _____. (*I'll be waiting for you.*)

Ciao! (*See you!*)

Book II, Chapter 3: Exploring the Outdoors, Sports, and Hobbies

In the following box, try to find the names of some plants and animals introduced in Chapter 3 of Book II. The English is provided; you supply the Italian.

Find and circle the Italian for these words: *horse, flower, bird, cat, wolf, oak, pine, cow, sheep, tree.*

A	J	A	R	O	C	E	P	O	S
U	I	V	S	W	S	O	P	A	B
A	H	C	E	M	L	U	Y	O	A
C	I	K	R	L	L	U	V	G	D
C	G	B	A	E	F	O	L	E	D
U	N	V	M	Z	U	I	N	S	D
M	A	R	X	J	C	Q	O	I	Y
C	G	A	T	T	O	E	I	R	P
A	L	B	E	R	O	P	S	T	E
F	R	H	O	L	L	E	C	C	U

Illustration by Wiley, Composition Services Graphics

Book II, Chapter 4: Planning a Trip

Fill in the missing words with one of the three possible answers that accompany each sentence.

1. **Quest'anno andiamo in** _____. (*This year we're going to the mountains.*)

    a. **albergo**

    b. **montagna**

    c. **aereo**

2. **Il volo parte** _____ **Palermo alle tre.** (*The flight leaves from Palermo at three o'clock.*)

    a. **da**

    b. **su**

    c. **a**

3. **Passo le vacanze in** _____. (*I spend my vacation in the country.*)

    a. **mare**

    b. **campagna**

    c. **montagna**

4. **Dov'è la mia** _____? (*Where is my suitcase?*)

    a. **stanza**

    b. **piscina**

    c. **valigia**

5. **È un** _____ **organizzato.** (*It's an organized trip.*)

    a. **viaggio**

    b. **treno**

    c. **volo**

Book 11, Chapter 5: Money, Money, Money

Here's a little game for you: First define each word in the following list, and then find the words in the word search puzzle.

1. **Banca** _____

2. **Bancomat** _____

3. **Cambiare** _____

4. **Carta di credito** _____

5. **Contanti** _____

6. **Documento** _____
7. **Dollaro** _____
8. **Euro** _____
9. **Kuna** _____
10. **Ricevuta** _____
11. **Spiccioli** _____
12. **Sportello** _____
13. **Sterline** _____

```
C  A  R  T  A  D  I  C  R  E  D  I  T  O  D
S  O  K  S  Z  N  B  O  Y  D  O  Y  Y  D  O
E  R  R  Y  P  A  Z  G  E  C  L  S  A  M  C
T  R  J  U  N  O  G  P  S  D  L  P  N  F  U
A  X  A  C  E  B  R  P  Q  Z  A  K  U  L  M
M  G  A  I  A  M  I  T  Q  S  R  X  K  J  E
O  L  W  A  B  C  T  O  E  Y  O  R  J  I  N
C  H  L  N  C  M  E  N  I  L  R  E  T  S  T
N  C  K  I  E  B  A  I  N  V  L  N  L  H  O
A  J  O  A  S  S  A  C  K  R  A  Q  Z  P  H
B  L  T  R  I  C  E  V  U  T  A  A  S  E  K
I  E  H  T  W  N  L  C  N  X  M  K  Q  G  V
Q  J  A  U  Y  C  V  O  Q  A  G  M  N  A  Q
Q  L  N  Q  E  K  C  Y  P  D  F  Q  L  V  W
Z  Q  X  X  B  E  J  M  W  F  Y  Y  A  L  N
```

Illustration by Wiley, Composition Services Graphics

Book II, Chapter 6: Getting Around: Planes, Trains, Taxis, and Buses

What a mess! This schedule is really jumbled. The Italian words for *train, bus stop, train station, track, ticket, one way, return trip,* and *surcharge* are hidden in the following puzzle. If you want to get to your train on time, you have to solve it. Hurry up!

B	S	M	T	A	T	A	M	R	E	F	O
I	T	U	D	H	G	L	T	X	L	N	C
N	S	Y	P	V	X	L	A	B	E	D	G
A	P	J	Y	P	B	E	I	R	S	H	D
R	K	D	A	J	L	G	T	X	F	X	V
I	V	D	U	Y	L	E	M	R	C	D	Q
O	I	D	Y	I	K	A	M	G	G	D	R
R	Z	J	E	L	X	S	T	E	E	L	K
B	C	T	C	P	M	D	Q	A	N	C	I
B	T	H	P	R	S	P	U	F	D	T	K
O	R	I	T	O	R	N	O	S	O	N	O
S	T	A	Z	I	O	N	E	Z	A	G	A

Illustration by Wiley, Composition Services Graphics

Book VI

Appendixes

Book 11, Chapter 7: Finding a Place to Stay

Unscramble the Italian words in the first column and then match them with their definitions.

1. **gorblea** _____   *bed*

2. **oinpnsee** _____   *luggage*

3. **rcaaem** _____   *suitcases*

4. **asznat** _____   *room*

5. **gilevia** _____   *bathroom*

6. **aneoepozirtn** _____   *room*

7. **tnloaireimma** _____   *small hotel*

8. **lucla** _____   *crib*

9. **aehicv** _____   *swimming pool*

10. **cniapsi** _____   *key*

11. **ttelo** _____   *room with a large bed for two*

12. **ricmeeaer** _____   *reservation*

13. **bgoan** _____   *waiter*

14. **ggbalaoi** _____   *hotel*

Book 11, Chapter 8: Handling Emergencies

Find out how many body parts you can remember by labeling as many of them as you can on the following picture.

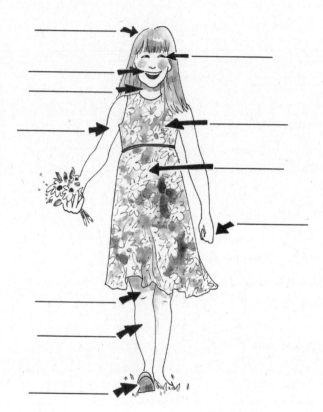

Illustration by Elizabeth Kurtzman

Book III, Chapter 1: What Do You Know? Parts of Speech

In the sentences that follow, identify the underlined part of speech and write it next to the sentence. Then translate the sentence into English. See the example.

> Q. **Mauro e Giovanna <u>ballano</u> il tango.**
>
> A. **Verbo;** *Mauro and Giovanna dance the tango.*

1. **<u>Ah</u>! Ci hai fatto una bella sorpresa!**

   _____

2. **Luigi non si sente <u>bene</u>.**

   _____

3. **Non mi è piaciuto <u>il</u> film.**

   _____

4. **Vado <u>con</u> lei <u>in</u> montagna.**

   _____

5. **Bianca mangia il pesce, <u>ma</u> non mangia la carne.**

   _____

6. **Hai comprato <u>le</u> uova?**

   _____

7. **<u>Siete partiti</u> in orario?**

   _____

8. **Mi hanno dato una buona <u>ricetta</u>.**

   _____

9. **Non <u>ci</u> hanno ascoltato.**

   _____

Book III, Chapter 2: Noun and Article Basics: Gender and Number

Decide whether the following nouns are masculine or feminine and mark an *M* or *F* on the corresponding blank lines.

1. **algebra:** _____

2. **biro:** _____

3. **corsa:** _____

4. **dialisi:** _____

5. **medicina:** _____

6. **colle:** _____

7. **pera:** _____

8. **pino:** _____

9. **sapienza:** _____

10. **pelle:** _____

Book VI

Appendixes

Book III, Chapter 3: All about Pronouns

Replace the direct object (underlined) in the following sentences with a direct object pronoun, making any necessary changes to the past participle, as the example does.

Q. **Franco ha trovato <u>i cuccioli</u> nella strada.**

A. **li ha trovati**

1. **La nonna ha mandato <u>baci</u> a noi.**

_____

2. **Mirella ed io abbiamo ricevuto <u>le cartoline</u> ieri.**

_____

3. **Il babbo ha pagato <u>il conto</u>.**

_____

4. **Loro hanno studiato <u>la biologia</u>.**

_____

5. **Tu hai visitato <u>la chiesa ed il museo</u>, vero?**

_____

6. **Gli studenti hanno ordinato <u>vino ed acqua</u>.**

_____

7. **Lei ha portato <u>pantaloni corti</u>.**

_____

8. **Lei ha comprato <u>una macchina</u>.**

_____

9. **I bambini hanno frequentato <u>una scuola privata</u> l'anno scorso.**

_____

10. **I gattini hanno mangiato <u>le piante</u>.**

_____

Book III, Chapter 4: Adjectives, Adverbs, and Comparisons

Choose the adjective in the gender and number appropriate for the word that it describes. Both the ending and the meaning of the sentence should help you choose the right word from the options provided. See the example.

Q. **Il film era lunga/interessanti/noioso.**

A. **Il film era <u>noioso</u>.** (_The movie was boring._)

1. **La canzone è bello/interessante/lunghe.**
2. **Paolo compra una macchina nuova/rosso/grandi.**
3. **Giuliana è intelligenti/noioso/brillante.**
4. **Loro sono giovani/importante/bella.**
5. **Le mie sorelle sono giovane/vecchi/stanche.**
6. **Le arance non sono mature/buona/cattivi.**

Book III, Chapter 5: Meeting the Challenge of Prepositions

Insert **di** (*of*), **a** (*characterized by*), **da** (*with the function of*), or no preposition at all between the following sets of nouns. Here's an example:

Q. **la camicia _____ notte**

A. **la camicia da notte** (*nightgown*)

1. **gli occhiali _____ sole**

2. **i pantaloni _____ righe**

3. **il giornale _____ ieri**

4. **la tazzina _____ caffè**

5. **il discorso _____ Giovanna**

6. **un saggio _____ trenta pagine**

7. **il forno _____ microonde**

8. **l'asilo _____ nido**

Add the appropriate preposition(s) to the following notes. Choose from **di, a, da, in, con, su, per, tra, fra, sopra, sotto.** See the example.

Q. **Parto _____ Amsterdam** (destination) **_____ Milano** (origin).

A. **Parto per Amsterdam da Milano.** (*I'll leave for Amsterdam from Milan.*)

9. **Roma è a ottocento chilometri _____ Torino.**

10. **_____ la Francia e l'Olanda c'è il Belgio.**

11. **Strasburgo è _____ Francia.**

12. **Per andare _____ Madrid** (origin) **_____ Berlino** (destination) **passiamo _____ Monaco.**

13. **_____ Capri c'è la villa di Tiberio.**

14. **L'università di Oxford è _____ Inghilterra.**

15. **Il treno _____ Parigi** (origin) **_____ Londra** (destination) **passa _____ la Manica.**

Book III, Chapter 6: Demonstrative, Indefinite, and Possessive Qualifiers

Revise the following sentences by replacing the **di** plus noun/name or the **essere di** constructions with the appropriate possessive. Here's an example.

Q. **Quel gatto appartiene a Paolo?**

A. **Quel gatto è suo?** (*Is that cat his cat?*)

1. **I genitori di Marisa celebrano le nozze d'oro.**

   _____

2. **La figlia di Federico e Piera ha quindici anni.**

   _____

3. **È il collega dell'avvocato.**

   _____

4. **Sono arrivate tre amiche degli zii.**

   _____

5. **Quella macchina appartiene a voi?**

   _____

6. **Non toccare quella bambola! Appartiene a noi!**

   _____

From the options provided, select the proper conclusion to each sentence and write it in the blank.

Ce n'erano cinquantamila!

No, non abbiamo incontrato nessuno.

No, ce ne hanno messe cinque!

Qualcuno di voi è disponibile?

Sì, grazie, ne vorrei mezzo litro.

7. **Abbiamo bisogno di tre volontari.**

   _____

8. **Avete incontrato qualcuno al centro commerciale?**

   _____

9. **Ci hanno messo tre ore da Bologna a Firenze?**

_____

10. **Quante persone c'erano al concerto?**

_____

11. **Vuole dell'acqua minerale?**

_____

Book III, Chapter 7: Making Connections with Conjunctions and Relative Pronouns

Join the following sentences by using the appropriate relative pronouns. Use both the invariable or variable forms; at times, both will be correct. (*Tip:* You need to place the relative pronoun after the word to which it refers, which means that you may have to change the word order of the new sentence, as the example shows.)

Q. **Ti ho parlato di quella persona. È arrivata.**

A. **La persona di cui/della quale ti ho parlato è arrivata.** (*The person I was telling you about has arrived.*)

1. **Ho fatto un sogno. Volavo sopra il Polo Nord.**

_____

2. **Il professore è famoso. Darà la conferenza.**

_____

3. **Ci siamo dimenticati di quei libri. Puoi portarli tu?**

_____

4. **Volevo regalare un CD di Pavarotti a quella amica. Ce l'ha già.**

_____

5. **Siamo passati dall'aeroporto di Oslo. È molto bello.**

_____

6. **Siamo passati da quell'aeroporto. Ci ha fatto perdere la coincidenza.**

_____

Book III, Chapter 8: Asking and Answering Questions

Match these answers to the following questions.

A. **Siamo di New Orleans.**

B. **No, gli affitti delle case vicino all'università sono troppo alti.**

C. **No, non è così lontano. A piedi sono soltanto dieci minuti.**

D. **Siamo arrivati due giorni fa.**

E. **No, infatti deve iscriversi urgentemente anche a un corso di italiano.**

F. **Piacere, io sono Alexa e lui è Paul.**

G. **Studiamo al DAMS. Io studio Antropologia culturale e Paul segue un corso di Danza.**

1. **Ciao, io mi chiamo Silvio, e voi?** _____

2. **Piacere mio. Non siete di queste parti, vero? Da dove venite?** _____

3. **Che bello! Da quanto tempo siete qui?** _____

4. **Benvenuti! Cosa fate di bello in questa città?** _____

5. **Abitate vicino il DAMS?** _____

6. **Non è scomodo?** _____

7. **Ma Paul non dice mai una parola?** _____

Book IV, Chapter 1: Jumping into Action with Italian Regular Verbs

Conjugate the verbs in parentheses according to the subject pronouns, as shown in the example.

Q. **Mario** _____ **(leggere) molto.**

A. **legge**

1. **Io** _____ **(scrivere) cartoline agli amici.**

2. **Noi** _____ **(vivere) ad Arezzo.**

3. **Tu** _____ (prendere) thè o caffè?

4. **Lui** _____ (chiudere) la porta.

5. **Loro** _____ (vendere) frutta e verdura.

6. **Voi** _____ (vedere) quello?

7. **Mirella** _____ (rispondere) subito.

8. **Gli studenti** _____ (ripetere) le parole.

9. **Lei** _____ (credere) di sì.

10. **Noi** _____ (prendere) sempre l'autobus numero 7a.

11. **Tu** _____ (sentire) qualcosa?

12. **Riccardo** _____ (dormire) fino a tardi.

13. **Noi** _____ (aprire) i libri.

14. **Loro** _____ (finire) le lezioni all'una.

15. **Voi** _____ (partire) domani, vero?

16. **Francesca** _____ (capire) sempre.

17. **Loro** _____ (seguire) gli altri.

18. **Io** _____ (preferire) i gatti ai cani.

19. **Tu** _____ (pulire) la casa il sabato, no?

20. **Io non** _____ (sentire) nulla.

Book IV, Chapter 2: Talking in the Present Tense with Irregular Verbs

Use the appropriate conjugated form of **essere** (*to be*) in the following sentences according to the subject. Here's an example:

Q. **Marco** _____ **un bravo studente.**

A. **è**

1. **Loro** _____ **simpatici.**

2. **Tu** _____ **americana?**

3. **Voi** _____ **insegnanti?**

4. **Giulia e Chiara** _____ **cugine.**

5. Io _____ felice.

6. I bambini _____ a casa.

7. Tu e Paola _____ amici.

8. Laura _____ molto giovane.

9. Io ed Emilio _____ in campagna.

10. Tu e loro _____ in montagna durante l'estate.

Fill in the appropriately conjugated form of **avere** (*to have*) in the sentences that follow. Here's an example:

Q. **Noi** _____ **molto da fare.**

A. **abbiamo**

11. **Luigi** _____ **un gatto che è vecchio vecchio.**

12. **Voi** _____ **una bellissima casa.**

13. **Lei, signora,** _____ **il biglietto?**

14. **Io non** _____ **una macchina.**

15. **Tu** _____ **un amico che si chiama Leonardo?**

Book IV, Chapter 3: Using Reflexive Forms and the Imperative Mood

Keeping in mind the clues that help you distinguish between use of the present perfect and the imperfect, complete the following sentences with the reflexive or reciprocal reflexive form of the verb in parentheses, using one of the past tenses. Here's an example:

Q. **Da bambini, loro** _____ **(volersi) bene.**

A. **si volevano**

1. **La domenica, lei ed i bambini** _____ **(divertirsi).**

2. **Io** _____ **(preoccuparsi) sempre.**

3. **Ieri noi** _____ **(vedersi).**

4. **Ogni giorno gli amici** _____ **(vedersi).**

5. **Giovedì, loro** _____ **(laurearsi).**

6. **Ieri sera, io _____ (addormentarsi) presto.**

7. **Mentre loro _____ (parlarsi), io leggevo un libro.**

8. **Io _____ (trovarsi) molto bene a Venezia.**

9. **Da bambino, tu _____ (lamentarsi) spesso.**

10. **Mentre parlavano con il poeta, Paolo e Francesca _____ (ricordarsi) del tempo felice passato insieme.**

Translate the following expressions into Italian; the subject pronoun is provided for you.

Q. (**noi**) *Let's read.*

A. **Leggiamo.**

11. (**tu**) *Don't talk.*

_____

12. (**noi**) *Let's eat.*

_____

13. (**voi**) *Sleep.*

_____

14. (**tu**) *Sing.*

_____

15. (**tu**) *Don't call.*

_____

16. (**noi**) *Let's talk.*

_____

17. (**voi**) *Buy the car.*

_____

18. (**noi**) *Let's not write.*

_____

19. (**tu**) *Don't look.*

_____

20. (**voi**) *Wait.*

_____

Book IV, Chapter 4: Declaring Your Likes (And Dislikes) with Piacere

Choose either **piace** or **piacciono** (to express *like*) to complete the following sentences. Remember that you use **piace** for one thing, as in *Paolo likes jazz music,* and **piacciono** for more than one thing, as in *Lara likes classical music and ballet.* Here's an example:

Q. **Mi** _____ **i libri.**

A. **piacciono**

1. **Gli** _____ **studiare.**
2. **Ti** _____ **i bambini?**
3. **Non mi** _____ **i ragni.**
4. **A loro** _____ **mangiare.**
5. **Ci** _____ **i fiori.**
6. **Le** _____ **scrivere poesie.**
7. **Vi** _____ **gli sport?**
8. **Gli** _____ **i vini italiani.**
9. **Ti** _____ **il caffè ristretto?**
10. **A Mario** _____ **la bistecca fiorentina.**

After filling in the forms of **piace/piacciono,** translate the sentences into English, as per the following example.

Q. **Mi piacciono i libri.**

A. *I like books.*

11. _____
12. _____
13. _____
14. _____
15. _____
16. _____

17. _____
18. _____
19. _____
20. _____

Book IV, Chapter 5: The Future Tense and the Conditional Mood

Conjugate the following verbs into the future, using the subjects provided. Here's an example:

Q. **Lei** _____. (**uscire**)

A. **Lei uscirà.** (*She will write.*)

1. **Giuseppe** _____ **il compito.** (**finire**)

2. **Riccardo e Emilia** _____. (**camminare**)

3. **La mamma** _____. (**alzarsi**)

4. **Mio padre** _____ **l'albergo.** (**prenotare**)

5. **Giorgio ed io** _____ **il negozio.** (**aprire**)

6. **Io** _____ **un cono.** (**prendere**)

7. **Tu** _____ **un aumento.** (**chiedere**)

8. **Mia sorella ed io** _____ **il 22 maggio.** (**partire**)

9. **Lui** _____. (**divertirsi**)

10. **Voi** _____ **come sassi.** (**dormire**)

Fill in this brief dialogue between two lovers by using the regular conditional conjugations. Here's an example to get you started:

Lei: **Mi** _____ **ogni sera?** (**telefonare**)

Lui: **Sì, ti** _____ **ogni sera.** (**telefonare**)

Lei: **Mi telefoneresti ogni sera?** (She: *Would you phone me every night?*)

Lui: **Sì, ti telefonerei ogni sera.** (He: *Yes, I would phone you every night.*)

11. Lei: **Tu mi** _____ **per sempre?** (**amare**)

12. Lui: **Sì, io ti** _____ **per sempre. (amare)**

13. Lei: **Ci** _____ **la mano sul fuoco? (mettere [tu])**

14. Lui: **Sì, ci** _____ **la mano sul fuoco. (mettere [io])**

15. Lei: **Tu** _____ **con me per scoprire il mondo? (partire)**

16. Lui: **Amore, sì che** _____ **con te per scoprire il mondo. (partire [io])**

17. Lei: _____ **solo con me? (uscire [tu])**

18. Lui: **Sì,** _____ **solo con te. (uscire [io])**

19. Lei: **E quando mi** _____**? (sposare [tu])**

20. Lui: **Non ti** _____ **mai! (sposare [io])**

Book IV, Chapter 6: Getting into the Subjunctive Mood

For this exercise, conjugate the verbs in parentheses into the regular present subjunctive mood. This simple substitution exercise should drive home the concepts of structure and conjugation. Try to establish a drill-like rhythm while you do them, and notice all the verbs and the expressions in the main clauses: **sperare** (_to hope_), **credere** (_to believe_), **È importante** (_It's important_), **sono triste che** (_I am sad that_). Follow the example:

Q. **È importante che tu mi** _____. **(capire)**

A. **È importante che tu mi capisca.** (_It's important that you understand me._)

1. **È importante che voi mi** _____. **(capire)**

2. **È importante che loro mi** _____. **(capire)**

3. **È importante che la mia ragazza mi** _____. **(capire)**

4. **È importante che noi** _____. **(capire)**

5. **È importante che tu** _____. **(finire)**

6. **È importante che io** _____. **(finire)**

7. **È importante che la bambina** _____ **a nuotare. (divertirsi)**

8. **È importante che voi** _____ **a nuotare! (divertirsi)**

9. **È importante che loro** _____. **(ascoltare)**

10. **Bisogna che loro _____. (partire)**

11. **(Io) Sono triste che tu _____. (partire)**

12. **(Io) Sono triste che lui _____. (partire)**

13. **La mamma è triste che voi _____. (partire)**

14. **Loro sono tristi che io _____. (partire)**

15. **Loro sperano che voi _____ il film. (vedere)**

16. **Loro sperano che la mamma _____ il film. (vedere)**

17. **Loro sperano che tu _____ il film. (vedere)**

18. **Loro sperano che il professore _____ l'italiano. (parlare)**

19. **Spero che Giancarlo _____ presto domani. (alzarsi)**

20. **I miei genitori sperano che io _____ presto domani. (alzarsi)**

Book V, Chapter 1: Been There, Done That: Talking in the Past Tense

Complete the following sentences by filling in the past tense of the specified verb. Remember that each answer has two words. Here's an example.

Q. **I ragazzi _____ (mangiare) troppi dolci oggi.**

A. **hanno mangiato**

1. **Tu _____ (leggere) il libro?**

2. **Ieri loro _____ (vedere) un bel film.**

3. **Riccardo _____ (perdere) i documenti.**

4. **Tu ed io _____ (rispondere) alle domande.**

5. **I bambini _____ (guardare) la TV oggi?**

6. **Mario e Paolo _____ (chiudere) il negozio.**

7. **Voi _____ (prendere) un caffè bello caldo.**

8. **I genitori _____ (dire) di no.**

9. **Tu _____ (avere) una risposta da loro, vero?**

10. **Le ragazze non _____ (trovare) il gattino.**

Book V, Chapter 2: Reflexive Verbs in the Past

Using the reflexive present perfect, fill in the sentences with the conjugated forms of the verbs in parentheses. Here's an example:

Q. **I bambini** _____ **(svegliarsi) molto presto.**

A. **si sono svegliati**

1. **La famiglia** _____ **(trasferirsi [isc]) in Italia.**
2. **Lui** _____ **(mettersi) la cravatta oggi.**
3. **Noi** _____ **(divertirsi) tantissimo ieri sera.**
4. **Io** _____ **(prepararsi).**
5. **Paolo e Francesca** _____ **(innamorarsi) subito.**
6. **Ieri gli studenti** _____ **(laurearsi).**
7. **Lei** _____ **(affrettarsi).**
8. **Voi** _____ **(alzarsi) tardi.**
9. **Loro** _____ **(pentirsi).**
10. **Tu** _____ **(lamentarsi).**

Book V, Chapter 3: Second-Guessing Actions with the Past Conditional and Past Perfect

Conjugate the following verbs in parentheses into the conditional past tense, adding the correct form of **essere** (*to be*) or **avere** (*to have*) along the way. You may not necessarily form complete sentences. For example, you could say **Io mi sarei alzata . . . ma/se . . .** and mean *I would've gotten up . . . but/if . . .* and then follow with something else, but you could also say (as you may in English) **Io mi sarei alzata** (*I would've gotten up*). ***Remember:*** The verb **avere** takes **avere** as its auxiliary verb, and the verb **essere** takes **essere** as its auxiliary verb. Follow this example:

Q. **Io** _____ . . . (alzarsi)

A. **Io mi sarei alzato/a** . . . (_I would've gotten up_ . . .)

1. **Guglielmo** _____ **il** . . . (**fare**)

2. **Giancarlo ed io** _____ . . . (**sposarsi**)

3. **Tu e Stefano** _____ . . . (**giocare**)

4. **Stefania e Michele** _____ . . . (**divertirsi**)

5. **Tu** _____ . . . (**partire**)

6. **Io** _____ . . . (**chiedere**)

7. **Davide** _____ **pronto** . . . (**essere**)

8. **Noi** _____ . . . (**mangiare**)

9. **Voi** _____ . . . (**nascondersi**)

10. **Casanova** _____ . . . (**sedurre**)

Book V, Chapter 4: 1 Hope That You've Had Fun! The Subjunctive Mood in the Past

Conjugate the following verbs in parentheses into the past subjunctive, like the example that follows:

Q. **Sembra che** _____. (**partire** [**loro**])

A. **Sembra che siano partiti.** (_It seems like they've left._)

1. **Sembra che la mamma** _____ **del freddo a Torino.** (**lamentarsi**)

2. **Sembra che voi** _____ **tardi.** (**alzarsi**)

3. **Non so se loro** _____ **a Napoli.** (**stare** [**mai**])

4. **Credo che** _____ **soltanto Capri ed Ischia.** (**visitare** [**loro**])

5. **È probabile che Emilia** _____ **queste parole a scuola.** (**imparare**)

6. **Cosa credi che** _____? (**succedere**)

7. **Mi dispiace che** _____. (**litigare** [**voi**])

8. **Mi dispiace che voi** _____. **(lasciarsi)**

9. **È bene che io finalmente** _____. **(capire)**

10. **Non mi pare che tu** _____ **così. (dire)**

11. **Non mi pare che tu** _____ **così. (fare)**

12. **Adriana e Rudi non immaginano che io** _____, **vero?
(arrivare)**

13. **Adriana e Rudi non credono che io** _____, **vero?
(telefonare)**

14. **È importante che Guglielmo** _____ **tanto. (impegnarsi)**

15. **Temo che gli avvocati** _____ **un errore. (commettere)**

Book V, Chapter 5: "If" Clauses, the Impersonal, and the Passive

Choose the verb tense and conjugation that completes the **se** clause in the
following sentences. Some questions may have more than one answer. Here's
an example.

Q. **Se tu** _____ **(desiderare), lo facciamo.**

A. **desideri**

1. **Se tu** _____ **(avere) del tempo libero, ci andremo
domani.**

2. **Se loro non** _____ **(volere), me lo potevano dire.**

3. **Se lui** _____ **(arrivare), mangeremo insieme.**

4. **Se lei non** _____ **(studiare), non riceverà buoni voti.**

5. **Se Angelo e Guido** _____ **(andare), andrò anch'io.**

6. **Se tu** _____ **(preferire), resta qui.**

7. **Se io** _____ **(trovare) i biglietti, verrai con me?**

8. **Se** _____ **(succedere) un'altra volta, griderò!**

9. **Se tu lo** _____ **(volere) sapere, gli ho telefonato.**

10. **Se loro** _____ **(partire), partiranno fra poco.**

Book V, Chapter 6: Progressing through Gerunds in Italian

For this exercise, transform the following infinitives into the present gerund form and then translate your answer. Here's an example:

Q. **diventare**

A. **diventando;** *becoming*

1. **andare** _____
2. **viaggiare** _____
3. **vedere** _____
4. **riflettere** _____
5. **lasciarsi** _____
6. **vestirsi** _____
7. **finire** _____
8. **avere** _____
9. **non sapere** _____
10. **morire** _____

Answer Key

The following sections provide answers and translations for the activities in this appendix. The answers appear in **boldface**.

Book I, Chapter 1: Exploring Pronunciations and Italian You May Already Know

Read the passage aloud. Here's the translation of the Italian:

> I'm American, but I consider myself a citizen of the world. I speak three languages, English, Spanish, and Italian, and I love to travel. I'm from Chicago and study art history at the university. I love contemporary art, so this summer I'm going to Venice for the Biennale. Do you know it? It is an international exhibition of contemporary art, which is famous all over the world. When I participate in events like these, I meet many young people who, like me, love art. They come from all over the world. Being able to communicate with them without barriers of language is exciting. True, many speak English, but not all. So my knowledge of foreign languages is very useful.

> When I'm in Chicago, I keep in touch with my friends through my blog "VagabondA," where we exchange information about cultural events in our countries. I must say that when I want to talk about a show or a concert, [knowing] Italian helps me a lot. It's amazing the number of words that this language has lent to the vocabulary of the arts! Now I am organizing an exhibition of contemporary art at my university, to which I invited many artist friends, met during my travels. If you are nearby, stop by. It's worth it!

Book I, Chapter 2: Dealing with Numbers, Dates, and Time

A. **inverno** (*winter*); **dicembre, gennaio, febbraio** (*December, January, February*)

B. **estate** (*summer*); **giugno, luglio, agosto** (*June, July, August*)

C. **primavera** (*spring*); **marzo, aprile, maggio** (*March, April, May*)

D. **autunno** (*fall*); **settembre, ottobre, novembre** (*September, October, November*)

Book 1, Chapter 3: Buongiorno! Salutations!

1. come sta
2. e Lei
3. Le presento
4. conoscerla
5. il piacere

Book 1, Chapter 4: Making Small Talk

1. mia madre; mio padre
2. mio fratello
3. i miei nipoti
4. mia nonna
5. mia zia
6. mio cognato
7. mia nuora
8. mia figlia
9. i miei cugini
10. mia suocera

Book 1, Chapter 5: Casa Dolce Casa: Home Sweet Home

1. il bagno (*the bathroom*)
2. la camera da letto (*the bedroom*)
3. il letto (*the bed*)
4. il soggiorno (*the living room*)
5. il divano (*the couch*)

6. **i fornelli** (*the stovetop*)
7. **la cucina** (*the kitchen*)
8. **la tavola** (*the table*)

Book 1, Chapter 6: Using the Phone and Talking Business

1. **Pronto**
2. **parlo**
3. **amico**
4. **C'è**
5. **appena**
6. **lasciare un messaggio**
7. **Prego**
8. **chiamato**

Book 1, Chapter 7: Food, Glorious Food, and Drink

1. **ananas**
2. **ciliegia**
3. **uva**
4. **pera**
5. **cocomero**
6. **fragola**

Book 1, Chapter 8: Shopping, Italian-Style

1. **cappello**
2. **camicia**
3. **cravatta**

4. **completo**

5. **pantaloni**

6. **scarpe**

7. **gonna**

8. **camicetta**

Book II, Chapter 1: Where Is the Colosseum? Asking Directions

1. **della Vigna Nuova**

2. **Ponte Santa Trinità; Ponte Vecchio**

3. **Arno**

4. **Palazzo Vecchio**

5. **Piazza Duomo** and **Piazza San Giovanni**

6. **Lungarno**

7. **Piazza della Repubblica**

Book II, Chapter 2: Having Fun Out on the Town

1. **festa**

2. **invitato**

3. **sabato**

4. **ora**

5. **verso**

6. **dove**

7. **perchè**

8. **aspetto**

Book II, Chapter 3: Exploring the Outdoors, Sports, and Hobbies

cavallo (*horse*), **fiore** (*flower*), **uccello** (*bird*), **gatto** (*cat*), **lupo** (*wolf*), **quercia** (*oak [tree]*), **pino** (*pine [tree]*), **mucca** (*cow*), **pecora** (*sheep*), **albero** (*tree*)

Illustration by Wiley, Composition Services Graphics

Book II, Chapter 4: Planning a Trip

1. b. montagna
2. a. da
3. b. campagna
4. c. valigia
5. a. viaggio

Book II, Chapter 5: Money, Money, Money

1. Bank
2. ATM

3. **To change**

4. **Credit card**

5. **Cash**

6. **Identity document**

7. **Dollar**

8. **Euro[s]**

9. **Croatian currency**

10. **Receipt**

11. **Small change**

12. **Counter**

13. **British pounds**

```
C  A  R  T  A  D  I  C  R  E  D  I  T  O  D
S  O  K  S  Z  N  B  O  Y  D  O  Y  Y  D  O
E  R  R  Y  P  A  Z  G  E  C  L  S  A  M  C
T  R  J  U  N  O  G  P  S  D  L  P  N  F  U
A  X  A  C  E  B  R  P  Q  Z  A  K  U  L  M
M  G  A  I  A  M  I  T  Q  S  R  X  K  J  E
O  L  W  A  B  C  T  O  E  Y  O  R  J  I  N
C  H  L  N  C  M  E  N  I  L  R  E  T  S  T
N  C  K  I  E  B  A  I  N  V  L  N  L  H  O
A  J  O  A  S  S  A  C  K  R  A  O  Z  P  H
B  L  T  R  I  C  E  V  U  T  A  A  S  E  K
I  E  H  T  W  N  L  C  N  X  M  K  Q  G  V
Q  J  A  U  Y  C  V  O  Q  A  G  M  N  A  Q
Q  L  N  Q  E  K  C  Y  P  D  F  Q  L  V  W
Z  Q  X  X  B  E  J  M  W  F  Y  Y  A  L  N
```

Illustration by Wiley, Composition Services Graphics

Book 11, Chapter 6: Getting Around: Planes, Trains, Taxis, and Buses

treno (*train*), **fermata** (*bus stop*), **stazione** (*[train] station*), **binario** (*track*), **biglietto** (*ticket*), **andata** (*one way*), **ritorno** (*return trip*), **supplemento** (*surcharge*)

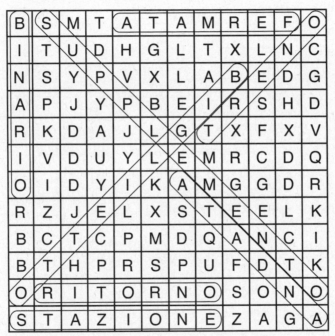

Illustration by Wiley, Composition Services Graphics

Book 11, Chapter 7: Finding a Place to Stay

1. **albergo** (*hotel*)
2. **pensione** (*small hotel*)
3. **camera** (*room*)
4. **stanza** (*room*)
5. **valigie** (*suitcases*)

6. **prenotazione** (*reservation*)

7. **matrimoniale** (*room with a large bed for two*)

8. **culla** (*crib*)

9. **chiave** (*key*)

10. **piscina** (*swimming pool*)

11. **letto** (*bed*)

12. **cameriere** (*waiter*)

13. **bagno** (*bathroom*)

14. **bagaglio** (*luggage*)

Book 11, Chapter 8: Handling Emergencies

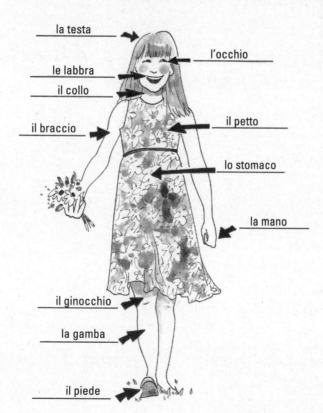

la testa

l'occhio

le labbra

il collo

il braccio

il petto

lo stomaco

la mano

il ginocchio

la gamba

il piede

Illustration by Elizabeth Kurtzman

Book III, Chapter 1: What Do You Know? Parts of Speech

1. Interiezione; *Ah! You prepared a nice surprise for us!*

2. Avverbio; *Luigi doesn't feel well.*

3. Articolo; *I didn't like the movie.*

4. Preposizione; *I'm going to the mountains with her.*

5. Congiunzione; *Bianca eats fish but she doesn't eat meat.*

6. Articolo; *Did you buy eggs?*

7. Verbo; *Did you leave on time?*

8. Sostantivo; *They gave me a good recipe.*

9. Pronome; *They didn't listen to us.*

Book III, Chapter 2: Noun and Article Basics: Gender and Number

1. **algebra** (*algebra*): **F**

2. **biro** (*ballpoint pen*): **F**

3. **corsa** (*run*): **F**

4. **dialisi** (*dialysis*): **F**

5. **medicina** (*medicine*): **F**

6. **colle** (*pass, hill*): **M**

7. **pera** (*pear*): **F**

8. **pino** (*pine tree*): **M**

9. **sapienza** (*wisdom*): **F**

10. **pelle** (*skin; leather*): **F**

Book III, Chapter 3: All about Pronouns

1. **li ha mandati**

2. **le abbiamo ricevute**

3. **l'ha pagato**

4. **l'hanno studiata**

5. **li hai visitati**

6. **li hanno ordinati**

7. **li ha portati**

8. **l'ha comprata**

9. **l'hanno frequentata**

10. **le hanno mangiate**

Book III, Chapter 4: Adjectives, Adverbs, and Comparisons

1. **La canzone è <u>interessante</u>.** (*The song is interesting.*)

2. **Paolo compra una macchina <u>nuova</u>.** (*Paolo is buying a new car.*)

3. **Giuliana è <u>brillante</u>.** (*Giuliana is brilliant.*)

4. **Loro sono <u>giovani</u>.** (*They are young.*)

5. **Le mie sorelle sono <u>stanche</u>.** (*My sisters are tired.*)

6. **Le arance non sono <u>mature</u>.** (*The oranges aren't ripe.*)

Book III, Chapter 5: Meeting the Challenge of Prepositions

1. **gli occhiali <u>da</u> sole** (*sunglasses*)

2. **i pantaloni <u>a</u> righe** (*striped pants*)

3. **il giornale <u>di</u> ieri** (*yesterday's newspaper*)

4. **la tazzina <u>da</u> caffè** (*demitasse [cup]*)

5. **il discorso <u>di</u> Giovanna** (*Giovanna's speech*)

6. **un saggio <u>di</u> trenta pagine** (*a 30-page essay*)

7. **il forno <u>a</u> microonde** (*the microwave oven*)

8. **l'asilo nido** (*nursery school*)

9. **Roma è a ottocento chilometri <u>da</u> Torino.** (*Rome is 800 kilometers from Turin.*)

10. <u>Tra</u> **la Francia e l'Olanda c'è il Belgio.** (*Belgium is between France and Holland.*)

11. **Strasburgo è <u>in</u> Francia.** (*Strasburg is in France.*)

12. **Per andare <u>da</u> Madrid <u>a</u> Berlino passiamo <u>da/per</u> Monaco.** (*To go from Madrid to Berlin, we'll go through Munich.*)

13. **<u>A</u> Capri c'è la villa di Tiberio.** (*Tiberius's villa is on Capri.*)

14. **L'università di Oxford è <u>in</u> Inghilterra.** (*Oxford University is in England.*)

15. **Il treno <u>da</u> Parigi <u>per</u> Londra passa <u>sotto</u> la Manica.** (*The train from Paris to London goes under the Channel.*)

Book III, Chapter 6: Demonstrative, Indefinite, and Possessive Qualifiers

1. **I suoi genitori celebrano le nozze d'oro.** (*Her parents celebrate their gold wedding anniversary.*)

2. **La loro figlia ha quindici anni.** (*Their daughter is 15 years old.*)

3. **È il suo collega.** (*He's one of his colleagues.*)

4. **Sono arrivate tre delle lore amiche.** (*Three of their friends have arrived.*)

5. **Quella macchina è vostra?** (*Is that car yours?*)

6. **Non toccare quella bambola! È nostra!** (*Don't touch that doll! It's ours!*)

7. **Qualcuno di voi è disponibile?** (*Is anyone available?*)

8. **No, non abbiamo incontrato nessuno.** (*No, we didn't meet anyone.*)

9. **No, ce ne hanno messe cinque!** (*Oh no, it took them five!*)

10. **Ce n'erano cinquantamila!** (*There were 50,000 people!*)

11. **Sì, grazie, ne vorrei mezzo litro.** (*Yes, thank you, I'd like half a liter.*)

Book III, Chapter 7: Making Connections with Conjunctions and Relative Pronouns

1. **Ho fatto un sogno in cui/nel quale volavo sopra il Polo Nord.** (*I had a dream in which I was flying over the North Pole.*)

2. **Il professore che darà la conferenza è famoso.** (*The professor who will give the lecture is famous.*)

3. **Puoi portare tu quei libri di cui ci siamo dimenticati?** (*Can you bring those books which we forgot?*)

4. **L'amica [a] cui/alla quale volevo regalare un CD di Pavarotti, ce l'ha già.** (*The friend to whom I wanted to give a Pavarotti CD already has it.*)

5. **Siamo passati dall'aeroporto di Oslo, che è molto bello.** (*We flew through the Oslo airport, which is beautiful.*)

6. **L'aeroporto da cui/dal quale, per cui/per il quale siamo passati ci ha fatto perdere la coincidenza.** (*The airport we went through made us miss our connection.*)

Book III, Chapter 8: Asking and Answering Questions

1. F. Piacere, io sono Alexa e lui è Paul.

2. A. Siamo di New Orleans.

3. D. Siamo arrivati due giorni fa.

4. G. Studiamo al DAMS. Io studio Antropologia culturale e Paul segue un corso di Danza.

5. B. No, gli affitti delle case vicino all'università sono troppo alti.

6. C. No, non è così lontano. A piedi sono soltanto dieci minuti.

7. E. No, infatti deve iscriversi urgentemente anche a un corso di italiano!

Book IV, Chapter 1: Jumping into Action with Italian Regular Verbs

1. scrivo

2. viviamo

3. prendi

4. chiude

5. vendono

6. vedete

7. risponde

8. ripetono

9. crede

10. prendiamo

11. senti

12. dorme

13. apriamo

14. finiscono

15. partite

16. capisce

17. seguono

18. preferisco

19. pulisci

20. sento

Book IV, Chapter 2: Talking in the Present Tense with Irregular Verbs

1. sono

2. sei

3. siete

4. sono

5. sono

6. sono

7. siete

8. è

9. siamo

10. siete

11. ha

12. avete

13. ha

14. ho

15. hai

Book IV, Chapter 3: Using Reflexive Forms and the Imperative Mood

1. si divertivano
2. mi preoccupavo
3. ci siamo visti
4. si vedevano
5. si sono laureati
6. mi sono addormentato/addormentata
7. si parlavano
8. mi trovavo/mi sono trovato
9. ti lamentavi
10. si sono ricordati
11. Non parlare.
12. Mangiamo.
13. Dormite.
14. Canta.
15. Non telefonare.
16. Parliamo.
17. Comprate la macchina.
18. Non scriviamo.
19. Non guardare.
20. Aspettate.

Book IV, Chapter 4: Declaring Your Likes (And Dislikes) with Piacere

1. piace
2. piacciono
3. piacciono
4. piace
5. piacciono

6. **piace**

7. **piacciono**

8. **piacciono**

9. **piace**

10. **piace**

11. *He likes to study.*

12. *Do you like children?*

13. *I don't like spiders.*

14. *They like to eat.*

15. *We like flowers.*

16. *She likes to write poems.*

17. *Do you like sports?*

18. *They like Italian wines. He likes Italian wines.*

19. *Do you like strong coffee?*

20. *Mario likes Florentine steak.*

Book IV, Chapter 5: The Future Tense and the Conditional Mood

1. Giuseppe <u>finirà</u> il compito. (*Giuseppe will finish his homework.*)

2. Riccardo e Emilia <u>cammineranno</u>. (*Riccardo and Emilia will walk.*)

3. La mamma <u>si alzerà</u>. (*Mom will get up.*)

4. Mio padre <u>prenoterà</u> l'albergo. (*My dad will reserve the hotel.*)

5. Giorgio ed io <u>apriremo</u> il negozio. (*Giorgio and I will open the store.*)

6. Io <u>prenderò</u> un cono. (*I will have a cone.*)

7. Tu <u>chiederai</u> un aumento. (*You will ask for a raise.*)

8. Mia sorella ed io <u>partiremo</u> il 22 maggio. (*My sister and I will leave on May 22.*)

9. Lui <u>si divertirà</u>. (*He will have fun.*)

10. Voi <u>dormirete</u> come sassi. (*You* [plural] *will sleep like a log* [literally: *like a stone*].)

11. Lei: Tu mi <u>ameresti</u> per sempre?

12. Lui: **Sì, io ti <u>amerei</u> per sempre.**

13. Lei: **Ci <u>metteresti</u> la mano sul fuoco?**

14. Lui: **Sì, ci <u>metterei</u> la mano sul fuoco.**

15. Lei: **Tu <u>partiresti</u> con me per scoprire il mondo?**

16. Lui: **Amore, sì che <u>partirei</u> con te per scoprire il mondo.**

17. Lei: **<u>Usciresti</u> solo con me?**

18. Lui: **Sì, <u>uscirei</u> solo con te.**

19. Lei: **E quando mi <u>sposeresti</u>?**

20. Lui: **Non ti <u>sposerei</u> mai!**

Book IV, Chapter 6: Getting into the Subjunctive Mood

1. **È importante che voi <u>mi capiate</u>.** (*It's important that you* [plural] *understand me.*)

2. **È importante che loro <u>mi capiscano</u>.** (*It's important that they understand me.*)

3. **È importante che la mia ragazza <u>mi capisca</u>.** (*It's important that my girl-friend understands me.*)

4. **È importante che noi <u>capiamo</u>.** (*It's important that we understand.*)

5. **È importante che tu <u>finisca</u>.** (*It's important that you finish.*)

6. **È importante che io <u>finisca</u>.** (*It's important that I finish.*)

7. **È importante che la bambina <u>si diverta</u> a nuotare.** (*It's important that the baby have fun swimming.*)

8. **È importante che voi <u>vi divertiate</u> a nuotare!** (*It's important that you have fun swimming!*)

9. **È importante che loro <u>ascoltino</u>.** (*It's important that they listen.*)

10. **Bisogna che loro <u>partano</u>.** (*It's necessary that they leave.*) (*They need to leave.*)

11. **Sono triste che tu <u>parta</u>.** (*I'm sad that you're leaving.*)

12. **Sono triste che lui <u>parta</u>.** (*I'm sad that he's leaving.*)

13. **La mamma è triste che voi <u>partiate</u>.** (*Mom is sad that you all are leaving.*)

14. **Loro sono tristi che io <u>parta</u>.** (*They're sad that I'm leaving.*)

15. **Loro sperano che voi <u>vediate</u> il film.** (*They hope that you* [plural] *see the movie.*)

16. **Loro sperano che la mamma <u>veda</u> il film.** (*They hope that mom sees the film.*)

17. **Loro sperano che tu <u>veda</u> il film.** (*They hope that you see the movie.*)

18. **Loro sperano che il professore <u>parli</u> l'italiano.** (*They hope that the professor speaks Italian.*)

19. **Spero che Giancarlo <u>si alzi</u> presto domani.** (*I hope that Giancarlo gets up early tomorrow.*)

20. **I miei genitori sperano che io <u>mi alzi</u> presto domani.** (*My parents hope that I get up early tomorrow.*)

Book V, Chapter 1: Been There, Done That: Talking in the Past Tense

1. **hai letto**
2. **hanno visto**
3. **ha perso**
4. **abbiamo risposto**
5. **hanno guardato**
6. **hanno chiuso**
7. **avete preso**
8. **hanno detto**
9. **hai avuto**
10. **hanno trovato**

Book V, Chapter 2: Reflexive Verbs in the Past

1. **si è trasferita**
2. **si è messo**
3. **ci siamo divertiti**
4. **mi sono preparato/preparata**

5. **si sono innamorati**

6. **si sono laureati**

7. **si è affrettata**

8. **vi siete alzati/alzate**

9. **si sono pentiti**

10. **ti sei lamentato/lamentata**

Book V, Chapter 3: Second-Guessing Actions with the Past Conditional and Past Perfect

1. **Guglielmo <u>avrebbe fatto</u> il** . . . (*Guglielmo would have done . . .*)

2. **Giancarlo ed io <u>ci saremmo sposati</u>** . . . (*Giancarlo and I would've gotten married . . .*)

3. **Tu e Stefano <u>avreste giocato</u>** . . . (*You and Stefano would've played . . .*)

4. **Stefania e Michele <u>si sarebbero divertiti</u>** . . . (*Stefania and Michele would've had fun . . .*)

5. **Tu <u>saresti partito</u>** . . . (*You would've left . . .*)

6. **Io <u>avrei chiesto</u>** . . . (*I would've asked . . .*)

7. **Davide <u>sarebbe stato</u> pronto** . . . (*David would've been ready . . .*)

8. **Noi <u>avremmo mangiato</u>** . . . (*We would've eaten . . .*)

9. **Voi <u>vi sareste nascosti</u>** . . . (*You* [plural] *would've hidden . . .*)

10. **Casanova <u>avrebbe sedotto</u>** . . . (*Casanova would've seduced . . .*)

Book V, Chapter 4: I Hope That You've Had Fun! The Subjunctive Mood in the Past

1. **Sembra che la mamma <u>si sia lamentata</u> del freddo a Torino.** (*It looks like mom complained about the cold in Torino.*)

2. **Sembra che voi <u>vi siate alzati</u> tardi.** (*It seems like you* [plural] *got up late.*)

3. **Non so se loro <u>siano mai stati</u> a Napoli.** (*I don't know if they've ever been to Naples.*)

4. **Credo che <u>abbiano visitato</u> soltanto Capri ed Ischia.** (*I believe that they've only visited Capri and Ischia.*)

5. **È probabile che Emilia <u>abbia imparato</u> queste parole a scuola.** (*It's likely that Emilia learned these words at school.*)

6. **Cosa credi che <u>sia successo</u>?** (*What do you think happened?*)

7. **Mi dispiace che <u>abbiate litigato</u>.** (*I'm sorry that you [plural] argued.*)

8. **Mi dispiace che voi <u>vi siate lasciati</u>.** (*I'm sorry that you left each other.*)

9. **È bene che io finalmente <u>abbia capito</u>.** (*It's a good thing that I finally understood.*)

10. **Non mi pare che tu <u>abbia detto</u> così.** (*It doesn't seem to me that you said so.*)

11. **Non mi pare che tu <u>abbia fatto</u> così.** (*It doesn't seem to me that you did that.*)

12. **Adriana e Rudi non immaginano che io <u>sia arrivata/o</u>, vero?** (*Adriana and Rudi don't know that I've arrived, right?*)

13. **Adriana e Rudi non credono che io <u>abbia telefonato</u>, vero?** (*Adriana and Rudi don't know that I phoned, right?*)

14. **È importante che Guglielmo <u>si sia impegnato</u> tanto.** (*It's important that Will worked so hard.*)

15. **Temo che gli avvocati <u>abbiano commesso</u> un errore.** (*I fear that the lawyers made an error.*)

Book V, Chapter 5: "If" Clauses, the Impersonal, and the Passive

1. **hai, avrai**

2. **volevano**

3. **arriva, arriverà**

4. **studia, studierà**

5. **vanno, andranno**

6. **preferisci**

7. **trovo, troverò**

8. **succeede, succederà**

9. **vuoi**

10. **partono, partiranno**

Book V, Chapter 6: Progressing through Gerunds in Italian

1. **andando;** *going*
2. **viaggiando;** *traveling*
3. **vedendo;** *seeing*
4. **riflettendo;** *reflecting*
5. **lasciandosi;** *leaving each other*
6. **vestendosi;** *dressing him/herself*
7. **finendo;** *finishing*
8. **avendo;** *having*
9. **non sapendo;** *not knowing*
10. **morendo;** *dying*

Appendix E

Audio Tracks

• •

*T*his appendix is a guide to the 29 audio tracks that accompany this book. We recorded many of the Talkin' the Talk dialogues found in Books I and II to help you sharpen your listening skills. You're sure to discover more about pronunciation and oral communication by listening to these Italian speakers.

If you've purchased the paper or e-book version of *Italian All-in-One For Dummies,* just go to www.dummies.com/go/italianaio to access and download these tracks. (If you don't have Internet access, call 877-762-2974 within the U.S. or 317-572-3993 outside the U.S.)

Discovering What's on the Audio Tracks

You can use the audio tracks to practice both your listening comprehension and your speech. If your goal is to work on pronunciation, start by listening to the tracks that accompany the first chapter of Book I and discover all those funny new sounds. Imitate the speakers and start to sound Italian.

Here are a couple of ways you can practice your listening comprehension:

✔ First, read a dialogue for comprehension. Then listen to the track without following the written script in the chapter to see how much you understand without visual support. Repeat this exercise as many times as you like.

✔ Before you even read a dialogue, listen to it a couple of times and extract as many ideas as possible from it. Then check the written dialogue in your book to confirm how much you understood.

Here are some ways to practice your speaking ability:

- ✔ Read the dialogue in the book. Say one sentence at a time aloud before listening to that sentence to check whether it sounds the way you thought it would.

- ✔ Pick one of the speakers and pretend to be that person, allowing you to interact with the other person(s) in the conversation. Say your lines aloud as you play the audio track. You can even take turns being different characters.

Track Listing

The following is a list of the audio tracks that accompany this book.

Track 1: The Italian alphabet (Book I, Chapter 1)

Track 2: Pronouncing numbers in Italian (Book I, Chapter 2)

Track 3: Specifying numbers and dates (Book I, Chapter 2)

Track 4: Expressing time (Book I, Chapter 2)

Track 5: Introducing people (Book I, Chapter 3)

Track 6: Discussing how to spend the day (Book I, Chapter 4)

Track 7: Talking about home (Book I, Chapter 5)

Track 8: Speaking with a friend on the phone (Book I, Chapter 6)

Track 9: Making arrangements over the phone (Book I, Chapter 6)

Track 10: Conducting a business call (Book I, Chapter 6)

Track 11: Having dinner with friends (Book I, Chapter 7)

Track 12: Getting ice cream (Book I, Chapter 7)

Track 13: Making restaurant reservations (Book I, Chapter 7)

Track 14: Asking for assistance in a store (Book I, Chapter 8)

Track 15: Shopping for clothing (Book I, Chapter 8)

Track 16: Shopping for shoes (Book I, Chapter 8)

Track 17: Asking for directions (Book II, Chapter 1)

Track 18: Following directions (Book II, Chapter 1)

Track 19: Giving an invitation (Book II, Chapter 2)

Track 20: Discussing sports (Book II, Chapter 3)

Track 21: Talking about vacation (Book II, Chapter 4)

Track 22: Discussing travel plans (Book II, Chapter 4)

Track 23: Changing currency (Book II, Chapter 5)

Track 24: Discussing currency exchanges (Book II, Chapter 5)

Track 25: Inquiring about train schedules (Book II, Chapter 6)

Track 26: Discussing city transportation (Book II, Chapter 6)

Track 27: Checking in at a hotel (Book II, Chapter 7)

Track 28: Consulting a doctor (Book II, Chapter 8)

Track 29: Reporting an incident to the police (Book II, Chapter 8)

Book VI

Appendixes

Index

• G •

• *Q* •

• *R* •

● *y* ●

Notes

Notes

About the Authors

Antonietta Di Pietro is a native of Rome. She holds an MA in Italian pedagogy from the Università per Stranieri di Siena and an MA and a PhD in Atlantic History from Florida International University. She is fully certified as an ACTFL OPI Tester and has conducted research on the cultural identity of Italian immigrants in Miami and Southeast Florida and on Italian folk traditions. Her extensive teaching experience has helped her develop tailored teaching strategies for a very broad range of students.

Francesca Romana Onofri studied linguistics and Spanish and English language and literature in university. After graduation, she lived abroad for several years to better understand the cultures and languages of different countries. In Spain and Ireland, she worked as an Italian and Spanish teacher as well as a translator and interpreter at cultural events. In Germany, she was responsible for communication and special events in a museum of modern art, but even then she never gave up on her passion for languages: She was an Italian coach and teacher at the Opera Studio of the Cologne Opera House and did translation — especially in the art field. Back in Italy, Francesca has edited several Berlitz Italian books, translates art books, and serves as a cultural events organizer and educator.

Teresa Picarazzi graduated with a BA from Skidmore College and an MA and a PhD in Italian Literature from Rutgers University. For many years, she taught Italian language, literature, and culture at several universities, including The University of Arizona, Wesleyan University, and Dartmouth College. She also directed the Italian language and study abroad programs at some of these schools. More recently, she has taught Italian at The Hopkins School in New Haven, Connecticut. In her spare time, Teresa likes to cook and read. She lives in Fairfield, Connecticut, with her daughter, her husband, Toby the dog, and Mittens and Governor the cats. The family spends every summer in Ravenna, Italy.

Karen Möller has studied Italian and English linguistics, literature, and culture. Before entering academia, Karen worked in the field of public relations and wrote articles for all kinds of fashion magazines and newspapers. Recently, she's worked with Berlitz Publishing on German-Italian projects, including verb, vocabulary, and grammar handbooks and Italian exercise books.

Daniela Gobetti is a native of Italy who has lived in the United States for more than 30 years. She holds a *Laurea in Lettere e Filosofia* from the University of Turin, Italy, and a PhD in Political Science from Columbia University. She has taught political theory for several years and has helped build the European Union Center at the University of Michigan. She's one of the founders of PROXIMA — Global Education Consulting Training, a consulting firm in the field of the internationalization of higher education and of cultural training. Daniela has taught Italian, translated books from Italian into English and from English into Italian, published peer-reviewed articles in both languages, and authored several books on learning Italian.

Beth Bartolini-Salimbeni teaches languages and literatures (Italian, Spanish, Latin, and English) and history at the high-school and university levels. Beth grew up in a household that valued languages, and her parents, Art and Ellie Gard, made it possible for her to travel, study, and work abroad. She has studied and carried out research in Italy, Spain, England, and Argentina (where she was a Fulbright Fellow). She holds a BA in Spanish literature and history and an MA in comparative literature. Beth has founded and directed summer programs for high-school students, university undergraduate and graduate students, and adults in Latin America and Italy since the 1970s.

Dedication

I would like to thank my editors at Wiley — Elizabeth Rea, Jennette ElNaggar, and Christy Pingleton — who were always kind and helpful, and the technical reviewers, Mario Costa and Elisa Lucchi-Riester. Special thanks go to my friend Elizabeth S. for her inspiration. —Antonietta Di Pietro

Author's Acknowledgments

For those who have a passion for all things Italian. —Antonietta Di Pietro

Publisher's Acknowledgments

Associate Editor: David Lutton

Project Editor: Elizabeth Rea

Copy Editors: Jennette ElNaggar,
Christine Pingleton

Technical Editors: Mario Costa,
Elisa Lucchi-Riester

Senior Project Coordinator: Kristie Rees

Supervising Producer: Rich Graves

Cover Image: ©Design Pics/jupitierimages

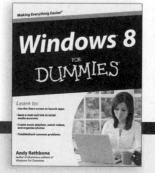

Math & Science

Algebra I For Dummies,
2nd Edition
978-0-470-55964-2

Anatomy and Physiology
For Dummies,
2nd Edition
978-0-470-92326-9

Astronomy For Dummies,
3rd Edition
978-1-118-37697-3

Biology For Dummies,
2nd Edition
978-0-470-59875-7

Chemistry For Dummies,
2nd Edition
978-1-1180-0730-3

Pre-Algebra Essentials
For Dummies
978-0-470-61838-7

Microsoft Office

Excel 2013 For Dummies
978-1-118-51012-4

Office 2013 All-in-One
For Dummies
978-1-118-51636-2

PowerPoint 2013
For Dummies
978-1-118-50253-2

Word 2013 For Dummies
978-1-118-49123-2

Music

Blues Harmonica
For Dummies
978-1-118-25269-7

Guitar For Dummies,
3rd Edition
978-1-118-11554-1

iPod & iTunes
For Dummies,
10th Edition
978-1-118-50864-0

Programming

Android Application
Development For
Dummies, 2nd Edition
978-1-118-38710-8

iOS 6 Application
Development For Dummies
978-1-118-50880-0

Java For Dummies,
5th Edition
978-0-470-37173-2

Religion & Inspiration

The Bible For Dummies
978-0-7645-5296-0

Buddhism For Dummies,
2nd Edition
978-1-118-02379-2

Catholicism For Dummies,
2nd Edition
978-1-118-07778-8

Self-Help & Relationships

Bipolar Disorder
For Dummies,
2nd Edition
978-1-118-33882-7

Meditation For Dummies,
3rd Edition
978-1-118-29144-3

Seniors

Computers For Seniors
For Dummies,
3rd Edition
978-1-118-11553-4

iPad For Seniors
For Dummies,
5th Edition
978-1-118-49708-1

Social Security
For Dummies
978-1-118-20573-0

Smartphones & Tablets

Android Phones
For Dummies
978-1-118-16952-0

Kindle Fire HD
For Dummies
978-1-118-42223-6

NOOK HD For Dummies,
Portable Edition
978-1-118-39498-4

Surface For Dummies
978-1-118-49634-3

Test Prep

ACT For Dummies,
5th Edition
978-1-118-01259-8

ASVAB For Dummies,
3rd Edition
978-0-470-63760-9

GRE For Dummies,
7th Edition
978-0-470-88921-3

Officer Candidate Tests,
For Dummies
978-0-470-59876-4

Physician's Assistant Ex
For Dummies
978-1-118-11556-5

Series 7 Exam
For Dummies
978-0-470-09932-2

Windows 8

Windows 8 For Dummies
978-1-118-13461-0

Windows 8 For Dummies
Book + DVD Bundle
978-1-118-27167-4

Windows 8 All-in-One
For Dummies
978-1-118-11920-4

Available in print and e-book formats.